PENGUIN BOOKS

THE PENGUIN HISTORY OF
THE UNITED STATES OF AMERICA

Hugh Brogan was educated at Repton School and Cambridge. He worked on the *Economist* for two years before his first visit to the United States as a Harkness Fellow in 1962. He was a Fellow of St John's College, Cambridge, for the period 1963–74 and thereafter, until his retirement in 1998, taught at the University of Essex (he was R. A. Butler Professor of History for the period 1994–8). His works include a study of Alexis de Tocqueville, *Tocqueville* (1973), *The Life of Arthur Ransome* (1984), *Mowgli's Sons: Kipling and Baden-Powell's Scouts* (1987) and *Kennedy* (1996). His most recent work is *Signalling from Mars: Selected Letters of Arthur Ransome* (1997).

HUGH BROGAN

*The Penguin History of
the United States of America*

Second Edition

PENGUIN BOOKS

PENGUIN BOOKS

Published by the Penguin Group
Penguin Books Ltd, 80 Strand, London WC2R 0RL, England
Penguin Putnam Inc., 375 Hudson Street, New York, New York 10014, USA
Penguin Books Australia Ltd, 250 Camberwell Road, Camberwell, Victoria 3124, Australia
Penguin Books Canada Ltd, 10 Alcorn Avenue, Toronto, Ontario, Canada M4V 3B2
Penguin Books India (P) Ltd, 11 Community Centre, Panchsheel Park, New Delhi – 110 017, India
Penguin Books (NZ) Ltd, Cnr Rosedale and Airborne Roads, Albany, Auckland, New Zealand
Penguin Books (South Africa) (Pty) Ltd, 24 Sturdee Avenue, Rosebank 2196, South Africa

Penguin Books Ltd, Registered Offices: 80 Strand, London WC2R 0RL, England

www.penguin.com

First published as *The Longman History of the United States of America* by Longman 1985
Published as *The Pelican History of the United States of America* in Penguin Books 1986
Reprinted as *The Penguin History of the United States of America* in Penguin Books 1990
Second edition published by Longman 1999
Published in Penguin Books 2001
5

Copyright © Addison Wesley Longman, 1985, 1999
All rights reserved

The moral right of the author has been asserted

Printed in England by Clays Ltd, St Ives plc

Contents

BOOK FOUR: *The Age of Gold*

BOOK FIVE: *The Superpower*

List of Maps

A Note of Thanks

This book has been fifteen years in the making – rather more, if the time taken for printing it is allowed for – and so my first thanks must be to my publishers, who have shown exemplary patience (they were expecting something much shorter, much sooner). Next I must thank my two academic homes, St John's College, Cambridge, and the University of Essex, not only for paying my salary but for providing excellent conditions for the pursuit of learning. One of the great advantages of belonging to such institutions is that at points of difficulty you can always turn to a colleague for reliable advice; an invaluable circumstance.

In so long a period, during which I have tried to master so enormous a subject as the history of the United States (I may say I grew rather weary of being told what an easy job I had, since America was so new a country), almost everything I have done or learned seems to have contributed to the making of my book; and I have benefited directly from innumerable conversations with learned and sharp-minded historians, both British and American. It would seem to claim too much if I were to name them all here: I hope I am not a name-dropper. Better to say, in general terms, that I have profited hugely from many lectures, seminars, classes, articles, monographs and stray encounters which, though uncited, have helped to strengthen this history in innumerable ways. I have learned a lot from my pupils, both through discovering what they really needed to know and (when they asked me questions I couldn't answer, or, in their essays, included information or references that were new to me) where my own ignorance lay. I have also benefited from various visits to the United States, from discoveries in academic libraries there, and from opportunities to get to know the various regions of that immense country. So I ought also to name the University of Chicago, Lewis and Clark College (Portland, Oregon), the University of Washington (Seattle) and the University of Tennessee, all of which greatly assisted my studies and my understanding of America, in return, at most, for a little summer teaching. And I must name the men who got me to the places: John Hope Franklin, Don Balmer, Dwight Robinson and

Milton Klein, my good friends. I am also well aware of how much this book owes to the two years which I spent as a Harkness Fellow at the Brookings Institution and at Yale between 1962 and 1964. Last but not least, indeed above all, I and my book are immeasurably indebted to my father, the late Denis Brogan. It will soon be ten years since he died, but the longer I live the more I am aware of how much I owe him; in particular I know that it was he who made me an Americanist, and he who taught me all the most important things I needed to learn about the United States. I wish he could have lived to see this result of his teaching (if only because he would have told me very frankly where it fell short); his memory and example have been with me ceaselessly as I worked at it.

Various people at various times read all or part of my drafts, and whether by correction or encouragement helped me along. I end this note by naming them with all gratitude: J. R. Pole, H. C. Porter, A. F. Rowlands, Rupert Sheldrake, Jill Steinberg, Howard Temperley, Hugh Tulloch, Alexander Tusa, Fiona Venn and Stuart Woolf.

Wivenhoe, 25 July 1983   Hugh Brogan

Note for the Second Impression

I am most grateful to the reviewers and correspondents who have enabled me gradually to correct various errors that disfigured the first edition of this history.

Wivenhoe, 12 November 1986   H.B.

Note for the Revised Edition

History does not stand still, as I was well aware when this book was first published in 1985, but neither I nor anybody else foresaw what radical changes it would bring forth in the next few years. The end of the Cold War was a gigantic series of events, the consequences of which are still making themselves felt; we must therefore wait for anything like a full understanding of its importance. But today, a full decade after the Soviet Union and its empire began to break up, it is none too soon to add to my chronicle a chapter recounting the last years of the Cold War, and to revise earlier chapters in the light of our new knowledge. To push the tale further, into the 1990s, would be possible but not really useful: the pattern underlying events is not yet clear, and in a book of this kind the pattern is what matters. So my narrative now goes down to the retirement of Ronald Reagan but (except incidentally) no further.

I have maintained my division of American history into five main epochs, but have changed the label attached to the last: once called 'The New World', it is now called 'The Superpower'. This reflects my conviction that the central theme of world history in the twentieth century, for good and evil, has been the emergence of the United States as a power and civilization that surpasses, in its reach and strength, all empires of the past, and that those who begin their analyses at other points – with the Russian Revolution, say, or the collapse of the old colonial empires – are profoundly mistaken.

The torrent of research into all aspects of American history has continued to flow throughout the past fourteen years, and the fashionable pre-eminence of social history (in the broadest sense) has been constantly reaffirmed. This makes less difference to the study of American history than might be supposed: as I hope is clear from what follows, the history of the United States has always been primarily the history of a society. But in this revised edition I have tried to take account of the most important discoveries and fresh hypotheses. And I continue to be grateful to the readers who have written to me with comments, criticisms, corrections and suggestions: I have taken careful note of all that they have said, and revised my text in many places as a result. I also wish to acknowledge help from Virginia Sapiro and Graham K. Wilson; Louis Claiborne; Tim Hatton; Ken Plummer and Tony Badger.

I have also revised the dedication, but in its new form it is still meant to express my thanks to all those students, at Essex, Cambridge and elsewhere, for whom this book was written, who over the years have taught me so much (perhaps at least as much as I have taught them) and who, from first to last, have made my professional involvement with American history so enjoyable.

Wivenhoe, January 1998   H.B.

Acknowledgements

We are indebted to author's agents on behalf of The National Trust for permission to reproduce extracts from 'Captains Courageous' and 'The White Man's Burden' both from *The Definitive Edition of Rudyard Kipling's Verse* published by Hodder & Stoughton.

For permission to reproduce we are grateful to the following: for loosely based adaptation of map on endpaper of text of R. A. Billington, *Westward Expansion*, published by Macmillan Publishing Co. Inc. 1949; for map loosely based on maps from A. M. Josephy, *The Indian Heritage of America*, published by Jonathan Cape Ltd 1973.

Dedicated to All My Pupils

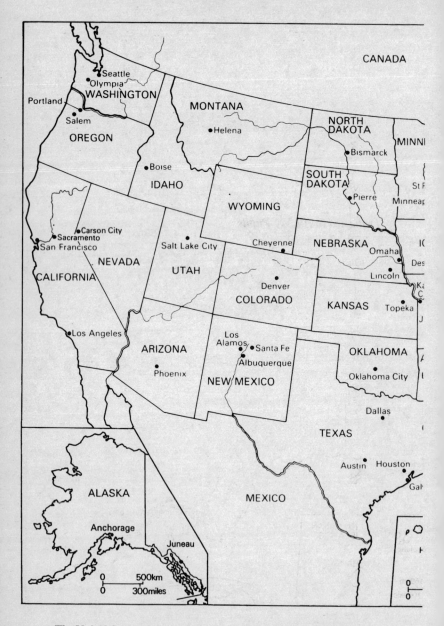

1. The United States of America: State Capitals and Principal Cities

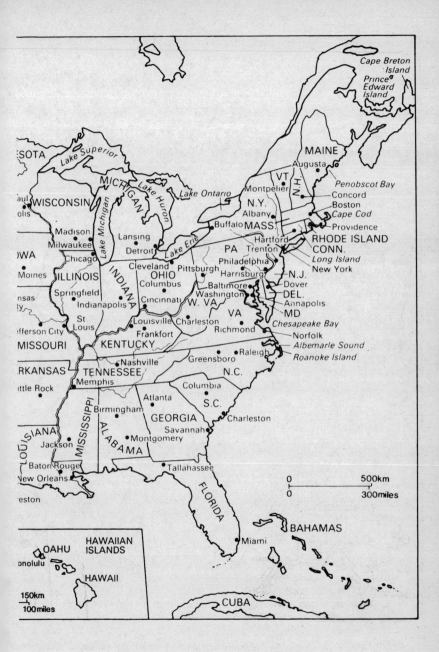

BOOK ONE

The Settlement

As in the Arts and Sciences the first foundation is of more consequence than all the improvements afterwards, so in kingdoms, the first foundation or plantation is of more dignity and merit than all that followeth.

Francis Bacon

1 *Prelude* c. 30,000 BC – c. AD 1600

Karlsefni and his men sailed into the estuary and named the place *Hope* (Tidal Lake). Here they found wild wheat growing in fields on all the low ground and grape vines on all the higher ground. Every stream was teeming with fish. They dug trenches at the high-water mark, and when the tide went out there were halibut trapped in the trenches. In the woods there was a great number of animals of all kinds.

Eirik's Saga[1]

Human history has been largely the story of migrations. The first crossings to the American continents seem to have taken place towards the end of the last Ice Age. So much water had gone to the making of the great northern ice-cap that the oceans receded from the shallow Bering Straits, and proto-Mongolians, it is thought, moved across the land-bridge thus formed. Then they gradually found their way, as generation followed generation, southwards down ice-free valleys. Their driftings went on for thousands of years. The Bering traverse may have begun before 30,000 BC. Patagonia, the extreme southern tip of South America, was reached by 9000 BC. Man established himself in all parts of the two continents and in the related islands of the Caribbean. His cultures grew to be many, varied and fascinating. None of them advanced to the use of iron or to complete literacy; by other measures of human progress the achievements were striking, especially those of the Mayan, Aztec and Inca civilizations of Central and South America. But by AD 1492 the New World, in its isolation, lagged substantially, in culture, behind the Old.

The trans-Bering migration probably ceased when the Ice Age ended and the sea rose, so that the straits appeared again, making any large movement of population impossible. Then civilization began to develop in

[1] From *The Vinland Sagas*, translated by Magnus Magnusson and Hermann Pálsson (Penguin Books, 1965), p. 98.

the great river-plains of China, India and the Middle East. That process
too went on for thousands of years. Cities were founded and destroyed and
re-founded, empires rose and fell, nomad hordes attacked, conquered and
were absorbed into more stable population groups; the stock of human
knowledge slowly increased. At length one fruit of that knowledge, the
perfected Scandinavian long-ship, gave such impetus to one particular
migratory group that it could dare to achieve the conquest of the ocean.
About AD 800 the Vikings reached the Faeroe Islands; in 870 they landed
in Iceland, and by the beginning of the eleventh century Leif the Lucky
had discovered Vinland the Good, part of the continent of North America.
Vinland was given its name and its epithet because it was far better suited
to human habitation than Greenland (settled in 981–2), or even Iceland,
but the Vikings were unable to settle it. The inhabitants, whom they called
Skraelings (roughly, 'wretches'), were numerous and soon became hostile;
the Vikings possessed no weapons that could compensate sufficiently for
their numerical inferiority. The distances to Greenland, Iceland and Europe
were too great to be conveniently and regularly crossed, even by long-ships.
So Vinland was never colonized, though knowledge of it and of the regions
to its north, Markland and Helluland – even a certain measure of intercourse
– persisted in the Norse lands for centuries, as is shown by, among other
things, the survival in Greenland of chests made apparently of larch wood
from North America.

In the end worsening climatic conditions destroyed even the Greenland
settlements. The Viking migrations led to nothing, unless (as is just possible)
Christopher Columbus learned of the Vinland tradition.

Europe had other dreams of the West. Islands lying far out towards or
beyond the sunset – the Islands of the Blest, the Garden of the Hesperides,
Hy-Brasil, Atlantis, Tir-na-Og, Estotiland, the Seven Cities of Antillia –
are omnipresent in legend. The Irish had traditions that St Brendan and
others of his kidney, travelling in leather boats, found peaceful retreats for
prayer across the seas (Irish monks do indeed seem to have got to Iceland
before the Vikings, though not necessarily any further). The Welsh at some
stage invented the saga of Prince Madoc, who sailed into the West, and,
they eventually alleged, there became either the ancestor of the Indians or
the begetter of their language (the quest for Welsh-speaking Indians was
to last into the nineteenth century). From time to time significant objects
were washed onto the coasts of the Old World: bodies of strange men,
wood carvings, branches of unknown trees. But these clues, like Vinland,
led to nothing: they were displayed to a world which for long had no
particular reason to bother about them.

The rediscovery of Vinland came about through coarser circumstances.
By the end of the fifteenth century the Portuguese were alarming their
neighbours by their success as navigators and ocean-travellers. They had
powerful motives: slaves, ivory and gold could be got from Africa, and they
hoped to gain a share in the lucrative spice-trade, monopolized until then

by the Venetians and the Turks. They succeeded in finding new routes to the Indies, by way of the Cape of Good Hope. Others determined to emulate them. In 1492 Isabella the Catholic, Queen of Spain, sent out a Genoese sailor of eccentric genius to find a westward route to the Indies, as he was sure he could. Instead he found the islands of the Caribbean. He made four voyages in all, on the last two of which, in 1498 and 1502, he discovered the mainland. Columbus called the Skraelings 'Indians' and supposed that the lands he had found were part of Asia; but at least he recognized the scope of his discoveries and prophesied their importance.

Now greed spurred on the Europeans to subdue the Americans. Even if gold and silver had not been discovered in Mexico and Peru, the quest for these metals or for a sea-route to Asia, or for such other wealth as America contained, would have drawn the white man into the New World, once he knew of its existence; but as it was, the resplendent civilizations of the Aztecs and the Incas were staggeringly effective advertisements for the enterprise. Total lack of scruple where heathen savages were concerned made the work of despoliation morally easy as well as agreeable, and conquest could further be justified by the universally accepted necessity of preaching the Christian God's word throughout the world. European diseases destroyed the American population more effectively than any weapons and demoralized the survivors by their scale: perhaps 90 per cent of the Indians died of these infections – smallpox, measles, malaria, yellow fever – in the first century after the discoveries. Lastly, European technology had advanced greatly since the Viking era. The Spaniards and Portuguese (who divided the western and eastern hemispheres between them) had guns, swords, armour, horses, improved sailing vessels and improved navigation. They also had first-rate military and political organization, perfected in the struggle against the Moors, and easy access to America along the Trade Wind latitudes. They could go where they wanted and do as they liked. By the middle of the sixteenth century they had effectively asserted their rule over most of Central and Southern America, and the Spaniards had also acquired, and were very slowly beginning to realize, claims to the dark continent north of Mexico.

But from the beginning, and even at the height of her power, imperial Spain faced competition, especially in the North. To understand why requires an awareness of many factors.

First must be mentioned the new European state system, with its built-in tendency to conflict.

The Renaissance state resulted from the complex interplay of many powerful forces, the relative strength of which varied from one country to another. Nevertheless it is clear that it existed primarily to protect its members from violence, above all from foreign and civil war, as was demonstrated in the brilliant writings of Niccolò Machiavelli and Thomas Hobbes. So long as the threat of war was real and pressing, and so long as a state could do its job by averting that threat, so long could it count on its subjects' support, although that support was severely qualified by a dislike of taxation so intense as to lead, frequently, to rebellion. But if the threat of war receded too completely the necessity of the state, at least in the highly centralized, oppressive, hierarchical form that it wore in the sixteenth century, would be questioned. Consequently, all those who had a stake in its continuance – kings, military aristocracies, bureaucrats and mercenary soldiers – had a vested interest, whether they admitted it or not, in perpetuating the evil that the state existed to correct. This paradox could only be resolved by an ethos which made permanent inter-state competition acceptable, if not to the poor peasants of Europe, at least to the consciences of their masters. That ethos was not lacking.

The history of each of the European states had been, during the period of its rise, a history of territorial extension. There seemed to be no reason why, in the Age of Monarchy, in the time of its maturity, a state should abandon the policy of aggrandizement. Reigning dynasties found it necessary to claim outlying provinces, ostensibly in order to maintain their legal rights and to increase the power, wealth and security of their states. Individual kings welcomed battles for new possessions, since they felt it was inglorious not to have fought valiantly in war. The aristocracy had for centuries been imbued with the idea of honour, and identified it with military virtues, which of course needed war for their display. Inferiors, ever prone to take their fashions from above, approved, or at least for the most part accepted, all these attitudes. It would have been difficult not to do so, since they were of very long standing and permeated the whole social structure. War thus seemed easy and natural to everybody.

So when Spain rose to her height as a result of the Columbian discoveries and the matrimonial expansionism of the Habsburg dynasty, all the other Old World states combined against her. In a world of inevitable war, her strength was too great to be tolerated safely. Nor did Spain do anything to conceal it, or to make it acceptable, for she too lived by the rules of the Renaissance game. And since men strike at their enemies wherever a blow is effective, Spain was challenged as much in the New World as in the Old. Her rivals hoped to win the treasure and trade of the Americas for themselves.

The English, led by another Italian, John Cabot, made the first anti-Spanish probes: they landed in Newfoundland in 1497 and discovered the great cod-fisheries, a treasure almost as precious as gold for medieval Europe, which suffered from a shortage of protein and, being Roman Catholic, needed fish to eat on Fridays and in Lent.

England laid claim to Newfoundland, but was at first too weak to make her claim good. French and Portuguese fishermen predominated on the Grand Bank.[2] The French made the first effective challenge to Spain. The pirates of François I were let loose in the Caribbean half a century before Hawkins and Drake. In 1524 François employed yet another Italian, Gio-

2 The Portuguese still know better than the English how to make cod palatable.

vanni Verrazano, to explore the Atlantic coasts of North America: this led to the discovery of Manhattan Island and the great harbour at the mouth of the Hudson river. The French had resumed the quest for the route to the Indies, and although the voyages of Verrazano and Cartier failed to find it, or to establish a French colony in the New World (attempts to wrest Florida from Spain also failed), they did lead to the thorough exploration of the north-east coast, especially of the Gulf of St Lawrence. Then the religious wars broke out, and French initiatives largely ceased.

The English returned to North America as sea-dogs, in the reign of Elizabeth I, as soon as that Queen felt it safe to challenge Spain. Their leader was Walter Ralegh. From his half-brother, Humphrey Gilbert, Ralegh had taken the notion that the region was one of the 'rich and unknown lands, fatally and it seemeth by God's providence, reserved for England'. Besides, the rich commerce and cities of New Spain were tempting prizes for piratical Englishmen: hence the exploits of Francis Drake in the Caribbean. On their side, the Spaniards planned to injure England by stirring up rebellion in Ireland. In revenge, Ralegh decided to establish a colony in what, in honour of the Virgin Queen, he called 'Virginia': that is, most of the eastern seaboard north of Florida and south of 'Norumbega' (the future New England). Such a colony, lying on the flank of Spain's communications with Europe, could with luck prey successfully on the Spanish treasure-fleets as they made their way home. He did not go to Virginia himself, but with the support of his Queen he placed settlers on Roanoke Island, on the coast of what is now North Carolina, in 1585; but at their own request Sir Francis Drake carried them home in the following year. The next attempt, in 1587, was even less successful. Neglected by the home government because of the Armada crisis, the little colony, or rather the colonists, had vanished by the time that Ralegh's ships next visited Roanoke. The only legacy of these efforts was the name, Virginia; some remarkable paintings of the natives and their villages; and a residual English interest in the area which bore fruit twenty years later.

Spain at first resisted the attempts on her American monopoly with considerable success. Time and the church eventually abated the savagery of the *conquistadores*; by gentler methods her devoted friars converted and pacified the Indians, so that her forts and missions could spread up the coast from Florida into what are now Georgia and the Carolinas; defences were strengthened in the Caribbean, so that Drake, in spite of all the damage he had inflicted, died at last broken-hearted after a final failure to capture and keep Panama. In time Spain weakened; but this merely increased conflict, for, as the power of the European states became more equal, one with another (as it did, on the whole, throughout the seventeenth century), so did their capacity and will to make trouble for each other. In turn, New France, New England, New Netherland, even tentative New Swedens and New Denmarks, imitated New Spain. Settlements in North America were fought and haggled over as if they were provinces in Europe: for example, the English took Quebec from the French, restoring it on payment of Queen Henrietta Maria's dowry in 1633; New Netherland changed hands twice before becoming New York for good. The unfortunate Indians – above all, French-backed Hurons and English-backed Iroquois – found themselves and their quarrels drawn into European disputes in which they had no interest.

It must not be supposed, however, that the inter-state conflicts, important though they were, were the only causes of North American colonization, or that they were innocent of religious or popular content, or that monarchical policy was always clear-headed and ruthless. None of these things was true. Furthermore, we have seen already how strong an influence was economic greed, and this affected peoples as well as rulers. The English and the Dutch alike dragged their governments behind them as they pressed into every corner of the world looking for profit. The Newfoundland fishing led to trade with the Indians. Fur, especially that of the beaver, was as valuable a product as cod, and the Indians were willing to barter it for such European goods as ironware and bales of cloth. Trading-posts were established, and by the beginning of the seventeenth century the returning French, led by Samuel de Champlain, were pressing further and further up the St Lawrence river and securing Canada for France. Quebec was founded in 1608, Montreal in 1642. The Dutch traded and settled up the river Hudson. The beginnings of English activities are discussed in the next chapter.

To another chapter may also be left an account of the effects of the ferocious religious disputes that tormented Europe between 1517 and 1689. Here it is enough to remark that these effects were dramatic. Along with hunger for trade and treasure, the political competition and the ever-improving knowledge of the Western seas, religion forced on the opening-up of North America.

And it was so easy. The riches that the continent contained were free, it seemed, for the taking. A few years of physical suffering were all that any part of it exacted as the price of conquest. The Indians were too few to do much more than fight a rearguard action. Modern scholarship cannot yet provide agreed estimates of the size of the population of North America before the Europeans came: guesses vary from two million to eighteen million. But whatever the truth, white diseases, to which the natives had at first no immunity, eventually reduced their numbers as inexorably as they had those of Mexico and Peru. Even so late as 1838 a smallpox epidemic would clear the way for white settlers across the Great Plains. So into the comparatively empty seven million square miles of the continent the densely settled Europe could pour its surplus sons and daughters in ever-swelling numbers.

The Indians were losers, but not the only ones, nor perhaps the worst. There were others, much more numerous, who made the country a happy hunting-ground. For them it had been paradise. Beaver, buffalo, Carolina parakeets, duckhawks, elk, great auks, grizzly bears, mountain-lions, passenger pigeons, sea-minks, sea-otters, whooping cranes and many other species that have since been either nearly or quite exterminated abounded in numbers that now seem literally unbelievable. According to a distinguished modern historian, at the time of the first settlement of Virginia there were

turkeys that weighed seventy pounds or more, and ducks so numerous that flocks seven miles long shut out the sunlight as they passed overhead. Streams swarmed with fish so large that ordinary nets would not hold them and so plentiful that a horse could not wade across a river when they were running.[3]

Until the sixteenth century men had been too few and too weak in weapons to diminish the abundance.[4] It was so enormous that for more than two centuries the Europeans were continually amazed by the beauty, numbers and novelty of the North American birds, beasts and fishes that they were destroying. Similarly, they proclaimed their admiration for the beautiful forests that they felled, the plains, rivers and mountains they despoiled. Nowadays their descendants lament a poisoned land and fear a silent spring.

---

3 R. A. Billington, *Westward Expansion* (New York, 1949), p. 38. Billington does not give his authority for this striking passage.
4 Though some now think that the earliest Indians may have hunted many great species to extinction immediately after the Ice Age – for instance, the American horse.

2 The Roots of English Colonization

This royal throne of kings, this scept'red isle,
This earth of majesty, this seat of Mars,
This other Eden, demi-paradise,
This fortress built by Nature for herself
Against infection and the hand of war,
This happy breed of men, this little world,
This precious stone set in the silver sea,
Which serves it in the office of a wall,
Or as a moat defensive to a house,
Against the envy of less happier lands . . .

William Shakespeare

Why then should we stand striving here for places of habitation (where many are spending as much labour and cost to recover or keep sometimes an acre or two of Land, as would produce them many and as good or better in another Country) and in the mean time suffer a whole Continent as fruitful and convenient for the use of men to be waste without any improvement?

John Winthrop

From the heights of Olympus the English conquest of North America, protracted though it was through a century and a half, must have seemed merely an incident in the movement which carried European power and European culture to every corner of the world. But those who try to understand the origins of the United States have to decide precisely what it was that so differentiated England from her competitors within the general European movement that she was able to outstrip them all. What were the special factors in Tudor and Stuart England that augmented the general outward tendency of the Europeans?

'Gold, trade, tillage represent the three stages in the history of colonization, and the greatest of these, because fundamentally essential to permanence, is tillage,' says the leading historian of the American colonies.[1] He is right; but it is important to notice that the Europeans did not discover this truth for over a century. Even Ralegh, most intelligent of the first English colonizers, thought of Roanoke primarily as an instrument for securing a large and early profit, either by gold-mining, plundering the Spanish, or by trade. As for the Iberian nations, they were at first content to hold Southern and Central America by force, living at ease off the labour of slaves imported from Africa (for Indians made bad slaves, dying more rapidly than they could be replaced). Yet the wealth of North America had to be worked for by Europeans, not only as traders or trappers, but as farmers and artisans also. This, as much as any of Columbus's, was a discovery that, once made, would change the history of the world. It was not enough to mine gold, to haul fish from the waters and to take beaver from the forest by barter with the natives.

This fact implied four things about the European advance. It meant that the country would succeed most completely which could most easily export the largest number of people; which could most easily keep them supplied – in other words, which was strongest at sea over the longest period; which had colonists who brought with them the most appropriate skills; and, lastly, which had the most adaptable culture, in the widest sense of that word.

That country turned out to be England. Inferior at various times and in various respects to her rivals, she possessed, overall, a stronger hand than any of them.

Her victory was ultimately due to the fact that she was the dominant entity in an island. She was thus spared the perils and temptations that afflicted the continental powers. Ireland, so near, so alien, so vulnerable to foreign fleets, was her weak point, but the Royal Navy guarded it successfully, on the whole, against foreign attack, and the Battle of the Boyne was merely the last of many victories which in the long run put an end to any danger from the inhabitants. Unlike one of her chief rivals, Holland, England was almost impossible to invade successfully while her fleet was in being. Unlike another, France, she would not succumb to the lure of continental hegemony, because her gentry, for their own reasons, kept the King in check, as they could not have done if a long land frontier, by making a large standing army necessary, had made him their master. In some respects Spain, isolated from Europe by the sea and the Pyrenees almost as effectively as England was by the Channel, shared the insular advantage; but this was neutralized by internal particularism and by the crushing, if spectacular, inheritance of the Habsburgs in the Low Countries, Germany, Italy, Hungary and Bohemia. Unlike this ancient enemy, England had no territorial

1 Charles M. Andrews, *The Colonial Period of American History* (New Haven, Yale paperback edn, 1964), Vol. i, p. 49.

or dynastic entanglements of a kind certain to involve her in continental land war. Calais had gone under Mary Tudor, Hanover would not come until the death of Queen Anne. The result of all this good fortune was a steady husbanding of vigour and capital. Compared to the Thirty Years War, or the Swedish wars, or the wars of Louis XIV, England's Civil Wars were mere episodes; and since their result, in the not-too-long run, was the remoulding and reinvigorating of English political institutions, which further increased the country's strength in all forms of international competition, they are not episodes to be regretted by Englishmen or English-speaking Americans. Lying across the sea communications of half Europe with the outside world, in a period when, as has been said, European culture was coming to overpower all other groups whatever, the scept'red isle needed only the will to use its various resources to take to itself whatever it wanted – sovereignty, loot or the world's commerce. Nor was the will lacking. On the contrary, many things fostered it.

More perils confronted England during the sixteenth century than in any other between the eleventh and the twentieth. In 1500 she did not seem well equipped to meet them. She was the weakest, militarily, politically and economically, of the leading Western states. Her trade was largely in the hands of foreigners. Her polity was still endangered by the rivalries of York and Lancaster. Her feudal institutions were in decay, her capital resources and geographical knowledge were small, Spain and Portugal were dominant in every ocean. Nor did things at once improve. Rather, the wool-trade declined, and after 1550 the cloth-trade did so too. Henry VIII involved the country in futile foreign wars to which he soon added a religious revolution. A disputed Crown and an even more bitterly disputed church settlement explain almost all the politics of Elizabeth I's reign. Imports of American bullion helped to produce a European inflation which, in turn, generated social conflict and tension.

But danger and misfortune sharpened the wits. Throughout the century the Tudor state strengthened its efficient grip on the country. The struggle with Spain, religious in origin, quickly grew nationalistic: Drake, the principal burglar of the Spanish Main, became, in the eyes of his countrymen, a leading Protestant and English hero, as did his fellow Devonian pirates, Hawkins, Gilbert and Ralegh. Not only did he show the way to honour God and vindicate his country's pride: his unlicensed but profitable war on the treasure-fleets of Spain seemed to point to the solution of English economic difficulties. His defeat of the Spanish Armada completed the fusion of motives. *Realpolitik*, covetousness and religious zeal fused in an apotheosis of patriotic triumph. Caribbean piracy was holy, lucrative and for a long time easy. It was resorted to more and more zealously, seriously weakening and deferring the first English attempts to colonize North America. Investment in buccaneering enterprises seemed surer and more pleasurable and more certainly God's will than investment in what were called 'plantations'.

Then in 1604 the new King, James I, made peace with the Spaniard, and English capital sought new outlets.

Thanks to various incidental factors, such as the exclusion of foreign traders and the dissolution of the monasteries, but, above all, thanks to the untiring enterprise of Tudor merchants, there had been a steady accumulation of wealth during the sixteenth century. New trading companies, regulated by royal charters, sprang up, partly to utilize, partly to increase, the new resources. The Muscovy Company, the Levant Company, the East India Company, the Guinea Company, the Eastland Company – their very names are evidence of how far English merchants were prepared to go in their search for markets. Efforts to manufacture new goods for export led to a primitive industrial revolution, which created yet more risk capital. It was certain that before long, having explored in all other directions, the companies would turn westward. Peace hastened the process, as war had retarded it.

Some had been encouraging it for years. In 1600 Richard Hakluyt, friend, counsellor and protégé of Ralegh, crowned nearly two decades of diligent propaganda by publishing the final version of his *Principal Navigations, Voyages, and Discoveries of the English Nation*[2] to rouse the English from their 'sluggish security', an aim in which he was largely successful. He prevented the achievements and projects of Gilbert and Ralegh from being forgotten, even when the one was dead and the other a prisoner in the Tower. Among his readers were the large number of influential men who had been involved with Ralegh and himself in their Irish and American enterprises, men now powerful in the companies – Sir Thomas Smith, for example, who dominated the East India Company.

Hakluyt made a complete case for colonization. In his pages it is easy to learn what the Elizabethans hoped to achieve in the West. Later propaganda confirms the lesson. From the whole corpus we can discover the appeal of America to all classes, and why the English made the great discovery, that tilling the soil – not gold, or even trade – would best bring permanence and wealth to the conquerors of North America.

To the rich, it seems, Virginia meant in the first place dreams of quick profit – if not from gold-mines, then from the North-West Passage to Cathay, which was no doubt close at hand,[3] or from timber, soap-manufacturing or the export of pitch. Investors were also tempted by the idea of producing Mediterranean commodities, such as wine and olive oil. Land on a scale no longer available in England was as attractive to squires pent in petty acres as it was to labourers with none.

Other factors played their part. There was the usual missionary excuse

2　The first edition had appeared in 1589, directly after the defeat of the Armada.
3　Ignorance of the North American interior was still almost total. The existence of the Appalachian mountains was known, but their length was not; and the vast extent of the continent was quite unguessed. Knowledge of Caribbean and North American waters, on the other hand, was much improved, thanks to the sea-dogs.

to sanctify the enterprise. Englishmen were professedly as ready as Spaniards 'to preach and baptize into *Christian Religion*, and by propagation of the *Gospel* to recover out of the arms of the Devil a number of poor and miserable souls, wrapt up in death, in almost invincible ignorance'.[4] The legend of Prince Madoc was useful reinforcement to the claim deriving from John Cabot, for it proved (at any rate to Englishmen and Welshmen) that 'that country was by Britons discovered, long before Columbus led any Spaniards thither'. Such were the sops to conscience, which made despoiling the Indians possible. More positive appeals could be made to the desire for glory in the high Roman fashion:

You brave heroic minds [wrote Michael Drayton]
Worthy your country's name,
That honour still pursue,
  Go and subdue!
Whilst loitering hinds
  Lurk here at home with shame . . .

And in regions far,
  Such heroes bring ye forth
    As those from whom we came;
    And plant our name
Under that star
  Not known unto our North . . .

(The poem ends with a puff for 'Industrious Hakluyt' and his *Voyages*.)

A less lofty motive was to be found in the general anxiety about the large vagrant population which wars, the rise in prices, enclosures and the growth of the towns had created in England. The well-to-do were vividly aware of the fragility of the social peace which the Civil Wars were soon to shatter. Hakluyt offered the New World as a literally God-given solution to the problem of 'valiant youths rusting and hurtful by lack of employment' – 'idle persons', John Donne called them, 'and the children of idle persons'. 'A monstrous swarm of beggars,' said others. Prisons could be emptied of the 'able men to serve their Country, which for small robberies are daily hanged up in great numbers'. Virginia and the voyage thither would not only free England of criminals, it would turn them into 'sober, modest persons', promised another authority. Unemployed soldiers could be used against the 'stubborn Savages' (no doubt in the intervals of preaching the gospel to them). It was all very tempting and convincing to a class which felt threatened from below. Transportation of convicts and, later, the encouragement of emigration became for centuries a settled policy of the government for dealing with this order of problems.

4 In the interests of consistency and general readability I have reluctantly modernized the spelling in this and all other quotations.

The upper classes were also encouraged by the precedent set in Ireland, which served as an experimental laboratory for identifying and solving the problems of colonization: the 'wild Irish' standing for the Indians. What seemed to be the absolute strategic necessity of securing Ireland to English rule, and the resistance of the inhabitants to that rule, had suggested the idea of colonizing the sister island; and what could be done there could be done in Virginia. By the same token, Irish setbacks inured the English rich to Virginian ones: they became prepared, in some measure, for a long haul.

The same could not be said of the English poor, who were the instruments of these schemes. Ireland as a place of settlement had little attraction for them. The soldiery knew it as a place of bad pay, food shortages, incompetent officers, native treachery and native cruelty. The civilians heard of it as a place where civilians were massacred. Both, therefore, 'had as lief go to the gallows as to the Irish wars'; Ireland and war were nearly synonymous terms.

All this applied, with the added terrors of the stormy Atlantic, distance and the unknown, to North America. Only the strongest motives could override a distaste for colonization based on a certain knowledge of some extremely unpleasant facts. How sensible that distaste was, how reliable that knowledge, was demonstrated when at last a permanent settlement was achieved in Virginia. The first inhabitants died easily and in large numbers; and 300 of the survivors returned to England in the first nine years of the little colony's existence.

The quest of the seventeenth-century capitalist was therefore the same as that of today's historian. What, both asked, could induce the labouring classes of England to abandon their homes for the dangers of the Virginia voyage?

The answer cannot, today, be taken direct from the men and women best capable of giving it. To us, the poorer social classes are dumb. They had few means to tell their thoughts to posterity, since they were largely illiterate and since the presses were mostly used for the purposes of their betters, which did not include making surveys of mass opinion. However, among those purposes was a wish to induce large numbers of the better sort of lowly Englishmen to sail for the West. Successful plantations could be built only out of human material superior to that which could be swept together from the prisons, brothels and slums of London and compelled to go to America. The result was a vast literature of propaganda and persuasion directed not so much at the man looking for an investment as at the man looking for a chance in life. From that literature can be learned what their contemporaries thought would move the working men. And on such matters contemporaries are likely to be broadly right. It is only a matter of using the evidence with caution. Who could not learn a lot about the motivation of England today from such a study of English advertising?

Hakluyt was the greatest author of promotion literature, but he had countless imitators. One theme dominates overwhelmingly in their appeals to the people: land-hunger. 'In Virginia land free and labour scarce; in England land scarce and labour plenty' was the slogan that summed it up. In a pre-industrial age land was bound to be the most precious commodity, while the labour of his body was often all that a man had to sell. Virginia could, therefore, easily be presented as a land of unique opportunity. To the very poor, a country where an illimitable forest provided an inexhaustible supply of free fuel and free housing materials was patently a land 'more like the Garden of Eden: which the Lord planted, than any part else of all Earth'. And, as has been noted, the very poor were very numerous in Tudor and Stuart England. So to them was sung:

To such as to Virginia
  Do purpose to repair;
And when that they shall hither come,
  Each man shall have his share,

Day wages for the labourer,
  And for his more content,
A house and garden plot shall have
  Besides 'tis further meant

That every man shall have a post
  And not thereof denied
Of general profit, as if that he
  Twelve pounds, ten shillings paid.

The better-off could best be tempted by larger, if similar, inducements:

With what content shall the particular person employ himself there when he shall find that for a £12 10s. adventure he shall be made lord of 200 acres of land, to him and his heirs forever. And for the charge of transportation of himself, his family and tenants he shall be allotted for every person he carries 100 acres more. And what labourer soever shall transport himself thither at his own charge to have the like proportion of land upon the aforesaid conditions and be sure of employment to his good content for his present maintenance.[5]

Not only was there plenty of the arable land that had grown so expensive, because so scarce, in England. In America there were none of the oppressive feudal laws that encumbered landholding in England: there, copyholders could become freeholders. No enclosing of common lands in America: there, men could eat sheep, not sheep men. It is little wonder that, according to Andrews, 'the bulk of the colonial population was of the artisan and tenant class which in England held by some form of burgage or copyhold

5 £12 10s was the price of a share in the Virginia Company. See below, p. 24.

tenure'.[6] Life in England held little charm for many such: they might reckon themselves fortunate to have a way of escape. Plague and famine are not pleasant things in themselves, and both were common; they also had disastrous effects on the economy, effects which, inevitably, bore hardest on the poorest. Misgovernment, as symbolized under James I by Alderman Cockayne's scheme, which wrecked the cloth-trade in the 1620s, or international tragedy, such as the Thirty Years War, which completed Cockayne's work, were only a little less inevitable. Human misfortune on a national or continental scale has been one of the most constant forces behind emigration to America from the seventeenth century to the twentieth.[7]

The promoters, in fact, were in a seller's market. All they had to do was to overcome memories of Ireland by doubling and redoubling their assurances that America was the true demi-Paradise. Nor did they fail. The Reverend Daniel Price displayed the true colours of Celtic fantasy when, in a sermon in 1609, he rhapsodized that Virginia was

Tyrus for colours, Basan for woods, Persia for oils, Arabia for spices, Spain for silks, Narcis for shipping, Netherlands for fish, Pomona for fruit, and by tillage, Babylon for corn, besides the abundance of mulberries, minerals, rubies, pearls, gems, grapes, deer, fowls, drugs for physic, herbs for food, roots for colours, ashes for soap, timber for building, pastures for feeding, rivers for fishing, and whatsoever commodity England wanteth.[8]

Not only Wales spoke in this strain. It was an English play which, four years before Mr Price gave tongue, asserted that in Virginia 'wild boar is as common as our tamest Bacon is here' (the wild boar is not an American species). Curiosity and ignorance about the New World could be advantageously manipulated in a hundred ways. Thus, in 1605 five Indians were brought over and paraded round the country, to its vast excitement.[9] They were an excellent advertisement for Virginia: the best sort of proof that it did actually exist. Pocahontas, the beautiful Indian 'Princess' whom John Rolfe married a few years later[10] and brought to England, must have been an even stronger stimulus to the imagination.

6 Andrews, *The Colonial Period*, Vol. i, p. 57.
7 See Carl Bridenbaugh, *Vexed and Troubled Englishmen* (New York, 1968), *passim*, and especially Chapter XI, 'The First Swarming of the English'. Professor Bridenbaugh estimates that 'between 1620 and 1642, close to 80,000, or 2 per cent of all Englishmen' emigrated. He makes the important point that about 20,000 of them went to the continent, not to America; and singles out economic conditions as the chief cause of restlessness.
8 Andrews, *The Colonial Period*, Vol. i, p. 55.
9 Probably giving Trinculo his idea for displaying Caliban at English fairs: 'when they will not give a doit to relieve a lame beggar, they will lay out ten to see a dead Indian' (*The Tempest*, II, 2).
10 For more about Pocahontas see below, p. 21. According to Rolfe, he married her 'for the good of this plantation, for the honour of our country, for the glory of God, for my own salvation, and for the converting to the true knowledge of God and Jesus Christ, an unbelieving creature'. She is buried at Gravesend.

It is true that another motive, the religious, played a major, indeed a heroic part in stimulating English settlement in America; but it can best be studied through the history of New England. And many years before the Pilgrims sailed, the twin desires of the capitalists for gain and of the poor for land, both stimulated by the tribe of Hakluyt, succeeded at last in planting Englishmen permanently in the New World. As a motive, materialism had proved sufficient. In 1605 two companies, for London and for Plymouth, were chartered, their business being to establish colonies in America. After some exploratory journeys and yet another abortive attempt by the Plymouth Company to establish a settlement (this time at Sagadahoc, in what is now the state of Maine) the London Company founded the first enduring English plantation, on 24 May 1607, on the James river in Virginia. It was small, and already unfortunate, since of the company of 144 that had embarked in three little ships (*Susan Constant, Godspeed, Discovery*) only 105 had survived the voyage. The place they founded, Jamestown, has long been abandoned.[11] But with Jamestown begins the history proper of the people known as Americans.

---

11 Except that it has been turned into an excellent historical museum.

3 The Planting of Virginia
1607–76

And cheerfully at sea
  Success you still entice
    To get the pearl and gold,
  And ours to hold
Virginia,
  Earth's only paradise.

Where nature hath in store
  Fowl, venison, and fish,
    And the fruitfull'st soil
    Without your toil
Three harvests more,
  All greater than your wish.

And the ambitious vine
  Crowns with his purple mass
    The cedar reaching high
    To kiss the sky,
The cypress, pine,
  And useful sassafras.[1]

Michael Drayton

Disaster dogged the first Virginians, and disappointment their patrons, for nearly twenty years.

The reasons were many and complicated.

Nothing, on a long view, could be said against the region that they had chosen for their experiment. The James river winds, wide and deep, fifty miles into the interior and is only one of a score of navigable waterways. The coast, in fact, is extravagantly indented and proved ideal for that

---

1 Sassafras was 'useful' because it was thought to be a cure for venereal disease.

seaborne traffic with the outer world without which the colony could not
have lived. The land itself, sloping gently upwards towards the foothills of
the Alleghenies, was extremely fertile, rich in game and timber.[2] The local
Indians, though fully capable of resenting and punishing injuries, were less
formidable and thinner on the ground (thanks to European diseases) than
many tribes to be encountered elsewhere, by others, later on. The frightful
American climate – jungle-hot in summer, tundra-cold in winter, unbearably
humid whenever it isn't freezing – is, as it happens, far more agreeable in
Virginia[3] than in most of the rest of the Eastern seaboard. Captain John
Smith summed it up accurately:

The summer is hot as in Spain; the winter cold as in France or England. The
heat of summer is in June, July, and August, but commonly the cold breezes
assuage the vehemency of the heat. The chief of winter is half December, January,
February, and half March. The cold is extreme sharp, but here the proverb is true,
that no extreme long continueth.

Certainly it is not the damp and mild climate of England;[4] but many could
be found to say that this is no disadvantage. Thomas Jefferson, for example,
at the end of the eighteenth century, exulted in the fact that whereas in
Europe one never saw a wholly blue sky, quite innocent of cloud, in Virginia
it was common.

So much is true; but it is equally true that the new colony more than
once came within a hair's breadth of sharing the fate of Roanoke and
Sagadahoc.

In 1610 the settlers had actually abandoned the site and were sailing
down-river when they met the new Governor, Lord De La Warr, sailing
up it, with men and supplies sufficient to allow the enterprise to be renewed.
At that time – only three years after its founding – Jamestown appeared

rather as the ruins of some ancient fortification, than that any people living might
now inhabit it. The pallisadoes . . . torn down, the ports open, the gates from the
hinges, the church ruined and unfrequented, empty houses (whose owners'
untimely death had taken newly from them) rent up and burnt, the living not able,
as they pretended, to step into the woods to gather other firewood.

And in 1617 a new Deputy-Governor found it much the same: '. . . but five
or six houses, the church down, the palisadoes broken, the bridge in pieces,
the well of fresh water spoiled . . .' The more the early history of Virginia

2 When the settlers' ships arrived off Jamestown, they 'moored to the trees in six fathom
water'.
3 The name Virginia, originally given to a much vaster area, was soon monopolized by
the Jamestown settlement, and the opening-up of New England began the long process of
differentiating the various regions of North America by name.
4 Damper and less mild in the seventeenth century than it is today.

is studied, the more it must (and did) appear miraculous that the colony survived.

Three things explain the miracle.

First, in time, importance and honour, must be placed the spirit of some of the colonists, and some of their leaders. Captain John Smith may be taken as the type of both, partly because he has left remarkable accounts of himself and his experiences, partly because of his general importance, as propagandist, to the colonization movement as a whole, partly because without him the Virginian settlement must have foundered within two years of its birth.

Captain Smith (1579–1631) was a soldier of fortune who sailed with the first settlers. A man with, as it proved, justified faith in his own abilities and no weak reluctance to make enemies, he was actually placed under arrest for mutiny before the little fleet reached the Canaries, and remained in duress until it was found that the London Company's sealed orders made him a member of the council that was to rule the colony. This, his high reputation among the settlers and the good offices of the Company's chaplain restored him to freedom, which he proceeded to make the most of. During the summer he bestirred the Company into building adequate shelters; he hunted on its behalf and intimidated the Indians into providing maize for it. A map-maker, he energetically explored the area, with never more than a handful of companions. On one of these expeditions, during the winter, he was captured by Indians and taken to Powhatan, chief of the confederacy of that name. Powhatan might have killed Smith, but at the last moment Pocahontas, 'the King's dearest daughter', 'got his head in her arms, and laid her own upon his to save him from death'. This led to a temporary reconciliation with Powhatan, who gave the Englishman the name 'Nanta-quaus' and received in return two cannons and a millstone from Jamestown. On his return to that place Smith found his fellow-settlers preparing to abandon the undertaking and sail in the pinnace for England or Newfound-land; but he, threatening the boat with cannon from the shore, forced them to stay or sink. It was his third such intervention: on an earlier occasion one of the would-be fugitives had been executed for mutiny. This time the leading mutineers were merely sent as prisoners to England.

By the spring Captain Smith, though still, officially, no more than a member of the council, had emerged as the master-spirit of the enterprise. No wonder. He seems to have been born with all the gifts of a frontiersman, including the knack of handling Indians, gifts such as were to prove their value again and again during the conquest of North America. The body of the settlers were sensible enough to recognize it. They chose him as their President in September 1608. His ascendancy was not to be seriously shaken until the accident that put an end to his Virginian career, although after that accident (the explosion of a bag of gunpowder, 'which tore the flesh from his body and thighs') a plot was laid to assassinate him. But 'his heart did fail him that should have given fire to that merciless pistol,' Smith explains. Some later Presidents were to be less fortunate.

Smith left in September 1609. The two preceding years had seen him face, and for the most part overcome, a multitude of hideous problems.

First and worst was the recurrent threat of starvation. There never were nor could be adequate food supplies from home; ships reached Virginia only four times between 1607 and 1609. The English were slow to master the arts of catching or killing American game, which was not, in any case, invariably plentiful. During the frequent quarrels with the Indians barter for food ceased. In 1608 Smith organized the successful planting and reaping of the colony's own corn; but rats, come into Virginia off the ships, devoured almost the whole, so that the settlers had to be boarded out with the Indians. Nevertheless, by the end of his Presidency he had secured the food supply. The colonists had enjoyed a second harvest, and their European livestock – pigs, hens, goats and some sheep – were proliferating satisfactorily.

Next only to starvation as an enemy was disease. Jamestown had been founded on an isthmus that was ideal for military defence,[5] but, surrounded by marshes, was fatal to the health of all too many. Malaria came with Caribbean mosquitoes, like the rats, in the first ships. Plague and yellow fever came with the later ships; so, apparently, did jail-fever. Bad diet bred scurvy. Bad water bred dysentery. The damps and colds of winter were no discouragement to rheumatic disorders. Finally, psychological ailments may have appeared: in 1619 one of the settlers (who, it is true, did not live at Jamestown) insisted that Virginia was healthy, and that 'more do die here of the disease of their mind than of their body by having this country victuals over-praised unto them in England and by not knowing they shall drink water here'. The contrast between conditions in their new and their old homes must surely have seemed unduly sharp to many. But in view of the physical predicament mental causes need scarcely be invoked to explain the fact that by the end of 1607 only thirty-eight men survived of the hundred or so who had originally landed.

Leadership could do little against bacteria or melancholy. It became accepted that it was necessary to 'season' settlers;[6] and, of course, the process of acclimatization often failed. So of the hundreds of settlers, including, from 1611 onwards, women and children, who were poured into Virginia, hundreds continued to die or to flee back to England, so that the population did not pass the thousand mark until the twenties; and still there were fluctuations. In 1628 there were reckoned to be 3,000 Virginians; in 1630 only 'upwards of 2,500'. By 1643, it is true, there had been a dramatic increase, to nearly 5,000. Seasoning remained a slow business.

5 This was thought to be important, as it was feared that the Spanish might attempt to snuff out the colony before it could be a trouble to them. So they would have, but for the somewhat mysterious forbearance of Philip III. Perhaps he thought the colony was certain to fail. The Virginians themselves were less passive. An expedition was dispatched in 1613 to extinguish a French settlement in Nova Scotia, which it did without undue fuss, tenderness or cruelty.
6 That is, they had to catch the diseases and survive – a kill-or-cure, 'natural', indeed Darwinian process of immunization.

Death, disease and the Indian were to stalk the frontier of settlement throughout its history; they imposed a corresponding necessity on the frontiersmen and women to be incessantly watchful, prudent and hardworking. Yet Smith's little band contained many who did their best to evade the necessity. Some, as has been seen, tried to abandon Virginia entirely; others deserted to the Indians; private trading undermined Smith's attempts to regulate relations with the aborigines, and laxness enabled these to steal from the Company's few precious stores. Mutiny was endemic, quarrelling incessant. And all too many of the settlers – 'drunken gluttonous loiterers' – were simply not prepared to turn their hands to the mundane tasks of obtaining food, either by hunting or agriculture, or of building shelters.

These last Smith eventually dealt with by swearing to turn off all who would not work to starve in the wilderness; but the moral he drew was that settlers who were merely gentlemen or soldiers were worse than useless. 'Good labourers and mechanical men' were what was wanted, and there were far too few of these among the first Virginians – perhaps some two dozen. 'All the rest were poor gentlemen, tradesmen, serving men, libertines, and such like, ten times more fit to spoil a commonwealth, than either begin one, or but help to maintain one.' 'When you send again,' he wrote to the London Company, 'I entreat you rather send but thirty carpenters, husbandmen, gardeners, fishermen, blacksmiths, masons and diggers up of trees, roots, well provided; than a thousand of such as we have: for except we be able both to lodge them, and feed them, the most will consume with want of necessaries before they can be made good for anything.' Smith, at least, rapidly learned the lessons of tillage, and saw through some of the delusive visions that were encouraging the Virginia voyage in England.

The Virginia Company of London was little quicker to learn than the generality of Englishmen, and Smith complained bitterly about the unrealistic orders it sent him, commanding him to find gold-mines, and the passage to the South Sea, and Ralegh's lost colonists, and not to fight the Indians, and to crown Powhatan King and vassal of James I. But though it is possible to sympathize with the Captain, it is not entirely possible to take his grievances as solemnly as he did himself. For the second factor, for lack of which Virginia would certainly have foundered, was the steady support that the parent company gave to its creation.

Smith left in the autumn of 1609. The incompetents whom he had superseded had returned, and the new rulers of the colony, Sir Thomas Gates and Lord De La Warr, had not yet arrived. Jamestown, which Smith had left tolerably well ordered, immediately began to fall to pieces, and there ensued the 'Starving Time'. Yet as we have seen, the colony survived, if only just. The London Company continued to find for it money, and women and men (of an improved quality). It sent out efficient and unsentimental soldiers, such as Thomas Dale and Samuel Argall, to govern it *à la* Smith (that is to say, autocratically) until it had found its feet, and then it began gracefully to relinquish its absolute control as private enterprise became desired and possible.[7] And when emergencies occurred it did all it could to come to the rescue. The worst such emergency was in 1622. By then the colony had spread far up both sides of the James, as far as the falls where Richmond now stands. Powhatan and Pocahontas were both dead, and the leadership of the Indians had devolved on the understandably bitter Opechancanough. On 22 March, 'at eight of the clock on that fatal Friday morning', he launched a carefully planned massacre which killed a third or so of the 1,200 settlers. On receiving the news the Company immediately applied to the King for leave to send to the beleaguered colonists 'certain old cast arms remaining in the Tower and the Minorites'. The arms were sent, and used to such effect that the colonists soon reduced the Indians to submission. There was to be no more serious trouble with them for twenty years; and the next uprising (in 1644) was the last.

It was not easy for the Company to be so steadfast. One of the necessities which most plagued both the colony and its promoters was that of, somehow, showing a profit for the adventurers (that is, stockholders). It is thought that the Company gained great strength from being based on the comparatively vast resources of London, rather than on the slender funds which were all that Ralegh and the out-ports (Plymouth, etc.) had been able to raise for Roanoke; nevertheless even Londoners did not like throwing good money after bad. And profit proved very hard to come by. Consequently, after the glorious dispatch (and apparent failure) of the first few voyages, investors grew wary. The Company, whose original members could not, by themselves, raise more money, had already expanded its membership, selling shares at £12 10s. each and granting special privileges to those who would buy two or four such shares. In 1612 it hit on the idea of running a lottery. Royal permission was given, and until 1621, when the permission was revoked, the lottery was 'the real and substantial food by which Virginia hath been nourished'. Its ending was a leading cause of the collapse of the Company, which came about in 1624. With a treasury emptied by the insatiable requirements of the colony and its leaders at bitter odds, the organization had outlived its usefulness. Virginia became a colony under the direct government of the King.

But before then the Company had redoubled its services to Virginia. During its first and greatest period its head, or treasurer, was Sir Thomas Smith, the old associate of Ralegh and the leading London merchant. He held office from 1609 to 1618 and conducted affairs ably and sensibly – much more ably than his successors. Several of the most valuable developments of the Company's policy seem to have originated in his time. But in 1618 he was dislodged by a cabal headed by Sir Edwin Sandys, a somewhat impetuous, visionary man. He and Smith had dominated the Company since its beginnings, and their quarrel, which rapidly became many other quarrels involving many other persons – an amoeba of a quarrel – was, when all is said, the

7 See below, p. 25.

root cause of the Company's fall. But perhaps the quarrel and the consequent fall of Smith were necessary. For Sandys, during his brief ascendancy, gave life to two policies which were to be of the very greatest importance for the future of America.

First, he launched the headright system of land allotment. Under this arrangement, which replaced the old system of Company monopoly, a prospective settler received fifty acres for himself and as much again for every additional person whom he brought with him to Virginia – family or servants. The land was to be his and his heirs' forever. In return, he had only to pay a fixed rent, to the Company, or towards the recruitment and support of the clergy, or towards the support of a college, depending on what portion of the public lands he had been allotted. This system spread from Virginia to many of the other colonies and became a Virginian right, as its name indicates, after the fall of the Company which had conferred it as a privilege. Under it, as the figures of population and occupation suggest, the growth of the colony was steady, if not swift: not even the great massacre could long interrupt it. The dream of landed independence in the New World began to come true, and accordingly the lure of Virginia was strengthened.

This reform was at least as important as the other with which Sandys' name is associated: the establishment, under the Company's patronage, of the General Assembly of the colony, the Virginian parliament, in which representatives of the settlers – called, for this purpose, burgesses – met, from 1619 onwards, to discuss and pass upon their common affairs. The rise of this body was very swift. It took almost fewer years than the House of Commons took centuries to reach maturity. By 1635, in which year the burgesses deposed a Governor of Virginia, it had become the central institution of the colony. Such precocity demands explanation.

The fact is that it would have been impossible to govern the colony, once private enterprise and private landholding had been sanctioned, without machinery for consulting the colonists and obtaining their assent to proposed measures. The mutinous strain in the earliest settlers – men who were facing death and whose only hope lay in cooperation – has already been stressed. The same strain was to express itself again and again in Virginian history, right down to the Revolution, if not beyond.[8] The King had no army in Virginia, while the Virginians not only had arms but a very lively sense of their own interests. When in difficulty, they could always vanish for a time into the unknown wilderness. The assertion of authority by force was thus even more difficult than it was in England. Some machinery of consent, of compromise, was therefore a governmental necessity, and was early recognized as such, first by the royal Governors and then by the King

8 When in 1861 Robert E. Lee agonized over the necessity of choosing between his country and his state and decided for the latter, he was acting in that state's oldest, and most insurgent, tradition.

himself (in 1639). Such necessity would have made itself felt even without the rather weak English representative tradition, or the originality of Sir Edwin Sandys. But he and the Company deserve credit for being the first to accept the facts; for the machinery of consent is, of course, the very essence of the Western tradition of freedom, and was to have an extraordinary flowering on American soil. The root and stem of that flower were the institutions set up in Virginia and New England in the early seventeenth century.

The hard-won arts of survival on the frontier and the wise dispositions of the Company largely account, then, for the success of the third attempt to colonize Virginia. But not all the intelligence in the world can prevail without the means of success. And until 1612 it seemed at times as if there were no such means. It was not just that Virginia seemed fatally lacking in those resources which would guarantee a profit to the Company's shareholders; it seemed lacking in the resources needed to support the colonists themselves. It was true that, given the fertility of the land, they might grow enough to feed and clothe themselves; but if subsistence farming was to be the destiny of Virginians, there was no sense in having come so far: it was available at home. Right until the end of the twentieth century, the chief lure of North America for prospective immigrants was the opportunity for a higher standard of living. So unless the colony could really promise such an opportunity, it would fail. And all promises would be delusory unless a way could be found by which Virginia could pay, with her exports, for the goods which she would for long be obliged to import. In the early seventeenth century these goods were almost everything, from books to whipsaws, from armour to vinegar, which the colonists could either need or desire.

John Smith and the Company alike tried to solve this problem by encouraging silk-manufacturing, glass-manufacturing, soap-manufacturing, the export of timber products, of grain, of wine, of anything but the one thing which proved to be the third necessity for the salvation of Virginia: tobacco. This they fiercely opposed, in the teeth of the colonists' insistence on producing almost nothing else. For the dangers of an economy absolutely dominated by a single staple crop were as clear in the seventeenth century as they are nowadays. Dependence on one primary product leaves the producers at the mercy of the market, with its recurring gluts and lowered prices, and its recurring shortage of money. Primary producers are normally at the mercy of their customers anyway: but if they have diversified their products they can at least hope to live off the sales of the others when the sales of one – say, cocoa – have declined, in volume or in value. To these theoretical objections may be added the detail that the seventeenth-century world market was far from encouraging to the Virginians. Smoking was by no means a novel disease. Indians, of course, throughout both Americas, smoked. From them the habit spread to Portugal (1558), Spain (1559) and, through the ubiquitous sea-dogs, to England in 1565. Inevitably, it was Sir Walter Ralegh who made tobacco fashionable. He started to smoke after the first Roanoke expedition and 'took a pipe of tobacco a little before he went to the scaffold'. His example meant that his dread sovereign's thunders against sotweed, as it was sometimes called, or 'this chopping herb of hell', were thunders in vain. John Rolfe, Pocahontas's husband, the first to grow tobacco in Virginia (1612) and to ship it to England, was himself a habitual smoker. He can have been under little illusion that the Virginian leaf would find it easy to compete with West Indian, Spanish or even English-grown tobacco. And in fact by 1630 the Virginians had helped to cause a glut on the world's market.

Rolfe and the others felt, however, that they had little choice. Tobacco could be sold at a profit, though the profit might be uncertain, irregular and low. Anyone could grow it. To the unskilled Virginians these two arguments were irresistible. They took the plunge, and soon the first great boom in American history was under way. At one stage even the streets of Jamestown were sown with tobacco; and the zeal to plant more and more greatly encouraged the spread of population up the James river and, in the thirties, up and down the coast, on every inlet between the river Potomac and the Dismal Swamp. This movement was in part caused by the fact that tobacco exhausted the soil in seven years, so that tobacco planters were constantly in search of new lands. This explains also the steady move westward of Virginians in the seventeenth and eighteenth centuries and the eventual ruin of Virginia when, at the beginning of the nineteenth century, the state had run out of fresh land suitable for cultivation.

Thus the destiny of Virginia was fixed. Prices went down, production went up: in 1619 the colony produced 20,000 pounds of tobacco at three shillings a pound, in 1639, 1,500,000 pounds at threepence. A year later the population of the colony was over 10,000, making Virginia the largest English settlement (which it remained until the Revolution). Its life, whether economic or social, was dominated by a numerous yeoman-planter class: not until the next century was tobacco to support an aristocracy.

Before that time it had become plain that tobacco had settled Virginia's fate in another fundamental matter. The history of agrarian society, until the coming of the machine age, was everywhere dominated by the tension between the desire of most men to be independent farmers and the power of a few men to compel them to be dependent labourers. From age to age, country to country, the upper hand lay now with one side, now with another, as geography, population and technological pressures determined. In Virginia the issue was long in doubt. On the one hand the most profitable growth of tobacco demanded, in the long run, large estates and cheap, plentiful labour. On the other hand the English population was very small, and every male member of it was determined to be, if not rich, then at least independent, through the cultivation of tobacco – if need be on plantations no bigger than could be worked by one family. This determination kept up the price of labour and held down the possible profits of tobacco, to the point, it might be argued, of endangering the colony's survival. Various remedies were tried, the most important being the system of indentures, by which servants were brought out from England at the planters' expense, bound to service for a term of years, and then given their freedom and a little land. But indentures proved unsatisfactory: the servants had constantly to be replaced, were frequently disobedient and unreliable, and as frequently ran away and made good their escape.

However, a solution was found, and it may be wondered why it was not found sooner, as Europeans had been buying African slaves since the fifteenth century and carrying them to the Americas since early in the sixteenth. Sir John Hawkins had shipped slaves to the Spanish colonies in the 1560s and found an eager market for them. Land, staple crops, and cheap labour – the three essentials of what became the central economic institution of the New World, the plantation (a word whose very meaning narrowed to fit the new facts) – were in place in Spanish and Portuguese America by the mid-sixteenth century, but it took a long process of trial and error before their joint potential was realized, and it was only in 1600 or thereabouts that Africans in tens of thousands began to be imported annually to work the great estates of Brazil and the Caribbean. Sugar, eclipsing silver and gold, became the most lucrative commodity of Atlantic trade, but tobacco, cotton and dyestuffs also figured largely from the start. The English soon got the idea: in the 1640s, Barbados emerged as their first, immensely profitable, sugar colony. It is no credit to their memory that the slave-labour system, as they adapted it, was even crueller than the Hispanic variety, and was debased further by prejudice against people who were black.

Dutch traders brought Africans to Virginia for the first time in 1619, and more followed, in tiny numbers, over the next few decades. For the first two generations, Africans were treated, it seems, much like other indentured servants, even (in some cases) to the distribution of land to them when their time of service was up. One of them, Anthony Johnson, is recorded as a freeman owning cattle and 250 acres in 1650.[9] Perhaps, while African-Americans were few, the Virginians did not think to treat them as anything other than fellow human beings. But after the Restoration of Charles II in 1660 the planters could no longer be blind to the opportunities suggested by the example of the Caribbean sugar islands, which now took African slaves in huge numbers with correspondingly huge profits. The price of tobacco was still falling rapidly as new lands came into production, for instance in the colony of Maryland, founded in 1632 to the great indignation of the Virginians, who saw it as a rival (which indeed it was). Because sotweed was so cheap, and because of the growing prosperity of the English people at large, smoking became an ever more general habit in England;[10] the market was limitless, and the producers could make vast fortunes,

9 Robin Blackburn, *The Making of New World Slavery* (London, 1997), p. 240.
10 Jordan Goodman, *Tobacco in History* (London, 1993), pp. 60–61.

provided that they kept their costs down – their labour costs above all.

The turning point came with the first of the great American uprisings, Bacon's Rebellion, in 1676. As leader of the poorer planters, Nathaniel Bacon, a distant relation of the great Francis, seized control of Virginia from the royal Governor, Sir George Berkeley, on the grounds that Berkeley opposed making war on the Susquehanna Indians and seizing their lands. Bacon and his following were true revolutionaries, planning to overturn the political and social structure of the colony, abolish the poll tax, and enlist poor freemen, indentured servants and African slaves in their forces. They burned Jamestown to the ground. But Bacon died of dysentery, and Berkeley then rallied enough strength to suppress the rebellion. To prevent any recurrence of these events, royal authority was placed firmly on the side of the richer settlers; their attempts to grab all the best land in Virginia were endorsed, and Africans were rapidly excluded from the privileges of civil society (if free) or thrust down into hopeless servitude (if slaves). A new gentry emerged, which quickly enriched itself by its effective monopoly of land, labour and political power. The price would be paid, for nearly two centuries, by the slaves. It was a tragic development, but given the combination of tobacco, a hierarchical social structure both in England and her colonies, and the greed of seventeenth-century Englishmen, it was probably inevitable.

4 The Planting of New England
1604–c. 1675

Who would true Valour see
Let him come hither;
One here will Constant be,
Come Wind, come Weather.
There's no *Discouragement*,
Shall make him once *Relent*,
His first avow'd *Intent*,
To be a Pilgrim.

John Bunyan, *The Pilgrim's Progress*

Those that love their own chimney corner and dare not go far beyond their own towns' end shall never have the honour to see the wonderful works of Almighty God.

The Reverend Francis Higginson, 1629

The accession of Elizabeth I to the throne of England in 1558 brought with it what proved to be the decisive victory of Protestantism; but scarcely was it won when the word *Puritan* began to be heard, in allusion to a party within the national church which held that the work of reformation was not complete when the Pope had been rejected, the monasteries dissolved, the mass abolished and the Book of Common Prayer imposed.

Inevitably the authorities saw the existence of this party as a political problem. As has been stated,[1] the Renaissance state existed to secure its subjects against civil war and invasion. The Tudor dynasty rammed home this point explicitly, endlessly. Anarchy, battle and usurpation had brought them the Crown of England; their propaganda against these evils – which found its most brilliant expression in certain plays of Shakespeare – was incessant. The Tudors also saw clearly that if subjects were left to themselves

1 See above, pp. 5–6.

they would make their sovereign's religious opinions the touchstone of their loyalty. To monarchs convinced of their right and duty to rule it was intolerable that civil peace, their reigns, perhaps even their lives, should be at the mercy of turbulent fanatics. The inference was clear. Not only must religion teach the duty of obedience to the prince and submission to the social order over which he (or she) presided. The national church must be, for safety's sake, of royal ordering both in form and doctrines; it must be subordinate to royal purposes. To Queen Elizabeth, at least, the rightness of the arrangement was clear. She was not, she knew, a demanding sovereign: she would make no windows into men's souls. Let her subjects swear allegiance to her as Supreme Governor of the church and all would be well. It was her duty, it was her God-given exclusive privilege, to rule the realm, to take the decisions necessary for its safety and her own. Therefore to disobey her too conspicuously, or to question her decisions too publicly, or too frequently to demand more than she was prepared to give, was to verge on disloyalty, if not rebellion.

Unfortunately many Englishmen and Englishwomen did demand more. Protestantism had a built-in democratic tendency in that it encouraged the literate to search the Scriptures for themselves and act in the light of what they found there. Thus strengthened by what they took to be God's word, the Puritans frequently refused to conform their conduct to the Queen's views: some of them dared to rebuke her to her face. Nor was even she wholly reasonable, consistent or realistic. Her own religious tastes (it would probably be excessive to speak of her convictions) were conservative, and as her reign continued she gradually found bishops who, sharing them, were happy to attempt to force them on her subjects. Hence the promotion to Canterbury of the bullying Whitgift and to London of the policeman-like Bancroft. Furthermore Elizabeth, like almost everyone else, clung to the old medieval dream of religious unity. The Church of England must be the Church of all Englishmen: the whole nation at prayer. She would not admit that the ideals of uniformity and comprehensiveness were at war with each other, but even in her lifetime Archbishop Whitgift's conservatism and rigidity drove many of the devout to 'separate' from the sinful national church – to resign from it, as it were, and organize little 'separatist' churches of their own (they were called 'conventicles'). Bishops grew more and more unpopular; and in the seventeenth century the ideal of a comprehensive national church crashed to the ground, bringing the dream of national religious uniformity (whether episcopalian or presbyterian) to ruin with it.

At the beginning of Elizabeth's reign the Puritans were, in a sense, no less (and no more) than the Protestant party itself. They saw that the country was still for the most part either Catholic or indifferent. Their business was to bring the full Reformation to pass; to achieve the conversion of England. For years and years they tried to persuade their Queen to join them in the work by reorganizing the church on presbyterian lines and by using her unquestioned right to compel her subjects to be saved. They quite agreed with her that a uniform, all-embracing national church was demanded by both reason and religion; only it must be governed on the lines that Calvin inferred from the Bible. Elizabeth, however, steadily refused to co-operate. So the Puritans were compelled, after some nasty brushes with the law, to turn from political to purely pastoral labours. As they were not to have the chance to compel their countrymen to come in, they tried to preach them in. By 1603 they were succeeding spectacularly.

The English Reformation had many causes, but its soul was the desire to renew the Christian life of the people, and Puritanism was that soul's instrument. Episcopacy was resisted because it acted as an umbrella for such abuses as pluralism, non-resident clergy, corrupt church courts and a 'dumb dog', non-preaching, unlearned ministry, all of which came between the English and the good news of salvation. Even before their rebuff at the Queen's hands the Puritan ministers had shown themselves adept at pastoral work; thereafter they moved through the land, devoted to uprooting sin from the hearts of the congregations. Their chief tool was the sermon. It had played little part in pre-Reformation church life. Now a conscientious minister would expect to have to preach once every day, and at least twice on the Sabbath; and preaching was extraordinarily popular. It was something new, and people flocked to hear good speakers – so much so that 'gadding about to sermons' was a vice much denounced by the conservative.[2] But the godly had the last word. Serious and intelligent, they had an influence on their communities out of all proportion to their numbers, though those increased rapidly. Like young Siegfried with the broken sword Nothung, the Puritans ground down the English soul to powder and then re-forged it to heroic temper. Nor is this only metaphor. The central Puritan experience was that of conversion, when a man's sins 'came upon him like armed men, and the tide of his thoughts was turned'. Conversion struck in many ways, as we learn from the innumerable fragments of autobiography left us: from a tract sold by a pedlar, from an insult hurled by a woman in the street (thus 'drunken Perkins' became 'painful Perkins', a celebrated preacher) – most usually from some 'affectionate' sermon. Conversion was the moment when God's grace entered the soul and began the work of its redemption. It was a moment predestined from Creation, as St Paul taught:[3] 'Whom he did predestinate, them he also called;' it was the moment when Hell's gates closed: 'Whom he called, them he also justified;' the moment when the doors of the Celestial City opened: 'Whom he justified, them he also glorified.' It was a moment that enlightened and rejoiced the lives of tens of thousands of plain people. It assured them

2 The successful Puritan insistence on a preaching ministry explains why in America, which has largely taken its religion from the Puritans, the term 'preacher' is so widely used as a synonym for priest, clergyman, parson or minister.
3 Epistle to the Romans viii, 30.

that although life would continue to daunt them with its problems and temptations, they had only to fight ceaselessly against sin within them and without them, and whatever wounds they took in the battle, victory was sure.[4]

It is easy to mistake the nature of this Puritanism. The word today generally connotes a loveless respectability, a Philistine narrowness, Biblical idolatry or a neurotic hatred of other people's pleasures. 'Show me a Puritan,' said H. L. Mencken, 'and I'll show you a son-of-a-bitch.' But while it would be absurd to deny that a certain censoriousness was present in Puritanism from the start, it would be equally absurd to let the degenerate aspect it wears today conceal the splendours of its prime. Certain of their salvation, the best Puritans were brave, cheerful, intelligent and hard-working. One of their preachers urged them to be 'merry in the Lord, and yet without lightness; sad and heavy in heart for their own sins, and the abominations of the land, and yet without discouragement or dumpishness'. The quality of Puritan piety is best savoured in *The Pilgrim's Progress.* John Bunyan, the old Ironside, knew how to make his simple image – one that had long been dear to Puritans, indeed to all Englishmen: Hakluyt's continuator called his book *Purchas, His Pilgrims*[5] – of life as a journey and a battle, not only true, but startlingly important. It is easy, reading Bunyan, to feel what immense strength those of his faith derived from their belief that the promises Christ made were literally true. For them, the trumpets were sure to sound on the other side.

What could kings, queens and archbishops do against such people? Very little; and for the most part they prudently attempted less. Puritanism was left to seep peacefully through England. But after the Hampton Court Conference in 1604 Policeman Bancroft, now Archbishop of Canterbury, was unwise enough to attempt a little persecution. 'Apparitors and pursuivants and the commissary courts' – the whole detested machinery of ecclesiastical officialdom – were turned against those, within and without the church, who were less than perfect conformists to the officially prescribed practices; among them a little band of Separatists living in villages on the borders of Lincolnshire, Yorkshire and Nottinghamshire. The leaders of this conventicle were educated, but its members were for the most part lowly, sincere, literate but otherwise untutored folk. Their irregular piety

---

4 New England Puritanism, for various reasons, decided that conversion was a slow process, not a lightning flash; but in this, as in several other important respects, it differed sharply from the mainstream – from its English predecessors, and its American successors.

5 See also Ralegh's lines written in prison under sentence of death:

Give me my scallop shell of quiet,
   My staff of faith to walk upon,
My scrip of joy, immortal diet,
   My bottle of salvation,
My gown of glory, hope's true gage!
And thus I'll take my pilgrimage.

was thus doubly offensive to the authorities, with their memories of Tyler, Cade and Kett.[6]

So

some were taken and clapped up in prison, others had their houses beset and watched night and day, and hardly escaped their hands; and the most were fain to flee and leave their houses and habitations, and the means of their livelihood.[7]

Understandably, these religious Lincolnshire poachers decided to emigrate. With some difficulty in 1607 and 1608 they slipped over in groups to Holland, 'where they heard was freedom of religion for all men', led by Pastor Robinson and Elder William Brewster.

Robinson and Brewster took their followers to Leyden, where with much difficulty they scratched a living for the next ten years or so. But Leyden could not be a permanent resting-place. There was a danger of Spanish conquest; the prospect of continuing grinding poverty was a discouragement; the children of these resolute English threatened to turn Dutch, not only as to language, which was bad enough, but as to religion, which was far worse (for the Dutch, though Calvinists, refused to keep a properly gloomy Sabbath). Finally, there seemed to be small chance in Leyden of achieving that really remarkable labour for God of which the more ardent Separatists dreamed, hemmed in as they were by the world. It would be better to move on again. Where to? England was still closed, its churches, for the most part, corrupt. Their minds began to turn to 'some of those vast and unpeopled countries of America'.

It was not really surprising. The idea of a religious refuge across the water was tolerably obvious. The French Protestant leader, Admiral Coligny, had sent a party to settle in Florida as early as 1560 (though as the Separatists knew, it had been speedily snuffed out by the Spaniards). More particularly, the exiles were by no means cut off from English news, and these were the great years of the Virginia adventure, as we have seen. The Virginia Company of London, in its quest for funds, was advertising itself far and wide. John Smith was still busy. In 1612 he published his map of Virginia, '*with a description of its Commodities, People, Government, and Religion*'. In 1614 he was employed by the Company to explore the North Atlantic coast from Penobscot Bay to Cape Cod. He learned enough to make another good map, to give the region a name, New England, and to begin a lengthy literary campaign extolling the excellences of those parts for settlement: thus in 1616 he published his *Description of New England* and in 1620 his

6 Nor, in view of what was to happen after 1642, can this theory, that popular religion was necessarily subversive, be regarded as altogether mistaken.
7 *Of Plymouth Plantation*, by William Bradford, edited by Samuel Eliot Morison (New York, 1966), p. 10. Bradford (1590–1657) was to be for many years the Governor, and the historian, of the first Separatist settlement in New England. I quote him extensively.

New England Trials.[8] In fact he became a full-fledged 'booster', a type we have met before and will again. Nevertheless, the Captain, as was his habit, told few lies, in spite of his enthusiasm. He could truthfully boast, for example, that

you shall scarce find any bay, shallow shore or cove of sand, where you may not take many clams or lobsters, or both at your pleasure, and in many places load your boat if you please; nor isles where you find not fruits, birds, crabs, and mussels, or all of them; for taking at a low water cod, cusk, halibut, skate, turbot, mackerel, or such like are taken plentifully in divers sandy bays, store of mullet, bass, and divers other sorts of such excellent fish as many as their net can hold: no river where there is not plenty of sturgeon, or salmon, or both, all which are to be had in abundance observing but their seasons: but if a man will go at Christmas to gather cherries in Kent, though there be plenty in summer, he may be deceived; so here these plenties have each their seasons, as I have expressed.[9]

In this and other passages throughout his work he gave vent to his settled belief that a fortune, indeed an empire, could be founded on the fisheries of New England: Portugal, Spain, Provence and Italy would all provide ready markets for 'our dry fish, green fish, sturgeon, mullet, caviare, and buttango'. 'Therefore (honorable and worthy countrymen) let not the meanness of the word Fish distaste you, for it will afford as good gold as the mines of Guiana or Tumbatu, with less hazard and charge, and more certainty and facility.'

The Leyden community might well be encouraged by such talk. Furthermore, these were the years of a burgeoning Dutch interest in North America. In 1609 Sir Henry Hudson, an English mariner in Dutch pay, had rediscovered Manhattan Island and, behind it, a huge river which now bears his name. He thus opened up a rich fur-bearing region to European trade, and was soon followed. In 1613 the Dutch sailed 150 miles up the Hudson and founded a trading-post called Fort Nassau (later, Orange; later still, Albany; today, the capital of New York state). They also began to trade on the Delaware river, whose mouth is 150 miles or so south of that of the Hudson. In 1621 their activities culminated in the foundation of the Dutch West India Company, much on the lines of the various English companies: it began to send out settlers in 1624, and in 1625–6 founded a colony on Manhattan Island, called New Amsterdam. To increase its security the director of the enterprise, Peter Minuit, bought the island from the local

---

8 The second edition of which (1622) contains interesting material describing the first days of the Plymouth settlement.
9 *The General History of Virginia, New England, and the Summer Isles*, Book VI. This passage was not published until 1624, after the Pilgrims had settled in New England and sent back accounts of the cold winters and shortage of food. Smith had the true booster attitude to such faintheartedness. If all was not Paradise today, it would be tomorrow.

Indians with sixty guilders' worth of miscellaneous goods. This transaction is now legendary as 'the best real-estate deal in history'.

The Leyden congregation was approached by the Dutch, looking for worthy settlers, when word of their plans got about. But Dutch stirrings were not very far advanced when Pastor Robinson's flock began its deliberations in 1616 or 1617. And neither Virginia nor New England could seem better than daunting. For the Separatists had none of the resources of the great companies; their only reliance could be on their own characters and on the God whom they were trying so earnestly to please. Trusting in that God, and in His blessing on such a great and honourable action, they refused to be daunted. They agreed on the principle of emigration to the New World and on an application to the Virginia Company of London for a patent to erect a 'particular plantation' on its territory. These plantations were the latest device of the London Company for encouraging, at small cost to its exhausted exchequer, more of the settlers of whom it was in desperate need.[10] In effect the organizers of a particular plantation were given such rights as to make it almost an independent colony. In return, it was hoped, they would provide supplies and colonists. The idea became a favourite of Sir Edwin Sandys. It so happened that Elder Brewster's father had been Sandys' brother's tenant at Scrooby (a relationship that was closer than it sounds); and that Sandys himself had puritanical sympathies. The conclusion was obvious to both parties, and matters should have gone swiftly forward to a conclusion.

They did not, even with royal encouragement;[11] the struggle to organize the desperate voyage went on for two years, far into the summer of 1620. News came that another Separatist congregation, from Amsterdam, sailing to America on a similar errand, had met with total disaster at sea, 130 perishing: this must have lowered spirits at Leyden, though voices were not wanting to attribute the disaster to the failings, moral and ecclesiastical, of the expedition's leader. Money was short, and Brewster, by tactlessly printing a religious tract attacking James VI and I's church policy in Scotland, alienated the authorities and had to go into hiding. But 'at length, after much travail and these debates, all things were got ready and provided'. They had bought *Speedwell*, a small ship of sixty tons, at Leyden, to carry them to England; they also hoped to make use of her in America. A larger ship, *Mayflower*, was hired to carry the greater part of the company and its stores across the Atlantic. She was to meet *Speedwell* at Southampton. Brewster would be the spiritual guide of the journeyers, for Robinson must stay in Leyden with the majority of the congregation who had declined the voyage, at any rate for the present.

---

10 At this date the Company owed £75,000: a debt incurred in its attempt to settle its own lands itself.

11 James I asked how the settlers proposed to live. 'By fishing,' was the reply. 'So God have my soul,' said the King, ' 'tis an honest trade, 'twas the apostles' own calling.'

And the time being come that they must depart, they were accompanied with most of their brethren out of the city, unto a town sundry miles off called Delftshaven, where the ship lay ready to receive them. So they left that goodly and pleasant city which had been their resting place near twelve years; but they knew they were pilgrims, and looked not much on those things, but lift up their eyes to the heavens, their dearest country, and quieted their spirits.

This was on 22 July 1620.

Even now there were more delays. *Speedwell* proved unseaworthy (Bradford thought her crew had sabotaged her), but it was long before hope of her repair was abandoned. Only on 16 September did *Mayflower* finally sail from Plymouth. She carried, besides the officers and crew, 105 persons, of whom thirty-five only were certainly Pilgrims (as the Separatists may now, following their historian, properly be called). The rest had been found by the London merchants whom the Pilgrims had induced to finance their voyage, and were indentured servants or persons of particular skills likely to be useful in the new colony (the lessons of Jamestown had sunk in, though the Pilgrims had dared to refuse John Smith's offer to come with them). The ship was heavily laden with furniture, pots, pans and provisions; some livestock, it appears – pigs, goats and chickens, two dogs (of course), no cattle. The ship herself is described as a 'staunch, chunky, slow-sailing vessel, square-rigged, double-decked, broad abeam, with high upper structure at the stern, the passengers occupying cabins or quarters between decks, or, in the case of the women and children, in rough cabins forward below the poop'.[12] She was about ninety feet long, twenty-five feet wide at her waist. She boasted twelve cannon. Her upper deck leaked in bad weather, and she was very overcrowded, having perhaps thirty more people on board than she should. During the voyage she encountered the autumnal gales, and her passengers were extremely seasick. At one point there was serious danger of the vessel foundering. Altogether, it was in conditions very like those of the later steerage, as well as those of the earlier Virginia voyages, that the Pilgrims crossed the Atlantic. In this sense they had a typical emigrant experience. The single advantage of *Mayflower* was that she was a 'sweet' ship: having been engaged in the wine trade, her hold was not rank with the smells and diseases left behind by animal cargoes. The result was a healthy voyage: of the entire complement of 149 persons, 'only' five died. But food was insufficient and not good, the voyage was overlong, confinement on shipboard was even longer. When the landing in America had been made and the winter had come, the mortality from scurvy and similar complaints was frightful, carrying off half the crew and half the passengers, including all but four of the eighteen married women. Many of these deaths must be attributed to what was suffered on *Mayflower*.

12 Andrews, *The Colonial Period*, Vol. i, p. 269 fn. 1. The description is based on likelihoods: no plan or picture of *Mayflower* survives, but she was a typical merchant ship of the period.

So when, at daybreak on 9 November, they made landfall, 'they were not a little joyful'. The tip of Cape Cod, fifty miles out from the mainland, must have looked much as it does today: a waste of tumbled white sand dunes, patchily held together by stands of scrubby oak and pine. The Pilgrims could not settle there, but they took water aboard and then set out to look for a friendlier shore. They hoped to sail south and settle on the Hudson, in what was then termed 'the northern parts of Virginia'; but wind and rocks forced them back into what is now Provincetown harbour on Cape Cod. From there various reconnaissance parties went out in search of food and a suitable site for inhabitation, and on 11 December a party led by Bradford found its way, in a blinding snowstorm, into Plymouth harbour (first discovered by John Smith, named by him and the future Charles I). Plymouth was chosen to be their new home, and on 16 December *Mayflower* entered the harbour.[13] On 25 December, ignoring any popish significance of the date, they set to work to erect 'the first house for common use to receive them and their goods'. Jamestown had acquired a sister.

The Pilgrims' case was grim enough. Bradford says:

And for the season it was winter, and they that know the winters of that country know them to be sharp and violent, and subject to cruel and fierce storms, dangerous to travel to known places, much more to search an unknown coast. Besides, what could they see but a hideous and desolate wilderness, full of wild beasts and wild men – and what multitudes there might be of them they knew not . . . What could now sustain them but the Spirit of God and His grace? May not and ought not the children of these fathers rightly say: 'Our fathers were Englishmen, which came over this great ocean, and were ready to perish in this wilderness; but they cried unto the Lord, and He heard their voice and looked on their adversity,' etc. 'Let them therefore praise the Lord, because He is good: and His mercies endure forever.'

The Pilgrims had to suffer: agony followed their arrival, an agony which did not abate until 1625, when, Bradford tells us, the settlers first tasted 'the sweetness of the country'. But in some respects they were lucky. The winter was mild for the region, and the Indians, having been immensely reduced in number by a plague, were less dangerous than those of Virginia. Near-contemporary accounts,[14] though admittedly written as encouraging propaganda, do make it seem that conditions were less unbearable in Plymouth than they had been, ten years previously, in Virginia. For one thing, the Pilgrims were made of better stuff than the Virginians. They survived, and thus achieved their historic mission.

13 Early in the eighteenth century a large rock was identified as the first bit of America touched by the Pilgrims' feet. Being unconvincingly far up Plymouth beach, it had to be moved down to the water's edge to satisfy visitors' notions of how history ought to happen.
14 For example, that in the second edition of *New England's Trials*.

For New Plymouth was not a colony that could easily or quickly grow. The Separatists were a minority of the inhabitants to begin with, but they early subdued their fellows to their ways; yet their ecclesiastical doctrines, which in effect denied the authenticity, the purity, of all other congregations whatever, except those of the remaining exiles in Leyden and Amsterdam, were bound to repel many, even many other Puritans, who might have joined them. Then, the economic basis of the colony was too weak and narrow to support any ambitious edifice: not until 1648 did the Pilgrims pay off the debts in which their voyage had involved them. Farming and fishing (the soil being thin and Plymouth far from the best fishing-grounds) alike at first disappointed the hopes that had been placed in them: only the fur-trade kept the infant colony in being. In a small way, it is true, it throve: in 1628 the town presented a respectable appearance to a Dutch visitor, who has left us details of the well-built wooden houses, the gardens, the stockade and the cannon; by 1630 its population stood at nearly 300, by 1637 it was nearly 550. But Virginia, at the same dates, had a population of more than 2,500 and more than 5,000 respectively. Plymouth, with its population of, in the main, unintellectual and socially undistinguished zealots, could save itself, indeed prosper, by its exertions; its influence could spread only by example. There would be nothing like the steady march of population across country from the first settlement that so strongly characterized the Virginian development; though it is worth noting that in other respects the common features of American experience made themselves felt. Thus, in Plymouth, as in Jamestown, an attempt to have all things in common was made, and failed. Bradford tells us:

So they began to think how they might raise as much corn as they could, and obtain a better crop than they had done, that they might not still thus languish in misery. At length, after much debate of things, the Governor[15] (with the advice of the chiefest among them) gave way that they should set corn every man for his own particular, and in that regard trust themselves . . . And so assigned every family a parcel of land . . . This had very good success, for it made all hands very industrious, so as much corn was planted than otherwise would have been by any means the Governor or any other could use, and saved him a great deal of trouble, and gave far better content. The women now went willingly into the field, and took their little ones with them to set corn; which before would allege weakness and inability.

Once more it had been shown that, whatever their faith in a common road to heaven, Jacobean Englishmen desired individual economic salvation on earth, and that the only way to secure their prosperity and cohesion in the New World was by assuaging their land-hunger: which, fortunately, was easy. In New England, as in Virginia, the most alluring advertisement for the colonies was to be that which we find in such remarks as William

15 Bradford himself.

Hilton's, made from Plymouth in 1621: 'We are all freeholders, the rent day doth not trouble us . . .'

And, as in Virginia, the political necessities of American life also made themselves felt promptly. When the *Mayflower* company contemplated its future after reaching Cape Cod it seemed plain that such a group, far from all the sanctions and blessings of regular English government, could not thrive without an agreed constitution. Accordingly the Saints (remembering the covenant by which they, like all Separatist churches, had established themselves) and the Strangers (that is, the non-Saints) agreed on the *Mayflower* Compact – signed on 11 November by most of the company's adult males. In content it was no more than a covenant constituting the signatories a body politic, which would issue and abide by its own laws; but the manner in which it was arrived at was, if not democratic, at least self-governing, like the Separatist churches;[16] and the constitution which evolved from it, though in substance paternalistic (for the Governor and his council made all decisions), had similar characteristics: notably the provision for the annual election of the Governor by all properly qualified adult males. Seen against a modern American background there is nothing very striking in the Pilgrims' political arrangements; but set against the background of Stuart England they are eloquent of what was different about the New World. Government, indeed survival, was possible there only with the consent of the governed; political institutions therefore became in the first instance instruments for securing that consent. The *Mayflower* Compact was the first of innumerable agreements arrived at by the American people as they founded new settlements. Its example was unconsciously but exactly followed in seventeenth-century New England, in eighteenth-century Kentucky, throughout revolutionary America, and everywhere on the nineteenth-century frontier: in Texas, California, Iowa and Oregon. These agreements enabled generations of settlers to feel that their lives, property and prospects were secure under the rule of law, and they conditioned American political assumptions, so that the leaders of revolutionary Maryland could assert without fear of contradiction that 'All government of right originates from the people, is founded in compact only.'[17] All this prepared the way for the greatest compact of all, the Constitution of the United States. The Pilgrims were thus forerunners of even more than was prophesied to them from England in 1623, when their associates wrote: 'Let it not be grievous unto you that you have been instruments to break

16 Or, indeed, any of the truly Reformed churches. Prof. Patrick Collinson, in his *Elizabethan Puritan Movement* (London, 1967, p. 94), has well remarked that 'Protestantism was at least potentially a levelling principle.' The history of New England shows this potential becoming actual. Henry Jacobs showed the significance of Puritan church organization when he wrote from Leyden in 1611 that 'each congregation is an entire and independent body-politic, endured with power immediately under and from Christ'. No wonder the descendants of these people turned into republicans and democrats.

17 See H. S. Commager, *The Empire of Reason* (London, 1978), pp. 178–84.

the ice for others who come after with less difficulty; the honour shall be yours to the world's end.' The Pilgrims had shown what could be done; and others soon profited from their example.

For England had now entered on a half-century of chronic trade depression, and her greatest export, cloth – especially in its traditional form, the so-called Old Draperies – was hardest hit of all. An ill wind blew throughout East Anglia and the South-West, where Puritanism, outside London, was at its strongest; and presently a new force began to make itself felt in the Church of England: the bigoted moderation of William Laud, created bishop in 1621, Bishop of London in 1628, Archbishop of Canterbury in 1633. Over-zealous and over-sure of himself he was, in the end, to do as much as any man (next the King) to bring down the old order in England; but before that he mightily helped to bring about another important work, the Great Migration of thousands of Puritans to New England, there to be free of him and hold up the model of a Reformed church to their unhappy countrymen at home.

Other impulses too pushed them westwards, as they had pushed the Virginians before: impulses which, throughout this time, were speckling the Atlantic coast, from Newfoundland southwards, with white men's habitations. As a result of the depression, land-hunger and the quest for trade were stronger than ever. Not only that, it was an era when mounting incompetence and remoteness were driving the Stuart monarchy into ruinously arbitrary courses: it was not so good to be an Englishman as it had been. But there can be no doubt that the religious impulse, as such, was predominant, indeed sufficient by itself to account for this 'Puritan Hegira'.[18] It was intimately connected, of course, with the other forces mentioned. Two-fifths of the emigrants seem to have come from the cloth counties. The King's incompetent despotism was a seamless web, oppressing the political and economic as well as the religious life of his subjects, with Star Chamber as well as High Commission, since religion, labour and politics were interfused. But none of this need have been true, and the Puritans would still have sailed. Laud silenced the godly preachers, enforced conformity, frustrated all attempts to puritanize the Church of England from within. More and more the Puritans found God's work to be hampered in England; they must pursue it elsewhere.

It is unnecessary to elaborate the process which led to the great decision. The propaganda of a generation had pointed the way, and the Pilgrims had made it seem practicable. Laud made the matter urgent. Earlier efforts were crowned and superseded by the foundation, in 1629, of the Massachusetts Bay Company, which inherited a struggling plantation at Naumkeag (now Salem) in New England; and in 1630 it put a fleet to sea of eleven ships, carrying 700 passengers, 240 cows, sixty horses, the royal charter of the

18 Bridenbaugh, *Vexed and Troubled Englishmen*, p. 434.

Company (so that self-government was legally possible in New England)[19] and a leader, the Governor of the Company and the colony, John Winthrop (1588–1650), the first great American.

Winthrop was of the same astonishing gentry generation as Pym, Hampden and Oliver Cromwell; nor was his achievement less than theirs. Like Cromwell, he was a decaying gentleman: his estate, Groton in Suffolk, was at the heart of the region injured by the decline of the Old Draperies. Like Cromwell, though he was far from being an ordinary man, an ordinary man could have been made out of him. His natural tastes were those of a straightforward countryman: he liked food, drink and field sports; was extremely uxorious (four wives, sixteen children); hated London. Like Cromwell, his soul had early been fired by Puritanism; like Cromwell, he had little or no sense of humour; like Cromwell, his chance came at the age of forty.

There the resemblance ceases. There were traces of a high generosity and an intellectual distinction in Winthrop which Cromwell never attained. There was no whiff of sulphur about him, none of the Cromwellian blind groping to his destiny. Winthrop was eminently reasonable. He wrestled intelligently with his temptations, in the process discovering the great strength of his character and the joys of a life of challenge. His days were marked throughout by an earnest and honest attempt to mould himself and his society according to the will of God. But he made no impossible demands of himself and his fellows. His religion reflected his character, as a man's religion always does, rather more than it shaped it.

Winthrop was able, hard-working, healthy and, until the call came, obscure: Puritanism enabled him to balance ambition and pleasure, and to accept the narrow confines of his life. Yet in 1629 he was known to a wide circle of Puritan gentry, merchants, lawyers and ministers as a man of great gifts, at peace with himself. He was clearly such a man as the Massachusetts Bay Company needed. Gradually he was drawn into its plans; gradually he accepted the part he might play in them. He set down on paper the arguments in favour of attempting a Puritan plantation in New England. Reasons of ambition and economics were stated; but over all predominated the feeling that, for the faithful of God, the times were bad and getting worse; that God was preparing a judgement against England, 'and who knows, but that God hath provided this place, to be a refuge for many, whom he means to save out of the general destruction'. However, if the old England were, in spite of all, to be saved, it might best be done from the new. 'It was a good service to the Church of the Jews that Joseph and Mary forsook them, that their messiah might be preserved for them against the

19 Great mystery surrounds this charter, the only one of its kind not to specify that the Company headquarters must be in London. How it was obtained with this omission remains unknown. But the matter is less important than many historians suppose. As the history of Virginia and Plymouth shows, self-government *de facto*, if not *de jure*, was inevitable in the North American colonies, whatever charters said or did not say.

times of better service.' And if this undoubtedly honourable work were to succeed, it would need to be undertaken by some men, at least, of education, ability and wealth. Winthrop at last agreed to be the chief of them. His friends had long insisted that they would not stir without him.

The decision once made, his spirit sang within him:

Now thou the hope of Israel, and the sure help of all that come to thee, knit the hearts of thy servants to thyself, in faith and purity. Draw us with the sweetness of thine odours, that we may run after thee, allure us, and speak kindly to thy servants, that thou may possess us as thine own, in the kindness of youth and the love of marriage. Carry us into thy Garden, that we may eat and be filled with those pleasures, which the world knows not: let us hear that sweet voice of thine, my love, my dove, my undefiled. Spread thy skirt over us and cover our deformity, make us sick with thy love. Let us sleep in thine arms, and awake in thy kingdom.

The joyous sense of a divine work to be done carried him on triumphantly to the building of the most remarkable of the English colonies and the establishment of a truly new society in the New World.

The times were with him. At their arrival, the Puritans found, like the Pilgrims before them, that the Indians were agreeably few; and there was no serious interference, let alone attack, from the Dutch or the French. The colony never lacked the essential for success, plentiful recruitment: during the 'Eleven Years Tyranny' some 20,000 Puritans are thought to have crossed to Massachusetts Bay. Many died, many lost heart and returned; but most stayed. The earlier arrivals supplied the later with corn, dressed timber, cattle; in return the latecomers provided the cloth, pots, gunpowder and so on which could not yet be manufactured in New England.

The debt of America to Winthrop and his associates (especially the ministers) can scarcely be overestimated (though it may be misstated). It was not merely that the Governor made all the great decisions of the early days, such as that to establish the seat of government on the Shawmut peninsula, thereafter famous as Boston; or that his cheerful faith sustained the settlers' morale throughout the starving winter after their arrival; or that he generously subsidized the colony from his own pocket. His faith, his programme, his method of government raised some questions, settled others; but overall the great work of the Puritans was the stamping of their character on American society. For the mark, though much altered by time, has proved indelible.

True, in the eyes of the Puritans themselves, their failure was almost as conspicuous as their success. We have seen that one aim of the Great Migration was to provide in the New World a new model of the due form of government, civil and ecclesiastical, by which, when the times mended, the Old World was somehow to be saved. 'We must consider that we shall be as a City upon a Hill,' said Winthrop to the first settlers, 'the eyes of all people are upon us.' A splendid and deservedly famous assertion. Unfortunately it remained a mere assertion. The eyes of all people – even of English people – proved to be looking elsewhere; and from that day to this, when they have from time to time turned to the Bible Commonwealth founded by Winthrop, they have seen more to blame than to admire. Seventy-five years of the Puritan spirit bore the New England settlements as their fruit; but the spirit continued to evolve with the years, leaving the ideas of Winthrop's generation behind, stranded, as it were, on the American shore: looking to a different harvest. Winthrop's city upon a hill was, nevertheless, actually built, organized and maintained against its enemies. Few other Utopias could ever boast as much. No wonder that, in spite of outer neglect and inner backsliding, its citizens continued to be proud of it and of themselves.

It was very much a Separatist Utopia. Not that, before their voyage, many of the Puritans had been of the Pilgrim stripe. As a matter of fact, nothing in the history of English Protestantism is more striking than the extreme and long-enduring reluctance of the Puritans under the Stuarts to be logical and separate from the national church. However zealous for the discipline, few of the ministers and lay Puritans had the martyrs' temperament; and many, even of the most earnest, of those least swayed by material considerations (the discomfort of prison, the comfort of a benefice) could not bring themselves to abandon comprehensiveness and their dear, if sinful, fellow-countrymen, even though they cherished the notion that a church ought only to be a local thing, an exclusive and independent congregation of the saved. The Massachusetts Congregationalists were not voluntary schismatics: they were driven out of their church by Laud.[20] It is not surprising that professed Separatists had been the first to make the greatest break of all, and leave, not just their church, but their country, seeking a new England; and it is a certain testimony to the despair settling like a winter fog over the Puritans in Laudian England that so many of them decided to follow the Pilgrim lead. For by doing so they conceded the Separatist case. They struggled against admitting it: Winthrop and his friends (protesting, maybe, a trifle too much) issued a fulsome declaration of loyalty to the Church of England just before sailing. They had no wish to seem deserters of God's cause in England. But the act of sailing was a sign that they had in fact abandoned it. Geography was too strong. Three thousand miles of ocean, they discovered, left them free (and therefore bound) to follow their religious principles to their logical conclusions without fear or regret. Bishops and the Book of Common Prayer were abandoned.

20 Nor were all Puritans Congregationalists. The other main tendency was Presbyterian and clung to the ideal of a comprehensive, national but Calvinistic church, tightly disciplined from the centre. Understandably, few Presbyterians sailed to Massachusetts, and those who did caused trouble, seeking more influence than they were allowed, and closer ties with England. These Winthrop did not want to allow, for they might hamper New England's freedom to follow its own path for its own good. 'We are bound to keep off whatsoever appears to tend to our ruin or damage,' he said. This attitude was to recur many times in American history.

Ties of sentiment and habit fell away, and non-separating Congregationalism ended. Every New England church was sovereign in its locality, amenable only to the advice of neighbouring churches and the strong arm of the civil authority.

This last was a very severe restriction on the sacred freedom of the churches. It was a much more total surrender to the state than anything which Charles I or Laud were able to impose on the church in England. But Winthrop and the ministers felt they had little choice but to try to square this circle. Heresy and sedition (that is, non-Congregationalist views) would sprout unless some power existed to check them. That power could only be the state, since no church might coerce another, and since the state existed only to further God's clear purpose . . . it was sophistry, but plausible enough. Heresy became a civil offence, like any of the others (such as witchcraft, profanity, blasphemy, idolatry, adultery, sodomy, Sabbath-breaking) with which the courts had to deal. Right liberty, Winthrop carefully explained, was liberty only to do God's will. All other forms of liberty were frowned on. So, arm in arm, the Puritan churches and the Puritan state forced men to be free. It was an enlightened despotism.

Such a system was more acceptable in the religious than in the secular sphere. The bulk of the settlers were happy to believe that the divines whom they had followed from England knew how to steer them all safe to heaven, and supported them and the enforcing secular arm contentedly against such challengers as Roger Williams (1603–83), the founder of Rhode Island colony in 1636, who argued for complete separation between the institutions of church and state, and Anne Hutchinson (1591–1643), who claimed direct inspiration from God. Politics was a different matter. Winthrop launched, and would have liked to continue, an enlightened despotism in this sphere too, but circumstances were too strong for him, and he showed his usual good sense in gracefully giving way to them. The colonists intended to run no risks of forced loans, ship money, billeting or any other arbitrary exactions now that they had got free of Old England. The preachers too, remembering Laud's heavy hand, were all in favour of a strictly limited government in non-ecclesiastical affairs. 'If you tether a beast at night,' said the Reverend John Cotton, 'he knows the length of his tether before morning.'

So in 1632 the settlers insisted on the principle of no taxation without representation (though not in those words). It was agreed that every town was to elect two deputies (like the borough members of the House of Commons) to confer with the Governor and other magistrates (known as assistants) and vote necessary taxes. They also successfully claimed the right to elect the Governor and Deputy. Then in 1634, at the May meeting of the General Court, 'it was ordered, that four general courts should be kept every year, and that the whole body of the freemen should be present only at the court of election of magistrates, etc., and that, at the other three, every town should send their deputies, who should assist in making laws, disposing lands, etc.'. The General Court was, under the charter, the sovereign body both of the Massachusetts Bay Company and of its colony, into which it had merged. Increasingly this court came to resemble the English Parliament. The resemblance was accentuated when, in 1644, it was formally divided into two houses, the magistrates and the deputies.

Winthrop, believing in a truly aristocratic government – 'the best part is always the least and of that best part the wiser is always the lesser', he said – deplored this evolution, but could not end it. The annual election of Governor and other magistrates had brought the joys of electoral politics to the sympathetic soil of North America. Winthrop was twice voted out of the Governorship for a period of years (in 1634 and 1640); and his belief in a flexible, organic government, to be guided by the precedents of its own decisions, was rejected by the colonists, who insisted on a code of written laws – the *Body of Liberties* (1641).[21] Within so few years of its establishment, the Massachusetts plantation had grown into a fully self-governing little republic, having only paper connections with the royal government in England – it was far outside both the protection and the power of Whitehall. But it was far from being a democracy, which Winthrop (reflecting the general educated attitude of his time) described as the meanest of all forms of government. There had been no democracy in Israel. The danger that 'worldly men should prove the major part' of the government had to be avoided, and was, by a decree (1631) that 'to the end the body of the commons may be preserved of honest and good men . . . no man shall be admitted to the freedom of this body politic, but such as are members of some of the churches within the limits of the same'. Since only those who could convince the other members that they had been converted were admitted to churches the danger of ungodly rule was thus eliminated; and since the number of the converted was always small, the danger of mere majority rule was eliminated at the same time.

An élite, then, of the elect, the Saints, governed Massachusetts; an élite which was itself dominated by men like Winthrop, as he desired, men of wealth, education and breeding.[22] It was not a class élite, all the same. God did not save or damn by income: poor as well as rich were admitted to the churches. Whatever the other inequalities, church members were equal in political rights. Yet in every class, in every town, they were in a minority. By the end of the century their monopoly of political power was exciting envy in the unregenerate. Long before that, it was proving inconvenient to the regenerate. Efficiency required wider citizenship. For freemanship entailed not rights only, but responsibilities, and all too many church members, obeying a natural instinct to shirk, were declining to apply for it. In order to keep the affairs of government running smoothly, it proved necessary to find ways round the rule restricting freemanship – let us say

21 Superseded by the *Laws and Liberties*, 1647 (second edn 1660).
22 Even when refused the Governorship, Winthrop was always elected to the magistracy.

citizenship – to the saved. (In the daughter colony of Connecticut – founded in 1635 – the rule was never adopted.) The purely local franchise was early opened to all men of mature years who had taken the oath of fidelity to the commonwealth. In this way the idea of political equality began to make itself felt.

It was not an ideal which could make much headway in a society whose prime preoccupation was religion. But (here the history turns comic) though the subject continued fascinating, the preoccupation did not last very long – certainly not so long as the ministers' obsession with the idea of New England's divine errand and covenant with God. Soon the men of Marblehead near Salem were coarsely telling their minister that he was mistaken as to their motive in travelling to America – 'our main end was to catch fish'. For fishing proved almost as lucrative as John Smith had foreseen. The New Englanders soon ventured to the Grand Banks and steadily improved the design of their fishing vessels. The result was that in 1641 alone 300,000 barrels of cod were exported; herring, mackerel, alewives and delicious bass also found ready markets. Great Britain had her own fishermen, but Europe was happy to take the best of New England's catches; the middling grades were sold to farmers of the American back-country, the worst fed slaves on West Indian plantations. Prosperity was fostered by the fur-trade too, which, lucrative in itself (though rapidly declining after the first decade of settlement), also opened up the back-country of New England to farmers. It proved impossible to export the region's plentiful timber, labour and transportation costs being so high, but the shipbuilders of Boston and the coast made good use of it, as they did of other marine stores. For overseas trade boomed. Some of its ingredients have been mentioned. Others were, for export: pipe-staves, barrel-staves, clapboard, sheep, goats, hogs, horses, barley, wheat, oats, rye, dried beef, pork, rum, cheese, butter, soap, frames of houses, peas; for import: from the West Indies, molasses (for making rum), sugar, cotton, tobacco, indigo, slaves; from Europe, wine, salt, fruits, raisins, silk, olive oil, laces, linen, cloth; from the southern English colonies, tobacco, corn, beans, meat. Trade became a fascination for the children of the Puritans, and the ministers found that they were distressingly ready to tell lies to help it, and their fortunes, along. There were even graver consequences. As early as 1634 a sumptuary law had to be passed forbidding the use of 'lace, silver, gold' in clothing, and 'slashed clothes, other than one slash in each sleeve and another in the back; also, all cutworks, embroidered or needlework caps, bands and rails'. To no effect: forty years later it was frequently necessary to fine humble persons for impudently wearing the fabric of their betters, silk. Then, drink, that staple of the trade, had distressing effects: in 1673 a minister lamented 'How has wine and cider, but most of all rum, debauched multitudes of people, young and old?' Most dreadful, however, was the distracting effect of mere prosperity itself. By 1660 Boston was a thriving town of 3,000 people, clear evidence of God's favour; but to what avail if it had forgotten its mission?

Ministerial outcries became incessant: 'It concerneth New England always to remember that originally they are a plantation religious, not a plantation of trade.' No use – the gloomy verdict could not be avoided: 'Outward prosperity is a worm at the roots of godliness, so that religion dies when the world thrives.'

Matters were no better in the back-country. On their arrival the Puritans had quickly sensed how well adapted the traditional English manor-village was to their purposes; so they organized the New England countryside accordingly. This was a superficially more significant importation than the Essex weatherboarding which covered their houses and barns; yet it has left less of a mark on the American landscape. Weatherboarding can now be found in quantity in every state of the Union; the godly township of the Puritans' plans, nowhere. Yet the idea had seemed so good! The nuclear village, surrounded by fields farmed in strips, such as the settlers had known in England, would be economically self-sufficient and keep the villagers close under the minister's eye. It would make easy the maintenance of a school, and the Christian training of servants and children. It would prevent the intellectual and moral stagnation in isolation of adults, and facilitate local self-government, since town-meetings could easily be arranged. Thus a congregation, whether meeting as a civil or as an ecclesiastical community, could observe the principles of its institution, and its members (powerfully egged on by a preaching minister's eloquence) could act against any back-sliding.

To a wonderful extent the New England township achieved all these things; and, in purely secular form, it lingers still, with its characteristic institutions, the town-meeting and the selectmen (annually elected administrative officers), in the quieter corners of New England. But land-hunger in Connecticut and Massachusetts continued to be strong. Land was plentiful; and, until the looming of the English Civil War dried up the supply of new immigrants, there was, as has been stated,[23] an eager market for agrarian products of all kinds. Prices collapsed, it is true, in 1642; but they gradually recovered as New England sailors found markets abroad. Soon the demands of the market made themselves felt again on the farm; and, thus assured of profit, the farmers opened up more and more new land. They could not be kept within range of the towns and the ministers, and their land-hunger made them somewhat unreceptive to exhortations. 'Outlying places', said one preacher, 'were nurseries of ignorance, profaneness and atheism.' Said another, 'The first that came over hither for the Gospel could not tell what to do with more land than a small number of acres, yet now men more easily swallow down so many hundreds and are not satisfied.' A third exclaimed, 'Sure there were other and better things the People of God came hither for than the best spot of ground, the richest soil.' No doubt: but the People of God chose to forget it. They chose to live in America, not as

23 See above, p. 47.

members of a close-knit community of piety, but as individualist farmers, each seeking his and his family's salvation, economically and spiritually, on his own. Had they cared to they could have argued that they were the truest Puritans, individual salvation being the central value of Puritanism; no wonder that, in propitious circumstances (and the frontier of settlement in North America was very propitious), the value was followed to its logical, 'he travels fastest who travels alone', conclusion. But by the perhaps excessively strict standards of its founders the city on the hill began to look less like Jerusalem than like a displaced Sodom or Gomorrah; and Bradford shook his head over the degeneracy of Plymouth, too.

So perhaps it was as well that the eyes of all people were directed elsewhere; but this, too, was a cause of distress and saddened John Winthrop before his death. First there was Laud: they had fled him. Then there was the Presbyterian Parliament: they defied it. Then Cromwell arose, an Independent, one of their own – and instead of adopting the New England way of compulsory Congregationalism, as exemplified in Plymouth, Massachusetts, Connecticut and New Haven, he took up the ideas of the black flock among them, Roger Williams's sheep of Rhode Island, that hotbed of religious liberty! 'Toleration' was all the cry.[24] The New England Puritans were rising to the peak of their political strength: Connecticut and New Haven were settled, and in 1652 Massachusetts asserted its dominion over the regions of New Hampshire and Maine to the north, where many of the ungodly had been rash enough to settle within reach of the saintly commonwealth's long arm. In the same year it assumed one of the chief attributes of sovereignty and began to mint its own money. But to what avail? The errand into the wilderness had failed. Very success was corrupting the new Canaan from within; and the Puritans they had left behind were neglecting the lessons of Massachusetts orthodoxy. What could it matter to an English Independent that Master Thomas Shepard, the minister of Cambridge, Massachusetts, had declared it 'Satan's policy, to plead for an indefinite and boundless toleration'? To the men of Bunyan's generation only the adoption of such a policy could save them from Bedford jail. To their eyes (some of them began to say so as early as 1643, when Roger Williams, seeking, successfully, to protect Rhode Island from Massachusetts expansionism, went to England for help) the compulsory orthodoxy of New England was cold and sterile. Later holders of this opinion were to talk of the 'glacial age' of the New England mind. The saga was over.

Had it nothing to show but anticlimax? The *diminuendo* of a commercial republic where the founders had intended to build the City of God? 'Thus stands the case between God and us,' John Winthrop had boasted in 1630, 'we are entered into Covenant with him for this work, we have taken out a Commission, the Lord hath given us leave to draw our own Articles, we

24 Oliver did not go so far as to offer it to Catholics, Anglicans, Levellers or Diggers. To offer it to Jews, Antinomians, Anabaptists and Presbyterians was bad enough.

have professed to enterprise these Actions upon these and these ends, we have hereupon besought him of favour and blessing.' He had earnestly warned his followers that there must be no backsliding, for fear of the Lord's judgement; and he had promised them God's blessing if they were faithful. Perhaps the promise was a presumptuous mistake. 'Thou shalt not tempt the Lord thy God.' They had backslid; and yet, to judge by all earthly standards, God had blessed them. It was more than a little awkward and absurd. A sense of humiliating failure haunted the ministers at the end of the seventeenth century. New England was no longer the land of the covenant. They could take no comfort in its sublunar achievements: a high, and improving, standard of living for all; a free and stable society; a thriving life of the mind and spirit.[25] Where was Zion?

Perhaps there was one answer which would have comforted them somewhat. At any rate it must be offered today. Puritanism, it must be said again, influenced the whole of English Protestantism, being only its most radical form. Its most characteristic note was one of intense introspection, intense concern with individual salvation. As it seeped through England and conquered America it deeply affected the lives of countless men and women, many of whom were anything but Puritans in the strict sense. The result was that, in spite of clerical jeremiads, the English and American character, at its best and most effective, was sober, respectable, self-reliant, energetic, content on the whole with decent, homely pleasures. Its dominant traits of earnestness and uprightness can be found as much in Jane Austen and Dr Johnson as in John Adams and Dr Franklin, and lay behind the greatest achievements of the Victorians. It was the most remarkable work of the English Reformation, and might, however reluctantly, have been accepted as a sufficient justification by those ministers who tried so earnestly to create a godly people. They well knew, after all, how inevitably far short of perfection all human endeavour must fall.

In America, the New England character became almost proverbial. We shall see it making the Revolution, the Civil War and the Industrial Revolution. Its greatness lay in its reasonableness, earnestness and zeal for righteousness; its weakness in a tendency towards hypocrisy, covetousness and self-righteousness. Through it Puritanism persisted into later times. The city on a hill failed; but it was one of greater authority even than John Winthrop's who promised that 'the Kingdom of Heaven is within you'. The course of American history would have given a Puritan reason to suppose that this promise, at least, had been kept.

---

25 A life which was fostered by the Puritans' belief in a learned ministry (to train which Harvard College was founded as early as 1636) and in a Bible-reading congregation, for which schools were founded in every township.

5 Indians 1492–1920

We were happy when he first came. We first thought he came from the Light; but he comes like the dusk of the evening now, not like the dawn of the morning. He comes like a day that has passed, and night enters our future with him . . .

Plains Chieftain, *c.* 1870

Friends, it has been our misfortune to welcome the white man. We have been deceived. He brought with him some shining things that pleased our eyes; he brought weapons more effective than our own. Above all he brought the spirit-water that makes one forget old age, weakness and sorrow. But I wish to say to you that if you wish to possess these things for yourselves, you must begin anew and put away the wisdom of your fathers. You must lay up food and forget the hungry. When your house is built, your store-room filled, then look around for a neighbour whom you can take advantage of and seize all he has.

Chief Red Cloud of the Oglala Sioux

Like the miner's canary, the Indian marks the shift from fresh air to poison gas in our political atmosphere; and our treatment of Indians, even more than our treatment of other minorities, reflects the rise and fall of our democratic faith.

Felix S. Cohen, 1949

Virginia and Massachusetts exacted the space devoted to them here, for not only did they retain their primacy among the English settlements down to the American Revolution and beyond, but between them they perfectly illustrate, indeed epitomize, the great colonizing movement and its roots. But the sister settlements that followed them rapidly must not be forgotten. As England put forth her strength in the seventeenth century her colonies spread further along the Atlantic coast of North America, and flourished in the West Indies. Massachusetts bred New Hampshire (finally created an independent province in 1692) as well as Connecticut and Rhode Island. The Dutch of New Amsterdam extinguished New Sweden (the future state of Delaware) only to fall themselves to English conquest in 1664, when New Amsterdam and New Netherland became the city and colony of New York. Further south three proprietary colonies were planted – 'New Caesarea or New Jersey' (1664), the work of Lord Berkeley and Sir George Carteret; Pennsylvania (1681), founded by William Penn to be a refuge for Quakers and to enrich his family; and Maryland (1632), founded by the first Lord Baltimore as a refuge (though it was not to be much used as such) for Catholics. Virginia sprouted North Carolina, on Albemarle Sound, first settled from the older colony during the 1650s, though its legal existence dates from 1663. South Carolina, on the other hand, though born legally of the same 1663 charter, acquired no settlers until 1670, when it began a thriving career. The last addition to this string of colonies was Georgia, founded in 1732, in part to serve as a place of rehabilitation for persons imprisoned for debt in England, partly as a plantation for the cultivation of silk, but chiefly as a buffer state against the Spanish in Florida and the French in Louisiana.

For while, to the north, the English colonies and their outposts – Nova Scotia and Newfoundland – jostled Canada, the southern boundary of English North America was a matter of continuous international strife from the foundation of South Carolina onwards. French enterprise linked the two areas of friction. Louis XIV's brave explorers, inspired partly by an imperial vision and partly by a hunger to monopolize the fur-trade, claimed the Great Lakes and the Mississippi for their King; and in 1699 founded a colony about the mouths of the great river which they named Louisiana in his honour. The Spaniards, by contrast, stood mainly on the defensive, having much to lose. They still had the energy to reconquer New Mexico (lost to a great rebellion of Pueblo Indians in 1680) and, so late as 1769, to enter and settle Upper California. But their policy was dominated by dread of English competition to the north and French competition to the west. On their side the English dreaded encirclement and extinction by the French, or by a Franco-Spanish combination. The French dreaded an English challenge for control of the Mississippi.[1] The obsessive rivalries of Europe had reached North America; for more than a century they would determine its history.

The three competing empires differed in character. Florida's value to Spain was chiefly strategic: the colony protected the Bahamas Channel and Spanish communications with Mexico and the sugar islands. Accordingly it was garrisoned rather than inhabited, though Franciscans did their usual excellent missionary work among the Indians. The English colonies, we have seen, were agrarian and commercial, and grew ever more thickly

1 To understand these anxieties, look at Map 2 (p. 54).

populated. New France gradually acquired a farming population, but its lifeblood, like that of Louisiana, was the trade in peltries – beaver fur and deer hides.

Such dissimilar entities, it may be thought, could well have afforded to co-exist. Unhappily they were not different enough. All had an interest in the fur-trade, for one thing; and the habit of suspicion, fear and rivalry, common to all three, did the rest. In this, we see, Old and New Worlds were much alike.

But in the means of competition the continents differed sharply. Not for many years could there be a conventional war of regular soldiers in North America, or even conventional commercial rivalry. The tangled forests were too wide, white numbers (for warfare) too few, European tactics too inflexible. All Europeans had to learn the lessons taught New Englanders by King Philip's War (1675–6), that 'it is one thing to drill a company in a plain champaign and another to drive an enemy through the desert woods'; and that Indian allies were absolutely necessary, to act as auxiliaries and scouts. The Indian, it emerged, was the key to dominion in the wilderness. When North America was at what passed for peace, imperial success was measured in terms of influence with the tribes. When, as repeatedly happened, peace was admitted to be war, the Europeans, it has been well said, showed themselves 'ready to fight to the last Indian'.[2]

Luckily for the intruders, the tribes were commonly happy to fight each other. They had the usual human grievances against their neighbours, and war was a principal occupation among them. Success in war was the leading source of individual prestige. Indeed, before the European arrival, wars seem to have been waged in many cases solely to provide chances for warriors to win this prestige. It was a lethal game, with elaborate rules, and so addicted were most of the Indians to it that in the early eighteenth century the Cherokees could remark, 'We cannot live without war. Should we make peace with the Tuscaroras, we must immediately look out for some other nation with whom we can engage in our beloved occupation.' The skill gained in this wilderness conflict proved invaluable for attacking or defending European possessions.

Furthermore, only Indians could provide the commodities of the peltries trade; and there was much money to be made out of them. For as time went on the Indians grew ever more dependent on European goods. By the same token they grew more and more manipulable. Those who controlled the supply of essential articles such as guns controlled their customers. And so the curtain rose on the tragedy of the native peoples of North America.

There had been a long prologue. It is easy to forget, when studying the comparatively gentle rule of Spain north of Mexico (at any rate after the Pueblo revolt), what the conquest of the Aztecs and the Incas had involved.

2 William Brandon, *The American Heritage Book of Indians*. As its readers will recognize, I have drawn heavily on that wonderful volume for this chapter.

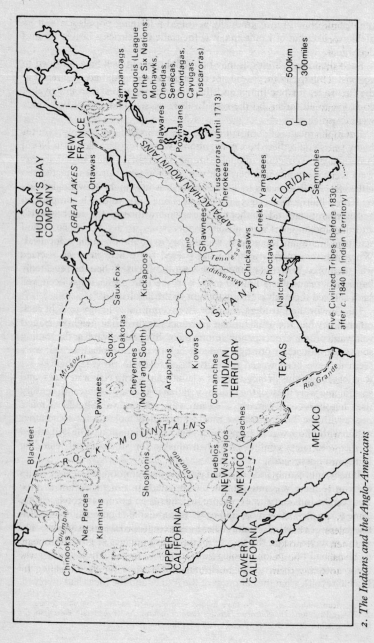

2. The Indians and the Anglo-Americans

The crimes of the Anglo-Americans pale beside those of Cortès and his successors. Hundreds of thousands of Indians were killed outright; even more were worked slowly and horribly to death as slaves. The fact that European diseases were even more destructive hardly excuses the conquistadores. One Carib Indian, about to be burned to death after a rebellion, refused baptism, though it could take him to heaven, because he feared he would find more Christians there. Genocide is an unpleasant word, but it seems appropriate here. If the North American Indians had known what had happened south of the Rio Grande, they might well have trembled at the future.

But they were blessedly ignorant. They did not even know how completely they were trapped in the destiny of the Europeans. Towards the end of their days of freedom and power one man of genius among them, the Shawnee Tecumseh (1768–1813), saw the truth and realized that only by uniting in one nation might the Indians save themselves. Tecumseh ('Crouching Tiger') was a great general, a compelling orator, a generous and humane man. But his vision came too late, the red men had thrown away their safety and their numbers in ceaseless wars among themselves; after delusive early success Tecumseh failed, and died in battle.[3] The Fates were not to be balked.

Few historical themes are of greater fascination than the tale of the North American Indian; but it cannot be told here for its own sake. A history of the United States must be a history of victors; the defeated are relevant chiefly for what they tell us of their conquerors. *Sed victa Catoni*; the sage Auden, however, tells us that

Few even wish they could read
the lost annals
of a cudgelled people.[4]

Honour to those few; but they must seek satisfaction elsewhere. Let us see what the cudgelled can reveal of their oppressors.

Names are revealing. What did the races call each other?

The Anglo-Americans had a long list of savoury adjectives and nouns for the Indians: for example, besotted, childish, cruel, degraded, dirty, diseased, drunken, faithless, gluttonous, insolent, jealous, lazy, lying, murdering, profligate, stupid, thieving, timorous, uncivilizable, vindictive, worthless; barbarians, demons, heathen, savages, varmints (vermin). The red men were no less definite. At first, by the gentle Caribs, the Europeans were called 'The People from Heaven'. Later, Indians to the north, who came to know them well, dubbed them 'People Greedily Grasping for

3 American soldiers are said to have helped themselves to pieces of his skin to keep as souvenirs.
4 W. H. Auden, *City Without Walls* (London, Faber, 1969), p. 58.

Land'. Members of the Algonquian group most commonly called the English 'The Coatwearing People'; next often, 'The Cut-Throats'.

In many respects the Indians badly needed to be discovered by Europe. The greatest intelligence[5] must be limited by the means available to it, and Indian technological backwardness was largely inevitable, because of the absence in the Americas of easily worked tin and iron deposits, and of draught animals (hence the principle of the wheel could not be exploited). The sacred book and higher mathematics of the Maya, staggering stone and metalwork achievements, the great Inca political system, might make Central and Andean America glorious: they could not nullify the Indians' weakness in other respects. So it was in part with delight and fascination that the intelligent red men greeted the coming of the People from Heaven and their marvellous possessions. When the Spanish entered New Mexico[6] in 1598 they brought with them sheep, goats and horses. Time, chance and the Pueblo rebellion gradually spread these things among the western tribes who thereupon began to evolve the dazzling Plains culture which has so long enchanted the world's imagination. Many Indians now became shepherds and horsemen (and brilliant horse-thieves);[7] mounted on piebald ponies and armed, originally, with spearheads made from old Spanish sword blades, then with guns got in trade from the East, they became mighty hunters of buffalo. No longer was it necessary to stampede a herd over a cliff, or to wait for a weak or injured beast to stray; now swift riders could select, pursue and bring down their prey whenever they chose. The result was health and wealth: finally abandoning almost all sedentary pursuits to the women, the men brought in meat in such vast quantities that there was more than enough for everybody. As a result the population grew strong and numerous. Male leaders of the Sioux, resplendent in eagle-feather war-bonnets, made the most picturesque appearance; but it is through the women's work that we can most clearly see what the new way of life amounted to. Men might be artists and paint pictorial calendars on buffalo leather; it was the women who, for example, jerked the surplus meat; that is, sliced it thin and dried it; or pounded it together with berries and poured melted fat and marrow over it to make pemmican. It was they who ornamented clothing and parfleche (bags made of raw buffalo hide) with porcupine needles, beadwork, elks' teeth and paint; they who made and painted the buffalo hide lodges (*tipis*). Meantime the men danced the annual Sun Dance, to win supernatural favour for the tribe; or ritual dances to secure a good hunt; or the war dance, after which they would go off to raid rival tribes and earn personal glory. The greatest feat was to count coup,

5 For what they are worth, IQ tests carried out in the 1940s showed groups of Indian children regularly performing better than the control groups of white children.
6 To be understood, before the Mexican War (1845–8), as, very roughly, the area bounded by the rivers Colorado, Gila, Grande and Pecos, and by the Sangre de Cristo mountains in the East.
7 Not the Pueblo, who remained sedentary agriculturalists, living in the adobe townships that got them their name (*pueblo*, Spanish, 'town').

that is, to touch a chosen foe with a special stick and get away without harming him or being harmed. At times war would be suspended. Then there would be great gatherings, for gambling, trade, foot races, horse races; it was thus that the sign language of the Plains developed, to make communication possible between tribes that spoke different languages. The problem of communication with fellow-tribesmen over a distance was solved by the device of signals made with smoke from buffalo-dung fires. It was a good life; small wonder that many tribes abandoned their settled villages for a nomadic existence. All was well so long as the buffalo herds lasted; and they teemed inexhaustibly until the white settlers came.

All the same, the Plains culture was the outcome of a meeting between the Indians and the Europeans. The same was true in the dense eastern forest. The horse was less valuable there, but brass kettles replaced earthenware cooking pots, English cloth replaced attire of fur and hide, and, above all, guns replaced bows and arrows. Everywhere the Indians welcomed the coming of European animals and artefacts with joy, and their cultures burst into brief, beautiful flower.

Even had that been all, a price would have had to be paid, some of it in currency: guns and powder could be obtained only by barter, and to get them eastern Indians had to hunt their woods bare of beaver and deer.[8] This in turn bred trouble. For example, when the Iroquois (or Five Nations)[9] had run through their local supply of furs they chose to secure a continuing flow of trade goods by becoming middlemen in the traffic which brought furs from the unexhausted West to the rivers Hudson and St Lawrence. This was simple to arrange: all they had to do was massacre the previous middlemen, Hurons and related tribes, which they duly did (1648–53); then they settled down for the next century as the lords of the North-East, one of the most formidable obstacles to French and English advance. Similar convulsions occurred everywhere beyond the frontier of white settlement. They were not too important: long before the coming of the European, tribes and confederacies had risen and fallen. And the presence of whites, in forts or townships, might stabilize, rather than inflame, a perilous situation. The coastal tribes of South Carolina welcomed the planting of Charles Town in 1670: it protected them from the wild Indians of the interior.

For the blessings of trade, such prices were not too high; but more was exacted. The Puritans, not content with earnestly trying to convert the Indians to Christianity, characteristically tried to impose the prim Sabbatarian manners of rural England on them: this was one of the contributory causes of King Philip's War.[10] The provincialism of Anglo-American

---

8 One buckskin or *buck* became so generally known as the basic unit of exchange in the traffic that it is now universal slang for a dollar.

9 Later, Six, when the Tuscaroras migrated north after a losing war with the colony of North Carolina, 1711–13.

10 'King Philip' was the English name for Pometacom, Chief of the Wampanoag Indians who had, in his father's time, done much to aid the Pilgrims.

culture, its complacency in front of the exotic, was a perpetual source of friction, and of misery to the Indians. Indian customs were condemned by successive generations as sinful, un-Christian, uncivilized, unprogressive. In the later nineteenth century the agent for the Yankton Sioux wrote:

As long as Indians live in villages they will retain many of their old and injurious habits. Frequent feasts, heathen ceremonies and dances, constant visiting – these will continue as long as people live together in close neighbourhoods and villages. I trust that before another year is ended they will generally be located upon individual land or farms. From that date will begin their real and permanent progress.

It is the voice of Gradgrind, condemning the intensely sociable Indians to dour, if virtuous, money-grubbing in freezing isolation; but the agent spoke for past and future, as well as for his own cold-hearted time. The obsession with private property which, as we have seen, made it impossible for the English to organize their original plantations on communist principles made it impossible for them or their descendants to respect, or even to comprehend, Indian communism, Indian clannishness, any more than they could respect or tolerate Indian polygamy or Indian religion; and in all too many cases this obsession makes such respect impossible today.

The social bigotry of the Anglo-Americans, then, was an affliction to the Indians; but their diseases were more punishing still. General Smallpox, General Cholera, swept the American plains as ruthlessly as their colleagues Janvier and Février did the Russian; and they were aided by measles, dysentery, scarlet fever, venereal disease, influenza and tuberculosis. The Europeans can hardly be blamed for spreading these infections,[11] from which, after all, they suffered, if less catastrophically, themselves. Nor should they be condemned *en masse* for the worst disease of all, alcoholism.

Fermented and distilled drinks were unknown to the pre-Columbian Indians, so they had as little resistance to alcoholism as to smallpox, and for some reason, yet to be explained, their social organization was incapable of developing customs by which drinking could be rendered as comparatively innocuous as it is among black and white Americans (not that that is saying very much). From earliest times the white governments saw the danger and made earnest efforts to keep firewater away from the Indians. They were supported by all the wiser heads among the tribes. But these efforts were largely defeated by the mania for booze and by the readiness of too many whites to supply it in the desired, limitless quantity. The English traders found that glass beads, hatchets, hoes, knives, shirts, coats, hats, shoes, stockings, breeches, blankets, thread, scissors, guns, flints, powder, bullets, tobacco, pipes, looking glasses, ostrich plumes, silver medals, yards

11 Except for the rare occasions when they passed them on deliberately, as in 1763, when an attempt was made to spread smallpox among the warriors besieging Fort Pitt in Pennsylvania.

of silk and bales of cloth (to name only some items of the trade) were often less desired than the means of getting dead drunk. 'Brandy goes off incomparably well,' they discovered, and was very easy to supply, particularly if adulterated. Drunk, an Indian was incapable of insisting on proper payment for his goods, and he seemed to be incapable of resisting the chance to get drunk. There were other consequences, however, than ruined Indians. Governor George Thomas of Pennsylvania summed the matter up in 1744:

Our Traders in defiance of the Law carry Spiritous Liquors amongst them, and take Advantage of their inordinate Appetite for it to cheat them out of their skins and their wampum,[12] which is their Money, and often to debauch their wives into the Bargain. Is it to be wondered at then, if when they Recover from the Drunken fit, they should take severe revenges?

Indeed not; again and again the frontier of settlement was scourged by flame and tomahawk as the Indians paid for their treatment by the traders.

But the traders were universally held to be the dregs of the white race: 'The Lewdness and wickedness of them have been a Scandal to the Religion we Profess.' They were supposed to be unrepresentative of their people.

Perhaps they were; for though many were indeed unscrupulous rogues, who sold the Indians drink, and, in the South-East at least, did not hesitate to egg them on to inter-tribal wars, so that prisoners could be captured to sell into slavery, at least all were ready to live among the Indians, to adopt their ways and to marry their women. It was possible to be an honest Indian trader, and those that were acquired great influence. They married into chiefly families, and their descendants – bearing names like Brant, McGillivray, Ross – became great leaders of their people. Above all, the traders, who depended on the Indians for their livelihood as much as the Indians depended on them, did not want their customers to disappear. They injured, but did not hate, the Indians; just as trade disrupted – in a sense, fruitfully disrupted – but did not destroy the Indians' way of life. Hatred and destruction were the specialities of the respectable, who taught the Indians that they were not to keep their independence when they were no longer required for use in the quarrels of the Spanish, French and British Empires.

For the respectable, typical, farming British wanted the Indians' land; and, as time was to show, they wanted all of it. In due course they gained the strength to take it. And without land, the Indian must cease to exist; or at least go under, become utterly dependent and dispirited.

12 Wampum consisted of bead-belts, beautifully patterned. It reached its height after the whites brought steel tools with which tubular beads could be fashioned. The patterns of the finest belts were symbolic, and were frequently used to record treaties and other important events.

Two needs clashed when red met white; and so did two great principles: the principle of private property and the principle of common ownership. The English attitude was well stated by John Winthrop, in words which look forward to the doctrines of Hobbes, Locke and Rousseau:

That which is common to all is proper to none. This savage people ruleth over many lands without title or property; for they enclose no ground, neither have they cattle to maintain it, but remove their dwellings as they have occasion, or as they can prevail against their neighbours. And why may not Christians have liberties to go and dwell amongst them in their waste lands and woods, leaving them such places as they have manured for their corn, as lawfully as Abraham did among the Sodomites? For God hath given to the sons of man a two-fold right to the earth; there is a natural right and a civil right. The first right was natural where men held the earth in common, every man settling and feeding where he pleased; then, as men and cattle increased, they appropriated some parcels of ground by enclosing and peculiar manurance, and this in time got them a civil right.

Thus the patriarch of New England, justifying the robberies he meant to commit by the best social science of his day. Perhaps his style betrays a slightly uneasy conscience; but even if it does not, he should not be blamed overmuch. The migration of forty million Europeans between 1607 and 1914 is too great a matter to be dealt with by elementary moral texts, such as the Eighth Commandment. Migration, we have seen, is natural to man. It cannot reasonably be maintained that, once the Atlantic had ceased to be a barrier, the Europeans were wrong to better themselves by sailing to inhabit the largely empty land. Even the Indians might have benefited greatly from it. Anyway, there was (and is) room enough on the vast continent for both peoples.

The Indians knew it. It was hard, of course, on the particular tribes which had to be squeezed or dislodged to make way for English villages; conflict was therefore inevitable, but since the whites suffered as acutely as the reds during its course, they could have been held to have purged the crimes committed on arrival. The two peoples might have developed side by side in peace. Certainly the Indians hoped so. Nothing is more striking, throughout the long tale of their agony, than the manner in which, again and again, they waited to attack until driven to desperation, and, again and again, failed to unite against the foe, and, again and again, held their hands at the last, when they had him at their mercy. Of course there was always dispute within the tribes, between conservatives and those Indians who sought to profit, both in goods and instruction, from the Coatwearing People. But by and large it may be said that later generations were intelligent enough to repeat Powhatan's reasoning, as he expressed it to John Smith:

Think you I am so simple, not to know it is better to eat good meat, lie well, and sleep quietly with my women and children, laugh and be merry with you, have copper hatchets, or what I want, being your friend: than be forced to fly from all, to lie cold in the woods, feed upon acorns, roots, and such trash; and be so hunted by you, that I can neither rest, eat, nor sleep; but my tired men must watch, and if a twig but break, every one crieth there cometh Captain Smith: then must I fly I know not whither: and thus with miserable fear, end my miserable life.

It is true that on too many occasions, as on this, such words were not uttered in good faith, or received in it; but the history of the Indian supports them. Again and again he made treaties with the white man, to last, in the picturesque phrase, 'as long as grass grows or water runs'; invariably the treaties were broken almost at once – by the whites.

Treachery was a principal theme in the whites' treatment of the red men. The use traders regularly made of whisky to cheat Indians of their fair payment has already been mentioned. It was as regularly adopted to cheat them of their lands. Nor was it the only method. Illiterate Indians were induced to put their names to documents transferring land-title which they did not understand and had, anyway, no right to sign, but which were used to justify the expulsion of them and their fellows from their hunting-grounds. In 1686 the Delaware Indians ceded to William Penn as much land to the north as a man could walk in three days. The upright and moderate Penn ('I desire to enjoy it with your consent, that we may always live together as neighbours and friends', he had remarked in 1682) took only what he covered in a day and a half of easy strolling; but fifty-one years later his successors had the rest of the ground covered by relay runners, and claimed the whole enormous extent under the so-called 'Walking' purchase. (This led directly to the war of the 1750s in Pennsylvania.) In later years bribing the chiefs – particularly half-breed ones – to part with tribal land was found to be a good method. Another was to recognize, for the purpose of land transactions, a pliant Indian as chief, or an otherwise unempowered fragment of a tribe as competent to act for the whole. And where straightforward trickery was inapplicable, humbug, its twin, proved invaluable. The two greatest wrongs ever committed against the Indians as a group, the Removal Act of 1830 and the Allotment Act of 1887,[13] were both made palatable to the Anglo-American conscience by sincere, semi-sincere and insincere assurances that they were passed chiefly to help their victims.

Cruelty was another leading theme. In extenuation it may be urged that the Indians (especially the sadistic Iroquois) were demons when on the warpath; but it should be observed that in their peacetime behaviour (unless demoralized by booze) they were, compared to the white men, models of decorum. They enjoyed a high degree of social cohesion and tolerance, and much about European manners astonished and distressed them. They could not understand child-beating, or indeed exclusive family loyalty: 'I don't

13 For both, see below, pp. 67–8 and 69–70. The Allotment Act is also known as the Dawes Severalty Act.

understand you Frenchmen – you love only your own children, but we love all children,' said an Algonquin to a Jesuit missionary.[14] Religious strife horrified them. An Indian chief who sheltered a persecuted Quaker in winter could only exclaim, 'What a God have the English who deal so with one another about the worship of their God!' Too often they showed themselves prejudiced against the black men, and at the beginning of the nineteenth century South-Eastern tribes owned many black slaves (of whom the whites were anxious to despoil them); but slavery under the Seminoles was a far gentler thing than under the whites. One witness was insistent that 'an Indian would as soon sell his child as his slave, except when under the influence of intoxicating liquor'.

But it is not necessary, even if it is fair, to condemn white behaviour by contrasting it with red. It stands condemned by its own standards. The records of the American past re-echo with denunciations of the fiendishness of the savages, just as Africans were accused of insatiable lust, bloodlust and criminal propensities of all kinds; but the Christians themselves raped, scalped,[15] looted, murdered, burned and tortured, the very deeds by which they justified their contempt and loathing for the Indian. Said US Lieutenant Davis, who fought against Geronimo, '. . . the Indian was a mere amateur compared to the "noble white man". His crimes were retail, ours wholesale.' Colonel Chivington (a Methodist minister) could, as late as 1864, organize the Sand Creek Massacre of 300 peaceful Cheyennes and Araphoes in Colorado. 'Kill and scalp all,' he said, 'big and little; nits make lice.' A US government commission subsequently commented:

It scarcely has its parallel in the records of Indian barbarity. Fleeing women, holding up their hands and praying for mercy, were shot down; infants were killed and scalped in derision; men were tortured and mutilated. No one will be astonished that a war ensued which cost the government $30,000,000 and carried conflagration and death to the border settlements.

No matter: in Denver, after the massacre, Chivington had exhibited a hundred scalps in a local theatre and had been hailed as a hero. The next year General Phil Sheridan gave a phrase to the language when he remarked 'the only good Indians I ever saw were dead'. A few years earlier, on the West Coast, the cry had gone up: 'Let our motto be extermination, and death to all opposers.' In Kansas, in 1867, the Indians were attacked as

14 Apache children were being kidnapped and enslaved in Arizona as late as 1871 – eight years after Abraham Lincoln had issued the Emancipation Proclamation, ending black slavery, and six years after the surrender of the South.
15 Scalping seems to have been the invention of the North-Eastern Indians. The Dutch of New Amsterdam first took advantage of the custom by offering a bounty for every scalp brought in. The English copied them, and then took to scalping themselves; they and the French ended by spreading it throughout the continent. Only the Nez Percés (see below, p. 69) were wise enough to eschew the practice.

'gut-eating skunks . . . whose immediate and final extermination all men, except Indian agents and traders, should pray for'.

Examples of such behaviour could be cited almost indefinitely. However, those given should be enough to account for the name Cut-Throats. It is more difficult to explain such inhumanity.

Certain considerations seem to be relevant. The North American Indians lived for the most part by hunting, and in the history of European colonialism it was always the hunters who were most exposed to exterminating practices. Mexico and Peru are still largely inhabited by descendants of the agricultural Aztecs and Incas; the hunting Caribs of the islands were completely wiped out. Secondly, it is noteworthy that while the Indian tribes were formidable – while, in other words, they occupied most of the continent and had French and Spanish allies – they were treated with considerable respect. It was before 1800 that the most magnificent promises were made; after, that the Americans, growing steadily bolder, committed their worst atrocities. Thirdly, there can be no doubt that the frontier area at all times had a high concentration of white rabble; and the further the frontier advanced away from the settled areas (which it did with enormous speed throughout the nineteenth century) the more completely did the rabble get out of hand. The Indians felt the effect. For example, although cruelty, humbug and land-hunger were conspicuous in New England at the time of King Philip's War, the Puritan conscience also made itself felt in word and deed, and effectively protected peaceful Indians from the vengeful mobs that might otherwise have lynched them, as Indians were lynched in Pennsylvania during the Pontiac uprising (1763–4). The Reverend Increase Mather, gloating over the capture of King Philip's wife and child ('It must be bitter as death for him . . . for the Indians are marvellously fond and affectionate towards their children'),[16] was more than counterbalanced by the Reverend John Eliot (1640–90), translator of the first Indian Bible, missionary to the tribes, who besides converting many to Christianity[17] argued strongly against selling Indians as slaves and tried in vain to save the life of an Indian he believed innocent of any crime, retorting to the Governor's assurances of guilt 'that at the great day he should find that Christ was of another mind, or words to that purpose, so I departed'. Such doughty defenders of the natives were happily to arise at all periods and in all places of American history; but they were never again to be so effective as in New England until after the First World War, and in the Wild West's palmy days they were repeatedly frustrated.

It may also be considered that it is only in the last fifty years or so that regular association with animals of many kinds – horses and cows as well

16 Wife and child were later sold into West Indian slavery.
17 The Reverend Cotton Mather, Increase's son (1663–1728), commented: 'To think of raising these hideous creatures into our holy religion! . . . Could he see anything angelical to encourage his labours? All was diabolical among them.'

as dogs and cats – has ceased to be universal. Today, it is easy enough for the white man to see red men, black men, yellow men, as human, for their likeness to himself strikes him instantly, their likeness to animals not at all, since he does not know many of these. The reverse was true during the settlement of America. The pre-Darwinian Englishman, supposing himself to be a little lower than the angels, his perceptions stultified by a narrow creed and culture, saw the differences between himself and other races as vastly important, and the same went for their likeness to the brute creation. The African was clearly a beast of burden, and might be enslaved; the Indian was a hunting beast, and might be shot (especially since on the whole he made poor material for slavery). The note of contempt (Prospero on Caliban) runs right through the literature and cannot be missed. It is to be found in Hakluyt ('more brutish than the beasts they hunt, more wild and unmanly than that unmanned wild country, which they range rather than inhabit'), in eighteenth-century Virginia ('Indians and Negroes . . . they scarcely consider as of the human species; so that it is almost impossible, in cases of violence, or even murder, committed on those unhappy people by any of the planters, to have the delinquents brought to justice'), Pennsylvania ('the animals vulgarly called Indians') and even in the enlightened nineteenth century, when the coming of Darwin merely encouraged the whites to hold that the law of the survival of the fittest had condemned the 'Vanishing Indian' to the usual fate of obsolete species ('they do accept the teaching that manifest destiny will drive the Indians from the earth,' said Bishop Whipple of Minnesota in 1881. 'The inexorable has no tears or pity at the cries of anguish of the doomed race.').

Mercifully, the time has come when, as Senator Frelinghuysen of New Jersey hoped in 1830, 'it is not now seriously denied that the Indians are men, endowed with kindred faculties and powers with ourselves'. Progress is possible. But its very fact makes the past more difficult to understand imaginatively. White contempt for the red man now seems so absurd as to be almost incredible. We can see that over a period of millennia the Indians, making use of very limited resources, had in every part of the Americas evolved ways of life that were almost perfectly adjusted to the environment, and in many cases held out high hopes of future evolution. More, we can see that in some respects – and those which were most universally to be found among the tribes – Indian culture too was superior to the European.

Thus, the idea of co-operation was central to Indian life, as competition is to ours. The Indians were highly individualistic, and vied with each other in the performance of brave deeds. They adored dressing up, and cherished favourite horses, favourite guns. And among the far tribes of the North-West there was even competition in the acquisition and display of personal wealth.[18]

---

18 Though as the favourite form of display was to give huge parties, known as *potlaches*, at which the host proved his wealth by giving much of it away, their acquisitive instinct must be reckoned to have been singularly innocent.

But their essential social belief was one of property-as-use. The Indians shared what they had, especially food: it was noted that while there was any to share, all shared it; when there was none, all starved. Most of all, they shared the land. The tribe had its territory. Any member might set up his lodge on any part of it and there grow his corn. The Five Civilized Tribes (Choctaw, Cherokee, Chickasaw, Seminole, Creek) explained in 1881:

Improvements can be and frequently are sold, but the land itself is not a chattel. Its occupancy and possession are indispensable to holding it, and its abandonment for two years makes it revert to the public domain. In this way every one of our citizens is assured of a home.

The Indian could no more understand the Europeans' conception of perpetual personal title than they could understand his conception of none. Nor could he understand the accumulating itch. Why did the People Greedily Grasping for Land want more acres than they needed to grow food on? Why did they build houses that would outlast their occupants? Why were Indians called thieves for helping themselves to what they needed, as they always had? Above all, why, even when he had acquired it honestly, did the white man insist that land he had bought became his exclusively, and for all time? How could he make such a claim? It was ridiculous. 'Sell a country!' exclaimed Tecumseh. 'Why not sell the air, the clouds, and the great sea? . . . Did not the Great Spirit make them all for the use of his children?'[19]

The issue of land cannot be shirked. Although, from one point of view, the mystery of the relations between the English settlers and the North American Indians cannot ever be understood, any more than any other great evil (for why should men oppress each other?), the temptation to which the settlers succumbed is all too plain, and all too familiar. It was the usual temptation to believe that what we want with passion must be right; and that the means of obtaining it cannot be sinful. The passion for landed property, that guarantee of independence, prosperity and prestige, which, as we have seen, uprooted the English and carried them across the Atlantic to Virginia and New England, also carried them and those who came to join them into the practice of atrocious crimes. Land-hunger is too weak a phrase, for hunger can be sated. It were better called land-lust: it was as insatiable as the sea. Like all great desire, it was fertile in rationalizations which satisfied those who felt it, if no one else. When the American Republic was established, its President became the Great Father of the Indians. Even in his most enlightened incarnations, he was swift to evade his paternal

19 In 1977, during a winter drought in the Pacific North-West, the states of Washington and Idaho began to quarrel about the division of rainfall obtained by 'seeding' the clouds. It was solemnly observed that it had never been settled who owned rainclouds.

obligations; and sometimes he committed infanticide. 'The hunter or savage state requires a greater extent of territory to sustain it, than is compatible with the progress and just claims of civilized life . . . and must yield to it . . . A compulsory process seems to be necessary, to break their habits, and civilize them' (James Monroe). 'Their cultivated fields; their constructed habitations . . . are undoubtedly by the laws of nature theirs. But what is the right of the huntsman to the forest of a thousand miles over which he has accidentally ranged in quest of prey?'[20] (John Quincy Adams). 'The game being destroyed as acknowledged by all, the right of possession, granted to the Indians for the purpose of hunting ceases, and justice, sound policy, and the constitutional rights of the citizen, would require its being resigned . . .' (Andrew Jackson). 'Is one of the fairest portions of the globe to remain in a state of nature, the haunt of a few wretched savages, when it seems destined by the Creator to give support to a large population and to be the seat of civilization?' (William Henry Harrison). It was the universal argument; its rightness was the universal feeling. No wonder, then, that the history of the Indian in the English colonies, and in the United States afterwards, can best be sketched in terms of the development of the white programme for depriving the red man of his lands.[21]

The tragedy had three acts, corresponding roughly to the three principal eras of American history. During the colonial epoch the Indian position remained, once the European coastal settlements had been established, surprisingly stable. The Iroquois League to the north, the looser Creek Confederation to the south, anchored as they were on the line of the Appalachians, markedly held up white expansion, particularly after the Iroquois had realized that the best way for the Indians to remain numerous and prosperous was to stay neutral in the Franco-British quarrel and not to fight each other more than they could help. There was a gradual erosion of the Indian position, but it remained a strong one so long as the English dared not attack the tribes for fear that they would go over to France. Even after the French defeat in the Seven Years War[22] and the expulsion of the British in the American Revolution, the Indians of the South could still play the same game, using Spain (now mistress of Louisiana as well as Florida) against the Americans. The last triumph of this period was the Creek War

20 The trouble with this formula was that the Americans habitually ignored its distinctions. The Iroquois and Cherokees were primarily farmers, but they were turned off their lands just the same. It was so easy to pretend that they were savage hunters.
21 A programme that could sometimes be enunciated with staggering frankness, as by the Indian Commissioner in 1872 who stated: 'No one certainly will rejoice more heartily than the present commissioner when the Indians of this country cease to be in a position to dictate, in any form or degree, to the government, when, in fact, the last hostile tribe becomes reduced to the condition of suppliants for charity.' But as we have seen, most men preferred to disguise their actions and their motives. For example, the seal of the Massachusetts Bay Company showed a naked Indian begging for the light of the Gospel in words adapted from the Acts of the Apostles (xvi, 9): 'Come over and help us.' The Puritans went over and helped themselves.
22 Known to Americans as the French and Indian War.

against the brigand state of Georgia (1786–90), which was masterminded by the great chief Alexander McGillivray,[23] who signed a treaty with George Washington in 1790 that protected the bulk of the Creek lands against encroachment for the next twenty-five years.

By the end of that period the second act had fairly begun. This was the epoch in which the American people, relieved of almost all international anxieties and gaining in wealth and numbers every day, asserted their complete dominance over the continent. To the Indians they proved their power by stripping the tribes of almost all they possessed, thus ensuring that the third act should show the Indians as paupers dependent on the harsh, irregular and frequently stupid charity of Uncle Sam. It is the process of spoliation as carried out in the second act that raises the most serious questions about the American national character. Thus under the Indian Removal Act of 1830 the 60,000 Indians of the Five Civilized Tribes were moved from the lands they had always occupied, lands which were guaranteed to them on the honour of the United States as pledged in treaty after treaty, to lands far across the Mississippi – lands which in due time were also to be filched from them. Many other Indians, until the very end of the nineteenth century, were to be uprooted. But the Great Removal sticks in the memory because of its scale, and because of the ostentatious bad faith of all concerned, from President Jackson down to Greenwood Leflore, a renegade Choctaw chief, and because of the immense human suffering involved. One example: when the Choctaw migration was arranged, the whites of Alabama and Mississippi descended on the unhappy tribe like so many horseflies, to bully and trick the Indians out of most of their movable property as well as their lands. The tribe then had to trek to Indian Territory (today, Oklahoma) during the winter of 1831–2 – the coldest since 1776. At least 1,600, or nearly a tenth of the entire tribe, died as a result of the hardships of the emigration and a cholera epidemic to which, in their starving, naked, shelterless, hopeless and unclean condition, the emigrants could offer little resistance. Most of those who died were children or old people. Another example: the 16,000 Cherokees[24] realized, long before 1838, when they were removed by force from their ancient homelands in the mountains of western Georgia and North Carolina, that the only way to survive the impact of the white man was to learn his ways. Accordingly they turned themselves into a successful farming people; Sequoya, a Cherokee half-breed of genius, invented an alphabet for their language, which rapidly spread literacy among them; they had a printing-press and a weekly newspaper, and in 1827 adopted a constitution modelled on that of the United States. All in vain: the usual cold, greedy hostility

23 Who was three-quarters white. McGillivray is an outstanding illustration of the point that it is culture, not colour, that makes a man an Indian, European or American.
24 This figure is solely for the eastern Cherokees; it does not take into account those (about 5,000) who had earlier moved to Indian Territory.

went to work, and the Cherokees had to labour along their own path of agony into the West. They called it the Trail of Tears; and at least 4,000 died, either in the concentration camps where they were assembled for deportation or during the removal itself.

Contemplation of these and all the other atrocities at length forces the historian to face fundamentals. He will remember the crusades, the religious wars, the Reign of Terror, the Russian purges, and the extermination of the Jews, and see that the treatment meted out to the American Indian was not exceptional, it was characteristically European, if not human, and gentler than many comparable manifestations. He will look with doubled and redoubled scepticism on all expressions of missionary zeal, remembering that though many good men set out to bring Christianity to the Indians, they were almost ludicrously fewer in number than the multitudes who, professing similar motives, were concerned only to gratify their lust for land at any price, and than the still larger numbers who apathetically allowed evil to triumph. More, he will doubt the depth and sincerity of most men's professions of civilization, democracy and benevolence at most times, since they have so often proved such feeble checks on conduct, and compatible with actions of the utmost injustice. Yet he will not despair either of humanity or of the possibility of progress. For even on the frontier the Europeans were not uniformly or perpetually vicious. Many (if too few) deeds of kindness and truth from white to red, red to white, are known, especially in the relations of the US army with the Indians. And the faithlessness, inhumanity and greed displayed by the whites to the Indians were to prove their own punishment. It was the operation of these characteristics in Georgia which, first, expelled the Cherokees and then, in 1864, laid the state open to Sherman's devastating march to the sea,[25] when the whites paid the penalty for their headlong course *via* the oppression of the Indians and the enslaving of the Africans into rebellion and bloody civil war. More generally, we can say that as the whites did to their red victims, so they did, and do, to each other and to the blacks – with what results the criminal statistics of the United States today make plain. Yet it must be added that as time has passed, more and more white Americans have come to see the folly and loathe the evil of this legacy of violence, and have tried, *pari passu*, to behave more justly and mercifully to the Indian as they have tried to be more just, more merciful, in their other social relations.

But this has been mostly a twentieth-century development. The nine-teenth century was the Indian's era of defeat, which was only made worse (for punishment followed) by each temporary victory: that, for example, of the Little Big Horn, when some Sioux, under Crazy Horse and Sitting Bull, wiped out an American regiment. The news reached the East, it is pleasant to report, on 5 July 1876, in nice time to spoil the celebrations of

25 See below, pp. 342–3.

a hundred years of freedom and independence; but the retaliation was all the more cruel.

A year later some of the Nez Percés, generally reckoned to be among the most intelligent and large-minded of the tribes, were forced off their homelands in the Wallowa valley in eastern Oregon,[26] and, after drunken outrages by a handful of their young men, were hunted by army detachments 1,500 miles across Idaho, Yellowstone Park and Montana. They fought a brilliant campaign which earned them the ungrudging respect of their antagonists: 'they abstained from scalping,' said General Sherman, 'let captive women go free; did not commit indiscriminate murders of peaceful families and fought with almost scientific skill'. But in the end they were caught at a place called Snake Creek, forty miles south of the Canadian border and safety, and realized, like Lee at Appomattox twelve years before, that they faced a choice between annihilation or surrender. Their war-leaders had almost all been killed, so it was left to Chief Joseph, the wisest man among them, to accept the inevitable. He came forward between the armies and spoke nobly of what broke the Indians:

. . . I am tired of fighting. Our chiefs are killed. Looking Glass is dead. Toohoolhool-zote is dead. The old men are all dead. It is the young men who say yes and no. He who led the young men is dead.[27] It is cold and we have no blankets. The little children are freezing to death. My people, some of them, have run away to the hills, and have no blankets, no food; no one knows where they are – perhaps freezing to death. I want to have time to look for my children and see how many I can find. Maybe I shall find them among the dead. Hear me, my chiefs, I am tired; my heart is sick and sad. From where the sun now stands, I will fight no more forever.

Nor did he; Chief Joseph spent the rest of his life (he died in 1904) in patiently effective diplomacy, the object of which was to get his people back to their homelands, or at least somewhere nearby. He surrendered, having received generous promises: all were broken, not by the officers who made them but by their superiors ('White men have too many chiefs,' was his comment). In the end, after years of suffering, he was able to lead the Nez Percés back to the North-West; but he never again lived in Wallowa.

Naturally enough, the defeat of the last Indian warriors (the Apaches under Geronimo, who 'came in' in 1886) did not end the spoliation. In 1890 the decennial census made it seem that there was no more unoccupied land available for white settlement in the United States; but in that very year the Indian tribes were robbed of a further seventeen million acres – one-seventh of the remaining Indian lands – under the Allotment Act of

26 General Harney: 'I have lived on this frontier fifty years and I have never yet known an instance in which war broke out with these tribes, that the tribes were not in the right.'
27 I.e., his brother, Chief Ollokot.

1887, which Congress had passed solely, its supporters averred, in order to hasten the civilization and happiness of the Indians. It resulted in the Indians losing eighty-six million acres altogether between 1887 and 1934. They were the most valuable acres. Yet the Indians, as they grew poorer, grew also, by a process common in 'underdeveloped' countries, more numerous. It had once seemed that the race would gradually cease to reproduce itself. Now more and more Indians came into the world to suffer. Their reservations, narrow and poor to begin with, were less and less able to afford them the means of life. They became ever more expensive charges on the government, which yet continued callous and incompetent – so much so that by the 1920s destitution was bringing about famine. It seemed that the last ruin of the American Indian was at hand. By the same token, the white conquest of the continent, which had begun so uncertainly, so small, so long ago, was complete.

BOOK TWO

The Old Order and the American Revolution

Novus Ordo Seclorum.

Motto of the United States of America

Many states and kingdoms have lost their dominions by severity and an unjust jealousy. I remember none that have been lost by kindness and a generous confidence. Evils are frequently precipitated by imprudent attempts to prevent them. In short, we never can be made an independent people except it be by Great Britain herself; and the only way for her to do it is to make us frugal, ingenious, united, and discontented.

John Dickinson, 1765

6 Imperial Britain 1660–1763

The obligation of each Briton to fulfill the political duties, receive a vast accession of strength when he calls to mind of what a noble and well balanced constitution of government he has the honour to belong; a constitution of free and equal laws, secured against arbitrary will and popular licence, a constitution in fine the nurse of heroes, the parent of liberty, the patron of learning and arts, and the dominion of laws.

George III

Here numberless and needless places, enormous salaries, pensions, perquisites, bribes, groundless quarrels, foolish expeditions, false accounts or no accounts, contracts and jobs, devour all revenue, and produce continual necessity in the midst of natural plenty.

Benjamin Franklin to Joseph Galloway, London, 25 February 1775

The American colonies are great to this country in general and indeed very justly, as being the principal sources of our balance in trade, and consequently of our riches and strength, by the great quantity of shipping employed, of manufactures vended and of the useful returns of their growth.

Horace Walpole, 1754

On 26 October 1760, King George II died at stool in his closet.[1] His grandson, enemy and heir, also named George, was twenty-two years old. His reign was to be the second longest in English history, and one of the most eventful; he himself was to play a more important part in politics than any of his successors, although his role in American history was by no means so crucial as legend maintains. A word about his character is in order.

George III was no tyrant, whatever his enemies said. He was devoted to

---

1 In modern idiom, on the lavatory.

the British Constitution, and his political virtues leap to the eye if we compare him with those other royal failures, Charles I, Louis XVI and Nicholas II, and explain why he kept his life and throne while they lost theirs. He was above all things open, honest and loyal. Ministers who were true to their royal master's person and policies could depend on his support. He was extremely hard-working, and gradually acquired an immense political expertise matching that of those other master-managers of eighteenth-century English politics, Sir Robert Walpole (1676–1745) and the Duke of Newcastle (1693–1768). His private life was blameless (that is, single-mindedly uxorious); and since he had the sense to stipulate that the woman chosen for his wife should be uninterested in politics, this trait helped his popularity. Finally, he was a stout English patriot. 'I glory in the name of Britain,' he remarked. Not for him the longings of his grandfather and great-grandfather for their dear native Hanover. To him, Hanover was 'that horrid electorate which has always lived upon the very vitals of this poor country'. His passion for agriculture and a country life earned him the nickname of 'Farmer George'. These attitudes could only endear him further to most of his subjects. He was an intelligent patron of the arts and learning, and gave a pension to Samuel Johnson.

The King had the defects of his virtues. As a backward, secluded boy he was racked by self-distrust and clung for reassurance to the Earl of Bute (1713–92). Poor Bute was as weak as the King seemed, and at length failed his friend completely. But by then George had matured, and his self-confidence became such that he could for years prop up an appallingly weak Prime Minister: Lord North. Unhappily self-confidence all too often shaded into obstinacy and wilfulness. Furthermore, George thought that change of any kind was incompatible with the survival of his country and her greatness. The convictions he defended with passionate stubbornness were those of a narrow, second-rate intellect. Again and again he employed his political cunning, his powers as King and the respect won by his character (later, the timidity inspired by his madness) to prevent essential reforms.

In 1760 his inheritance was as magnificent as that of any monarch in history. No wonder that George and his bold Britons were full of self-glorification. But the spendour was transient. The next five chapters will explain how the English-speaking world came to split into two great but utterly distinct polities – how Farmer George's biggest farm was lost.[2]

He could not have expected to lose it, coming to the throne, as he did, during an enormously successful war of expansion; and even before that war started in 1756, the British Empire was something to marvel at. The wildest visions of Ralegh, Hakluyt and Captain Smith had long been surpassed. At the mid-point of the eighteenth century Great Britain was strong

2 A phrase lifted from Eleanor and Herbert Farjeon, *Kings and Queens* (London, 1932), the first book to interest me (at the age of eight) in history.

enough to crush her last rival and become the leader and arbiter of the world.

Hers was, above all, an Atlantic empire. British ships ventured to China; the East India Company fostered a lucrative trade in South Asia and would soon win the rule of Bengal; but India was to be the heart of the second, not the first, British Empire. George III's principal overseas possessions stretched in a gigantic bow round the grey ocean from Newfoundland, down the east coast of North America, across the Caribbean and the precious sugar islands to the west coast of Africa: a curve of some eight thousand miles. It was an empire built on, by and for trade; and in 1750 that trade was worth more than £20,000,000 annually. The imperial merchant marine was the largest in the world; King George's subjects enjoyed the highest standard of living. There were fifteen million of them: fewer than the inhabitants of the kingdom of France, but, if various calculations proved sound (as they did), the empire was destined rapidly to overhaul the ancient rival in population as in everything else. Unlike its nineteenth-century successor, and in spite of the presence within its borders of Irish, Africans, American Indians and East Indians, it was strikingly homogeneous, the bulk of its people being white, Protestant and English-speaking. The wide seas acted, not as a barrier, but as a link – for water transport was, in the pre-railway age, far easier, and far cheaper, than land.

Yet revolution was to break out – first in the British Empire, then in the kingdom of France: in other words, in the two most modern, richest, best-governed polities in the world; and it broke out in the more advanced of them first. This was not a coincidence, but historians are still groping for, and quarrelling over, the explanation. It is a large and difficult question. No answer can be final.

Still, the point must firmly be made that it was growth, not decay, victory, not defeat, that touched off the American and French Revolutions. Alexis de Tocqueville long ago pointed out that

It is not always the going from bad to worse that causes a revolution. It happens more often that a people who have borne without complaint, and apparently without feeling, most oppressive laws, throw them off violently as soon as their weight lightens. The system that a revolution destroys is almost always better than that which immediately preceded it, and experience teaches that the most dangerous moment for a bad government is usually that in which it begins to reform.[3]

With modern historical knowledge, we would have to modify these remarks before ourselves applying them to the French old order; and they would have to be still more sharply qualified before they could be applied to the first British Empire; but there is still much relevant truth in them, worth

3 A. de Tocqueville, *L'Ancien Régime et la Révolution* (first published in 1856), Book III, Chapter 5. My translation.

pondering. For Tocqueville points to the phenomenon now known as 'the revolution of rising expectations'. It was such a revolution that undermined the old order throughout the West.

No social system can ever be perfect, and the failings of the old order early became manifest. But it was destroyed by its success. It had been given its final shape by the English and French of the seventeenth century and their greatest statesmen. Their work had been far from fruitless. They had not merely solved, in rough and ready fashion, the problems of religious and civil strife which had plagued their countries; they had not merely made those countries the mightiest and most progressive states in the world. They had created the modern French, British and American nations, whose overriding characteristic turned out to be a restless creativity. This creativity could not long be confined within the political, economic, intellectual and social structure which generated it. The men of the eighteenth century came to expect, and inexorably to demand, more than the seventeenth-century ordering of their world could possibly provide. A home and refuge thus became a prison. Only in the British Isles did it prove possible to break out fairly peaceably, and even there the Irish had a ghastly history. Overseas, the mighty edifice which George III inherited collapsed in tumult and war, and the fate of the French kingdom needs no retelling here.

To be sure, periods of self-criticism were frequent even while the old order was at its height. Montesquieu was only the greatest name among the critics who rose up against the French monarchy between the death of Louis XIV and the Seven Years War. In Britain, the long ascendancy of Robert Walpole drove opposition politicians of all stripes into frenzied denunciations of 'Robinocracy' and the decline of British liberty. The classic phrase 'bribery and corruption' began to be heard – in North America, among other places. The cry went up that an oppressive Parliament had succeeded the oppressive Stuarts. 'Power' (we would say 'the state' or 'bureaucracy') must be brought under control again by such devices as manhood suffrage, parliamentary reform and freedom of the press. Opposition writers spread abroad an oppressive anxiety, a mood reinforced by the long, undistinguished years of the War of the Austrian Succession. In 1750 fear and worry were growing as another great struggle with France drew near, for many doubted the capacity of the ruling clique to achieve victory, or even to avert defeat. Henry Pelham (1695–1754), the chief minister, was better fitted for reducing the national debt and the size of the navy than for conducting a war.

In spite of all, the underlying mood of mid-century Britain – the right little, tight little island – was one of unlovely and almost bottomless complacency, bred by sixty years' success in all fields of life. The realm of Great Britain[4] was the heart and chief beneficiary of the lucrative Empire. The

---

4 Legally, at first, England, Ireland, 'the dominion of *Wales*' and the town of Berwick-on-Tweed. Scotland became a full partner in 'the realm' under the Act of Union (1707). Ireland never enjoyed more than a tithe of British privileges and prosperity.

gross national product was worth some £48,000,000 annually, £15,000,000 being exported. The countrymen and heirs of Newton, Marlborough, Pope, Hogarth, Chippendale, Kent and Locke, contemplating themselves and such monuments as Parliament and the Bank of England, saw little to criticize. On the contrary, they brooded on their innumerable virtues and on the compliments they incessantly paid themselves. The national mood was well symbolized by the toilsome lawyer Blackstone, whose *Commentaries* attempted to demonstrate the wisdom, consistency and rationality of the Common Law of England, that extraordinary hodge-podge from the deep past. The lower orders congratulated themselves on being freeborn, and on not wearing wooden shoes like backward foreigners. The anthem of the age proclaimed:

To thee belongs the rural reign;
  Thy cities shall with commerce shine;
All thine shall be the subject main
  And every shore it circles thine.
Rule, Britannia! Britannia rule the waves!
Britons never never never shall be slaves!

You may, therefore, boldly defy the best-read historian to assign a single reign in all our annals when these great ends of government were more religiously intended or more generally obtained than under his present Majesty's auspicious, mild, and steady administration: nay, you may boldly challenge the most discontented and querulous of all his subjects to point out that nation under Heaven where he will venture to assert, that he could live so happily, in all respects, as he does in England.

Thus an anonymous admirer of the constitution in 1748. His views are representative. Yet the Hanoverian – perhaps one ought to say the Walpolean – political system was, as has been said, the solution to the problems of Stuart England. To deal with the problems of Georgian Britain it would have had to be flexible and adaptable. Unhappily it was dangerously rigid.

For one thing, it was deeply aristocratic and oligarchical. On the eve of the great changes that collectively are known as the Industrial Revolution, landed wealth was still the supreme source of power and prestige. The gentlemen of England were wiser than the French *noblesse*: less insolent, spendthrift, exclusive, military, Court-oriented, selfish and crass. But (or perhaps therefore) they had an even firmer grip on their country. The great families of the Whig aristocracy had palpably gained most from the Glorious Revolution. Since 1689 the British political system had reflected their influence, their acres, their rent-rolls; but the lesser gentry, the squirearchy, secure in their manor-houses and their justiceships of the peace, were quite as deeply committed to the system as the grandees. Their lesser status only made them less intelligent, for it kept them mostly in the countryside with none but dogs, horses and huntsmen for company. In everything, individually and collectively, they showed the effect of narrow horizons. Shooting, hare-coursing, fox-hunting and port were their pleasures; church-going was their religion; farming and gamekeeping their only business. Snobbish by vocation, for they were compelled to cherish the values of blood, land and cash which kept them at the top of the heap, they were also as besottedly insular as any of their most ignorant inferiors. In politics, whether in Parliament or out of it, they were deeply conservative; reluctant to pay, or to vote, taxes, though conscientiously doing so when obliged by law; contemptuous of merchants and of fortunes won in trade (unless lucky marriages brought such fortunes their way); loyal to the King, the Protestant religion and old customs; more reluctant than any duke or businessman to contemplate radical change, except perhaps for the enclosure of the common fields.

As to the Whig grandees, they had wealth, worldliness and intelligence enough to be rakes or reformers if they chose without much risk. Their basic conservatism did not become conspicuous until they were frightened by the French Revolution. They were as reluctant as the squires to contemplate the loss of power, or any alteration in the scheme of things which had given them ascendancy. But their position was complicated by this very instinct for power. According to the Whig tradition, they had wrested authority from the Stuart kings to exercise it themselves, in the name of Protestantism and the landed gentry; this left them with a residual suspicion of the Crown, no matter who wore it. All went fairly well while George I and George II let themselves be guided by the oligarchs; but the emergence of the active, opinionated George III soon revived the divisions and tensions within the oligarchy itself that had marked the reigns of William III and Queen Anne. A vigorous king made a vigorous opposition likely: it only needed an issue, which the times swiftly provided. Then, as long before, the role of the monarchical executive again became a leading question of British politics.

The tradition of such a full-bloodedly aristocratic society was bound to be that office was primarily a form of property, a source of income. No higher end could be imagined for the public service than that of providing for the dependants of the gentlemen and peers of Britain, men whose position entitled them to insist on decent provision, out of the national purse, for their younger brothers and other poor friends and relations. Hence the power wielded by the King, or his trusted Minister (a Walpole, a Pelham), through the medium of deaneries, bishoprics, clerkships, commissions in the army, colonial governorships, etc. – the whole vast machine of patronage. Even this was only part of the social system that it symbolized; for example, the municipal government of England had been falling into the hands of little local oligarchies since before the Civil War. But it was the part that mattered, for politics largely consisted of squabblings over the allocation of the patronage plums, and it was the part through which the Empire was governed. Inevitably we must ask, how efficient was it?

No simple answer can be given. Clearly, a system which could bring the British, in war and peace, to the pinnacle they had attained by the end of the Seven Years War was both vigorous and efficient, if only by the skin of its teeth. But it had conspicuous failings, for all that.

In the first place, the patronage machine, skilfully used, gave whoever commanded it an almost unbreakable hold on the politicians. The House of Commons could and did rebel from time to time, bringing down such long-dominant Ministers as Walpole and Lord North; but it did not do so often, and seldom or never succeeded in forcing an unwanted Prime Minister on the King, at any rate for very long. Throughout the Georgian age no ministry ever lost a general election. So it was dangerously possible for a government to persist in ruinous policies long after public opinion would have sanctioned their abandonment, and still longer after their unwisdom should have been clear to Ministers – or to the King.

Secondly, a system so riddled with jobbery, so studded with sinecures – a government service which had as so prominent an object the protection of politicians' clients, or of retired politicians themselves,[5] was not very capable of putting the right man in the right place. This affected offices high and low. An exceptional man at the head of affairs, like the elder Pitt (1708–78), might know how to find the right person (say, General Wolfe) for the right job (the conquest of Canada); nevertheless there was all too much likelihood that an emergency would find a man of only passable competence in the place of urgency. More important, the everyday level of knowledge and capability in the middle and lower ranks of the public service was adversely affected. We need not take too seriously the case of the member of the Board of Trade who thought that Virginia was an island; but his like proliferated, and made it difficult to conceive and carry out wise policies. Surveying the Age of Walpole and the Age of Chatham,[6] we may think that the wonder was that the imperial and domestic administration was so well conducted; but its deficiencies were real, and were soon to emerge as fatally important.

Third, and last, we must note the most insidious, and perhaps the worst, evil of the system, which was that everyone – King's friends, civil servants and Whig reformers alike – had a stake in it. Boards, committees and incompetents might proliferate to the general confusion. Everyone was conditioned, almost unconsciously, to avoid the thought of fundamental alteration. Some politicians' actions might carry them and their countrymen

---

5 This was of no little importance in an era when a politician might well leave office far poorer than he entered it. The Duke of Newcastle was estimated to be £300,000 worse off at the end of his political life than at its beginning; George III came to North's rescue by paying his debts and making him Lord Warden of the Cinque Ports; the enormous debts of the younger Pitt (as reckless as his father in his personal finances) had to be settled by his friends after his death.

6 Sir John Plumb, whose categories these are, dates them as 1714–42 and 1742–84 respectively. See his *England in the Eighteenth Century* (Harmondsworth, 1950).

long leagues towards radical change: thus the younger Pitt greatly enlarged the scope and effectiveness of Edmund Burke's 'economical reform', transmuting what had started as a mere attempt to curb royal patronage into a true modernization of English government. But the politicians' vision remained bounded by horizons beyond which not even the Pitts, Burke or Charles Fox could look. This made them curiously helpless when a crisis arose which posed fundamental challenges to the old order. There is no sure evidence that even Chatham, in office and in health, could have settled the American question peaceably, to the enduring satisfaction of both sides. His assumptions were too much those of George III.

In view of the foregoing, it is not surprising that the attitude of the British to the Empire which they had acquired was not very enlightened. Distinctions must be made. Some Britons still regarded the New World as potentially a most lucrative investment; others still hoped to find a better life by going there; others, especially in the political class, saw the Empire, east and west, as both a burden and a glory. But it seems safe to say that on the whole a profound indifference to, almost an unawareness of, the colonies' existence was the commonest stance, even during the excitements of the Seven Years War. The colonists could thus count among their blessings a complete security against interference from British public opinion. The ending of this security was to make a great difference for the worse. The waking of the American Revolution in the Stamp Act crisis awoke the slumbering English too, impelling them to ask themselves what they thought of the colonies. They replied, as men always do in such cases, with a torrent of cliché, on this occasion about the Mother Country. They took great pride and pleasure, they decided, in owning an empire (provided it cost them nothing), and their tone (caught from their betters, the politicians) became highly patronizing. They could make nothing of the American view that the colonists owed allegiance, not to their British fellow-subjects, but to George III as their common King. As Benjamin Franklin said, 'Every man in England seems to consider himself as a piece of a sovereign over America; seems to jostle himself into the throne with the King, and talks of *our subjects in the Colonies*.' It was shallow, foolish and harmless – until the explosion of 1774, when the North ministry was able to fan this feeling into a flame of support for its severe American measures, and thus sweep aside all opposition in its drive to disaster.

But the great emergency was far below the horizon in 1750. In that year the Empire was still very much what it had always been, with nothing worse to perplex it than the perennial problems of the French, the Spanish and the Indians, and organized according to the set of economic and political principles commonly known as mercantilism.

The term is convenient, but treacherous. It was never a coherent, universally practised creed, and to present it as an obsolete economic theory, or, contrariwise, as a forerunner of the economic policies of modern nation-states, is to over-simplify. The word itself is nineteenth-century; Adam

Smith, in *The Wealth of Nations* (published in 1776), was the first commentator to identify the thing – he called it 'the mercantile system'. Different
countries adopted different varieties of it at different times. Generalizations
about mercantilism are therefore certain to be unsound, and in what follows
I confine myself to the British variant. Still, there was nothing unique about
the English system, except the size of its success. Identifiably mercantilist
doctrines were widely popular for many centuries, and at some time or
other were adopted as government policy by every important state in
Western Europe. In fact mercantilism was one of the most universal
expressions of the old order of the West. Its rise and decline corresponded
closely to the rise and decline of that order. It was scarcely coincidental that
1776 saw the emergence not only of Adam Smith, the critic of mercantilism,
but also of Jeremy Bentham, the critic of Blackstone, and Thomas Jefferson,
the critic of the old politics. A moment of general crisis had arrived.

Yet the British mercantile system, if judged by its own tenets, was one
of the old order's most solid successes. In the mid-eighteenth century its
achievements were clear for all to see. The Empire was the chief of them,
for it encompassed, explained and made possible all the others.

Such a monumental structure could never have been erected by a purely
economic theory. Mercantilism was a political as well as an economic
doctrine. As one of its supporters asked, 'Can a nation be safe without
strength and is power to be compassed and secured but by riches? And can
a country become rich anyway but by the help of a well-managed and
extended traffic?' Mercantilism reflected the realities of a world in which
inter-state competition in all fields was deadly and incessant. It also intensified that competition: a large part of a mercantilist ruler's purpose was to
deny to his rivals, and secure to himself, as big a piece as possible of what
was thought to be a largely static quantity: the wealth of the world. It was
in part a system of defensive commercial regulation; but was also the continuing, institutionalized expression of the ambitious, aggressive, outward-
looking spirit which had inspired the first American settlements, the first
quest for the world's trade. Other considerations had played a part in
colonization, but commercial greed had never been lacking, and as greed
was rewarded by success, the ever-wealthier merchants of an ever-wealthier
England rose in influence. Their views began to colour those of statesmen
and theorists. The great Earl of Clarendon (1609–74) urged the need
for a strong navy, as encouraged by the Navigation Acts, to check the
'immoderate desire' of other states 'to engross the whole traffic of the
universe'. When the Second Dutch War broke out in 1664, General Monck
commented on its origins, 'What matters this or that reason. What we want
is more of the trade the Dutch now have.' Fifty years later John Withers,
author of *The Dutch Better Friends Than the French*, remarked, 'If those
Froglands were once crushed the trade of the world would be our own.'
Such men demanded wars, plantations and Acts of Parliament to help on
the quest for riches; the rulers of England, looking to the military strength,

prosperity and quiet of the realm, were happy to co-operate; and so mercantilism was born, to put its stamp indelibly on the Atlantic Empire, both in its creation and government.

The earliest theorists were not especially interested, for the most part, in colonies: they hoped to extinguish Dutch competition (for a time their chief problem) by other means. But by the late seventeenth century the English overseas possessions had come to play an essential part in mercantilist thought. Economic self-sufficiency was, as always, the aim, but now it was conceived on an imperial, not merely national scale. All members of the Empire – colonies and mother country – would contribute to the prosperity of all; outside supply, of skills or produce, would not be needed. From this basis the trade of the world would be captured, and thus the wealth and glory of England would be splendidly augmented. The colonies were merely an expedient. Not for a moment were they supposed to have any purposes of their own. They existed for the sake of the mother country which had founded and nourished and now protected them. There was no room for sentiment or imagination in the great maritime and commercial struggle. The colonists' interests could never be allowed to take precedence over England's. According to a commentator in 1696, 'The same respect is due from them as from a tenant to his landlord.' Their role was simply to provide, cheaply, those things – chiefly crops such as sugar, rice and tobacco – which the English could not or would not grow at home. They would thus emancipate England from dependence on foreigners. They would furnish the English merchant with a market which he could profitably monopolize, once effective laws had been passed excluding foreign competitors; and such laws, the celebrated Navigation Acts, were passed between 1651 and 1696.

The Navigation Acts were many, and the system they established was never wholly symmetrical or thoroughly efficient. But their principal provisions, as set out in the Acts of 1660 and 1696, were clear and practical enough. Their purpose was to restrict the colonies to the functions listed in the last paragraph and to monopolize the profits of the carrying trade, indeed of all forms of economic activity, so far as was possible: no foreigner should grow rich as a result of activities carried on within the English realm or colonies. Under penalty of forfeiture of ships and goods it was laid down that all vessels importing or exporting goods to or from any English 'lands, islands, plantations or territories' in Asia, Africa or America, or carrying goods from such possessions to the English realm, or carrying exports out of the realm, must be 'truly and without fraud' English, with English masters, and crews three-quarters English. Foreign goods might come to the realm in such vessels only, or in vessels of their countries of origin (a blow against Dutch middlemen, this). Any ling, stock-fish, pilchard, cod-fish, herring, whale-oil, whale-fin, whale-bone, whale-blubber, etc., imported in foreign bottoms 'shall pay double aliens custom'. The American colonies might export certain specified, or 'enumerated', products (sugar, tobacco, cotton, indigo and other dyes, specklewood)[7] only to each other or to England; customs officers in the plantations were to have the same powers as those in the realm, and plantation laws which clashed with the Navigation Acts were declared to be 'illegal, null and void, to all intents and purposes whatever'. The system was rounded off by some lesser provisions, and in 1696 the Board of Trade was set up to administer it.[8]

It is impossible to decide exactly how successful the system was. According to British merchants, times were always bad, foreign competition was always dangerous, even under the Navigation Acts (and since those acts were defied by vast numbers of smugglers, the merchants may not have been entirely wrong). However, some observations may be ventured.

The mercantile system was selfish and nationalistic – arising from a condition of conflict, no doubt, but making that condition worse. According to C. M. Andrews, the greatest historian of colonial America, 'It fomented war in provoking an economic struggle among the commercial and industrial nations for place, power, and wealth.'[9] It sacrificed the Empire's periphery to its centre, and all loftier considerations to those of commerce and power. Against this it can only be urged that rulers in the seventeenth and eighteenth centuries had to deal with the world as they found it, and mercantilism was at least a rational and in many ways a beneficial response to trying circumstances.

More particularly, the British system turned, as we have seen, on tropical and sub-tropical staple products. They were raised by plantation owners in the mainland colonies south of Pennsylvania and in the British West Indies, whose prosperity was made possible by the importation of vast numbers of African slaves, in itself a lucrative staple trade.[10] There were some crucial differences between the mainland and island planters. The mainland planters, whose crops were less profitable, bought fewer slaves, a much higher proportion of them women, and treated them better (since replacements for the dead or incapacitated were expensive). The proportion of black slaves to free whites was far, far greater on the island plantations, and so was discontent. The planters were to a great extent absentees. Consequently imperial protection, against rebellion as well as invasion, was much more important to the islands than to the mainland. Secondly, sugar was so incomparably the most valuable colonial crop that the absentee planters were able to buy themselves into Parliament and the ruling class of landed gentlemen, to form, in alliance with the sugar merchants,

---

7 Specklewood was a product of Jamaica, used in fine cabinet-making. Many additional products were to be enumerated during the eighteenth century: cacao (or cocoa), rice, molasses, naval stores (listed on p. 84), copper, beaver and other furs. After 1763 the enumeration was extended still further.
8 Officially the Lords Commissioners of Trade and Plantations – a title too easy to confuse with that of the Board's forerunner, a Privy Council committee known as the Lords of Trade.
9 C. M. Andrews, *The Colonial Background of the American Revolution* (Yale paperbound edn, 1967), p. 93.
10 A fuller discussion of slavery and the slave-trade will be found in Chapter 7.

a powerful lobby known as the West India interest. By contrast, tobacco planters were content to be colonists. They regularly exceeded their incomes in the attempt to live magnificently at home. Their credit was good, but they over-strained it: by the outbreak of the Revolution, it is estimated, they owed more than £4 million sterling to London.

Britain throve on the system as she was meant to. She had become the staple for her colonies: all colonial produce passed through her ports in its quest for European customers, and she reaped the middleman's reward. She enjoyed a monopoly of the colonial market for manufactures, which stimulated her industries, and was independent of potentially hostile sources for supplies of such essential commodities as naval stores: tar, pitch, rosin, turpentine, hemp, masts, yards, bowsprits. The slave-trade was a risky and often unprofitable business to individuals, but it helped to make the fortune of Bristol and Liverpool. The merchant marine benefited from the Navigation Acts, as planned, and thus furnished a reserve of trained seamen and seaworthy vessels, most useful to the Royal Navy in time of war. The various customs duties brought in handsome revenue returns for the government, and places in the customs service were useful additions to patronage. The trade and tax structure meant that there was a constant drain of bullion from the colonies to the realm, which appeased the constant mercantilist anxiety about a shortage of precious metals. Finally, the fences which Britain erected round her Empire denied its products to her rivals. Decidedly the mother country seemed to have little reason to complain of mercantilism.[11]

Nor was it so oppressive to the colonies as it may seem. Great Britain wanted her plantations to be contented and prosperous, and took steps to make them so. The tobacco colonies of the south mainland – Virginia, Maryland and North Carolina – were allowed to trade only with Britain; but they were given a monopoly of the British market, heavy duties being placed on foreign leaf and British farmers being forbidden to grow any.[12] Similar advantages were given to South Carolina, which grew rice and indigo; and of course to the sugar islands (which otherwise would have suffered from the competition of cheap French sugar). The colonies of the north mainland – Pennsylvania to New Hampshire – had their own profitable place in the system. The British West Indies became dependent on them for provisions. New Englanders were encouraged by the imperial government to build and sail ships, and eventually supplied nearly a third of all British

11 Though from the beginning there were critics who argued that, economically at least, Britain would have gained more by free trade. Certainly the British greatly exaggerated the value to them of the colonial trade and undervalued that of the trade with France which, deeming it immoral and unpatriotic, the government denied them.

12 Even so, the colonial tobacco planters never managed to perfect their monopoly of the British market, and they had to pay duty on their exports to Britain – duties imposed, and from time to time increased, solely to raise revenue. In fact it was the ease of taxing tobacco brought in by sea, and the impossibility of taxing tobacco grown in the realm, which lay behind the ban on British leaf.

bottoms, owning half of the 3,000 vessels involved in the colonial trade. Perhaps the colonies' chief gain was in the political and military sphere. Britain, a careless mother, expected her children to be self-supporting; they were to be a source of profit, not expense; but, with some consistency, and whether the Navigation Acts were obeyed or not – they often were not, for an illicit trade with the French and Spanish colonies became a valuable source of income to the North Americans – she did not interfere with their internal government, beyond occasionally disallowing a colonial law; and she protected them against France and Spain. The colonies were well aware of political and military problems, and that islands and plantations could change hands at peace conferences. To them therefore it mattered little that no large British force was sent to America until the Seven Years War: they were protected equally, or better, by the mother country's victories on European battlefields, or at sea. For the rest, they were sure of some assistance and support in their perennial struggle against the French- and Spanish-supported Indians. The Board of Trade could plan intelligently, and sometimes rescue a desperate situation. For example, the incompetent heirs of the founders and proprietors of South Carolina, declared under Queen Anne to be 'the frontier colony of all Her Majesty's plantations on the Main in America', might have been left to ruin their province and enjoy their charter in peace for far longer, had not the Yamasee Indians in 1715, in a war arising out of the misdeeds of the Indian traders, shown vividly how a weak government in one colony could injure the whole British position in North America. The war wiped out the Indian trade of the Carolinas for a time and revived French and Spanish strength in the area. The southern flank of the British might be turned, or their traders and settlers confined to the coastal plains. The colony survived – just – but its defence had clearly become too important to be left to incapable private management, so the Board of Trade endorsed a revolt of the settlers in 1719, and in 1729 the proprietors were bought out, South Carolina being 'taken into the King's hand' – that is, becoming a crown colony of the usual type, with a Crown-appointed governor.

On the whole, then, the mercantilist system must be reckoned to have fulfilled the purposes of its makers: it made the prosperity of all parts of the Empire possible. Its drawbacks were its inefficiency and incompleteness – the Board of Trade could never induce Parliament to make it watertight, and the customs officers were too few, too ill-paid, too corrupt to plug the gaps. It was, economically, increasingly obsolescent. But its destruction was to come from quite different causes.

In 1756 the war that had been threatening between France and Great Britain since their last peace (1748) burst into life; and before long the helm of British government had been seized by the man of genius, Pitt the Elder, vaingloriously but truly saying, 'I know that I can save the country and that I alone can.' For the war had not been going well; and Pitt incarnated the logic of mercantilism – logic which, ruthlessly pursued, would bring victory.

Pitt was not afraid of the harsh international conflict, the scramble for power and profit, from which mercantilism sprang. On the contrary, he rejoiced in it. Faith in Britain's divine mission inspired him, as it had inspired those earlier pirates, the Elizabethan sea-dogs. He had long correctly identified France as Britain's last rival, and now he fell upon her with wild ferocity. Her capacity for sea trade and sea warfare must be destroyed. Britain must be aggrandized with France's spoils. As to the cost of such an onslaught, of such a daring bid for pre-eminence, it could (Pitt thought) be met, ultimately, from the proceeds of war; until they were realized, his colleague, Newcastle, might usefully struggle to raise money by loans and taxes. Meanwhile the French sugar islands, Canada, India and the Floridas were seized, and the French navy was destroyed at Quiberon Bay. Overnight, it seemed, Pitt had doubled the extent of the British Empire with one hand, while sustaining with his other Frederick of Prussia's struggle in Europe against hopeless odds. Frederick's role was to keep the French too busy to defend their Empire. 'I have conquered Canada in Germany,' Pitt boasted.

Then victory showed its disappointing side. The mercantile system touched the summit of its glory, and glory proved too much for it. First, George II died, and the new King, longing for peace, like most of his people, got rid of the great war minister. In 1763 George III and Bute signed the first Treaty of Paris. Next, the government began to face the problem that Pitt had so airily dismissed. The war had run up the National Debt to £129,586,789, carrying an interest charge of £4,688,177 per annum. The land-tax stood at four shillings in the pound. Glory and power now had to be paid for. How was it to be done? And how was an empire grown suddenly so large, so heterogeneous, to be harmoniously governed?

7 *Thirteen Colonies* c. *1675–1763*

England already possesses an uninterrupted line of well-peopled provinces on the coast successively begun within less than 150 years. She sees them every year augmented by an accession of subjects excited by the desire of living under governments and laws formed on the most excellent model upon earth. In vain do we look for an equal prosperity among the plantations of other European Nations . . . This surprising increase of people is a foundation that will bear a mighty superstructure.

John Bartram of Philadelphia, 1751

'Tis here Apollo does erect his throne;
This his Parnassus, this his Helicon.
Here solid sense does every bosom warm;
Here noise and nonsense have forgot to charm,
Thy seers how cautious, and how gravely wise!
Thy hopeful youth in emulation rise;
Who, if the wishing muse inspired does sing,
Shall liberal art to such perfection bring,
Europe shall mourn her ancient fame declined,
And Philadelphia be the Athens of mankind.

Anon, *Titan's Almanac*, 1730

I do not see how we can thrive until we get into a stock of slaves sufficient to do all our business, for our children's children will hardly see this great Continent filled with people, so that our servants will still desire freedom, to plant for themselves, and not stay but for very good wages.

Emanuel Downing to John Winthrop, *c.* 1645

At the centre of the Empire and the Empire's problems lay the mainland colonies of British North America.

In 1763 there were eighteen of them. Thirteen were later to turn rebel and claim the lion's share of attention. But it is important to remember that, feeble, underpopulated and insignificant though Nova Scotia, Newfoundland, East and West Florida were, Georgia was scarcely any better. Only the newly won Quebec and the seventeenth-century English foundations could claim to be mature societies. Nor were even the twelve senior English plantations uniform or united. Economic, religious, political and cultural differences cut them off from each other. Massachusetts was apparently loyal to the Crown; neighbouring New York simmered with agrarian revolt. The pattern of coming events cast no shadow before it.

So long as settlers moved west into the wilderness the agonies of Jamestown and Plymouth would be repeated, but in the mid-eighteenth century the westward movement was only just beginning to cross the Appalachian mountains. In the coastal towns the first feeble settlements and their sufferings were only memories. Even the site of Jamestown had been abandoned after a disastrous fire in 1699, and Massachusetts had swallowed up the Pilgrim colony in 1691 when, in the aftermath of the Glorious Revolution, it acquired its second charter (the famous first having been overthrown in 1684, when the English government at last gave way to its mounting irritation at the Puritans' obstinate refusal to conform to royal policies).

The years since then had at first seen Boston's continued development on the lines indicated in Chapter 4. Its population had risen from 7,000 in 1690 to 17,000 in 1740, and throughout the years between it had been the largest city in the colonies. It and the other towns of New England retained their characteristic instrument of self-government, the town-meeting, which made even the smallest township a city-state, a direct democracy of the purest classical kind. The town-meetings were more and more dominated by the well-off at the expense of the poor and the 'middling sort', but they still sharply differentiated the New England from the Old and provided essential training in self-government.

The religious and social tendencies discussed at the end of Chapter 4 also continued. The New England conscience, the New England mind, had many victories ahead before their submersion in the vast society of twentieth-century America. But ministerial denunciation of the too-evident backsliding went on. A visitor in 1740 might say that the Bostonians' observation of the Sabbath was 'the strictest kept that ever I yet saw anywhere', and indeed the day seems still to have been a properly miserable one, with no public pleasures of any kind allowed, not even walking in the streets. All else declined from godliness. To a Huguenot visitor in 1687 it was clear that 'the English who inhabit these countries are as elsewhere, good and bad'. This was no consolation to the surviving Puritans. One of them, Judge Samuel Sewall (1652–1730), denounced 'affectation and use of gaiety, costly buildings, stilled and other strong liquors, palatable, though expensive diet ... sensuality, effeminateness, unrighteousness, and confusion' and tried to restrain his acquaintance from wearing periwigs.

Another, Cotton Mather, deplored the appearance on the streets of Boston of beggars, whom 'our Lord Jesus Christ himself hath expressly forbidden us to countenance' (it was God's law that men work, not beg), and lamented that 'idleness, alas! idleness increases in the town exceedingly; idleness, of which there never came any goodness!'[1] Worse was to happen, in spite of all efforts. The General Court of Massachusetts had three times to pass laws forbidding 'extraordinary expense at funerals'. Women got out of hand: some dared to run away from disagreeable husbands, others set up in the oldest profession on Boston docks. Most unfortunately, a leading business of the town came to be the manufacture and export of rum, which was drunk throughout the Empire as well as by the Royal Navy. Boston, exporting some 600,000 gallons annually,[2] was herself, if anything, less boozy than other places. In 1752 Pennsylvania, an agrarian colony with many thirsty harvesters, distilled 80,000 gallons of rum and imported 526,700 gallons. A Philadelphia poet, J. Dumbleton, wrote a *Rhapsody on Rum*. Right-thinking Bostonians were not comforted. In 1726 they had to denounce in the press 'the birth of so formidable a monster in this part of the world' as dancing, and to announce that 'the abuse of strong drink is becoming epidemical among us, and it is very justly supposed . . . that the multiplication of taverns has contributed not a little to this excess of riot and debauchery'. Taverns were indeed much more numerous than churches, and probably more influential: it was in their hospitable rooms that news was exchanged and opinions formed. Bostonians, we are told, sat 'tippling and sotting for whole evenings, or perhaps for whole days'.

Much of the ministers' outcry seems to us, with our different beliefs and values, irrational and disproportionate, or simply elderly. The bulk of the colonial population, above all in Massachusetts, was as grimly conventional in its morality as could be wished. Real crime, on the other hand, was a concrete problem on which the ministers could offer little guidance, one which the American cities were as unable to solve in the eighteenth century as they are in the twentieth. Already complaints were heard at New York that 'it seems to be now become dangerous for the good people of this city, to be out late at nights, without being sufficiently strong or well-armed, as several attacks and disturbances have been lately made in our streets'. To deal with the sprinkling of footpads, housebreakers, shoplifters, pickpockets, etc. – many of them no doubt transported from England – the colonists had to rely on the old English system of watches and constables that, in Boston at any rate, had improved very little since the days of Dogberry.[3] Thus in 1742

---

1 The number of poor quadrupled in Boston between 1687 and 1771, though the population merely doubled: part of the reason may have been the refusal of the country towns to do anything for each other's poor, who therefore tended to drift to Boston.

2 The Boston article competed successfully with West Indian rum because, though much nastier, it was also much cheaper, which was a decisive consideration with the poor and frugal consumers of North America.

3 See *Much Ado About Nothing*.

some malicious and evil-minded persons took off the hinges and carried clear away, the door of the watch-house at the town dock, while our Guardians were at their natural rest, to the great endangering of their health, if not their lives, there being nothing more pernicious to persons asleep, than nocturnal air. There has been a proposal made in the neighbourhood, to raise a guard for the defence of the said house, to prevent the like enormity for the future. But all generous proposals meet with opposition from contracted spirits, some object and say, that the watch-men ought at least to take care of their own lodgings.

To no avail: this was not the first time the watch had slept on duty, nor was it the last, for a month later the door was stolen again. The truth was that all watches tended to be what they were called in New York: parcels of 'idle, drinking, vigilant snorers, who never quelled any nocturnal tumult in their lives (nor as we can learn, were ever the discoverers of a fire breaking out,) but would, perhaps, be as ready to join in a burglary as any thief in Christendom'. It was usually impossible to find enough strong, responsible men for the watch, and equally impossible to erect prisons strong enough to keep criminals until their trial – and the incident at New Jersey in 1745, when, after a politically motivated jail-break, the jail-breakers mended the hole they had made in the wall before dispersing, was quite as exceptional in colonial America as it would be anywhere else. The crime rate rose everywhere, because increasing wealth increased temptation; because more and more immigrant felons arrived; because the size of the cities increased, offering the protection of urban anonymity; because, even in America, it was possible to be unemployed or underfed; because the size of the continent helped getaways; and because innocent Americans, not yet attuned to the times, were still easy gulls.

The ministers could be excused for dismay when contemplating such a world and for sighing that things did not use to be so in New England. They also had professional grounds for anxiety. There could be no doubt that the Congregational churches were losing their hold on men. Perhaps it all began in the mid-seventeenth century, when it had unfortunately seemed necessary to persecute the Quakers, then intent on disturbing the peace of Zion with their own version of divine truth. Some had been flogged ferociously, some imprisoned or driven from the colony, some hanged. This sort of thing encouraged the home authorities to annul the Winthrop charter, for it was Whitehall's opinion, expressed by the Board of Trade in 1750, that 'as toleration and a free exercise of religion is so valuable a branch of true liberty, and so essential to the enriching and improving of a trading nation; it should ever be held sacred in his Majesty's Colonies'.[4] So the

---

4 The Board was also shrewd enough to see that the prospective migrants were attracted as well by colonies which enjoyed a fair measure of self-government. Accordingly it bowed to the inevitable, tolerated the colonial assemblies and carefully provided local legislatures when it came to make constitutional arrangements for new colonies such as Nova Scotia and the Floridas.

pernicious practice of religious freedom came to Massachusetts, and with it, Anglicanism, which proved shockingly attractive to some of the better-off.[5] Then there was the bad business of the Salem witches in 1692, when in a wave of superstitious hysteria twenty people were hanged for crimes of witchcraft that the judges and the jury later became convinced they had not committed (Judge Sewall nobly made public confession, in the meeting-house, of his fault). This did nothing to strengthen public respect for the ministers. Finally, the age of science was at hand and many men were growing less susceptible to the old Biblical evangelism: more interested in the world about them, less in the world to come. In his old age Cotton Mather devoted himself to the introduction of inoculation against smallpox; while the young Benjamin Franklin sold his set of Bunyan's works to buy history books.

Not that the age was irreligious. In spite of science, belief in a magical universe was still fairly general. Presbyterianism revived in America as a crusading creed, with the fire that had once been the Congregationalists' and the Quakers'; and in the thirties the Great Awakening, first and fiercest of religious revivals, swept across the colonies. It was connected with the birth of Methodism in England: George Whitefield himself visited America to preach the new word. He, and American revivalists like him, such as Jonathan Edwards of Northampton, Massachusetts (1703–58), dealt with the degenerate times by reviving the old Puritan concern with the con-viction of sin, the necessity of conversion and the certainty of salvation. Spectacular results were achieved. Members of Edwards's congregations fell to the floor in fits as he announced that God,

though he will know that you cannot bear the weight of omnipotence treading upon you, yet he will not regard that, but he will crush you under his feet without mercy; he will crush out your blood, and make it fly, and it will be sprinkled on his garments so as to stain all his raiment. He will not only hate you, but he will have you in the utmost contempt.

This sort of thing convinced tens of thousands that they must change their wicked ways; but, as in all such cases, a few years later the effect had largely worn off and the good people of Boston and Philadelphia felt free to dance again.[6] The Awakening doubtless saved souls, but it split churches; indeed, its emphasis on the importance of individual experience may be said to have democratized American religion. Many men of good sense, good nature or good education disliked its emotionalism and turned to deism,

5 So real seemed the threat of Anglicanism that the Congregationalists thought it prudent to appeal to the English Act of Toleration lest their religious order be overturned as their political one had been and an Anglican Establishment be forced upon them.
6 Said Whitefield, 'It grieves me to find that in every little town there is a settled dancing-master, but scarcely anywhere a settled minister.' He was talking of North Carolina; but dancing was just as popular in the other colonies.

unitarianism or infidelity. Many congregations split into New Light (ranting) and Old Light (respectable) portions; and a gulf opened, which has not yet closed, between the liberal, rationalizing prosperous religion of the town and the fundamentalism of the economically and intellectually backward countryside; and also between the religion of the urban rich and the urban poor. It was an Old Light Presbyterian minister who sniffed that 'the vulgar everywhere are inclined to enthusiasm'. In Connecticut the dispute spilled over into politics and became a quarrel of secular parties that was still bitter during the Revolutionary period.

In other respects Boston, and the New England which it dominated and represented, flourished notably. The Boston Latin School, Harvard College and mighty Yale College (founded at New Haven, Connecticut, in 1701, by strict Congregationalists, when Harvard showed alarming signs of liberalism) were merely the most conspicuous of many excellent educational institutions which gave New England the highest literacy rate in the colonies and quite probably in the world. Inoculation for smallpox caught on after some resistance: before long the colonies had outstripped Britain in generally adopting it. Disastrous and repeated fires forced Bostonians to replace their wooden houses by brick as much as they could, and to develop an efficient fire-service. Town sanitation made great advances; so did printing and the book-trade. If Boston built fewer and fewer ships, other towns in Massachusetts and Rhode Island built more and more.

There was the rub. Worldlier men than the ministers could reasonably worry about Boston after 1740. The narrow and agriculturally unpromising hinterland ceased to attract settlers, who found more tempting prospects to the South-West. Newer colonies (above all, Pennsylvania) began to cut into Boston's early monopoly of the trade to the West Indies. The town's shipbuilding did indeed decline, and so did that accurate barometer of her prosperity, her population, while the other leading American cities continued to gain. The rum-trade became the only dependable staple, and that in turn depended on importing molasses from the French West Indies, where it was cheaper than in the English, a practice ineffectively forbidden by the Molasses Act of 1733. The merchants of Boston turned smugglers rather than obey the law, but other, heavier blows were in store for them. Britain drifted into war with France in the forties, and Massachusetts bore most of the burden in the colonies. Her sailors were pressed into the Royal Navy; many of her young men were killed; and heavy taxes hampered economic life still more. Worse, it was decided to fall in with the imperial government's desire to replace the inflationary and unsound paper money then current with a metallic currency; accordingly in 1749 the paper money was called in and coins became the only legal tender. But they were in very short supply, so that there was no money to finance new ventures. As a result, merchants were soon lamenting that 'trade is quite dead' and that 'all trade seems to be stagnated; and little else goes on but drinking'. In 1760 Boston was devastated by the worst of all the many fires she endured during the colonial period. 'This once flourishing metropolis must long remain under its present desolation', sighed the *Boston Post Boy*, a local newspaper. It is not very surprising that, in their attempt to recoup their losses, Bostonians traded freely with the enemy during the Seven Years War. Nor is it surprising that the first events of the Revolution struck sparks out of a city which had been in a bad way for twenty years.

For a picture of thriving urban life we have to turn to Boston's successful rival, Philadelphia. In her relation to the province surrounding her, the younger town may stand for all that was new, hopeful and vigorous in colonial America.

In the causes which brought it about, in the causes of its subsequent successes and in the nature of its ultimate failure, the foundation of Pennsylvania[7] in some respects recalls that of Massachusetts. William Penn (1644–1718) intended 'a holy experiment', a state to be run on Quaker lines, as John Winthrop had planned his city on a hill. Like the older dream, the Quaker vision faded. In 1721 a rapidly increasing crime rate induced the Friends to abandon their mild penal code for an extremely stiff one: the crime wave continued to mount. One historian has unkindly remarked that eighteenth-century Quakers preferred the counting-house to the meeting-house. He might equally well have remarked that they preferred the family farm, for the settlers in Pennsylvania brushed aside, quite as firmly as the New Englanders had done and even more promptly, all attempts to make them live in compact villages, centring their lives on the meeting-house and cultivating their lands co-operatively. They were resolute individualists; and it was to be in large part from their settlements that the tradition of the small farm was eventually to spread into the Ohio and Mississippi river valleys, thereby becoming a sacred, because so universal, detail of the American way of life.

Like the Puritans, Penn had been spurred on by the fear of religious persecution in England. Friends who shared his anxiety emigrated to the new colony in large numbers: by 1690, a mere seven years after her foundation, Philadelphia was the second city of the colonies, with a population of 4,000 (in the same year Boston's was 7,000). The spectacular rise of Pennsylvania was accelerated by persecution in another place than England (where, as it turned out, the Quakers were left in peace). The Friends had established contacts with European religious groups of the same quietist, undogmatic stripe in the days of George Fox, their founder; and William Penn himself had visited such groups in Germany. Accordingly he took pains to advertise his project by having his promotional pamphlets translated into German and distributed in the Rhineland, where they had a great success. For the incessant wars of Louis XIV in that region, and rigid oppression of the new sects by native rulers who, whether Lutheran, Calvinist or Catholic, were

7 Named by Charles II after his dead friend Admiral Penn, the founder's father, not after the founder himself.

all equally unsympathetic, made the idea of a fresh start in a new world irresistible, though the journey to America was even more beset with difficulty and hardship than it had been for the Pilgrims. Poor peasants for the most part, the sectarians had somehow to find their way down the Rhine, past innumerable tolls and customs barriers, first to Holland, then to England, then to America. At every stage they encountered cheats and oppressors, and the ships which carried them to America (in return for the privilege of selling them as indentured servants when they arrived) were all too often what were later known as 'coffin-ships' – vessels quite unfit for the voyage: unhealthy, overcrowded, liable to founder. Whereas the Pilgrims had at least enjoyed a comparatively quick crossing, these Germans (or Palatines, from the Rhenish Palatinate, as they were called in Pennsylvania)[8] often were confined at sea for months, waiting for favourable winds to carry them into harbour. Sometimes they found assistance or revenge when they arrived. When one such ship, the *Loving Unity*, sailing from Rotterdam, arrived in Boston, the authorities discovered that half the 142 passengers had died on the voyage and the other half had been monstrously oppressed by a brutal captain and crew. Judge Byfield of the vice-admiralty court punished the scoundrels heavily. But the Palatines cannot even so have been very happy to be in Boston, for there was little land left to take up in New England, where the soil was anyway none too good. New York might have attracted them, but the great proprietors, Dutch and English, who dominated that colony had no intention of endangering their titles to the land by admitting too numerous and vigorous a farming population, even as tenantry.

Pennsylvania was the place. Penn had laid it down from the first that there should be no religious test for the holding of office or the exercise of political rights, let alone molesting or prejudice in person or estate because of 'conscientious persuasion or practice'. With him, it was a matter of noble religious principle: 'How can any man's conscience be at another's dispose?' he asked. This was in line with the practical colonial policy of the Board of Trade; but the policy of religious freedom was so zealously carried out in Pennsylvania that a German traveller in 1750 reported:

Coming to speak of Pennsylvania, that colony possesses great liberties above all other English colonies, inasmuch as all religious sects are tolerated there. We find there Lutherans, Reformed, Catholics, Quakers, Mennonites or Anabaptists, Herrnhuter or Moravian Brethren, Pietists, Seventh Day Baptists, Dunkers, Presbyterians, Newborn, Freemasons, Separatists, Freethinkers, Jews, Mohammedans, Pagans, Negroes and Indians. The Evangelicals and Reformed, however, are in the majority. But there are many hundred unbaptized souls there that do not even wish to be baptized.

8 Or Dutch, a corruption of *deutsch* – hence 'Pennsylvania Dutch'. They can still be heard speaking German in the Pennsylvanian countryside today.

The attractiveness of such a state of affairs to the Palatines amply justifies, in a worldly sense, both William Penn and the Board of Trade; but Pennsylvania had charms for everybody. The coastal plain, gently sloping a hundred miles inland from Philadelphia to the feet of the Appalachians, watered by three great rivers – the Susquehanna, the Schuylkill and the Delaware – was ideal country for European farmers, whether Palatines, English, Scottish or Irish. The temperate climate made it possible for them to grow the crops they were used to: wheat above all, but also rye, oats, barley, hemp and flax; maize was the only new grain they attempted. The immense fertility of the soil, and the large acreage to be had for the asking, ensured large harvests for everyone, although Pennsylvanian methods of agriculture were distinctly backward, compared to English or even south German ones. Some settlers had money enough to get land, implements and housing immediately; others served out indentures, learning the way of the new country, and then set out westward. However it was, development was rapid. The first settlement of any size to be founded after the Quaker city herself was Germantown on the Schuylkill (1683). Others soon followed. Big German barns, spreading orchards and fertile fields soon gave a new character to the back country. Before long a vast and ever-increasing tide of farm produce began to pour into Philadelphia; and a city's fortune was made.

This story illustrates, as well as any other, how hugely America was to benefit from her immigrants (she would also be shaped and changed by them in non-economic, non-utilitarian ways).[9] The rise of Philadelphia illustrates another general truth about American history: the importance of the cities, and of the processes of urbanization.

Philadelphia had great advantages. The city acted as the essential export–import channel for Pennsylvania, for the 'Three Counties' (the future state of Delaware), for 'West Jersey' (the lower area of New Jersey) and, until the belated rise of Baltimore, for Maryland, though the areas were all politically distinct. The Great Philadelphia Wagon Road was built to bring the farmers' produce swiftly to market: it was transported in the famous Conestoga wagons,[10] forerunners of the covered wagons in which the pioneers were to settle the Great West in the nineteenth century. The corporation of Philadelphia spent large sums between 1720 and 1736 on building, improving and regulating the city market, until it was the envy of other towns and was

---

9 By 1775 there were approximately 100,000 Germans in Pennsylvania. In the early eighteenth century Irish Protestants in large numbers, driven out by the economic subjection of their country, had come to add their numbers and energy. Other ethnic groups, who were either survivals from earlier attempts at colonizing the region or were attracted by William Penn's pamphlets, were Finns, Swedes, Dutch, Welsh and Huguenots (French Protestants).

10 Named after Conestoga Creek in Lancaster County, a centre of German settlement on the Susquehanna due west of Philadelphia. The farmers there not only perfected the covered wagon, but bred the sturdy horses needed to draw it.

allowed by foreigners to be the best of its bigness in the known world, and undoubtedly the largest in America; I got to this place by 7 [our informant continues] and had no small satisfaction in seeing the pretty creatures, the young ladies, traversing the place from stall to stall, where they could make the best market, some with their maid behind them with a basket to carry home the purchase, others that were designed to buy trifles, as a little fresh butter, a dish of green peas, or the like, had the good nature and humility enough to be their own porters.

The wagoners, once they had sold their produce, bought what they needed, and so trade went on merrily. By the eve of the Revolution it was thought that there were no fewer than 20,000 wagons in Pennsylvania, and they went down to Philadelphia in hundreds. More than eighty carriages for the gentry added to the hurly-burly. The din and danger of the streets were sometimes unendurable.

On this solid economic foundation city life flourished. By 1760 Philadelphia had a population of 23,750, and was the largest town in the colonies, leading its nearest rival, New York (swelling from wartime profits), by more than 5,000. By 1775 it had nearly doubled, having 40,000 inhabitants, and left all others behind.[11] At the top, dominating the city, were the mercantile gentry, revelling in their wealth, their pomp, their power, their town and country houses. Many were still Quakers, but a drift into the more showy and aristocratic Anglican communion had begun, as in Boston. These merchants enjoyed and patronized, though they did not create, an intellectual life which was threatening to surpass Boston's. The great Linnaeus, for example, founder of modern botany, called the Quaker Dr John Bartram of Philadelphia 'the greatest natural botanist in the world'. At the bottom was a comparatively small class of the poor, the unemployed, the transient. Their condition was appreciably less pitiable than that of their more numerous English and European counterparts, but such Old World evils as unemployment, slums, beggary, prostitution, hunger and the degradations of poor relief were present in the New, and the very poor were miserable enough.

Between the extremes came the great bulk of the citizens, 'the middling sort', the intelligent, energetic, thriving artisan class, the real beneficiaries of America, who gave the city its character and did most to exploit its opportunities. Honest, earnest workmen could be sure of making a good living in Philadelphia, where skills were always in demand; and many could do better, rising to fortune and sometimes to fame. It was such men whom Justice William Allen had in mind when he cheerfully asserted: 'You may depend upon it that this is one of the best poor man's countries in the world.' It was most fitting that the first world-famous American should

11 It may have been the second largest city in the British Empire, from which it was about to secede, and was certainly one of the four biggest (the others being London, Dublin and Edinburgh).

spring from among them, and that he should still be the symbol at once of his city and his country.

Benjamin Franklin (1706–90) is, of all great Americans, the one I should most like to dine with in heaven. He was physically unremarkable, though he had a sagacious, twinkling face, a strong, sturdy build, and spectacles. His character was an enchanting blend of simplicity, drollery, shrewdness, energy, intellectual curiosity, benevolence and integrity. Apart from touches of endearing vanity, his only weakness was for women: he confessed that in youth he could not resist them, and in old age he was still an incorrigible flirt. He was middle-class to the core: the prophet of the cult of rising in the world by hard work and honest worth. I can see nothing wrong in this, though others have professed to do so. Franklin had a genius for enjoying life without ever failing in his duty to society and to his conscience. He was a walking paradox: a hedonistic Puritan. Thus his life well illustrates, among other things, an extraordinary transformation that was threatening Puritanism in the eighteenth century.

For though Franklin early became a deist, he was born in Boston of perfectly orthodox parents. They could not afford to keep him at school for more than a year, but 'I do not remember when I could not read': he educated himself, with great success, eventually mastering French, Italian, Spanish and Latin, as well as some degree of arithmetic, and reading extensively in everything English that came his way, which, as he was a printer by trade, was a great deal. In due course he became a more than competent natural scientist. At first he worked for his elder brother James in Boston; but young Benjamin grew weary of his apprenticeship and ran away to New York. There was no work for him there, so he found his way to Philadelphia, where, after a few years, he began a rapid rise to great prosperity.

His printing business throve, and by 1748 he was rich enough to retire, young though he was, and do as he pleased – a fact which in itself tells us much about the growth of his chosen city; but it is the extraordinary variety and number of his occupations that best convey the nature of life in eighteenth-century Philadelphia. His most famous ventures, next to his political career, were his experiments with electricity, in the course of which he proved the single nature of the 'fluid', demonstrated the identity of lightning and electricity, and with characteristic, and characteristically American, practicality invented the lightning-rod – no small thing this, for American thunderstorms are ferocious and the largely wooden towns[12] of colonial America suffered again and again from devastating fires. Franklin well knew this: he had pioneered a volunteer fire-fighting society at Philadelphia, an example which was widely followed. (This was also characteristically American in that a private group of citizens undertook to do what

12 Brick was increasingly used, but it was a comparatively rare and expensive material, and the supply could not keep up with the demand for new buildings.

elsewhere was left to the authorities.) It was as an electrical scientist that he first attained international celebrity and was awarded honorary degrees at St Andrew's (1759) and Oxford (1762), so that it is only proper to speak of him in later life as Dr Franklin. (He loved the title.) His great reputation at home was founded on his journalism. At this time the power of the newly mature press to influence opinion and conduct was immense, and growing. It threatened to rival, if not to eclipse, that of the pulpit. Like his brother James and most other colonial printers of any importance, Benjamin Franklin, as part of his printing business, ran a newspaper (the *Pennsylvania Gazette*), most of which consisted of advertisements and reprints from English and colonial papers, but the original part of which he chiefly wrote himself. He also, again following usual practice, published an almanac, under the pseudonym of Richard Saunders. As *Poor Richard's Almanac* it soon became immensely popular, selling 10,000 copies annually, and was, says the author, 'generally read, scarce any neighbourhood in the province being without it'. Franklin peppered it with proverbs, invented or improved by himself, which passed into the language: 'Great Talkers, little Doers'; 'God heals and the doctor takes the fee'; 'Necessity has no Law: I know some Attorneys of the name'; 'Neither a fortress nor a maid will hold out long after they begin to parley'; 'Lost time is never found again' (one of the Puritan axioms of behaviour). The plain people of America, in need about equally of amusement and good advice, delighted in this sort of thing, and in the author, who encouraged the taste for reading (good business to do so) by founding first a book-club (it arose out of a discussion group called the Junto that he started in Philadelphia) and then an academy which soon grew into the College of Philadelphia (chartered 1755; later the University of Pennsylvania – the first university, as distinct from a college, in America).

Franklin had always been interested in public affairs: his zeal for improving himself and the world around him implied as much. He had a hundred schemes which needed political action: there was one for reforming the night watch, and one for building a public hospital (both succeeded).[13] Inevitably he was drawn into politics, in the first place by the needs of military defence. Pennsylvania had two fundamental problems: the political power of the pacifist Quakers, and that of the Proprietors, the Penn family. Both were restricting the free growth of the colony; the former threatened its life. The Friends relied on God and their treaties with the Indians, so in 1747 French and Spanish vessels were able to enter the Delaware and attack plantations and shipping. Another time they might descend on Philadelphia

---

13 His other activities included: organizing the American post so that it was for the first time efficient and profitable; launching a scheme for paving the streets of Philadelphia; inventing an improved stove for mitigating the effects of the American winter, which sometimes froze the ink in inkwells (Franklin refused to patent this useful invention); inventing the armonica, an improved form of musical glasses, for which Mozart and Beethoven eventually composed pieces (all good musical dictionaries describe the instrument); acting as secretary to the first Masonic Lodge in Philadelphia; devising an abortive scheme for spelling reform.

itself. Franklin proposed a voluntary association, like his fire-fighting one, for the defence of the province. As usual, his scheme was a great success, and after that he was irretrievably set on a public career. In 1748 he entered the Pennsylvanian assembly. His influence and his popularity grew; he formed a political party which in time defeated the Proprietors and incorporated those Quakers who were ready to fight in self-defence (the Indians devastated the frontier in 1756, so the number was large). In 1757 he was sent to England to act as Pennsylvania's London agent in the attempt finally to crush the Penns. The apprenticeship of a statesman was complete.

All this shows how Pennsylvania was maturing. The process, and the direction in which it was moving, were clear to some contemporaries. So assertive had the assembly grown, even so early as 1707, that the then Governor remarked 'it plainly appears that the aim is to revise the method of government according to our English Constitution, and establish one more nearly resembling a republic in its stead'. He was defending William Penn's prerogatives, but the assertiveness was a fact all the same. In 1755 the Deputy-Governor wrote:

They have been most remarkably indulged, both by the Crown and Proprietaries, and are suffered to enjoy powers unknown to any assembly upon the continent, and even such as may render them a very dangerous body hereafter; but not content with privileges granted to them by charter they claim many more and among others an absolute exemption from the force of royal and proprietary instructions.

The Pennsylvanians, like other Americans, were now numerous and strong enough to insist on their own interests; they expressed themselves vigorously through their assembly and began the evolution of the American party system. They were well used to looking after themselves; they were not at all used to paying taxes. In all these respects they were typical of most of their fellow-colonials.

In one respect, however, they were highly atypical. 'We do not like Negro servants,' said Franklin firmly (although he allowed advertisements concerning such to appear in the *Pennsylvania Gazette*). His objection was largely the outcome of European self-interest: he did not want to see the province overrun, as the southern and Caribbean colonies had been, by Africans. He was eventually to take a much higher view of the question. But his original attitude was as characteristically Pennsylvanian as it was untypical of mid-century America in general. Few Philadelphian merchants entered the slave-trade, which was the staple of Newport, Rhode Island, an equally Quaker city. Pennsylvania originally accepted slavery and promulgated a harsh code of regulations to govern it. Free Africans were attacked as 'idle slothful people . . . who often prove burthensome to the neighbourhood, and afford ill examples to other negroes'. But from the start there were doubts. The earliest anti-slavery petition came from Germantown in

1688. Memories of the persecutions they themselves had suffered, and their central doctrine of the Inner Light (God working in the hearts and consciences of men), slowly led the Quakers of Philadelphia to see things as they were. A rise in white immigration, making black labour less necessary, was a great help. The Quakers began to move to the position that no member of the Society of Friends might be a slave-trader. They sent emissaries over to England with the message, which soon found willing hearers. Thus began one of the most important developments in the history of humanity: organized anti-slavery. But it did not achieve maturity or success overnight. In the eighteenth century slavery and the slave-trade were at their height. It is more than time to examine these most tragic of American institutions.

Slavery is a form of service imposed and maintained by force: no more, no less. It treats men as things, as pieces of property.[14] To define it is to condemn it. It violates the Golden Rule. As Abraham Lincoln is said to have replied to a pro-slavery argument, 'What is this good thing that no man wants for himself?'

So much is clear to us; but it has only become clear during the past 250 years. The historical problem is that of deciding why slavery was abolished, not why it arose, for it seems to have existed continuously since the dawn of history. In some societies it was mild or limited in scope, or eventually died out. The English in England, for example, had lost all the medieval forms of servitude by 1600 at the latest. But they did not hesitate to introduce slavery into their new empire a few years later; and the system of indentured servitude, which paved the way for that of African enslavement, was evolved out of Tudor methods of dealing with the unemployed and beggars which in their harshness resemble the colonial slave codes.[15] In spite of their Christianity and growing civilization, the English were still (myths of Merry England to the contrary) ceaselessly cruel in their social relations.

The old British Empire, like its rivals, was built on slavery. This means not only that the Atlantic slave-trade, centring on the Guinea Coast, was a large part of the world trade which the Empire was designed to capture, but that most of the Empire's commerce was in the produce of slavery. Sugar was the chief imperial commodity: the sugar plantations of the Caribbean were worked by slaves.[16] Part of the sugar went to England, to enrich the merchants there; part in the form of molasses to New England,

14 For example, a Boston court case listed as goods 'Two negroes, four casks of brown sugar, two casks of cocoa and two Pateraroes [*sic*]'.
15 This is especially true of the statute of 1547, which provided for the branding and enslaving of vagrants, whom their masters might beat, chain, half-starve and put to labour 'how vile so ever it be'. But this statute was so harsh as to be unenforceable, and was repealed within three years.
16 Not that the English were first in the field. As a matter of fact the first sugar island worked by African slaves was Cyprus under the Venetians.

to be made into rum.[17] The sugar islands grew very little of their own food, so merchants found ready markets there for the produce of Ireland, Pennsylvania, New York and the New England fisheries. The significance of this trade is unmistakable: as Richard Pares put it, 'Without it the sugar colonies could not have existed and the North American colonies could not have developed.'[18] Exposed to new diseases, overworked and underfed, a slave on a sugar plantation had a life-expectancy of only seven years; this, and the shortage of women (which implied a shortage of children), meant that the planters had to replenish their labour force by regularly importing new slaves, which of course was good business for the slave-traders. The East India Company and the English manufacturers got a share of the profit by producing iron, coarse cloth, beads and other items with which to tempt African traders with victims to sell. This triangular trade was, in fact, the symbol of the Empire. *Sic fortis Etruria crevit*: the countryside round Bristol soon gleamed with country palaces for the merchants; Glasgow became a great city; Liverpool added to its indirect profits by operating a small slave-market of its own. The guilt of living off the misery and oppression of fellow human beings spread throughout prosperous and virtuous British society. To take two random examples: a slave-based fortune paid for the splendid buildings by Hawksmoor at All Souls College, Oxford; and although Jane Austen made a hostile reference to the slave-trade in *Emma*, she also made the Bertram family in *Mansfield Park* largely dependent on a slave-plantation in Antigua for their wealth, apparently unconscious of the evil they were exploiting.

Nor was any part of the North American colonies free of guilt. By 1720 one-sixth of Boston's population was black. Cotton Mather was once presented with a slave-boy by his grateful parishioners: he turned this to good account by baptizing the boy Onesimus[19] and learning from him the practice of inoculation. Mather spoke up for the religious equality of blacks and advocated their education; but he also urged Africans to give up their foolish 'fondness for freedom' and to recognize that they were better off as slaves.[20] In 1760 there were 16,340 blacks in New York, most of them slaves. Pennsylvania, New Jersey and the Three Counties throve on their exports to the slave-islands; and the southernmost colonies – Maryland, Virginia, the Carolinas and Georgia – all enjoyed, if that is the word, slave-based agrarian economies.

It is still a matter for learned argument what effects the slave-trade had

17 See above, pp. 89 and 92.
18 Richard Pares, *Yankees and Creoles* (London, 1956), p. 1.
19 See Philemon, 10–20.
20 A naval officer, 'lieutenant of a man of war, whom I am a stranger to, designing to put an indignity upon me', Mather complained, 'has called his *negro slave* by the name of COTTON MATHER'. The lieutenant was perhaps as much annoyed by Mather's attempts to clean up the sexual morality of the port of Boston as by his advocacy of inoculation and friendliness to Africans. The racial attitudes in all this defy elucidation.

on the various African societies that were touched by it; but there is no dispute about what happened after the slaves were brought to the markets on the coast. After lengthy haggling, often complicated by rivalries among the slavers of different nationalities, some of the victims were bought and taken on board, while the rest were left rotting on shore, waiting for the next customers. The cargo slaves were meanwhile manacled with heavy iron chains in pairs. They were taken below and laid out, we are told by a reformed slaver,

in two rows one above the other, on each side of the ship, close to each other, like books upon a shelf. I have known them so close that the shelf would not easily contain one more. And I have known a white man sent down among the men to lay them in these rows to the greatest advantage, so that as little space as possible be lost . . . And every morning perhaps more instances than one are found of the living and the dead . . . fastened together.

For the slave-decks were not only hellishly uncomfortable, but also spreading-grounds for the diseases that many of the victims brought aboard with them. Ships sometimes sailed with hundreds on board and arrived having lost two-thirds of their complement, though the usual loss on British ships in the eighteenth century seems to have been more commonly in the region of 10 per cent, and the figure tended to decline, for it was considered prudent to take some measures to preserve the lives of the slaves: they were valuable property.[21] It was usual to bring them up on deck and force them to dance and sing for the sake of their health. Some slavers bought instruments on the coast for the cargo to play; in this way African music was carried to the New World. The songs were usually laments: the slaves did not much enjoy these occasions, nor was it meant that they should. Too great liberality might lead to a successful uprising, and it was always necessary to be on guard against suicide attempts; so a brutal constraint was universal. At last the ship would complete the Atlantic crossing ('the Middle Passage') and the slaves would be sold again, again with every additional circumstance of indignity. If they were lucky they were shipped to the North American mainland; if they were not (and it is now thought that only 5 per cent of the total, or approximately 400,000, in the whole history of the trade were carried to British North America) they quickly rotted away in the mines, ranches and plantations of Brazil, Spanish America and the sugar islands.

In this fashion the African population of the colonies grew until just before the Revolution (and for some decades after it). It was, next to the

---

21 The longer the voyage, the higher the mortality among both slaves and slavers. Ironically, if justly, the attempts to lower the death-rate of the cargoes were somewhat successful, but the death-rate of the crews remained constant, and constantly high. Not for nothing was the West Coast of Africa known as the white man's graveyard.

English, the largest ethnic group. The total number of slaves imported to the thirteen colonies or states before 1790 is thought to have been between 250,000 and 300,000 (our information is at present too scanty for greater precision), but very early, outside South Carolina at any rate, the African population began to show a natural increase which by the end of the century was approaching that of the Europeans. By 1775 there were approximately half a million African-Americans, many of whom had first-hand experience of the horrors of the Middle Passage.

A comparison of the birth-rate and death-rate of the North American plantations with those of plantations elsewhere, not to mention a comparison with the death-rate on shipboard, shows that conditions in the thirteen colonies, even in the tobacco- and rice-growing regions, were better than they might have been; but they were horrible enough. The system was one of forced labour and depended on the most brutal sanctions. Witches were not burned to death, but slaves were. So late as 1805 a slave suffered this punishment in North Carolina for poisoning her master, mistress and two other whites; the next year another, a man, was burned in Georgia for killing an overseer.[22] Burning was a punishment that had earlier been fairly common, and it was resorted to on a grand scale in New York in 1740–41, when, in a scare that was the precise equivalent of the Salem witch-hunt, the city convinced itself that it was in imminent danger of being burned to the ground by a horde of popish blacks. Four whites were hanged, fourteen blacks were burned, eighteen were hanged, seventy deported. Everywhere the codes regulating slavery as a social institution authorized the harshest punishments and gave masters a free hand, up to and including the power of life and death, with their slaves. For private regulation, however, the whip was usually deemed sufficient: the diary of William Byrd, a cultivated Virginian gentleman, the colony's most learned judge, shows him lashing one or more of his 'servants' every few weeks.[23] Fearing to put ideas into their chattels' heads, slave-owners would not let them be taught Christianity (not that the church had often baulked at recognizing the legitimacy of slavery) or be taught to read and write. Slaves were used casually as concubines, so much so that it has been thought that there was more inter-racial mingling in the eighteenth century than at any time since; the feelings of fathers, mothers and children were not respected, families being frequently broken up when the master wanted to sell. Slaves were outside the protection of the common law: even in Pennsylvania they were denied trial by jury. Above all the Africans were employed ruthlessly and incessantly to perform the heavy labour that the Europeans would not. To be a great tobacco planter in Virginia two things were required: plenty of cheap land

22 The British must not make too much of these incidents. At late as 1763 a white woman was burned in England for murdering her husband.
23 Herbert Aptheker, *The Colonial Era* (second edn, New York, 1966), pp. 41–3. The most humane entry Aptheker quotes from Mr Byrd's diary reads: 'I had a severe quarrel with little Jenny, and beat her too much, for which I was sorry.' Nine days later he was at it again.

to replace the acres wasted by soil-exhaustion and soil-erosion, the marks of inefficient agriculture, and cheap labour (otherwise the overheads of running a large plantation would price its product out of the market). Oppression of the Indians provided the first, oppression of the Africans the second. On this foundation a splendid civilization was erected.

Or so it is conventional to state. Certainly it cannot be denied that for a short time Virginia produced numbers of men as remarkable for their character as their intellect. George Washington (1732–99), Thomas Jefferson (1743–1826) and John Marshall (1755–1835) are only the greatest names among them. They were high-spirited, well-educated, rich, intelligent and responsible gentlemen, who broke a kingdom and created a republic. Many of them deeply disapproved of slavery, though few of them could think of anything to do to end it, save emancipating their own slaves in their wills, as Washington did. Meantime they planned to clear the Indian tribes from the lands west of the Appalachians and seize for themselves new fields to exploit through the labour of their bondsmen. They lived in handsome houses on tidal creeks and rivers, exporting tobacco to England, and in return importing the means to lead a civilized life as the English gentry understood it: port, porcelain and mahogany furniture. They sent their sons either to the Inns of Court to acquire a smattering of law and manners, or to Williamsburg, Jamestown's successor as the capital of Virginia, where they could attend the college of William and Mary (founded in 1693) and later study, as Jefferson did, under the lawyers practising in the town. Their cultural achievements were real. William Byrd had one of the largest libraries in the colonies in his generation, as Jefferson had in his. And Monticello, Jefferson's great dream house, designed by its owner, remains the most extraordinary building in the United States, as Versailles is in France. It was begun in 1770 and not finished until 1809, and incarnates a lifetime of steadily improving taste and skill. But like Versailles it has a profoundly ambiguous meaning. Jefferson, an architect and interior designer of genius, imposed his vision of the noble life on a Virginian hilltop as completely as the Sun King imposed his on the heaths of the Île de France. Posterity does well to admire and cherish both monuments: posterity has not had to pay for them. Yet each glory was made possible only by a deeply oppressive society which ruthlessly exploited the weak.[24] Jefferson, it is true, was a humane slave-master, where Louis XIV was a supremely callous king; but he was the beneficiary of a system which was the negation of humanity. And like the French monarchy, the Virginian system, because of its strength and weakness alike, carried the seeds of its own certain destruction within it.

For the greatest achievement of the Virginian gentry was unquestionably political. It is possible to exaggerate its originality. Gentlemen in England

24 Versailles and Monticello also have this in common, that each was the grandest gesture of a chronically bankrupt regime.

were equally monarchs of the countryside, and every community in the colonies was necessarily self-governing. But there is no denying that in Virginia, more than anywhere else, the theory and practice of American republicanism grew to maturity. The gentlemen of the colony were said to be 'haughty and jealous of their liberties, impatient of restraint, and can scarcely bear the thought of being controlled by any superior power'. The great planters and their families – Randolphs, Byrds, Harrisons – dominated the region; the lesser planters and white farmers moved obediently in orbit, and the franchise, being restricted to freeholders with at least a hundred unimproved acres (or twenty-five improved, with house), could not place power in dangerous – for example, in black – hands (though some black freemen voted as late as 1723).[25] It was, in short, a highly class-structured society. The gentry expected to be consulted about the organization and politics of their communities; they served conscientiously if, in many cases, reluctantly, on the vestries, commissions of the peace and other institutions by which their hold on church and state was maintained, and treated the voters to rum punch[26] and barbecued beef at election time, to make sure that the right men continued in command (it once cost George Washington £50 to be elected to the House of Burgesses). Officially Anglican, they allowed no bishop to challenge their control of ecclesiastical patronage; although a Crown colony, Virginia was really ruled by its assembly, the House of Burgesses, which, in an epoch when all the colonial assemblies were rising in power and vigour, had no rival for self-assertiveness. The ruling class had in a few decades achieved a position of unchallenged authority and had not yet bred out of its system, by marriage exclusively within a confined circle, the qualities of intelligence, drive and judgement which had brought it to the top. Its commonwealth was as much a model of the aristocratic republic dear to Montesquieu as Boston was a model of the city-state. The great planters were as casually certain of their right to make all important decisions without interference from above or below as they were certain of their benevolence and wisdom. If challenged, they would and eventually did rely on their self-evident maturity and skill to justify their desire to govern themselves and others. And within the aristocratic pale, all was equality, duty and responsibility.

Unhappily for the gentry, aristocracy was, in the eighteenth century,

25 In practice sheriffs often ignored restrictions, allowing white tenants to vote, which was a gesture to democracy, but frequently led to disputed elections.
26 This technique was once described as 'swilling the planters with bumbo'. It could be employed too enthusiastically. In 1758 a Mr Marrable poured 30 gallons of rum down the voters' throats in Lunenburg County. This was held to be going too far, and he was unseated by the assembly. On the other hand, in the same election George Washington dispensed 66 gallons and 10 bowls of rum punch, 58 gallons of beer, 35 gallons of wine, 8 quarts of hard cider and 3½ pints of brandy: and nobody objected. In 1777 the young James Madison, standing for re-election to the revolutionary assembly, was defeated because, in a fit of republican virtue, he refused to set up barrels of free whisky in the courthouse square of Orange County.

showing signs of obsolescence. The most important slogan of the age was that of the ambitious, intelligent, educated young *bourgeois*: 'careers open to talent'. All the traditional justifications of aristocratic rule proved useless when challenged, in one nation after another, by men who desired and were able to take and wield power, whether intellectual, economic or political. It is true that all was not plain sailing for these new men. In England they had a hard time of it until the 1832 Reform Act, and later. In France it took three revolutions to displace the nobility. All the same, their monopoly of power was doomed, and nowhere more than in America. There, the urban gentry was by definition raw, *bourgeois* and *arriviste*, like the towns themselves; and even the tobacco aristocrats were new men. Their power and position were too recently gained, by methods too imitable, and were too completely undermined by economic failure, to create a permanent noble caste like those which held up progress in France and Germany. The tobacco barons were soon supplanted, in true American fashion, by men as energetic and as newly rich as their own grandfathers had been. Even their political practices worked against them, as a Pennsylvanian writer pointed out in 1776, saying that 'a poor man has rarely the honour of speaking to a gentleman on any terms, and never with familiarity but for a few weeks before the election . . . Blessed state that brings all so nearly on a level! In a word, electioneering and aristocratical pride are incompatible.' Finally, in order to defend their power from a challenge from above and abroad – from Britain and the British King – they had been obliged to become self-conscious and explicit republicans; they had found it necessary, as will be shown in the following chapters, to justify rebellion by appealing to the rights of man. Extreme emergency had produced an extreme remedy, one which was a powerful example to others besides gentlemen. It proved impossible to keep the slaves from English, Christianity and literacy for ever; soon they found friends whose consciences were newly awakened to the implications of their religious and political principles (many of the latter having been learned from the Virginians); and in due course it was discovered that the rights of man were seditious. They undermined George Washington's Virginia as thoroughly as they had undermined George III's empire, and the leadership of the South passed, disastrously, to South Carolina, where men were still growing rich by slavery and were not ashamed to admit the force on which their political and social system rested. Men were still living who remembered Jefferson when, in 1861, a war broke out between those who adhered to his principles and those who adhered to his practice. Thus the Virginian formula was exposed as self-contradictory.

Nor was that all. It cannot be denied that Virginia was based on slavery; equally, it was based on race-prejudice. From the beginning of the trade slavery and racism had gone together. It is impossible to say that either came first. The Portuguese, in carrying the slave-trade into the Atlantic, were merely extending a practice which had been continuous in the Mediterranean since the remotest antiquity. And in all epochs men of one creed, class, race or state have tended to despise, hate and fear men of alien identities. Few societies, furthermore, have been more parochial, self-satisfied, greedy and cruel than Europe in the age of the discoveries. So the fate of the Africans was as certain and unpleasant as that of the Red Indians with whom it was linked. They were to be enslaved, put to menial tasks and despised, as the masters have always despised the mastered. As time went on the neat reasoning that the African was enslaved because he was inferior, and was inferior because he was a slave, came to be supported by other, equally mischievous, if not always mutually consistent, syllogisms. Slavery was a punishment for the Fall of Man and therefore part of the natural order, not to be tampered with. The slave-trade conferred a benefit on the African, since it removed him from the sin and heathenism of the Dark Continent. The same African was a savage who could not be Christianized, and because he was not a Christian had no rights. Being black, heathen and enslaved the African was different, and therefore wrong, for to be European, and especially English, was to be right; to be heathen and enslaved was clearly to be inferior to a free Christian; since all Africans were black, heathen and enslaved perhaps their colour was inferior too. Indeed it quite clearly was, because black was the colour of night, of evil, of the curse of Ham (imposed on him for looking at his father Noah drunk and naked);[27] and it was well known that black men preferred white women to their own, just as apes (it was alleged) preferred black women to mates of their own species.[28] Possibly the black man was not human at all, but a lesser creature, a link in the Great Chain of Being between humanity and the apes. After all, he lived, and was first encountered by the European, in the same part of the world as the chimpanzee (known at that time as the orang-outang)[29]. . . an immense farrago of evil nonsense slowly multiplied as men, otherwise of good conscience, found that they had to justify the continuing wrong they were inflicting on their fellow-men; and fear of rebellion or other retribution, fear inspired by guilt and the occasional violent expression of black resentment, made hatred inevitable and increased the will to justify the root of all evil. The result was the deeply entrenched, pathological enmity between the races which is the ugliest and oldest problem of American society; an enmity to which the light of Virginia, Mr Jefferson, gave revealing expression in those parts of his book on his native land, *Notes on Virginia*, where he expatiated at length on the ugliness of Africans. It

27 See Genesis ix, 20–27.
28 In this particular myth we may detect a strong undertone of bitter envy of the black man's strength and alleged sexual licentiousness.
29 See Winthrop Jordan, *White over Black* (Chapel Hill, NC, 1968), pp. 28–32. Professor Jordan's discussion of what may be called the orang-outang fallacy throws a flood of curious light on such legends as Tarzan of the Apes and King Kong, and on those apparently innocent cartoons that used to amuse me so much in the *New Yorker*, showing variants of the ape-carrying-off-blonde situation. All, it may be suggested, derive, consciously or unconsciously, from white fear and envy of the black, and a desire to see him as at once dangerous and contemptible by presenting him as a great ape.

makes one look with a sceptical eye on his rhetoric, his architecture and the wooden plough he invented, and prefer, to his rustic paradise, cities such as Boston and Philadelphia where hope for the future was really being born.

Rural America, the ideal to which the Virginians were religiously committed, was never, even in the eighteenth century, the thing of absolute joy that they depicted. Social mobility – the means of rising from one class to another – was far greater in colonial America than in Europe, but it was greater in the towns than in the country. In some areas there was substantial social and political equality between the farmers, but these were the poorer regions. The richer areas showed sharp and rigid class divisions. But (a big but) geographical mobility – the chance to move west to virgin land and start a new, more prosperous career – offered hope to agrarian Americans on the make. The future lay that way for many. Before the Peace of Paris the French began to lay out a town where the rivers Missouri, Mississippi and Illinois meet; though it was to be under Spanish sovereignty for the next forty years, St Louis from its beginning attracted English-speaking traders and settlers. To the north-east, at the Forks of the Ohio, after the defeat of Pontiac, another wilderness town, Pittsburgh, began to grow up on the site of former Fort Pitt (or Duquesne). This westward movement soon created problems of the highest policy for the imperial government.

Meanwhile the great planters of Virginia were falling deeper and deeper into debt to London and Scottish merchants: the world price of tobacco was collapsing and the soil of Virginia was becoming exhausted. Planters in South Carolina, while more prosperous, lived for the few months in the year when they could flee from the dangers of yellow fever and slave rebellion on their rice and indigo plantations to Charles Town or, better still, to the cool breezes of Newport, Rhode Island, just then beginning its long career as the rich man's playground.

The back-country, from Georgia to Maine, struggled against Indians, agrarian inefficiency, indebtedness and remoteness, already displaying a provincialism and a hatred for more prosperous Easterners ('city slickers') which were to scar American society until well into the twentieth century. Even Dr Franklin, who in 1764 nobly defended the rights of some Indians against a mob of rural lynchers ('the Paxton Boys'), succumbed sufficiently to bucolic prejudice to worry about the incoming tide of Germans as well as that of Africans, fearing that the English settlers and their culture would be lost, and persuading himself that Swedes and Finns were darker than, and therefore inferior to, the English.

Almost every province had territorial claims that were unrealistic but not to be relinquished,[30] and hence quarrelled with its neighbours over boundaries. The war between debtor and creditor interests which was to

---

30 'Virginia is bounded by the great Atlantic Ocean to the east, by North Carolina to the south, by Maryland and Pennsylvania to the north, and by the South Sea to the west including California' (Colonel Thomas Lee to the Board of Trade, 1750).

figure for so long in American history was beginning, and taking its standard form of a dispute about paper money. Maryland, driven by economic necessity, had imported 20,000 transported convicts, as indentured servants, to the dismay of adjacent colonies.[31] A sense of common interest, if not of common nationhood, was slowly, almost surreptitiously growing, but even in the face of the greatest emergency the colonies had yet known, the war with France, was not strong enough to sustain Franklin's 1754 Albany Plan for colonial union. The peace, it was hoped, would bring renewed prosperity with it, as war had brought vigour and self-confidence; but everywhere there were discontents and grievances which very little would enflame. Rapid growth had made the colonies strong, and therefore potentially dangerous. They were not the sleeping dogs of Sir Robert Walpole's favourite phrase: they were sleeping dragons.

31 Though Virginia imported convicts too.

8 The Waking of the Revolution
1759–66

That our subjects in the American colonies are children of the state and
to be treated as such no one denies; but it can't reasonably be admitted
that the mother country should impoverish herself to enrich the children,
nor that Great Britain should weaken herself to strengthen America.

Charles Davenant, 1698

If the Colonies do not now unite, and use their most vigorous endeavours
in all proper ways, to avert this impending blow, they may for the future,
bid farewell to freedom and liberty, burn their charters, and make the
best of thraldom and slavery. For if we can have our interests and estates
taken away, and disposed of without our consent, or having any voice
therein, and by those whose interest as well as inclination it may be to
shift the burden off from themselves under pretence of protecting and
defending America, why may they not as well endeavour to raise millions
upon us to defray the expenses of the last, or any future war?

Eliphalet Dyer of Connecticut, 1764

A great empire and little minds go ill together.
Edmund Burke, 1775

War, next only to technology, is the most certain solvent of modern society.
Reforms miscarry, revolutions are prevented or perverted; war is always
with us and seldom or never fails to bring sweeping change. So it was with
the Seven Years War.

Its immediate work was striking enough: the expulsion of the French
from India and North America, the confirmation of Prussia's expansion in
Europe, the raising-up of British power, the casting-down of the ancient
rival dynasties of Habsburg and Bourbon, the appearance of Russia as a
principal factor in the balance of power. The war left behind it, like all wars,
a set of new alignments for the next round: France and Spain clung together

in hope of a common revenge on Britain and, more ominous for the islanders, Frederick of Prussia, needing them no more, turned to collaboration with the Tsarina Catherine in the partition of Poland. Britain found herself without an ally on the continent.

But it was the economic consequences of the Seven Years War, above all, that were to shape the future. The usual wartime boom (produced by military purchasing) was followed by the usual post-war slump. All the former belligerents had to grapple with monster deficits left by the struggle, and to do so with very inadequate means. The governments of the old order, in fact, were in an impossible situation. As Norman Hampson has remarked, 'It was the cost of warfare, irrespective of its success, in an age when the destructive capacity of government had got ahead of the economic productivity of societies, that subjected all the Powers to new stresses. The attempts of governments to raise more money in turn set off new social conflicts.'[1] Louis XV's efforts to solve his money problems led him on to his final and most dramatic clash with his *parlements*. The deficit incurred by the victorious power was to lead to revolution in North America.

In April 1763, two months after the Peace of Paris, Lord Bute resigned. His nerve (always feeble) had been destroyed by ill-health, by the outcry of the mob, by the abuse hurled at him as a Scotchman,[2] as a royal favourite, as the architect of a pusillanimous treaty (William Pitt's pet allegation) and above all (though of course it was not said openly) as the man who had dislodged the Walpolean Whigs from the seats of power and profit which they had enjoyed for forty years. George III was bitterly disappointed at thus losing his 'Dearest Friend', who, after encouraging his King to believe that, together, they would bring back the reign of public virtue, had despaired of the project and was now leaving him in the lurch;[3] but he made the best of it in welcoming Bute's chosen successor as First Lord of the Treasury (in effect, prime minister), George Grenville (1712–70). Grenville was a rising star whom George and Bute had earlier brought into power as leader of the House of Commons in succession to Pitt – which had caused Pitt, who was his brother-in-law, to disown him. The King no doubt supposed he was taking on a loyal ally. He and his unfortunate subjects were to pay dearly for this natural mistake.

Grenville was one of the most formidable politicians of his day. After Pitt's elevation to the Lords in 1766 he dominated the Commons as no one else could. This was not because of his charm or eloquence, for he was quite without either quality: his speeches went on for ever, and a discerning

1 *Historical Journal*, 1968, No. 2, p. 384.
2 The English hated the Scots because, as Henry Fox explained, 'Every man has at some time or other found a Scotchman in his way, and everybody has therefore damn'd the Scotch: and this hatred their excessive nationality has continually inflam'd.'
3 It proved extremely difficult for the public, whether in England or America, to believe that the favourite had fallen for good and was not acting as a 'minister behind the curtain'. The sinister influence of 'this mysterious THANE' was detected everywhere. See below, p. 130.

follower said that 'he was to a proverb tedious'. But the same man noted that 'though his eloquence charmed nobody, his argument converted'. Logical, accurate and overwhelmingly well-informed, he was always the expert. He had further virtues as an administrator, being cautious, upright and, above all, ceaselessly hard-working. He was too greedy for personal profit from office, otherwise we could say that today he would have made an excellent senior civil servant under a strong minister. As a statesman in any age he would have been a disaster, for he was an impolitician, entirely lacking that sagacity which was, for example, a leading characteristic of Dr Franklin. He was tactless, unimaginative, stubborn, void of judgement and self-satisfied as only they can be who never stop talking: they have time to hear, but not to listen to criticism. His worst trait from the King's point of view was that, having been kept out of power for years, he was now determined to be master, and badgered his wretched sovereign ceaselessly for tokens of subjection. In the end George got rid of him, and summed him up as no better than a clerk in a counting house. But by the time of his fall he had done irreparable damage.

As a good clerk he had a horror of debt and immediately set about reducing the country's vast liabilities. He pared cheese with the zeal and folly that England expects of the Treasury. If he lacked Mr Gladstone's hawk's eye for detail, he had all his recklessness in military and naval affairs, starving the army of men and the navy of money. The evil results of this policy were to become evident in the War of the American Revolution: meantime Grenville grew very popular with backbenchers hoping for reductions in the land-tax. Nothing would have pleased the minister more than to be able to oblige them; but he was well aware that at the moment it looked as if he would be obliged to raise another tax instead (for he refused to borrow). Peace has its deficits as well as war.

Grenville may not have had the imagination to realize that a militarily enfeebled England invited attack, and another expensive war; but he could not overlook one that was actually raging. In America in May 1763 the North-Western Indians went on the warpath, inspired by the Ottawa leader Pontiac; the whole frontier, from the Great Lakes far southwards, was in flames, and the British army had to stamp them out. The Pontiac rising was just the sort of sudden crisis that the Empire might expect in the future and for which, therefore, it would have to be always ready (as it had not been in 1763) – ready with soldiers, ready financially. The French and Catholic colony of Quebec had no settled form of government and might rebel at any moment. British soldiers in America were needed to keep the older colonies in order, should they get restive. They might also be used to make the fur-traders behave, deter squatters on Indian land and put down smuggling. In the opinion of General Amherst, the British commander in North America, garrisons ought to be maintained in Newfoundland, Cape Breton, Prince Edward Island, Nova Scotia and the Floridas. 'The Whole,' he rightly commented, 'is an Immense Extent.' There were also the garrisons of Gibraltar and Minorca to think of. Grenville estimated that the annual cost of supporting these forces would be £372,774, most of which would be spent in North America. The only questions that remained were, where and how to raise this sum?

It was easy to decide that the British taxpayer, already the most heavily mulcted in the Western world, should not be further burdened. Had Great Britain been a militarist absolute monarchy like France, her government might have calculated that the power and wealth accruing from the empire of North America would in the end richly repay the Treasury for any immediate outlays: further taxation or further borrowing might have seemed easily acceptable policies. But the achievements of the previous century and a half made such calculations impossible. Paradoxically, the comparative modernity of British institutions made adaptation to modern needs harder. In an absolute monarchy glory, power and profit (if any) redounded in the first place to the King, who could thus take the long view, if he chose, or was able to (two conditions not often fulfilled); but in a constitutional monarchy, where the purse was firmly controlled by a tax-paying gentry, it was much harder to see what would be gained by sacrificing the present to the future. It was not a case of choosing to lose America rather than spend £372,774 per annum: it had not come to that yet, though it shortly would. Rather it seemed to the English neither just nor necessary that they alone should bear all the cost of an imperial organization from which the Americans profited, in immediate terms, so much more than they (it was not Yorkshire which Pontiac threatened, after all). The notion that they ought in prudence to sacrifice their immediate rights and interests to the larger good of the Empire had no attraction for them. The taxpayers' strike which was to bring the Empire down may be said to this extent to have begun on the eastern Atlantic shore.

Besides, the existing governmental machinery made further taxation in England almost impossible. Great Britain enjoyed unusually advanced financial arrangements (one of the reasons for her triumph over France); but, like all other states of the old order, she could never make her full economic resources available to her rulers. In 1763 she was at the end of such resources as were available. A tax on cider, determined upon by Bute, provoked 'tumults and riots' in the West Country.[4] It incorporated an excise, a hated name since the storm which had forced Walpole to withdraw his similar scheme in 1733; more important, it seemed extraordinary, to a country newly at peace, that additional levies should be imposed. Times were bad, and for some years got worse: it was thought that some 40,000 persons were in prison for debt in 1764. Decidedly, further exactions were out of order. In the view of Grenville, and indeed of most people who thought about the matter, it was high

---

4 Nothing ever occurs for the first time. Taxes on cider and perry were among the grievances which provoked the peasants of Normandy to rebel in 1639; a stamp tax provoked a rebellion in Brittany in 1675.

time that the Americans assumed a share of the burden of their own defence.

There remained the question of what duties to levy, and how. Here another matter was relevant. It had not escaped the government's notice, during the war, that it was not only very difficult to get the colonies to pay anything directly for the war effort – Pitt had had to promise reimbursement before even Massachusetts would raise a penny – the extensive colonial trade with the enemy had probably prolonged the long and expensive war and had certainly strengthened the foe significantly. This mightily enraged William Pitt. Never mind that the New Englanders' traffic with the French was essential to enable them to exist, let alone play their part in financing the great struggle: Pitt could only see that it gave the French the essential supplies they needed to continue to fight. It was a paradox of the kind that ministers hate to face: without New England the French in the New World must have collapsed much sooner; yet without the French the Americans could not have fought at all. Pitt, instinctive autocrat that he was, could not endure the thought that the Navigation Acts were being systematically flouted; worse, that the customs officers in the New World eked out their miserable pay by accepting fees from smugglers in lieu of full payment of the tariff (the going rate at Boston was 1d. a gallon of rum when the duty was notionally 6d.); he may even (while in office) have had some sympathy with Grenville's view that the whole system was very expensive to administer and brought in next to nothing to cover the costs. He and others denounced this 'lawless set of smugglers' and their 'illegal and most pernicious trade', and the Royal Navy was ordered to enforce the Acts. It seemed a necessary step towards victory. But like other wartime measures in other wars, this decision was to have a long peacetime history. Without realizing it Pitt had diverted the mercantile system from its role as an instrument for regulating and encouraging trade – the only one in which it made any sense – to one of raising a revenue. It was an example eagerly followed by the Grenville ministry. 'Preventing smuggling is to be a favourite object of the present administration,' announced Thomas Whately, Grenville's Man Friday at the Treasury. The navy was kept at work, and strict administrative measures were taken to enforce the Navigation Acts (not before time: colonial administration had grown dreadfully slack). And the Acts were now definitely to be exploited for raising a revenue, the money gained to be spent on the imperial establishment in North America. To increase the take, new articles of trade were enumerated.

It was estimated that this new policy, embodied in the so-called Sugar Act (1764), would bring in some £45,000 per annum – a good return, but not nearly enough to cover the costs of empire. To fill the gap Grenville took up a measure that had often been proposed – a colonial stamp duty. Legal documents, such as wills and conveyances, could be required, to be valid, to carry a stamp,[5] for which the party involved would have to pay

---

5 Not to be confused with a postage stamp: see p. 116.

the government. Such a duty had been imposed in England for years and had proved a dependable, cheap and easy source of revenue. In America too it would, no doubt, prove, Grenville thought, 'equal, extensive, not burdensome, likely to yield a considerable revenue, and collected without a great number of officers'. Accordingly, in March 1764, at the same time as he announced his other colonial measures, Grenville proposed, and carried, a resolution in the House of Commons that a stamp tax might be imposed by Parliament on the colonies; and he explicitly asserted, without being challenged, that Parliament had the right thus directly to tax the colonists. He was unambiguous: 'Mr Grenville strongly urg'd not only the power but the right of Parliament to tax the colonies, and hop'd in God's Name as his expression was that none would dare dispute their sovereignty'; he added that if a single man doubted Parliament's right, 'he would take the sense of the House, having heard without doors hints of this nature dropped'. No one responded.

This was the first great error which brought on the American crisis. It was even more tragic than fatuous. Whom the gods wish to destroy they first make unsound of judgement. Grenville had clearly noted – how could he not? – the restiveness of the colonies under his policies and the criticisms of his course that were already current in England 'without doors'. Instead of taking warning, he decided to brazen it out – a reaction that was to be all-too-universal among the English in the coming years. To the colonists' cry, just beginning to be heard, that they might not be taxed by a Parliament in which they were not represented, he would answer with a Stamp Act, which the faithful Whately hailed as 'a great measure . . . on account of the important point it establishes, the right of Parliament to lay an internal tax upon the colonies'. Smugly insular, administrative and self-assured, incapable of questioning his own rectitude, he next committed another mistake. His stamp duty resolution, by committing Parliament to an assertion of its right to tax the colonists, made it difficult, if not impossible, for that proud and touchy institution even to consider changing its mind if challenged; while by deferring the introduction of a bill for a year (that is, until 1765) he gave himself time to draw up a good measure based on reliable information about colonial conditions, in which his administrative abilities could display themselves to advantage. It was a clever scheme, but unfortunately open to misconstruction. Jasper Mauduit, the agent in England of Massachusetts, misunderstood it. He wrote home to tell the assembly that 'the stamp duty you will see, is deferr'd till next year. I mean the actual laying it: Mr Grenville being willing to give the provinces their option to raise that or some equivalent tax. Desirous as he express'd himself to consult the ease, the quiet, and the goodwill of the colonies.' Mauduit's mistake is understandable: Grenville's wisest course would have been to behave in just this way. Some of the colonies (notably Massachusetts) were willing at least to discuss alternative means of raising the needed monies: Pennsylvania's agent, Dr Franklin, thought they might meet in a 'general

Congress' for the purpose. (Presumably he was hoping to revive his Albany Plan.) But nothing could be done without a clear and official statement from Grenville of how much money he wanted. No such statement was ever forthcoming. Grenville had made up his mind to have a stamp tax.

It never seems to have occurred to him that by failing to consult those colonial leaders most sympathetic to his problems and policies he was helping their opponents. He thought he could afford to ignore the petitions of protest that poured in from every colony as the year of grace ended. His clerks produced, and he laid before Parliament, a sweeping measure, which might have been designed to affront the urban colonial élite – lawyers, merchants, editor–printers – and thus to provoke unanimous resistance, for it taxed not only legal but also commercial transactions and documents (liquor licences, mortgages, insurance policies, customs clearances and so on) and pamphlets, almanacs, newspapers, newspaper advertisements – a printer's whole business, in fact. These necessary stamps were to be embossed on sheets of paper in England and sold only by the stamp commissioners – thus injuring the printers still further, since many of them, like Benjamin Franklin, were accustomed to manufacturing their own paper. On 22 March 1765 the Stamp Act became law, and the American Revolution began.

For the Stamp Act was a catalyst, touching off fundamental change. The reasons for its immense unpopularity are simple enough and (except for the straightforward grievance of the lawyers and businessmen) are summed up in the famous slogan, 'no taxation without representation'. As the earlier chapters of this book should have made clear, the American colonists were a vigorous, thriving, independent-minded people. They had enjoyed most of the essentials of self-government from the time of the earliest settlements, and were well aware of its benefits. Furthermore, they regarded themselves as still retaining and enjoying the rights of Englishmen, which had been codified and made explicit at the Glorious Revolution in 1688. Among the most fundamental of those rights was the right to be taxed only with the consent of themselves or their representatives. This right of representation, they came to think, was beyond the power of kings to give or to withhold. The power of the purse, it was held, had enabled the seventeenth-century Parliaments to wrest a free constitution from tyrannous rulers; to relinquish that power was to risk, or rather to ensure, a return of slavery. This much was agreed on both sides of the Atlantic; but whereas the English Whigs were content to leave it at that, to assume that victories won by Parliament were best and sufficiently safeguarded by Parliament, the colonists (more attached to rights than to institutions) went further. They were not, and probably could not be, properly represented in Parliament by their own MPs, so Parliament could not lawfully tax them. Some politicians (among them Grenville) held that they were 'virtually' represented in Parliament because men whose interests coincided with theirs sat there: they brushed aside this cobweb. In their situation, they held, only their assemblies could truly represent them; the assemblies exercised the power of the purse in the colonies. The Stamp Act encroached on that power. The colonists had never been overtly taxed from Britain before, though, as they soon discovered, the new Sugar Act was essentially a taxing device too. But the Sugar Act, though possibly unwise, was clearly constitutional in their eyes, since it was ostensibly concerned only with the regulation of trade, a legitimate concern of the imperial Parliament, whereas the Stamp Act illegally taxed the colonists without their consent, for that consent could be given only in the little parliaments, the assemblies.[6] It was a light tax, true; but to consent to a light tax was to give warrant for the subsequent imposition of a heavy tax – possibly, O horror!, to risk the transfer of the complete tax burden of the Empire from British shoulders to colonial ones. (Besides, light though it was, it would actually double the amount paid by Americans in taxes.) 'The same principles which will justify such a tax of a penny will warrant a tax of a pound,' they said, 'an hundred, or a thousand pounds, and so on without limitation.' This was an encroachment of power on liberty: some of the protesters may have noticed that for some time past Whitehall had steadily been encroaching on the independence of colonial governors, especially in the matter of patronage. Now it was the assemblies' turn. The government might go on from there to pay the governors, at present dependent on the assemblies for their salaries, with the proceeds of the Stamp Act, and thus make them wholly independent of the will of their subjects. (In fairness we should note that Grenville had 'warmly rejected' this allegation.) No wonder the cry against the Act was almost unanimous.

The Act had been passed after the most energetic, intelligent, earnest and loyal protests and remonstrances from the colonies. 'The boldness of the minister amazes our people,' wrote a New Yorker. 'This single stroke has lost Great Britain the affection of all her colonies.' The blow to American confidence in British wisdom, justice and goodwill was indeed very heavy if not mortal; and the subsequent discovery that resistance could prevent the Act's operation gave the colonists a heady sense of their own strength. Only years of patience and good temper could have made good the damage: and they were not forthcoming.

Bad though it was, the Act could not have had such a devastating effect in isolation. Had Grenville held his hand, there might never have been a quarrel between Britain and her colonies; but to say this is to say that the Stamp Act was the last straw, confirming suspicions and fears which had been steadily mounting since 1759. To understand them it is necessary to look again at the colonial policies adopted by England after the fall of Quebec.

Colonial grievances made up a formidable but mixed bundle. Some were more or less chronic, arising from the day-to-day difficulties of governing

---

6 As the controversy developed, Americans drew a distinction (adopted also in the House of Commons by William Pitt) between Parliamentary legislation and Parliamentary taxation. The former, for the good of the Empire, they were, they said, willing to submit to; the latter, in every case, they would resist.

an empire, and had little significance beyond the highly important result of producing a general loss of temper. Of such a nature were the complaints peculiar to particular provinces. Thus, New Hampshire bitterly resented the White Pine Acts, which reserved white pine-trees growing outside private property for the use of the Royal Navy. These laws were ill-thought-out, not distinguishing between trees which were useful to the navy and trees which were only useful to the colonists: all were reserved. An ill-advised effort at strict enforcement in 1763 roused the whole of the Connecticut valley[7] against the Acts, just when the more general crisis was brewing.

A nagging grievance concerning judges affected four colonies in this period – New York, New Jersey, Pennsylvania and Jamaica. Each wanted their judges to sit, in accordance with post-1701 English practice, during good behaviour, thus giving them security of tenure and political independence. The Crown, however, insisted on appointing colonial judges during pleasure, so that it could, in theory, dismiss them at will (in practice it never did so). Its motive was to retain political control, for otherwise the judges, dependent, like the Governors, on the assemblies for their salaries, might be too tender to certain types of criminal – smugglers, for example. The Crown would not relinquish this control, even when Pennsylvania and Jamaica wanted to give judges permanent salaries as well as tenure during good behaviour, thus making them independent of both Crown and assemblies. The colonists disliked what they saw as an attempt to rob them of their Revolutionary heritage.

In South Carolina disaffection was caused in the early sixties by a clash between the assembly and a blockheaded royal Governor, who abused his power of dissolving the assembly.

These local grievances, more or less important in each case, all involved a disturbing rigidity in the official British attitude to the problems of colonial life and government: in all three cases the basic trouble was a refusal on the part of the authorities to take sufficient note of the colonists' point of view. More serious were a set of complaints that affected all the colonies, more or less.

There was the bishop question. The Anglican church in America had never known a bishop, so that colonial clergy had to cross to England to be ordained. There were other sound ecclesiastical reasons for thinking the appointment of an American bishop desirable, but sounder political reasons against it. To the descendants of the Puritans the idea of a bishop was inseparably connected with the idea of persecution. The planters of Virginia, as we have seen, liked to run the church themselves. There would certainly be a storm in the colonies if a bishop was appointed (though the Dissenters

---

7 The Connecticut river forms the boundary between the present state of New Hampshire and the state of Vermont, which were one province in the colonial era. It flows on south through Massachusetts and Connecticut. The White Pine Acts thus affected three of the four New England colonies.

would not, apparently, have objected to a visit from one of the English bishops). For once the government was sensible enough not to stir up a hornets' nest: no bishop was appointed in the pre-Revolutionary period. But Thomas Secker (1693–1768), created Archbishop of Canterbury in 1758, was not so sensible. Born a Dissenter, he had a convert's misplaced zeal, various expressions of which seriously alarmed the colonists. He backed the opening of an Anglican missionary church at Cambridge, Massachusetts, seat of Harvard College and centre of New England Congregationalism: this looked like an attempt to undermine Puritanism in Massachusetts, and probably was. He induced the Privy Council to disallow a Massachusetts Act setting up a Congregationalist society for missionary work among the Indians. He pressed for the appointment of a colonial bishop and stirred up a pamphlet war on the topic in New England. These activities of so powerful and influential an Englishman did nothing to endear the mother country to American Dissenters – who were still in an overwhelming majority in New England.

Even more unsettling was the question of the British army in North America. Basically, this was a matter of two right opinions clashing. The British noticed that during the late war the colonial militia had proved strategically and tactically useless – a point reinforced by its performance during a war with the Cherokees (1759–61) and Pontiac's rising. With some honourable exceptions, above all Massachusetts, the colonies had failed to supply either sufficient men or sufficient money for prosecuting the war, and yet all had repeatedly and urgently summoned help from the regular army: help which had always been forthcoming. It had in fact been proved again and again that without some central, organizing military authority and a body of trained troops, some engaged in building and garrisoning forts in the wilderness, others embodied in a strategic reserve, for use where necessary in Amherst's 'Immense Extent', the colonies, particularly the westernmost settlements, were helpless and indefensible. Further proof of the point, if it be needed, is furnished by the fact that after the Revolution the newly independent Americans found that, however unmilitaristic and anti-taxation they were, they still had to set up and pay for a national army. This became one of the inescapable responsibilities of the federal government. In the colonial period it was the inescapable responsibility of the imperial government; which naturally wanted gratitude, co-operation and financial help in bearing it.

On the other hand, the colonists had all the distrust of a standing army traditional in England since the time of Cromwell's major-generals. They could not forget that it was their efforts which had conquered the French fortress of Louisbourg on Cape Breton Island, the only serious British gain during the War of the Austrian Succession (nor that Louisbourg had been returned to France at the peace); that in 1755 the British General Braddock, far from saving the Pennsylvania frontier, had led his army to disaster; and that the regulars who eventually won the war in America had largely been enlisted there, and employed tactics devised in the colonies out of long experience of battle in the woods. Nor could they overlook Amherst's large part in provoking Pontiac's rising[8] – any more than Amherst could overlook the part which the persistent movement of settlers westward, across the mountains, into the Ohio river valley, played in alarming the tribes. On military matters, in short, the Americans and the British could each plume themselves on their success and each justly accuse the other of incompetence. What both tended to overlook was that both were carrying out essential tasks. The colonists furnished the troops, the tactics, some funds and many supplies; the British furnished the organization, the discipline, the training, the strategy, the rest of the supplies and funds, and above all, the sustaining energy to keep the army in being and prepare for future contingencies.

Linked to the military question, as I have indicated, was that of the Indians and the Western lands. The imperial government took the view that unless there was to be endemic, expensive and bloody war on the frontier of settlement, pledges made to the Indians had better be kept, and all transfers of land from red men to white had better be made with due legal propriety, including fair payment of the Indians. It was the policy of the Quakers in Pennsylvania, and was to be that adopted, on the whole, by the federal government in the post-Revolutionary era, thus again illustrating the continuity of American history. The settlers, or pioneers as they would come to be called, took, the reader will not be surprised to learn, a bolder and crueller attitude, and bitterly resented the Royal Proclamation of 1763 which drew a line along the map from north to south and stated that thus far might they go, and no further, in their quest for land, 'until our further pleasure be known'. Their indignation, and willingness to defy the Proclamation, would have been much increased had they known that the Board of Trade wished to pen them up between the Appalachians and the sea so that they would be forced to emigrate to the new and empty colonies of Nova Scotia, Georgia and the Floridas, 'where they would be useful to their mother country, instead of planting themselves in the heart of America, out of the reach of government, and where from the great difficulty of procuring European commodities they would be compelled to commence manufactures to the infinite prejudice of Britain'. Not knowing this, the colonists consoled themselves with the thought expressed by George Washington to his land agent, that the Proclamation was only 'a temporary expedient to quiet the minds of the Indians'. As such, it could of course be ignored. 'Those seeking good lands in the West,' said Washington, 'must find and claim them without delay.'

It is plain, then, that there were many matters of controversy between the

---

8 Amherst thought of the Indians as Colonel Blimp thought of the Fuzzy-Wuzzy: they 'never gave him a moment's concern', being incapable of 'attempting anything serious'; being mere savages they could be easily punished with 'Entire Destruction' if they tried any tricks. So he denied them the powder and shot which were essential to them, and was surprised when they went to war and devastated the West.

colonies and the imperial government in the early sixties which were enough to keep everyone busy for a long time seeking mutually acceptable solutions, but which were unlikely to lead to a rupture between the two sides. The Board of Trade had become rather too set in the old ways, still seeing the colonies and colonists as 'merely factors for the purposes of trade'; it was, after all, an instrument of the old order, wholeheartedly dedicated to the interests of the English merchants, pillars of that order; but the disagreements could have sputtered on for years in perfect safety until Whitehall mustered enough statesmanship to deal with them. Indeed, there is plenty of evidence of prudent and creative thought about the Empire's future at this period: slowly, we may feel, the more manageable colonial grievances could have been attended to. They were only dangerous in the context of the highly unmanageable controversies developing in other parts of the forest.

These other issues all began in economics and ended in politics. This was so because, in every case, the two sides, without being fully aware of what they were doing, were seeking to modify the institutions and practices of the old colonial system – in itself an integral part of the European old order – seeking to adapt them to the needs of a new age, without being agreed on either the means or the ends of the exercise. British and Americans alike were struggling in a net of circumstances which they had not woven and could not escape; they could not fully understand what was happening to them, or to each other. C. M. Andrews suggested that the British Empire was already beginning to evolve towards its nineteenth-century pattern, while the thirteen colonies were moving towards what they eventually became, an independent, unitary North American nation. This is, perhaps, a view too dominated by hindsight to be wholly convincing; but it does at least catch the feeling which overwhelms the historian from time to time, that the economic, social, cultural and therefore political destinies of the two peoples were leading them inexorably apart; perhaps, in the end, to follow parallel paths, but, indubitably, to follow different ones. Something very deep, something quite central, was at issue between Great Britain and her colonies; it follows that to discover what it was we must look at the central problems of men's lives, and at the metropolitan areas of the colonies – not at the wilderness, whether in New Hampshire or the Ohio valley or Georgia, but at Boston, Rhode Island, New York, Philadelphia and Virginia. It was in these places that the great drama unfolded, enlightening the participants by its course as to its full importance and implications. We too can best understand it by watching it develop: can see how it grew before Mr Grenville's unfortunate experiment, how that experiment proved to be the fatal turning-point, and why its failure did not bring the drama to an end, but merely to the opening of a new phase.

Pitt, as we have seen, began the proceedings, diverting the mercantilist system from its generally acceptable role as the more or less impartial regulator of imperial trade to the much more questionable one of determining

3. British North America, 1765

the economic life of the Empire to suit the military and political designs of London. Grenville eagerly followed him, passing the Sugar Act at a time when his action was certain to be sharply resented in New England in general, and in the towns of Boston and Newport in particular; for each depended on an unimpeded trade with both French and British West Indies.

Dislike of the new strictness was in fact so general that the Bostonians seized the first opportunity of sabotaging the laws, which occurred long before the Sugar Act was passed. In 1761 the customs officers of Boston applied for writs of assistance to enable them to carry out the searches for contraband that were part of their job. The technicalities of these writs need not detain us: it is enough to record that the court found in favour of the officers, but the temper of Boston was such that the writs could never again be used in Massachusetts. In 1766 writs of assistance in the colonies were disallowed by the English Attorney-General.

The case has great symbolic importance, for not only did it, in the end, lead to a successful defiance by the colonists of an Act of Parliament (the 1696 Navigation Act authorized writs of assistance), but it made the lawyer James Otis (1725–83) famous as a radical leader. Otis appeared as counsel for the merchants of Massachusetts. Other lawyers in the case argued dry points of law; he passionately denounced the writs, which sanctioned the entry and search of private houses, as against natural law and therefore against the British Constitution and therefore illegal whatever Acts of Parliament said. His speech was in the anti-prerogative tradition of the common law, but it was perhaps more notable for its eloquence than its learning, and none the less effective for that. It was an extraordinary achievement, for in it Otis leapfrogged all the issues that were to perplex the British and Americans in the years to come and arrived at the simple appeal to natural law, right and justice which, in 1776, the Declaration of Independence was to use as the basic justification of the colonies' rebellion. The speech electrified its hearers, one of whom, another radical Bostonian lawyer, young John Adams (1735–1826), was to date the Revolution from its utterance. 'Otis was a flame of fire,' he recollected in old age. '. . . Every man of an immense crowded audience appeared to me to go away, as I did, ready to take arms against writs of assistance. Then and there, was the first scene of the first act of opposition, to the arbitrary claims of Great Britain. Then and there, the child Independence was born.'

No doubt there is some exaggeration in this account, but there is no doubt that the speech was remarkable and carried James Otis to a position of radical leadership. A year after his emergence another legal orator in another colony rose to fame in the same way. Again a clash between colonial and British economico-political interests lay in the background, this time in the form of a debtor–creditor controversy about the currency. The planters of Virginia, confident in the marketability of their tobacco, had, as we have seen, felt free to finance a luxurious way of life by running up enormous debts. Unfortunately they had failed to reckon with the weather, and some bad harvests in the fifties plunged them into difficulties with their creditors, the Scottish and English merchants, who wanted to be paid, either interest or principal, in good currency – preferably in tobacco, which could be sold at a profit. In order to find tobacco to satisfy the merchants the planters passed a law at the expense of the Virginian clergy, whose stipends were supposed to be paid in tobacco, but who were now required to accept Virginian paper money instead. Again we need not follow the details of the dispute which ensued (it was compromised eventually), and the so-called 'Parsons' Case' which arose out of it was only a side-issue; but Patrick Henry (1736–99), a Scottish Presbyterian lawyer from the back-country, made a constitutional drama out of it. The King, acting through the Privy

Council, had disallowed the law forcing the parsons to accept paper money, had he? Then he had broken the compact between him and his people, degenerated into a tyrant and forfeited all right to his subjects' obedience. Understandably, this provoked cries of 'Treason!' but Henry swept on to denounce the clergy as rapacious harpies and was carried shoulder-high from the court-room. The plaintiff (the Reverend James Maury) was awarded damages of one penny.

Nor was that the end of the controversy. The parsons dropped out, but the underlying difficulty was still there: the planters owed more than they could pay, and with considerable spirit and cunning contrived to evade their obligations, in spite of their creditors' pressure. Yet while this pressure from Britain continued, feeling in Virginia grew more and more embittered. By the time of the Revolution, L. H. Gipson has pointed out, tempers were so high that none of the planters were loyalists and none of the merchants were rebels.[9]

What is striking about these incidents is that they occurred before the end of the Seven Years War (though not before victory was in sight). They show how dangerously easy it was to stir up anti-governmental feelings in the two leading colonies, even without undue provocation. But provocation, of course, was not long in coming. In 1764 Grenville pushed the Sugar Act through Parliament.

No other incident in the making of the Revolution has been more widely misunderstood than this. The Sugar Act made the change in the imperial system apparent to all. Revenue, not trade regulation, was now to be the purpose of the Navigation Acts. A shout of indignation went up from the colonial merchants. The duty on molasses imported to the mainland colonies from the non-British West Indies was reduced from the notional 6d. to 3d., but Grenville made it plain that from now on the full duty would be collected. In other words, for reasons already given,[10] he was really raising the duty by 2d. a gallon. So in a torrent of pamphlets, newspapers and letters the merchants predicted that they would be utterly ruined;[11] and on the whole historians have taken them at their word. Only Gipson has pointed out that the molasses was required for making rum and that the entire history of taxation imposed on booze shows that, whatever the duty, drinkers will pay it. In other words, it is very easy for brewers and distillers to pass on their costs to their customers. Hence the *sang froid* with which modern Chancellors of the Exchequer raise the duty on Scotch from time to time. Grenville, in fact, had chosen an almost painless way of raising revenue; but the distillers of America shrieked as if they had been stabbed.

9 L. H. Gipson, *The British Empire Before the American Revolution* (New York, 1939–70), X, p. 179.
10 See above, p. 114.
11 It is a notably curious feature of American history that the merchants and businessmen have always foreseen ruin whenever a tax has been imposed on their commercial activities, or has been threatened. Yet somehow they have managed to thrive.

The truth is that the prosperous days of war had, contrary to the colonists' expectation, been followed, in America as in Europe, by a peacetime slump.[12] Times were bad for traders on both sides of the Atlantic, and it was impossible for the American merchants not to believe that the Sugar Act would make matters worse. Compared to this belief it was of less, but still great importance that the Act, loosely and inconsiderately drafted (as tended to be the case with Grenville's measures), hampered the whole maritime trade, and especially coastal traffic, with a set of intensely irritating, because inconvenient and unfair, regulations, and created what looked like a patronage machine, 'hordes of petty placemen', to enforce them. Some, like Chief Justice Thomas Hutchinson of Massachusetts (1711–80), even saw that the sugar duty was essentially a tax on the people, and thus clashed with what Hutchinson called 'the so much esteemed privilege of English subjects – the being taxed by their own representatives'. The uproar was enormous, and a vigorous movement was launched to boycott British goods until the government came to its senses. The row had not subsided when the Stamp Act was passed. It is small wonder that there was an unprecedented explosion, or that, because of the Sugar Act, solid merchants, the most influential and normally among the most conservative elements of colonial society, associated themselves with it. The decisive proof of Grenville's massive frivolity is that he was so unfit for his post as to be unaware that to the colonists the Stamp Act really was the last straw – was really like a match to gunpowder.

In partial extenuation it can be pleaded that even the colonial agents in London, even Benjamin Franklin, did not foresee the dimensions of the reaction; but it is the business of governments to be well informed and to know what they are about. To urge that Grenville could have done no better (though this is highly doubtful) is only to say that Britain was incapable of governing America; which was, of course, what the colonists came to think and to prove. But much had to happen first.

Scarcely a soul could be found in America to defend the Stamp Act; but nevertheless the colonists were far from united. On the contrary, they quickly split into moderate and radical factions, with the radicals carrying the day. This in itself indicates how much the movement of resistance to British prerogatives was to change America, for until 1765 well-connected and well-off conservatives had ruled the roost in every colony.

They were swept away in the Stamp Act crisis. Patrick Henry and his followers rushed the Virginian assembly into passing a set of anti-Stamp resolutions, the essence of which was their assertion of the principle of no taxation without representation. By an absurd accident,[13] the idea got

12 For instance, in the autumn of 1763 Yankee traders found there was a glut of flour (their principal export) throughout the West Indies.
13 The editor of the *Virginia Gazette* (there were four papers of that name in the colony by 1776 – it must have been very confusing) disapproved of the resolutions so strongly that he would not even print the four that the assembly had actually passed, for fear of their

about in the other colonies that Virginia had gone much further, urging disobedience to the Act and proscribing, as an enemy, any man who supported it; and they were quick to follow the supposed example. Before the news arrived in Boston, the Massachusetts assembly, the General Court of the colony, had launched a proposal for a conference of delegates from all the colonies to discuss measures of resistance; and this meeting, the celebrated Stamp Act Congress, did in fact open on 7 October. By then matters had taken an even more dramatic turn. The mob had gone to work.

The crowd in the American Revolution badly needs a historian. The traditional picture, of a uniquely discriminating, moderate, politically motivated mob, led or manipulated by, if not consisting entirely of, members of the middle or even the upper classes (one hears repeatedly of workmen's clothes and blackened faces serving as ineffective disguises), has been discredited, but as yet no complete substitute has been provided. There was considerable upper-class participation in some of the disturbances: a mill-owner and militia officer led a rising against the White Pine Acts in New Hampshire in 1754; 'all the principal gentlemen' in Norfolk, Virginia, were alleged to have assisted at the tarring and feathering of a customs official in 1766; other instances could be supplied. In the Revolutionary mobs, participation and a measure of direction by the 'better sort' were universal: English policy united the Americans and made it possible for the prosperous to sanction lawlessness which in other times horrified them. But the crowd existed independently of its leaders, sometimes (for example, in Rhode Island) getting out of their control, and we know that the comparative restraint and respect for legality of the American mob also characterized the mobs of London during the Wilkes and Gordon riots, and even the Parisian mob during the French Revolution: the eighteenth-century crowd knew what it was about, even its worst orgies of violence were not pointless, and its simultaneous impact on the history of France, England and America is one more piece of evidence showing how uniform was the history of the Atlantic world during this period. The very low death-rate in colonial disturbances was due less to the restraint of the crowd than to the weakness of the authorities, for in Europe it was usually they who did the killing, not the rioters.[14] We can infer from all this that the American mob was like its European counterparts in other respects:[15] above all that it was largely self-directing, most of the time.

---

inflammatory effect. This left Henry and his friends free to circulate their most extreme proposals, which the assembly had rejected, as resolutions actually passed, without fear of effective contradiction.

14 In England the authorities could call out the militia or the regular army. In America there was no regular army to speak of, and the militiamen were usually to be found rioting with their fellow-citizens.

15 George Rudé, describing the leading characteristics of the English and French political, urban crowd in the eighteenth and early nineteenth centuries, draws a composite profile which strikingly resembles the Stamp Act mob in Boston (see his *The Crowd in History*, Chapter 15). The likeness is all the more interesting as he nowhere takes America into account.

However, there is much that we do not yet know about the crowd, much that we need to know that at present we can only guess. There had always been riots in the American towns and countryside, but what touched them off?' What was the relation of the economic to the political in a crowd's sense of grievance? Above all, who and what were the rioters?

Some valuable work has been done on this last topic[16] which throws some light on the others as well. Apart from a group of carpenters who formed part of a New York mob in 1765, the chief identifiable components of the urban crowd were 'armed seamen, servants, Negroes . . .'; 'seamen, boys, and Negroes'; 'saucy boys, Negroes and mulattoes, Irish teagues and out landish jack tars' – this last being John Adams's account of the mob that rampaged through Boston after the Massacre in 1770. We need to be on our guard here – Adams was describing one incident only, in a speech, furthermore, as defending counsel. Studies of French popular history suggest that the well-off were very prone to exaggerate the importance of ungrateful servants in revolutionary movements, though the likelihood that, here, indentured servants are meant makes the analysis more acceptable. No doubt many of the 'Negroes' were whites with blackened faces (it was certainly a respectable mob – it Puritanically refused to riot on Sundays). Nevertheless there is no need to be entirely sceptical, since there is ample confirmatory evidence that sailors formed a large element in these mobs, and since the lists present a consistent picture of a crowd formed of the severely disadvantaged, little attached to their communities and their rulers. The population of the colonial cities and towns was highly mobile at the lowest level: if a man could not earn a decent living in, say, Boston, he went elsewhere. Many 'saucy boys' chafed, like the young Franklin, at the restraints of the apprenticeship system and ran away from their native places, like him, to try their luck in another colony – or in England – or at sea. Africans, whether free or enslaved, were profoundly disadvantaged, in the North as in the South, in the cities as in the countryside; but they were least amenable to coercion and control in the towns. As to the seamen, the largest element in the urban working class, they had a host of grievances and a long experience of rioting. Every colony with seaboard traffic knew what a press-riot was; every sailorman went in dread of the press-gang.

We tend to look back on impressment as a picturesque necessity of the Age of Hornblower. Actually it was a savage practice of a savage service: legalized kidnapping. Not until the mutinies (more properly, strikes) at the Nore and Spithead during the French Revolutionary wars did the working conditions of the Royal Navy begin to improve. In mid-century they were horrible. Life on the ocean blue was no picnic in the merchant fleets: whaling was a particularly bitter and dangerous occupation. Life in the Royal Navy

16 For example, by Mr Jesse Lemisch. See his 'Jack Tar in the Streets: Merchant Seamen in the Politics of Revolutionary America', *William and Mary Quarterly*, Vol. XXV, No. 3, July 1968.

was far worse. Discipline was harsh and irrational; cruel punishments far from unusual (merciless flogging was the rule); the pay was bad, and, apart from the dangers of war, a man's health was constantly imperilled by scurvy, fever and the wet and filthy living conditions of the lower deck. On one point Doctors Johnson and Franklin were agreed: the sea was no life for a man. Dr Johnson rescued his black servant from it, Dr Franklin his son. Dr Johnson remarked that 'no man will be a sailor who has contrivance enough to get himself into a jail; for being in a ship is being in a jail, with the chance of being drowned'. Dr Franklin observed that illness was even commoner in the Royal Navy than in the merchant marine, and more frequently fatal at that. Death from drink, madness or disease was indeed so common that we cannot wonder that the navy was incessantly plagued by the problems of desertion and undermanning. Some captains tried to avert desertion by withholding their crews' pay for years, calculating that a man would hang on to collect, eventually, what was owed him, rather than lose all hope of his pay by taking to flight; but this only added one more evil to a life already too full of them, and was ineffective. So, rather than treat sailors decently, impressment was constantly resorted to.

It was of very uncertain legality in America between 1708 and 1775, but that could not stop the navy. Its ships haunted the coast, its gangs regularly went ashore or boarded merchant vessels in search of deserters or of extra hands. The people of the colonies reacted to the quest for deserters and men to press much as their descendants in the North were to react to the quest for fugitive slaves in the mid-nineteenth century; and indeed sailors were no better off than slaves in all too many respects, being totally at the mercy of their employers: there is even a tale of one of the too-numerous corrupt captains pressing men and then selling them to other ships. Wives feared for their husbands, parents for their sons, parsons for their flocks, merchants and skippers for the crews of their trading vessels. Even the argument that the Royal Navy protected the Empire and the trade routes lost force: Franklin commented, at the height of the war in 1759, that 'New York and Boston have so often found the inconvenience of . . . station ships that they are very indifferent about having them: the pressing of their men and thereby disappointing voyages, often hurting their trade more than the enemy hurts it.'

It is not surprising, therefore, that men were often so desperate to avoid impressment that they preferred to fight rather than come quietly. Consequently press-riots, in which deaths occurred on both sides, were regular occurrences. Nor would it be surprising if, as may have happened, sailors and the poorer inhabitants of the ports conceived a sense of the rights that were denied them, a hatred of the navy[17] and a scepticism about the claims

17 Which also earned a bad name among the more prosperous, and not only for impressment. There were numerous cases of naval thieving and marauding. One such involved HMS *Gaspee*: see below, p. 155.

of the authorities. Like the poor of London and Paris, they had suffered too much to be natural supporters of the *status quo*. When they rioted they wanted justice, or, if that was unattainable, revenge. Plunder, even alcoholic plunder, seems to have been a minor inducement: they were not soldiers.

The question remains, what brought them out against the stamp tax? Being a charge on legal and commercial business, it could have little direct effect on the poorer classes; and the cry of 'no taxation without representation' could mean little to those who were not represented even in the colonial assemblies. But in the thirteen colonies in 1765 (and outside them too: several of the West Indian islands opposed the tax) all conditions worked to one end. The economy was still depressed, so unemployment was high. Sailors were cast on shore with the coming of peace: no more privateers, and a slump in maritime trade, cut the job-supply.[18] During the war prices had risen; in the peace the money supply was cut back, but prices did not fall and the wage-earner was worse off than ever. The Sugar Act brought the fear that the price of rum would rise (and rum was a food as well as a drink to many poor people): a similar fear had touched off the riots against the cider tax in the apple-counties of England. Finally, it may be argued, someone lifted the lid. Never before had trouble spread so rapidly or so universally from colony to colony – not even in 1689, when the news of the Glorious Revolution had touched off rebellion against half-a-dozen unpopular governments. The English might well regret alienating the printers: through their newspapers and pamphlets they now helped to unite opinion, from top to bottom and north to south, in opposition to the Stamp Act. Even the conservatives in Massachusetts echoed James Otis's language of natural rights in denouncing it. Radicals urged resistance. Secret groups met to concert plans, for it was generally felt that desperate measures were needed. These groups formed contacts with the leaders of the crowd.

The storm broke in August, in Boston. Andrew Oliver had been appointed Distributor of Stamps for Massachusetts; so on 14 August the mob hanged him in effigy from a tree in Boston (known thereafter as the Liberty Tree); levelled a new brick building he had built as a speculation; broke the windows of his private house, which it later sacked; and burned the effigy at a great bonfire. The colonial government could do nothing but wring its hands; so the next day Oliver, impressed by this clear expression of public opinion, announced that he would resign his post. 'Everyone agrees that this riot exceeds all others known here,' the Governor reported, '. . . never had any mob so many abettors of consequence as this is supposed to have had.' But it was quickly outdone. For twelve days later the crowd decided to vent its anger against all those involved in enforcing the trade laws. It destroyed

---

18 The same cause produced trouble in England. Professor Rudé states that in the autumn of the peace year, 1763, 'The justices of the Tower Division were ordered by the Secretaries of State "to take proper measures for suppressing the riots of sailors and others at Shoreditch".' Sailors' disputes continued to be endemic, culminating in a great strike in May 1768. (See G. Rudé, *Wilkes and Liberty*, Oxford, 1962, p. 93.)

the records of the vice-admiralty court and wrecked the houses of the register of the court, of the Comptroller of Customs and of Chief Justice Hutchinson – who, as he was too well aware, had done nothing to deserve this punishment.

Yet the attack on Hutchinson is probably the most significant of these episodes. He was easily the most distinguished man in the colony: a descendant of Anne Hutchinson; a leading merchant; an excellent historian; Lieutenant Governor. More to the point, he had devoted himself to the public welfare as a leading official for twenty years or more, and had done great service, first, in the reform of Massachusetts' currency immediately after the War of the Austrian Succession, a reform which had given the colony the soundest money in America;[19] second, by his conduct of the colony's finances during the Seven Years War; thirdly, by his administration of those finances since 1763. Unfortunately he was also something of a monopolist of government office. He was related by marriage to Andrew Oliver, and the families of the two men, closely intertwined, found few posts beneath their dignity. The rising tide of imperial ordinances and imperial enforcement led to an increase in the number of posts available to such collectors. Accordingly, when the mob attacked Hutchinson it was attacking the perfect symbol of Anglo-American imperial orthodoxy. It was attacking the economic policies which kept many of its members out of work; the political structure which involved them in war or the exigencies of war (especially impressment); and the aristocracy, part-mercantile, part-official, which was slowly forming (Governor Bernard of Massachusetts, a close ally of Hutchinson's, dreamed of creating a colonial peerage, in which his friend would no doubt have enjoyed a place). So it is hard to believe that the crowd needed much incitement; but if it did, there was an action committee of middle-class tradesmen, known at first as the Loyal Nine and then as the Sons of Liberty, to egg it on through its leader, Ebenezer Macintosh, a shoemaker.[20] The Loyal Nine had been behind the riot of 14 August, and it is hard to doubt that they had a hand in that of the 26th. Yet it also seems clear that some of the men behind the second affair had little interest in stamps but a great one in destroying evidence that they were smugglers which, they feared, had come into Hutchinson's hands. If so this completes the picture of an uprising against all aspects of the traditional order.

The example thus given quickly spread to other colonies. It became a favourite pastime to burn the effigy of a stamp distributor (often, as in the Oliver incident, with a boot, to stand for Lord Bute, tied to its shoulder), to pull down houses and to terrorize the respectable.[21] The New York

19 See above, p. 92.
20 Characteristic of the American Revolution was the presence among the Loyal Nine of Benjamin Edes, printer of the *Boston Gazette*, which published 'a continuous stream of articles to stir up feeling against the Stamp Act' (E. S. and H. M. Morgan, *The Stamp Act Crisis*, Chapel Hill, 1953, p. 122). Edes also printed many radical Whig pamphlets.
21 Pulling down houses was also one of the traditional riotous activities of the London eighteenth-century mob; and Hutchinson's experience at the hands of the Boston mob was strikingly like that of Joseph Priestley, the scientist, Unitarian minister and friend of Thomas

distributor was driven to resign on the night of the Hutchinson riot; two days later, a mob at Newport, fortified by 'strong drink in plenty with Cheshire cheese and other provocations to intemperance and riot', forced the resignation of the Rhode Island distributor; September and October saw the distributors in most of the other colonies resigning too. The distributor in Connecticut was threatened with lynching if he didn't; so was the distributor in the Bahamas; both took the hint.

The countryside was as roused as the town – in Massachusetts, more so. 'They talk of revolting from Great Britain in the most familiar manner,' the Governor reported, 'and declare that though the British forces should possess themselves of the coast and maritime towns, they will never subdue the inland.' In Georgia it was the country people who forced the merchants of Savannah not to use the stamps.

It was against this turbulent background that the Stamp Act Congress met at New York on 7 October. We must not exaggerate the significance of the meeting. Only nine of the continental colonies were represented, and of those New York, New Jersey and the Three Counties of Delaware sent only unofficial or irregularly chosen delegates.[22] The resolutions passed by the Congress, though firm, indeed incontrovertible, statements of the American case, were all moderately, even conservatively, couched, and events rapidly outran its deliberations, as the Whig or patriot party which was forming evolved a programme, first, of refusal to use or allow the distribution of the stamps; second, of non-importation – that is to say, of cutting off all trade with Great Britain; third, of allowing legal and commercial life to go forward without stamps, though this risked heavy penalties at the hand of the authorities, especially the Royal Navy, which was standing by to intercept unwarranted cargoes. Nevertheless the Stamp Act Congress was important. It was no abortive Albany conference. Its members exercised for the first time on a continental scale those arts of organization, compromise and conciliation which were eventually to make a continental legislature possible. It had a national tinge: as one of the South Carolina delegates, Christopher Gadsden (1724–1805), remarked,

we should all endeavour to stand upon the broad and common ground of those natural and inherent rights that we all feel and know, as men and as descendants of Englishmen, we have a right to ... There ought to be no New England men, no New Yorker &c; known on the continent, but all of us Americans.

For the first time an inter-colonial body met whose authority was accepted, not rejected, by all the colonies.

Jefferson, at the hands of the Birmingham mob in 1791. Hutchinson eventually went into exile in England; Priestley took refuge in the United States.

22 The other colonies represented were Massachusetts, Rhode Island, Connecticut, Pennsylvania, Maryland and South Carolina. There were twenty-seven delegates in all.

The events of the winter confirmed the drift of events. It was of no account to be opposed to the Stamp Act, as Thomas Hutchinson had been from the beginning: the question was, what was a man prepared to do about it? The moderates were hopelessly overtaken by events and passions. It was well for Dr Franklin that he was in England at the time. He had opposed the passage of the Act, but had seen no harm in acquiescing afterwards, and had secured the post of distributor in Pennsylvania for his friend John Hughes, who was soon forced to resign it and eventually to leave the colony. Franklin was at first opposed to 'the madness of the populace' and 'acts of rebellious tendency'; but his foreign residence gave him time to change his tune and emerge as a leader of the opposition: his representations to the House of Commons were to be influential in persuading Parliament to repeal the Act. Moderates in America were less fortunate: they lost political control to the radicals and could only count themselves lucky if they were left in peace.

By the New Year, then, the imperial government was confronted with an acute problem. The Stamp Act had been effectively nullified, to use a term with a long future.[23] Except in Georgia, and there not for long, no stamps had been distributed; the Sons of Liberty in the various colonies (for the name had spread with the agitation) had effectively superseded the regular administrations; life was otherwise proceeding in its normal, unstamped channels;[24] and there was simply not force enough available to compel obedience to the law. (We can now see that to have tried would merely have precipitated the War for Independence nine years earlier.) Common sense suggested that the Grenville programme must be abandoned: Whitehall and Westminster would have to climb down. It was easier for them since George III had got rid of Grenville in July.

The new ministry, headed by the Marquis of Rockingham and composed of men sympathetic to the colonies, soon came to the view that there was nothing for it but repeal.

Unhappily there was no way of disguising the fact that this was a humiliation for Britain: one much resented in the proud Parliament. Many were the warnings that to give way on the Stamp Act was to necessitate giving way on everything else; the scarecrow of a colonial bid for independence, which had been alarming ministers since the beginning of the century, flapped again. And for once the prophets of doom were right. The choice, in all ugliness, was between war and abdication: there was no room for compromise. To such a pass had Grenville's statesmanship reduced the

---

23 See below, pp. 295–6.
24 Except that, the civil courts being closed, debts and rents could not be collected. This distressed English merchants, making them long for repeal, as the Virginian George Washington had, for one, foreseen; the reopening of the courts distressed the debtors and touched off a chain reaction of evictions, riots and the restoration of order by troops in the Hudson Valley, NY.

great Empire. The Act was repealed, on 18 March 1766, and London church bells rang out in joy; but first a Declaratory Act was passed, stating that nothing had changed, that Parliament had an absolute right and power to do what it liked with the colonies whenever it chose. This was of course a face-saver, and, it may be thought, an unconvincing one; but the Rockinghams could not have persuaded Parliament to swallow repeal without it. Ministers' chief fear seems to have been that war with the colonies would necessarily involve a renewal of war with France and Spain (again, an accurate foreboding); they also encouraged the merchants of England to petition Parliament for repeal, on the grounds that trade was being ruined by American non-importation (and it was in fact in a parlous condition). Thus the English were furnished with two good practical excuses for climbing down, and the question of principle was side-stepped; but as the Declaratory Act showed, the matter was not as simple as men of good will wanted it to seem.

For questions had been raised on both sides of the Atlantic to which there were, in eighteenth-century terms, almost certainly no answers. The richer colonists, reared on the traditions of the Glorious Revolution, and indeed on the tradition of the Cromwellian Revolution before that, injured or annoyed by many misguided British policies and feeling themselves to belong to mature societies, with a limitless future, refused to be held in leading strings any more. 'No taxation without representation' was a cry that expressed more than it said: it was really an insistent refusal to be governed without proper consultation by a remote and frequently incompetent, if well-meaning, mother country. The poorer colonists were, we may hazard, sick of being oppressed in the name of an empire, citizenship and international trade which brought them little perceptible benefit. Both parties, though suspicious enough of each other, could unite over the good old sentiment that 'Britons never never never shall be slaves', and slavery, it seemed, was what the Britons' government had in store for them. Day by day that government seemed more and more like the tyrannous regimes of Charles I and James II, and pamphlets poured from the presses to enforce the parallels. It would have taken, in the wake of the Stamp Act crisis, some extraordinary gesture of generosity and reform to win back the confidence of the colonists in the British Parliament.

Such a gesture was impossible. The statesmen of Westminster had no desire to tyrannize anybody, but equally they had no desire to upset the applecart in which they had ridden so happily for so long. Like the American upper and middle classes, they faced a challenge from below. The Wilkes affair, during the years leading up to the Revolution, was bringing political institutions under serious attack in England as well as in her colonies, and it was probably impossible to reform Parliament and the imperial government along lines equitable enough to satisfy the colonies without having to make similar concessions at home. This the oligarchs were in a position to refuse to do. They fought off reform as long as they could; some are fighting a rearguard action still.[25] In the Declaratory Act they nailed their colours to the mast:

The said colonies and plantations in *America* have been, are, and of right ought to be, subordinate unto, and dependent upon the imperial crown and parliament of *Great Britain* . . . the King's majesty by and with the advice and consent of the lords spiritual and temporal, and commons of *Great Britain*, in parliament assembled, had, hath, and of right ought to have, full power and authority to make laws and statutes of sufficient force and validity to bind the colonies and people of *America* subjects of the crown of *Great Britain*, in all cases whatsoever.[26]

No argument here; no appeal to Whig or Revolution principles; indeed, in one of the debates on repeal Lord Mansfield, the eminent lawyer, went so far as to deny that 'no taxation without representation' applied even in England itself.

  The peers and squires who governed the realm also feared that concessions to the colonies must ultimately lead to independence, independence to economic ruin, and economic ruin to the end of Britain's greatness. They could not, in fact, abandon the logic of mercantilism, and in so doing threw themselves across the natural development of the times. Even Grenville, in his clerk's way, had seen that the Empire must change and adapt to survive: his mistake was in the changes that he favoured. But after the Declaratory Act and the fall of the Rockingham ministry (which took place in June 1766) this salutary attitude was forgotten. The British people persuaded themselves that concessions to the Americans ultimately meant their own ruin; and on that ground, on the sole principle of self-defence, they took their public stand. Their attitude was pathetically unrealistic, as the Americans could see. In the end it made war inevitable.

25 Rockingham was not to be forgiven for betraying his side by calling in 'opinion without doors' – the petitioning merchants – to force the repeal of the Stamp Act. Two generations were to pass before his following recaptured real power and pushed through the Reform Act of 1832.

26 Professor Palmer points out that only two weeks before the passage of the Declaratory Act the French King made an equally ringing assertion of his rights before the disobedient *parlement* of Paris (R. R. Palmer, *Age of the Democratic Revolution*, I, p. 164). In the crisis of the old order, Britain and France kept strictly in step.

9 The Road to Ruin 1766–75

What do we mean by the Revolution? The war? That was no part of
the Revolution; it was only an effect and consequence of it. The Revolution was in the minds of the people, and this was effected, from 1760
to 1775, in the course of fifteen years before a drop of blood was shed
at Lexington.

John Adams, 1815

I know it is expected that the more determined the Colonies appear, the
more likely it will be to bring the Government here to terms. I do not
believe it.

Thomas Hutchinson, London, 1774

Governments [derive] their just powers from the consent of the governed.

Declaration of Independence, 1776

Repeal was even more welcome to the Americans than to the English. Dr
Franklin sent his wife fourteen yards of pompadour satin in celebration. The
Sons of Liberty in Boston resolved to display 'such illuminations, bonfires,
pyramids, obelisks, such grand exhibitions and such fireworks as were never
before seen in America'. The New York assembly voted the erection of an
equestrian statue of George III and a statue in brass of William Pitt. Countless ministers hurried into their pulpits to preach sermons of thanksgiving.
And then everyone tried to get back to normal as fast as possible.

Not that normality was synonymous with tranquillity. The vigour of
colonial life had from the start led to contentious politics. Even if the imperial
government had behaved with the utmost circumspection and wisdom, the
increasing maturity of American society must have brought about *de facto*
independence before the end of the century. It would simply not have been
possible to keep the colonies in tutelage indefinitely. Nor could the separation
have been accomplished wholly without friction. The question before

historians is only whether there also had to be violence and a complete break, and the answer tends to be no, in theory. Seen in this light, the Stamp Act crisis, like later ones, was merely a needlessly acute phase in a chronic disease. When it had passed, the patient was not healed, but she was more manageable.

In New York, for example, a fresh controversy immediately took the stage, but was eventually compromised. Among Grenville's measures had been the Quartering or Mutiny Act of 1765. This had been passed in response to the urgent pleas of General Thomas Gage (1721–87), the Commander-in-Chief in North America, who was plagued by problems of disciplining, quartering and transporting his troops in the existing defective state of the law. Peace having come, Americans who had been quite co-operative in wartime would, Gage thought, grow contumacious. 'It will soon be difficult in the present Situation,' he grumbled, 'to keep Soldiers in the Service.' He was probably an alarmist, but nevertheless an Act was passed providing that, where there were no barracks, the colonial governments were to quarter the soldiers in taverns, uninhabited houses, barns or other such buildings; provide them with bedding, fuel, pots and pans, candles, vinegar and salt, and with a ration of small beer, cider or rum. It was one of Grenville's better laws, for he had had the sense to consult the colonial agents, including Franklin, and they had seen to it that the Act contained ample provision for preventing and correcting any abuses. As a result the law was quietly accepted in most of the colonies.

New York, however, made a fuss. The assembly was quite willing to look after the soldiers, who came in very useful just then, for there were agrarian riots in Dutchess County: threats were actually being made to burn New York city to the ground. As a British officer noted in his diary, 'Sons of Liberty great opposers to these Rioters as they are of opinion no one is entitled to Riot but themselves.' At the root of this affair was a dispute about land-titles between New York and Massachusetts. The army gained no kudos in the latter province for interfering on the side of the former. And the Quartering Act made even New York ungrateful. It seemed to be another attempt to tax the colonists unconstitutionally. Accordingly the assembly resisted it for over a year, and finally, in June 1767, passed a Billeting Act (renewed annually thereafter) which, while doing all that Parliament had required, studiedly did not mention Parliament's role, thereby implicitly denying the Parliamentary right to tell the colonial assemblies what laws to pass. The government prudently ignored this silent challenge, and was rewarded when, in 1770, New York applied for (and got) Parliament's consent to an issue of paper money, thus acknowledging Parliamentary supremacy. In both cases good sense prevailed. By comparison it mattered little that (also in 1770) one Alexander McDougall, a New York Son of Liberty, being imprisoned for publishing what the assembly called 'a false, seditious and infamous libel', was dubbed by his fellow-radicals 'the Wilkes of America'. This was not going to bring about a civil war.

Nor was it originally of revolutionary significance that the popular party in Massachusetts Bay exploited its success in the Stamp Act crisis to consolidate its power. As Thomas Hutchinson remarked, 'Power, once acquired, is seldom voluntarily parted with.' The radicals' prospects of retaining it for long were not, after repeal, very good. They still had a majority in the Council and the House of Representatives, but there was now no urgent issue with which to stir up the crowd and induce solid citizens to overlook their excesses. It seemed likely that at the 1767 elections the conservatives would make large gains: they might even win a majority, as they had regularly done until 1765. The only political question of importance was that of compensating Hutchinson and the other victims of the mob. None dared openly deny the equity of this, but few were willing to do it just because Parliament had ordered it (as part of the repeal measures). On the other hand failure to obey would alienate the friends of the colonies in England and embarrass William Pitt, who had just formed a new administration. A complicated struggle followed, much like that concurrently proceeding in New York, the upshot of which was that Hutchinson got his compensation under an Act of the Massachusetts assembly (the General Court) which was in British eyes outrageously unconstitutional and was accordingly disallowed by the Privy Council. But by the time that news reached Boston, Hutchinson had been paid, so the matter was allowed to drop. In the same conciliatory vein Governor Bernard decided to overlook some small-scale rioting which had prevented searches by customs officers in Boston and in Falmouth, Maine (then a part of Massachusetts). The outlook for agitators seemed poor.

This was scarcely a matter for grief. It is impossible to feel unqualified respect for the self-styled 'patriot' leaders of Massachusetts. Even the best of them, plump and passionate John Adams (1735–1826), was, rather evidently, a young lawyer and politician on the make, who, with a notable capacity for self-deception, hero-worshipped James Otis and whitewashed his other associates, while looking on Thomas Hutchinson as little better than a fiend. As to the other leaders, James Otis had been alarming his friends with insane symptoms for some years before a cut over the head in a tavern brawl with a conservative sent him really mad in 1769. Otis, even when sane, was self-tortured, never happy in the role of patriot, unable to reconcile himself with the conservatives. There can be no doubt of his brilliance – he furnished many of the best arguments used by the patriots in the years to come. He was frequently a restraining influence on his associates. But he was also, when the demagogic mood was on him, a reckless liar, as in his statement that the Stamp Act had been concocted in Boston, that he knew the very room in Governor Bernard's house where it had been conceived, the time, and the company responsible. Such fantasies served only to inflame the mob, and so did Otis's occasionally wild language, as when he denounced the members of the House of Commons as 'a parcel of button-makers, pin-makers, horse jockeys, gamesters, pensioners, pimps and whore masters'. John Hancock (1736–93), Boston's richest merchant (and arguably its leading smuggler), seems, throughout his career, to have been a mixture of vanity, pique and cowardice. His chief use to the patriots was his wealth and social standing: he made opposition smart.

Of them all the most effective was Samuel Adams (1722–1803). He has been called the last of the Puritans. He might just as well be called the first of the politicians, or even the first democrat. He must be given more than a cursory comment.

He had a genuine vocation for politics, which was just as well, since he was incompetent at everything else. His father, a successful man of business, having seen his son reject both the ministry and the law as professions, lent him £1,000 to make a start in trade. Sam lent half of it to a friend, and was never repaid; the rest somehow vanished. On his parents' death he inherited cash, real estate and a thriving brewery: ten years later he was again penniless. Elected tax-collector for Boston, he turned what was usually a lucrative post into a liability, ending up some £8,000 down in his account and more than suspected of being legally, if not morally, an embezzler. It was only by political manipulation that he kept himself out of jail. The causes of this string of failures are easy to find. Adams neglected business for politics; he was helplessly improvident and muddle-headed where money was concerned; above all, he was far too fond of making friends, far too unwilling to make himself unpleasant, either in exacting what was due to him or what was due to Boston, to be a successful tradesman, let alone an effective tax-gatherer. His second cousin John Adams reinforces the impression of excessive amiability by describing Sam as a man 'of refined policy, steadfast integrity, exquisite humanity, genteel erudition, obliging, engaging manners'. No doubt there is exaggeration here: John Adams saw men, for good or ill, as he wanted them to be, and Sam was his ally as well as his cousin; but the description fits very well with what else we know of the elder Adams.

He was in everything extremely old-fashioned. He was a strict Calvinist in religion and made a cult of the founders of New England; he never had much time for the rising generation and was conservative even in dress (he wore a three-cornered hat to his dying day). In public life he modelled himself on the more disagreeably virtuous Romans of Plutarch, such as the elder Cato. In spite of the tax embezzlement, his personal integrity was never called in question: he could rightly say, when in his extreme old age he at last retired from politics, that he had never made a penny from office, and indeed it is usually hard to see what he lived on. In early life he was also conventionally patriotic. There was no better constitution than the British, except the Charter of Massachusetts. He saw it as his mission in life to preserve the good old ways, in fact: until he was over forty it would have seemed fantastically unlikely that one day Thomas Hutchinson would seriously ask whether there was 'a greater incendiary in the King's dominion or a man of greater malignity of heart'.

Adams's views were for a long time much less important than his occupation. For his talents made him the first of a long line of professional American politicians, or bosses.

He was a fluent and ingenious journalist, who knew, whether as chief contributor to the *Boston Gazette* or clerk to the House of Representatives, exactly how to draft articles, speeches or official papers in such a way as to further his ends. Even more impressive was his command of the other arts of democratic politics. Like many a later enthusiast of the Left, he had been born to his trade: his father, also an active politician, had secured his early admission to the Caucus Club of Boston, which, besides bequeathing its name to a long progeny of political organizations,[1] was the original 'smoke-filled room' where, over tobacco and strong drink, the leaders of the Boston opposition fixed the business, especially the elections to office, that would come before the next town-meeting. It was through the Caucus Club that Sam Adams became, first, clerk of the market, then town scavenger and finally, as we have seen, tax-collector. It was at the club that he learned the arts of getting along with people (for which his pliability gave him a natural aptitude), arts which he could practise further in the taverns, where, his cousin John once remarked, 'if you set the evening, you will find the house full of people drinking drams, flip, toddy, carousing, swearing, but especially plotting with the landlord to get him, at the next town meeting, an election either for selectman or representative . . .'. Something of a bigot, Sam Adams was nevertheless prepared to overlook any religious or moral failing in allies, or potential allies, if they voted right. Sam was ready to haunt taverns because, as John said, in taverns 'bastards, and legislators, are frequently begotten'. It was there that he acquired the reputation of being the friend and spokesman of the meaner sort, for whom he had a genuine respect. He was not a Freemason, liking only those societies in which he was the ruling spirit; but he exploited his musical talents to found a musical society through which he could convert more Bostonians to his school of patriotism. He was not much of an orator or administrator: he left that side of the game to others. But his influence spread through the town by means which every subsequent generation of politicians would have recognized: he was building up a machine.

It was this activity which, perhaps, led him to the misjudgement that was to have so profound an influence on the course of American history. When things began to go wrong, Adams and the other patriots looked about for someone to blame, and, following the lead of James Otis, blamed it all, as we have seen, on the secret machinations of Hutchinson. They suspected Hutchinson of the sort of underground activity they were so good at themselves. It was long before Adams accepted that the chief difficulty was with London, and still longer (not until January 1776) that he accepted that

---

1 H. L. Mencken claims an Indian origin for this word. Others, perhaps less plausibly, connect it with the caulkers who, along with other sorts of shipwright, made up the bulk of the club's membership in its early days.

independence was the only remedy; but years and years previously he and the others had torn Massachusetts apart in their vendetta against the Hutchinsons and Olivers; the feud strengthened the tendency, on both sides, to see everything in the most lurid colours; and several times (above all during the Boston Massacre and the Boston Tea Party crises) events were given a marked turn for the worse, or at least the more violent, by the suspicions and passions of the patriot party, which Adams assiduously and sincerely fostered.

Yet he was, in one sense, no leader. He thought that the job of a politician was to advise the people, to acquiesce in majority decisions, to try to carry them out. In this rather passive notion we can see a reflection of Adams's own character. We can also see a foreshadowing of one of the chief doctrines of nineteenth-century party politics.

Adams was not the sort of man to initiate trouble, though there was no saying how far he would go if he thought that citizens' rights were being endangered. A man of such purely local influence was not likely to cause much trouble when times were quiet, trade good and the British not obviously oppressing the Americans, however tiresome he might make himself to the Governor of Massachusetts. Once more it took events initiated in London to arouse America.

In the summer of 1766, despite their success in repealing the Stamp Act, the Rockinghams fell from power, largely because they were pushed by William Pitt. He had first refused to join their administration, and then induced his followers to withdraw from it. The Rockinghams, at odds with everyone else (especially Grenville and the waning power of Bute), could find no other support and were duly superseded by the Great Commoner. He had large ideas of his mission, as formerly. This time he would rescue the King from faction by setting up the 'able and dignified ministry' that George desired – a ministry based on solid royal support and his own imperious authority. He would be the patriot minister of a patriot king, in fact, and smash the selfish bonds of faction which entangled all other politicians. This done, he would engineer a grand alliance between England, Prussia and Russia as a counterbalance to the Bourbon powers' family pact; and he would solve the country's financial problems by plundering the East India Company as it had plundered Bengal. All that was needed to ensure success was a totally subservient government. By filling the Cabinet with weaklings, satellites and odd-men-out he thought he had secured this *desideratum*.

It was all fantasy. Pitt was too old and ill to carry out the duties of one of the great executive offices: instead he took the sinecure job of Lord Privy Seal and transferred to the House of Lords, as Earl of Chatham, thus abandoning the Commons where he had always found the basis of his power. The shift was more important as a confession of weakness than anything else. Still, it diminished his popularity and authority in both England and America. Next, it turned out that Prussia and Russia could not be interested in a British alliance, and that it was far more difficult to settle the affairs of the East India Company than Chatham assumed. The financial problem remained very pressing, but Chatham was not well suited to grapple with it – he had always left money matters to Newcastle in his first ministry. Budgets and estimates were not his style: as Horace Walpole remarked unkindly, 'the multiplication table did not admit of being treated in epic'. By early 1767 the administration was already far into shoal-water.

Chatham ought not to have taken office. Physically broken, he could not do the work. And then he went mad. His associates, from the King down, found it almost impossible to believe or accept, but it was true. After months of desperate struggle he succumbed: in March 1767 he disappeared from society for more than two years, unable to bear human contact or apply his mind to business of any sort.

Yet this shattered man remained prime minister! Nothing more strikingly illustrates the fragility and incompetence of the old order. The government of England was still a personal, not a party matter. The King depended on Chatham to rescue him from the tyranny of such faction leaders as Grenville and Rockingham, who proposed to deal with the alleged undue influence of Bute over the King by wielding such an influence themselves; and given the constitutional and political realities of the mid-eighteenth century, George was wholly justified in propping up Chatham as long as possible, in self-protection. The country might not have been any better governed if the factions had succeeded in their attempts to 'storm the Closet' – that is, force themselves on the King. Besides, in the last resort they could not do so, as they always started to quarrel about the spoils. So, until George could find a better shield, Chatham, with his darkened mind, was safe in office. It was a hopeless way to rule an empire.[2]

Had the ministry been strong enough to replace Prime Ministerial with Cabinet government, its chief's collapse might not have mattered. Cabinet government is just as viable as Prime Ministerial, and was an art well understood in eighteenth-century England. Unhappily, Chatham's Cabinet, without Chatham, was second-rate. It had been put together in defiance of party principles and looked like a stretch of crazy paving (to compress one of Burke's most famous flights of invective). Chatham thus left a gap indeed.

It might have been filled by Lord Shelburne (1737–1805), one of the Secretaries of State, the ablest of the Chathamites; but he was universally disliked and distrusted. So a stormy petrel – Charles Townshend, the 'splendid shuttlecock' – Chancellor of the Exchequer – eloquent, brilliant, unstable, untrustworthy – was able, for a few months, to dominate the administration, with disastrous consequences for England and America.

2 It is worth pointing out the contrast between England and America in this respect. When Chatham went mad, the government of his country was paralysed. When James Otis went mad, the patriot party of Massachusetts Bay simply turned to the alternative leadership of John Hancock and Sam Adams. Clearly the advantage lay with the colonials.

Townshend (1725–67) is a figure to whom it is difficult to be fair, and most historians have not tried. His faults and his talents were equally glaring. Horace Walpole, at various times, hit him off best: 'His figure was tall and advantageous, his action vehement, his voice loud, his laugh louder. He had art enough to disguise anything but his vanity.' Walpole noticed that in eloquence, energy and unpredictability Townshend had much in common with Chatham, and explained that, in his great war ministry,

Pitt did not choose to advance a young man to a ministerial office, whose abilities were of the same kind, and so nearly equal to his own. Both had fine natural parts; both were capable of great application: which was the greater master of abuse could not easily be determined: and if there was something more awful and compulsive in Pitt's oratory, there was more acuteness and more wit in Charles Townshend's.

Pitt's distrust of Townshend continued: he did his best to keep him out of his 1766 ministry, and, just before his own collapse, tried to replace him with Lord North. He had every reason. If he himself was an impossible master, Townshend was an impossible subordinate. He was in flat disagreement with Chatham on the East India question and agreed with Grenville about America. As Chatham declined, Townshend successfully sabotaged his policies by his energy, ability and hot-tempered threats to resign. He was no more loyal to his colleagues than he was to their chief. By the late summer of 1767 nobody trusted him any more; his future was highly unpromising; there was nothing for him to do but die, which he duly did, leaving his private affairs in great disorder.

Yet in the act of policy for which alone he is now remembered Townshend acted, though with his usual flamboyance, more as a statesman and less as a showman than in anything else he attempted. He had served a long apprenticeship in American affairs at the Board of Trade, and where colonial questions were concerned, was a champagne version of Grenville. He had always been an exponent of imperial centralization, criticizing the Albany Plan, for example, because it would have developed a devolved federal structure in North America. He was too intelligent to accept the distinction between internal and external taxation which had eased the way to the repeal of the Stamp Act, and, like all other British politicians, upheld the principles of the Declaratory Act. Then, as Chancellor of the Exchequer he was sharply aware of the financial problems that, the Stamp Act and the raid on the East India Company both having failed, were as pressing as ever. It was true, of course, that Chatham was identified in the public mind, both in England and the colonies, as America's staunchest friend, and that no ministry bearing his name could decently abandon his policy for Grenville's; but what was that to Townshend? He saw his opportunity, and took it. On 26 January 1767, Grenville, who was now fixated with the idea that America should be taxed, introduced a motion to that end in the House of Commons. The motion was defeated, but Townshend, replying for the government, accepted the principle involved by announcing 'that he knew the mode by which a revenue might be drawn from America *without offence*'. Shelburne rightly commented that such a speech was not the way to make anything go down well in North America; but worse was to come. A month later the opposition carried a motion to reduce the land-tax by a shilling in the pound: 'The joy in the House of Commons was very great,' Grenville recorded, 'all the country gentlemen coming round Mr Grenville, shaking him by the hand, and testifying the greatest satisfaction.' Now the fat was in the fire: for it was reckoned that the government needed more than £400,000 a year to pay for overseas military establishments in North America alone.

Accordingly Townshend felt emboldened to fulfil his pledge. One of his talents as a politician was that he always knew which way the wind was blowing: according to Burke, 'He conformed exactly to the temper of the house; and he seemed to guide, because he was always sure to follow it.' He knew the general irritation caused by the antics of Massachusetts and, even more, of New York; even Chatham had called New York infatuated, the victim of a demon of discord, and believed that it would have to be disciplined. The House of Commons, being even more reluctant than usual to vote taxes on itself, would welcome levies on America, so long as they did not bring with them Stamp-like troubles. This Townshend promised to arrange. He also meant to put the whole government of North America on a radically new footing, of the centralizing kind he favoured.

On 13 May 1767 he introduced his measures. The last was signed by the King on 2 July. All had an easy passage through Parliament. They were helped on by a general resentment of New York's ungrateful behaviour, as is shown by the fact that one of them (the New York Restraining Act) invalidated all Acts of the New York assembly until the Quartering Act was obeyed. This particular measure remained a dead letter, because the New York assembly had complied with the Quartering Act in June,[3] but its mere passage was resented as an act of arbitrary usurpation. It was to be remembered. And the other Townshend laws were also directed against the colonial assemblies. For whereas the Stamp Act had been carefully limited to the purpose of providing funds for the imperial military establishment, Townshend exploited the financial problem and the unpopularity of the Americans to strike at institutions which he had long held to be the real originators of all Anglo-American troubles. His Revenue Act revived the question of taxation by imposing new duties on glass, lead, painters' colours, paper and tea, and explicitly authorized writs of assistance in their collection; while another act set up an American Board of Customs Commissioners at Boston to expedite the collection of these and other, older duties. The following year four new vice-admiralty districts (Halifax, Boston,

3 See above, p. 136.

Philadelphia, Charles Town) were set up to act as further instruments of mercantilist control and law-enforcement. These, since they operated without juries, were seen by Americans as encroaching further on sacred rights: 'What has America done to be . . . disfranchised and stripped of so invaluable a privilege as trial by jury?' It was worse than the Stamp Act. Above all, Townshend earmarked the proceeds of the new duties to set up a colonial civil list, which would enable the King to pay the salaries of colonial Governors, customs officers and other officials without recourse to the assemblies which had hitherto paid them. In short, here was a direct assault on the power of the colonial purse. It was bold, intelligent and exceedingly unwise – so unwise that the most mysterious thing about the affair is that Townshend apparently never asked himself seriously if and how his Acts could be enforced.

Even without the Stamp Act precedents the challenge must have been resisted. I have already tried to make it clear that representative self-government was a principle coeval with the English settlements. The eighteenth-century assemblies embodied this principle and by 1767 were doing so very effectively indeed. Thanks partly to British neglect and partly to the stresses of local politics, in every colony the lower, popularly elected house had gained an ascendancy over both the executive (the Governors) and the upper house (the Council).[4] It had constantly been represented to Whitehall that as long as the Governors depended on annual votes of the colonial assemblies for their salaries the assemblies would have the whip hand: but Charles Townshend was the first minister ever to listen, and by the time he acted it was too late. Even in Virginia, where the Governor's salary was safe from opponents in the House of Burgesses, the assembly had grown used to running the colony, quite as the House of Commons was to run nineteenth-century England (here, as so often, colonial development had raced ahead of that of the mother country). As to the upper houses, the Councils, these had declined for various reasons. In Massachusetts Bay, under the 1691 Charter, the House of Representatives elected the Councillors, and it is only surprising that not until 1766 and the Stamp Act crisis did it designedly choose men who would do its own bidding rather than the Governor's; but the Council had been weakening for sixty years previously. Other colonies reached the same goal by different paths, but all reached it. The purest Whig doctrine came to prevail: the right of no taxation without representation had been successfully exploited to make each province essentially self-governing, and Townshend should have known enough to realize that any challenge to the assemblies' powers was certain to provoke a ferocious reaction.

This was so for more reasons than one. Not only were the assemblies essentially sovereign by the mid-eighteenth century: each had become the instrument of a particular group, or interest, which used them to wield and

4 For the particular case of Pennsylvania, see above, pp. 98–9.

keep local power. Planters to the South, merchants to the North, those living on or near 'tidewater' had flourished mightily in the past century, and in a hundred ways their interest in continuing to do so affected their politics. In Massachusetts, typical of the New England colonies, everything turned on the townships, with which men identified themselves before they thought of themselves as citizens of Massachusetts, certainly before they thought of themselves as subjects of King George. Representation in the General Court was weighted in favour of the seaboard, mercantile towns, and the fact that the Court met at Boston, where the mob was always at hand to intimidate inland representatives, did nothing to correct the balance. Important though these factors were, tidewater ascendancy in Massachusetts Bay was chiefly the result of the fact that the merchants and shopkeepers of Boston knew what they wanted and how to get it: they were the most dynamic elements in the colony's politics, and the Stamp Act crisis had united the colonials in views most congenial to them. Subsequent British blunders refreshed the union. Thus the Revolution in Massachusetts was chiefly to be shaped by Boston, capital of commerce and patriotism. In Pennsylvania the great fight was between the Penn family, still exploiting its position (for example, its enormous landholdings were untaxed), and the so-called Quaker party – which, by the time Franklin and his friend Galloway came to lead it, was misnamed, being essentially the party of the merchants and eastern landholders. These men looked on themselves as the true representatives of the people of Pennsylvania. They based their claim partly on their descent from the first Quaker and Anglican settlers, partly on their wealth (for property was increasingly coming to be seen as a necessary qualification for participation in politics) and partly on the kudos they felt they had earned by their long struggle against the oppressive and aristocratical Penns. But the Quaker party was nevertheless at odds with the hinterland, now filling up with German and Northern Irish aliens: its control of the assembly, and so of Pennsylvania, had to be defended on two fronts, and indeed was, by many advanced political methods, including that of gerrymandering.[5] In Virginia an advance to the West was a matter of desire, not alarm, to the great planters: they hoped to make a fortune out of it, and were happy in principle to extend the suffrage to Western settlers if this induced them to play their part in opening up new territory. But the planters had, of course, no intention of relinquishing control. They were quite at one with the Pennsylvanians in holding that property was a prerequisite for political power. As a 1670 Virginian law stated, a voice in elections belonged only 'to such as by their estates real or personal have interest enough to tie them to the endeavour of the public good'. Even between

---

5 *Gerrymandering* – the manipulation of constituency boundaries to maximize the effect of votes for the manipulating party. Named after Elbridge Gerry (1774–1814), a patriot in the Revolution and successful politician thereafter, whose activities as Governor of Massachusetts (1810–12) suggested the need for a new word. He died while Vice-President of the United States.

property-holders there was no democracy. The mere right to vote was not worth very much, since local government was in the hands of the oligarchs, who also ensured that no candidates from outside their ranks ever got elected to the House of Burgesses, or even came forward. Controlling the assembly, on the other hand, was well worthwhile, and the oligarchs' prolonged success in doing so (going back to the seventeenth century) naturally fortified their belief in themselves and their attachment to Whig principles. Few of them had read Harrington, Sidney or Locke, but those writers' insistence that, both in nature and in right, governments could be founded only on the will of the people, which will was best expressed through representative institutions (related notions which together made up the doctrine of legislative supremacy), like their failure to support universal suffrage, was very compatible with American conditions. The ideas of these writers had, over time, become widely diffused in the colonies, even if their works had not.

Accordingly, when news of the Townshend Acts reached America, the only question was what form resistance should take this time. So clear was the challenge, whether to the rights of the citizens or the powers of the assemblies, that some sudden, single, vigorous outburst like that which had defeated the Stamp Act might have seemed a probable response. If, instead, the reaction was prolonged over three years or so and varied greatly in intensity from place to place and time to time, it was, paradoxically, because opposition to Townshend touched even more people than had opposition to Grenville; because the patriot leaders saw, and seized, the opportunity to devise new and even more formidable organizations of resistance, which necessarily took time; and because this last development began seriously to alarm certain American interests, so that where the Stamp Act crisis had, on the whole, united the colonials (for even Thomas Hutchinson had objected to British policy) the Townshend crisis, just because it ran deeper, divided them.

Massachusetts, as might have been expected, led the way. The radical patriots, led by Sam Adams, were most concerned with the political implications of the Townshend Acts: here was renewed taxation without representation, here was a plot to make the colonial governments independent of the governed, here was the thin end of the wedge. Before long colonial money would be used to support the standing army in America and (Adams did not scruple to add) a bishop over New England. The customs commissioners, now on their way to take up their duties in Boston, should be given as hot a reception as had greeted the would-be Stamp collectors. But this advice fell on deaf ears. For the moment it was the economic aspects of the Townshend Acts which most dismayed the merchants and shopkeepers: the merchants because stricter customs regulation would put an end to the smuggling in which so many of them (especially John Hancock) so profitably engaged; the small men because they were frightened that the rise in prices which the new duties would bring about would put them out of business. There may have been some substance in their fears. For example, the duty on tea was threepence a pound, a not inconsiderable sum in the eighteenth century. There were said to be 'deluges of bankruptcies' in Rhode Island that autumn; the *Massachusetts Post-Boy* spoke of an 'alarming scarcity of money and consequent stagnation of trade' in that province. Conditions were much the same in New Hampshire. Whatever the real cause, the Townshend duties were blamed for this state of affairs, and a spontaneous movement sprang up to counteract them. 'Save your money and save your country,' said the *Post-Boy*. On 28 October the Boston town-meeting launched a non-consumption agreement, the subscribers to which pledged themselves to boycott a large number of goods that were usually imported (for example, 'loaf sugar, cordage, anchors, coaches . . . Men and women's hats . . . shoes . . . snuff, mustard . . . glue'), to buy colonial produce instead, and to observe frugality in mourning (since the yards and yards of black cloth necessary to lament the dead in the usual style had to come from England). Tea was not officially boycotted, but it became a patriotic duty to shun it; besides, it was a 'most luxurious and enervating article', probably to blame for all the new-fangled ailments ('tremblings, apoplexies, consumptions') that were going round.

This sort of thing proved popular, and the non-consumption movement spread throughout seaboard Massachusetts; but it could not be expected to have much effect on imperial policy, being neither universal nor dramatic. Accordingly, radicals and shopkeepers (of course the two categories often overlapped) began to look for more assertive measures, as did many of the leading merchants. These, through their mouthpiece James Otis, had ensured that the customs officers were unmolested when they arrived in Boston on 5 November 1767; but they were so forbearing only because they were anxious not to alienate opinion in the other colonies by riotous behaviour. What was hoped for was a renewal of the non-importation agreements of 1765: a hope that was much encouraged by the publication of John Dickinson's *Letters from a Farmer in Pennsylvania*, which appeared in the *Pennsylvania Gazette* between December 1767 and February 1768. These *Letters* were immensely successful: officially commended by town-meetings, republished in newspapers throughout the colonies and also in pamphlet form, they became the Bible of American patriotism until the eve of independence. With cool good temper and good sense Dickinson (1732–1808), a prosperous Philadelphian lawyer, acknowledged the sovereignty of the Crown and the authority of Parliament to regulate the trade and industry of the Empire, but attacked everything else: the New York Restraining Act, the Townshend Acts and, root and branch, all attempts to tax the colonies without their consent or govern them otherwise than through their assemblies, which, deprived of the power of the purse, might '*perhaps* be allowed to make laws *for the yoking of hogs,* or *the pounding of stray cattle.* Their influence will hardly be permitted to extend *so high,* as the *keeping roads in repair,* as *that business* may more properly be executed by those who receive the public cash.' Americans must resist, or become mere slaves; and, strongly deprecating violence, Dickinson advocated a non-importation movement as the best means.

This was music to Massachusetts, though no sweeter, presumably, than Dickinson's remark in a letter to James Otis that 'Whenever the cause of American freedom is to be vindicated, I look towards the province of Massachusetts Bay.' Thus encouraged, Otis and Sam Adams worked with a will at the winter session of the General Court. On 20 January 1768 the House of Representatives agreed on a petition to the King seeking the repeal of the Townshend Acts, and on 11 February, after many of the western conservatives had gone home, the House voted to send a circular letter to all the other colonial assemblies, affirming American rights, denouncing the Townshend Acts and reporting what the Massachusetts assembly had done by way of protest. Then on 1 March the merchants of Boston (that is, everybody who traded directly with England) met in conclave and pledged themselves to refrain for a year from importing anything but a few fishing essentials from Great Britain, provided only that New York and Philadelphian merchants would agree to abstain too.

The merchants' action was just what John Dickinson had recommended, but the circular letter had the first success. This document was written chiefly by Samuel Adams and is a monument to his literary skill. Unalarmingly polite, moderate and logical in its language, it nevertheless stood rock-firm on the question of taxation:

what a man has honestly acquired is absolutely his own, which he may freely give, but cannot be taken from him without his own consent.

Since Americans neither were, nor, in practice, could be, properly represented *in* Parliament, they could not be lawfully taxed *by* Parliament. It was becoming a familiar doctrine, and was welcomed throughout the colonies. The Virginia General Court, for example, sent off a petition to the King, a memorial to the House of Lords and a remonstrance to the Commons. This action (16 April 1768) prompted the acting Governor to prorogue the assembly. This, or an even stronger measure, was just what the British government would have required of him.

For during the previous winter the government had been reconstructed (though Chatham did not resign until October 1768). The supporters of the Duke of Bedford now dominated the Cabinet, and, like the King, indeed even more enthusiastically, believed that a policy of 'firmness' was what the situation required. A new post of American Secretary had been created, and its first occupant, Wills Hill, Lord Hillsborough (1718–93), read the circular letter with great rage, though he was not a Bedfordite. Massachusetts, it seemed to him, was attempting to form an 'unwarrantable combination' to resist the law and revive the 'distractions' of the Stamp Act crisis; so he sent a circular letter of his own to the royal Governors, telling them to dissolve any assembly that looked like acting favourably on the Massachusetts proposals, which the assembly of that colony must withdraw. All to no avail. As 1768 went on, one assembly after another defied Hillsborough and the Governors and was accordingly dissolved, New Jersey in April being the first, New York in January 1769 being the last. Hillsborough's letter had done no more than make matters worse: in Pennsylvania it was denounced as 'the ministerial mandate, by which it seems we must bow our neck to the yoke, without uttering one groan'.

Meanwhile the non-importation movement could not be said to be flourishing: New York had been ready to follow Boston's lead, as had the minor towns of Massachusetts, but Philadelphia hung back, and without it nothing could be attempted. Fortunately for the cause the British again intervened with ill-advised decisions and (for them) disastrous results.

During the winter of 1767–8, as Massachusetts Bay tried to rally the colonies for common action, Samuel Adams had kept the Boston crowd on a short rein, so that the customs commissioners had been able to work comparatively unmolested, though their life was far from pleasant. A favourite trick of the 'disorderly boys' of the city was to lay night-time siege to the commissioners' houses, with drum-beating, horn-blowing (through conches) and the 'most hideous howlings as the Indians, when they attack an enemy'. This unnerved the commissioners, and the knowledge that the crowd went no further only because Adams had laid it down that for the time being there were to be 'NO MOBS – NO CONFUSIONS – NO TUMULTS' was scarcely comforting. Then on 10 June 1768 there was at last a real riot when the customs seized John Hancock's sloop *Liberty* on the grounds that she was smuggling madeira. The mob stoned the commissioners and broke the windows of their houses, so that they had to flee to the protection of HMS *Romney*, a warship recently stationed in Boston harbour. On 30 September the British government rashly sent two regiments of regular soldiers to Boston, to restore and maintain order.

In part this was possible because Lord Hillsborough had abandoned all attempts to police the West, in view of what he called 'the enormous and ruinous expense' involved. Since it had so far proved impossible, on either side of the Atlantic, to raise a revenue for imperial purposes, the authorities had perforce fallen back on a policy of reckless penny-pinching. General Gage had launched economies that were to leave the army in a poor way to fight the War of the American Revolution. Now Hillsborough decided that the regulation of the fur-trade and the prevention of another Indian war were policies that no longer justified their cost, so most of the interior forts were abandoned. It was another British abdication; but this most significant fact was overlooked because it was immediately followed by the military occupation of Boston.

This development had a very bad effect on American opinion. For five years the government had insisted that the standing army was in America only for imperial defence, yet now it was declared to be for the purpose of enforcing obedience to Parliament, and was to police Boston. How could Crown or Parliament ever be trusted again? Sam Adams, who regarded a standing army in peacetime as a sure sign of impending tyranny, talked of organizing armed resistance, but there were no volunteers. However, he did persuade the House of Representatives to meet (unofficially, since Governor Bernard refused to summon it), calling itself a convention, on the favourite seventeenth-century English model. This convention gathered in the week before the troops landed, and did little, except to scuttle out of town 'like a herd of scalded hogs' on the day the troopships appeared off-shore: no one wanted to be the first martyr for liberty. Furthermore, during the convention it became plain for the first time that there was a solid opposition to Bostonian extremism in country Massachusetts, which sufficed for the moment to keep Adams in check. But it was sufficient for the grossly unconstitutional convention to have met: British law was thus again flouted, and in a new way.

It is scarcely surprising that the talk in London, even among the Rockingham Whigs, began to be about isolating and punishing Massachusetts, that 'ringleading province'. However, this was easier to will than to do, and in the upshot this frustrated feeling grew into an obsession that was to prove very harmful. In the winter of 1768–9 it issued in new provocations – or, as American conservatives would have argued, in mere gestures which annoyed without disciplining the patriots. In August 1768 New York joined the non-importation movement, and in March 1769 Pennsylvania at last did likewise, all its attempts to extract concessions or redress from the British government having failed. What came over instead was a report of eight Parliamentary resolutions. Sponsored by Hillsborough, they were all sound and fury, denouncing all the proceedings – riots, circular letter, convention – of Massachusetts and Boston, and asking the King to take what steps he could to prosecute any treason or misprision of treason that had occurred, if necessary by carrying the culprits to England for trial. No more was done or attempted, but the colonies were greatly provoked, and both the Virginia and South Carolina assemblies prepared counter-resolutions stoutly supporting Massachusetts. The plantation colonies (those lying south of Pennsylvania) had not previously been much touched by the agitation of the commercial colonies: Boston was too mobbish for them; but now they took alarm. For instance, George Washington of Mount Vernon, Virginia (1732–99), a prosperous (for a wonder) planter, a retired militia colonel who had seen much service in the Seven Years War, was convinced by the Hillsborough Resolutions that 'our lordly masters in Great Britain will be content with nothing less than the deprication [*sic*] of American freedom', and that a resort to arms might prove necessary, if only as a last defence. In the meantime he advocated Virginia's entry into the non-importation movement, and enough of his countrymen agreed with him for Virginia to do just that, though only after a year of painful negotiation. All the other Southern colonies had done the same by the end of 1769 (the agreement was but ill-observed in Georgia) and by the spring of 1770, of the leading English provinces, only New Hampshire was holding aloof.

By that time sense was returning to Whitehall. It was, indeed, a perfectly pointless quarrel, and as early as May 1769 the Cabinet decided, in view of American hostility, to repeal the Townshend duties, except for the one on tea. This was to be retained for the principle of the thing, as the Declaratory Act had sweetened the pill of Stamp Act repeal. The about-turn took time to arrange, for the Westminster winter (1769–70) was preoccupied with the retirement of the Duke of Grafton, the notional Prime Minister. He was replaced by Frederick, Lord North (1732–92), the son and heir of the Earl of Guilford, and the sort of chief minister that George III had been looking for since the beginning of his reign. Not for North the abrasive policies of a Grenville, the abrasive personality of a Pitt, the weakness of a Bute, the factiousness of a Rockingham. Like his king, whom he resembled, physically, so closely that the story got around that they had the same father[6] – they both looked like bullfrogs, only in North the frog was more apparent than the bull – his strengths and weaknesses were those of the old order at its best. Hence his failure, for, except in matters of public finance, he was incapable of creative innovation, however necessary. He fumbled from expedient to expedient, which has its points in quiet times, but is a quite inadequate response to great emergencies. Yet if the old order could have responded to the challenge, North might well have been the instrument. For one thing he was utterly devoted to it, especially to the rights, powers and prestige of the old, unreformed Parliament, in which he would never find any flaw. He was 'the complete House of Commons man',[7] bland, humorous and occasionally eloquent in debate, a masterly political tactician, a competent administrator and personally more than acceptable to George III, whom he served loyally. He was steadfast in emergency, and if he was irresolute when great decisions were to be made, the King was always there to stiffen his nerve. He put together a stable ministry and a permanent Parliamentary majority, and was successful for years: only gradually did his weaknesses cripple him. To begin with, all went well. On 5 March 1770, in the first great measure of his administration, he moved the repeal of the Townshend duties, arguing that they were commercially nonsensical. He said nothing about the crucial fact that they had stirred up more trouble than they were worth.

They were still doing so. Across the Atlantic, on the very day of North's speech, Boston erupted again.

The British had been too ready to mock the city's peaceful acquiescence in the arrival of the troops. Since that time relations between the townspeople and the soldiers, never good, had got worse and worse. The humaner sort

6 Frederick, Prince of Wales.
7 John Cannon, *Lord North* (London, 1970, Historical Association pamphlet), p. 9.

of Bostonian was horrified at the brutal floggings by which officers tried to maintain discipline; everybody was inconvenienced by the challenging sentinels who were posted on Boston Neck to catch deserters; the presence of the army was widely resented as a check on liberty;[8] and the soldiers and officers themselves, while not perhaps exceptionally brutal and licentious, were too much so for the staid manners of Boston.[9] Harassment of the troops became a patriotic duty, to be combined if possible with those other duties, evading the trade laws and intimidating the merchants so that they dared not break the non-importation agreement (even Thomas Hutchinson's sons were forced to comply). Sam Adams kept up a constant storm of inflammatory journalism. And the boys of Boston, reacting as children always do to prolonged periods of unrest, plunged headlong into the good work with all the recklessness of those who are still too young to know the difference between game and grim earnest. They took to rioting every Thursday – market day, when the schools were shut. On Thursday, 22 February 1770, some of them besieged a conservative in his house; he, in terror, fired into the crowd, wounding one boy and killing another, the eleven-year-old Christopher Snider, who was honoured with an enormous public burying. 'My eyes never beheld such a funeral,' wrote John Adams in his diary, 'the procession extended further than can well be imagined.' This was thrilling enough, but baiting soldiers was even better. There were several ugly incidents, and gangs had come to dominate the streets of Boston, before the assaults of a mob led by Crispus Attucks, a half-Negro working man, forced the guards of the Customs House to fire in self-defence, on 5 March. Five Bostonians were killed, including Attucks. This 'massacre' was quickly elevated into legend. It was used as evidence that the British would stick at nothing. It was held to vindicate a hundred times the traditional Whig belief that a standing army was necessarily a threat to civil peace and liberty, which the people should always be on guard against. The dead became martyrs, and, more prosaically, Sam Adams and the other radicals were able to use the incident to force the authorities to withdraw the troops from Boston to Castle William down the harbour. This, indeed, had probably been the purpose of the riot which had touched off the 'Massacre', for it was almost certainly instigated by the radical leaders. Next, New Hampshire was shocked into temporary acquiescence in the non-importation movement, and the rest of America resounded to cries of horror, especially after Adams's grossly untrue accounts of the affair got round.

As tempers cooled again, however, it could be seen that the extremists had done themselves more harm than good. It was tolerably plain that they had provoked the 'Massacre', and the spectacle of seething Boston had little

---

8 'To have a standing army! Good God! What can be worse to a people who have tasted the sweets of liberty!' Thus the Reverend Andrew Eliot, on 27 September 1768.
9 Though there is wisdom in John Shy's remark that 'soldiers tended to be drunken and disorderly, but then so did many Americans' (*Toward Lexington*, p. 394).

appeal to the respectable elsewhere. This was especially true of the richer merchants, who, on learning that the Townshend measures had been repealed, rushed to dissociate themselves from their dangerous allies. New York resumed importation in July, Philadelphia in September, Boston in October. The other ports did likewise, and once more an uneasy peace descended on the thirteen colonies.

Thomas Hutchinson was sworn in as Governor of Massachusetts in March 1771 and was welcomed with great warmth throughout the province. He was, after all, native-born and an ornament to the land he had served long and well. Normality of a different kind manifested itself at the same time in North Carolina, where the feud between the western and eastern areas culminated in the rebellion of the so-called Regulators,[10] the men of the West, who after overturning the government in the back-countries in late 1770 were met and defeated in battle at the Alamance river by Governor Tryon and the tidewater militia on 16 May 1771. It was not a very impressive battle: the Regulators, lacking effective military organization, were easily routed, many having been wounded though only nine were killed; amnesty was granted to the rest, on condition that they took an oath of allegiance to the King. Yet it was the most thrilling event between the collapse of non-importation and the summer of 1772 – a period of nearly two years.

This appearance of restored calm was deeply misleading. The period since the Stamp Act had transformed American attitudes to Great Britain. The slightest action of the mother country was now regarded with automatic suspicion: any major initiative might well re-open the volcano. Nor was that all. In eleven of the thirteen colonies – all, that is, except New Hampshire and Georgia – the Sons of Liberty retained power, and in Massachusetts, under the command of Sam Adams, they were organized to extend and exert it – if necessary by stirring up trouble instead of tamely waiting for it to arise.

There was for a moment a chance of driving Adams from the stage. In Governor Hutchinson he at last had a worthy foe. Hutchinson was in the end to be the one great tragic figure of the Revolution: a moderate, patriotic, able and devoted man, whose virtues as much as his limitations (he had no vices to speak of) would lead him to disaster; but during the first two years of his Governorship he had some appreciable successes. A reaction set in among the country people against the agitations of their long-distrusted capital. Even in Boston itself Sam Adams lost ground: he ran[11] for Registrar of Suffolk County (which includes Boston) and lost. His vote at the elections for the House of Representatives sank to a dangerously low level. Hutchinson rejoiced to report to Lord Hillsborough that there was more 'general appearance of contentment' in Massachusetts at the beginning of 1772 than at

10 This word had appeared earlier in England, where in 1766 rioters against the high price of wheat in Dorset 'declared they were Regulators'. See George Rudé, *The Crowd in History*, p. 42.
11 In England, of course, we stand for election: in more dynamic America they run, and it is obviously best to use the American idiom here and throughout the book.

any time since the Stamp Act. All the same, Adams's control of the General Court was never seriously threatened, and he kept up his strategy of picking quarrels with authority on every occasion.

Events in Britain also belied the appearance of calm. The great Wilkes affair is too long a subject to be detailed here. Suffice it to say that John Wilkes, prosecuted, banished, imprisoned and expelled from the House of Commons, had become by the late sixties a heroic symbol for all those forces which, in Britain as in America, were struggling, for all manner of reasons, against the ossification of the old order. Potentially Wilkes was for Britain what Patrick Henry and Sam Adams were for America. His weaknesses were twofold: he was a conservative, or at any rate not a revolutionary, at heart (else he could hardly have become Lord Mayor of London); and his personal character, that of a reckless, if attractive, gambler and rake, tended to alienate the Puritan element, then as now an essential part of any British reform movement. Franklin, that incarnation of late Puritanism (even though he was himself something of a rake on the sly), dismissed Wilkes as 'an outlaw and an exile, of bad personal character, not worth a farthing'. More perceptive was somebody's remark that if Wilkes had had the unblemished personal reputation of George III, he could have dethroned the King: it gives an exact idea of his importance.

Americans watched the drama, from their distance, with fascination. It seemed their own battle, as indeed to some extent it was. Wilkes's fight against general warrants was the same as their fight against writs of assistance. They sympathized instinctively with his stand for freedom of the press, free elections, the rights of man, and some measure of Parliamentary reform (a cause, it is worth noting, that their other great English hero, Lord Chatham, would soon endorse). The Wilkite crowd was much like the Bostonian one in composition, aims and behaviour: it too was led by sailors and pulled down houses, though it was much more good-humoured. It had the same enemies: the standing army shot down Londoners in the St George's Fields Massacre as it shot down Bostonians. Accordingly American patriots toasted 'Wilkes and Liberty' at many a banquet and subscribed liberally to Wilkite funds. They mourned the hero's defeats, cheered his victories, read his pamphlets. And thus a new poison entered the American bloodstream.

English radicals strongly sympathized with their American counterparts, and anyway found the American question a useful stick with which to beat the government. But being closer to the scene of action than the colonials, and being even more deeply impregnated with Whiggish notions deriving from the struggle between King and Parliament in the seventeenth century, they were much quicker to blame George III as well as his ministers for the plot against liberty that they detected in every act of the administration. In his great philippic against the King of 19 December 1769, the pamphleteer 'Junius' assumed that the colonials had seen the point:

They were ready enough to distinguish between *you* and your ministers. They complained of an act of the legislature, but traced the origin of it no higher than to the servants of the crown: They pleased themselves with the hope that their sovereign, if not favourable to their cause, at least was impartial. The decisive, personal part you took against them, has effectually banished that first distinction from their minds. They consider you as united with your servants against America, and know how to distinguish the sovereign and a venal parliament on one side, from the real sentiments of the English people on the other . . . They left their native land in search of freedom, and found it in a desert. Divided as they are into a thousand forms of policy and religion, there is one point in which they all agree:– they equally detest the pageantry of a king, and the supercilious hypocrisy of a bishop. It is not then from the alienated affections of Ireland or America, that you can look for assistance . . .

This was a self-fulfilling prophecy. The Americans read it, and others like it, and began to wonder if it was not true. Were their affections alienated? Was the King their real oppressor? They began to study his behaviour, and soon discovered the obvious, that George, far from being the victim of misleading and oppressive ministers, was their energetic and willing ally. He snubbed Wilkite petitions and led the battle against Wilkes himself. An American merchant in London wrote home that 'the *Best of Princes* had taken care to offend all his English subjects by a uniform and studied inattention which irritable men like myself construe into more than neglect and downright insult . . .'. The image, once dear even to John Adams, of a patriot King, the benevolent scion of the House of Brunswick, the guarantor of the Protestant succession, began to crumble, and memories of the legendary Stuart tyrants to revive. One more link with Britain was snapping.

Matters were not helped in the summer of 1772 when the merchants (that is, the smugglers) of Newport, Rhode Island, captured and burned the revenue schooner HMS *Gaspee*, whose commander, it was alleged, had not only pressed men in the colony, but stolen sheep, hogs and poultry, and cut down fruit-trees for firewood. He had also been inconveniently diligent in enforcing the Navigation Acts. This outrage compelled some imperial reaction, since the local officials made not the slightest attempt to bring the criminals to justice. When it came, the reaction was significantly feeble, showing that the British had learned a few lessons. They had learned, for example, to keep out of quarrels between, or within, colonies, and to move cautiously, one might say timidly, when involvement was inescapable. Their response to the *Gaspee* incident was to set up an investigatory commission consisting of the Governor of Rhode Island, the Chief Justices of Massachusetts, New York and New Jersey, and the judge of the vice-admiralty court for the New England district. These men were all far too American and far too cautious to take any risks, so the commission was ineffective, as might have been foreseen. All in all, it was a pitiful way of dealing with what was, in one sense, a deadlier challenge than the Boston

Tea Party itself was to be, since it involved the destruction of one of the King's ships, not just of some private property. Such feebleness was another sign of abdication, even though the commission was too strong for radical stomachs and was treated everywhere by the Sons of Liberty as a tyrannical interference. For among its instructions was the fatal provision that persons arrested as a result of its findings were to be transported to England to stand trial. The alarm occasioned by this 'court of inquisition, more horrid than that of Spain and Portugal' (!) led the Virginian House of Burgesses in the spring of 1773 to propose the establishment of a chain of inter-colonial committees of correspondence, for the concerting of common measures against acts of oppression. This proposal was eagerly taken up by the other colonies.

So failed the policy of feebleness. But its alternative, 'vigour', failed even worse when it was at length applied to the most mutinous of the colonies, Massachusetts Bay.

There, months before Virginia acted, Sam Adams had recaptured the initiative. Using as his pretext the new policy by which the proceeds of the American customs were used for the salaries of government officials, including judges, he painted a frightful picture of liberty and justice in America being subverted by 'pensioners, placemen and other jobbers, for an abandon'd and shameless ministry; hirelings, pimps, parasites, panders, prostitutes and whores' (this use of extravagant sexual abuse was common with Adams and his associates).[12] He was able, by much hysteria and not a little trickery, to induce Boston town-meeting to start a chain of committees of correspondence within Massachusetts, each township to have one. These committees were eventually to usurp the government of the province. By 1774, 300 towns had been drawn into the network. Each committee reported directly to Boston; and at Boston a connection was established with the committees of the other colonies.

Working for the imperial government was men's natural desire for a quiet life and a return of prosperity. In Virginia, George Washington, forgetting his talk of armed resistance, was devoting himself entirely to the management of his plantations and the pursuit of rich land-grants in the new country opening up across the Allegheny mountains. There were many like him in every colony. But on the whole conditions for British policy were getting slowly, imperceptibly, but definitely worse.

Lord North did not notice: Parliament did not discuss America for two years. He had other problems on his mind, the foremost being India. Like everything else it was connected with the difficulties of government finance.

The East India Company was another victim of the decaying mercantilist system. Chatham, it will be remembered, had hoped to pay for the Empire not by taxing the West but by squeezing the East: the Company was saddled

12 John Adams compared England to imperial Rome: both were the prey of 'musicians, pimps, panders, and catamites'.

with the requirement to pay an annual £400,000 to the government. It was also burdened with rising administrative costs in India, with competition in the tea-trade from English and American smugglers, and with the consequences of a great famine in Bengal. Its purely business affairs were being badly managed, the price of its shares had collapsed, and a financial panic, followed by a twelve-month trade depression, which made the collection of money owed to the Company very difficult, started early in 1772. By September in that year, with debts amounting to more than £1,300,000, it was nearing bankruptcy, and the government had to intervene.

The resulting legislation took the first step on the road that led eventually to supersession of the Company in India by the Crown. North also adopted an ingenious idea, put forward by Company officials, for aiding it commercially. He prepared an Act of Parliament (the so-called Tea Act) by which all mercantilist burdens on the export of the Company's tea to America were lifted. Company tea would thereby be able to compete effectively with the smuggled sort, which at the time was selling in the colonies at 2s. 7d. per pound. The appearance on the market of fine East Indian teas at 2s. per pound would force the smugglers' prices down in a rush (though they would still enjoy a 6 per cent profit). Furthermore, under North's arrangements the Company would be allowed to act as its own retailer, selling direct to the colonial consumer, not, as previously, through middlemen. This was manna to the East Indiamen. They expected to accumulate, in 1773–4, a surplus of thirty-one million pounds of tea, and before the Tea Act (which became law on 10 May 1773) they had not expected to sell more than thirteen million pounds. Now they were free to dump as much as they could on the American market, being required only to keep back ten million pounds in case of some national emergency (a very British piece of foresight). No wonder Lord North spoke of the Act as 'prodigiously to the advantage of the Company'.

He had not consulted any of the American merchants or colonial agents in London before legislating. To judge by his later statements, he had assumed that the Americans would rush to buy cheap tea and given the matter no further thought. It certainly never occurred to him that the ordinary American tea-drinker would make common cause with the smugglers and legal importers to protest against a measure which substantially lowered the price of the stuff, just because it did not abolish a duty which had been accepted in practice, at any rate in New England, for the previous five years. He took no warning from the fact that the colonies south of Connecticut had never accepted the duty. In 1770 the amount of dutied tea imported to New York was only 147 pounds; Philadelphia took only sixty-five. Both cities drank enormous quantities of contraband tea instead. The plantation colonies showed a similar pattern. The duty was never accepted in principle anywhere, of course: the colonies had continuously petitioned against it. North's blindness to all this demonstrated, as had Grenville and Townshend, how little fitted British ministers were to govern the Empire. The Tea Act would, unless nullified or repealed, gravely injure American smugglers, a not inconsiderable force in colonial life, as the *Gaspee* incident had proved; by eliminating the middlemen it would also injure merchants in the legitimate tea-trade; and as the Townshend tea-duty of 3d. a pound was to continue, the revenue of the Crown in America would be greatly enhanced while the great principle of no taxation without representation went by default. North should have known, or should have found out, that the colonials would be most unlikely to accept the Act: to barter the principles of their liberty for cheap tea. He did not, and thereby missed a great opportunity. Benjamin Franklin had suggested, vainly as usual, that merely by repealing the duty North would enable the American market to absorb four million pounds' worth of the surplus tea in the East India Company's warehouses. Such a repeal, combined with the Tea Act, would have been a masterstroke of policy. North would have greatly aided the East India Company and removed an American grievance, the latter quite without compulsion or agitation. He might have won the government some much-needed popularity, as well as the political initiative. Such a move would have angered the mercantile but not the consuming interest in the colonies. It would have opened the way to replacing mercantilism by free trade, the most pressing of necessary imperial reforms. But these grand ideas never crossed North's mind. Muddled and complacent, he rejected the Rockinghamite suggestion that the Townshend duty, not the British duty on exports, should be abolished, for he saw no need to gratify the Americans, whose temper, he said, was 'little deserving favour from hence'. He refused to listen to William Dowdeswell's warning, made in the debate on the Tea Act, that 'if he don't take off the duty they won't take the tea'. The East India merchants were equally obtuse and sanguine. In vain John Norton, an American trader in London, warned them 'not to think of sending their tea till Government took off the duty, as they might be well assured it would not be received on any other terms'. Bright visions of immediately exporting 600,000 lb. of tea to America danced before their eyes. More could follow . . . they pressed ahead.

Dr Franklin, writing to the Speaker of Massachusetts Bay, sounded the alarm. It was, he thought, a plot to bribe the Americans to acquiesce in the tea-duty and thus submit to the principle of Parliamentary taxation. Bitterly giving vent to a long-mounting disgust with the English, he commented

They have no idea that any people act from any other principle but that of interest; and they believe, that 3d. in a lb. of tea . . . is sufficient to overcome all the patriotism of an American.

The British government had made no such calculation, but should have known that this was how its actions would appear, even to an experienced man like Franklin. As the news of the Act and of the East India Company's plans crossed the Atlantic, alarm spread and resistance mounted. The patriot party seized the opportunity to rally opinion on yet another great symbolic issue. In October, as inter-colonial committees of correspondence were set up in Pennsylvania, Delaware and Maryland, Philadelphia and New York passed resolutions denouncing the Tea Act. But as usual it was Massachusetts which took the lead.

That summer Sam Adams had at last effected the political destruction of Thomas Hutchinson, for Dr Franklin had sent him ill-gotten copies of some letters that the Governor had written to England several years before, containing opinions that, with judicious twisting, could be made to prove that Hutchinson was an enemy to his country. The twisting was done, the letters, against Franklin's wishes, published, and the Governor was condemned by all sections of Massachusetts. His popularity vanished for ever. He was thus helpless to check the tide of events now rushing to a climax.

On 21 October the Massachusetts correspondence committee called for common action by all the colonies against the Company. Boston town-meeting (assembling unofficially) passed anti-Tea Act resolutions on 5 November. The first tea-ship arrived on 28 November, and the next day the town heard the first suggestion that her cargo should be dumped in the harbour. There followed nearly three weeks of bitter contention. Under the laws of trade the tea could not be sent back to England, as Sam Adams wanted, without a clearance from the Governor, and that clearance Hutchinson refused to give, since the re-exportation duty had not been paid and he would not let himself be forced into acquiescing in Adams's scheme. Besides, he thought he had the upper hand: if the duty had not been paid by 17 December, the tea could legally be seized by the customs, landed and sold. At length, on 16 December, at a mass-meeting in Faneuil Hall, John Rowe, one of Sam Adams's associates, asked pointedly, 'Who knows how tea will mingle with salt water?' In the first gloom of a winter evening, after candles were lit, news came in that Hutchinson was still adamant, and cries for 'A mob! A mob!' went up. Adams came forward and announced that 'This meeting can do nothing more to save the country.' It was a signal, taken up with a war-whoop in the gallery, which in turn was answered from the door by a band of men roughly disguised as Indians. 'Boston harbour a teapot tonight!' they shouted, and a huge crowd rushed down to the waterfront, the 'Indians' in the lead. The harbour was now bathed in bright moonlight. The three tea-ships were boarded, the 342 or so tea-chests were hauled on deck and broken open, and the tea was poured into the dark waters, nearly choking them (it was low tide). No other damage was done, and the Tea Party ended with a triumphal march through Boston to fife and drum.

It was the apotheosis of the Boston mob, and Sam Adams's masterpiece. Many of the 'Indians' were his followers from the North End of Boston – sailors, shipwrights and other artisans. Others had come from the allied Massachusetts towns, summoned, no doubt, through his committees of correspondence. He was in ecstasies at his success. 'You cannot imagine the height of joy that sparkles in the eyes and animates the countenances as well as the hearts of all we meet on this occasion,' he wrote a few days later, 'excepting the disappointed, disconsolated Hutchinson and his tools.' The disconsolated Hutchinson, in his *History of Massachusetts*, was to call it the 'boldest stroke which had yet been struck in America'; and the other Adams, who had been inexplicably absent from Boston during the culminating stage, exulted in his diary:

This is the most magnificent moment of all. There is a dignity, a majesty, a sublimity, in this last effort of the patriots, that I greatly admire. The people should never rise, without doing something to be remembered – something notable and striking.

The news flew through the colonies, rousing and uniting patriot Americans and establishing the unquestioned leadership of Massachusetts. Further resistance to the Tea Act was greatly encouraged. Ten days later Philadelphia returned its tea-ships to England; tea was landed at Charles Town but not distributed; on 9 March 1774 Boston destroyed thirty more chests; on 22 April New York city also had a tea party.

The affront to the royal government was staggering. The Tea Act had been nullified and the legitimate Governor spurned, but the matter went deeper than that. Said John Adams,

The question is whether the destruction of this tea was necessary? I apprehend it was absolutely and indispensably so . . . To let it be landed, would be giving up the principle of taxation by Parliamentary authority, against which the Continent has struggled for 10 years.

Another question was developing from the old one: not Parliamentary authority to tax, but Parliamentary authority at all was in question. Challenged by Hutchinson ('I know of no line that can be drawn between the supreme authority of Parliament and the total independence of the colonies') the Massachusetts House of Representatives had already claimed, less than a year before, that the American colonies, by virtue of their charters, were 'distinct States from the mother country', independent of Parliament though owing allegiance to the King. Even this theory could hardly justify the assault on the property of the King's subjects in the East India Company.

The news of the Tea Party was published in London on 20 January 1774, and the majority in Parliament instantly turned to the question of how to chastise, once and for all, the insurgent province and 'secure the dependence of the colonies on the mother country'. It was not so much a calculated response as a loss of temper. For the desire to punish Massachusetts had been felt, probably with increasing power, at least since 1768, when Lord North had observed that some of Boston's actions had approached treason, when Lord Hillsborough had proposed the alteration of the Massachusetts Charter, and when Lord Camden, a wise friend of the colonies, had held that the Townshend duties ought to be repealed everywhere, except perhaps in Massachusetts Bay, to bring that unruly province to heel. Nothing had since mitigated British hostility. The Tea Party was the last straw. The British now blamed themselves for having repealed the Stamp Act. In their own unphilosophical way they had come to see the full, fatal implication of that abdication. It had been, they decided, an act of weakness. They were now resolved on very different measures. It had become a duty to crush Boston. Lord North ranted,

I would rather all the Hamilcars and all the Hannibals that Boston ever bred; all the Hancocks, and all the sad-Cocks, and sad dogs of Massachusetts Bay; all the heroes of tar and feathers, and the champions, maimers of unpatriotic horses, mares and mules, were led up to the altar, on to the Liberty Tree, there to be exalted and rewarded according to their merit or demerit [he meant hanging] than that Britain should disgrace herself by receding from her just authority.

So the Coercive Acts (to be known in America as the Intolerable Acts) began to make their way through Parliament. The first, the Boston Port Act (signed by the King on 31 March), provided that the port of Boston should be closed to trade until the townsmen had paid compensation for the tea to the East India Company. The next two Acts were processed more or less simultaneously, becoming law on 20 May. Of these, the Act for regulating the government of Massachusetts made the provincial council appointive, as it was in most of the other colonies,[13] rather than elective; gave the Governor sole power to dismiss inferior judges, sheriffs and other lesser officers of the law; gave him powers to control and restrict the activities of the town-meetings; even the institution of the jury was tampered with. The Act for the impartial administration of justice tried to protect revenue officers and other servants of the crown in Massachusetts: it provided that if they were accused of capital crimes in the performance of their official duties, they might be tried in another colony or in Great Britain, at the discretion of the Governor. Next came the Quartering Act, signed by the King on 2 June. This attempted to settle an ancient controversy by empowering the Governor to quarter troops more or less wherever he saw fit. Finally, on 22 June, the King signed the Quebec Act. This measure, which was long overdue, was an honest attempt to settle the future status of the French-speaking inhabitants of Canada: its chief features were that it set up a non-elective legislative council to make laws; extended the authority of Quebec into the Ohio and Illinois regions, where there were already some French communities; and recognized the traditional rights of the Catholic Church in Canada. The Act was not designed to be one of the

13 All except Connecticut and Rhode Island.

Intolerable Acts, but the accident of its timing and the unpopularity of its contents in the thirteen colonies[14] made them lump it in with the rest. To enforce the new laws, Governor Hutchinson was to be replaced by General Gage, long an advocate of stricter measures towards the colonies. He had boasted that he could restore order in Massachusetts with four regiments. He was now given the chance to try, and landed at Boston on 17 May. A fortnight later Thomas Hutchinson left for an exile in England from which he was never to return.

The opposition had tried in vain to deter North from these, he hoped, devastating counter-moves. Fox hammered, glittering Burke ridiculed a government which had contrived that 'so paltry a sum as threepence in the eyes of a financier, so insignificant an article as tea in the eyes of a philosopher, have shaken the pillars of a commercial empire that circled the whole globe'. 'Why will you punish Boston alone?' asked Dowdeswell. 'Did not other towns send your tea back to England, and refuse the landing?' The former Governor of West Florida warned that the Port Act would be 'productive of a general confederation to resist the power of this country'. It was no good. Opinion was immovable, and Franklin despaired of colonial petitions: 'The violent destruction of the tea seems to have united all parties against our province.' It was too true.

As usual, the news was slow to leak over the Atlantic. It was greeted with rage and astonishment when it did arrive, but with no weakening. On the contrary, the ranks of the radicals were much increased, for now it seemed clear that they were right, and that there was afoot, as young Thomas Jefferson of Virginia put it, 'a deliberate and systematical plan of reducing us to slavery'. Such was the universal language. It was used in connection with the Intolerable Acts by John Dickinson and George Washington as well as by all hotter heads. Andrew Eliot wrote of 'a deep-laid and desperate plan of imperial despotism'. 'The Parliament of England have declared war against the town of Boston,' one patriotic young Virginian, Landon Carter, confided to his diary. '. . . This is but a prelude to destroy the liberties of America.' So thought the *Boston Evening Post*, commenting that 'It is not the rights of Boston only, but of ALL AMERICA which are now struck at. Not the merchants only but the farmer, and every order of men who inhabit this noble continent.' All America seemed to agree. In March the men of Massachusetts had begun military training. News of the Boston Port Act arrived on 10 April. As it spread along the coast, Boston's appeal was heard, and farmers throughout the colonies sent provisions to the beleaguered town. In late May the Virginia House of Burgesses appealed for public support of the Bostonians and was dissolved for its pains; but on 27 May it met extra-legally at the Raleigh Tavern in Williamsburg and invited

14 Roman Catholicism was by now abhorred less for its supposedly erroneous doctrines than for its association with 'slavery and arbitrary power': it was the religion of despots – Habsburgs, Bourbons, Stuarts – and as such had to be kept at bay in America.

delegates from all the other colonies to meet in a general congress to discuss the crisis. The idea had already been aired and was eagerly taken up. During the months that followed, in one colony after another, assemblies and Governors clashed, and delegates were appointed to the proposed Congress, which opened, amid vast enthusiasm, in Philadelphia on 5 September. Meanwhile in Massachusetts Gage found that the Intolerable Acts were unenforceable outside Boston, though inside the city their operation was effective enough to put hundreds of men out of work. The committees of correspondence were by now well able to defy him, and he had not troops enough to crush them or reduce the province, as North and the King were eagerly expecting. He dared not even arrest the radical leaders, who went unconcernedly about their business under his nose.

The First Continental Congress was an infinitely more impressive body than the Stamp Act Congress which was its forerunner. This time, of all the colonies, only Georgia hung back. The others had each sent their brightest talents and best characters to speak for them, and all were welcomed at Philadelphia with fitting ceremony, rejoicing, wines and dinners – 'Turtle, and every other thing – flummery, jellies, sweetmeats of 20 sorts, trifles, whipped syllabubs, floating islands, fools, etc . . . Wines most excellent and admirable.' Not all the delegates were radicals, by any means: in fact the contingent from Massachusetts was regarded with some distrust, on account of its advanced views; but radical ideas dominated, above all the repudiation of Parliamentary supremacy. This was an important, perhaps a crucial step, for, James Madison was to assert in 1800, 'The fundamental principle of the Revolution was that the colonies were co-ordinate members with each other and Great Britain of an empire united by a common sovereign, and that the legislative power was maintained to be as complete in each American parliament as in the British parliament.'[15] This seemed the merest good sense to such delegates to the Congress as Christopher Gadsden of South Carolina, who, according to John Adams, was 'violent against allowing to Parliament any power of regulating trade, or allowing that they have anything to do with us. – Power of regulating trade he says, is power of ruining us – as bad as acknowledging them a supreme legislative, in all cases whatsoever.' The Congress showed its radicalism by approving the so-called Suffolk Resolves, resolutions passed by the Bostonians and their neighbours on 9 September 1774, refusing obedience to the Intolerable Acts and detailing measures of defiance to be taken against them; by rejecting the ingenious and statesmanlike plan of Joseph Galloway, the Speaker of the Pennsylvania Assembly, for reconciliation with Britain; and above all when, on 18 and 20 October, a few days before dispersing, it agreed to a policy of immediate

15 Lord North, for one, would have agreed. As early as 1770 he was saying: 'The language of America is, We are the subjects of the King; with Parliament we have nothing to do. That is the point at which the factions have been aiming: upon that they have been shaking hands.' It was precisely the point which Lords and Commons would resist most strenuously.

non-importation and eventual non-exportation and set up a 'Continental Association' to enforce it. It was in one sense not new: there had been non-importation agreements before; in every important sense it was unprecedented. Never before had a pan-American body like the Congress appeared and laboured so effectively and so long; never before would its behests have been so strictly enforced. The committees of correspondence, by familiarizing the radical leaders with the techniques of inter-colonial co-operation, had been the first step towards political union. The Continental Congress was a long second step.

Meanwhile in Britain Lord North had prepared for the coming storm by holding a general election, which returned a Parliament much like the old one and no less resolved to reduce America to obedience. The radicals, led by Wilkes, made some effort to rouse the country against the ministry on the American question, but without success. As Burke had bitterly remarked in February, 'Any remarkable robbery on Hounslow Heath would make more conversation than all the disturbances of America.' Even the radicals thought America less important than Parliamentary reform. But the news, whether from Massachusetts or Pennsylvania, was now so alarming that in the midst of further aggressive preparations the minister tried to launch a conciliatory proposal, and the opposition roused itself for further mighty efforts against the fatal policy which, it seemed more and more likely, was leading straight to civil war. Chatham took the lead. On 1 February 1775 he brought forward proposals for settling the imperial question. They were sweeping: possibly even sweeping enough. Almost all the recurring colonial grievances were to be appeased by such measures as repealing every act abhorrent to the Americans, beginning with the Sugar Act; and the Continental Congress, which was planning to reconvene in May, was to be erected into what was, in effect, an American Parliament. The proposal was voted down in the Lords, 61–32; Lord North's gestures of conciliation were approved, inadequate though they were and ineffective though they were doomed to remain; then Parliament hurried through the Restraining Act, which, in answer to the Association and non-importation, forbade any trade between the New England colonies and any British dominions (under the Navigation Acts they were already restrained from trading anywhere else) and forbade them access to the Newfoundland fisheries until the dispute was settled. Again a harsh bill became law (on 30 March) but again not until it had been fiercely attacked. Burke made one of his greatest speeches, calling for peace with America; but it was Lord Camden who uttered perhaps the gravest and wisest warning:

To conquer a great continent of 1,800 miles, containing three millions of people, all indissolubly united on the great Whig bottom of liberty and justice, seems an undertaking not to be rashly engaged in . . . What are the 10,000 men you have just voted out to Boston? Merely to save general Gage from the disgrace and destruction of being sacked in his entrenchments. It is obvious, my lords, that you cannot furnish armies, or treasure, competent to the mighty purpose of subduing America . . . but whether France and Spain will be tame, inactive spectators of your efforts and distractions, is well worthy the considerations of your lordships.

Again in vain; the Act was passed, and on 13 April a second became law, which extended the restraints to the other colonies.

By that time the gap between war and peace was vanishing. Gage had long been virtually besieged in Boston, while the countryside hummed with drilling militiamen and military stores were piled up. The money for these activities had been voted by a Massachusetts provincial congress, which had in effect completely superseded the old General Court. Soon similar revolutionary governments would seize control in the other colonies, as the royal Governors fled to the safety of His Majesty's ships and the conservatives prepared to defend themselves as best they might against the all-conquering patriots. But first General Gage, spurred on by a letter from the American Secretary, Lord Dartmouth, reluctantly set out to challenge the insurgent farmers. On the night of 18 April 1775 he sent what he hoped would be a secret expedition to seize or destroy a military store at Concord, twenty miles or so by road from Boston. The radicals in Boston found out; night-riders hurried ahead to warn the people that 'the British are coming!' At the village of Lexington, therefore, the 700 British infantrymen found in the morning a line of seventy-five volunteers, or Minute Men as they were called, drawn up to resist them. A shot rang out – fired by which side is unknown – and in a moment the redcoats had opened fire and driven the Minute Men from the field: eight had been killed, ten wounded. The British then re-formed and went on to Concord. But they accomplished nothing there, for the stores had been removed or hidden before they arrived and they were successfully attacked at the North Bridge by a force of local militiamen (the 'embattled farmers' of Emerson's poem[16] who 'fired a shot heard round the world'). The long march back to Boston was a nightmare. British casualties were heavy . . . So began the War of the American Revolution. It was characteristic of the way in which the British Empire had slid into ruin that the last step was taken because a minister in London thought he knew better than the man on the spot.

The war spread rapidly, or perhaps it would be more accurate to say it flared up simultaneously in many places. In Virginia the British managed to seize the colonial store of gunpowder at Williamsburg. This was more than offset by the fall of Fort Ticonderoga to the rebels on 10 May, which opened the road to Canada. On the same day the Second Continental Congress met.

It had several decisions immediately forced upon it. Since war had come, it had to be organized, and it was of the highest importance that all the colonies should have a stake in the conflict. Already there were volunteers

16 Ralph Waldo Emerson, 'Hymn Sung at the Completion of the Concord Monument'.

from beyond New England in the force that, following Lexington and Concord, had sprung up outside Boston. The Congress took this force under its wing and voted to raise more troops. The command of the army was a question that had to be settled. It should go, Congress felt, to a Southerner, for the sake of American unity – a decision which greatly disappointed John Hancock. George Washington was the inevitable choice. He came from the right colony, and what was known about his military experience suggested that he had at least as much capacity as anyone else at the Congress – not that that was saying very much. He thought himself unfit for the post and took it only as a duty: he told Patrick Henry, with tears in his eyes, that 'From the day I enter upon the command of the American armies, I date my fall, and the ruin of my reputation.' He was wrong, of course. No greater stroke of good luck ever befell America than the availability of that remarkable man at that crucial juncture, except the availability, eighty-five years later, of Abraham Lincoln. Washington's entry on the stage opened a new act in the history of the Revolution.

An old era ended symbolically some months later. As late as the debate on the Intolerable Acts the country gentlemen of England sitting in Parliament were deluding themselves that, if they supported the government, funds would be extracted from America that would avert the need for a threatened rise in the land-tax. They were appalled by the succeeding turn of events. Then, in the autumn of 1775, the Americans invaded Canada, thus turning, it seemed, their defensive war into an offensive one. The duty of Englishmen was obvious. Lord North moved that for 1776 the land-tax should stand at four shillings, and the country gentlemen patriotically acquiesced. The ghost of George Grenville did not know whether to laugh or cry.

10 The War of the Revolution 1775–83

And to the angel of the church in Philadelphia write ... I know thy works: behold, I have set before thee an open door, and no man can shut it: for thou hast a little strength, and hast kept my word, and hast not denied my name.

Revelation iii, 7–8

It is the will of heaven that America be great – she may not deserve it – her exertions have been small, her policy wretched, nay, her supineness in the past winter would, according to the common operations of things, mark her for destruction.

General Henry Knox, 1777

Under a full persuasion of the justice of our cause, I cannot entertain an idea that it will finally sink, though it may remain for some time under a cloud.

General George Washington, 1776

From the moment that war broke out, British rule in the thirteen colonies was at an end. The fighting that followed was, from one American point of view, irrelevant, for it proceeded merely from the British attempt to recapture and hold by force what had been created and maintained, before 1765, by consent; and the attempt failed. The genie of American independence could not be put back in the bottle. But from another, equally American and more humane point of view, the war was as important in American history as the movement which preceded it. It was the second saga (the first being that of the settlers at Jamestown and Plymouth, the third the Civil War). In it a nation was born and discovered its identity, its destiny. Without the disasters (the several occasions when all was nearly lost) and the suffering, as well as the triumphs, the American people as such, the entity which is the subject of this book, might never have come into being. Too early success might have left a handful of squabbling little states, under the informal and treacherous tutelage of France and Spain, clinging to the seaboard while the great continent behind them was developed by the peoples of Canada, Louisiana and Mexico. As it happened, the war produced a more remarkable outcome than any of the might-have-beens. The purpose of this chapter is to show what that was, and how it came about.

The British lost, but it took seven years and a world war to beat them. The effects of the military struggle thus had time to make themselves felt in every corner of the colonies (or states, as they soon began to call themselves). Soldiers, sailors, members of Congress, farmers, town-dwellers, men, women and children, all experienced the war, whether as a bloody struggle on their doorsteps, or as a terrible inflation which upset all the familiar patterns of trade, or as a general scarcity of goods (which was fine for those who produced them, and especially for the farmers who grew the food the armies needed), or, most of all, as a revolution: an overturning of all the old political ways and means. War hurried on change and in many cases determined its direction. It could not have done this if victory had come to either side as promptly as was hoped at Philadelphia and Westminster. The first question to settle, then, is why the war lasted so long.

British incompetence helped. It will not do to make too much of this. In terms of ships, men and money, Great Britain put forth a greater effort than she ever had before, even in the Seven Years War. The war ministers (Lord George Germain for the army, Lord Sandwich for the navy) were able and conscientious, whatever legend says, even if they were not the equals of Chatham or Churchill. The old order in England might be corrupt, but it had always been at its best as a war-machine, at any rate since the reign of James II, and modern notions of rationality were in fact making themselves felt first in the fighting services.[1] Army and navy had alike been allowed to decay to danger point since 1763; but they were restored to a surprisingly vigorous condition surprisingly soon. (By contrast, the new order emerging in America found almost anything easier than the organiz-ation and support of an army, unless it was the organization and support of a fleet.) If British generals were, at best, merely competent, and were all too often less than that,[2] there was one great admiral, Rodney, and one who was later to prove himself great, Lord Howe.[3] Although, in the end, the British had to give up all their holdings in North America south of

---

[1] The navy, for instance, had just begun the practice of copper-bottoming its ships and was introducing the use of lemons as an anti-scurvy measure.

[2] Contemporaries could be much more critical: 'I indulge a hope that I shall yet have a chance of seeing a General that's neither a Rebel nor a Hysterical Fool,' said a New York Loyalist with bitter irony in 1779.

[3] Though the most ludicrously incompetent British officer was a sailor – Sir Peter Parker, who managed to lose the seat of his trousers during his unsuccessful attack on Charles Town in 1776.

Canada, they kept their empire everywhere else. They were defeated, but not conquered.

Still, defeated they were. Partly it was a matter of morale. There was no middle ground for the Americans: for them it was either victory or total submission. They were fighting for their fundamental interests in a way that the British, for all their huffing and puffing about their greatness and glory being at stake, were not. Consequently there was a limit to the islanders' exertions. As Piers Mackesy puts it, '. . . in England before the French Revolution the line was sharply drawn by concern for individual liberty and low taxation'.[4] Of course the Americans also drew this line, and very hampering their leaders found it; but, with their backs to the wall, they were unlikely to be the first to give up the struggle because it was oppressive and expensive. George III and his ministers thus had, in the last analysis, a narrower political base than George Washington and the Continental Congress. And, as the great quarrel had been begun, so it was continued: again and again the British high command, whether at home or in the colonies, made disastrous blunders and threw away victory. The war was long partly because the British did not know how to win and would not admit that they had lost.

The rebels committed similar errors (they were British too, after all). Having appointed George Washington, Congress did at least have the sense to stick with him. But it made his task difficult to an extent that would have driven any less iron-souled man to throw in his hand. Again and again his army dissolved about him because the civilian authorities did not keep it paid, clothed, fed, sheltered, armed or reinforced. In large part this failure arose from the jealousy that festered between Congress and the state governments, itself an inevitable consequence of the primitive organization of this, the first attempt at an American Union. The state governments regularly left Congress without funds or authority, often because they themselves were abandoned by their citizens. But explanations and excuses never justify incompetence. It is impossible to follow the history of Washington's campaigns without indignation at the inhumanity of the politicians and astonishment at their short-sightedness. They assumed – correctly, as it happens, though the arguments they put forward were absurd – that the American strategic position was, basically, very strong. That of the British, condemned as they were to attempt the conquest of thirteen energetically self-governing states at the end of a 3,000-mile supply-line (since they never gained enough American territory to secure an adequate foraging area) while constantly looking over their shoulders for fear of the French, was very weak. They were always short of manpower, and so could not endure losses in battle: 'Our army is so small that we cannot even afford a victory,' said one of their commanders, truly enough, though he was speaking of the largest force Great Britain had ever sent to North America. There was hope

4 Mackesy, *The War for America* (Cambridge, Mass., 1965), p. 170.

of victory only if Washington's army could be utterly destroyed. For that army could not be replaced, and without it there was nothing to stop the British from taking all the principal cities, controlling the seaboard and eventually breaking up the Revolutionary governments, including the Continental Congress. There would, no doubt, have been prolonged and bitter guerrilla resistance; British victory might well have been fruitless; but the great experiment launched in 1776 would have been aborted, and with it many a hope. At the very least, the Americans would have suffered even more grievously than they did. The survival of Washington's army as an effective force was therefore the first, or should have been the first, of rebel war-aims. Instead it was, or seemed at times to be, the last. Again and again nothing but luck, or that Providence which is proverbially supposed to protect idiots, drunkards and the United States of America, stood between Washington and undeserved destruction. The Derby favourite had entered the race with a bag of cement up.

Fortunately he also carried the champion jockey. George Washington cannot honestly be called a great fighting general, though he was a capable and aggressive one. He made some bad mistakes in his campaigns, especially in the first year or two. Matched as he was against such limited opponents as Gage, William Howe, Clinton and Cornwallis, it scarcely mattered: they made more and worse mistakes than he. What did matter was that he possessed various other qualities that made him, if not unique among commanders, at any rate highly unusual.

He had never been an especially conspicuous figure in Virginia, but he had always taken the place to which his large and well-run estates entitled him. During the first fifteen years or so in which he had farmed at Mount Vernon and gone down regularly to Williamsburg for the meetings of the House of Burgesses, he had slowly been recognized by his fellow-members of the Virginian élite (and later by the Continental Congress) as the sort of invaluable man that every enterprise needs. His judgement, if a little slow-moving, was invariably sound; he had a strong will and immense application: no detail was ever too small for his attention; yet he seldom lost his sense of proportion. Above all, his size and strength (he was a very big man) went with a tenacious, dignified, conscientious mind which never allowed difficulties, however great or disagreeable, to deflect him from the path of duty. It was as if his extra inches, like Abraham Lincoln's, had endowed him with a spiritual shock-absorber. At any rate, no amount of unfair criticism, inadequate support, poor supplies, incompetent or treacherous subordinates, bad weather, inexperienced soldiery or any of the other thousand-and-one plagues that afflict generals was ever allowed to overwhelm his spirit; with equal resolution he kept his naturally hot temper under rigid command. Many were the occasions when a loss of nerve by the Commander-in-Chief would have meant the ruin of the American cause; indeed, on the one occasion (during the retreat from Manhattan Island in 1776) that Washington's nerve did falter, all was very nearly lost. But on the whole his temperament proved equal to the strain, and throughout the war, whoever else was delinquent, however justly depressed he felt ('Fifty thousand pounds should not induce me again to undergo what I have done'), General Washington was always at his post.

The same could not be said of the men he commanded. Desertion was one of the principal causes of the chronic shortage of regular, 'Continental' soldiers which was always the General's worst problem. Militiamen, untrained, reluctant to serve outside their native provinces, determined to go home as soon as their time was up, whatever the military situation, exacerbated it. It is hard to blame these reluctant heroes. Underpaid, when paid at all, in a constantly inflating currency, the Continental paper money authorized by Congress that soon became proverbially worthless; badly officered for most of the time (Washington never found enough good subordinates); unfed, unsheltered, unclothed, unequipped, through the callous neglect of the civilians, who could look even on the army's sufferings at Valley Forge, Pennsylvania, in the winter of 1777–8 with indifference; oppressed by 'Commissaries, Quartermasters, Surgeons, Barrack Masters and Captains' whose own low pay too often led them to make illegitimate deductions from that of the men: why should they alone have martyred themselves for the American cause? It is much to their credit, as to Washington's, that the army never melted away completely.

And, gradually, it learned the art of war. By 1777 an English officer was writing home that

though they seem to be ignorant of the precision, order and even of the principles by which large bodies are moved, yet they possess some of the requisites for making good troops, such as extreme cunning, great industry in moving ground and felling of wood, activity and a spirit of enterprise upon any advantage. Having said this much, I have no occasion to add that though it was once the *ton* of this army to treat them in the most contemptible light, they are now become a formidable enemy . . .

The Continental Congress can have had little idea, at the time, of how well it had acted in appointing Washington, but it soon found out. He went north to Boston in July 1775, and from his arrival there the war began to assume a tidier appearance; the American forces were set in order for a long haul.[5]

Before the General left Philadelphia the British had made one of their blunders. If Gage was to keep control of Boston, let alone reconquer New England from that base, he needed to control the heights to north and south

<hr />

5 Washington also helped the cause by the excellent personal impression he made on Massachusetts civilians. Mrs John Adams wrote enthusiastically: 'Dignity with ease and complacency, the gentleman and soldier, look agreeably blended in him. Modesty marks every line and feature of his face.' The General was harder to please. The men of Massachusetts, he wrote, were 'exceedingly dirty and nasty'.

of the town which commanded it and its harbour. Having neglected to secure these vital points while they were undefended, he launched an infantry attack on the northern one, Bunker Hill,[6] on 17 June 1775. Once again the British learned, the hard way, that they were up against a formidable foe. They carried the position, but at such fearful cost that ever since the battle has been remembered as an American rather than as a British victory.[7] Popular memory is right: exhausted and intimidated by this battle, Gage could attempt no more. Washington settled down to besiege him while trying to shape an army out of his very miscellaneous forces. In due course he saw that the key to Boston was now the southern position, Dorchester Heights. In the face of fearful difficulties[8] he and his staff gradually mustered sufficient artillery (most of it captured at the fall of Ticonderoga) and by early March 1776 it was plain that the British would either have to admit defeat and withdraw, or endure an assault which could only have one end. Wisely, they decided to withdraw – to Halifax, Nova Scotia – thus sparing Boston a bombardment. With them went many Loyalists, the first of an ever-swelling body of refugees which the war was to create. Washington, almost bloodlessly, had won his first victory. The British army never returned to Massachusetts.

They might have taken this setback as a warning to make terms with the Americans while these were yet nominally subjects of King George. Instead, the bulldog redoubled its efforts. Gage had already been superseded (he made a convenient scapegoat for the blunderers who had forced him to order the Lexington expedition). His successor was William Howe. The so-called 'Olive Branch Petition', Congress's last attempt at a reconciliation, was rebuffed contemptuously; a naval blockade of American ports was proclaimed; British volunteers being in very short supply, 18,000 mercenary soldiers were hired from minor German princelings;[9] and a grand assault on New York was planned as the first step in the reconquest of America.

All this took time, and Howe was anyway a sluggish commander. When at last he and his admiral brother, Lord Howe (commanding the naval squadron), arrived off Long Island in the summer of 1776, the rebels had taken the final, irrevocable step.

It had been long in the making. Voices urging the complete independence

6 This is the traditional name, but the battle was actually fought on the adjacent Breed's Hill. Here is a point where it would be confusing to be accurate.

7 The Americans were commanded by Israel Putnam, who gave the famous order, 'Don't fire, boys, until you see the whites of their eyes.' They obeyed to such effect that 226 British soldiers and officers were killed, 828 wounded. The Americans lost 140 killed, 270 wounded, thirty prisoners.

8 Not the least of which were the indiscipline and inexperience of the troops. Washington imposed savage punishments, usually whipping, for such offences as desertion. But he also had to recognize, as he said himself, that '. . . a people unused to restraint must be led, they will not be drove, even those who are engag'd for the war, must be disciplined by degrees'.

9 Chief among them, the Landgrave of Hesse-Cassel; hence the soldiers were generally known as Hessians. They were especially detested by the Americans, for they plundered and destroyed with professional conscientiousness.

of America had grown steadily louder and more numerous ever since Lexington. Every battle since then had strengthened the feeling that reunion was impossible. So did the renewed British war-effort. Every new outrage by the mother country strengthened the desire to have done with her, the belief in her fatal corruption, the aspiration to create a new refuge, a new empire for liberty in America where her ancient flame still shone. In January 1776, a recent immigrant from England, Tom Paine, had published a pamphlet, *Common Sense*, that sold 120,000 copies. It anticipated many of the themes of United States history, and put the case for independence in savagely brilliant language:

Can we but leave posterity with a settled form of government, an independent constitution of its own, the purchase at any price will be cheap. But to expend millions for the sake of getting a few vile acts repealed, and routing the present ministry only, is unworthy the charge, and is using posterity with the utmost cruelty; because it is leaving them the great work to do, and a debt upon their books, from which they derive no advantage. Such a thought is unworthy a man of honour ...

Government, said Paine, was at best a concession to man's fallen state, 'a mode made necessary by the inability of moral virtue to govern the world'. Where was the true King of America? 'I'll tell you, friend, he reigns above, and doth not make havoc of mankind like the Royal Brute of Great Britain.' This sort of thing seemed excellent teaching to the Calvinist ministers of New England, already denounced by the Tories as a 'black-coated regiment' of rebels, for they had happily sunk their innumerable doctrinal quarrels to unite in the patriot cause against the British and their bishops. They read out *Common Sense* from their pulpits. Washington commended Paine's 'sound doctrine and unanswerable reasoning', and doubtless they made nearly as many converts as the author later claimed. Perhaps more decisive was the fearful uncertainty of life while the great question was unresolved. Until it was settled who was to govern America, and by what authority, there was an ever-growing risk that no one would, or could. At the same time, the enormous advance that the colonies had made towards national self-consciousness is shown by the willingness of the provincial governments to wait for the decision of the Continental Congress. As early as the autumn of 1775 they had begun to seek and obtain permission from Congress to set up new constitutions. The cry went out for 'revolutionizing all the governments', and in May 1776 Congress, to speed the laggards, passed a resolution recommending each colony 'where no government sufficient to the exigencies of their affairs hath been hitherto established' to set up a new one; in response new governing bodies appeared in what must hereafter be called the states; and one by one they instructed their Congressional delegations to vote for independence. By that instruction they again recognized the authority of Congress, and, more important, that Americans were one people and must behave as such: if Congress could not act without the states, the states could not, in this matter, act without Congress; which body wrestled with the problem throughout the early summer at Philadelphia. Some stout patriots, such as John Dickinson, held out against independence to the very last;[10] but in spite of them the great resolutions were at length adopted. Early in June a committee was set up to carry out one of Tom Paine's suggestions, by drafting a declaration of independence in succession to the Declaration of the Causes and Necessity of Taking Up Arms, compiled by Dickinson and promulgated exactly a year earlier. The members were: Benjamin Franklin (Pennsylvania); John Adams (Massachusetts); Roger Sherman (Connecticut); Robert R. Livingston (New York); and Thomas Jefferson (Virginia). Of the three accomplished penmen on the committee, Franklin was laid up with gout, Adams came from New England, which was lying low in Congress at the moment so as not to alarm less revolutionary regions, and Jefferson came from the most populous and important state. To him, then, fell the task of composition.

It could not have fallen to better hands. Superficially Jefferson looked like an untidy farmer. He was tall, red-haired, careless in his dress and a lover of the outdoors (next to George Washington he was reckoned to be the best horseman in Virginia). Under this commonplace exterior was the most passionately inquiring mind ever to be born in America; a mind of dazzlingly diverse talents, among them a gift for writing transparently lucid and attractive prose; a mind on fire with republican enthusiasm. He was a child of the European Enlightenment as well as of aristocratic Virginia; he had learned in a good law office how to make a case; best of all, he had been pondering and testing all the arguments for at least two years. By the end of June he had a draft ready for his colleagues.

On 2 July Congress approved the decisive resolutions, previously framed and presented by Richard Henry Lee on behalf of Virginia,

That these United Colonies are, and of right ought to be, free and independent States, that they are absolved from all allegiance to the British Crown, and that all political connection between them and the State of Great Britain is, and ought to be, totally dissolved.

That it is expedient forthwith to take the most effectual measures for forming foreign alliances.

That a plan of confederation be prepared and transmitted to the respective Colonies for their consideration and approbation.

Two days later, that is on 4 July, Congress voted its approval of Mr Jefferson's document.

John Adams was never really reconciled to the adoption of 4 July as his

---

10 Nevertheless, when the decision was made, Dickinson proved to be one of the very few members of Congress who actually went off and fought for the cause.

country's great holiday. The actual break with Great Britain was undoubtedly effected by the resolutions of 2 July, and if that were all that
counted July the Second should have become America's great day, as Adams
at the time predicted it would. Besides, he had played a leading part in the
orating and arguing which had brought Congress to the sticking-point,
answering Dickinson, for instance, in a notable speech on 1 July; not to
mention his valuable services at an earlier date in the murky waters of
Massachusetts politics. It was hard on him that his countrymen determined
to commemorate, not an action, but a document, and one in which he
had had so little hand. Jefferson himself at the time thought the fact of
independence was more important than the words he had so carefully strung
together, and thought, furthermore, that the few changes made in his text
by Congress[11] had ruined it. But both he and Adams were wrong.

For he had produced a masterpiece: one of the great achievements of
the human spirit. Its form may seem to belie this statement, for the greater
part of it (it is only some fifteen hundred words long) is a list, spirited in
expression admittedly, of the chief grievances which the Americans had
been denouncing since the Intolerable Acts. Today a knowledgeable reader
will note that among many just complaints are some (for example, a protest
about the Quebec Act) which are less than convincing; and it is impossible
not to regret the degree to which Jefferson's acceptance of the American
Whig myth distorted his account of historical reality. Everything was blamed
on George III (Parliament was not named once in the document, and was
alluded to indirectly as sparingly as possible) and the long tale of British
crimes and blunders was presented as evidence that 'the present King of
Great Britain' had 'in direct object the establishment of an absolute Tyranny
over these States', 'a design to reduce them under absolute Despotism'.
There is no doubt that by 1776 this was the almost unanimous belief of
the Revolutionaries; but it was not a true belief, for all that. Had the Declaration been no more than an opportune and eloquent political manifesto its
blemishes, and its occasional character, would have ensured that it was long
ago forgotten: it would have diminished beside the enormous fact which it
asserted, the independence of America.

Instead, it remains an inspiration to all democrats today, and especially
to Americans. That is because Jefferson, by a process like that which
engenders poetry, was able to distil in his preamble, as eloquence, centuries
of historical experience.

We hold these truths to be self-evident, that all men are created equal, that they
are endowed by their Creator with certain inalienable Rights, that among these

---

11 Apart from deletions in the closing section, of the kind which cause all authors agony but
which always improve their texts, the most important, ominous change was the removal of
Jefferson's denunciation of the slave-trade, 'in complaisance to South Carolina and Georgia,
who had never attempted to restrain the importation of slaves, and who, on the contrary, still
wished to continue it' (Jefferson, *Autobiography*).

are Life, Liberty and the pursuit of Happiness. That to secure these rights, Governments are instituted among Men, deriving their just powers from the consent of the governed. That whenever any Form of Government becomes destructive of these ends, it is the Right of the People to alter or abolish it, and to institute new Government, laying its foundation on such principles and organizing its powers in such form, as to them shall seem most likely to effect their Safety and Happiness . . .

These splendid assertions were indeed self-evident to the revolutionaries – to all Americans: how could they doubt them? They expressed attitudes which everything in their experience as settlers had tended to stimulate and reinforce. Side by side, their grandfathers had set up new polities; their fathers, and then they themselves, had enjoyed the consequent responsibilities and rewards of self-government. Side by side, Americans had tamed a wilderness, or begun to, practically experiencing the fact that on the frontier all men (and women too) had equal needs and (said the Puritans) souls equally precious and equally in need of salvation, whether religious or economic (depending on whether one agreed with the minister or the fishermen of Marblehead). The marvellous abundance of their new world had proved in the most satisfactory manner that everyone could be prosperous, and therefore that everyone had a right so to be. Their republican (we would say democratic) habits were so ingrained that one of the reasons for the failure of the rebel invasion of Canada in the winter of 1775–6 was that whenever the New England volunteers were given orders to attack, they held an *ad hoc* town-meeting to decide in the manner they were used to, that is by voting, whether to obey or not. And even revolution was to them a practical matter, almost an institution, since they had been trained, not only by the controversy with Britain since 1764, but by the endless feuds with noble proprietors and royal Governors and between the diverse interests within the colonies themselves – say, between tidewater and piedmont – ever since the foundation of Jamestown.

The challenge to the governing principles of the British Empire and the British realm which America incarnated could not have been articulated with greater sharpness; but that was not all. The Americans were the vanguard of the West. They were, after all, the progeny of the Old World: an Old World whose social order was based ultimately on force, hierarchy and a religion which condemned the secular pursuit of happiness as delusory, since the only happiness really worth having was that awaiting the faithful beyond death. The thirteen colonies no longer accepted these principles. Original sin – that is, social inequality of various kinds – existed in America, but conditions were vastly more egalitarian and hopeful than anything in the Old World. Even if, with the growth of wealth and numbers, certain new tendencies were arising (one of the reasons why oligarchs such as Thomas Hutchinson had to be opposed by rising young men like John Adams was that the oligarchs were the forerunners of a very subversive change) on the whole the thirteen colonies were still comparatively pristine, their challenge still untainted. Soon that challenge would find an echo in Europe itself. For America was only one of Europe's offspring. The Protestant Reformation; the rise of literacy; the dawning of modern science and industry; the vortex of change summed up in the words Enlightenment, trade and whiggery – these were the forces which had made the successful emigration to America possible and were now fostering its work. They were also preparing new upheavals in their homeland. Jefferson's words spoke of the European experience as well as the American; they crystallized certain thoughts to which many minds were moving (the phrase about 'inalienable rights' might have come straight out of Jean-Jacques Rousseau); the Declaration was a protest and a programme, not only for Jefferson's countrymen, but for civilized mankind.

For the preamble, in the name of the people, denies that the strong may legitimately oppress the weak; and asserts that all men and women, whatever their age, condition or origins, shall not be cheated of their birthright into misery; that this theme, of human freedom and dignity, is what politics is about. As this message was heard, it seemed to many Europeans – perhaps especially to the French – that there was a new star in the West to steer by. It seemed as if John Adams's favourite prophetic dream would come true. 'I always consider the settlement of America with reverence and wonder,' said he, 'as the opening of a grand scene and design of Providence for the illumination of the ignorant, and the emancipation of the slavish part of mankind all over the earth.' This soon became the universal faith of the Revolution.

Ever since 1776 Americans have returned to rekindle their patriotic self-dedication at the flame of the Declaration. For it answers a question which was to trouble the new nation throughout its history: what is America *about*? History and geography had forestalled any such question for most of the other peoples of the world; but the immensity of the nearly empty continent, and the break with the past which every settling family had made, posed it acutely for the Americans and would necessarily do so at least until all the wilderness was conquered. The problem of political institutions and of a national identity could hardly wait until then. America needed a blueprint, and by luck the long processes of her colonial history, which had already made so many inexorable decisions, fathered one on the genius of Thomas Jefferson. 'All men are created equal . . . life, liberty and the pursuit of happiness.' These words have never ceased to sound in America; as one historian has said, 'The history of American democracy is a gradual realization, too slow for some and too rapid for others, of the implications of the Declaration of Independence.'[12] The future to which they pointed was not all bright. It contained chains, cannon-fire, fiery crosses and the

12 Ralph Barton Perry, *Puritanism and Democracy* (New York, 1944), p. 133; quoted by Dumas Malone, *Jefferson the Virginian* (Boston, 1948), p. 227.

sign of a clenched fist as well as the Bill of Rights and the New Deal; but for weal or woe, the Declaration had shown the way. No wonder the Fourth of July is still a high festival.[13]

Lee's Resolutions and Jefferson's Declaration (neither writer's name was announced) were enthusiastically welcomed throughout the states, from Philadelphia, where, according to John Adams, the church bells were rung and the local militia fired 'the Feu de Joy, notwithstanding the Scarcity of Powder', to the backwoods of South Carolina, where a nine-year-old boy named Andrew Jackson was deputed to read the Declaration to 'thirty or forty' of his less literate fellow-citizens. General Washington, who had long been urging the final step, paraded his regiments at six in the evening to hear the Declaration read out. To the patriots, it was clear what the great departure meant. At last the incubus had been thrown off, and a bitter debate was ended. The happy era of patriotism and republicanism had arrived. There would be no more 'jars and contentions'; no more English meddling, and hence no more disputation between town and country, Whig and Tory, Governor and assembly. These hopes were not entirely realistic. Although acceptance of the Declaration, which, with its pledge of 'our lives, our fortunes, and our sacred honour', was among other things a loyalty oath, did put a formidable barrier in the way of any backsliding, so that compromise with Britain was virtually ruled out, there were still plenty of Tories and traitors to make life difficult, not to mention the British army; but for the moment the Declaration swept all before it. Congress, amid much wrangling, drew up Articles of Confederation to act as an instrument of government for the new Union of States.[14] They formalized the *ad hoc* arrangements which had already emerged: the alliance of the states in Congress assembled was confirmed as a government, and Congress was empowered to appoint ministers to execute its policies. Eight of the states proclaimed new constitutions for themselves; in the enthusiasm of the moment these documents were mostly extravagantly democratic, whether in the twentieth-century or the eighteenth-century meanings of that word. State legislatures were to be supreme; the people they represented were to be consulted as often as possible on as much as possible; the executive power was kept deliberately weak; and the very soul of the old order was throttled by provisions in several of the constitutions expressly outlawing class privileges and hereditary public offices (there was to be no opportunity for a revival of the Oliver–Hutchinson oligarchy and its counterparts). Whether any of these instruments (including the Articles of Confederation) would work in practice remained to be seen.

Apart from these institutional arrangements, a general liberalizing pro-

---

13   Today it is probably regarded chiefly as one more opportunity to get down to the beach, but throughout the nineteenth century it was celebrated with the utmost patriotic fervour: flags, parades and torrents of oratory; fireworks, cannon and gallons of drink. Daniel Boorstin amusingly describes the rise of the Fourth in his *National Experience* (London, 1965), pp. 375–90.

14   For further particulars, and a discussion, see Chapter 11.

gramme was widely undertaken. Established churches were stripped of their privileges (except in New England); bills of rights, securing the liberties of the individual citizens, were passed into law; land was redistributed (at the expense of refugee Loyalists); the 1763 British Proclamation was formally overthrown, thus opening the trans-Allegheny West to legal settlement; and voices began to be heard asking if slavery could be reconciled with patriot principles. As early as 1773 Dr Benjamin Rush of Philadelphia, a patriotic physician, who later became one of the signatories of the Declaration of Independence and a friend of Jefferson's, had attacked what he called 'Slave Keeping', and urged his fellow 'advocates for American liberty' to be consistent. 'The plant of liberty,' he wrote, 'is of so tender a nature that it cannot thrive long in the neighborhood of slavery. Remember, the eyes of Europe are fixed upon you, to preserve an asylum for freedom in this country after the last pillars of it are fallen in every other quarter of the globe.' Jefferson himself, slave owner though he was, attacked the institution in the following year; and the Reverend John Allen of Massachusetts took up the cry:

Blush ye pretended votaries for freedom! ye trifling patriots! . . . for while you are fasting, praying, nonimporting, nonexporting, remonstrating, resolving, and pleading for a restoration of your charter rights, you at the same time are continuing this lawless, cruel, inhuman, and abominable practice of enslaving your fellow creatures.

News of the nascent anti-slavery movement in England travelled to the West, and so, perhaps, did a report of Dr Johnson's scornful opinion of slave-holders who rebelled in the name of liberty. At any rate, by 1776 a powerful preacher of Rhode Island could argue that the patriot cause could never win God's blessing and prosper until the sin of slavery was removed: the 'Sons of Liberty' were nothing but fathers of oppression. These arguments were not without effect: Puritan New England, Quaker Pennsylvania and Pennsylvania's little pendant, Delaware, all outlawed the slave-trade. Still more important was the non-importation agreement. In April 1776, Congress directed that, as a war-measure, no slaves were to be imported into any of the thirteen colonies.[15] It thus became possible for enlightened Americans to hope that in the not-too-distant future their new country would live up to its liberal slogans.

The war, meanwhile, went on. General Howe moved late and sluggishly, but also effectively. He fought and manoeuvred Washington off Long

15 It is worth underlining the point that this important decision, which proved to have dealt a mortal wound to the American slave-trade, was justified as an emergency measure, just as Lincoln's Emancipation proclamation, which gave the death-blow to slavery itself, was justified eighty-seven years later.

Island, out of New York city, off Manhattan Island, across and out of New Jersey. By December 1776, it seemed all too likely that the British would celebrate the New Year in Philadelphia, while the continental soldiers, their time expired, left their commander and went home. The New Jersey Loyalists came out to celebrate and collaborate with the victor – rather too soon, for at Christmas Washington turned, and in two lightning attacks across the Delaware river defeated the royal forces at Trenton and Princeton. In terms of the numbers engaged these battles were tiny; but, as at Boston, their strategic effect was important. They saved Pennsylvania for the time being and cleared most of New Jersey. Patriot morale, which had been very low, made a rapid recovery. Washington could live to fight in the spring (supposing only that his freezing, tatterdemalion army survived that long). He had won precious time and prestige for America: time for an alliance to ripen, prestige to clinch it.

The French, looking for revenge on England, had been covertly sending munitions to the rebels almost since the rebellion started. The longer it lasted, the likelier their full-scale intervention became. Dr Franklin, most urbane of Americans, arrived in Paris on 20 December 1776 to use his charm and scientific prestige to lure Louis XVI and his ministers into the war.

He had a staggering personal success. The ladies of Paris were enchanted by him,[16] the scientists welcomed him as a brother, he was ceremonially embraced by Voltaire at the Académie des Sciences and impressed everyone as another, nicer Rousseau because of his (somewhat studied) simplicity of manner and dress. Fur hats *à la* Franklin became the fashion. He was hailed as '*le bon Quacker*' (of course he was nothing of the kind), as a child of Nature, father of his country, worthy representative of the virtuous foresters who were struggling for liberty against corrupt England. More important, he had the goodwill of Vergennes, the Foreign Minister and leader of the war-party, who encouraged the Doctor in his activities as propagandist, diplomatist and spy. Some at Versailles, notably the great Turgot, recently fallen from his post as Controller-General of the Finances, foresaw the danger to France, not yet recovered from the Seven Years War, of another struggle; but Franklin worked up the general French enthusiasm for his cause, and at Court the war-party was dominant, only waiting for an excuse to fight. Such an excuse the British quickly provided.

From George III's point of view the war had already gone on much too long. Already he was having to bolster the fainting morale of his Prime Minister with his own robust courage. This impatience in London led to the disastrous adventure of Burgoyne at Saratoga. That general – a norm-ally complacent, dilatory British officer, despising the Americans, always intriguing for his own advancement, rash in action – 'a vain, very ambitious man, with a half-understanding which was worse than none', according to

16 And he by them: he proposed marriage to one of them, the widow of the great Helvétius.

Horace Walpole – hoped that by plunging south from Canada with 7,000 men until he reached the line of the Hudson river he could cut the rebellion in two. Thus to break Washington's line of communication with New England would have been a notable stroke, but Howe's unbusinesslike dispatches to London confused the planners, and there was none of the co-operation with Burgoyne that was essential if the latter's scheme was to succeed. Howe went off to capture Philadelphia while Burgoyne's army, laden down with superfluous equipment, moved too slowly southwards, losing touch with its base as it did so. The word went forth, 'Now let all New England turn out and crush Burgoyne.' There was a hearty response by the militia: this was ideal country for the sharpshooters of the wilderness. It was the retreat from Concord on a far larger scale. Burgoyne's flanks were mercilessly harried. Too vain to admit failure, he struggled on when he should have turned back, and at last, his rations nearly exhausted, his retreat cut off, his army badly mauled after a couple of pitched battles, he had to surrender what was left of his force (which he saw fit to blame for his mishap) to General Horatio Gates at Saratoga on 17 October 1777. Gates had done well; his second-in-command, Benedict Arnold, with whom he was always quarrelling, had done better; but the real glory belonged to his irregular levies. They were the American people in arms, and by their crushing victory they made clear the real nature of Britain's intractable problem: with handfuls of mercenary troops to crush a society, a nation. Counter-revolutions need stronger foundations. Saratoga was most inadequately counterbalanced by the fall of Philadelphia to Howe, although Washington and his men were thereby compelled to endure their darkest hours at Valley Forge, a bleak encampment near the city where they had somehow to survive another bitter, foodless, shirtless winter, without blankets, in huts which gaped to wind and snow from every quarter. No matter: Saratoga convinced France that this was a war in which Great Britain really could be beaten, and the following year she entered it, followed shortly by her ally, Spain.[17]

This altered the whole nature of the war. Hitherto the balance of battle in America had swung this way and that according to the local strength of the belligerents. Even Saratoga could not be said to prove that, left to themselves, the British lacked the strength to win some sort of victory in the long run, though it surely demonstrated the need for better generals. With France and Spain in the fight matters looked very different. In the first place British supply-lines across the Atlantic would now be threatened by French as well as American ships. Much worse was the general vulnerability of the British Empire. During the Seven Years War the French had

17 The Spaniards were reluctant belligerents: their King, anxious about his own transatlantic possessions, was most unwilling to help George III's rebels. The King of France, Louis XVI, also had an accurate royal intuition: he showed what he privately thought of the Americans by presenting one of Franklin's noble lady friends with the Doctor's portrait painted on the inside bottom of a chamber-pot.

been beaten in India, Canada, the West Indies and at sea while Frederick II kept them busy in Germany; Spain entered the war only when France was already defeated, so that England could turn her undivided strength on the lesser Bourbon power. Furthermore, war seemed to finance itself: at any rate the conquest of various sugar islands greatly helped the military budget. In the War of American Independence none of these considerations applied. Frederick stayed at home; it was England's turn to worry about the loss of sugar islands (so much was this the case that the Caribbean actually replaced North America as the principal theatre of the war); and she was thrown on the defensive in Europe, for not only was she threatened ineffectively with a French invasion but her high-handedness at sea drove the Dutch to war and provoked the formation of a League of Armed Neutrality, led by Catherine II of Russia. It seemed touch-and-go whether George III might find himself fighting the whole of Europe. Secondly, the very extent of the Empire gave the initiative to the French, who could choose when and where to attack and mounted offensives in the Caribbean, North America and the Indian Ocean at the same time as they threatened England herself. The Spanish took Minorca and besieged Gibraltar; Yankee privateers swarmed in the Atlantic, eventually doing Britain £18 million worth of damage; the *Bonhomme Richard*, a vessel of that puny infant, the US navy, commanded by John Paul Jones, captured HMS *Serapis*, a much stronger vessel, on 23 September 1779. It was no wonder that Lord North had the vapours again.

The King ('If others will not be active I must drive'), Lord George Germain, the Admiralty and the generals held on. The prospect of French intervention had induced them to offer terms to the rebels. Everything would be conceded, except independence. The offer was rejected, the Bourbon powers declared war and the British resigned themselves to a continuing struggle. They attacked American commerce as effectively as the Yankees raided theirs and mounted devastating raids on coastal towns such as New Haven and coastal districts such as tidewater Virginia (in January 1781 Thomas Jefferson, now Governor of Virginia, was temporarily driven out of Richmond, the state's new capital, by a force led by Benedict Arnold, who had previously changed sides in every circumstance of contemptible treachery). General Clinton, in command at New York, in the spring of 1780 launched a successful expedition against Charles Town (or Charleston, as it was coming to be called), the principal port of the Southern states; his energetic subordinate, General Cornwallis, overran Georgia, where some sort of royal government was re-established, and invaded the Carolinas. Doggedly, the British high command stuck to its original strategic doctrine: if enough force was mustered and if Washington's army could be caught and made to fight (a big if, since it had become very adroit at dodging its pursuers), it must surely be crushed; and then the Americans would despair. The King was ready to go on fighting indefinitely. 'This war like the last will prove one of credit,' said he. He was sure that the French political and financial system could not stand the strain nearly so well as the British,[18] and once France was beaten the rebels could be dealt with at leisure.

It is more than doubtful if, in the seventh year of the war, these calculations were sound any longer. True, in April 1781 Washington capped an endless gush of justified complaints about the state of affairs with the simple phrase, 'We are at the end of our tether,' but his position conditioned him to look on the gloomy side. It seems likeliest that, when the war broke out, there was a large patriot party, a substantially smaller Loyalist party and a majority of the population that was neutral. Subsequent events radically changed matters. The mere fact of war, the promulgation of independence and the survival of the Revolutionary governments tended to win recruits to the patriot party, which grew larger throughout the war, in spite of a dangerous war-weariness. Very foolishly, the British enlisted the Iroquois in the North-West. They did little for the imperial cause, but their depredations, carried out with their usual relentless cruelty, horrified and aroused every settler who had crossed, or was about to cross, the Appalachians in search of new land. (It was tales of Indian atrocities as much as anything else which brought out the New Englanders against Burgoyne.) Wherever the British won a temporary victory the Loyalists came out for them, only to find, at any rate in the North outside New York, that after a little while the British went away again,[19] leaving their collaborators with no choice but to flee. This of course put military and political power even more firmly in the hands of the patriots, while the Loyalists became a mere floating refugee population.[20] The most effective Loyalist, Banastre Tarleton, who raised a substantial and efficient fighting force for Cornwallis, fought with such savagery (the American way of war is, perhaps, more cold-blooded than the British) that he not only added the fullest horrors of civil war to the Revolution, but inspired active hatred and patriotism in equal amounts throughout the South. The terror of his name drove the timid to seek the protection of General Washington and his subordinates, while the patriots vengefully hunted out Tories from their jobs, property and country. The American general, Nathanael Greene, commented sadly in South Carolina that

The animosity between the Whigs and Tories, renders their situation truly deplorable. The Whigs seem determined to extirpate the Tories, and the Tories the Whigs. Some thousands have fallen in this way, in this quarter, and the evil rages with more violence than ever. If a stop cannot be soon put to these massacres, the country will be depopulated in a few months more.

18 He was quite right: the old order in France was wrecked by the war. In this sense we can say that Saratoga caused the French Revolution.
19 Philadelphia, for example, taken in 1777, was evacuated the following year.
20 Most of them (80,000 or so) eventually settled north of Lake Erie and there founded English-speaking Canada. A few went to England, where they suffered innumerable slights from English snobbery and jingoism.

After years of this sort of thing it grew less and less likely that any military victory would enable the British to reconstitute their rule. Their supreme war-aim had become unattainable long before they were forced to stop fighting for it.

A good example of what all this meant to ordinary people is provided in the continuing career of young Andrew Jackson. When he was thirteen (1780) the war came to his neighbourhood. He and all his relations were soon made fugitives by Tarleton's terrible incursions, and then turned to fight. The boy saw service as a mounted orderly, was captured by the British and nearly died of smallpox in jail. His mother and his two brothers did die, his mother of 'ship fever' while nursing prisoners of the British at Charleston. None of this endeared the invaders to young Jackson. But the episode that was to become legendary when he became famous was that of the English subaltern who commanded his young prisoner to clean his boots. Jackson, standing on his rights as a prisoner of war, refused, and got a cut on his head from the officer's sword for his insolence. It left a scar which, as his biographer says, he was to carry through a life 'that profited little to England or any Englishman';[21] more to the point, it was characteristic of the innumerable small strokes that were cutting the few remaining bonds between Britain and America. There must have been thousands of young sparks like Jackson. And George Washington was now a hero to all his countrymen; their admiration for him was uniting them as little else could. None of those who had learned to venerate him – least of all those who had fought under him – would abandon the struggle before he did. However dark the outlook from time to time, it was always too early to talk of the Americans despairing.

However, the assumptions underlying British strategy were never to be thoroughly tested, for the rashness of a general made them irrelevant. Cornwallis proved to be another Burgoyne. He began well, but in his quest for the decisive victory over Nathanael Greene he allowed the Americans to lure him further and further north, losing men and supplies all the way. Finally he realized that he could neither retreat nor go forward in face of the resistance he was meeting, so he dug in where he was, at Yorktown in Virginia (a few miles from Jamestown and Williamsburg), and waited to be rescued by the Royal Navy.

Washington saw that this was the sort of opportunity that only comes once. His army had long been stationary in the North, pinning down the British in New York. Now was the time for it to move, if only because of the increasing war-weariness of the Americans and the desperate financial straits of the French, who had nevertheless sent him an army of some 6,700 regulars under the Comte de Rochambeau. A French naval squadron under Admiral de Grasse was at sea. Washington had been trying to concentrate all these forces for an attack on New York; but now he saw a chance, probably a last chance, for a decisive victory over the British. British carelessness

21 Marquis James, *Life of Andrew Jackson* (New York, 1938), pp. 25–6.

had given the allies temporary naval superiority in Virginian waters: De Grasse was able to seal off Chesapeake Bay, thus putting himself between Cornwallis and his relief. Washington and Rochambeau marched briskly south. Before Cornwallis quite knew what was happening to him he was trapped. The inexorable work of an eighteenth-century siege went forward; and at last Cornwallis gave in. On 17 October 1781 – four years exactly since Burgoyne's misadventure – he asked for terms. Two days later he surrendered unconditionally. Legend has it that as he and his soldiers marched out, prisoners, their regimental bands played 'The World Turned Upside Down'.

Rightly, if so, for Yorktown was a decisive victory, though Washington could not at first believe it. It did the French little good (a few months later Admiral Rodney drubbed De Grasse in the Battle of the Saints); but it settled the question of American independence. The news provoked the House of Commons to mutiny at last. 'Oh God! It is all over,' said poor Lord North. His government fell, and a Whig ministry led by Rockingham, and after his death by Shelburne, lasted just long enough to negotiate a new Treaty of Paris (3 September 1783).

This treaty gave the United States excellent terms (far better than France and Spain were to get), for which the American negotiators (Franklin, John Adams, John Jay) deserved most of the credit. Not only did the British recognize American independence and make peace, and grant valuable concessions to American fishermen in Canadian waters; they conceded most generous boundaries to the new republic. Up to a point, this only confirmed what was already clear on the ground. In a series of desperate campaigns against the British and the Indians, the Americans had already made good their claim to the trans-Appalachian West. Still, the British controlled large areas there, in the Great Lakes region, and their Indian allies were still unbroken; but they had no stomach for continuing the struggle and formally recognized northern and western frontiers for the United States on the Lakes and the Mississippi. America thus became the legally undisputed mistress of an immense territory. Next to independence itself it was the most notable gain from the War of the Revolution.

At last General Washington was able to unbuckle his sword. He had had to repudiate a proposal that he make a bid for kingship, and to suppress a threatened mutiny over pay, which he did with a personal appeal to his officers. ('Gentlemen, you must pardon me,' he said, putting on his spectacles to read his manuscript. 'I have grown grey in your service and now find myself going blind.' That did the trick.) Sadly, he saw his cherished veterans going off to their homes like a 'set of beggars', still unpaid, though a body of mutinous soldiers had actually besieged the ungrateful Congress in State House at Philadelphia. Joyously, in November 1783, he entered New York as the British evacuated it; and in that city, on 4 December, he bade formal farewell to his officers, shaking each one by the hand, before he set off to the longed-for repose of Mount Vernon. Poor man: he was not to enjoy it for very long.

11 *The Peace and the Constitution 1783–9*

The Americans are the first people whom Heaven has favoured with an opportunity of deliberating upon, and choosing, the forms of government under which they shall live. All other constitutions have derived their existence from violence or accidental circumstances, and are therefore probably more distant from their perfection, which, though beyond our reach, may nevertheless be approached under the guidance of reason and experience.

John Jay, 1777

Let us raise a standard to which the wise and honest can repair. The event is in the hand of God.

George Washington, 1787

Having got rid of the British, the Americans had to cope with the difficulties that had baffled George III and his ministers. The victorious rebels had one advantage: the American Empire (a favourite phrase of the time) was smaller, more compact and more homogeneous than the British, so there was much less inducement to break it up. In fact most Americans wanted to make a success of their new Republic, and maintain their Union. But the obstacles were, in practice, daunting.

The second Peace of Paris left many problems unsolved. It defined America's place in the international system, but that place was an unsatisfactory one, at any rate to the Americans, and reflected the country's weakness and unimportance in the scheme of things. Independence was qualified by the necessity of a French guarantee, of French protection. Until the United States could do without France, she would be no more than a satellite, unable to achieve or attempt much without permission. This might prove a disastrous position if, for example, she should clash with Spain. The Spanish alliance was a major component of French foreign policy; it would certainly not be sacrificed to the interests of an upstart little protégé. Yet

Spain was now a principal obstacle to the growth and, perhaps, to the continued existence of the United States. The first Peace of Paris, in 1763, had given her Louisiana, which included New Orleans and all the country between the Mississippi and the Rocky Mountains. By the second, in 1783, she had regained Florida, which then stretched right along the Gulf Coast across what is now southern Alabama. She disliked the republicans, and had two effective weapons against them. By her control of the Mississippi navigation and the market of New Orleans she could dictate terms to the western Americans, who had begun to settle the valleys of the Ohio and Tennessee rivers, for the only practicable outlet for their produce lay down the great rivers, since land carriage back across the Appalachians was so expensive; and she could stir up the powerful Indian tribes of the South-West – the Creeks and the Cherokees – against the weak new settlements of the Tennessee. By the winter of 1786–7 a full-scale frontier war was raging, and Spanish agents were at work plausibly suggesting to the Westerners that for protection in future they ought perhaps to look to the King of Spain rather than to the United States. Congress was as helpless as the individual state governments to do anything about these highly undesirable developments, which might end by robbing the United States of half her splendid Western heritage.

Relations with Great Britain were even more important, and equally unsatisfactory. George III received John Adams in London as the first American minister to the Court of St James, in a ceremony that both men found deeply moving; but such occasions had little or nothing to do with the making of high policy. The English Cabinet had its own ideas. First, it discovered that more had been given away at the peace than had been intended or than was, perhaps, quite necessary. If the Great Lakes country was handed over to the United States the fur-trade would go with it, to the great impoverishment of Canada. England decided not to vacate Fort Detroit just yet, nor the other six frontier posts which she was pledged, by her signature of the treaty, to give up (the excuse was that America had not fulfilled some of the other terms of the peace). So for the time being much of the North-West would remain in British hands, while £200,000 worth of furs per annum found their way to London through Montreal, not through New York. As if that were not enough, England set out systematically to crush America's maritime rivalry. The Navigation Acts were revised by Orders in Council. With seeming generosity, all duties were lifted from North American goods coming to Britain in British or American bottoms. This was a great encouragement to American producers to look to the British market. The catch was that at the same time the Americans were strictly forbidden to trade with the British West Indies; yet it was there that the colonists, before 1775, had always found their best customers. Now British ships alone would carry the produce of New England and Pennsylvania to the Caribbean and the produce of the sugar islands to Britain. With this immense advantage, British merchants soon began to drive out their American competitors from all the Atlantic routes, for they could afford to charge lower rates. It looked as if the British merchant marine would soon have a monopoly of Atlantic trade, and thus Great Britain would be able to dictate the economic future of the ports of her former colonies. Her statesmen looked with complacency on the bickering and feebleness of the US government; some began to speculate that before long economic pressure would force the New Englanders, at least, to see sense and come back to their true allegiance. Instead, the individual American states imposed discriminatory tariffs on British goods and passed navigation Acts to shut out British shipping; but although these measures were helpful, they could not of themselves defeat British policy. Besides, they set American merchants (who welcomed the navigation laws but disliked the protective tariffs) against American artisans (who were most interested in the tariffs). And, as in the matter of Spanish relations, there seemed to be nothing that Congress could do.

The young Republic, then, endured something like an economic cold war in the first years of peace. Bad as this was, the internal situation was if anything worse. At times it seemed that the peace, by removing the British, had removed the one force capable of inspiring an effective Union. Each state began to go her own way. Even more depressing, the end of the war was followed (as has usually been the case with America's wars) by an economic crisis.

It will not do to exaggerate this. Benjamin Franklin, coming home for good in the autumn of 1785, was delighted with the evident prosperity of Pennsylvania, and wrote to all his friends in Europe telling them not to believe English assertions that the United States was on the brink of ruin. George Washington did the same. 'It is wonderful to see how soon the ravages of war are repaired,' he wrote:

Houses are rebuilt, fields enclosed, stocks of cattle which were destroyed are replaced, and many a desolated territory assumes again the cheerful appearance of cultivation. In many places the vestiges of conflagration and ruin are hardly to be traced. The arts of peace, such as clearing rivers, building bridges, and establishing conveniences for travelling &c. are assiduously promoted. In short, the foundation of a great empire is laid.

All this was no doubt true: America was and is an intrinsically rich country, and the inhabitants have never been backward in exploiting her resources. But in the wake of the Revolutionary War even this natural abundance could be an embarrassment, or at any rate of little use to the producers. The Americans were oppressed by all manner of debts, and the means of paying them seemed to be lacking. The foreign debt alone, including both capital and interest, went up from \$7,885,085 in 1783 to \$11,858,983 in 1789.[1] Most of

1 Because of their proximity to the West Indies and the Spanish Empire the only coinage which the Americans had used at all commonly in colonial times was Spanish, though reckonings were usually given in pounds, shillings and pence. Metal currency was driven out of circulation by Continental paper money during the Revolutionary War; thereafter Spanish

this was owed to France, which did not press for her money; but domestic creditors were less forbearing. They wanted to be paid, and to be paid in good currency, that is, in gold or silver: they spurned the grossly devalued paper money issued by the states and Congress. At the same time many debtors found it impossible to earn the necessary specie, for it could only come from abroad, and Great Britain, as we have seen, had cut off American farmers from their foreign markets. Their unsellable produce piled up in their barns, and their creditors took them to court. Matters were made worse all round by the pressure of the state governments. Public credit was exhausted, and could be renewed, so that government might continue, only by a determined, successful effort to redeem the paper currency; and the only way by which such redemption might be achieved was by higher taxes. At the back of the queue came Congress, desperately pleading for enough money to pay the running expenses of the national government, if not to pay off the national debt.

In the circumstances it is not surprising that there was a revival of the bitter battles between debtors and creditors that had marked the late colonial era. Defying the peace treaty, the Virginia legislature passed laws to stop British creditors suing to collect their pre-war debts, for, as George Mason wrote to Patrick Henry, 'If we are now to pay the debts due to the British merchants, what have we been fighting for all this while?' In Rhode Island, the debtor party won control of the state government, and tried by law to compel creditors to accept the depreciated paper currency in settlement of debts: this led to complete economic dislocation. Things were even worse in Massachusetts. There the debtor–creditor struggle merged with the long-standing feud between the eastern part of the state, dominated by Boston, the lesser ports and mercantile interests generally, and the farming west. To pay the public debt the Boston-influenced legislature decreed taxes which the West found intolerable. For the farmers of the up-country were not in the least like those of Pennsylvania, or the planters of the South. Their land was poor; they could not produce for the market, but only for their own subsistence, as is shown by the fact that they were not very eager customers for expensive things like imported cloth. Their contribution to trade lay only in the small amounts of tea and sugar for which they bartered what they could spare of their harvest. Some had done well from the sale of provisions during the war, but others were badly hit by the dislocation of the times: here and there land went out of cultivation and began to revert to wilderness. Harvests were good in 1784, but hardship grew worse as the pressure from the state government increased. As one sympathizer pointed out,

coins (pesos, pieces of eight, dollars) slowly returned. In 1792 Congress made a silver dollar the basic unit of American currency; it was divisible into the now-familiar quarters, dimes, nickels and cents. However, it took years to get used to the change, and many of the leading Revolutionaries continued to think in terms of the old English money.

. . . when a farmer brings his produce to market, he is obliged to take up with the buyer's offer, and is forced, not infrequently, to take merchandise in exchange, which is totally insufficient to discharge his taxes. There is no family that does not want some money for some purposes, and the little which the farmer carries home from market, must be applied to other uses, besides paying off the [tax] collector's bills. The consequence is, distraint is made upon his stock or real estate.[2]

The westerners had no sympathizers in the East: Sam Adams had long since lived down the indiscretions of his youth and was as hot against defaulting agitators as if he were Thomas Hutchinson himself. Business conditions were very bad for the time being: the peace had brought a rush of goods to the United States, which had quickly glutted the market. As a result many importing merchants had been ruined; trade was now at a standstill, even for the rum distilleries (according to an English traveller). It was time to put the public finances on a sound footing, so as to diminish inflation, restore confidence and thus, perhaps, initiate an economic revival. So the legislators relentlessly hounded the farmers to pay their taxes. At length it was more than the westerners could bear. In the autumn of 1786, led by a former Continental officer, Daniel Shays (1747–1825), a veteran of Lexington, Bunker Hill and Saratoga, they rose in rebellion, closing down the county courts which were sending so many of them to debtors' prison,[3] and threatening to march on Boston. But they were unarmed, except for pitchforks, the federal arsenal at Springfield was successfully defended against them, and so they were easily dispersed by the state militia. There was not going to be a second revolution in Massachusetts; and anyway the state government showed itself to be more wise and lenient than George III. The rebels were punished lightly, and some of their demands were granted: there were no Intolerable Acts. In 1787 prosperity began to return, and discontent died down.

None the less, Shays's Rebellion was a terrible shock to respectable Americans. The nature of the uprising was largely unknown to people outside Massachusetts; all they could see was that an armed revolt against a duly constituted republican government had come dangerously close to succeeding; that property was in danger; and that nowhere in America was there sufficient force to defeat another such challenge, either internal or external (Chief McGillivray was just now beginning his successful depredations on the Georgian frontier).[4] George Washington's reaction, as so often, was entirely representative:

2 James Swan, *National Arithmetick*, 1786. Quoted by Merrill Jensen, *The New Nation* (New York, 1967), p. 240, from which book most of this paragraph is derived.
3 This revolt against the courts is strikingly similar to other episodes in American history, such as the tumults in Iowa at the depth of the Great Depression a hundred and fifty years later. See below, p. 536.
4 See above, p. 67.

What a triumph for the advocates of despotism, to find that we are incapable of governing ourselves, and that systems founded on the basis of equal liberty, are merely ideal and fallacious. Would to God that wise measures may be taken in time to avert the consequences we have but too much reason to apprehend.

The important thing to understand here is what Washington meant by 'wise measures'. He saw the problem as essentially political, not economic; and therefore the cure he looked for was also political. He decided, like many another solid citizen, that the time had come to amend the Articles of Confederation.

The remedy may seem somewhat remote from the disease. Perhaps it was, for Massachusetts was not the only place where economic conditions began to improve long before any effective political action at the national level had been taken. But a number of well-placed gentlemen had been agitating for a reform of the Articles for some years; and in a crisis men tend to adopt whatever programme is on offer, without scrutinizing its fitness too nicely. The great point is to be doing something. The economic argument for a reform was not wholly implausible: the underlying causes of American debility were British mercantilism, which only a strong national government could challenge successfully, and the collapse of the national credit, which only such a government could restore. Washington's brilliant young protégé, Alexander Hamilton of New York (1755–1804), believed in these propositions passionately. To his mind 'the three great objects of government, *agriculture, commerce and revenue*, can only be secured by a general government', and he was prepared to say so, in season and out of season, and recommend a pretty strong general government into the bargain – certainly a much stronger one than that set up by the Articles. Others were less single-minded on the point than Hamilton; or they had entirely different reasons for wanting a reform. To them, Shays's Rebellion was more an opportunity than an argument.

American government under the Articles of Confederation has no doubt been unfairly attacked, both in its own time and since. The Confederation Congress had some real triumphs to its name. It had conducted the revolutionary war feebly but successfully and secured a generous peace treaty through its chosen emissaries. In the years since 1783 it had achieved a settlement of the Western land question that was to be of incalculable importance to the American future. To get the Articles ratified it had been necessary to induce Virginia and other states with charter claims to relinquish them and concede that the vast stretch of territory between the Appalachians and the Mississippi, between the Great Lakes and the borders of Florida, should be held by Congress on behalf of all American citizens. The existence of this heritage did much to cement national loyalties and to diminish the importance of state identities. Next, in 1785, Congress had passed the Land Ordinance first drafted by Thomas Jefferson, which laid down, with all the brilliant rationality of its author, how and on what terms the national lands should be disposed of. Jefferson was indeed the Father of the West: as President he would purchase Louisiana and send out the Lewis and Clark expedition; but the Land Ordinance was his masterpiece. If most of America is today a chessboard it is because of his plan, by which the public lands were surveyed and divided into townships (as in New England) six miles square. Each township was subdivided into thirty-six further rectangles, known as sections; and these sections were to be sold whole, at not less than a dollar an acre, to developers. Not many American farmers could pay $640 for a whole section, so the Ordinance was a boon for the speculative land companies; but even they had to subdivide their sections and sell at fairly low prices eventually, if they were to find customers and make a profit; meantime the Ordinance secured an orderly growth of the West. Finally, in 1787, when settlement of the Ohio river valley was about to begin, Congress passed the North-West Ordinance, which provided for the political organization of the new lands. Under this law three stages were envisaged for the North-West. First, it would be ruled by a governor and judges appointed by Congress. Then, when it had acquired 5,000 free male adult inhabitants, it would become a self-governing 'territory', a colony, as it were, with its own legislature and a non-voting delegate in Congress, but still with an appointed governor. Finally, when any part of the territory had acquired 60,000 free inhabitants it could (Congress consenting) become a state of the Union, on an equal footing with the old thirteen. To prevent the old states being totally swamped by the new, it was laid down that no more than five (and no less than three) states might be carved out of the territory. Various other provisions of the Ordinance guaranteed to the Westerners what would one day be known as the American way of life: civil rights and liberties, religious freedom, education – even, or especially, personal freedom: for it was laid down that 'there shall be neither slavery nor involuntary servitude in the said territory'.

The North-West Ordinance became the pattern by which all future territorial acquisitions were regulated, and it shows conclusively that the Confederation Congress could act wisely and effectively on some matters. But its diplomatic and military strength was nil; its financial affairs were hopeless. Under the Articles, Congress had as little power to tax American citizens as George III had after the repeal of the Stamp Act – less, in fact, since it could not even impose a duty on tea. It had to rely on the system of requisitions employed by the English government during the Seven Years War: that is, it asked the state governments for money and, if it was lucky, got some (it never got all it needed). Various unsuccessful attempts were made to solve the problem: one promising notion was the imposition of a 5 per cent import duty; unfortunately the Articles required the unanimous consent of the state assemblies to make such proposals effective, and the impost, as it was called, was always one state short of ratification. The strictest economy could not make up for the resultant shortage of funds, and brought other disadvantages. For instance, at one point the standing army was reduced to eighty men. Even those Americans who most passionately distrusted this potential instrument of tyranny could see that this was an unsatisfactorily small force. Its numbers were allowed to grow; that of course meant that its cost rose too; even so it never became effective: during Shays's Rebellion it was the Massachusetts militia which saved the Springfield arsenal, much to the mortification of General Knox, the Secretary of War.

By 1786, then, it was clear to all well-informed men (especially to those who had served in Congress) that the national government needed a thorough overhaul if it was ever to be worthy of the name. Not everybody wanted it to be worthy of the name: the smaller states were nervous about their future in a strengthened federation, and in all the states there was a reluctance to sacrifice the joys of quasi-independent power. In one sense American unity had weakened in the years since Lexington: Congress had come to exist almost on sufferance, as the mere instrument of the state governments, which ran themselves without interference – except from each other, and in some cases their bickering was getting out of hand. They erected customs barriers and taxed each other's trade where possible: for example, New York imposed a tax on all vessels trading through her waters to New Jersey or Connecticut. This sort of thing generated a great deal of ill-feeling, leading some observers to expect an inter-state war in the near future.

The men who had fought the British regarded all this with ever-increasing dismay, but also with a determination not to let their achievements be undone. Far away in London John Adams wrote a long, able, ill-organized work on the principles of republican government, which at least forced its readers to think. Nearer at hand, Alexander Hamilton, so early as 1780, suggested that 'a Convention of all the States, with full authority to conclude finally upon a General Confederation' ought to be summoned. This was the plan eventually adopted, but political talents of a different order from Hamilton's were required to bring it about.

Hamilton served in Congress in 1782–3. While there he got to know a promising Virginian, a few years his senior, a small, quiet man called James Madison (1751–1836). They struck up an alliance, for their strongly nationalist views were, at this period, largely identical, although Hamilton already favoured a much more powerful, aristocratic government than did Madison. For the rest, their talents were complementary. Hamilton was the more dazzling and eloquent, depending less on information than on intellectual power. Madison was deeply learned in public law and constitutional theory; a man of pellucid intellectual clarity; a most hard-working, conscientious public official, whether as a member of Congress or of the Virginian assembly; above all, a man whose human warmth and reliability won him friends and allies wherever he went. He was a consummate politician, and, as Jefferson's right-hand man (they first joined forces in the strenuous and successful battle to disestablish the Anglican church in

Virginia), was always sure of good advice when his own subtlety failed him. It was he, more than anyone else, who made sure that when the opportunity for reform occurred it was seized. He began by bringing about a conference between Maryland and Virginia to settle problems arising out of the joint navigation of the river Potomac. The conference did little for the Potomac navigation, but it popularized the idea that a larger conference, between all the states, might be useful in sorting out the Union's commercial entanglements. Virginia sent out an invitation to the other states to meet at Annapolis, Maryland, in September 1786 to confer on 'the trade of the United States'. Only five states in the end sent delegations, but that was all to the good. Hamilton and Madison were among those present; so was Edmund Randolph, a cousin of Jefferson, governor of Virginia, and much influenced by Madison. Thanks to Madison's diplomatic skill Hamilton was induced to write a moderate, and therefore acceptable, letter to the states arguing that the problems of trade could never be solved until the Articles of Confederation were re-drafted; and Randolph approved it. Hamilton's document called for a convention, to meet at Philadelphia on the second Monday in May 1787. Its purpose was

to take into consideration the situation of the United States, to devise such further provisions as shall appear . . . necessary to render the constitution of the Federal Government adequate to the exigencies of the Union; and to report an act for that purpose to the United States in Congress assembled as, when agreed to by them and afterwards confirmed by the Legislatures of every State, will effectually provide for the same.

The three clever young men then persuaded their nine colleagues at Annapolis to adopt this report; and went home to persuade the state governments too.

At this point Shays's Rebellion occurred. For a moment all, or almost all, were convinced: Mr Madison's scheme must be given a trial. Twelve states (Rhode Island was the exception) agreed to send delegates to Philadelphia; Congress approved the plan; and on 14 May 1787 the convention officially opened.

It was a unique occasion in American history (indeed, it is not easy to think of a parallel anywhere: perhaps the closest is the Council of Nicaea). It was the crowning act of the American Revolution; next to the decision for independence, it was the most important; and it was a huge, though not unqualified, success. Add to this the personnel of the convention, and it is not surprising that Americans have traditionally regarded it with religious awe. Thomas Jefferson, the American minister in Paris, set the tone when he wrote from afar that 'it is really an assembly of demigods' (a remark which he later regretted). At times the air of reverence has grown so thick as to be stifling, notably at the end of the nineteenth century; this in turn has provoked a healthily sceptical reaction. Still, the truth must not be overlooked: the constitutional convention of 1787 was indeed an astonishing and impressive affair; history's business is to characterize and explain its success, not to question it.

The problem that the delegates had to solve was daunting but finite: how to devise a permanent framework for the government of the American nation. So put, it is obvious that one of the reasons for their success was that this problem had been in the offing ever since the foundation of Jamestown. Various expedients had been tried, including substantially complete independence for each new settlement (during the seventeenth century) and government from Westminster (during the eighteenth); their failure had convinced almost all Americans that their future must lie together, as one confederated body politic. Even during the convention, various other suggestions would be made, but usually only as debating points. The great decision was implicit in the history of the previous 180 years and had been amply confirmed by the events of the Revolution: the United States would be a nation. The framers of a new constitution would only have to settle the details.

Their success in this task was undoubtedly due to their own exceptional qualifications for the work. The political and social conditions which had bred such a generation of wise, capable and public-spirited men have already been sufficiently described: the long experiment in self-government, whether as attempted in Massachusetts, Pennsylvania or Virginia, now reached its logical culmination. Equally important was the personal experience of the delegates. They were not a random group, but the cream of the Revolutionary leadership. There were some notable absentees: Jefferson; Adams; Patrick Henry, who was elected, but refused to serve, explaining later that he smelt a rat; Sam Adams, who was not elected. But for the rest, the great makers of the Revolution were all present, from John Dickinson, who had attended the Stamp Act Congress, to Rufus King of Massachusetts, one of the chief architects of the North-West Ordinance. Alexander Hamilton was a New York delegate. Connecticut had sent a strong team, dominated by Roger Sherman, who according to Jefferson never said a foolish thing in his life: he had signed the Declaration of Independence. But for star quality, no state could rival the Pennsylvanian and Virginian delegations. Pennsylvania sent its President, Dr Franklin, now a martyr to gout and stone, but still alert and acute; James Wilson, Scottish-born, one of the ablest men in the convention; Gouverneur Morris, one of the most forceful; and Robert Morris (no relation), who had suffered nearly as much in his attempts to handle the finances of the Revolutionary War as had Washington in the field, and for the same reasons. Virginia sent Washington himself (it had taken the most earnest efforts of Randolph and Madison to persuade the General to accept his election); George Mason, the patriarch of the state's politics, the indispensable adviser of his more visible countrymen, Washington, Jefferson, and Madison; Edmund Randolph; and James Madison. The convention was a surprisingly young body: nearly half its members were under forty, and one, Charles Pinckney of South Carolina, was under thirty. But almost all of them had been seasoned in the great drama of the Revolution. In the early days of their deliberations the learned Madison showed a tendency to dwell on the lessons to be derived from the Amphictyonic League of ancient Greece; but such musty reasoning was never usual and was soon almost entirely abandoned. Instead the records of the convention are full of allusions to American experience, whether before or after independence; at war or at peace; at state or at national level. These veterans of the army, of the Continental Congress, of the Revolutionary state assemblies and of high diplomacy had been too profoundly shaped by their service ever to forget that what they produced must fit Americans, and be justifiable in terms of the American experience and American aspirations. Only Alexander Hamilton, the high flyer, wasted the convention's time by orating at length on the beauty of principles that had no chance of popular acceptance. The rest were intensely practical, though some of them wasted time in other ways: Luther Martin, of Maryland, brilliant, drunken, was a notable bore.

Many of them had worked together before; if they had not, they quickly learned how, for they knew the value of time, the necessary arts of compromise and the importance of not expecting other people to be angels. In many cases they were agreeably surprised to find that colleagues from strange parts of the country were as sensible as themselves. The convention's deliberations were secret, and were not published in any form for twenty years afterwards; this meant that there was no temptation to play to the gallery. There was comparatively little loss of temper, and no discourtesy.

What above all helped the business along was the fact that these were revolutionaries who wanted their revolution to succeed for ever. Their basic agreement on the meaning and purpose of the American Revolution was complete; they were all nationalists and republicans, and most of them were on the way to becoming democrats. They could debate practicalities so incessantly because they shared the same principles. There was no ideological rift, no left, right and centre. In fact it is extremely difficult to settle who was conservative and who progressive at the convention: everyone seemed to be both. They all dreaded 'anarchy and confusion' (another recurrent phrase), which would result if the Articles were not reformed; they all believed, with George Washington, in a 'Government of respectability under which life, liberty, and property will be secured to us'. In their own opinion they were radical, for were they not aspiring to consolidate the old Whig programme, deriving from the Puritan Commonwealth, and dispense with kings, nobles, militarism and privilege? To us they seem conservative, for they did not propose to remodel the foundations of society. Whichever description is apter, there is no doubt that it covers them all.

But their agreement was not perfect, which was also all to the good. They represented the variousness of America, as well as her unity; probably each of them had to sacrifice some cherished belief or proposal before agreement was possible. For the convention was wiser than any one of its members, since no one member could know the American people and the American continent as well as the whole did. Only by long discussion could it become clear whether a particular idea would be acceptable throughout the republic. It had to be chewed over by men from the North as well as from the South, by men from small states as well as men from large, by men from the country as well as men from towns. What finally emerged, after nearly four months' debate, stood a very good chance of being acceptable to the people, for it had been thoroughly tested in argument by men who were truly their representatives. If one single explanation of the durability of the Constitution is needed, this is it.

All through May the delegates drifted into Philadelphia: a quorum was finally formed on the twenty-fifth. George Washington was promptly and unanimously elected President of the convention, a post which he accepted in his usual anxious style, sure that he was unfit for it. As usual he was a great success, and the prestige of the convention and its product owed not a little to the fact that Washington, of all Americans the most universally trusted, had in this fashion lent it his prestige. Franklin's presence was an asset too, though the Doctor was now too old to make any great mark on the proceedings: his chief contribution was to keep people in a good humour with his sayings, jokes and stories.

This was Virginia's hour. No state had done more to carry the Revolution to victory; no statesmen had done more than her delegates to summon and prepare for the convention. Madison resolved, not only to take an active part in the deliberations, but to be their chronicler. He sat in the front row, under the President's nose, and recorded what everyone said, fairly and fully: without him posterity would know very little of what went on. Before the other delegates arrived, the Virginians caucused, and concocted the so-called Virginia plan: suggestions for a new constitution which Randolph got to his feet to propose as resolutions on 29 May; and the real work of the convention started.

To begin with, the delegates made remarkably rapid progress. All agreed that, as a matter of fact, the chief defect of the Articles was that the confederated Congress represented states, and because of the unanimity rule one state, even a very small one, could frustrate the will of all the others. They agreed in principle that the remedy for this infirmity was to set up 'a national government . . . consisting of a supreme Legislature, Judiciary, and Executive' which would operate directly on individuals, not just on states. It was agreed that the legislature ought to consist of two chambers; some progress was made towards settling the details of the judiciary and the executive. But it soon became clear that a fundamental problem gaped before the convention. The delegates from the large states held that, as a matter of republican principle, direct elections should be held for both legislative houses, and that representation in both should be proportioned to population, ignoring the states; while the small states, though ready to give up the equal rights they enjoyed under the Articles, insisted on some protecting privilege under the new system. Throughout June and early July the point was debated; anxiety mounted that it might wreck the whole convention; Hamilton left in despair, and his colleagues from New York in disgust (they were committed small state men); by early July Washington was looking as grim as he had at Valley Forge;[5] but eventually the large states conceded, as they had to if they wanted to make progress. It was agreed that the lower house would be elected on a population basis, though every state was to have at least one representative; while the upper house, or Senate, would be elected by the state assemblies, and each state would have an equal vote there. This was the Great Compromise; without it the Constitution would not have been agreed, and it was a price worth paying. Yet essentially it was a price paid by the future to the past. Major political conflict has never, since 1787, raged between large states as such and small states; so the Constitutional protection has been neither a help nor a hindrance. Madison foresaw this at the time; he insisted that the real disputes would in future arise between the regions, or sections – between North and South, say; but he too acquiesced in the arrangement. The essential points of the compromise were adopted on 16 July.

This matter having been settled, the convention was free to get down to the hard work of settling the details of their grand design. It was agreed, for example, that each state would have two representatives in the Senate, who would vote as individuals, not as a unitary state delegation; that the new Constitution would be the supreme law of the land; and that executive officers might be impeached for high crimes and misdemeanours. The debates were long and earnest, and not always very enlightening: during the discussion of that dangerous institution, the standing army, Gerry of Massachusetts actually proposed that the Constitution limit the size of the army to two or three thousand men. Fortunately, Washington killed the idea by muttering audibly from the chair that they should next make it unconstitutional for any enemy to attack with a larger force.[6]

The next important crisis arose towards the end of August. It was complicated and messy, for it involved two very different questions, trade and slavery. As to trade, one of the New England delegates remarked bitterly that 'the Eastern states had no motive to Union but a commercial one. They were able to protect themselves. They were not afraid of external danger, and did not need the aid of the Southern States.'[7] For that reason they demanded that Congress be given the power to pass a navigation law by a

5 The observation was made by one of Washington's former French officers, just then visiting Philadelphia.
6 A contemporary described Gerry as 'a man of sense but a Grumbletonian . . . of service by objecting to every thing he did not propose'.
7 At this period, before the line of settlement had spread deep inland, what were later known as the Northern states, and still later as the North-Eastern, were generally called Eastern. The custom survives of referring to Maine as 'down East'.

simple majority. Such a law would at last enable American merchants to fight back effectively against British discrimination. Unfortunately, it might also make them masters of the South, enabling them to charge what they liked for carrying products such as rice and tobacco (soon, cotton) to market. So South Carolina, in particular, resisted the proposal, but then found herself attacked on her other flank, for the delegates from Virginia and Pennsylvania wanted to renew the wartime ban on the slave-trade, arguing that the continued importation of Africans was only storing up trouble, in the shape of a slave rebellion, for the future.

Georgia and South Carolina reacted to this with cold violence. Virginia they thought hypocritical: she wanted to ban the import of Africans only so that she could sell her own superfluous slaves at a good price. It was drummed into Pennsylvania, very firmly, that neither state would ever agree to any shackle on slavery. Left to themselves, they said, the far Southern states might possibly abolish the institution one day; but they would never do so if bullied.

It was a naked challenge, of a kind that was to become fatally familiar in the next seventy years. It would have been better for the United States if it had been taken up and disposed of in 1787, once and for all; but it was not possible. Anyway, the resistance of the middle states was overcome by New England, which agreed to support the slave-trade if the Carolinas and Georgia would abandon their proposal that a navigation Act could only be passed by a two-thirds vote of both houses of Congress. This bargain satisfied each side; and the slave states won some other guarantees, of which the most important was the provision that 'representatives and direct Taxes shall be apportioned among the several States . . . according to their respect-ive Numbers, which shall be determined by adding to the whole Number of free Persons, including those bound to Service for a Term of Years [that is, indentured servants], and excluding Indians not taxed, three fifths of all other persons' – in one word, a word carefully excluded from this free Constitution, slaves.[8] It is really no wonder that a nineteenth-century aboli-tionist called the Constitution a covenant with hell: the net effect of these various provisions was to deeply entrench slavery in the American political system. In return all that the liberals got was the provision that Congress might forbid the Atlantic slave-trade after 1808 – not before.[9]

All this was too much for old George Mason, who wanted to end slavery by educating the slaves, then freeing them, and giving financial compensation to the owners. There were other things he objected to about the Constitution as it emerged: it did not include a bill of rights to protect citizens and states against encroachments by the national government (he had drawn up such a document for the state of Virginia, and it had been widely admired and copied) and he had doubts about some of its lesser provisions. But by the

8 *Constitution of the United States*, Article I, section 2.
9 It was in fact abolished in that year.

beginning of September the convention was too weary to listen to him. Its work was almost complete, an overwhelming majority of members supporting its plan; they wanted to go home, let Mason snort as much as he chose about their precipitate, intemperate, not to say indecent haste. The committee of style, led by Gouverneur Morris, cast the agreed points into plain yet elegant language; on 15 September the eleven remaining state delegations unanimously agreed[10] on the Constitution as amended; and on the 17th they signed the official parchment version.

It was a great occasion. Benjamin Franklin opened it with his last public speech, an exceedingly wise one, read for him by James Wilson, in which he pleaded for his colleagues to swallow their rancour and their vanity and accept the Constitution as the best that could be devised, in which spirit he accepted it himself. His plea fell on deaf ears, so far as Mason, Randolph and Gerry were concerned: they refused to sign; but everybody else did so, and as the last members were signing,

Doctor Franklin looking towards the President's chair, at the back of which a rising sun happened to be painted, observed to a few members near him, that painters had found it difficult to distinguish in their art a rising from a setting sun. I have, said he, often and often in the course of the session, and the vicissitudes of my hopes and fears as to its issue, looked at that behind the President without being able to tell whether it was rising or setting: but now at length I have the happiness to know that it is a rising and not a setting sun.

Madison, who tells this story, must have heartily agreed with him, for the Constitution that emerged, which greatly strengthened the national government while protecting the rights of the states and the individual citizens, was pretty much what he had worked for for five years; but he also knew that the battle to make the sun rise was still not over. To come into operation the Constitution would have to be approved by at least nine states; everybody knew that Rhode Island would continue to hold aloof; it would be a stiff battle to make sure that no more than three other states joined her. Special conventions were to meet; after a farewell dinner at the City Tavern in Philadelphia the delegates fanned out across America to persuade their constituents that what they had done was necessary and right. Already the enemy was at work: Luther Martin had gone off in a huff early in September, like Yates and Lansing of New York earlier;[11] and now the anti-Federalists, those who had never liked the convention, would work up a huge clamour of opposition.

The pen was a weapon. Washington seems to have thought that his name

10 That is to say, every state recorded its vote *for* the Constitution; but there were individual dissidents, for the way a state would vote was settled by majority voting among its delegates.
11 Their absence meant that Hamilton's signature on the Constitution could only be that of an individual, since the New York delegation did not have a quorum.

on the Constitution was publication enough (at any rate he was much distressed when an informal but sincere paragraph of endorsement from one of his private letters was printed); but he filled his enormous correspondence with praise of the Constitution and remarks on the progress of ratification. Franklin made sure that his last speech was widely available. Dickinson wrote a series of pamphlets as 'Fabius'. But the younger men bore the heat of the battle. Federalists and anti-Federalists (that is, pro-Constitutionalists and opponents) rushed into print, as if the great days of 1775 and 1776 were back. Some used their own names, some, pseudonyms: 'Cato', 'Centinel', 'Landholder', 'Roderick Razor', 'Constant Reader', 'Rough Hewer'. From the heap of ephemera one publication shines out: *The Federalist Papers*, by 'Publius', published in New York state between October 1787 and August the following year. 'Publius' was really Hamilton, Madison and (for five of the papers) John Jay, the Confederation's Foreign Secretary. Its importance to posterity, as an authoritative interpretation of the intentions and meaning of the framers of the Constitution and as the one classic of political thought so far produced in North America, overshadows its usefulness in the battle for ratification, which may not have been very great. At least the papers were quickly republished in book form and used as sources of Federalist ammunition in the ratifying conventions of Virginia and New York; while if they did no more than clarify the authors' thoughts they were a worthwhile enterprise, for it was by virtue of sheer intellectual superiority that Hamilton and Madison were to steer their home states to ratification. However, it seems likely that the irresistible logic and good manners of 'Publius' influenced more people than can be proved; certainly he was a classic by the autumn of 1788, and praised as such by Washington and Jefferson (who were both let into the secret of the authorship).

All the same, it would be words spoken rather than written that most affected the outcome. In this respect James Wilson was first to the fray. Sure of their ascendancy, the Federalists of Pennsylvania hurried their state into ratification, in a manner which caused a lot of ill-feeling: Wilson was beaten up by an angry Western mob just after Christmas, 1787. But before then he had argued before both the legislature and the state convention with such success that Pennsylvania was the second state to ratify (by forty-six votes to twenty-three in the state convention) – on 12 December. Delaware was the first, doing it unanimously on 7 December.

Next came New Jersey, Georgia ('If a weak state, with the Indians on its back and the Spaniards on its flank, does not see the necessity of a general government, there must I think be wickedness or insanity in the way,' General Washington had remarked) and Connecticut. The small states were making no difficulties: they well understood the value to them of the Great Compromise. For that very reason it was uncertain what the big states would do; yet without them the whole experiment would fail. Massachusetts deliberated throughout most of January and the first week of February 1788. Her delegates began as mostly anti-Federalists; but the men of the Bay State had had a sounder political training than those of any other: they knew good arguments when they met them; and besides, Sam Adams changed his tune. He had disliked the convention and, at first glance, its handiwork. 'I stumble at the threshold,' said he. 'I meet with a National Government instead of a Federal Union of sovereign States.' But the sweet reasonableness that, except in Pennsylvania, marked the Federalists' tactics everywhere won him over; and he then made it his business to win over the Governor, John Hancock, who meant to remain ill in bed with gout until it was clear which way the wind was blowing. A little flattery, a little reason, the alluring idea that, if Virginia failed to ratify, he might be the first President of the United States, and the trick was done: still flaunting his bandages, Hancock went down to the state convention, threw his weight behind the Federalists, and Massachusetts ratified; holding, in the words of one of her 'plough jogging' delegates, that 'there is a time to sow and a time to reap. We sowed our seed when we sent men to the Federal Convention. Now is the harvest.'

Three to go. Maryland ratified on 26 April, sixty-three to eleven: the anti-Federalists, led by Luther Martin, were repudiated largely because they were paper money men and the voters were tired of inflation. Two to go. On 12 May the South Carolina convention met, and once it was satisfied that the proposed Constitution was no threat to slavery, ratified by a crushing majority, one hundred and forty-nine to seventy-three. The minority, here as in several other states, was chiefly made up of men from the western areas. One to go: would it be New Hampshire or Virginia? In the event, it was nearly a tie: New Hampshire ratified on 21 June, Virginia on 25 June. That meant that ten states had agreed – one more than necessary to bring the Constitution into force. New York could no longer resist: she ratified on 26 July. Only North Carolina and Rhode Island held out – for the time being.[12]

This smooth tale conceals the fact that it was occasionally a very near thing. In practice, the Constitution would not be able to work, or only with damaging difficulty, if either New York or Virginia stayed out, for without them the Union would be cut into segments. Yet it was touch-and-go in both places. Governor Clinton of New York was strongly anti-Federalist; fortunately he did not dare assume the responsibility of rejecting the Constitution and so, perhaps, breaking up the Union, of which he was a supporter. So he procrastinated, hoping that some other state – Virginia or Massachusetts – would do the work for him; and when that dodge failed, though he had a large majority in the state convention, he could not keep it. 'Willing to wound, and yet afraid to strike,' he let leadership fall into Hamilton's hands. Never was that gentleman more charming, more eloquent, better-informed, more irresistibly logical. Single-handed, he kept the Federalist minority together, wore out some of the anti-Federalists and converted others. The news that Virginia had ratified was all he needed to secure final

12 In the end, North Carolina ratified on 21 November 1789, Rhode Island on 29 May 1790.

victory. His great services were acknowledged by the New Yorkers: when they hauled a model ship of state through the city, in celebration of the great event, they named her the *Hamilton*. She was quite the most spectacular thing in a great parade, which also included a banner showing Adam and Eve naked, except for fig leaf aprons, and bearing the motto, '*And they sewed fig leaves together.*'

The drama in Virginia was even more tense – largely because the debate was at a loftier level. Except for the anti-Federalist in New York who objected to the proposed Presidency because General Washington would no doubt be succeeded by General Slushington, the anti-Federalist arguments in New York were neither very funny nor very good. But in Virginia the anti-Federalists on the whole had greater prestige than the Federalists: they even claimed Thomas Jefferson for their own, though Madison, correctly, denied it. Patrick Henry, who took the lead in opposing the Constitution, was not above mendacious assertions, for the benefit of Virginians west of the Appalachians, in what was soon to be Kentucky, that the new government would give away the Mississippi navigation to the Spanish (as if the old government had not actually done so). His speeches were incessant storms of eloquence that do not read very well now and were not apparently perfectly convincing even then. Still they had to be answered, and Madison, with his feeble voice, his ill-health, his colourless manner, scarcely seemed the right person to do it. But his lucidity, knowledge and patent sincerity prevailed in the end, aided by the popularity of Edmund Randolph (who, rather like Hancock, had decided to back the winning horse) and the intellectual force of John Marshall, the future Chief Justice of the United States, and as such the man who, next only to Madison himself, would have most influence on the Constitution's development. Even the high character and good arguments of George Mason could not prevail. At last Madison let it be understood that when the new government met he would go to work to have a bill of rights passed as a Constitutional amendment. Such an amendment was in every state the honest anti-Federalists' chief demand. The promise was enough: by a small margin Virginia voted to ratify (eighty-nine to seventy-nine) and America gave herself up to rejoicing.

For it had slowly sunk in that the new Constitution really would achieve its purpose and safeguard the gains of the Revolution. National independence first: with a well-organized executive and the power of direct taxation, the United States could raise an effective army and even, if it chose, a navy. It would soon be unnecessary to play the satellite to either France or Britain; soon Spain could be challenged for control of the West. Political stability: only George Mason could go on believing that the popular representation allowed for in the Constitution was a sham; the new public authorities would still be subject to the control of repeated elections, which would give them legitimacy; secure in that legitimacy, they would have more power with which to protect themselves and the people from their enemies than had ever been allowed to the old Congress. Prosperity: the credit of the new government would underpin every agricultural, commercial or industrial enterprise. The pursuit of happiness: as Dr Benjamin Rush remarked, it would now be possible for those who, like himself, wished to be passengers on the ship of state to leave off the work of the sailors and get back to such equally valuable pursuits as science (or making money).

So everyone was pleased, and the anti-Federalists pledged themselves to do what they could to make the new frame of government a success. The dying Congress fixed the dates of the first elections; the electoral college, voting for the first time in February 1789, unanimously chose George Washington to be the first President; and on 30 April he took the oath of office in New York, after a journey from Mount Vernon which was turned by the enthusiastic citizens into one long carnival.

Nobody supposed that the Constitution was a perfect document; and nobody today, one Civil War and twenty-six amendments later, will argue that it was. But it has in practice worked exceedingly well. Some of the reasons have already been given, but the list must be completed; and the influence of the Constitution in shaping American history has been so profound that a plain statement of its structure and shaping principles is the very least that it deserves, even if it makes a long chapter longer. The degree of one's understanding of the Constitution is to a large extent the degree of one's understanding of the United States.

It is a nationalistic document. As such it was far in advance of its time, which explains why Patrick Henry and many others were so alarmed. The idea of a national government meant to them simply alien, selfish and oppressive power. After all, the last authority to insist on the Americans' nationality had been George III, whose ministers had tried to make them live up to their responsibilities as citizens of the British Empire. The anti-Federalists need not have worried: American nationality was no imperial fiction; but it is not surprising that they should have done so. For, until the American Revolution, the nation-state was a very uncommon thing, only fully achieved, perhaps, in England. Otherwise the Atlantic world was made up of dynastic states and ramshackle republics like Holland or Poland: all were polities held together partly by the pressures of the international power competition, partly by custom, partly by an intricate and fragile net of religion, privilege, dialect and so on. Yet nationalities existed: France, Spain, Italy and Germany were more than mere geographical expressions. America was newer than they, that was all. She too was defined by her borders, her language, her religion, her customs and her enemies. The easy way in which, for instance, the boy Franklin left Boston to live in Philadelphia, or Madison left Virginia to go to college at Princeton, New Jersey, shows how spontaneously Americans regarded themselves as part of each other. Their great achievement was the realization that they had a chance to avoid the fate of France, Germany or Spain: to avoid the chaos of a weak confederation on the one hand or the tyranny of a traditional monarchy on the other. The will to find a middle way drove forward the Founding Fathers (as they came to be known) to devise a national government for a new nation; and in so doing they opened the door of modernity.

The constitutional provision, then, by which the new government was to act directly on the individual instead of mediately, through the states, was absolutely crucial to its success. Experience had shown that there was no way to coerce a state short of civil war;[13] but individuals might be controlled through the normal mechanism of the courts. The states therefore had to sacrifice their claim to the undivided allegiance of their citizens. They might have avoided this loss of power if they had shown themselves willing to treat the requisitions of the Confederated Congress as binding laws; but they never did, and they would never have done so. And they had to make other sacrifices. They had had to give up their claims to the West to get the Articles of Confederation; the Constitution exacted even more fundamental sacrifices, and directly impaired state sovereignty. From now on the states, and state identity, would be secondary to the nation, to national identity. The idea, then, that a state might secede from the Union, as if it was a mere expedient alliance, was absurd, and was not contemplated in the terms of the Constitution; indeed the very quantity of states' rights built into the Constitution made little sense – spelling them out was unnecessary – if the states retained the sovereign remedy and could break up the machine at will by secession. It was only as the sectional quarrel developed over slavery that the South committed itself to a different view. To be sure, even if that had not occurred, there would still have been some reaction against the nationalism of the Founding Fathers: state identities were for long far too strong to be ignored, and too many politicians would find it convenient from time to time to exploit them (Madison himself was to do so in the 1790s). But the fact remains that the Constitution was and is a nationalistic document and a nationalist programme, and attempts to make it anything else have never been successful and have usually been dishonest, for they fly in the face of social reality.

The central government could not be conceded the right to make laws and policy without being given the means to enforce them. This implied courts, soldiers, sailors, diplomatic officers, ministers to supervise them and a dependable source of revenue to pay for such an establishment. That in turn implied taxation and tax-collectors – the very things which the thirteen colonies had resisted in 1765 – and, money being such a sensitive subject and the Anglo-Saxon tradition being what it was, it also implied a national assembly to make the laws, vote the taxes and oversee the executive. The main points of the Constitution can already be seen emerging from this list of requirements.

However, they are also the main points of the Articles of Confederation, at least as that instrument had evolved in practice by 1787. It could be

13 See Madison to Jefferson, 24 October 1787.

argued that all that was necessary to make the Confederation an effective modern government was to give it an effective taxation power. The Secretary of Congress saw to the correspondence with the states and to the coordination and continuity of administration. There was also the nucleus of a cabinet: the Board of Treasury, the Secretary for Foreign Affairs, the Secretary of War, the Postmaster-General. Congressional decisions could be enforced by the state courts. Replace the system of requisitions, which was patently not working, and all that was necessary had been achieved. (Patrick Henry was even prepared to rhapsodize on the requisition system – 'I will never give up that *darling* word, requisitions' – but Patrick Henry, sweeping away on the wings of his oratory, could say anything.)

The nationalists, or Federalists, replied that because of the unanimity rule, the Articles could not be amended on the point of taxation: efforts had been made to incorporate a rational finance system, and failed. This answer would be more convincing if the course the Federalists actually took had not been so revolutionary: sweeping the old system aside altogether and substituting a completely new one. It is hard (I find it impossible) to believe that if as much energy, devotion and ability had been put into a mere amendment of the Articles, it would not have passed into law. The unanimity rule need have been no obstacle. After all, support for the new Constitution was by no means unanimous; and yet North Carolina and Rhode Island soon came to terms. The same could have happened in the other case.

So it seems that the real issues lay rather deeper; nor can there be much doubt what they were. The anti-Federalists essentially wanted a Burkean, one might almost say an English, future: let American institutions evolve as necessity dictated; meantime, let there be as little government as possible, and let what there was be as close to the people as possible. This, to their mind, was what American freedom was all about; and it cannot be denied that their suspicion of government, the distrust some of them expressed for the well-off and well-educated, or the dread that others among them felt that, without a religious test, papists might come to rule America – heavens, the Pope might be elected President – were also in the authentic American strain.

But so were the Federalists. Hamilton saw, with brilliant clarity, better than anyone else, how enormous were the opportunities opening before the American people, with an untouched continent waiting to their west; he spoke for the pioneer impulse, and was determined to give the country a government which could make sure that the opportunity would not be wasted. Washington and Madison certainly shared this vision to a degree (both were speculators in Western lands); but the deepest thought lying behind the new Constitution was expressed by James Wilson. No one could pretend that this canny Scottish lawyer, whose unsuccessful land speculations were eventually to bankrupt him, wreck his judicial career and cause him to die in poverty-stricken exile from his home state, was a radical.

He was palpably the spokesman of the commercial classes of Philadelphia and eastern Pennsylvania. His support of majority rule was not even wholly sincere, for he came from one of the largest states, where the suffrage was unjustly weighted in favour of the region he represented – the East. Yet when all is allowed for, no one at the federal convention, or in the state conventions afterwards, put the case for American democracy better. The business of the convention, he said, was to frame a government

not only to thirteen independent and sovereign states . . . but likewise to innumerable states yet unformed, and to myriads of citizens who in future ages shall inhabit the vast uncultivated regions of the continent. The duties of that body therefore, were not limited to local or partial consideration, but to the formation of a plan commensurate with a great and valuable portion of the globe.

Such a plan could only work if it were grounded on the people.

For I insist, if there are errors in government, the people have the right not only to correct and amend them, but likewise totally to change and reject its form; and under the operation of that right, the people of the United States can never be wretched beyond retrieve, unless they are wanting to themselves.

The principles of the new Constitution were and had to be 'purely demo-cratical'; and Wilson meant what he said so much that he was one of those who held out longest for popular, not state, election of the Senate, and resisted all attempts to restrict the suffrage. Madison took the same line. To both men it seemed that the Articles conceded too much to the states; both at first had fears that the same was true of the Constitution, after the Great Compromise; and both have been vindicated by time. The democratic thrust of the American Revolution has compelled many amendments to the Constitution, but none, it is likely, that would have given greater satisfaction to Wilson and Madison, could they have foreseen it, than the Seventeenth, which took the election of the Senators away from the state assemblies and gave it to the people.

The belief that the government of the American Empire, to be permanent, had to be democratic, and that the Articles were not, or not sufficiently so, must seem thoroughly respectable to the modern mind; not so the equally prominent belief of the Founding Fathers that the people could not be wholly trusted, and that another of the main tasks of the Constitution must be to hold their dangerous impulses in check. The men of 1787 were in some respect alarmists. They were mocked for it in the Virginian state convention:

Pennsylvania and Maryland are to fall upon us from the north like the Goths and Vandals of old . . . the Indians are to invade us from our rear . . . And the Carolinians from the south, mounted on alligators, I presume, are to come and destroy our cornfields and eat up our little children! These, Sir, are the mighty dangers which await us if we reject the Constitution.

More characteristic of the Federalists was their fear of inflation, expressed as a loathing of paper money and stay laws. Paper money was a direct means of robbing persons of property; stay laws, by which the payment of debts might be more or less indefinitely postponed, were indirect robbery. Worse might lurk behind. They had all read their ancient history and knew that the poor had in the past risen to compel the passage of agrarian laws, to divide up the land of the rich between themselves: and that this had been the first act of the drama leading to dictatorship. When the poor became sufficiently numerous in America, the same drama might threaten, so it was necessary to take precautions. In this matter the chief instrument of demagoguery was the state: look at Rhode Island, look at what would have happened in Massachusetts if Shays had won. So the states were stripped of the power to issue paper money, and the central government was given the power to intervene to suppress rebellion if asked to do so by the legitimate authorities.

Yet the Founding Fathers remained American liberals. They were just as concerned to protect the states against illegitimate interference from the central government as the other way round. Again and again they insisted to themselves and to critics that the Constitution left all powers to the states that were not specifically removed or reduced; eventually the point was made specific in the Tenth Amendment. Anyway, it seemed obvious that the state governments must be strong and vigorous if the immense expanse of America was to be governed as a unity. A big country, whether measured by area or population – and the United States was going to be big on both counts – needs a central government, but if it is to be either free or efficient, let alone both, that central government cannot make all, or even most political and administrative decisions. Power, a great deal of power, must be left with regional and local governments. This principle of decentralization can go too far, as the history of the United States has demonstrated all too often, but then so can the principle of centralization. To preserve freedom, equality, peace and prosperity, the best way is the middle way, and that is what American federalism means: a dynamic combination of nationalism with localism. A federal republic, James Wilson explained, was one in which the freedoms of a republic were combined with the external dignity and force of a monarchy. The essence of the case (as so often with the Constitution) was common sense. The experience of the Articles of Confederation showed the dangers of too weak an association; America did not want to dwindle into something as futile as the Holy Roman Empire. A wholly centralized republic would concentrate too much power in one place, and was politically impossible; neither the states nor the people would agree to such a thing (the same holds true today). The Constitution successfully holds these considerations in balance.

So the first and second characteristics of the Constitution are its essential democracy and the horizontal separation of powers between the federal and state governments. The third, and perhaps the most conspicuous characteristic, is the vertical separation of powers: Executive, Legislative, Judiciary – or, Presidency, Congress, Courts. This principle was, as we have seen, one of the first matters agreed by the convention. It had become a cliché in the writings of Montesquieu and a dozen other thinkers deriving from Locke. It corresponded very closely to the formal structure of colonial politics, though colonial practice, as in the case of Massachusetts, was rather different. The alternative doctrine, of the rights of a sovereign legislature, had been given a fair trial in the Continental Congress, to general dissatisfaction, and to the particular dissatisfaction of those, like Madison and Hamilton, who had tried to make Congress work. As we have seen, under the Articles there had already begun some evolution towards the separation of executive from legislature, though the new ministers were firmly subordinated to the Congress. All in all, this fundamental decision was quickly taken because it was so obvious. Yet with hindsight it is easy to see that of all the arrangements of the Founding Fathers it was the most revolutionary.

British readers may best understand what is involved by giving a moment's thought to the constitution of their own country. It is built round a dogma of the absolute sovereignty of the King in Parliament, a dogma that emerged as a result of the civil wars of the seventeenth century and gave the sanction of immemorial tradition to the compromises that ended those wars. The myth of the King in Parliament has lasted for centuries, and is not quite done for yet. It cannot be defended on any grounds except that it happens to be the way that the British do things, yet all political transformations, all radical programmes, have had to adjust to it (at least until Britain entered the European Union). The American Constitution has had an even more overwhelming effect on American history. The Presidency, for example, the embodiment of the executive in one man, was invented partly for the reasons given, and partly because, in George Washington, the ideal President happened to exist. Had Washington died suddenly in the middle of the convention Wilson might have got his way and the United States have acquired a three- or four-man executive, like the five-member Directory in Revolutionary France. The convention had enormous difficulty in settling how to elect the President, and fixed on a method of indirect election, through an electoral college chosen by the voters, only after every other expedient had been considered at length. In the event the electoral college became a mere rubber-stamp for the people's choice; and so this purely practical expedient could become the towering symbol without which no American can imagine his country. Thanks to the first, very distinguished men who occupied the Presidency (Washington, John Adams, Jefferson, Madison); thanks to President Andrew Jackson's insistence on the overriding authority of his mandate from the voters; thanks to the Civil War and the martyrdom of Abraham Lincoln; thanks to the rabble-rousing of Theodore

Roosevelt, the crusading zeal of Woodrow Wilson and, above all, the dynamic leadership of Franklin Roosevelt, the President is now a popularly elected monarch; even the scandals of a Grant, a Nixon or a Clinton cannot strip the office of the mystique that has slowly accrued to it since 1789. There are only two really sacred things in America: one is the flag, the other is the White House. Nothing about this state of affairs would have gratified the Founding Fathers, who had no intention of setting up a monarch of any kind. Yet the institution they actually created has proved too strong for their philosophy (which held that the executive ought to come a decided second to the legislature, and expressed itself by putting the President in the second Article of the Constitution, the Congress in the first); and its glamorous example has of late filled the world with imitations.

If the Founding Fathers did not anticipate the spectacular development of the Presidency and pooh-poohed the warnings of those who feared the worst, they did provide institutions to keep it in check. 'Checks and balances' was a notion particularly associated with John Adams and his book; but it very well expressed the universal assumption. Power was too tempting to fallen man; the exercise of power must never be free from question, debate, exposure, possible defeat. Indeed, it was too likely that any exercise of power would lead to evil: quite as much as Lord Acton did the Fathers believe that 'power tends to corrupt'. So they piled check on balance, balance on check, until they arrived at what Richard Hofstadter so felicitously termed 'a harmonious system of mutual frustration'.[14] When Jefferson, back from France to be the first Secretary of State (foreign minister), asked Washington why the convention had thought a Senate necessary, the President in turn asked him why he tipped his coffee from his cup into his saucer. 'To cool it.' 'Even so we pour legislation into the senatorial saucer to cool it.' In practice the Senate has cooled the President: since every proposal he wants to get through the House of Representatives has also to pass the Senate. Two chambers make Presidential usurpation more than twice as difficult. The Constitutional convention expressly conferred the power to declare war on the Congress, and although the evolution of war in the industrial age has made this power increasingly nominal, the power of the purse, by which Congress alone can vote the money to pay for wars and armies, has meant that the President has always had to try to take Congress into partnership on foreign and military policy, or face calamitous consequences. And no treaty can come into effect until it has been ratified by two-thirds of the Senators present. Domestic legislation is peculiarly the province of Congress; and the power of Congressional investigation and review means that the executive always has to bear the views of Capitol Hill in mind. Since it is through their Representatives and Senators in Congress assembled that the views, ambitions, prejudices, passions and ideals of the ordinary American people most regularly make themselves felt in modern

14 Richard Hofstadter, *The American Political Tradition* (New York, 1948, Vintage edn), p. 9.

Washington, this is all to the good, as otherwise the President would tend to be over-impressed by the fact that he was elected to office by a large number of his fellow-citizens (not always, or even, of late years, often, a majority of those citizens who actually vote, and very seldom a majority of those citizens with the right to vote, since American voter turnout nowadays is low compared with that in other democracies).

The most impressive and original of the checks and balances is to be found elsewhere, in the courts, in the institutional doctrine known as 'judicial supremacy', or, in other words, the maxim that the Constitution is what the Supreme Court says it is. This was something entirely new.

Yet the legal tradition which the Constitution enshrines was the most English thing about the whole document; and intimations of judicial review – that is to say, of the role of the courts in deciding whether a given law or action is legal or constitutional – abounded in the earlier eighteenth century; the most famous English case being Camden's finding in favour of Wilkes in the general warrants judgement, and the most famous American case, perhaps, being Thomas Hutchinson's finding in the opposite sense in the matter of writs of assistance in 1761. The English-speaking world in the eighteenth century rang with appeals to the rights of men and Englishmen, and to the Anglo-Saxon Constitution; who but judges learned in the law could deal with such appeals in the last resort? The pre-eminence of statute law, though a thing accomplished, was not yet a thing generally acknowledged; indeed, the chief eighteenth-century legal monument is Blackstone's *Commentaries*, a panegyric on the common law that was intensely popular in America; and the common law is essentially judge-determined law.

This was the background; but as usual the members of the convention had more practical concerns at the forefront of their minds. They were anxious to entrench the judiciary in the political process, seeing the judges, rightly, as pillars of the settled order of things; but in the end caution, common sense and their own disagreements led them to abandon the idea of setting up a Constitutional Council of Revision, in which the President and the Supreme Court together would have passed on the constitutionality of the laws proposed by Congress. Indeed, so cautious were they that although they clearly understood the idea of judicial review, they refrained from mentioning it in the Constitution; its inevitability and desirability were first brought out by Hamilton in *The Federalist*. The utmost the Founding Fathers did was to declare (Art. VI, sec. 2) that the Constitution and treaties made under its authority were 'the supreme law of the land'. The wise might well infer that a law must be interpreted by judges, to be effected, and imposed by their decisions; the matter remained to be spelled out, the theory to be tested.

This was first done twelve years after the Constitution came into operation, in the case of *Marbury* v. *Madison*.

One of John Adams's last actions as President was to appoint John

Marshall Chief Justice of the United States; he also appointed members of his party to a dozen other judgeships that had just been created. The incoming Secretary of State, none other than James Madison, found these lesser judges' appointment warrants waiting on his desk; he refused to deliver them (since the judges were all his political opponents) and so the judges could not take up their appointments. One of them, William Marbury, sued for his job; and the case eventually came up before the Supreme Court. The Court found in favour of Madison; and Chief Justice Marshall wrote the opinion explaining why. The law under which Marbury sued, he declared, was unconstitutional.

The politics of the problem need not concern us; what remains important about Marshall's opinion in *Marbury* v. *Madison* is that he took the opportunity of laying down the principles of judicial review and judicial supremacy.

It is emphatically the province and duty of the judicial department to say what the law is. Those who apply the rule to particular cases must of necessity expound and interpret that rule. If two laws conflict with each other, the courts must decide on the operation of each. So if a law be in opposition to the constitution; if both the law and the constitution apply to a particular case . . . the court must determine which of these conflicting rules governs the case. This is of the very essence of judicial duty.

He thus made the Supreme Court the umpire of the Constitution. President Jefferson and Secretary Madison, who were rather more radical in 1801 than they had been in 1787, greatly disliked this doctrine; but they could not very well fight it, since it was embodied in a decision in their own favour. So the Supreme Court got away with its claim, a claim that was reinforced by the line of further important decisions that Marshall wrote in the rest of his long tenure of the Chief Justiceship (1801–33).

The consequences of all this can hardly be overstated. Again and again the Supreme Court has used its power to change the course of American history. The results have not always been acceptable. For instance, next to *Marbury*, the most famous Supreme Court decision was that in the case of *Dred Scott* v. *Sanford* (1857) when the justices rashly declared, not only that the slave Dred Scott had not been freed by being taken through a free state, but that the Missouri Compromise of 1820 was unconstitutional.[15] This enraged the North, and was one of the chief incidents which brought on the Civil War. Later in the nineteenth century the Court, by its decisions, hampered the struggle of labour against capital, legitimized racial segregation and disallowed a federal income tax. It made a cult of property, and showed a perverse ingenuity in twisting the meaning of the law to help the rich. It learned the error of its ways during the Presidency of Franklin Roosevelt, but during the years immediately following the Second World

15 See below, p. 306.

War it disgraced itself again by its acquiescence in the unjust, cruel and absurd anti-communist witch-hunt. However, under the leadership of Earl Warren (Chief Justice 1953–69) it reversed itself and became the most effective opponent of the witch-hunt.

On the whole the record since 1801 has been enormously impressive. 'Checks and balances' have been maintained and extended. Cynics have always been found to remark that 'the Supreme Court follows the election returns' (not necessarily a bad thing in a democracy) but they have usually exaggerated. The Supreme Court's chief task, perhaps, like that of any such body, has been, acting as the place of last resort, to uphold and clarify the law and maintain the high standards of the legal profession; but in its heroic periods it has also acted as the chief guarantee that the ideals of the American Revolution should never be abandoned.

Those ideals, as George Mason tried to point out to the impatient Fathers, were not completely expressed in the original document. However, the anti-Federalists, as we have seen, made their case for a Bill of Rights; and one was duly added to the Constitution, in the form of ten amendments, during the first years of the new government. The amendments looked after the rights and interests of the individual, as the earlier parts of the Constitution protected those of the national government and the states. The individual had not been wholly neglected in the original Constitution; nor were the rights of the states neglected in the amendments (they were strongly reasserted in the ninth and tenth of the list); but on the whole the emphasis fell on such things as freedom of speech, freedom of worship, freedom from cruel and unusual punishment, freedom from unreasonable searches and seizures,[16] freedom not to incriminate oneself. Like the main part of the Constitution these articles expressed a fundamental part of what the American Revolutionaries had fought for. They were not only democrats, in the sense that they believed in the rights of the people, as opposed to kings and nobles; they were liberals, in the sense that they believed in the inalienable rights proclaimed in the Declaration of Independence – and now these rights were spelled out. The right of revolution was tacitly dropped: the process of Constitutional amendment was supposed to remove the need for any such doctrine.[17] No President since Jefferson has believed that a revolution every twenty years is a good thing; and it is not clear that even Jefferson was dissatisfied with revolution through the voting-booth. The right to individual property was so intrinsically part of eighteenth-century thought that it was not made explicit in the Constitution, or even

16 This is a provision of the Fourth Amendment. It well illustrates the extent to which experience shaped the political thought of the Revolution, and, consequently, the Constitution. The authors of the Fourth Amendment wanted to avert any recurrence of the threat posed by writs of assistance.

17 The last President to reaffirm the right of revolution, so far as I know, was Abraham Lincoln in his first inaugural (1861). But although he affirmed the right, his whole argument was against the proposed exercise of it by the South.

in the Bill of Rights; but it is hard to see how it can be much endangered while the ten great amendments are enforced. For they are predicated on the assumption that the pursuit of happiness is effective only if the individual has the means to defend his interests through the press, the churches and the courts, as well as through the political process; and it is impossible to see how, in a society so organized, a citizen can lose the right to his economic independence (the power to maintain it is another matter) – which is what the eighteenth century really understood by property. In short, the Bill of Rights puts a sharp limit to the legitimate claims on the citizen of government, majority, minority and collectivity of any sort; given the immense conformist pressures that have from time to time built up in America, this has been just as well. True, the courts have not always interpreted and enforced the Bill of Rights as, today, we may think they should have done (a glaring case was the persecution of Japanese-American citizens during the Second World War); but there would have been far fewer victories for the ordinary man or woman without the Bill; and, at least since 1953, it has been the foundation for most of the solid advances towards greater liberty which American society has made. Given the grim record of so many other twentieth-century governments, of a world in which, for example, cruel punishments are so very usual, this is no small praise. The principle of checks and balances thus continues to flower; it continues to give us good reason to honour the men of the American Revolution; in a way, it defines what is politically best and most promising in the United States; what it means to be American.

The Constitution as it emerged between 1787 and 1791 crowned the American Revolution and provided a safe compass for the future. In theory, it settled all those problems – whether of taxation; of foreign relations; of collective duties and individual rights; of political and legal organization – which had proved so intractable that they had brought about the downfall of the old British Empire. It strongly resembled the old order to which Americans, as inheritors of English traditions and settlers in a wilderness, were accustomed; but it had eliminated from that order all those features which seemed obsolete or unjust in the New World. The political thought on which it was based was realistic, accepting that men were not angels, but that their aspirations were mostly legitimate, and it was the business of the political framework to give them scope. Liberty and law were its two inescapable guiding lights; as understood by the Founding Fathers they have served America pretty well. One thing the Constitution could not provide of itself: permanence. The world – not just America – was on the brink of an age of tumultuous change; of accelerated evolution. Madison was properly confident that the instrument which he and his colleagues had devised could ride any storm; but the will to work it had to be there, and the intelligence to supplement and amend it when necessary. During the next eighty years both will and intelligence were at times to falter; the vessel nearly foundered. Such is the process examined in the next book of this history. Yet even with that thought in mind it seems best to end this section by pointing once more to the astonishing fact that so wise and effective a settlement emerged from thirty years of revolution; and to the equal marvel of its adaptability. The new order has not gone the way of the old; the sun which Franklin hailed has not set. No other revolution, worthy of the name, has ended so happily.

BOOK THREE

The Age of Equality

I know of no country where the conditions for effecting great changes in the settled order of things, for the development of right ideas of liberty and humanity, are more favourable than here in these United States.

Frederick Douglass, 1857

12 The Planting of the West

Oh don't you remember sweet Betsy from Pike
  Who crossed the big mountains with her lover Ike,
With two yoke of cattle, a large yellow dog,
  A tall Shanghai rooster, and one spotted hog;
  Saying, goodbye, Pike County, farewell for a while,
  We'll come back again when we've panned out our pile.

Folk song

By the Peace of Paris in 1783 the United States gained a vast domain in the West, which in the course of the next seventy years was to be extended as a great empire to the Pacific, dislodging the French and Spanish from North America and forestalling British designs on Oregon. The Land Ordinance and the North-West Ordinance had given it flexible and efficient machinery for governing and developing this empire, and in the Declaration of Independence and the United States Constitution it had two excellent manuals for governing itself. Unfortunately, as everybody knows, technical manuals will only take you so far. The Americans believed that their ideology and their institutions were better than adequate for any problems that might arise, but even if they were right they still had to learn how to apply them. In a sense, the rest of this history shows them learning; this chapter and the two which immediately follow it describe the process in its earliest days, when perhaps it was most important. The Americans were an imperial, westering people; democrats; liberals, many of whom were slave-holders; a nation of immigrants; part of a burgeoning industrial civilization. Any one of these traits would have exposed them and their beliefs to a severe testing. Together, they produced a ferment so remarkable, and so nearly ruinous, as to make the nineteenth century even more dramatic and revolutionary than the eighteenth. The story is best told one theme at a time, beginning with the earliest, the movement west; for in ways which will be shown it largely conditioned everything that followed.

A great change overtook the Americans in the years after 1789; a change as profound in its consequences as the Revolution itself. Previously their society had looked seawards. Every settlement in the New World had depended for success on finding functions in the great Atlantic economy of seaborne trade. Maritime links were to remain strong during the nineteenth century, but their controlling importance soon ended. Until 1815 the leaders of the republic were still defensively preoccupied with Europe; but more and more their fellow-citizens looked westwards. They felt the pull of the land.

Of course it had always been there, that vast, tempting, unexplored wilderness; but until the late eighteenth century the advance upon it had necessarily been slow. Demography, politics, diplomacy, economics, technology and the Indians had seen to that. By the second quarter of the nineteenth century the balance had tipped dramatically to the other side, and the race for the Rockies and the Pacific was fairly begun. With it also began the great age of the Wild West.

Here a difficulty arises. The legend of the West, the Matter of America, is that country's greatest gift to the imagination of the world, and a historian neglects imagination only at excessive cost. So it must be acknowledged that somewhere in everyone's dreams Sulky Sam Snake, the fastest gun in Rattlesnake County, wearing a black hat, is cheating at poker in the Crooked Dollar Saloon. Diamond Lil looks over his shoulder. Meanwhile James Stewart, in a white hat, rides into town, a tin star twinkling on his chest. Elsewhere smoke rises off the mesa: the Apache have bad hearts, and are preparing to attack Fort Laramie, residence of a golden-haired heroine in a grey print dress. A thin blue line of US cavalry rides to the rescue. Elsewhere again, the wagon train crosses the Divide by South Pass: looking back east you can just see Natty Bumppo disappearing into the forest. Cowboys, the great drive over, whoop it up, more than ready for Lil and the Crooked Dollar. Someone, somewhere, is picking out 'I ride an old paint' on a mouth-organ. Frankie and Johnny are lovers.

Yet unchecked legend is the greatest enemy of historical truth. The precious insights it conveys are all too easily lost in fantasy, irrelevance and downright falsification. Epic takes space that ought to be devoted to statistics. Its glamour very frequently obscures the less showy but even more moving record of what really happened. American historians of the West perhaps enjoyed their subject too much. They have not always been careful to make the necessary distinction between the West as a point of the compass, as a certain region of the United States, and the moving West of the past – the West of exploration and settlement, that began at Jamestown and crept across the continent in the following centuries: the so-called frontier. Their works have been rich in suggestions and richer still in information; but they have not always avoided the trap of implying that the frontier was always much the same, from century to century; or the opposite error, that it was entirely different from generation to generation, region to region. There was uniformity; there was diversity; continuity and new departures. Both must be brought home to the understanding, for otherwise legend prevails.

The complexity of the real frontier experience can perhaps be most easily conveyed through sketches of the true life stories of half a dozen legendary Western leaders. Their biographies do not by any means include all aspects of the development of the American Empire; but in limited space it is impossible to deal completely with so huge a topic. We must be content with such drama and such truths as these lives can convey. Let us begin with Daniel Boone, the Long Hunter; for as he himself remarked, 'the history of the western country has been my history'.

He was born of Quaker parents in 1734, and although, once he had reached manhood, he stopped going to meetings, or indeed to any church, that particular religious background perhaps in part explains the notable patience and serenity of his character. More certainly, his life's course was shaped by a certain restlessness that seems to have been native to all the enormous tribe of Boones, and by an upbringing on the Pennsylvania frontier. He learned farming as a boy, but his natural instrument was the American long rifle, developed for the needs of frontiersmen by German gunsmiths in south-eastern Pennsylvania. Boone was from the first a marvellous shot. He was fascinated by the local Indians – they were Shawnees, a tribe he was to spend many years fighting – and learned his phenomenal woodcraft from them; they called him Wide Mouth. He became a hunter. When he was in his teens his father, having quarrelled with the Quakers, sold his farm and set off down the Great Valley of the Appalachians, a course taken by tens of thousands in the mid-eighteenth century. The land dictated which way he should go, as it had dictated to the beasts and the Indians before. The mountains lie on a slanting axis: the Boones soon discovered that the easiest road and the best land lay always to the south-west. Presently they reached the Yadkin river in North Carolina and settled. There, at the age of twenty-two, Daniel married.

But first he had an adventure. In 1755, the year before his wedding, he went, as did the young George Washington, with General Braddock's army to attack the French Fort Duquesne at the forks of the river Ohio. The expedition was a frightful failure: Braddock, ignoring all warnings, walked into an ambush and, with most of his men, was killed. Boone, serving as a waggoner ('teamster', in American English) had a narrow escape. But the direction of his life was settled: he had gone into the country beyond the mountains for the first time. In 1758 he went there again with the expedition that avenged Braddock and founded Fort Pitt (soon to be Pittsburgh) on the site of Duquesne. He did not forget.

He tried hard to settle down as a farmer on the Yadkin. Life was anything but dull. Indian raids had to be fought off during the Cherokee War, and afterwards he and his fellow-citizens had a sore struggle to restore order to a countryside stiff with horse-thieves and other robbers, oppressed also by

4. *The expansion westward*

corrupt government and crooked lawyers. This was the seedbed of the Regulator movement,[1] but Boone began to hold himself aloof. For him, the lure of the dark woods was paramount: he was forever prowling off along the trails after bear and buckskin, to the neglect of his family and his business. Small debts accumulated. He involved himself with an ambitious land speculator, one Richard Henderson, who had dreams of founding a proprietorial colony in 'Transylvania' across the Appalachians. He made an excursion down to Florida, newly annexed to the British Empire, but decided that he preferred the West. By 1767 his restlessness was too much for him: he set out to cross the mountains into the longed-for Kentucky.[2]

He was unlucky in the course he took. The uplands of eastern Kentucky and Tennessee are poor farming country: their only wealth is coal, which Boone did not know about and could not have used if he had. He saw, killed and ate his first buffalo (the liver, raw, and the hump, roasted, were reckoned to be particular delicacies on the frontier) but the hills were covered with a tangled forest of laurel. In the spring of 1768 he gave up the struggle and went home.

In 1769, with Henderson's financial backing, he tried again, and this time, guided by an old frontier pedlar, his party found the Cumberland Gap, the all-important, relatively easy route through the last eastward barrier of the Appalachians. A broad south–north valley (Boone approached it from what is now Tennessee) sloping gently up and down, ten miles long (1,665 feet or so above sea-level), it cut through the Cumberland mountains to the crossing of the Cumberland river. Others had seen it before Boone (the Indians called it Ouasioto) but none had made much use of their discovery. Now came the pathfinder: not the first, but the best explorer. Boone, though he did not know it, was pioneering a trail (not for the last time) along which, eventually, enormous numbers of settlers would pour. They would call it Boone's Trace, or the Wilderness Road. For twenty years it would remain the same boggy, rocky, narrow, tortuous path that he hacked out of the forest in 1775: passable only by pack-horses and travellers on foot.

In 1769, once past the Gap, Boone followed an Indian trail which skirted the laurel jungle and led to the great Kentucky bottomlands of which he had heard. Lying on either side of the river Kentucky, which flows north into the Ohio, these lands had already been colonized by another arrival from Europe – the famous bluegrass, *phleum pratense*, a native British plant. If the *Narrative* of Boone's adventures is to be trusted – and though not written by him, as it pretends, it is based on information that he supplied – it was then that he fell in love with the country. He passed through the forest noting only the beauty of its fruits, leaves and flowers, and the abundance of its game, especially the wild turkeys; coming to the bluegrass, he was amazed by the vast droves of buffalo feeding in the meadows; his

1 See above, p. 153.
2 The name is apparently derived from the Iroquois, *Kanta-ke*, 'great meadow'.

trained frontiersman's eye told him how good the soil was. He ignored the innumerable biting insects. He was intensely happy. He spent the next few years exploring the entire region, until he knew it intimately. He had many escapes and adventures, of which the best to tell is perhaps that in which some Indians stalk and trap him on the edge of a high cliff. He jumps out of their clutches into the air, landing sixty feet lower down in the topmost branches of a maple tree.[3] His knowledge of the back-country became famous, and many settlers were willing to follow him; but the Indian menace was daunting. In 1773, when he tried to lead a party into Kentucky, it was ambushed, his eldest son James was cruelly killed, and the party hurried back in dismay to the Yadkin. Only in 1775, after Henderson had bought off the Cherokees with trade goods and whisky, was the way open; but chief Oconostota took Boone by the hand and warned him: 'Brother, we have given you a fine land, but I believe you will have much trouble in settling it.' Boone said later that these words often came back to him in the next twenty years, for the war for the conquest of Kentucky and Ohio was the longest and bloodiest of all the struggles between the Americans and the Indians. But in 1775 Boone, his family and other pioneers pressed up the Wilderness Road until in April they reached the banks of the Kentucky, where they founded the fort and village of Boonesborough.

Even in this Boone was not quite the first: a little place called Harrodstown (today, Harrodsburg) had already been founded not far away by settlers coming down the Ohio. It was in the years to come that he earned his unique fame. They were years of battle, when the Shawnee Indians fought to retain their hunting-grounds and got plentiful assistance from the British, fighting to retain their Empire. At times the pitiful line of wilderness settlements was all that stood between the enemy and the fat back-country of Virginia and the Carolinas, and but for Boone's cool courage, dauntless leadership and unmatched woodcraft the settlements would have been wiped out. They came near to it when Boone was captured by the Shawnees; but instead of killing him the old Shawnee chief, Black Fish, adopted him, under the name of Big Turtle, as his son. Boone had to go naked (save for a loin-cloth), shave his head (save for a scalp-lock), paint his face and wait for months; but in the end he was able to escape from his captors and carry warning to Boonesborough that an attack was imminent. He compelled the demoralized and disorganized settlers to prepare their defences, so that when the siege came the Indians were finally beaten back, though it was a close thing.

Then, incredibly, Boone was court-martialled on charges of treachery. He was said to have secretly aided the Indians, and to be a British agent. It was the first of a long series of insults that he was to receive at the hands of the Kentuckians who owed him so much. He was acquitted, but the

3 Unfortunately John Mack Faragher, Boone's latest and best biographer, does not accept this story.

incident dramatizes the fact that Boone was a divided soul, like so many of those who first opened up the wilderness. He wanted to be rich in land, chiefly for his wife and children's sake; he sought out good acreage on the frontier as eagerly as anyone, and knew that it could only be secured from the Indians by a mass movement of population; so he led his countrymen through the Cumberland Gap. But at the same time he was in love with the untouched wild; happiest when, clad in deerskin shirt and moccasins, he was stalking deer, bear or buffalo, his rifle ready to his hand, his senses alert for any sign of Indian danger. He was, by instinct, more than half an Indian himself: the settlers sensed this and disliked him for it. The filling up of the new country, which he did so much to further (not least by killing off the game) was always a sad process for Boone, and he never made any money by it, being an extremely poor businessman. Kentucky appointed him a colonel in her militia, named a county after him, made him a territorial legislator, granted him wide lands – and then stripped him of them. Neither decency nor gratitude deterred the land sharks who poured into the region before and after it became a state of the Union in 1792; by systematically exploiting their influence, the uncertainties of land-surveying, and the inexactitude of legal records, they were able to rob Boone of every acre and then claim that he was still their debtor.

By 1799 the old hero had had enough: he left Kentucky in a dugout canoe, vowing never to return, and settled across the Mississippi under Spanish suzerainty, bringing with him a large party, which gained him an award of 9,000 acres from the Spanish government, in a form of head-right. He was thus one of the founders of Missouri, as formerly of Kentucky; and as in Kentucky he soon lost everything after the area became part of the United States in 1804. But he proved amazingly resilient. His children were able to support him, and old though he was, he could still, for some years, explore. He travelled and trapped far up the river Missouri, and died happy, at the age of eighty-five, in 1820.

Boone had long since become a legend, one which reached Europe, where Byron put him into some stirring stanzas of *Don Juan*. Fenimore Cooper, the first great American novelist, assimilated his fictional hero, Natty Bumppo, to what he knew of Boone. As self-sufficient master of the forest trails, he still haunts the American imagination, and his pithy sayings still have power: 'I wouldn't give a hoot in hell for a man who isn't sometimes afraid. Fear's the spice that makes it interesting to go ahead.' And, when teaching his son deer-stalking: 'Wisdom comes by facing the wind. Fools let it carry them.'

Andrew Jackson[4] differed from Boone in everything save courage. After a wild year or two in North and South Carolina, passed in scraping a legal education and losing his small but useful inheritance at the race-track, he got himself appointed, in 1788, at the age of twenty-one, public prosecutor in

4 We have met him before: see above, pp. 178 and 184.

the trans-Appalachian province of North Carolina. This was an immensely significant step. It illustrates the rapid emergence of a new ruling group in the West. Jackson was the son of one of the many Ulstermen[5] who, driven out of Ireland by oppressive English policies, landed at Philadelphia and found their way down the Great Valley of the Appalachians as the Boones had done. But the Irish had none of the craving for the woods that marked Daniel Boone (Andrew Jackson's only recorded aesthetic emotion was his admiration of British army drill as displayed before the Battle of New Orleans): they settled together in the back-country, and as one rose to fame and fortune he pulled up all his cousins with him. That was how Jackson got his job: thanks to his more prosperous relations he moved in influential circles, where he made a friend of the judge who was to be his superior officer in the West, a young fellow not much older than himself. Together they rode through the Cumberland Gap. Already Kentucky, to the north, was too full and competitive a place for a beginner; besides, it belonged to Virginia: Carolina connections would have been no good there. So Jackson was happy to head west along the newly opened Cumberland Road to Nashville, Tennessee. Apart from a hot temper, a steely will and a sort of shrewdness that was half intuition, half common sense, his only assets were a girl slave he had bought for $200, a saddle-bag full of elementary law books, and his friends. The combination did not fail him, the less so as he promptly married into the dominant clan at Nashville. It was a marriage of love, not uncomplicated by drama, for Jackson's Rachel had to be rescued by divorce from an unhappy marriage before she could become Mrs Jackson, and in the process she unintentionally committed bigamy, a misfortune that was to be the cause of much suffering to both man and wife in the years to come. The fact remains that by his marriage Jackson painlessly made the transition from one burgeoning aristocracy to another. He lived hard for most of his life, but he never lived small.

He was a second-wave frontiersman. He got his start in the West by exploiting his connections. He was paid for his labours as public prosecutor with deeds to public lands – in effect, in paper money, for he could not possibly develop all the thousands of acres involved by himself; he would have to sell most of his holdings and live off the proceeds. He proved an adroit businessman for some years, buying and selling land and slaves; then he decided to set up as a merchant. That was a potentially lucrative line. Manufactured goods came west over the mountains from New York, Philadelphia, Baltimore or Charleston to the Ohio and Tennessee valleys; there they were exchanged for Western farm produce (flour, whisky, tobacco) which in turn was transmitted, in flatboats or keelboats, down the Mississippi to New Orleans, to join Louisiana sugar in shipments from that rising port. The final stretch of this Circular Trade took Western produce to the East Coast cities. Unluckily for Jackson he exchanged his title deeds

5 Invariably called Scotch-Irish by American historians.

not for cash but for the notes of a Philadelphia merchant who failed, leaving Jackson with heavy debts which he could pay only by sacrificing his store. After that, for many years, he contrived to keep afloat financially only by breeding racehorses.

In other respects he was fortunate. When the Cumberland region was admitted to the Union in 1796 as the state of Tennessee, Jackson served as its first Representative in Congress and then as a Senator. Young, well connected and justly respected for his energy and ability, his only weakness seemed to be a propensity for fighting duels in defence of his wife's honour ('Great God! Do you mention *her* sacred name?') which Rachel would much rather he had avoided. He served as a judge for some years, with great success ('Do what is *right* between these parties,' he used to tell juries, idealistically, 'that is what the law always *means*'); on his Nashville plantation, the Hermitage, he grew cotton, as everyone was beginning to do; above all, he turned himself into a soldier by years of service as a militia general. The militia was a good route to influence and popularity: its musters provided much-needed social entertainment, and there were perpetual scuffles with the Indians throughout this period in Tennessee, in which many bold men earned reputations for courage. What is striking about Jackson is that he was not content with these easy triumphs or with the elementary knowledge of military science and discipline that was all most militiamen bothered to acquire. He studied books on the art of war more carefully than, in his youth, he had studied his law books. He came of the same stock as the Duke of Wellington, and his blood was beginning to have its way with him.

His chance arrived in 1812, when the Creek Indians, under the prodding of Tecumseh, went to war, just as war again broke out between the United States and Great Britain. Jackson quickly proved himself to be the ablest of the American generals, and the most successful. He marched against the Creeks. An attack of agonizing dysentery was not allowed to stop him, and he exacted similar resolution from his soldiers, who consequently nicknamed him after the toughest wood they knew – 'Old Hickory' – which stuck to him for the rest of his life. He crushed the Indians in battle, despite the best efforts of slothful, incompetent politicians and suppliers to prevent him; and in the subsequent peace treaty, the harshest ever made with the Indians, he not only stripped the Creeks of half their lands, but wrenched great tracts away from tribes who had actually fought on his side. The Indians called him Sharp Knife after that, but the Western settlers, to whom he had opened half Alabama and large stretches of Mississippi and Georgia, applauded him. When later he bid at public auction for some of the lands in the area no one would bid against him, and he got them at the lowest possible rate (the contrast with Daniel Boone's fate is cruel).

Next, President James Madison made him a major-general in the regular army; as such it fell to him to defend the South-West against British attack. Again he performed brilliantly. The British were preparing to capture New Orleans. Jackson mounted an effective defence; he was greatly helped by the British commander, one Pakenham, the Duke of Wellington's brother-in-law, who would have been perfectly at home in Flanders during the First World War. He devised a magnificent plan of attack that had the single disadvantage of being unworkable; then he hurled his devoted troops against Jackson's well-prepared trenches. All the Americans had to do was to shoot down the assailants as they came. The two armies were roughly equal in size (each had approximately 5,000 men). Total casualties were less symmetrically proportioned. Pakenham (who was himself killed) lost 291 killed, 1,262 wounded and 484 missing. Jackson lost thirteen killed, thirty-nine wounded and nineteen missing. The British crawled off to the safety of their ships, and America rejoiced. What did it matter that the Battle of New Orleans (9 January 1815) was fought after the signing of the Peace of Ghent, which ended the war on 24 December 1814? The latest British assault on the integrity of the United States had ended as ludicrously as the earlier ones: Old Hickory had given Wellington's veterans bloody noses. From now on Jackson could do no wrong in the eyes of most of his countrymen.

The myth that grew up round him was a most revealing distortion of the reality. He was seen as a child of nature, a wild man of the woods, a spontaneous untutored American democrat, splendidly victorious over an effete European aristocrat. Later on, when popular enthusiasm and cunning organization swept him into the White House, he was seen as the leader of a great democratic uprising against the oligarchs of the East. In fact Jackson was an oligarch himself; he was by temperament an autocrat; and as I have said, had made a serious study of the profession of arms. His restless ambition for fame and fortune were counterbalanced by a kind heart and a certain simplicity of character where women were concerned: he had a Quixotic belief in their chaste perfections. But none of this justifies his legend. True, he had an Irish contempt for correct spelling, but it is absurd to describe this lawyer, businessman, politician, military administrator and planter as illiterate (it is still sometimes done): he probably spent more time at his desk than on horseback. His political views were far too inconsistent to make him a convincing ideological leader as Jefferson and Hamilton had been, and as Lincoln was to be. He was a stout nationalist because he had fought the British and the Indians. He approved of the loose political structure of the West because it suited him: it had eased his rise to affluence and power, and he hoped it would do the same for other poor men in their turn. He distrusted Eastern merchants and politicians because he suspected (with some reason) that they were unwilling to share their wealth and authority with new men from the frontier. His experience as a trader had left him with a deep suspicion of paper money and the banks which printed it: a prejudice that was neither universal nor uncommon on the frontier, and one which would eventually change the economic history of the United States. He had no objection to robbing red men of their lands or black men of their liberty, but regarded himself as a friend of both races.

In spite of his beginnings, he was no backwoodsman. Rather, he was one of the land speculators who dislodged the backwoodsmen and tried to reproduce the political and social structure of old Virginia in the new country. Fatally, he was a large slave-holder. It was men like him, dominating frontier politics, exploiting their public position to seize the best lands for cultivation by slave labour, who dislodged thousands of small white farmers and sent them drifting off north and north-west in search of a better frontier. It seemed that flush times had come for good to the South-West. As an insatiable demand for cotton made itself felt in the world market (Lancashire was launching the Industrial Revolution by making cotton goods by steam, in factories) the Circular Trade was mightily stimulated. The long-fibre cotton of the Carolina Sea Islands was in great demand; and in 1793 Eli Whitney, a New Englander visiting Georgia, invented an improved cotton gin which made it much easier to separate the seed from the fluff of the short-fibre cotton which was all that could be grown in the vast Southern interior. For great planters like Jackson a golden age was at hand. What did it matter if small men found it difficult to stay afloat? In 1814 cotton sold at 15 cents a pound, and only 146,000 bales were produced (a bale weighed 500 lb.). Two years later cotton sold at just under 30 cents a pound, and 259,000 bales were produced: that year, the crop was worth $38 million, or nearly four times what it had been in 1814. Never again until the Civil War was the price of raw cotton to be so high, and in one catastrophic year, 1845, it was to go as low as 5½ cents; but though such fluctuations could be excessively painful, they scarcely mattered, in the not very long run, compared to the immense increase in the cotton harvest and the ease with which it was marketed. In 1820, 335,000 bales were produced, worth $28 million; in 1830, 732,000 bales, worth $36 million; in 1840, 1,348,000 bales, worth $60 million; in 1850, 2,136,000 bales, worth $131 million. Such a rising curve of income and production seemed fully to justify the South's self-confidence, and it mightily stimulated the transformation of the wilderness. In 1811, for instance, the first steamboat on Western waters was launched; and soon myriads of them hurried up and down the Mississippi as best they could (their course often being impeded by sandbanks, floating timber, and exploding boilers), carrying cotton and the imports that it earned.

No wonder that the cotton lords were confident (though before the end of his life Jackson began to wonder if dependence on one crop made any better sense in Tennessee than it had in Virginia). Yet the South-West eventually lost more than it could possibly gain by the westward movement of the plantation system. It was not only that the planters staked the future on a single card. It was not only that they squeezed so many ordinary people out of their native section[6] and into anti-slavery, though that was to prove

6 The word *section* has three connotations in American history, which must not be confused: (i) the strictest: a *section* under the land survey regulations – see above, p. 192; (ii) the geographical: when writers use terms such as the *South Atlantic section* or the *South Central*

bad enough, from their point of view, for one of their victims was Thomas Lincoln of Kentucky, who migrated first to Indiana and then to Illinois. His father, Abraham, had been a friend of Daniel Boone. His son, also Abraham (1809–65), was to be the nemesis of almost everything that Jackson stood for, except his nationalism, thus avenging the Long Hunter. The heart of the tragedy was that the cotton plantation tied the South-West to the South-East, so that the poison of race-hatred and class exploitation, with their fatal train of violence, backwardness and corruption, spread westward and condemned an otherwise buoyant and promising region to prolonged defeat.

Those southern yeomen who were not content to be shouldered onto the poorest lands of Trans-Appalachia either crossed the Mississippi, as Boone had done, or headed for the Old North-West, as it came to be called: Ohio, Indiana, Illinois, Michigan, Wisconsin – the area covered by the North-West Ordinance of 1787. There they met another stream of the displaced, coming west from New England.

Times were hard in that province throughout the years of the French wars, and afterwards. The towns on the seaboard did well enough; indeed, in the early years of the nineteenth century, even before the Peace of Ghent and all the more after it, American shipping rapidly overtook European and British, becoming the dominant mercantile fleet on the Atlantic until the Civil War and the rise of steam and iron. Even in the towns, the call of the frontier might suddenly be heard. 'One would think that Pawtucket offered as strong inducements, and as great facilities for industry as any place on the continent,' said the *Fall River Monitor* in 1830, shaking its head in wonder over the decision of some of the township's citizens to move to Illinois. Nineteen years later the lure of the gold-fields carried many Yankees to California. As the century wore on, many of the immigrants who landed at Boston or New York went straight on to the new country. But this drainage did not hamper urban growth. In Rhode Island, for instance, the urban population quadrupled between 1790 and 1840; in Massachusetts it more than quintupled in the same period. In both states the growth of rural population lagged: in Rhode Island it went up by only 11 per cent.

Life for the farmers of the backwoods in New England, particularly in western Massachusetts, upstate Connecticut and Vermont, was now becoming a desperate struggle to pick stones off the hillsides in an attempt to grow foodstuffs at prices which could compete with the produce of the lands coming into use in the West. Inevitably the attempt failed. Soon the forests and the deer were winning back the homesteads which had been wrested from the wilderness with such pains, while the New Englanders, with that hopefulness which characterized the American farmer until late

---

area they have the physical configuration of the United States in mind; (iii) the loosest: historical-political (with which this book is mostly concerned); 'the South', 'the Middle West', 'the West', 'New England' are *sections* in this sense.

in the nineteenth century, sought better lands and life elsewhere. 'Our New England prosperity and importance are dying away,' sighed Daniel Webster of Massachusetts (1782–1852), the section's rising statesman, in 1820. But he was wrong to lament, although sheep runs were replacing ploughed fields. The rise of the woollen industry meant that defeated Yankee farmers could sell their lands for a good price, and with the money build a Greater New England on the south shores of the Great Lakes. This had enormous consequences. No longer bottled up between the sea and the hills, the New England conscience, the New England way – Puritan religion and Yankee ingenuity – could now shape the whole future of America by their implacability, assiduity and intelligence. New England churches, white paint, wooden steeples and all; red-painted New England schoolhouses; seminaries and colleges on the New England model; family farms and businesses run on New England ideas of thrift – these (reinforced by similar traditions emanating from the Quaker state of Pennsylvania) soon marked the North-West even more deeply than the slave plantation was marking the South-West. The self-confidence of the section matched that of the great planters. These free farmers could imagine no better way of life.

It all seems so rapid and fated in retrospect, taking scarcely a generation. Yet it did not seem so at the time. For many, it was difficult to shake off a sense of failure, which first became pronounced, perhaps, when Shays's Rebellion collapsed. Many of these frontier Yankees – for example, those who had moved into the Green Hills between Massachusetts, New York, and New Hampshire, and there created the first post-Revolutionary state, Vermont – were as ill-educated as Daniel Boone himself, and far less well-adapted to their environment. Their ignorance made them easy prey for charlatans of all kinds, and their Puritan inheritance made it certain that the biggest field for charlatanry would be the religious one. The Bible retained all its old authority and fascination for these poor and anxious people, but they saw no harm in looking for additional revelations. Perhaps they needed religious reassurance all the more because they were uprooting themselves. At any rate, the years of the great exodus from New England were also the years of a new wave of religious enthusiasm. The flames of penitence and conversion, lit by urgent and dramatic preaching, flared over upstate New York[7] so often in these years that it became known as the Burned-Over District; not that the religious revival stayed within those bounds. It burned over into western Pennsylvania and into Ohio. It exploded in the South-West, touched off in part by a Presbyterian minister from Pennsylvania, James McGready: it was his example which led in 1801 to the first of the great camp-meetings, at Cane Ridge, Kentucky, where ten to twenty thousand people gathered for days at a time, to be stimulated by a team of preachers into religious delirium – everything from visions of

7 A glance at the map will show that upstate New York lay across the New England migrants' westward path.

heaven to barking like a dog. In Tennessee a minister was brave enough to call General Jackson to repent and be saved (the invitation was declined). The wave passed over the seaboard, north and south. In short, the phenomenon which had dismayed the respectable sixty or seventy years earlier was now renewed. To distinguish it from the Great Awakening it is known as the Great Revival.

In the Burned-Over District it produced a willingness to take up novel creeds that far outstripped the interest in Methodism and Presbyterianism of the earlier period. Joseph Dylks of Ohio proclaimed himself the Messiah and promised to found a holy city at Philadelphia. One of his followers discovered that Jesus Christ was a woman. Another prophet proposed to save the world by walking the streets of New York with a sword and a seven-foot ruler. John Chapman of Massachusetts (*c.* 1775–1847) took up the faith according to Emanuel Swedenborg, the eighteenth-century Swedish visionary. He hit on a highly original manner of diffusing it. He went off to the Old North-West and bought up odd corners of land, never more than an acre or two, here and there, which he planted with appleseeds and apple-slips. When his little orchards matured, he sold them; bought more land and more seeds; and, with what was left of the profits from these transactions, obtained and distributed Swedenborgian tracts. He did not have much success in converting his countrymen; but his gentle selflessness (spending nothing on himself, he went about in rags, with a tin dish for a hat) and, above all, his orchards won every heart on the frontier. It was so pleasant, after hacking your way through the wilderness, to arrive at your holding, where you expected nothing but back-breaking toil, to find well-grown apple-trees waiting for you. As a result, Chapman is immortal: his original name forgotten, he is known to every American child as the forest demi-god, Johnny Appleseed.

Of all these enthusiasts, Joseph Smith (1805–44) and his follower Brigham Young (1801–77) left the deepest mark on history. The Smiths and the Youngs were poor families from Vermont, who drifted like so many others into the Burned-Over District. There young Joseph Smith was visited by the angel Moroni[8] and given an account of the pre-Columbian history of North America which has not so far been confirmed by archaeology. More important, Moroni indicated that Smith was the Prophet of the Lord, destined to redeem the world. He led the Prophet to certain sheets of solid gold buried in a hill near Palmyra, NY, on which were inscribed the text of the *Book of Mormon*. Mormon, Moroni's father, had written in ancient Egyptian, but fortunately Smith (who had received only a minimal education) was given some angelic machinery which enabled him to translate his author into a quasi-Biblical English disfigured by anachronisms. Eleven admirers (including the Prophet's father and brothers) signed affidavits to the effect that they had seen the golden pages, and one of them actually

8 'I am not making this up, you know' (Miss Anna Russell, in her guide to Wagner's *Ring*).

mortgaged his farm to pay for the publication of the book, in July 1830, which Smith then began to peddle round the countryside. Previously it had come to him that the elect of God must gather themselves into a new church, in a new place, under one leadership, turning their backs on the Gentiles, to carry out Moroni's programme. On 6 April 1830 he founded the Church of Jesus Christ of the Latter-Day Saints, who are known to the rest of the world as Mormons. He soon made converts, among the earliest being Brigham Young and his family.

The church developed rapidly from these small, eccentric beginnings. Partly this was because Joseph Smith, in spite of many failings, was a religious genius, a man of huge creativity, who never let things get dull. Like all such leaders he assured his followers that they were the chosen people of God, which was excellent for their self-respect; he received a constant flow of divine revelations, and was forever creating new bodies of government, inspiration and privilege – the Twelve Apostles, led by Brigham Young, 'the Lion of the Lord', the Sons of Dan, the Council of Fifty. Even the doctrine of polygamy seems to have been introduced, in part, to keep the pot boiling. But more important than Smith's dynamism (and good looks) was the suitability of his new creed to the frontier society which gave it birth. *Mormon* had the answers to all the questions which tormented the pioneers. Most of the original converts, including Brigham Young, were barely literate, but they came from New England and had a deep respect for anything that could pass for learning or take on the authority of Scripture. It was therefore very necessary to found a new church on a new Testament. And this particular Testament ministered to the fact that although Americans of the time were enormously proud of their country, they also felt inferior when they heard about the history and achievements of the Old World. It was very soothing to be assured by Joseph Smith that the Garden of Eden had been in America – to be precise, in Missouri. Then, *Mormon* answered questions that many were asking. For instance, one of the Indian cultures of the pre-Columbian age had left huge sacred mounds as conspicuous monuments in the Ohio country. Settlers there were naturally curious, and as they had no means whatever of learning anything true about the history of the mounds, they invented various unsound theories. One, that the mounds were the work of a non-Indian race which had since vanished, found its way not only into the *Book of Mormon*, but into Alexis de Tocqueville's great commentary on American society, *Democracy in America*, which was published five years after *Mormon*, a work with which it otherwise has nothing in common.

It was also understandable that the Mormons went in for faith-healing. Medical science, even at the centre of civilization, was still in its infancy; in the American West it was almost non-existent. Yet people could not submit to pain and illness without a struggle; and it was natural for them to seek physical as well as spiritual salvation from their religion. This was the root of the Church of Christ, Scientist, founded in 1879 by Mary Baker Eddy

(1821–1910) as well as many other nineteenth-century experiments in alternative medicine. So it is not surprising that this movement found expression among the Mormons. Heber Chase Kimball, Young's brother-in-law, could cure the sick by sending them a handkerchief which he had blessed or by throwing his old cloak onto their beds. It was at least as much in order for him to do this as for more conventional practitioners to offer useless bleedings, purgings and pills. Indeed, a religion which did *not* offer medicines for the body as well as for the soul was not going to get very far.

Even polygamy, the most contentious of Mormon practices, should be looked at in the same light. The practice is quite unacceptable in an advanced society, such as the United States was becoming; but the old Puritan sexual morality had become an intolerable burden to many, and something had to be put in its place.[9] The literature of nineteenth-century America is suffused with sexual guilt and longing; significantly, one of its most powerful and convincing expressions, Nathaniel Hawthorne's *The Scarlet Letter* (published in 1850), is set in seventeenth-century Massachusetts. The misery caused to many by the iron code of Puritanism was an evil to be fought; and Joseph Smith, a decided womanizer, by heeding his own impulses and then universalizing them, opened the way to reform of a kind. It was not an easy victory. Brigham Young, for instance, longed for death when commanded by the Prophet to take extra wives to himself; but he got over the difficulty, and in the end was 'husband' to seventy women. Few other Saints approached such a total; the practice was generally condemned by the Gentiles (as non-Mormons were called); but given the frequent association at this time of religious and sexual radicalism, it cannot be doubted that this too, or something like it, was what many male Americans wanted. And virtuous New England wives and spinsters were amazingly ready to fall in with polygamy. Perhaps they too were tired of Bostonian sexual primness.

Polygamy remained a scandal nearly to the end of the nineteenth century; in the infancy of the church other accusations were heard. Yet they too show how much Mormonism was a thing of the frontier. Smith was said to be a swindler because in 1837 he established a Mormon bank which issued large quantities of virtually worthless bank notes. In January 1838 he had to flee from Ohio in the dead of night to escape his creditors; but if he was dishonest it was only in the fashion of the West, where everyone counted on getting rich so quickly that all promises would be redeemed without effort. Smith was one of hundreds who launched banks with insufficient capital. Like many others he fell a victim to the panic of 1837, which closed banks and shattered fortunes throughout the country. He had done his best for his followers. In the same way his deep involvement in the more squalid processes of American party politics, which ended as

9 Looked at in detail, the intricacies of Mormon polygamy strikingly resemble those of twentieth-century American divorce, especially as to wife-swapping.

disastrously as his financial speculations, may be excused: corruption, in a way, was only an extension of land speculation, and at first it rewarded the Mormons handsomely.

Land, indeed, was the key to Mormon success: land and organization. It was an egalitarian, democratic age, and at first sight the extremely autocratic rule of the Prophet was inconsistent with it; but in fact Smith's autocracy ensured that the Mormons would enjoy equality in the one respect that really mattered. This was still the People Greedily Grasping for Land. Mormon towns and villages were laid out by authority; Mormon business ventures were all co-operative; Mormons could have dealings with Gentiles only through the church. A Mormon settlement, in other words, was somewhat like a company town, the company being the hierarchy of apostles and bishops. Mormon discipline and unity created a monopoly. In the free-and-easy conditions of the frontier, where it was usually each man for himself, the operations of this phalanx of co-operative farmers were irresistible. The resultant prosperity naturally encouraged members of the church to convert others. Missionary work thus proved another strength, for promises were made which could be kept. As Brigham Young was to boast in 1855, after the settlement in Utah,

We have taken the poor and the ignorant from the dens and caves of the earth and brought them here, and we have laboured day and night, week after week, and year after year, to make ourselves comfortable, and to obtain all the knowledge there is in the world, and the knowledge that comes from God, and we shall continue to do so. We shall take the weak and the feeble and bring them up to the standard that God requires.

In 1838 Young carried this glad message to England, which like America was suffering from an economic crisis; he made many converts, and from then on a stream of recruits crossed the Atlantic. When they could not come immediately, they sent money. Either way, it was a welcome addition. In return, the converts got economic security for the first time in their lives. Here, once again, the influence of the time and place can be seen. Smith had picked up the communist ideas that were so popular among reform enthusiasts in the early nineteenth century. Not much good in that: the Pilgrim Fathers had tried to hold property in common and been beaten by the desire for individual property. So were most of the humanitarians and early socialists (among them the Welshman Robert Owen) who tried out their ideas in the American back-country. Mormon arrangements were more successful, by luck or by skill.

Or perhaps by persecution. The Mormons were extremely unpopular. Life on the frontier was dominated by the struggle for the best land: wherever the Latter-Day Saints appeared, the best land rapidly became theirs (rather as slave plantations competed successfully against free farmers in the South). Furthermore, Mormon practices revolted those whom they did not entrance.

Psychologically, the total surrender of the individual will to the church seemed deeply un-American.[10] Polygamy was immoral. Smith and Young seemed to be men whose capacity for deceiving themselves was only surpassed by their taste for deceiving others. As if all that were not enough, Mormons further affronted their neighbours by their total cynicism about democracy. This was the period when the American political system was maturing;[11] men took their duties and privileges as citizens very seriously. It was no light matter that the Mormons abandoned their political rights and freedoms to the Prophet, who sold their votes unscrupulously to political leaders, as if he were the boss of a late nineteenth-century city machine. When, for instance, the Mormons established themselves in Illinois, at the place on the Mississippi they named Nauvoo, Whigs and Democrats in the state legislature fell over themselves to grant a city charter and various unusual privileges, both parties hoping to get the solid block of Mormon votes in return.

That was in 1841. Before then the Saints, growing in numbers but not in acceptability, had wandered from the Burned-Over District to Kirtland, Ohio, and Jackson County, Missouri.[12] Wherever they went they met ferocious hostility; in Missouri, indeed, a state rent by violent passion on many issues (including slavery), there had been something like a miniature civil war: blood had been shed on both sides. Joseph Smith eventually cursed Jackson County, prophesying its destruction (a prophecy that came true during the great Civil War). Matters were soon as bad in Illinois. Nauvoo and its neighbourhood acquired a population of 25,000 Mormons who prospered exceedingly. They began to throw their weight around, politically, economically and morally: the secret of polygamy began to leak out. They formed their own militia, the Nauvoo Legion, answerable only to Smith, and a secret society, the Sons of Dan, not unlike a secret police or the Ku Klux Klan. The Gentiles resorted increasingly to violence, which reached a climax in the summer of 1844. Smith and his brother Hyrum were arrested for destroying the printing press of an apostate Mormon newspaper. They were thrown into jail and lynched there.

After that the feeling was that it was open season on the Mormons, and only their willingness to resist by force of arms taught their enemies a little prudence. Thanks to Brigham Young, who instantly asserted his authority

10 Similar tensions have arisen between American society and totalitarian sects in the twentieth century. The most appalling demonstration of the clash of values occurred in 1978. Jim Jones, the mad, charismatic leader of the People's Temple sect, which had left California to establish itself in Guyana, murdered an investigating Congressman; immediately afterwards all 900 members of the sect, on Jones's orders, committed suicide by ritually drinking lemonade laced with cyanide. Jones died with them.

11 See next chapter.

12 Jackson County is to be the gathering place of the Saints in the Last Days. They are commanded to build a temple there, in the chief town, Independence, which happens to be also the place where the Oregon and Santa Fe trails started, and where Harry Truman was born.

as Smith's *de facto* successor, the church stayed together, though there were some alarming defections. Yet if it remained at Nauvoo there would be war on the frontier. Closing ranks, the Saints ran dissidents out of town and (literally) whipped others into line; a leading Son of Dan ambushed and shot one of Smith's assassins. But the Gentiles were more numerous and reckless. Many of them had come up the Mississippi from the slave South, where violence was all too common a technique. They took to burning down Mormon houses. The state authorities indicated that they could not and would not protect the Mormons indefinitely (not that they had ever done so very effectively). The Saints were just completing the Nauvoo temple; but in the circumstances it is not surprising either that Smith, before his death, had begun to talk of moving on again; or that Young now took the great decision.

His task was formidable, and probably he alone of all Mormons could ever have accomplished it. For all his gifts, Smith had also something of the knowing rogue about him: he could smile even at polygamy. The earthier Young had no sense of humour, great executive ability and an indomitable will. Now he had to organize the journey of 16,000 or so Saints to some refuge in the Far West where they would be safe from the citizens of the United States for long enough to build up an unassailable position. The cost in money would be enormous: could he raise the funds? The religious costs might be higher: could he maintain the faith and discipline of the people on the long journey?

This business of finding 'the White Horse of safety' of which Smith had spoken in prophecy might not have been possible but for a great widening of prospects which had come about in the previous half-century. American settlers had begun to cross the Mississippi into Spanish Louisiana (the territory between the great river and the crest of the Rockies) even before the end of the eighteenth century, as we saw in the story of Daniel Boone; the process had been hugely accelerated when, in 1803, Napoleon Bonaparte first cozened the Spanish out of Louisiana and then sold it to the United States for $11.5 million – a useful sum for his war-chest – and for $3.75 million with which to settle the claims of private US citizens against France. The Louisiana Purchase was one of the most important episodes in American history. It not only eliminated the French from the imperial competition, it roughly doubled the size of the trans-Appalachian American empire and correspondingly enhanced its prospects. It began to seem certain that the United States would one day stretch from the Atlantic to the Pacific, and President Jefferson immediately sent out an expedition led by Meriwether Lewis and William Clark to explore the new domain and find, if they could, a good route to the Pacific. Lewis and Clark had succeeded magnificently, ending their transcontinental journey by sailing down the Columbia river to the sea; and they soon had many followers. By 1845 the West had been pretty thoroughly explored. It had been criss-crossed by hundreds of mountain men – the last generation of old-style fur-trappers and traders –

and military missions. It was known that the valley of the Columbia in Oregon territory was a good place for farm settlements, and there were already the makings of the Oregon Trail to lead pioneers there. Explorations were going ahead to open a practicable route to California, which was also very promising country. But for that very reason the Mormons could not go to either region: too many other migrants would press in before them and beside them; and, although California was still legally Mexican territory, and the British claimed Oregon, it would probably not be long before the United States took both.

Yet there was a place, and, thanks to earlier explorations, Brigham Young had heard of it. What he wanted would probably be found in the Great Basin, just across the continental Divide, where, travellers reported, there were high barren mountains and a great salt lake; also good farming land and fertile valleys full of timber – none of which was yet claimed.

A cold going they had of it: just the wrong time of the year for prairie travel. On the eastern rivers the late winter was the most usual season for pioneers' departure. It meant that they got to the new settlement in time to get the ground cleared and seeded at the earliest possible moment. On the banks of the Ohio and its tributaries it was common in March to see a big raft floating down the waters, a cow or two forward, a haystack amidships, and, aft, a family trying to lead a normal life. The Mormons were to have a different experience. They had no choice: as soon as the news got about that they were really leaving, the Gentiles hurried to make sure that they did not change their minds, using methods that had already been perfected for dislodging the Cherokees from their ancestral lands (indeed the Mormons too were driven to take a Trail of Tears, though it led to a happier destination). A favourite device was to force a family to leave its house, carrying what it could in the way of furniture and belongings, and then set fire to the building while the owners watched, standing miserable in the snow. It was clear that it would be unsafe to linger; so on 4 February 1846 the first emigrants began to cross the Mississippi. It was very cold, but the huge river, between three-quarters of a mile and a mile-and-a-half wide at the Nauvoo bend,[13] though full of floating ice, was not yet frozen over, and several of the Mormons' craft capsized in the water, all passengers drowning. A day or two later the Mississippi froze completely, so the crossing was safer; but frost and blizzard made conditions for travel quite appalling. Nevertheless the Saints moved on westward through Iowa, at a snail's pace. In March the snow ceased, but they were not much better off, for the rains came, fearful spring torrents, turning the ground into 'shoe-mouth deep' mud, slowing progress to a minimum, sometimes to no more than a mile a day. In the steady downpour it was often impossible to get food cooked or keep clothes and bedding dry. When at last summer came the people

13 I am grateful to Mr Jonathan Raban for supplying this piece of information, which I had long looked for in vain.

and the oxen drawing their covered wagons were plagued by black clouds of mosquitoes, and some were killed by the bites of rattlesnakes. Preparations for the journey had gone on for more than a year; but few of the Saints had really understood what such a journey required of them. At times Brigham Young was almost at his wits' end for money to support them even as far as the river Missouri; cattle and babies, children and the elderly began to die. The starving time of Utah occurred when its settlers were still nineteen months and a thousand miles away.

The survival of these new Pilgrims must finally be explained by the fact that their heroic virtues outweighed their vices. Many were idle, backsliding, quarrelsome or just plain silly, but most found in themselves the qualities necessary for survival. At bottom they were honest plain Americans; brave, patient and practical; stiffened and disciplined by their apocalyptic faith. Little things helped them: there was an English brass band among the converts, to whose music they danced in the evenings, after prayer, at every stopping-place (weather permitting). And as Bernard De Voto shrewdly remarks, every pioneer train was a village on wheels;[14] the villagers had the usual consolations of the frontier to keep them sane. When the women had done with their sewing, patching and cooking, and with trying to teach their children the alphabet, they could gather for gossip; when the men rested from driving the herds and the wagons and from the endless round of maintenance that prairie schooners required, they could enjoy a game of cards or dominoes, or a practical joke (once, towards the end of the long trek, Brigham Young gave them a fearful dressing-down for enjoying them too much). Both sexes liked the dancing, the prayers and the priests' harangues. These things seem paltry enough, but they strengthened the spirit to endure.

All the same, they would never have come through but for the great gifts of their Prophet.[15] For one thing, they were desperately poor. They had managed to escape from Nauvoo with a surprisingly large number of horses, mules, sheep and 30,000 head of cattle, but the Illinois mob had forced them to sell most of their property at minimal prices; sometimes there had been no buyers at all, even for a good house or a flock of sheep. Yet it was usually reckoned that a pioneer outfit, one adequate to carry a family from Independence to Oregon or California, cost at least 500 dollars. Until the passage of the Homestead Act in 1862, which in effect made the public lands free for the taking, money would also be needed to buy a farm on arrival, and even after that it might be some time before they could support themselves in the new country. Further supplies must be brought along against that contingency, or at least some good specie dollars. The Mormons, even the best-off among them, and after a year's preparation, and allowing

14 Bernard De Voto, *The Year of Decision: 1846* (Boston, Sentry edn, 1961), p. 159.
15 Young was not actually acclaimed by this title until 1848, but by then the ceremony was only a recognition, by God and the people, of a *fait accompli*.

for the fact that they would not have to pay for the land they proposed to settle, were quite without resources on the necessary scale. So Young set about fund-raising. He encouraged the men to hire themselves out at any odd jobs as the wagon-train passed through the scantily settled Iowa prairie (1846 was the year Iowa won its statehood). He put Mormon communities everywhere – Ohio, Mississippi, England – under contribution. He exploited the needs of the United States government: while the Mormons were on the march another war broke out, this time with Mexico (by this means the Americans meant to make sure of Texas, recently annexed from Mexico, and the whole of the Pacific West), and Young was happy to supply 500 indifferent soldiers to serve the country's need. The Mormon battalion won no military glory, but the money paid it for wages and expenses was impounded by the Prophet and kept the emigration alive.

Forward planning was essential. Young soon accepted the fact that the Saints would not get to the Great Basin in 1846. It would be as much as he could do to get them from the Mississippi to the Missouri. So his advance party was set to establishing a transit camp, Winter Quarters, near the site of the present city of Omaha, Nebraska, on the western bank of the Missouri. It was really a town, carefully laid out according to the Mormon passion for town-planning, with streets, mills, wells. The houses were not much – mostly mere huts; but they were better than nothing, though the mortality rate during the winter of 1846–7 continued to be appalling. Most important of all, fields were dug, tilled and sown: the Mormons from now on would have an independent and sure food-supply. Young saw to it that tillage was also undertaken, on a smaller scale, at the string of lesser camps that he planted across Iowa, though their prime purpose was to provide rest and repair facilities for the rearguard. (The last of the Saints did not get away from Nauvoo until September 1846, and they were the most destitute party of the lot, for the Gentiles grew ever bolder and more violent as the number of Mormons in Illinois dwindled.) Beyond all this it was necessary to learn all one could about the road to the Salt Lake and about conditions on its shores.

That Young did not fail or falter in doing all this, as well as governing the whole Church of the Latter-Day Saints throughout the world and organizing the necessary lobbying at Washington, is proof enough of his abilities.

The 1847 journey was much easier than that of the year before. After they left Winter Quarters they soon reached the river Platte, where they joined the Oregon Trail pioneered by more ordinary emigrants. The Trail went along the south bank; the Saints kept to the north, to avoid contamination from their fellow-adventurers. They had been able to wait until April and May before beginning their journey: that was the right time for crossing the Great Plains, when the grass was growing again for the cattle to eat. Indeed, Mormon discipline and training meant that they could now show the Gentiles a thing or two. Those unenlightened souls were fiercely individualistic, questioning all orders, or rather suggestions, of the wagon-train captain and constantly delaying themselves to indulge in another favourite occupation of the village on wheels, politics. (They had left state and federal elections behind them, but they were still Whigs and Democrats: so they organized elections of their own.) There was no such nonsense in Brigham Young's flock. He had it well in hand, so it made excellent time; though like all pioneer parties it had to struggle against many difficulties, of which perhaps the white alkaline dust of the Wyoming desert was the worst. It damaged eyes, sometimes to blindness, corroded the skin, smothered the lungs and was a sure sign of bad water to poison men and beasts. Yet the advance party won through, crossed the Divide by South Pass (the Rockies equivalent of the Cumberland Gap: beyond it you drink from streams which flow to the Pacific) and reached the Salt Lake in July 1847. The main party of that year's migration got there in August. By winter, 1848, Brigham Young was settled in Salt Lake City, which was rapidly taking shape, with 5,000 Saints around him. And more were coming. For the next thirty years Deseret (as they named what the United States called Utah – the word is supposed to mean 'land of the honeybee') filled up steadily with Mormons, summoned by their Prophet from all quarters, especially England and Wales.

The country could never have prospered but for Young's last great innovation. It was obvious to all that the Great Basin could only yield crops if it was extensively irrigated.[16] Young's inspiration was to see how this might be arranged in Mormon fashion. Clearly the old law of riparian rights, by which the water of a stream or river belonged to the owners of the banks, would not do: such was the reckless, self-serving individualism of the American nineteenth-century temperament that it was quite certain that such rights, if conceded, even to Saints, would be abused. So Young laid it down firmly that 'there shall be no private ownership of the streams that come out of the canyons, nor the timber that grows on the hills. These belong to the people: all the people.' The system he adopted was not unlike that of the Spanish, first rulers of an empire in the West, or the ancient Egyptians. Water, it was laid down, would be allotted for their use, like land, by the community's officials, who had to swear oaths to do so fairly. To construct and maintain irrigation ditches, the Mormon families were organized by their bishops into groups, the men of which were required to contribute their labour, in proportion to the amount of land they wanted to water; when the system was ready, water was allotted in proportion to the amount of labour contributed. The use of timber was regulated on the same principles, and strict discipline enforced its conservation.

16 The same might be said of the entire West between the Cascade and Sierra Nevada mountains and the eastern edge of the High Plains, or short-grass country, which runs roughly north and south down the middle of the Dakotas and Nebraska, defining the western third of Kansas, and the panhandles of Oklahoma and Texas. In the whole of this vast region the politics of water (a source of energy as well as food) is as important as the politics of oil, and much more so, nowadays, than the politics of silver.

This arrangement worked excellently, and in modified form continues in the Mormon West to this day. It set an example which other Americans would have done well to heed: instead of which they persisted in the ruinous individualistic scramble until the coming of the New Deal. This was, in fact, the most successful co-operative experiment ever undertaken in the United States. It is impressive for many reasons, not least that it was managed with next to nothing in the way of outside capital. 'We shall need no commerce with the nations,' said Brigham Young. 'I am determined to cut every thread of this kind and live free and independent, untrammelled by any of their detestable customs and practices.' And when Brigham Young was determined on a thing, it happened.

He was in many ways an unattractive character. He had an instinct for power, for the surest means of getting it, wielding it and cutting down rivals with it. Smith communed with God and His angels, but Young was more concerned with economic advantage, especially in his later years. He was also bloodthirsty in a peculiar, vicarious way. He often preached sermons that were naked incitements to violence; he was capable of dropping hints, much subtler than Henry II's, when he wanted someone put out of the way. The result was a long series of murders, which he sometimes deplored, but could not talk about without a sort of gloating. Unpleasant; yet it must be allowed that even in Deseret the Mormons continued to suffer from the ferocious aggression of their fellow-Americans, and if Young defended his society in part by violence, so did many other nineteenth-century frontier communities, whether in mining camps or cattle towns like Dodge City. And the community which the heroic labours of Young and his followers built was unique. It was an achievement to compel respect.

The rules laid down by Smith and revised by Young stood the test of time and use. There was always Young's absolute authority to fall back on if Saints grew restless; for the rest of the time there were the common principles of social organization in the church to rely on. Joseph Smith had decreed an in-gathering of Saints, so the population of Deseret grew steadily: from 11,000 in 1850 to 87,000 in 1870. The Mormon village was as compact as the first Puritan villages in New England, which not only ensured that the church officials would be able to enforce their regulations, but also made possible the most efficient and egalitarian use of the common lands. The principle of stewardship on behalf of the Kingdom of God, a fundamental Mormon tenet, made the practice of co-operation easy; and the pursuit of prosperity was sanctioned by the duty of the Saints to redeem the earth from the primordial curse brought on it by Adam's fall, and so to use it as to make it fruitful, like Eden, for man's use. The emphasis on plain living (not only alcohol but also tea and coffee are forbidden indulgences) made sure that every spare penny was reinvested.

It was a unique system, bordering on socialism, but still it was less un-American than, superficially, it seemed. The pioneers who were pressing westward to Oregon and California differed from the Saints in their individualism, but shared the belief that a better life could be found toward the setting sun: they too were looking for a white horse and self-sufficiency. Above all, the fundamental commitment to equality which was so essential a mark of nineteenth-century America was manifest among the Mormons. It was subordinate equality, enforced by authority; it was certainly not complete economic equality (Brigham Young believed in the parable of the talents) but the same might be said of the United States itself. As the irrigation regulations show, every Mormon was expected to contribute his labour to society, and every Mormon could claim a stake in return: land, security, prosperity. Nor were even the two most objectionable features of life at Salt Lake City without parallels. Brigham Young's power as Prophet, Seer, Revelator, Trustee-in-Trust and, for four years, Governor of Utah Territory (appointed by President Fillmore) and the informal power he wielded over executive, legislature and judiciary resembled that of a big city boss, or of Huey Long in Louisiana in the 1930s. Even his use of violence, of which the most disgraceful episode was the Mountain Meadows massacre of 1857, when a party of Mormons commanded by one of Young's closest henchmen slaughtered 120 Gentile men, women and children, can be likened to massacres of the Indians (the Sand Creek massacre occurred only seven years later). And to Americans in the 1850s polygamy was important, once the sexual titillation of it had been allowed for, because it raised exactly the same questions about states' rights, individual rights and that instrument which so delicately combined the two, the US Constitution, as did slavery. Did not the philosophy of equal individual rights entitle the federal government to intervene to protect women and slaves alike? The new Republican party thought that it did, and in its 1856 platform denounced slavery and polygamy together as 'twin relics of barbarism'. Or did the philosophy of states' rights bar the government from meddling in state matters? That was the view of the South, which hoped to win the support of the Mormons for its own 'peculiar institution' if it showed itself ready to accept theirs. Brigham Young saw which side his bread was buttered. He welcomed Stephen Douglas's doctrine of popular sovereignty[17] and made no secret of his opinion that slavery was just what the Negro deserved.[18] Deseret was neutral in the Civil War, since although it was part of the North a Southern victory would probably have cleared the way to a successful secession by the Mormons. The anti-polygamy case strikingly resembled the anti-slavery one: polygamy, it was said, was anti-Christian, it destroyed family life, it made its victims degraded and unhappy, it encouraged the worst propensities in males, it was economically antiquated and it threatened to impede the glorious progress of the great American nation by dissolving the Union. Abraham Lincoln might as well have said of polygamy what he did of slavery, that if it was not wrong, nothing was wrong. There was even

17 See Chapter 14.
18 Not until 1978 was the first Negro elder appointed in the Church of the Latter-Day Saints.

an impending crisis which led in 1857 to a miniature civil war, when an army expeditionary force was sent against Salt Lake City. Young, a much wiser man than Jefferson Davis (and in a much weaker military position), prudently defused the crisis by peaceful submission, which left him master of the situation; but the difference in outcome scarcely weakens the force of the overall similarities.

Opinions differ as to just how many polygamists there were among the Mormons. It is at least clear that, like the Southern slave-holders, they were in a minority, and not a large one; but they dominated their people. And Brigham Young knew very well that polygamy effectively cut off the Mormons from their countrymen, thereby rendering them all the more dependent on each other and on him. What does not seem to have concerned him was the corrupting effect it had on the position of Mormon women, even those who were not plurally married. They were fully as devout and brave as the men, and did as much to build up Deseret; in return they were reduced, in the eyes of their menfolk and even their own, to the status of chattels. They were deemed to be naturally inferior, as blacks were by their masters. Their function in life was to be household drudges. Poor farmers found it cheaper to marry several wives, who would get no wages, than to hire male labourers. Young, who did not believe in intellectual aspirations for anyone (there were no books in his houses and he was always at feud with the best educated of the Mormon leaders, Orson Pratt), saw nothing wrong with such a state of affairs. He preferred, however, to stress the spiritual advantages that plural marriage brought. A man with more than three wives was certain to enter the highest heaven (he himself, as a prophet with seventy wives, was going to rule that heaven, or part of it); a wife of such a man would also be sure of heaven, and if she had children, to multiply the Saints on earth, would be given an honourable place there. In exchange for this promise, Mormon women gave away their self-respect and their hope of love. In a way it was a worse bargain than slavery itself.

It seems that even women who accepted or defended polygamy did not on the whole thrive in these conditions. The consolation is that the system did not last long. Victory in the Civil War immeasurably strengthened the federal government, legally as well as materially, and the coming of the transcontinental railroad in the years immediately after the war not only brought Gentiles in large numbers to Utah but made it possible to pour in troops in large numbers at the slightest sign of trouble. And the federal government was implacably anti-polygamist. So the choice before the Saints was again to be submission or flight. Young succeeded in postponing the moment of choice, but after his death it was laid down: abandon polygamy or suffer the consequences. In 1890 the church repudiated the practice; six years later Utah at last became a state of the Union. The struggle to preserve plural marriage had very nearly wrecked the church, and had come near to destroying its wealth; but at least Mormon women could now enjoy the rights which their sisters elsewhere had already begun to win for themselves; though still, in remote country places, polygamy persists.

The verdict on Brigham Young must in the end be ambiguous. He did great good, and great evil. He was a quintessential figure of the frontier West. His career illuminates its most heroic phase. Its final act may be studied through the career of a simpler, better man.

William Frederick Cody was born on the Iowa bank of the Mississippi on 26 February 1846, a hundred miles or so north of the place where the Mormons were crossing from Nauvoo. His father was a pioneer from Ohio who in 1852 moved with his family to Missouri. Frontier violence there had taken a new turn, getting caught up in the rapidly developing conflict between the free and slave states. Isaac Cody was a Free Soiler, opposed to any new westward extension of slavery. As such he was stabbed, and eventually harried to death in 1857, leaving his eleven-year-old son to be the family's breadwinner. Young Will was precociously ready for the job. He could already ride and shoot competently; in the years to come, as he grew, so did his skills. He was a child of the West, haunted by the legend of the great mountain men, Kit Carson and Jim Bridger; by tales of Indians and wagon-trains. He was never to lose this boyish enthusiasm: it was to be the secret of his immense success. Inevitably, he was drawn along the Plains trails.

His career was never so heroic as a mountain man's, but it had adventure enough for any lesser mortal and well represents various phases of Western history.[19] He was a trapper. He went prospecting for gold in Colorado when he was thirteen. He was a rider for the pony express which relayed messages right across the continent (until it was killed by the electric telegraph) when he was fourteen. He spent the Civil War in Kansas, fighting at first as a Jayhawker, that is, as one of the Union raiders who gave tit-for-tat to the Bullwhackers, Confederate raiders from Missouri. Neither force had a good reputation and it was as well for young Cody that in 1864, after his mother's death, he enlisted as a scout with the Ninth Kansas Cavalry, seeing action in Tennessee, Mississippi and Missouri. After the war he married (it was a tempestuous and in the end an unhappy union). He tried to maintain his family by working as a stage-coach driver and (unsuccessfully) as a hotel-keeper; then he took service as a scout for the US army, which was beginning its long struggle to tame the Plains Indians. The railroads came to the West, and Cody found new employment as a buffalo hunter, slaughtering the huge beasts for the rail workers to eat. He had a horse called Brigham (after the Prophet) which he bought from a Ute Indian; together they performed prodigies. Cody would herd a number of buffalo to a point conveniently near the workers' camp, then, galloping alongside on Brigham,

19 The biographical details given in my text are mostly derived from Victor Weybright and Henry Sell, *Buffalo Bill* (London, 1956), which does as well as can be expected in sorting out fact from fiction in the records of Cody's life; but I would take my oath for very few of them.

would bring them down as quickly and economically as possible: he is reported to have regularly killed eleven buffalo with twelve bullets as they stampeded. It was better than a circus to watch. In the seventeen months that he worked for the railroads he killed 4,280 buffalo, and thus earned the sobriquet 'Buffalo Bill' under which he became immortal.

He worked as the chief army scout for a few years more. He served during the Sitting Bull campaign in 1876, and immediately after the Battle of the Little Big Horn won a duel with an Indian called Yellow Hand. 'First scalp for Custer!' he cried, brandishing the dead chief's war-bonnet before fitting action to words. In spite of this bloodthirsty episode Buffalo Bill's attitude to the Indians was always intelligent and (in peacetime) friendly. The Indians liked him, and he defended them against calumny: 'The defeat of Custer was not a massacre. The Indians were being pursued by skilled fighters with orders to kill. For centuries they had been hounded from the Atlantic to the Pacific and back again. They had their wives and little ones to protect and they were fighting for their existence.' Perhaps he was the more sympathetic because, as the famous rhyme indicates, he was losing his world as surely as the Sioux were losing theirs:

Across the plains where once there roamed
The Indian and the Scout
The Swede with alcoholic breath
Sets rows of cabbage out.

The army would not need him much longer. The farming frontier was spreading steadily across the plains, while the mining frontier annexed the hills (it was a gold rush in the Black Hills of South Dakota which had touched off the Sitting Bull war). The railroad and the telegraph were stretching across the land, cutting up the great buffalo range; and the buffalo themselves were being slaughtered with staggering thoroughness, not for food or even for sport, but to destroy the basis of the Indian way of life. Soon the Indians would be forced onto reservations, and the last few buffalo would be preserved in zoos, while cows and sheep usurped their pasture and cowboys drove the longhorns on the trails from Texas to the railheads at Abilene or Kansas City, whence they could be shipped to the stockyards at Chicago for slaughter. The life had its own high romance, and its own hard-working, underpaid reality; but it was not the life for Buffalo Bill.

News of his prowess as a hunter and warrior had reached the East some years before. There, urban Americans were entranced by the same magic of the West as had allured young Will Cody. They devoured cheap novels about cowboys and Indians, many of which featured Buffalo Bill as the hero. Rich men found their way by the transcontinental railroad to the West, where their hero in person taught them how to hunt buffalo so long as any were left. Crude melodramas about Bill began to be staged. On a visit to the East, Cody saw one of these shows and saw also that he could make a lot of money by appearing in them himself, as himself. So with a few Western cronies he toured the cities for several years in a preposterous farrago called *Scouts of the Plains*, in which he slaughtered hundreds of Indians with every bullet, while simultaneously courting, as a tender swain, a tender-hearted lassie. He was vastly successful everywhere, but when his sister saw the play he rebuffed her congratulations: 'Oh Nellie, don't say anything about it. If heaven will forgive me this foolishness, I promise to quit it for ever when this season is over.'

He enjoyed appearing on the stage, he found, and making and spending large sums of money; but he yearned for something better than tawdry exploitation. At length he saw his way. He would present an open-air show from the real West: the dreams of town-boys, fed by dime novels, would now be satisfied by something better. And the world which he had lived in and loved would have a last moment of glory.

Buffalo Bill's Wild West was a runaway success for fifteen years or more. It made millions, and it played not only in America but in Europe: Queen Victoria loved it, and everywhere crowds flocked to see it. It was really a circus, but like none that had ever existed before. It was crammed with legendary goodies: buffalo, bucking broncos, Indian scouts, and Indians: among others, both Red Cloud and Sitting Bull made appearances in the show. There were: Annie Oakley, the best shot in America; living representations of Custer's last stand and a cattle round-up; an attack by outlaws on the Deadwood Stage Coach; a train of prairie schooners; Indian dances; and above all, Buffalo Bill himself. As the show opened, a torrent of horsemen would pour into the ring: Indian braves – Sioux, Araphos, Cheyennes; Texas rangers, cowboys, Mexicans, gauchos; detachments from the US cavalry and artillery; also, when they could be got, cossacks, Arabs, British Lancers, German troopers, French chasseurs; they would enter thunderously, but with perfect discipline, following their banners, and then, when all was ready, the music would quicken, and Cody himself would ride in, tall, strong and graceful, his long curls flowing, and, doffing his sombrero to the audience, would announce 'a congress of the rough riders of the world'. Later in the show he would gallop into the ring accurately shooting glass balls tossed into the air by another horseman, and he took an active share in many other parts of the performance; but his real contribution was his own appearance. Looking at Buffalo Bill in his buckskin coat with his ready gun and admiring his matchless horsemanship, customers could feel that they had seen the West in action. He stood not only for his own career but for the whole romance of winning a continent. He had seen and done what Easterners could only dream of, and when they cheered him they were acknowledging not only his personality and performance, but something larger and more impalpable: something that would be a part of the meaning of America for ever. The hunters of Kentucky were in his train; the courage, faith and endurance of the pioneers, men and women, were manifest in the vision he displayed to the stay-at-homes; they might even glimpse some of the truth of the still remoter world of the Indians.

His end was sad. The show outstayed its welcome, for Buffalo Bill could not afford to retire. He had no head for business, and was an easy, generous spender; and then, he was a booster of the West. Like so many other men of the time he was convinced that every prospect in the Rockies was pleasing; he carried the message far and wide; but his own investments, even when they were sound in principle, never paid off for him. Racked with pain from an untreated prostate gland; heavily in debt to the man who had taken control of the Wild West from him; old, fat and inclined to drink too much, he yet dragged himself through his last performances, with undaunted courage and optimism. Tomorrow was always going to bring the pot of gold, yet he did not even have the satisfaction of Daniel Boone: he was still a debtor when he died, in January 1917, at Denver, Colorado.

His legend survived these later disappointments. He was buried on Lookout mountain outside Denver, and the place became a shrine; yet his true memorial was to be made of celluloid. He had played with film in his last years, and some footage still survives showing Buffalo Bill as a scout riding through the underbrush on the alert for Indians; but the greatest days of the movie Western still lay ahead. Nevertheless it was Cody who had first indicated to what dramatic heights and power the myth of the West might be raised, and how it might best be displayed; and he did it in the simplicity of a boyish heart, which had always longed for wonders, for centaurs. When he died, he, and cowboys, Indians, fur-traders, pioneers, Long Hunters, were one with those legendary creatures.

13 The Development of a Democracy 1789–1841

Let me now take a more comprehensive view, and warn you in the most solemn manner against the baneful effects of the spirit of party generally.

President George Washington, Farewell Address, 1796

Every difference of opinion is not a difference of principle. We have called by different names brethren of the same principle. We are all Republicans, we are all Federalists.

President Thomas Jefferson, First Inaugural Address, 1801

By the Eternal! I'll smash them.

President Andrew Jackson, 1832

After a year or two of their new government, Americans felt able to congratulate themselves on its complete success. They were beginning to enjoy just that solid economic progress for which they had hoped in vain under the Articles of Confederation. Thomas Jefferson, Secretary of State[1] in President Washington's Cabinet, summed it up best:

In general, our affairs are proceeding in a train of unparalleled prosperity. This arises from the unbounded confidence reposed in it by the people, their zeal to support it, and their conviction that a solid Union is the best rock of their safety, from the favourable seasons which for some years past have co-operated with a fertile soil and a genial climate to increase the production of agriculture, and from the growth of industry, economy and domestic manufactures; so that I believe I may say with truth, that there is not a nation under the sun enjoying more present prosperity, nor with more in prospect.

1 That is, foreign minister.

This passage shows that Jefferson could reason like an economist when he chose to do so; why he did not choose to do so more often, and why, in enumerating the causes and nature of America's prosperity, he did not mention commerce, or the wise measures of the Washington administration, will presently be made clear. For the moment, it is enough to note that he was right. The United States was entering on a long-lasting economic boom. A few statistics should make its dimensions plain. The population went from just under four million in 1790 to just over eight million in 1814. Exports, worth $20 million in 1790, were worth $61 million in 1811, the last full year of peace with Britain. In the same period imports rose from $23 million to $53 million. It is difficult to be both precise and accurate as to prices, but it seems clear, from the data available,[2] that in spite of fluctuations the price of farm products went up by between 50 and 100 per cent between 1790 and 1814 – very satisfactory for a nation still overwhelmingly committed to agriculture. And in these years work began on the extremely difficult but extremely important problem of transport, which had to be solved if America was to realize her economic potential. Beginning with the Lancaster Road, in Pennsylvania in 1792, turnpikes[3] were built everywhere to supplement the rivers; and in 1807, portentously, Robert Fulton launched the first steamboat. All promised very well. It is not surprising that the New York Stock Exchange was founded as early as 1792.

Even the news of revolution in Europe did not, at first, alarm. 'The close of the eighteenth century . . . shall teach mankind to be truly free,' said a New Hampshire clergyman complacently. 'The freedom of America and France shall make this age remarkable.' True, in a way; but the underlying optimism of such remarks would nevertheless be severely tested, and any assumption that the new Constitutional system, which made American prosperity possible, would enjoy an easy, quiet infancy was quickly destroyed. France slid from revolution into the gulf of war, where all the other European nations soon joined her. French armies drove north and east; the revolutionary convention decreed the beheading of Louis XVI; a month later Britain went to war. She and her allies soon showed themselves unable to resist France effectively on land, but at sea it was the old story. Once more the Royal Navy closed the ports of Europe by blockade; once more it carried British soldiers to the conquest of West Indian islands and to death from yellow fever; once more its principal fleets met those of France, Holland and Spain and, luckier this time than in the War of American Independence, defeated them decisively, one by one, in a series of great sea-battles. The implications of all this for the United States were unpleasant and inescapable.

To be sure, there were those who argued that Europe's distress was

2 See *The Statistical History of the United States*, pp. 201–6.
3 Roads which charged their users tolls.

America's advantage, pointing to the enormous increase in the value and extent of America's carrying trade on the Atlantic, as the commerce of the belligerents and their colonies sought the security of a neutral flag; pointing also to the purchase of the immense territory of Louisiana in 1803, which Napoleon, who had forced the King of Spain to give it up to him, relinquished chiefly because he had no hope of retaining it in the war with Britain that was about to resume. These are weighty arguments, but it will not do to forget that Europe's distress was also America's *dis*advantage. The great wars were to loom as a threat to the prosperity, the solvency, the political independence and tranquillity of the United States as long as they lasted. Nor, in the end, could America even stay at peace.

This struggle between foreign powers could so much affect so remote a neutral as the United States only because in many respects the work of the war of independence was incomplete. Vital American interests were still involved in relations with Britain, and British policy from 1793 onwards was necessarily determined, in this matter as in all others, by the priorities of national survival and the quest for final victory. Good relations with the United States were scarcely even a secondary objective. Britain still did not take the new republic seriously; forgetting all the lessons of the Revolution she assumed that in the last resort the Yankees had too much at stake to risk a conflict with her; besides, with no navy and next to no army, America did not seem a very formidable foe. This was to overlook the fact that the Americans were mostly devoted patriots, who would be prepared to put up with a good deal in the interests of peace and in the hope of securing a decent settlement of their differences with Europe; but who had ambitions of their own and who would certainly not forever swallow insults and injuries. National honour was not a mere phrase to them; it meant their determination to be respected and left alone in the enjoyment of their hard-won rights. It would have been well for John Bull if he had grasped this.

Instead, from the moment war began, he harried American shipping. As a neutral, the United States had the theoretical right to trade with all other nations; in practice Britain, dominant on the Atlantic, allowed only such traffic as suited her. Nor did the French waste much solicitude on the interests of a feeble bystander. So the British tried to strangle American trade with France; France sent out privateers to interrupt American trade with Britain.[4] The manpower needs of the navy drove desperate British officers to dangerous excesses. They boarded American ships in quest of British subjects, either deserters or merely seamen employed by the Americans; too frequently they carried off US citizens, ignoring their

---

4 A privateer was a private vessel, crewed and commanded by men who in peacetime were fishermen or merchants, which received 'letters of marque' from its government permitting it to attack the shipping of the national enemy in time of war. The trick was to dodge the blockading squadron in a small, light boat and then find a fat merchantman to prey upon. It was a licensed piracy, and France's only effective naval weapon against Britain.

protests, to service in British warships (conditions in which were so bad as to generate widespread mutiny in 1797). They had the less scruple in daring the hostility of the United States because of their resentful memories of the American Revolution and because they believed that they were defending the liberty of the world against French tyranny. American ships trading to enemy ports were seized as prizes of war; American goods were confiscated.

America's leaders, from George Washington downwards, were anxious to avoid war, if possible, and contrived to do so for nineteen years. But their response to the long crisis was at first complicated by an ideological division within the United States itself. Some men took the British view: the French Revolutionaries were bloodthirsty fanatics whose lunacy, unless checked, would destroy the foundations of civilized society. Some took the French view: corrupt monarchies were vainly resisting the heroic efforts of those engaged in bringing to birth a new order of liberty, equality and fraternity. As has been so common in American history, few on either side knew much about the countries whose merits they were debating. Neither side overbore its opponents for very long. In 1793 a tactless envoy, still remembered as 'Citizen Genêt', hoping to bring the United States into the war on the French side, stirred up wild enthusiasm for his cause, until his many indiscretions provoked a swing of opinion in the opposite direction. By 1798–9, such was French behaviour (including, in the XYZ Affair,[5] an attempt to extort bribes from American envoys) that it looked as if the United States was going to fight France. At the last moment a kind of settlement was achieved with the French republic's new ruler, General Bonaparte; and then for a short time (1801–3) war ceased in Europe.

These experiences amply vindicated George Washington's warnings, in his Farewell Address, against getting embroiled in foreign quarrels; warnings endorsed by Jefferson, when in 1801 he became President, in a famous phrase: 'Peace, commerce, and honest friendship with all nations; entangling alliances with none.' Unhappily this principle was easier to state than to secure, as had already been shown, and was now to be shown again. Britain and France, to their own detriment, were not interested in peace and commerce with the United States; they started to fight each other again in 1803, and subordinated every consideration to the most short-sighted notions of doing each other injury. This was particularly foolish in the British case. To be sure, America's neutral flag was a refuge for French maritime commerce, and in various ways British trade suffered grievously from American competition, which injured the war effort. On the other hand, the United States was now Britain's best customer; Americans were on the whole drawn to the British side of the great quarrel (Mr Jefferson, in particular, had no time for Corsican dictators); imports from America

5 So called because when President John Adams sent the papers concerning the business to Congress, he suppressed the names of the French officials involved, giving instead these initials.

were of the greatest importance to rising British industrialism, and added to Britain's war-making capacity. Put at its crudest, peace with America on any terms was cheaper and less troublesome than war. Yet in the end, by British fault, war it was to be. The Americans did everything they decently could to avoid it, although the provocation was as endless as it was unreasonable. In 1807 a British frigate, the *Leopard*, opened fire on an American frigate, the *Chesapeake*, which was suspected of harbouring British naval deserters. *Chesapeake* fired only one shot before surrendering, having endured twenty-one casualties and having sustained twenty-two shots in her hull. The British took off four deserters. This incident provoked intense indignation in the United States and led President Jefferson to try what commercial warfare would do, since he was not ready to try the real thing. In December 1807, Congress passed into law an embargo, which amounted to a self-blockade: America was to have no commercial dealings with any foreign country until her rights were recognized and respected. It was a bold early experiment in what would nowadays be called sanctions; unfortunately it was also a case of cutting off your nose to spite your face. The United States suffered far worse than her customers, and it was found that enforcement required ever more rigorous, authoritarian, un-American methods. So early in 1809 Congress passed an Act repealing the embargo, which Jefferson reluctantly signed two days before leaving office. A toothless Non-Intercourse Act was substituted.

The diplomatic proceedings of the next three years are too tedious and sterile a subject to be worth more than summary treatment. Napoleon did everything he could to bring on a quarrel between the United States and Britain. It slowly dawned on British statesmen, diplomats and manufacturers that such a quarrel was not in their country's best interests. The Americans, having patiently negotiated and endlessly waited for the victory of common sense, finally gave up and declared war in June 1812, just as Britain altered her policy by suspending the notorious Orders in Council which had substantially shut off American trade with Europe and the West Indies.

The War of 1812 was one of the most unnecessary in history, and reflects as little credit on Britain as any she has ever fought. It was in keeping with its character that it should break out just as one of its chief causes was removed, and that its greatest battle (New Orleans) should be fought just after peace was signed.[6] But though the war was unnecessary in the sense that the British could and should have prevented it by concessions, it was also, from the American point of view, inescapable. The Royal Navy kidnapped 3,800 American sailors and pressed them into that service. The Orders in Council ruthlessly subordinated American economic interests to the political interests of the British Empire: American farmers blamed the Orders, perhaps unfairly, for a fall in agricultural prices that produced a

6 See above, pp. 227–8.

depression in the West in the years immediately before the war. On the frontier, it was universally believed that Indian restlessness – this was the epoch of Tecumseh's great project[7] – was stirred up by British agents, though American oppression was the real cause. The choice before America, Jefferson sadly agreed with his successor as President, James Madison, was war or submission – to fight, or to undo one of the main achievements of the Revolution by accepting total subordination in international affairs to Britain. Looking back over the period since 1783, American leaders could not falter. Britain really had to be taught a lesson. As John Quincy Adams put it,[8] it was not just a matter of dollars and cents; no alternative was left but war 'or the abandonment of our right as an independent nation'. So thought President Madison when he sent his war message to Congress; and so thought the rising generation of politicians in Congress, the so-called War Hawks, led by Henry Clay of Kentucky (1777–1852) and John Caldwell Calhoun of South Carolina (1782–1850). Never in American history was a war entered on in a more sober frame of mind, even though Clay cheerfully promised the early conquest and annexation of Canada.

The war lasted for two years and a half and was not very satisfactory for either side. Canada was not taken, but nor was the United States successfully invaded: British expeditions were checked on the Great Lakes, at Baltimore and, by Andrew Jackson, at New Orleans. The British had much the best of things at sea, but the Americans, with next to no navy, won several creditable victories (as in the celebrated duel between the frigates USS *Constitution* and HMS *Guerrière*, in 1812) and raided the British merchant marine very profitably. Both sides occasionally disgraced themselves. The British mounted a series of destructive raids on coastal towns and villages, which only inflamed the patriotic anger of their civilian victims. The Americans lynched one general of the Revolutionary War and crippled another (Light Horse Harry Lee, the father of Robert E. Lee) because they were opposed to the present struggle. The British captured Washington and burned its public buildings down (not its private ones): when the Presidential Mansion was restored, it was painted white, and has been known as the White House ever since. General William Henry Harrison broke the power of Tecumseh and the Indians of the North-West at the battles of Tippecanoe (1811) and Thames river (1813), while General Jackson did the same for the Indians of the South.[9]

New England, or the dominant faction in that region, sulked near-treasonably throughout the war, because maritime trade was disrupted. In the autumn of 1814 representatives of the New England states met in a convention at Hartford, Connecticut. At the back of their minds was the

7 See above, p. 55.
8 John Quincy Adams (1767–1848) was the son and heir of John Adams. When the War of 1812 broke out he was US minister in Russia.
9 See above, p. 227.

project of seceding, or threatening to secede, from the federal Union, but the demands they actually sent to Washington were only for some amendments to the Constitution. Unluckily for them, but luckily for America, their messengers arrived in the federal capital at the same time as the news of the Battle of New Orleans and the signature of the Peace of Ghent (December 1814); the Yankees had to go home looking very silly.

The peace treaty (negotiated by Albert Gallatin, John Quincy Adams and Henry Clay) was little more than an agreement to stop fighting: neither side made any explicit concessions. Its inconclusive language concealed an important truth. England had at last learned that war with the United States was almost invariably not worthwhile. By her behaviour since 1764 she had alienated the respect and affection of her quondam colonies so thoroughly that it would take her more than a century to get back onto solidly friendly terms with them; she had also taught the Americans, much too thoroughly, that the only means to get on in the harsh world of diplomacy was by bullying and inflexibility; but still, the two countries had much more in common with each other than they had disagreements, and ever after 1814 both, in the last resort, were able to accept the fact. In spite of repeated war-scares during the nineteenth century, there has never been another Anglo-American conflict; and the credit for that may in large measure be given to the lessons taught the British by President Madison and his officers.

So thoroughly were the lessons learned that in 1823, during the next administration, that of President James Monroe (1758–1831), George Canning, the British Foreign Secretary, actually proposed a formal alliance between England and the United States for the purpose of resisting any attempt by the powers of the Holy Alliance (France, Prussia, Austria and especially Russia) to re-conquer the colonies of the Spanish Empire, then in revolt against their metropolis. The idea was tempting, and the now ancient Jefferson advised agreement; but John Quincy Adams, Monroe's Secretary of State, thought otherwise, and persuaded the President. A message was drafted and sent to Congress that showed with absolute clarity what American statesmen had learned from the long era of perilous neutrality and what they thought was to be their country's place in the world:

the occasion has been judged proper for asserting, as a principle in which the rights and interests of the United States are involved, that the American continents, by the free and independent condition which they have assumed and maintain, are henceforth not to be considered as subjects for future colonization by any European powers.

This is the famous Monroe Doctrine. Canning thought it a piece of impertinence, for the United States was far too weak to enforce it against any determined challenge from a great power; it was the Royal Navy which, for good British reasons (the preservation of global primacy, and of ascendancy in the markets of the New World), would for the rest of the century stand between North and South America and any aggressors; but it was nevertheless an effective warning to Great Britain that another war might follow if any serious attempt was made to extend the British Empire over, for example, the Isthmus of Panama; a warning that acted as an effective deterrent. The Doctrine also contained, in germ, the aspiration of the United States to wield its own hegemony over the New World – an aspiration that would in due course ripen into action.

There was another important passage in Monroe's message, a *quid pro quo* for the Doctrine:

Our policy in regard to Europe, which was adopted at an early stage of the wars which have so long agitated that quarter of the globe, nevertheless remains the same, which is, not to interfere in the internal concerns of any of its powers.

It was the doctrine of Washington's Farewell Address, of Jefferson, of what came to be called isolationism. It expressed a deep wish to be left alone and a rather pathetic belief that the United States would actually be so left if it made its wishes and intentions plain. Had not the Farewell Address pointed out that 'Europe has a set of primary interests which to us have none or a very remote relation'? And that Europe was a long way away? Such utterances should be protection enough, and Americans clung to them long after they had lost whatever value they had ever had (and, as we have seen, it was never much). To repeat, the real guarantor of American peace and isolation was the Royal Navy; if that shield should ever crack, the American people would be faced with some very unpleasant problems, for which their favourite diplomatic doctrines did little or nothing to prepare them.

Meantime the shield was intact, and the Americans were free to turn their backs on the Atlantic and carry out the conquest of their continent.

The international dilemmas of the 1790s left a permanent mark on American domestic history, for reasons that had as much to do with personalities as with politics.

The leadership of the American Revolution had been singularly homogeneous, singularly united and singularly durable. Quarrels and debates made little difference: no guillotine waited for those who were on the losing side in either case. John Dickinson, who had voted against the Declaration of Independence, played a valuable part in the 1787 convention. Patrick Henry, who voted against the Constitution, remained influential enough to secure the adoption of the Bill of Rights. Samuel Adams and John Hancock were genteel rivals for political power in Massachusetts until Hancock's death in 1793, which cleared the way for Adams to enjoy the Governorship at last. George Washington was quite reasonable in his hope that his administration would reflect this underlying harmony. No doubt there would be disputes about policy, clashes of personal ambitions, collisions of interests. What George III had called 'that hydra, faction', and which Washington disliked as much as his former sovereign, would perhaps raise its many poisoned heads. There might even be a tendency for society to break up into rival parties – another dreadful word – of rich and poor. But surely all such tendencies could be overcome with the aid of stout John Adams, his Vice-President; of James Madison, expected to display the same leadership in the new House of Representatives that he had in the Constitutional convention; of Washington's old comrade-in-arms, General Knox, who was to continue as Secretary of War; of Thomas Jefferson, reluctantly giving up his ministership to the Court of France (like all good Americans, he had fallen in love with Paris) to be the first Secretary of State; of Alexander Hamilton, Secretary of the Treasury. The leadership which had held together in war would do so in peace, equally to the country's benefit.

Within a year of Washington's assumption of office these hopes were falsified. It was not the President's fault. Hamilton was the rock of offence. The policies which he pushed through were profoundly divisive, however beneficial they proved in the long run; how divisive was demonstrated by the fact that the splits they provoked showed themselves first in Washington's official family.

Perhaps a family quarrel was inevitable. The two Virginians, Jefferson and Madison, differed fundamentally from Hamilton as to the present and future destiny of the United States. Coming from a populous farmers' republic, where equal aspirations for all white men was the general creed, they wanted no radical changes. Jefferson supported the extension of the United States across the continent, but he thought it would take a thousand years or so. Let the Americans grow more prosperous and civilized, by all means; but let them do so like Virginians; let them shape their own lives in manly independence and have as little government, state or national, as possible. Above all, let them eschew the sort of economic activity which led the population to huddle in great cities. Jefferson had been happy in Paris and professed a strong, optimistic belief in the virtue of the common man, but he viewed great cities, he said, 'as pestilential to the morals, the health and the liberties of man'. They must never arise in America to corrupt the people. Nor must growing national wealth lead to a growing class of the wealthy. He had no more use for merchant princes or financial titans than he had for Napoleon (gentlemen farmers were another thing). A concentration of wealth would bring about a concentration of political power; and then let the republicans of America beware.

This vision was perhaps equally marked by prescience and wishful thinking. Hamilton regarded it as so much moonshine, and was shocked as he gradually discovered that his old friend Madison shared it. He himself, having been born in the West Indies (he arrived in New York as a young man on the make at the age of seventeen), was immune to the claims of the states on the first loyalties of their citizens, claims which were so powerful with most other Americans. His own loyalty was given exclusively to the nation as a whole. He was immensely exhilarated by the possibilities that he saw arising from the creation of a new national state on a vast and virgin continent. The federal government's first business, he thought, was by every appropriate means to increase its strength and thus safeguard the glorious future. His understanding of the economic forces at work in the world was profound, and he relied on them to build up the United States. In a sense, he was the heir of the mercantilists. At any rate he believed that a strong unitary American commonwealth could encourage trade and industry far more effectively than the old loose federation of small states, and would in turn be strengthened by the new wealth it fostered. A class of rich men – merchants, financiers, manufacturers – linked with the governmental system by such institutional devices as a funded National Debt and a national bank like the Bank of England, could immensely benefit all their fellow-citizens by their energy, foresight and riches. True, such a system would be inegalitarian and undemocratic (since power would remain in the hands of those with property). Hamilton did not care. He never pretended to be a democrat: he thought democracy, which put power in the hands of the unenlightened multitude, was a disease. Human nature, in his opinion, was basically selfish, and talk of republican virtue was so much cant. 'Ambition and avarice' were the most reliable pillars of the state. None of the prophets of disinterestedness would be satisfied with a mess of porridge, even a double helping, when they might get a decent salary for their services. No, the art of government was to curb and guide men's greedy appetites into useful courses, so that, as the Scottish economist Adam Smith proposed, private vice could be public gain. Hamilton was a prophet of capitalism and passionately believed that a political and economic system dominated by capitalists would in the end produce the greatest happiness for all.

In theory, the Jeffersonian and Hamiltonian views of life were and are incompatible; in practice they can be reconciled, at least in part. Much of American social and economic history has been taken up with the attempt to blend them. For the weakness of the one was the strength of the other. Jeffersonism was too static, too backward-looking; Hamiltonism was too narrowly cynical about human nature. And the two creeds have this in common, that they both encouraged the economic individualism and the national ambitions of the new republic. Jefferson himself, in the course of his long political career (which extended even after his retirement from the Presidency in 1809), assimilated many Hamiltonian policies and ideas. Hamilton never returned the compliment; but then, in spite of his intellectual brilliance, he was greatly Jefferson's inferior as a practical politician. He was not wholly unlike George Grenville. He carried on public affairs with a high hand and trampled on too many people's toes: Jefferson was always bland and friendly, at least to men's faces. Furthermore, Hamilton's views of human nature were anything but flattering to American voters, and voters love to be flattered. In the end they were bound to prefer Jefferson's sincere, if imperceptive, compliments on their honesty to Hamilton's sharp truths.

In 1790 George Washington, a practical politician himself, was probably more concerned with the personal than with the ideological antipathy between his two ministers, but he was perfectly competent to contain it. The result was that while Jefferson set up the American diplomatic service, Hamilton left his mark on the first Washington administration with a series of dazzling achievements.

If the United States was to survive in a dangerous world, he said, its government must be strong and above all 'energetic' (a favourite word). To be so, it must have solid finances and a good name in the world's money markets. So the Secretary of the Treasury courted the speculators. These were not popular men; they were widely suspect as unscrupulous operators who knew how to get rich when everyone else was getting poor. But Hamilton thought them essential collaborators; and, having studied the methods of the younger Pitt (then at the peak of his fame as England's youngest Prime Minister and wizard financier), he knew how to attract them. He hoisted a signal that the United States government was anxious to favour them by proposing, in his Report on the Public Credit (9 January 1790), not only to pay the national debt (there had been talk of repudiating it) but to fund it, that is, to make arrangements by which the payment of the principal and interest of the debt should always, automatically, have first charge on the public revenues (which would come from a tariff and an excise). This was reassuring; he further proposed that the federal government should add the outstanding debts of the states from the Revolutionary War to its own debt, and pay them off in the same way. In short, £80 million of worthless, or nearly worthless, paper debts suddenly became very attractive investments indeed, and speculators who had not already bought a large holding hastened to do so before the innocent realized what was involved. Hamilton's final achievement was the establishment of the Bank of the United States (1791) to facilitate both government borrowing and private finance. He was rewarded with a sudden burgeoning of national prosperity.

He also aroused voluble opposition. The assumption of state debts meant that those states (such as Virginia) which had paid what they owed now had to bear part of the burden of the debts of those states (such as Massachusetts) which had been dilatory or inefficient. The decision to make payments from the national funds only to actual holders of national paper, such as speculators, not to the original purchasers, who had often been forced to part with their holdings at a huge loss, seemed unfair, especially in the case of the Revolutionary War veterans, who had been paid with certificates instead of cash and, to avoid starvation, had had to part with the certificates for whatever they would fetch, which was never their face value. Hamilton was inflexible: to secure the national credit it was necessary to make no exceptions, no concessions, even if the 'improvident many' suffered. When in 1794 the excise provoked a rebellion among the small whisky producers of western Pennsylvania, Hamilton led an army across the Appalachians against them. No wonder he became unpopular, so much so that, as he admitted himself, only Washington's great name protected him. He was also a restless and ruthless political intriguer, which alienated many political leaders. Jefferson had endorsed the assumption of the state debts and secured the acquiescence of Southern Congressmen in it by winning a promise that the federal capital city should be set up on the banks of the river Potomac, on the border between Maryland and Virginia; but when, a year later, a Bank of the United States was proposed, he opposed it as unconstitutional. He thought that its real purpose was to establish 'an engine of influence' by which Hamilton could recruit members of Congress to his capitalist phalanx; or, in plain language, corrupt them; nor was Jefferson wholly wrong. He began to resist Hamilton steadily within the administration; Madison was already doing so in Congress. Two new factions began to form: the followers of Hamilton took to themselves the honoured name of Federalist; his opponents began to call themselves Republicans.

Thanks to its proliferation of elections, the multiplication of its interest groups, the great extent of its territory, the assertiveness of its citizens and, not least, the ambitions of its politicians, the United States has always been fertile ground for party politics; but it is doubtful if even Alexander Hamilton could have provoked the emergence of a full-scale national party system had there been no other developments. The Anglo-French war changed everything. Everyone, as has been remarked, favoured neutrality; but neutrality, as has also been shown, was horribly difficult to maintain. The question before the American people therefore tended to become, not how might neutrality be preserved, but which side should the United States favour?

This question dovetailed all too easily into the controversy between the Federalists and the Republicans. Even the retirement of Jefferson from the Cabinet in 1793, and that of Hamilton in 1795, did not assuage the conflict. For here was a major issue of principle and policy. On the one hand (argued Hamilton) was the chance to use the great crisis to settle the outstanding issues with Great Britain. The need for American co-operation would induce the old country to remove her troops at last from American soil by vacating Fort Detroit and the other posts she still held in the North-West; an agreement would prepare the way for American traders to gain access to the markets of the British Empire, officially closed to them since 1783. All this, for the price only of quarrelling with the dangerous French Jacobins. On the other hand (said the Jeffersonians) was the Republic's truest ally, France, now a great sister-republic, who had thrown open her West Indian possessions to American traders. The way to get similar concessions from corrupt, monarchical Britain was not by alliance but by stern measures. Madison proposed discriminatory duties against British commerce; others advocated an embargo, or the sequestration of British debts. Andrew Jackson, who entered the House of Representatives as a fiery Republican in 1796, looked forward to the day when a French invasion would transform Britain herself into a republic.

The first great trial of strength between these views came when Jay's Treaty was laid before the Senate for ratification in 1795. This instrument had been negotiated in London by the Chief Justice of the United States, John Jay: it was an attempt, inspired by Hamilton, to arrive at an understanding which would preserve peaceful relations between Britain and America. The British made minimal concessions, but they did agree to vacate the North-Western forts. They might have conceded more had not Hamilton secretly informed them of the minimum terms that Jay was empowered to accept – an action which was tantamount to treason. Naturally, the British held out for the best terms they could get; and the result was a treaty which President Washington himself accepted only with the greatest reluctance. It was four months before he could bring himself to submit it to the Senate, which very nearly rejected it; and then it was two months more before he could bring himself to sign it (August 1795). The country was bitterly divided: as one Federalist had rightly predicted, 'the success of Mr Jay will secure peace abroad, and kindle war at home'. For in effect the treaty required the Americans to acquiesce in Britain's arrogant maritime polices for the duration of the war: it seemed to many an intolerable national humiliation. The fight against the treaty drew Jefferson back into public life from his unsuccessful struggle to bring some order into his personal finances, and marks the real beginning of the American party system.

Yet many of the issues which were so hotly debated do not look very real today. The Federalists did indeed include, as their enemies alleged, some fanatical anti-democrats; men who maintained, in almost caricature form, the traditional eighteenth-century distrust of 'the swinish multitude'. The majority were sensible men. So were the majority of Republicans, though a few were posturing pseudo-Jacobins and a great many were noisily egalitarian Westerners. The two groups had far more in common than they would admit, and alike had the good of their country at heart. This is well symbolized by the relations between Thomas Jefferson and John Adams.

These two old friends and collaborators were rivals for the Presidency in 1796, after Washington had insisted on escaping at last to Mount Vernon. Jefferson was the inevitable Republican candidate, Adams the only Federalist who could beat him. Adams's long and outstanding record as a patriot, especially his service in the Continental Congress and as revolutionary emissary to Holland and France; his courage and integrity; the reliance which Washington had increasingly come to place on him; his prickly intelligence and warm heart; above all, the fact that he was sure to carry the states of New England, his native region, compelled his adoption as the Federalist candidate, to Hamilton's great annoyance; for the very qualities which would make him a worthy successor to Washington, including the fact that he was no party man, meant that he would be nobody's tool, and certainly not Hamilton's. So the former Secretary of the Treasury embarked on a desperate intrigue to keep both Jefferson and Adams out of the Presidency. He hoped to foist the insignificant Federalist Vice-Presidential candidate on the country. As it turned out, he nearly gave away the election to Jefferson, who came within three electoral votes of Adams (sixty-eight to seventy-one); and when news of his treachery leaked out Adams was bitterly angry. He never forgave Hamilton; the Republicans crowed that 'when a *little Alexander* [Hamilton was only five feet seven in height] dreams himself to be ALEXANDER THE GREAT... he is very apt to fall into miserable intrigues'. The way seemed open for collaboration between Adams and Jefferson, who was now Vice-President.[10] For one thing, Adams disliked the Hamiltonian financial programme as much as Jefferson did, for the same reasons. He was particularly distrustful of the Bank of the United States.

However, the behaviour of the French made a reconciliation between Adams and Jefferson impossible and postponed the day of an open breach between Adams and Hamilton. In 1797 revolutionary France thought herself on the brink of final victory over all her enemies. Only Britain and her satellite (which is what the United States seemed, since Jay's Treaty, to be) still held out; the time had come to finish with both. Plans matured for an invasion of the British Isles and privateers were dispatched to wreck American maritime trade: over 300 merchantmen flying the Stars and Stripes were sunk or captured; and French diplomatic insolence brought the two countries to the very edge of war. So while Jefferson at Monticello drank success to General Bonaparte, Adams and his Cabinet (which he had inherited from Washington: it was packed with Hamiltonians) began to make plans in a very different spirit. The navy must be strengthened and an army recruited, which General Washington was summoned from retirement to lead (to Adams's intense vexation he insisted on Hamilton as his second in command). Jefferson gave up Adams as an 'Anglomane' and a 'monocrat'. By 1800 the President and the Vice-President were no longer on speaking terms.

Meanwhile the hastening march of the country to the brink of war produced ever-deeper political divisions. In 1798 an Alien Act and a Sedition Act were passed by the Federalist-dominated Congress, the ostensible purpose of which was to protect the country against French intrigue, but which were really meant to assail Republican journalists and politicians. By way of counter-stroke, in 1799 Jefferson and Madison secretly drafted the Kentucky and Virginia Resolutions (adopted by the legislatures of those states) which denounced the Alien and Sedition Acts in the name of the Bill of Rights, and proclaimed that the state governments had the right to settle, in the last resort, the question of whether actions by the federal

10 Under the original Constitutional arrangement, the runner-up for the Presidency was elected Vice-President. This resulted in repeated difficulty and intrigue, especially in 1800 when Jefferson and Burr, the Republican candidates, got exactly the same number of electoral votes, thus throwing the election into the House of Representatives. So in 1804 the Twelfth Amendment to the Constitution was adopted, by which a citizen may be a candidate for either the Presidency or the Vice-Presidency, but not for both at the same time.

government were constitutional or not. (This provoked counter-resolutions by all the states north of Virginia, asserting that the right of interpretation rested with the courts.) Then the spectre of war with France began to recede: to the intense indignation of the High Federalist war-party, Adams dismissed Hamilton's allies from his Cabinet and sent a new envoy to France, who was able to negotiate a settlement. It was a notable stroke of policy, but it determined Hamilton to get rid of John Adams. The election of 1800 was a lively one.

Party feeling was indeed bitter, and party organization reached a peak not seen again for a generation. After his victory, which the Federalist split made more or less inevitable, Jefferson liked to talk of the 'Revolution of 1800'; but the upshot was much less dramatic than such a phrase implies. Albert Gallatin became Secretary of the Treasury and carried out his duties with extreme Republican frugality, but the Hamiltonian system was not dismantled. This was just as well: President Jefferson's greatest achievement, the purchase of Louisiana, was made possible only by foreign loans, which would not have been forthcoming if Hamilton had not established the credit of the United States so solidly. Madison, as Secretary of State, found that foreign policy was no easier for a Republican than it had been for Federalists; and Jefferson quarrelled quite as bitterly with Vice-President Aaron Burr, the leader of the New York Republicans, as John Adams had quarrelled with Alexander Hamilton, leader of the New York Federalists. Then a duel between Hamilton and Burr in 1804 resulted in the death of the one and the disgrace of the other. In 1809, when Jefferson retired, Madison succeeded him; the Republicans were solidly entrenched in power; yet still everything went on much as it had under the Federalists. An old friend presently reconciled Adams and Jefferson.

The underlying agreements of the American political élite had at last reasserted themselves. Once the disturbing influence of Hamilton was removed and the intransigence of Britain had finally settled the question of what America's foreign policy should be, there was very little to quarrel about. So the first blossoming of national party politics was coming to an end by, at latest, the 1816 Presidential election, the last which the Federalists ever contested, for they were overwhelmed. Still, the American people had taken to party warfare with significant eagerness. The journalists of the two factions had proved themselves champions at scurrility and abuse (for example, it was alleged that Jefferson had fathered a large illegitimate family on one of his slaves).[11] The minor politicians of the various states had shown boundless energy and ingenuity in working for each other's downfall, and some of them were of the opinion that politics was as good a way of getting rich as any other. Ordinary Americans enjoyed the carnival aspect of politics: the speeches, the processions, the banquets, the racecourse excitement; they had also shown that they could be deeply stirred when

11 Modern scientific research has established that he begot at least one child in this way.

they thought that great issues were at stake. The triumph of the Republicans had been due as much to their ability to rouse their fellow-citizens, and to the Federalists' disdainful reluctance to compete, as to any intrinsic virtue in their cause.

So the lull that followed the collapse of the Federalists did not last for very long. The old Revolutionary elite was disappearing. The Father of his Country had died in 1799; Adams and Jefferson lived on and on (eventually dying on the same day, which by a wonderful coincidence was 4 July 1826 – the fiftieth anniversary of the Declaration of Independence) but they held no office. Presidents Madison and Monroe followed Jefferson into complete retirement as they had followed him in the Presidency. Inevitably, new men came to the fore: men without shared memories of the great struggle.

The country itself was changing too rapidly to be managed any longer by the arts of gentlemanly politics. By 1820 there were twenty-two states in the Union, and the population was 9,638,453. Loyalty to individual states, as against the Union, had perhaps waned somewhat; but Americans were becoming increasingly conscious of their identity as inhabitants of the various sections (principally, North, South and West). New economic interests were arising, old systems were decaying; new attitudes to life were forming, and the ideology that may loosely be described as Americanism – democratic, nationalist, capitalist, individualist – was coming to maturity. Inevitably a new sort of politics emerged.

The constitutional system both required and induced such a development. The system of checks and balances perpetually threatened to be too successful: President, courts, Congress and state governments might be so efficient at thwarting each other that nothing, however necessary, could get done. Means of inducing them to co-operate had to be sought, and party discipline, it turned out, was just what was wanted. Another factor was the basic principle of election. American life had been permeated with the elective spirit from its beginnings. Puritans had known no other way of securing their congregations against the horrors of prelacy, and practical settlers had known no other way of ensuring that new laws and infant authorities would be respected. The habit of elections was substantially reinforced by the battles of the 1790s. The same conditions which had necessitated elections in early New England now necessitated them as settlements sprang up in the West; while in the older parts of the country they held it to be an essential part of the American liberty which had been vindicated against King George, that all office-holders, whether state, national or merely local, should be answerable to the people at election time. True, there were many posts under the Constitution (most notably federal judgeships) which were appointive, not electoral; but it was elected officials – the President and the Senators – who made the appointments.

Such patronage increased the importance of Presidential and Senatorial elections, but that importance was already large. While governments exist they will be supposed to do so for the good of the governed, and early nineteenth-century Americans were clamorous in demanding that their government deliver the goods. Manufacturers in the East demanded higher tariffs for protection against British competition; settlers in the West demanded the protection of the US army against Indians and its help in driving the tribes from their lands; others wanted federal assistance in the building of roads and canals to carry produce to market. All these interests had opponents, of course: voters who wanted the federal government to do little of anything, and nothing that involved direct or indirect taxation (in this they showed themselves the true descendants of the Sons of Liberty). All alike turned to the professional politicians for assistance in winning their ends; and the politicians were very willing to co-operate. For they had noticed that elected offices carried salaries with them; so did appointive ones; judicious exertions could, by these means, keep an honest man solvent for the length of his natural life (for dishonest men, it was soon to emerge, the opportunities were even more glorious). All that was required was to make promises to the voters and then find means either of keeping those promises, or of seeming to do so; or to teach the voters that the art of compromise (with reality and one's opponents) is the essence of adult politics; or, if all else failed, of persuading them that the promises were broken because of the corrupt and treasonable activity of the opposition. In return, loyal partisans would sustain a man in office, where he could earn a good wage and where he could obtain additional rewards by handing out such jobs as postmaster or government clerk to the deserving. Underlings proved they were deserving by contributing part of their salaries to the war chests of the politicians.

This was the politics of patronage, of the so-called spoils system, of the lobby[12] and the special interest. It is familiar, in one form or another, to everyone who has grown up in a Western democracy, and so need hardly be explained further. The principle of favours given for favours received provides the staple of Atlantic politics. It does not make up the whole of the system. American voters, at least as much as European ones, can be decisively affected in their behaviour by great events; and they may have loyalties or interests which transcend the petty concerns of day-to-day living. Politicians are not mere greedy automata. The best and ablest among them cherish their self-respect; they feel the need to legitimize their personal ambitions by linking them to great causes. So American politics have always presented a complex and fascinating web of immediate personal

12 The 'spoils system' is explained below (see pp. 267–8). The lobby, as shorthand for pressure groups, derives, like so much else, from New York politics. Under the Albany Regency in the late 1820s it was noticed that men who wished to extract favours, or otherwise to influence state legislators, waited in the lobby of the state Capitol (since they were not allowed onto the floor itself). This gave rise to all sorts of new words: *lobbyists* forming *the lobby* or a particular lobby (e.g. the *railroad lobby*, the *labour lobby*) exist *to lobby* elected politicians. In English political usage, by contrast, the lobby consists of highly regarded newspaper correspondents who are accepted by Parliament as a convenient means of telling the world what it wants the world to believe.

and economic interests, national, sectional, class or racial rivalries, and individual careers – comical, tragical, heroical or villainous – on the largest scale.

These generalizations will take on more meaning if we look at the transformation of American politics that occurred in the 1820s and 1830s. For those decades saw the emergence of the classical pattern of the American party system, as a result of the combined activities of great statesmen, ordinary politicians and the mass of the American people.

The great statesmen had their eyes fixed on the highest offices of all: on governorships, senatorships, overseas ministries, Cabinet posts and above all on the Presidency. Such leaders were few, and they dominated the national scene for thirty years, forming a new elite to succeed the Revolutionary one. Their personal agreements and disagreements were not unlike those of the earlier day: at some time every one of them collaborated with every other one, and every one of them quarrelled with every other one. (The exception to this rule was the permanent enmity between Andrew Jackson and Henry Clay.) When they were neither quarrelling nor electioneering they went to each other's dinner-parties. But whereas the Revolutionary generation had been, in principle, united, the new men were, in principle, divided into two groups: on the one hand, followers of Andrew Jackson (Martin Van Buren, Thomas Hart Benton, James Knox Polk); on the other, his rivals (John C. Calhoun, Henry Clay, John Quincy Adams, Daniel Webster).

Had the system been essentially a matter of personalities, like the Jefferson–Hamilton rivalry, it would not have survived the death or retirement of its leaders. Instead, it proved to be the most stable feature of America's political history, next to the Constitution, and today's major parties, the Democrats and the Republicans, evolved from the Jacksonians and anti-Jacksonians of 1830. To understand this evolution, it is necessary to look at the American social structure and the great issues of the period, as well as the ambitions of individuals.

The rise of the party system was an intricate, slow process that began even before the War of 1812, perhaps when Jefferson settled that his successor should be nominated by the Congressional 'caucus' of the Republican party. Then there arose the War Hawks, Clay and Calhoun. Both were successful young lawyers (most American politicians have had legal training) who linked their ambitions to the particular interests of their states. They were not much alike otherwise, for Clay was an abounding, smiling extrovert, while Calhoun was a stern intellectual – somebody said that he looked as if he had never been born. They were bound to be rivals, since both wanted the Presidency; in the course of their long careers they would also, not infrequently, be partners; in 1812 their common patriotic stance brought them great prestige. Even more prestige was won by General Jackson. Towns and counties were named after every prominent American as settlement spread westward but songs were made about Jackson:

I s'pose you've read it in the prints
  How Pakenham attempted
To make Old Hickory JACKSON wince,
  But soon his scheme repented;
For we with rifles ready cocked,
  Thought such occasion lucky,
And soon around the general flock'd
  The Hunters of Kentucky!

He had become the supreme living national hero, taking the place left vacant by Washington. A young country, whose incessant bragging ill-concealed its acute inferiority complex, badly needed such a man. His emergence did not bode well for other people's ambitions.

More significant still was the impact of the war on the politics of New York. That state had been changing rapidly since independence. The ancient dominance of its great landed families was challenged, and the challengers marched under the banner of Thomas Jefferson. Adopting the Republican name and creed, they stoutly attacked the oligarchical governmental machinery which was the key to the ascendancy of the old families: the Livingstons, Clintons and Van Rensselaers. Another rising young lawyer, Martin Van Buren (1782–1862), whose family had been clients of the Van Rensselaers, now succeeded in pinning the charge of treason, or at any rate of lack of patriotism, on the aristocrats, because they opposed the war. Van Buren was an unlikely demagogue, being always quietly urbane and amiable and faultlessly dressed; but he was an intelligent and tireless political organizer (he was nicknamed the Little Magician) and with such a cry there was no resisting him. By 1820 he and his friends dominated New York state politics, and were to continue to do so for the next eighteen years.

They were a new phenomenon, and recognized as such. Their cohesion, and their success in controlling the government of New York in Albany, the state capital, earned them the nickname of the Albany Regency. Their followers, they said, were quite safe if they faced the enemy, but 'the first man we see *step to the rear, we cut down*'. The purpose of elections was to win public office; party unity was the means to victory; any who voted wrong would be denied all share in the rewards. For, as William E. Marcy, a leading Regent, proclaimed, 'To the victor belong the spoils'[13] – thus giving its name to the spoils system which was to dominate American politics until the twentieth century. Under this system every election in which power changed hands, whether local, state or national, was followed

13 It is worth quoting him in full: 'It may be, sir, that the politicians of New York are not so fastidious as some gentlemen are, as to disclosing the principles on which they act. They boldly *preach* what they *practise*. When they are contending for *victory*, they avow their intention of enjoying the fruits of it. If they are defeated, they expect to retire from office. If they are successful, they claim, as a matter of right, the advantages of success. They see nothing wrong in the rule that to the VICTOR belong the spoils of the ENEMY.'

by the dismissal of all office-holders of the wrong stripe and their replacement by adherents of the new administration. Some security for civil servants was provided by the possibility that the party which had appointed them would win re-election, and they toiled earnestly to bring about such a happy outcome; but basically their situation was unenviable. William Crawford, an ambitious Georgian who was President Monroe's Secretary of the Treasury, in 1820 put through Congress the first Tenure of Office Act, which gave the President and the Senate the power to re-appoint to every office in the gift of the United States government (except judgeships) every four years – that is to say, after each Presidential election. This law was justified by a principle much beloved of the Jeffersonians – the 'rotation of office', according to which government jobs ought to be passed around as often as possible so that there could not emerge an official aristocracy, holding government jobs for life and possibly passing them on to its children. In practice the Act undermined the civil service and sharpened the appetites of office-seekers, of whom there was soon to be a permanent horde; it enhanced the power of the Senate and diminished that of the President. As a result it soon came about that after every Presidential inauguration the new executive was besieged by office-seekers and had to spend weeks of valuable time pondering the political advantages and disadvantages of appointing Robinsons or Smiths to the hundreds of posts that Joneses and Browns wanted. Even when he had made his nominations, they had to go before the Senate, where horse-trading among the Senators ('You vote for my man and I'll vote for yours') ensured that the final decision would be theirs, not his. By the late nineteenth century, indeed, the power of appointment had largely passed out of the President's hands: Benjamin Harrison (President 1889–93) complained (not quite truthfully) that he had not himself chosen a single one of his Cabinet officers. Benjamin's grandfather, William Henry Harrison (President 1841), is unique in having been hounded to death by office-seekers (he caught pleurisy while delivering a long inaugural address in freezing weather, and could not find a single room in the White House where he could recuperate unmolested), just as President Garfield (1881) is unique in having been shot by a disappointed aspirant; even if unique, neither episode can be called a satisfactory advertisement for the system. Worst of all, the quadrennial scramble could distract attention from really urgent affairs of state: thus in the vital weeks between his inauguration and the attack on Fort Sumter in 1861 Abraham Lincoln had to spend at least as much time worrying about appointments as about the impending Civil War.

The spoils system did, however, have one huge advantage which twentieth-century reformed arrangements do not possess: it paid for democracy without putting power in the hands of the very rich. Democracy, at any rate as practised in the United States, is an inherently expensive process. Voters have to be induced to cast their votes, and to cast them for the right candidates. This necessitates, not merely a large outlay on posters, leaflets, campaign buttons and so on (and, nowadays, on airplanes, radio, television, opinion polls), but an active, labour-intensive political leadership which will shepherd citizens into the voting booths. The problem is enhanced by the fact that in America every year is election year: somebody is always running for something somewhere. The spoils system paid for election campaigns by taxing everyone who made a living out of politics. Office-holders were ruthlessly required to make regular donations to the party funds from their salaries. It was, in its way, a fair bargain, and if society never needed honest, efficient and hard-working administrators there might be more to be said for it than against it. It could even be argued reasonably that during most of the nineteenth century the United States needed little more competent, uncorrupt government than it got. Both the country and the political system survived the Civil War, which shows how strong they were. Only it is no use pretending that American politics in the nineteenth century was clean. It was as thoroughly, recklessly, unscrupulously and joyously corrupt as the politics of wicked old eighteenth-century Britain (from which many of its practices were inherited).

All this was in the future when Van Buren and his allies set up their Regency. They stood for reform. Their first business was to summon a convention which thoroughly democratized the New York state constitution, for example by abolishing the old, venal Council of Appointments and enacting that in future officials would either be elected by the people or (in 4,000 cases) appointed – in most cases by the state legislature. Either way was jam for a well-disciplined, popular party that usually won all elections. Their next enterprise was to spread the new doctrines and practices to the national level. Van Buren had himself chosen Senator by the legislature, and went down to Washington. He did not admit that he was an innovator; instead he said, and probably believed, that he was simply trying to revive the flagging Jeffersonian alliance between the planters of the South and the plains farmers of the North on the basis of the old Jeffersonian ideology of cheap, weak government and strict adherence to the letter of the Constitution. This stance served him well. Everyone still effective in politics described himself as a Republican – the old slogans still commanded much lip-service – and Van Buren took care to be seen making a pilgrimage to Monticello, where he went out with Mr Jefferson in a carriage. Nevertheless he was launching a new era.

Material conditions required it. The Industrial Revolution was erupting in Britain, the world's greatest manufacturing nation. Yet her businessmen were alarmed by such progress towards industrialization as the Americans had made during the War of 1812, when imports had been cut off. A vast quantity of goods had piled up in British warehouses. Now they were dumped on the American market, according to the policy recommended in the House of Commons by Henry Brougham: 'Stifle in the cradle those rising manufactures in the United States, which the war has forced into existence contrary to the natural course of things.' This development was briefly damaging, but its ill-effects were much mitigated by a series of appalling harvests in Britain and Europe, which generated a demand for American wheat and maize, paid for in hard cash. A boom developed, eagerly helped along by a surge of financial speculation: new banks, all anxious to lend money, multiplied like spring flowers. American and British goods sold extremely well. Then the weather improved in Europe: cash began to flow from the West to the East. There had been much thoroughly unsound dealing: for instance, the banks had printed far more paper money, as they were legally free to do, than their reserves of gold warranted. The result, in 1819, was the first of the long series of nineteenth-century crashes, in which all branches of the American economy suffered grievously.

The political consequences were twofold. First, it seemed to many voters that Jefferson's warnings had been fulfilled. Congress had not renewed the charter of the First Bank of the United States, Hamilton's creation, when it expired in 1811, but the extreme financial difficulties into which the War of 1812 plunged the government had persuaded President Madison, with many misgivings, to permit the foundation of a Second Bank, which started to function in 1816. It did not perform well. It plunged recklessly into the speculative enthusiasm of the post-war period, and then, in its battle to save itself from the effects of the 1819 crash, called in its loans so ruthlessly that many smaller concerns, not to mention individuals, were ruined. Add to this the suspension of payments in gold and silver (then universally regarded as the only 'hard', or real, form of money) by the lesser banks, and their widespread bankruptcies (which hurt their customers) and it is not surprising that 1819 convinced many Americans that all banks were untrustworthy, and the big national bank most of all. Thomas Hart Benton (1782–1858), about to become one of the first Senators from the new state of Missouri, discovered his life's cause, which was to earn him the nickname of 'Old Bullion': hard money and down with the BUS. 'All the flourishing cities of the West are mortgaged to this money power,' he cried. 'They may be devoured by it at any moment. They are in the jaws of the monster!'

Second, the economic contraction generated huge tensions between debtors and creditors. They were especially acute in the West, where hard money was difficult to come by at the best of times, the economy of that region being so new that it was still largely based on barter. Yet cash was needed to pay debts and taxes. In Kentucky the contention grew so acute that a debtor party fought and won the state elections on a programme which allowed it to suspend the payment of debts and to abolish the old courts of law whose judges had denied the legality of such 'stay' measures. Henry Clay, the hero of the state, who had accepted a part-time job with the Second Bank of the United States, lost much popularity. In Tennessee the debtor sweep was neither so extreme nor so complete, but the radicals did succeed in overthrowing the 'junto' of rich men who had dominated the state since its foundation. The junto fought back. Its most notable member was Andrew Jackson: he was induced to declare himself a candidate for the Presidency in 1824. Instantly this became the question of the hour in Tennessee. Jackson was the universal idol, and no one could afford to oppose him on anything, lest opposition hamper his drive to the White House. The new radical Governor quickly came to heel, making a compromise agreement with Jackson's friends; as a result he and they together governed the state for the next ten years. It was not just New York which was generating complicated party politics.

The 1824 election promised to be exciting. There were four worthy candidates besides Jackson. John Quincy Adams, Secretary of State (a post which three Presidents – Jefferson, Madison and Monroe – had held before him), was America's most successful and experienced diplomatist. Henry Clay, 'Harry of the West', was the proponent of the 'American System'. Under this scheme high tariffs would have protected American infant industries against British competition, while bringing in revenue to pay for new roads, canals and other public works of a kind to bind the country together, especially the West to the East. The wonder of the age was the Erie Canal. It was 363 miles long and cost $7,000,000 to build. It was opened in 1825 and, by linking the Great Lakes to the Hudson river, linked the Western interior with the Atlantic, to the great benefit of trade. Clay hoped to promote many more such enterprises. John C. Calhoun, Secretary of War, was a strong nationalist as well as the paladin of the South. William Crawford of Georgia, Secretary of the Treasury, was Van Buren's choice. However, Crawford was soon put out of the question by an incapacitating illness, and Calhoun recognized that he could not win. He secured the Vice-Presidency (which no one else wanted) and announced that he supported Jackson.

The election turned out to be something of a fiasco. There were no exciting national issues, and none of the candidates had devoted enough time to stimulating the electorate, so turnout was low. The election had to go to the House of Representatives, because although Jackson had the largest share of the popular vote neither he nor anyone else had a majority of the votes in the electoral college. The House had to choose among the three top candidates. Clay was not one of them: Crawford had retained enough followers to edge out the Kentuckian. But an invalid could not be President; the real choice lay between Jackson and Adams.

Clay, the highly popular Speaker of the House, was in a commanding position. He used his great influence to help Adams, who got the necessary majority on the first ballot. All might have been well had Clay not then accepted appointment as Secretary of State. It was natural enough for him to do so, but Van Buren was right in calling it his death warrant. There was a vast uproar, especially in the West. Jackson jumped to the conclusion that there had been a 'Corrupt Bargain' between Adams and Clay. He rode home from Washington to Tennessee in a rage and began to plot his revenge. He soon found fellow-conspirators.

Martin Van Buren for one. Perhaps he did not yet think he could be

President himself, but he did deeply desire political power. Besides, Adams and Clay stood for policies that he could not accept. New York was a large, rich state with an interest in free trade. It could not accept a high protective tariff as proposed by the American System, and did not see why national revenue should be used to pay for local public works. New York had paid for the Erie Canal by itself: let others do likewise. So Van Buren soon made overtures to General Jackson. They discovered in each other the two most adroit politicians in America.

John C. Calhoun certainly thought of the Presidency, and his part of the world, the strongly Jeffersonian Atlantic South, was as much opposed to the dangerously Hamiltonian American System as was New York. Calhoun calculated that if Jackson won the election of 1828 he himself, as Vice-President, would be well placed for the succession when the old gentleman stepped down. So the South Carolinian became a rival to the New Yorker for Jackson's favour. Meanwhile Henry Clay, determined to re-elect Adams and then to succeed him, tried to organize a resistance to this takeover bid. He did not have much success, because President Adams took a thoroughly eighteenth-century view of 'faction' and refused to cadge votes from the mob.

The election of 1828 was the first mature Presidential battle in American history, foreshadowing all that have followed it. For the rival teams of politicians the stakes were high, and all (with the exception of John Quincy Adams) flung themselves heartily into the fray. The decision would be made by the mass of adult white males, for the choice of Presidential electors was now in the hands of the ordinary citizen in every state except South Carolina, and all property restrictions on the right to vote had been swept away. There were no unpledged electoral candidates: all were committed either to Jackson or Adams. No means to victory was neglected. Shocking scurrilities, like those once circulated about Jefferson and the elder Adams, were freely published: Jackson was accused of bigamy, Adams of having pimped for the Tsar of Russia. But the secret of empire, now revealed, was organization. The methods of the Albany Regency were applied on a nationwide scale. Jackson co-ordinated the efforts of his followers by letter: correspondence committees, like those of the Revolution, were formed throughout the Union. Like so much else in this campaign, these committees were to prove permanent additions to American life. They were the skeleton of the future Democratic party. Newspapers – daily, weekly, monthly – propagated Jacksonian opinions; the party battle was waged with model discipline and fury in Congress (Senator Van Buren commanding). Everything which might secure the loyalty of office-holders or dazzle the simple was tried. In imitation of the Liberty Trees of the Revolution, for instance, hickory trees were planted, with due ceremony, in honour of Old Hickory. Clay struggled in vain against all the hullabaloo and the grand alliance of the West, the South and New York. The Adams administration was successfully labelled corrupt, inefficient, aristocratic and Federalist, even though in at least one state, New Jersey, the old Federalists were Jacksonians (which perhaps explains why the state went for Adams). The truth or falsehood of the label scarcely mattered: people made up their minds on the oddest grounds. The Irish immigrants of New York, for example, remembering that they had been ill-served in the time of the President's father by the Aliens Act, voted for Jackson – thus beginning one of the more permanent affiliations in American politics. The important thing was to make sure that Jackson supporters voted, which the campaign succeeded at brilliantly. Old Hickory's nationwide popularity; his unassailable hold on the South, where he was born, and the West, where he made his career; 'song, slogan, and nonsense'[14] – these explain the victory. Jackson won 178 electoral college votes to Adams's eighty-three, and in March 1829 he entered Washington like a conqueror, to the alarm of the genteel and the hysterical joy of everyone else. On inauguration day the White House was invaded by a triumphant mob, which snatched all the refreshments meant for its betters and was only ever got outside again because tubs of punch were placed alluringly on the lawns. 'I never saw such a crowd here before,' said Daniel Webster in grave amazement. 'Persons have come five hundred miles to see General Jackson, and they really seem to think that the country is rescued from some dreadful danger!'

Webster had put his finger on more than the secret of one election victory. From 1828 until the Civil War the most successful political parties would always be those which discovered some fearful threat to American liberties and persuaded the citizens that to vote for them was the right way to meet the danger. Underneath the self-importance and incessant boasting about the glories of republicanism which so many hostile foreign visitors noticed, the Americans were deeply insecure. They knew that they were conducting an extraordinary experiment, that of democracy, in a world that was in many ways inimical to it; and though they proclaimed, and believed, that its universal victory over monarchy and aristocracy was inevitable and near at hand, they were also perpetually nervous that it might at any moment be subverted. The politicians found it most profitable to play on these fears.

But for the moment General Jackson and democracy were victorious, and the people rejoiced. Jackson's election did not mean that America had become a democracy overnight, though many of his supporters talked as if she had, to the confusion of historians. That particular innovation had been coming on ever since the Revolution. The 1828 election merely proved that the process was complete. Men who, in the eighteenth century, could have expressed themselves only through a riot (as they so often did) could now do so through the electoral process. Although rioting continued, and continues, to be part of American life, the mob, in the old sense – the mob which had a place in the constitution, so to speak, both of colonial Massachusetts and imperial Britain – the mob which Sam Adams had

14 Robert V. Remini, *The Election of Andrew Jackson* (New York, 1963), p. 181.

manipulated – has disappeared. A cynic might argue that the shift was of form, not substance; that while the rights and power of the people were acclaimed, real control remained with the rich, who cared only for the protection of their property; but it makes more sense to see the transfer of power as real. For it was not only the urban rioters who became voters; by 1828 all the farmers, in every section, had the vote and used it effectively. It became ever more necessary for orators to flatter the sovereign people: proof enough, perhaps, that something really had changed, a first step on the road to effective human equality. At the least it must be admitted, even by cynics, that elections remain the road to office in America; and it is the many who decide them, not the few.

The election of 1828 also settled another important matter. On the surface it was a sectional affair: New England was as solid for Adams as the South and West were for Jackson. But in the Middle Atlantic states matters were by no means so cut and dried. Jackson had won, overall, but it was a near thing. Van Buren had had to strain every nerve to be sure that the ticket would carry New York, even to the extent of running himself (successfully) for Governor of the state. In Pennsylvania it was the same story. The Jacksonian agitation had stimulated the admirers of Adams and Clay as well as those of the General. The implications of this were about equally encouraging and discouraging for the two sides. In future, wherever there was not a strong local candidate, there was a good chance of victory for either party; to secure it they would both have to fling in all the resources they had mobilized in 1828. There was no chance that the sublime rightness of one party's cause would be universally and permanently apparent to most American voters. The system foreshadowed by the rivalry of the Federalists and Jeffersonian Republicans had at last emerged; two party politics had come to stay.

The story of the twelve years following Jackson's famous victory is thus largely the story of the consolidation of the Democratic party (as it soon came to be called) and the emergence of the nationwide opposition party which the very process of consolidation provoked. For example, one body could not long contain both Van Buren and Calhoun, rivals to succeed Jackson. The Little Magician's skill was the greater, and his political position stronger, since, to preserve his political base, Calhoun had to associate himself with the anti-nationalist tendencies of his state, which Jackson, an arch-nationalist, could not abide. So in 1832 Calhoun resigned the Vice-Presidency and went home to South Carolina to mastermind the Nullification movement,[15] while Van Buren was chosen to be Old Hickory's running-mate when he ran for re-election in 1832.

In the same year Jackson found it necessary to launch an all-out attack on the Bank of the United States. He had never liked banks, and he particularly disliked this one, whose cause Henry Clay had made his own.

15 See below, pp. 295–6.

So had the ex-Federalist, Senator Daniel Webster of Massachusetts, in return for a fat fee, frequently refreshed, which he cast away at the gaming-table. When Clay, as candidate for the new National Republican party, thrust the question of re-chartering the Bank into the Presidential campaign by inducing Congress to vote in favour of it, although the old charter had four years still to run, Jackson responded with a veto message that rang like a summons through every poor or Jeffersonian home in the land:

... most of the difficulties our Government now encounters and most of the dangers which impend over our Union have sprung from an abandonment of the legitimate objects of Government by our national legislation, and the adoption of such principles as are embodied in this act. Many of our rich men have not been content with equal protection and equal benefits, but have besought us to make them richer by act of Congress. By attempting to gratify their desires we have in the results of our legislation arrayed section against section, interest against interest, and man against man, in a fearful commotion which threatens to shake the foundations of our Union. It is time to pause in our career to review our principles.[16]

What did it matter that the rich, even in his own Tennessee, now began to abandon Jackson? The many (further stimulated by the folly of the President of the Bank, Nicholas Biddle, who behaved like the bullying aristocrat that Jackson said he was) rallied to the President. Jackson won re-election triumphantly, and continued the Bank War by refusing to deposit any more of the federal revenues with the BUS. He had to dismiss his Secretary of the Treasury to do it, but that merely strengthened the authority of the Presidency, the powers and prestige of which Jackson notably extended during his tenure. The Bank War also reinforced his authority as a party leader, and the buoyant prosperity of the mid-1830s was unaffected by his economic experiments (although their long-term results were disastrous). Jackson seemed to be more than ever the nation's leader and the people's President; the National Republican party evaporated; and Martin Van Buren, Jackson's chosen successor, was elected without the slightest difficulty in 1836. Old Hickory cheerfully went off to retirement in the Hermitage, remarking that his only regret was that he had not shot Henry Clay and hanged John C. Calhoun.

Jackson's enemies were too much in earnest to give up. By 1836 they had formed a new party, which they called the Whig, after the Sons of Liberty of the Revolution who had defended American freedom against King George III as their self-appointed heirs were defending it against 'King Andrew the First'. Still in its infancy, the party could not agree on a single candidate to run against Van Buren; but the omens of that election were good. With Jackson off the ticket the Democrats failed to carry Tennessee,

16 Jackson put the case rather more succinctly to his Secretary of State: 'The Bank, Mr Van Buren, is trying to kill me; *but I will kill it.*'

Ohio, Georgia and Indiana, though they won by a landslide in Van Buren's New York. They might be conquered yet.

The Little Magician proved an unlucky President. The year 1837 was another one of bankruptcies and financial panic. Things improved somewhat in 1838, but in 1839 trouble was renewed. A long depression set in. As always in such cases, the President got the blame – not very justly, for the nineteenth-century Atlantic commercial economy moved in a cycle of approximately twenty years, affected by such things as the state of the European and American harvests, the accumulation or exhaustion of financial credit, and the state (alternating glut and scarcity) of the world market for raw materials and industrial goods. In the late 1830s matters seem also to have been complicated by the movement of silver, which, mined in Mexico, desired in China (where it was used to pay for imports of opium from the British Empire) and managed in London, was almost entirely outside the control of any US administration: New York (not to mention Washington) was a long way from attaining the predominant influence on world trade that it was to acquire in the twentieth century.[17]

In the crisis, Van Buren's chief concern was to save the national credit: he wanted no repetition of the emergencies of the 1780s and the War of 1812. It was the most he could do: the federal government was quite without the means to mitigate hard times for ordinary Americans. But the Democrats had happily accepted the credit for good times. Inevitably, they were now blamed. The Whigs captured New York in the state elections of 1838. One of their young leaders, W. H. Seward (1801–72), won the Governorship, in the teeth of the Albany Regency, which was never the same again. Van Buren bid fair to be the Democrats' John Quincy Adams; so the Whigs decided to back their own Andrew Jackson: General William Henry Harrison (1773–1841), the victor of Tippecanoe. He lived in Ohio, but was descended from one of Virginia's leading families: his father had been a signatory of the Declaration of Independence. He was a shrewd old thing, and had done better than any other Whig in 1836, when he got seventy-three electoral votes. He would do. The only person who objected to his candidacy was Henry Clay. He waited in Washington for news from the Whig Presidential convention, gulping down glasses of wine to relieve the suspense and cursing his enemies the while ('That man can never be my political idol again,' said an onlooker sadly). When he heard of Harrison's nomination his fury and despair boiled over. 'I am the most unfortunate man in the history of parties,' he cried. 'Always run by my friends when sure to be defeated, and now betrayed for a nomination when I, or any one, would be sure of an election.'

Nevertheless, the election of 1840 was not one of those which are conceded in advance. The Democrats made their thoroughly experienced machine function as never before, and were rewarded by winning more votes for

17 For a detailed analysis of the subject, see Peter Temin, *The Jacksonian Economy* (New York, 1969).

Van Buren than they had ever got for Jackson. But the Whigs did even better: Harrison won by 234 electoral votes to 60 for the President, although the margin in the popular vote was fairly narrow (1,274,624 to 1,127,781). At bottom, the outcome was settled by the depression. Other factors explain the scale of the victory. Hard work by the Whigs: they did not miss a trick, for example nominating for Vice-President a renegade Jacksonian, John Tyler of Virginia (1790–1862), to strengthen the ticket's appeal in the Upper South. The vague but powerful feeling that the Democrats had been in power long enough. Van Buren's personal vulnerability: he was distrusted as a Northerner in the South, where he was little known, and regarded as altogether too polished a gentleman by many rough voters. A devastating mistake by the Democrats: one of their aggressive journalists, ignoring Harrison's genteel antecedents, wrote that he was unfit to be President, he should stay in his log-cabin with his tobacco pipe, his jug of hard cider, and his latch-string hanging out to let strangers in at the door. This snobbish remark was too much for the Americans. If the Whigs were the party of log-cabins and cider, they must be the right party to vote for. Soon every Whig parade, barbecue and clambake (of which there were hundreds) displayed log-cabins borne aloft on sturdy shoulders. Hard cider[18] was dispensed in large quantities. Whig leaders rapidly discovered that they had all, or almost all, been born in log-cabins; Daniel Webster explained that he had been born in a house only because, being the youngest, he had come into the world when his family had earned a little prosperity. His elder brothers had done the right thing. Some surrealistic genius constructed a gigantic ball made of tin and began to roll it along the roads of Ohio. Its point was expressed by a chant:

As rolls the ball
Van's reign does fall
And he may look
To Kinderhook.

(Kinderhook was Van Buren's home town.) Whig papers reported that the Siamese twins were going to vote for the Cincinnatus of Cincinnati.[19]

In vain the Democrats fought back, explaining (erroneously) that OK stood for 'Old Kinderhook' – that great and good man, Martin Van Buren.[20] The slogan 'Tippecanoe and Tyler Too' hammered them into the ground.

The election of 1840 was the climax of a long evolution. Even more than

18 British travellers to the United States need to be aware that what Americans call 'cider' is mere unfermented apple-juice; only 'hard cider' is alcoholic.
19 The Siamese twins were Chang and Eng (1811–74), who were united at their waists by a tube of cartilage. As children they were sold by their parents to a British merchant and exhibited as freaks in England and America. Before long they began to make money by exhibiting themselves. They married sisters and settled as farmers in North Carolina. They died at sea: Chang of drink, Eng, a few hours later, of fright.
20 'Okay' is thought to be a word brought to America by slaves from West Africa.

that of 1828 it expressed the new nature of American politics. That Jefferson had beaten Hamilton, and the republic was now a democracy, was patent to all the world. But it was a democracy of a particular kind. Every white male adult citizen was, or could be, involved (the percentage of the electorate voting in 1840 was 80.2 – a proportion to be surpassed only in 1860 and 1876): a legal revolution could occur every four years. A permanent contest had sprung up spontaneously between the Ins and the Outs: whatever the good luck or good management of the reigning party, there would always be an opposition ready to fight. The spoils system gave it something to fight for; the prospect of another election gave it something to hope for; and though a party might be defeated nationally, it would have great reserves of strength in the states, cities and counties which it still controlled – for no party victory has ever been absolutely complete – and, throughout the history of the American party system, local victory has always seemed, to some politicians, more important than a national one. The contest was by no means wholly cynical. Whigs and Democrats stood for significantly different economic programmes, and although both parties tried to appeal to all parts of the country equally, they did not sink all their beliefs in order to do so. The Democrats stuck by the doctrines they had inherited from Thomas Jefferson and Andrew Jackson. The federal government, they believed, should be weak, the states strong. There should be no national bank, nor paper money, but instead a currency of gold and silver, and an independent Treasury where federal revenues, derived from the sales of public lands rather than the tariff (the Democrats were a party of free-traders), could be kept safe from aristocratic speculators and corrupters. The Whigs were equally loyal to the memory of Hamilton's reports on manufactures and banking, and to Henry Clay's American System, which contradicted the notions of the Democracy at every point. The Whigs wanted to build up American national strength by building up the economy; if that meant creating a class of rich men, so much the better. But they were not undemocratic, in the political sense: they enjoyed the game too much for that; nor were they illiberal or reactionary as to social policy. This was a great era of experimental reform, and of noisy egalitarianism. The Whigs, or some of them at any rate, espoused both. Seward, for example, began his career as a leader of the so-called Anti-Masonic party in New York state, which in the early thirties suspected the Freemasons of dreadful conspiracies against democracy; and as governor of New York he showed himself to be a humane supporter of prison reform.

These differences gave the Americans an objective means by which to judge between the parties. But there is much sense in Tocqueville's remark that 'almost all the Americans' domestic quarrels seem at first glance either incomprehensible or childish'.[21] The two parties performed a great service

21 Alexis de Tocqueville, *De la Démocratie en Amérique* (first published 1835), Part II, Chapter 2.

to the republic, by making it seem to the citizens that grievances could be met within the constitutional system; you simply chose your side, worked for its victory and got justice in return. The party leaderships tended to lose sight of all such important considerations in the heat of the battle. Victory was all: it took even a man so able and upright as Martin Van Buren a lifetime to learn that there might be a higher good than party advantage. Whigs and Democrats alike went out to win the support of the common man by any means: whether by appealing to his prejudices or his sympathies, by libelling the opposition in the cheap newspapers that the advance of technology was making universal, or by haranguing crowds from the stumps of newly felled trees in western forest clearings (which gave the language the term 'stump-speaking').

The Democrats, once the sole champions of the people, were forced to accept the legitimacy of the Whigs. 'We have taught them how to beat us,' they sighed after the 1840 returns were in: they could not plausibly allege any longer that they had been defeated by the corrupt wiles of aristocratic Federalists. Both parties embodied the principle of compromise, for otherwise the different groups of which each was composed could never have stayed together; and by accepting the limitations of the Constitutional system and each other's existence they made compromise, which is one good way of accepting reality, a basic ingredient of American politics outside, as well as within, the parties. Both were extravagantly nationalistic, casting covetous eyes on Texas (which broke away from Mexico in 1836), on the Pacific coast, on Canada. Both were at bottom alliances of smaller groups from all parts of the Union. And if the rich as a class tended to vote Whig, having been frightened by Jacksonian rhetoric, there were nevertheless plenty of wealthy men who thought better of the Democrats. America was anyway not yet a society in which the moneyed class wielded disproportionate power. Numbers were everything, as every foreign visitor was told again and again; the zest for democracy was such that many of the citizens began to think that it might be extended yet further: say, to women. The first important meeting to demand universal suffrage was held at Seneca Falls, NY, in 1848.

But one of the similarities between the parties boded no good for what was otherwise a very promising political system. There was one urgent question which neither Whigs nor Democrats would willingly raise; both knew that they would split if it was asked too insistently, and that even the Union was not safe; yet, again and again, it obtruded, in spite of all the politicians could do. The question was that of slavery.

The tragedy of nineteenth-century America was to be that in spite of the heroic exuberance which tamed a continent, launched an industrial revolution and set up the first true modern democracy, the problem of the South and its 'peculiar institution' was to prove so intractable as to put all America's achievements in mortal danger.

14 Slavery and its Consequences 1800–1861

I tremble for my country when I reflect that God is just.

Thomas Jefferson, *Notes on Virginia*, 1784

Harper's Creek and roaring river
There, my dear, we'll live for ever
Then we'll go to the Indian Nation.
All I want in this creation
Is a pretty little wife and big plantation.

Plantation song

Everybody, in the South, wants the privilege of whipping somebody else.

Frederick Douglass

Slavery in nineteenth-century America is best understood as a survival. It had begun as a device for securing cheap labour to work raw land on the edge of civilization. It outlived its time because soon after men discovered that it was an evil they also discovered that they could not bear to part with it. They could not imagine a tolerable future without it – could not endure to acknowledge the pace and direction of the changes which the world was hurrying upon them. White Southern men, that is. Most of the blacks of course hated it; white Northerners gave it up with comparative ease in the twenty or so years that followed the Revolution: the last Northern state to put an end to the institution where it had previously existed was New Jersey in 1804. White Southern women were divided about slavery. No matter. Anti-slavery whites were too weak, blacks too few, to overthrow the system. Even in 1800, when one inhabitant in five of the United States was an African-American, the slaves – dispersed, socially backward, militarily feeble – could not have organized a successful uprising; and by 1860, though there were nearly four million slaves, there were nearly twenty-seven million free whites, and only 488,000 free blacks. The question of the persistence of slavery in the United States can be answered only by examining the attitudes of the ascendant race and its ascendant sex; the same is true of the question, why did the system end so calamitously? There was something inexorable about the trend of events to rebellion, war and emancipation; but this could not have been the case if the pro-slavery whites had not been so hopelessly provincial; that is, so caught up in slave society that they became, willy-nilly, its victims and its tools. The abolition of slavery was not an experiment that most of them would ever have felt free to try. Their courage, compassion and intelligence failed. Slavery frustrated the desires and abilities of the blacks; it perverted the whites. When slavery vanished, no one mourned it for long.

For the blacks, slavery was a regime of sorrow, of degradation, of unremitting toil, dreadful personal insecurity and perpetual frustration. Yet the enslaved Africans might have been worse off. They retained their self-respect, fragments of their ancestral culture, memories of their origins, and achieved some measure of fulfilment even in their bonds. Their essential victory is demonstrated by their religion and by the great music evolved from their plantation work songs; from the celebration songs, born in those revels which white gentlemen such as Mr Jefferson regarded with cool disdain; and above all from the spirituals, with their message of human sorrow, divine consolation and ultimate joy. Some of the most poignant themes of the spirituals arose directly from the slave experience: above all, perhaps, the feeling that life is a burden, and death the opportunity to lay it down. 'Never to be born is best,' said Sophocles: everybody knows that mood, occasionally. It predominated in the slave spirituals – so markedly that it even shaped the pastiche plantation songs of Stephen Foster (1826–64), such as 'Old Black Joe':

No more rain fall for wet you, *hallelujah.*
No more sun shine for burn you,
There's no hard trials
There's no whips a-cracking
No evil-doers in the Kingdom,
All is gladness in the Kingdom, *hallelujah!*

Slavery as a regime of incessant labour was nothing abnormal. There had been incessant labour in Africa; indeed, North American slaves were mostly descended from tribes among whom harsh agricultural toil was traditional: the hunting tribes successfully resisted enslavement. The nineteenth-century Atlantic world paid for its numerous leisured classes by merciless exactions on everybody else. The story of industrial workers in Britain (or, a little later, in Pennsylvania) was as bad as anything which could be told of the plantations, as defenders of slavery liked to point out. The ending of the importation of slaves from Africa, which became federal law in 1808, forced masters to look after their property better. 'The time has been that the farmer could kill up and wear out one Negro to buy another; but it is not so now,' one planter remarked in 1849. 'Negroes are too high in proportion to the price of cotton, and it behooves those who own them to make them last as long as possible.' Slaves were often whipped to work; and, a crucial point, their working day was of appalling length ('from day clear to nightfall' was the phrase); but otherwise their conditions of labour were little worse than those of many whites. The abundant evidence of the grinding nature of work for slaves is best understood as showing what slaves had in common with free men – or free women and children, for that matter. Cruel toil was as much the law in the factories of New England, the slums of New York and on the farming frontier as it was in Alabama.

Still, the fact remains that workers in New England were *not* whipped, they did have a shorter working day, they were legally free to change masters and they were free to spend their wages as they saw fit. Slaves without wages had to accept such clothing, housing and food as their owners doled out to them: none were of the best. 'Negro cloth' and 'Negro brogans' (shoes) were of the cheapest, poorest manufacture, and were seldom provided in enough quantity, so most slaves went dirty, barefoot and in rags. Most slave cabins were badly built, leaky and unglazed and unhealthy. The slave diet was chiefly maize and bacon, or pork, eked out by what could be hunted or stolen; it was deficient in vitamins and variety. Things were better than this on some plantations; but a plantation might also be more like a prison run by sadists than any Northern factory ever was. Such laws as existed for protecting the slaves were frequently unenforced, in the cause of white solidarity. Even if a master whipped a slave to death he might escape punishment, for it would never do if the blacks began to think that there were any limits to their owners' power over them. Also, masters often delegated responsibility to hired overseers, who, as one planter in Mississippi observed, were, 'as a class, a worthless set of vagabonds'.

The overseers might have retorted that most masters cared for nothing except production and profit, and thought that the best overseer was the one who produced the largest number of cotton bales or sugar hogsheads per slave. So no wonder the slaves were overworked. 'I'd rather be dead,' said one overseer, 'than a nigger on one of those big plantations.' The fact was so inescapable that even pro-slavery writers sometimes acknowledged it. 'It is this unrelenting, brutalizing, *drive, drive*, watch and whip, that furnishes *facts* to abolition writers that cannot be disputed, and that are infamous' – so said one Southern journal on the eve of secession.

Another difference between slaves and factory workers was in the matter of personal insecurity. In Victorian England, for example, the rise of the trade unions was a natural response to bad food, atrocious housing and dread of hard times – of unemployment, and the workhouse where families could be broken up, where husbands and wives, after a lifetime together, could be separated. No such response was possible under slavery. At the very time when the restrictions on union activity were slackening in England, the slave codes were tightening in America. Husbands might still be sold away from their wives, children from their mothers; a casual decision might uproot a man for ever from the place and people that he loved. Worst of all was the fate dreaded by slaves in the Upper South (Maryland, Virginia and Kentucky), where conditions were easiest: they might, for a dozen reasons, suddenly be sold 'down the river' – down the Mississippi to the Black Belt of central Alabama or Mississippi state; or to the coastal swamps, the regions of malaria and yellow fever; to the endless exhaustion of the cotton fields and sugar plantations. Even some of the slave-owners deplored this internal slave-trade; yet without it the Cotton Kingdom could not have prospered, for the trade was the chief means by which the labour supply was adjusted to the demand, and workers were shifted from the exhausted lands of the Atlantic coast to the fresh fields of the interior. Many a great gentleman of South Carolina owed his standing to his plantations and slaves in the West. There was always an acute labour shortage on the Southern frontier; consequently voices were often raised to demand the re-opening of the slave-trade with Africa. Therefore the planters' dislike of the internal slave-trade need not be taken any more seriously than their contempt for the overseers. They sold slaves away from their homes and families without compunction when they thought it necessary. What the slaves thought can be guessed from the large number of runaways, most of whom, if not simply treating themselves to a few days' holiday in the woods, paid for on return with a whipping, were trying to rejoin their wives and children.

Not that the wives were legally recognized as such. Even when a master agreed to say the marriage service for two slaves, he always left out the essential words, 'Till death us do part' – he might want to part them much sooner. The abolitionists certainly exaggerated in the appeals they made to the prurience of the righteous, but the stark fact remains that slave women belonged to their masters, and the result was a great deal of sexual exploitation. The best that could be said was that prudent masters acknowledged the validity of slave marriages in practice, because it was good for morale and labour discipline.

Frustration of the personality is something more difficult to measure or even to demonstrate than the more material forms of oppression; it is not necessarily less harmful. Slavery wasted generations of talent and energy. Slaves might not be taught to read or write, lest they read 'incendiary publications'; they could not own property; it was commonly thought unwise to teach them industrial trades, because, as *De Bow's Review* remarked, 'whenever a slave is made a mechanic, he is more than half freed'. They were given only the most limited responsibilities. A man so talented as Frederick Douglass (1817–95) might be condemned to pass his life as little more than a beast of burden unless, like Douglass, he succeeded in escaping to the North. To this particular form of humiliation was added a systematic attempt to cow the slaves by force and insult. Slave testimony would not be accepted in court against white; all blacks, slave or free, must accept close restrictions on their movements, being, typically, confined to quarters after dark and forbidden to go any distance except under orders; they were answerable to the slave patrols, a white gendarmerie which rode about at night maintaining order; must put up with whatever treatment they got; and must endure the knowledge that their oppressors, when not frightened of them or sentimental about them, regarded them with contempt as an inferior order of creation. They even found it convenient to pander to the racialist view by posing as so many Sambos – bewildered darkies with child-ish joys and fears, lazy, affectionate and stupid. It was safer to be seen as a Sambo than as a marauding ape, lusting for fire, slaughter and white women.

Finally, men and women cannot be unfree in a free society without knowing that they are wronged – even if their masters try to keep the fact from their attention.

So the African-Americans hated slavery. Decent treatment could not buy acquiescence – rather the contrary, as Frederick Douglass pointed out. 'Beat and cuff your slave,' he said, 'keep him hungry and spiritless, and he will follow the chain of his master like a dog; but feed and clothe him well, – work him moderately – surround him with physical comfort, – and dreams of freedom intrude. Give him a *bad* master, and he aspires to a *good* master; give him a good master, and he wishes to become his *own* master.' Yet the slaves on the whole did not try to alter their hated condition. They knew their injuries, but they also knew their weakness. It is a striking fact that in the half-century before the Civil War there were no slave risings of any great account, and those that did occur – the abortive Denmark Vesey conspiracy at Charleston in 1822, the Nat Turner rebellion in Virginia in 1831, in which some sixty whites were murdered – owed their notoriety chiefly to the terror which they inspired in the master race. From time to time there would be outbreaks on solitary plantations; or a white family might be slain, suddenly, by its slaves, with poison or knives.[1] These were isolated events, leading to nothing, meaning nothing, except that in one place, at one particular time, matters had reached a crisis point. Nevertheless, the slave-owners could not afford to take such affairs coolly. They too knew insecurity: they dared not trust the people they lived among. Periodically something would terrify them into renewed excesses of cruelty. After the Turner rebellion they hanged not only the murderers but also scores of the innocent.

Indeed, the drawbacks of slavery from the point of view of the whites were so glaring that it sometimes seems astonishing that it lasted so long. The women – some of them – saw clearest. One of them, Mary Chesnut (1823–86) of South Carolina, put the case most trenchantly, and with such

---

1 Kenneth M. Stampp, *The Peculiar Institution* (New York, Vintage edn, 1956, p. 131), records that 'a slave who had been promised freedom in his master's will, poisoned his master to hasten the day of liberation'.

frankness that her limitations, of class and personality, are as palpable as her insights. So her testimony is doubly valuable to historians. She disliked living among slaves, and some of the reasons she gives (black faces, woolly heads) show that she was racially prejudiced. But she was also bitter because many Southern women had to pretend not to notice the resemblance between their own offspring and certain little black children on the plantations: proof that their husbands and brothers had been dallying in the slave quarters. She greatly resented the strictures made by such Northern ladies as Harriet Beecher Stowe (1811–96), author of the immensely celebrated anti-slavery novel *Uncle Tom's Cabin* (published in 1852):

On one side Mrs Stowe, Greeley, Thoreau, Emerson, Sumner. They live in nice New England homes, clean, sweet-smelling, shut up in libraries, writing books which ease their hearts of their bitterness against us. What self-denial they do practice is to tell John Brown to come down here and cut our throats in Christ's name. Now consider what I have seen of my mother's life, my grandmother's, my mother-in-law's ... They live in Negro villages. They do not preach and teach hate as a gospel, and the sacred duty of murder and insurrection;[2] but they strive to ameliorate the condition of these Africans in every particular. They set them an example of a perfect life, a life of utter self-abnegation. Think of these holy New Englanders forced to have a Negro village walk through their houses whenever they see fit ... These women I love have less chance to live their own lives in peace than if they were African missionaries.

The resentment in this diatribe is genuine, but misdirected. The slight note of persecution mania is significant, for it illustrates one of the traits, general among white Southerners, which brought about secession from the Union and, hence, the ultimate destruction of the slave society. But Mrs Chesnut was not prevented from living the life she wanted either by the slaves or by the abolitionists. She was the victim of the planters, who, in a sense, owned the whites as well as the blacks. Certainly they owned their own wives and daughters. Mrs Chesnut loved her husband, or told herself she did; but he treated her abominably. Once he locked her up in her room rather than allow her to keep an appointment to meet a gentleman of whom he disapproved solely, it seems, because his wife liked him. On another occasion Mrs Chesnut congratulated herself: she had acquired a secret supply of money, which meant that for a time she wouldn't have to run to her husband for every penny she needed. She had no children, and found the work of supervising her house-slaves insufficiently challenging: she had no hope of a career.[3] The myth of slavery exacted this unnatural life. White ladies had

2 It ought perhaps to be said that Mrs Stowe, Horace Greeley and the others did not preach hate and murder either.
3 One of the many merits of the celebrated novel *Gone with the Wind* (by Margaret Mitchell, published in 1936; Edmund Wilson, the critic, called it the South's answer to *Uncle Tom's Cabin*) is that it shows its heroine, the spirited Scarlett O'Hara, in instinctive perpetual revolt

to be idle, else they would not have needed slaves to work for them. They had to be sexually cold and rigidly chaste, or there could be no justification for their husbands to chase after black women. They had to abandon their function as mothers to black 'mammies', so that they could parade before the world perpetually in fine dresses, jewels and carriages – the fruits of slavery, advertisements of their menfolk's success. White women had to be denied education and political rights, so that no challenge could be made to the supremacy of the white male: one challenge might breed another, and if men once conceded that they had no right to tyrannize over women, what right could they claim to tyrannize over slaves?

It was a violent world. In part this was the legacy of the frontier, which persisted longer in the South than in the North (not until the 1830s were the last Indian tribes cleared out of Alabama and Mississippi). And whereas in the North-West the family farm was the most efficient unit for developing the country, and entailed a supporting network of roads and market towns by means of which farm-produce could be got to the customers (there was besides the village tradition of New England to fortify civilizing tendencies), in the South, where vast cotton plantations would be hacked out of the virgin forest, their produce being sent to market down untamed rivers, the density of the population – especially the white population – continued much lower, though the financial yield of agriculture might be as great, or greater. Growth, that is, was too rapid to be smooth. But the time span in question (some seventy years, from the invention of Eli Whitney's cotton gin to the attack upon Fort Sumter) is too long for this explanation to be sufficient. The North too was raw country for most of the nineteenth century.

No, Southern violence owed most to the persistence of slavery. Young men had to be trained to ride and shoot so that they could effectively play their part in the slave patrols. As a result a strange, barbarous culture grew up which quickly annihilated (for example) Jefferson's dream that the University of Virginia, which he founded in 1819, would be a great light of republican civilization. The colleges of the South remained jokes until the twentieth century. Instead of science and Greek, the young gentlemen learned to hold their liquor, or at least not to mind getting blind drunk; how to use a knife in a brawl; how to handle duelling pistols and to play cards; how to race and bet on horses. They were provincial, ignorant and overbearing: excellent cannon-fodder, as it turned out, but lacking the desirable peacetime qualities of a sense of reality and responsibility.

An eye for profit did something to substitute for academic education. The graces with which the planters liked to adorn their way of life and their great white mansions deceived many at the time, and more since, into

---

against the insipid norms imposed on a 'lady' in the Old South. In Scarlett's world a lady forfeited caste by even such a small thing as drinking alcohol, however moderately. No wonder Scarlett became a secret tippler. In this as in other ways she cannot have been unique.

accepting them as a class of well-bred gentlemen, strictly comparable to the nobility of Europe. Their account books tell a different story. Experience sobers the wildest blade, if he lives long enough; in the Old South the demands of plantation management turned innumerable roaring boys into disciplined capitalists. They had little in common with the gilded lords of England, whose talent lay in spending rather than getting. Their true affinity was with the restless merchants and manufacturers of Pennsylvania, New York and Massachusetts.

For the great planters, at their height, it was a good life, so long as new lands could be found for tillage (incessant cotton-growing exhausted the soil as badly as tobacco) and more slaves could be bought from Virginia, and the meddlesome abolitionists of the North could be kept at bay, and the hands in the houses and the fields did as they were told, and the weather was good, and the world market for cotton was buoyant. But for the other white men of the South – the great majority – matters were never so simple.[4] Their moral position was weak, for they had taken part in the expulsion of the Indians and were indifferent to the sufferings of the Africans; but they were injured by slavery all the same. The profits of the peculiar institution were so enormous that the slave-holders were always able to outbid the white yeomanry for the choicest lands. As a result a sharp class division grew up in the South, which was to some extent also a geographical division, the poorer whites being thickest on the ground in the upland and mountain areas, the planters and their slaves in such rich lowlands as the Black Belt. In an age as stridently democratic as the early nineteenth century this growing gulf within the white population naturally had to find expression in politics (the yeomen were mostly enthusiastic followers of General Jackson) and might have been expected to lead to an attack on slavery as giving some whites an unfair advantage in the race for riches; but no such thing occurred. Planters exacted the utmost labour from their bondsmen; revelled in the wealth which resulted, and boasted of the skill of their slaves; appeased their consciences by inconsistently asserting the ignorance, shiftlessness and helplessness of blacks – a race so inferior that it needed enslavement; and made themselves affable to the yeomanry at election time. Poor whites shared to the full the contempt for and fear of African-Americans which were felt by their betters; they could not contemplate liberating slaves who, as free men, would compete on their own behalf for land and profit; they deeply resented any scheme which might place blacks on the same footing as themselves, however nominally (it was much more agreeable to feel that, however unfortunate and ignorant you were, there were always a large number of others even worse off); many among them cherished a hope, however unrealistic, that they too would rise into the planter class; and they

4 The total white population of the slave states in 1860 was 8,098,000 (black, 4,204,000); 385,000 were slave-holders, of whom only 46,000 owned more than twenty slaves and are thereby known as planters.

dreaded the revenge which, they thought, free blacks would take on their former oppressors. These views forged a strong bond between the yeoman farmers, the 'poor white trash' and the rich planters: they formed an alliance that was to survive all vicissitudes until the late twentieth century, and do incalculable damage to America and Americans. This alliance removed what might have been the strongest force making for abolition.

So far as Southern whites were concerned, then, slavery was an evil because, whether they realized it or not, it thwarted progress: in spite of its wealth the slave South lagged further behind the rest of the United States, not to mention Europe, every year. Some Southerners perceived some of its evil consequences; perhaps all its evils were noticed by someone or other in the South at some time in the years before the Civil War. Many voices were heard lamenting the backward state of Southern agriculture and the failure of the South to industrialize, or even to build enough railroads. The great men of the eighteenth century – Washington and Jefferson above all – had freely recognized slavery for an evil; they had been quite prepared to admit that it was inconsistent with the Declaration of Independence, and looked forward with confidence to its eventual disappearance. The tragedy of the South was that it ceased to listen to these prophetic voices. As time went on the assertion was made ever more frequently that slavery, far from being an evil, was 'a positive good', bringing all sorts of benefits with it.

It could not have been otherwise. The planters were in a hereditary trap, just as much as the blacks. They had inherited a labour system which, though extremely profitable,[5] was also degrading, dangerous and unstable. Towards the end of his life Jefferson, the eternal optimist, despaired and, speaking as a Southerner and a slave-holder, remarked:

I can say, with conscious truth, that there is not a man on earth who would sacrifice more than I would to relieve us from this heavy reproach, in any *practicable* way. The cession of that kind of property, for so it is misnamed, is a bagatelle which would not cost me a second thought, if, in that way, a general emancipation and *expatriation* could be effected; and, gradually, and with due sacrifices, I think it might be. But as it is, we have the wolf by the ears, and we can neither hold him, nor safely let him go. Justice is in one scale, and self-preservation in the other . . .[6]

He had once hoped that a new generation, brought up in republican liberty, would complete the work of the Revolution by abolishing slavery; in his old age he sadly recognized that he had been wrong. And today it is clear that he himself was hopelessly entangled in the contradictions of slavery. He too

---

5 The question of the profitability or otherwise of slavery has been fiercely debated since the eighteenth century. An excellent digest of modern work on the subject is to be found in R. W. Fogel and S. L. Engerman (eds), *The Reinterpretation of American Economic History* (New York, 1971), Part VII.

6 Jefferson to John Holmes, 22 April 1820. Note how Jefferson wavers between the belief that gradual emancipation might be effected and the belief that self-preservation made it impossible.

was a victim of fear and guilt. Because he could not trust African-Americans, he persuaded himself that they were racially inferior to whites; that God did not intend them to have any share in the bounties of the New World, reserved for enlightened Europeans; that therefore any scheme of emancipation must include provision for sending the Negroes back to Africa, or to Haiti; and that until such a scheme was in operation, slavery must remain, indeed expand. He was not consciously influenced by the consideration that James Henry Hammond of South Carolina (1807–64) put so bluntly when he asked if any people in history had ever voluntarily surrendered two billion dollars worth of property; but the racism which did influence him was at least as responsible for maintaining nineteenth-century American slavery as greed. Guilty slave-holders could not believe that their victims would not take a horrible revenge at the first opportunity. Slaves were sly enough for anything:

He died – the jury wondered why?
The verdict was, the blue-tail fly.

So it was emotionally very difficult to contemplate emancipating the blacks; and as the number of slaves increased, so did the difficulty.

Not that the economic argument was neglected. Slavery meant power and prosperity for the planter class; a huge amount of capital had been invested in it; and no white believed that the crops of the South could be grown and harvested except by slave labour. Free blacks, it was assumed, would abandon the cotton-fields, or insist on working only for themselves, as happened in the British sugar islands after emancipation in 1833. And then what would happen to the planter and his family?

In these circumstances there was no chance that the majority of voters in any Southern state would support abolition. Even enlightened Virginia, after long and anguished debate, rejected the idea in 1832. Private acts of manumission (never very numerous) came to be frowned on as irresponsible. What right had a man to undermine his neighbour's safety and prosperity merely to gratify his private conscience? Besides, a free Negro population was not only anomalous in the slave South, it was unsettling to discipline. Consequently, in state after state, manumission was outlawed, and the status of the free black was reduced. In this way the South bound itself anew to slavery and to the proposition that slavery was to be eternal. Thereby, Southerners excluded the possibility that black servitude could be ended peaceably, an exclusion that they were well able to enforce. They also denied that it would be ended violently. This they were not so well placed to command.

As we have seen, the slaves themselves were in no position to rebel successfully, and on the whole declined to do so unsuccessfully (though whether such restraint would have continued for ever may be doubted). It is also true that the United States Constitution permitted slavery and that there was never majority support in the North for armed emancipation until halfway through the Civil War at earliest. The South was a citadel, walled with law, force and opinion. To many it seemed impregnable. Yet its fall was rapid, and the process which destroyed it was a fairly simple, almost a predictable one. The castle's foundations were rotten. Its defenders proved incompetent, and their incompetence was as much a result of slavery as was any other aspect of Southern life.

This was proved by the fact that the enemies who first touched the fatal weakness had no idea of what they were doing. They did not understand the South at all. The abolitionists were as much the children of the North as the planters were children of the South, and in their way just as purblind. But they were much luckier.

Perhaps they deserved to be. Obsessed with their own experience, the slave-holders constantly misjudged other Americans. For instance, one of the worst mistakes made by such apologists for slavery as Calhoun and Hammond – a mistake prompted, no doubt, by the ever-increasing amount of cotton which New England mills were buying from the South – was to assume that the Industrial Revolution already dominated Northern society. They drew parallels between the chattel slavery of the South and the wage slavery of the North, and appealed for an alliance with the financiers and manufacturers who were beginning to form a new, moneyed aristocracy. But they were misguided, for rapidly though industrialism was rising,[7] there were far too few factories in the North as yet to determine the distribution of political power. The North, like the South, was predominantly agrarian. Its towns were growing more rapidly than at any other period of their history, but they were as yet chiefly commercial, rather than manufacturing: they provided goods and services for the surrounding farms and forwarded agricultural produce to the world market. Never, perhaps, has the city dominated American society less than in this period.

Family farms spread westward as far as the prairies of Iowa, Wisconsin and Minnesota. Times were mostly good, and when they were not the farmer was better placed than the townsman to sit them out. He could feed and clothe himself, and equip himself for the still comparatively simple needs of agricultural production (expensive machinery such as the mechanical reaper was not to become indispensable until after mid-century), and if his debts became heavy he possessed enough political power to stave off his creditors by one means or another. The tradition of the American Revolution gave him immense pride in being a free citizen and a keen sense of his rights. The rapid spread of modern means of communication (canals, newspapers, the post office) kept him in touch with his countrymen and the new ideas of the age. A brisk appetite for dollars (every foreign visitor noticed that Americans had an inordinate respect for riches) fostered his energy, his commercial astuteness and his relish for innovation of all kinds.

7 See below, Chapter 17.

There was nothing of the cautious, slow peasant about the successful Northern farmer, any more than there was about the Southern planter. He believed that the future was his, and boasted about the glorious destiny of whatever place he inhabited – every small settlement was going to outdo London and Paris – as if mere assertion (it was called boosting) would make all dreams come true. And his institutions were deeply marked by the heritage of New England. Education was highly valued, so that it would be hard to say which was most typical of the North-West, the proverbial little red schoolhouse where a basic literacy and patriotism was whacked into the souls of young Americans; or the small country college, where slightly higher attainments could be acquired; or the Lyceum, a hall maintained by subscription where adults could spend their evenings listening to travelling lecturers, who covered an amazing miscellany of subjects. The central institution remained the church or the meeting-house. To those New Englanders who moved west, Puritanism remained a living force, setting its stamp as deeply on the nineteenth century and the Mississippi valley as it had on the seventeenth century and Connecticut. It made Mid-Westerners both serious and passionate, though no less given to self-importance, self-deception and the seven deadly sins than other men. The same was true of many Southerners: there was never a more joylessly dutiful Calvinist than John C. Calhoun. But as time went on, Northern culture, not forced into sterile conformity by the need to defend the indefensible, slavery, began to deviate markedly from the ancient norms. In the old centre of the faith, Boston, heterodoxy had long ago reared its successful head. The leading minds of Massachusetts, while remaining deeply Puritan in the best sense – men and women of austere, aspiring lives, of lively consciences and highly trained intellects – were yet abandoning the theology which had once brought Puritanism to birth. They discarded traditional Christianity and became Unitarians; or, with their representative sage, Ralph Waldo Emerson (1803–82), and inspired at a distance by Wordsworth, turned to the cult of Nature. But their influence was restricted. Emerson was barred from Harvard College for thirty years because of his unconventional religious views, though Harvard itself was Unitarian; Unitarianism, in turn, was of little or no attraction to the masses of Northern Protestants. Not that they were necessarily frightened of novelty: this was the period of the birth of Mormonism and of numerous other equally experimental, if less durable creeds. But the bulk of Americans were more susceptible to the call to conversion than to intellectual deliberations. As the eruption of the Great Revival demonstrated, for them the key-experience of life was still that desired by their ancestors under Elizabeth I: the confrontation of the individual soul with the challenge of God. Conversion again became a common episode in the lives of earnest Americans, even such unlikely ones as W. H. Seward, whose career as a distinguished politician does not give much evidence of a religious sense. Most of the conversions either wore off after a time (as was the case with Seward) or led the converts only to greater introspective concern with the state of their souls and the conduct of their daily lives. But the instinct to make over the world, an instinct clearly owing everything to the sense of boundless opportunities which the opening of the continent entailed, and which was already a deeply established trait of the American character, led a great many of the converts to feel God's challenge as a spur to undertake social and political reform. With missionary zeal they threw themselves into the task. Some tried to save Americans from the slavery of alcohol ('the demon Rum' in their jargon); others undertook, with even less success, to turn American prisons into humane institutions for reclaiming criminals; yet others became campaigners for women's rights, or for world peace. Others set to work to abolish Negro slavery. They saw it as offensive to God and destructive to American claims to the world's respect. They brought a terrifying determination and single-mindedness to the task of ending it.

Abolitionism, as distinct from anti-slavery, emerged as a clear movement in 1831, the year in which William Lloyd Garrison (1805–79) founded his journal, the *Liberator*, in Boston. He has not, on the whole, had a good press, North or South (Georgia once offered a reward of $5,000 for his arrest and conviction as a seditious agitator). In some ways his personality recalls that of the arch-enemy, Calhoun. Both men were ruthlessly logical in following out their beliefs, and both, like so many fanatical leaders, spent as much time quarrelling with their associates as in attacking the opposition. As a political tactician Garrison suffered from two fatal weaknesses: he saw, all too clearly, how all the reform causes were intertwined, so that he could not support one without supporting all; and he refused the slightest compromise with what he saw as evil. His business was to cleanse the American soul, to purge it of the sin of slavery: nothing less would be acceptable to God. But Garrison's function was not really that of a politician. He was a born journalist, and he kept the slavery issue alive by the eloquence and courage of his writings. It was inconvenient to the more conventional, no doubt, that he supported women's rights and associated with African-Americans (whose subscriptions were the *Liberator*'s main support); but today we must surely find these eccentricities rather noble, and Garrison's instinct for the central issue positively magnificent:

. . . there are, at the present time, the highest obligations resting upon the people of the free States to remove slavery by moral and political action, as prescribed in the Constitution of the United States. They are now living under a pledge of their tremendous physical force, to fasten the galling fetters of tyranny upon the limbs of millions in the Southern States; they are liable to be called at any moment to suppress a general insurrection of the slaves; they authorize the slave owner to vote for three-fifths of his slaves as property, and thus enable him to perpetuate his oppression; they support a standing army at the South for its protection; and they seize the slave, who has escaped into their territories, and send him back to

be tortured ... This relation to slavery is criminal and full of danger: IT MUST
BE BROKEN UP.[8]

Massachusetts was once more sending out a signal to America.

The next thirty years were marked by ceaseless struggle; constant denunciation of the abolitionists; striking successes for their opponents; and defeats,
mostly for the good side. Hope always proved delusive. Theodore Weld
(1803–95) made triumphant speaking tours through the Middle West and
won hundreds of supporters to the cause, especially in Ohio; but in doing
so he wrecked his health, and no one was able to widen the foundations he
had laid by bringing in communities where he had not spoken. His wife,
Angelina Grimké (1805–79), who with her sister Sarah fled from their
house in Charleston out of horror of slavery (having first freed the slaves
they had inherited), proved to be an effective abolitionist writer and speaker
and a sure platform draw; but she did more for the feminist cause than for
abolitionism, since many anti-slavery males could not stomach feminine
leadership, and the movement split over the question of women's participation. Abraham Lincoln told Harriet Beecher Stowe that *Uncle Tom's
Cabin* had caused the Civil War. But for years after its publication there
was no sign that it had brought the death of the peculiar institution any
closer, though it undoubtedly made it even more hateful to Americans in
the free states. In 1837, in southern Illinois,[9] a Negro-hating mob murdered
Elijah Lovejoy, a white abolitionist who was persisting in publishing an
anti-slavery newspaper, although his press had been wrecked four times.
In 1835 a mob in Boston set upon Garrison and dragged him through the
streets at the end of a rope; an incident which, coupled with the murder of
Lovejoy and his own wife's influence, brought Wendell Phillips (1811–
84), the most brilliant speaker of the age, into the movement. Frederick
Douglass ran away from Maryland and became abolition's most notable
black orator. But all his speeches, and those of Phillips, seemed to leave
slavery intact. The abolitionists could not, they found, preach or pamphleteer the South into repenting its sin; and in the North, when they were not
being attacked as 'nigger-lovers', they were avoided as bores, and denounced
as agitators whose activities threatened the existence of the American Union:
for Garrison and Phillips attacked the slavery-sanctioning Constitution as
a covenant with Hell, while Calhoun and his followers said that unless the
abolitionists were silenced, it might be necessary, in self-defence, for the
South to secede. Even when Western and New York abolitionists broke
with Garrison (for, being an anarchist, he believed that all government was
wrong, all politics corrupting) and ran a candidate in the 1840 Presidential

8 *Declaration of the Sentiments of the American Anti-Slavery Convention*, 1833.
9 Southern Illinois, like Indiana, was largely settled by emigrants from the South, who brought
their racial attitudes with them; and Alton, where Lovejoy died, was just across the Mississippi
from that violent, slave-owning Missouri which gave so much trouble to the Mormons and
Buffalo Bill's father (see above, pp. 236 and 245).

election (James Birney, a repentant slave-holder) he only got 5,000 votes. It was not, all in all, an impressive record. Nevertheless the abolitionists changed the course of American history.

For without conscious analysis they had found the weakness in the citadel. The slave-holders rejoiced in the profits of slavery and exhibited the utmost arrogance in personal behaviour; but underneath they were profoundly insecure. They were on the defensive, as had been shown long before the abolitionists appeared on the scene, in 1819–20, during the Missouri Crisis, which turned on the question of slavery extension. Thanks to the North-West Ordinance and the pattern of migration, the new states – Ohio, Indiana, Illinois – carved out of the North-West territory had all been set up as free; the South had been able to balance them with Louisiana, Mississippi and Alabama. In 1819 it was proposed to admit the territory of Missouri as a slave state. The Northerners in Congress objected to this, even though Maine, an outlying area of Massachusetts, was ready for admission at the same time as a free state, so that the balance between the North and South in the Senate could be maintained. Congressman James Tallmadge of New York proposed that Missouri should be accepted only if it undertook to forbid further slave immigration and to emancipate its slaves gradually, as the Northern states had done in the years after the Revolution. Tallmadge and his associates had two objects in view: to reserve as much of the Louisiana Purchase as possible for free, white labour, and to weaken the political ascendancy in the Union which the South had enjoyed since independence. Naturally the Southern leaders in Congress opposed Tallmadge; more significant was the passion with which they did so. Fear and hatred of the black people whom they were oppressing led them (and, alas for enlightenment, old Thomas Jefferson too) to predict the most appalling consequences for America if the spread of slavery were checked, and to impute the proposal to an unholy alliance between Northern greed and Northern fanaticism. They said that a plot was afoot among the tyrant majority of free states to destroy the South: it must be resisted at all costs. This allegation was wide of the mark: there was no Northern plot, and the North-West Ordinance was ample precedent for Tallmadge's proposal. Southern hysteria merely annoyed the North. In the end Henry Clay's skilful leadership pushed a series of bills through Congress which together amounted to the so-called Missouri Compromise: in future slavery would be excluded from all parts of the Louisiana Purchase north of the line of latitude 36° 30', but it would be allowed in Missouri after all; Maine would be admitted simultaneously. Then Missouri nearly overset the bargain by adopting a constitution which forbade free African-Americans to enter the state, thus denying them the right, undoubtedly enjoyed by all white Americans, of moving freely about their country, although all such rights were guaranteed by the US Constitution;[10] Missouri was in fact implicitly

10 Art. IV, Sec. 2: 'The Citizens of each State shall be entitled to all Privileges and Immunities of Citizens in the several States.'

denying that blacks were citizens (a denial which would be made explicit in the *Dred Scott* decision in 1857). Congress, again under Clay's leadership, dealt with this defiance by forcing Missouri to declare that nothing in her constitution should be interpreted as abridging the privileges and immunities of US citizens, but everyone knew that this question-begging, face-saving measure would never be enforced. From the libertarian point of view it was an abject affair and its settlement was squalid; but it helped to keep the peace in America for the next decade. The outlook for anti-slavery was never bleaker. Abolition societies died out in the South, even in Virginia, whose economy now depended on exporting slaves as once it had depended on exporting tobacco: 300,000 would be sold out of the State between 1830 and 1860. Many people of goodwill involved themselves in the mare's nest of the American Colonisation Society, which hoped to ship the Negroes back to Africa – a futile hope, if only because of the numbers involved. It was against this background that Garrison first lifted his voice ('I WILL BE HEARD'). Unsurprisingly, to anyone who had studied the Missouri affair, the South reacted to his challenge with all the calm and common sense of a scalded cat.

It also exhibited its neurosis in the Nullification Affair. This opened in 1828, when Congressional politicians, beginning a game which was to keep them amused for the next century and more, decreed a new tariff – promptly dubbed the Tariff of Abominations, for it was more concerned to assist the Presidential candidacy of Andrew Jackson than to protect burgeoning American industry or make any other economic sense. Heavy duties on British imports put the South in an uproar, for they might provoke British retaliation, and the cotton regions were dependent on their ability to trade freely with Lancashire. But that was not all: as Calhoun made clear, cotton was valued not only because it was a profitable export, but because it provided a paying occupation for the slaves. It underpinned the peculiar institution, which most Southerners now agreed was the only possible system by which the two races could live together. So the tariff was denounced as a threat to slavery as well as to prosperity. The reaction went to extraordinary lengths: following Calhoun, and using the jargon he invented, South Carolina 'interposed her state sovereignty' and in its name 'nullified' the tariff – refused, that is, to allow United States customs officials to enforce it within the state boundaries. President Jackson proclaimed this to be treason and rebellion; since no other state joined South Carolina he was able to threaten a march on Charleston with perfect confidence, and actually began to make military preparations; but meanwhile Congress, again led by Henry Clay, pushed through a much-reduced tariff which Calhoun deemed acceptable. Jackson's view of nullification was generally adopted, and for the time being the policy of a protective tariff was abandoned. So far so good: but the fragility of the American Union had again been convincingly demonstrated. Calhoun, who dreamed of the Presidency, had devised nullification as a substitute for secession. Now nullification was dead. There was too much reason to suppose that if the South ever again felt itself in danger, it would break up the Union.

Next, the abolitionists began their work of inducing a siege mentality in the slave-holders. Pamphlets denouncing slavery were mailed in large quantities to the South. Southerners, enraged and terrified at the idea that these works might fall into the hands of the slaves and touch off a rebellion, intercepted and destroyed them with the collusion of Amos Kendall, Jackson's Postmaster-General. There was outrage in the North at such tampering with the mail: petitions of protest poured into Congress from the abolitionists. The South induced Congress to refuse to receive the petitions. This seemed to frustrate the First Amendment right of the people to petition for redress of grievances, and brought the aged John Quincy Adams into action. Retirement had had few charms for the ex-President; he had returned to Congress in 1831 as Representative from Boston; and now embarked on a relentless campaign for lifting the so-called 'gag rule' and thus restoring the right of petition. It was all priceless propaganda for the abolitionist cause, and it reinforced the suspicion of the South that there was a serious conspiracy against it.

The expansion of slavery into fresh territory, if it could be obtained, would strengthen the defence of the institution by increasing the planters' representation in Congress. Furthermore, Southerners were still patriotic, indeed nationalist, Americans: like most of their fellow-citizens they thought that the great republic would and should eventually expand to cover the whole of North America. So covetous eyes were cast on the northernmost provinces of Mexico (which had thrown out its Spanish rulers in 1822). American settlers, with their slaves, had been drifting into the largest province, Texas, for years. In 1833, alienated by the Mexican government, they launched a revolution, and in 1836 their leader, General Sam Houston (1793–1863), a close associate of Andrew Jackson, defeated the Mexican President, General Santa Anna, at the Battle of San Jacinto. He declared Texas to be an independent republic, of which he became the first President.

This touched off a storm in the United States. Instructed by the abolitionists and the rant of the South, many Northerners regarded the whole affair as a conspiracy of slave-holders intent on grabbing immense stretches of territory that might have been developed by free labour. This view gained colour from the fact that slavery was actually illegal under Mexican law, which Houston's movement overthrew. Jackson himself did not dare to recognize Texan independence until the very last hours of his Presidency, for fear of seeming a party to conspiracy; he only acted at all to spare his successor, Van Buren, a great difficulty. A greater immediately sprang up in its place. For the next seven years there was a steady agitation for the annexation of Texas to the United States: a project much favoured by the Texans themselves, by the South, and by eager American nationalists everywhere; but one regarded with deep suspicion by Northern liberals and with deep concern by many American statesmen, who correctly feared that annexation would bring much trouble with it. But the high tide of westward expansion was flowing ('Manifest Destiny' it was called[11]): in the election of 1844 Van Buren lost the renomination of his party, and Henry Clay lost the election (he was the Whig candidate) because they would not support annexation unequivocally. The political situation was confused. President Harrison had died after a month in office, and been succeeded by Vice-President John Tyler, a no-party man. Tyler was as unsuccessful as Van Buren and Clay: James K. Polk of Tennessee, a veteran Democrat, sometimes known as Young Hickory, won the election; but before he took office Tyler and his Secretary of State, none other than John C. Calhoun, had taken the decisive step of admitting Texas to the Union. Soon an American army under General Zachary Taylor had advanced 150 miles south of the Texan frontier to the Rio Grande. In short, Mexico was invaded, and war followed.

It was a disgraceful affair; the contrast with events in the Pacific North-West at the same time, where President Polk, confronted with the much more formidable rivalry of the British, compromised American claims and settled the frontier with Canada where it runs today, merely makes it more painful. The Mexicans were militarily far too weak to stand up to the enthusiastic volunteer armies of the *gringos*; General Taylor beat them at the Battles of Palo Alto, Resaca de la Palma and Buena Vista; General Winfield Scott captured Mexico City and forced them to make peace; other American intruders tore away California and what are now the states of Arizona, Utah, Colorado, Nevada and New Mexico. Mexico formally relinquished these lands in the Treaty of Guadalupe Hidalgo (1848); and then the chickens came home to roost.

To the poet Walt Whitman, editor of the *Brooklyn Eagle*, it was for the interest of mankind that the power and influence of the United States should be extended – 'the farther the better'. To wiser Americans, such as Emerson's friend Henry David Thoreau (1817–65), the war of naked grab which Whitman supported was obscene. Thoreau refused to pay the taxes that were to finance it. New England moralists, already much influenced by abolitionism, found it impossible to forgive the South for the business. Still more ominous for the South was the response of North-Westerners, such as Abraham Lincoln, one of the many Whigs who were swept into the House of Representatives in 1846 in reaction against the Democrats' war. Lincoln regarded slavery as a great wrong, but he was no abolitionist, and, though personally the gentlest of men, he came from Illinois, the state where mobs had murdered Joseph Smith and Elijah Lovejoy. Lincoln, an instinctive and profoundly skilled politician, was not the man to get too far

11 'Manifest Destiny' was a phrase launched by the Democratic journalist, John L. O'Sullivan, who in 1845 proclaimed that it was America's 'manifest destiny to overspread the continent allotted by Providence for the free development of our yearly multiplying millions'. It was 'manifest destiny' that the United States would one day soon come to possess not only Texas but also California, Oregon and Canada.

ahead of his constituents if he could help it: the key to his entire career is
to be found in the remark he made, as President, in 1864: 'I claim not to
have controlled events but confess plainly that events have controlled me.'
The events he usually had in mind were political. Illinois farmers, he knew,
were prone to violence and unsympathetic to blacks: many of them, like
Lincoln himself, were immigrants from the South, and the state laws were
notoriously hostile to free African-Americans. But the plantation South
was an economic competitor, already far too powerful in the national
government: in 1846 it had pushed through Congress another tariff revision,
which in effect committed the United States to free trade; Polk's Oregon
compromise had denied free Northern farmers access to the rich country
of what is now British Columbia; while the Mexican War looked like opening
up a huge new area to slavery expansion. George III had done nothing as
bad, and consequently the old Revolutionary rhetoric began to be heard
again: the whites of the North were, it was said, threatened with slavery
themselves – not chattel slavery, but slavery in the sense that all the important
economic and political decisions in America might soon lie with 'the Slave
Power', which seemed able to sway Congress and Presidency as it pleased.
No wonder that the Northern Democrat, Congressman David Wilmot of
Pennsylvania, in order to save his seat in the 1846 elections, introduced, in
August of that year, the so-called Wilmot Proviso, by which slavery would
be forbidden in any territory annexed to the United States as a result of the
Mexican War; no wonder that Congressman Lincoln not only supported
the Proviso, but spoke and voted conspicuously in favour of the Whig
slogan, 'No Territory!' It was becoming necessary to demonstrate that white
Americans still really enjoyed self-government, by checking the South.

The Wilmot Proviso, as such, never passed Congress: the South saw to
that, and seemed to be the only gainer by the Presidential election of 1848,
for the Democratic party in the North split on the slavery issue, Van Buren
and his followers temporarily fusing with the abolitionists to form the Free
Soil party, so that Zachary Taylor, the Whig candidate, won narrowly –
and Taylor was a slave-holder. Abraham Lincoln did not return to Congress.
But this was only the first of many hollow victories that the South was to
win in the next twelve years. Underlying the rivalry between slavery and
free farming was the stubborn geographical fact that the new territories
were mostly quite unsuitable for plantation farming, and therefore for either
cotton or slavery, while economic prospects within the South proper were
never more alluring; cotton production and cotton profits were to rise to
unprecedented heights during the fifties. There was, in fact, no real economic
or social impetus behind the plans for slavery expansion: no planter was
going to transport his slaves hundreds of miles to a less certain economic
future than he was enjoying in Georgia or Mississippi. The planters might
have gone to California, but they were denied the chance: in 1848 gold was
discovered on the banks of the Sacramento river, and during the subsequent
Gold Rush the free white population rose (by 1850) to 92,000, and was

more than four times as large by 1860. Slavery would never be allowed to get a foothold there. And meantime, from the South's point of view, Taylor turned out to be a grave disappointment. He saw no point in quarrelling over territories that could not possibly be won for slavery, and besides he had his re-election to think of. He had only carried New York, and so gained the Presidency, because of the Democratic split: he might not be so lucky next time. To the horror of Southerners generally, and Southern Whigs in particular, he began to work closely with Senator Seward of New York, who was the leader of the Northern anti-slavery Whigs. It really seemed as if, at Seward's prompting, the President was going to adopt the Wilmot Proviso.

In Southern eyes this was intolerable: even if the slave South could not, in actuality, expand, it must be conceded the right to do so, or lose its equal standing in the Union: were Southerners to be denied their share of territory that they had been the chief instruments in winning? If so, they were no better than slaves themselves (they too could use the Revolutionary vocabulary). 'Will you submit to be bridled and saddled and rode under whip and spur?' asked the *Montgomery Advertiser*. On the other side, there was equal determination not to be downtrodden by a set of aristocrats. 'I am jealous of the *power* of the South,' wrote David Wilmot to a friend, '. . . the South holds no prerogative under the Constitution, which entitles her to wield forever the sceptre of power in this Republic, to fix by her own arbitrary edict, the principles and policy of this government, and to build up and tear down at pleasure.' With this temper prevailing on both sides, it began to look as if anything might happen. Calhoun, from his deathbed, was urging the South to unite and stand firm in defence of 'Southern Rights': and what might not that entail? Secession? War?

With luck and good management, both were avoided. Henry Clay worked his magic for the last time. He evolved a programme which in the end consisted of five measures: California to be admitted to the Union as a free state; New Mexico and Utah to be organized as territories, but without saying whether they were to be free or slave (let the inhabitants settle that, according to the Democratic party's doctrine of 'popular sovereignty'); the boundary dispute between Texas and the United States, left over from annexation, to be settled, and the Texan republic's debt to be paid by Congress; the slave-trade in the District of Columbia to be abolished; and a new, stricter Fugitive Slave Law to replace that of 1793.

At first, as was said, Clay's proposals united the opponents instead of securing the friends of his measures. But Calhoun died, and so did President Taylor, to be succeeded by his Vice-President, Millard Fillmore (1800–1874), one of Seward's chief rivals in the New York Whig party. Daniel Webster threw his vast authority behind the proposals; Stephen A. Douglas (1813–61), a Democratic Senator from Illinois, took up the hard work, when Clay faltered, of getting the votes needed to pass the legislation through Congress, and succeeded triumphantly with an ever-shifting coalition of

Northern Whigs, Southern Democrats, Northern Democrats, Southern Whigs. The Union men triumphed in the South, the conservatives in the North, 'the Compromise of 1850' everywhere. By 1852, the next Presidential year, it seemed that normality had been restored, the territorial question settled, and with it the greater question of the future of slavery: for it had long been assumed that unless slavery could expand, it would die.

The price of this achievement, even if it was what it seemed, was fearfully high. The South was bitterly opposed to the explicit exclusion of slavery from California and its implicit exclusion from the territories under the popular sovereignty formula: was this equality within the Union? And the abolition of the District of Columbia slave-trade seemed to be an ominous exercise of national power, directly attacking slavery: worse might follow. On the other side, the new Fugitive Slave Law was denounced, above all in New England, as an intolerable affront to the rights of Northern states and the consciences of Northern men and women. For the small-meshed network of its provisions not only bound all public officers to assist slave-holders to recapture runaway slaves, but entitled them to call on the assistance of bystanders, imposed terrific fines and up to six months' imprisonment on all who were convicted either of helping the runaways or trying to rescue them from custody; and, worst of all, by forbidding persons claimed by slave-holders from testifying in their own defence and accepting almost any evidence that slave-holders chose to present as valid, made possible the kidnapping of Northern free Negroes. Emerson wrote bitterly in his journal, 'the word *liberty* in the mouth of Mr Webster sounds like the word *love* in the mouth of a courtesan'. In Cincinnati Mrs Stowe was moved to write *Uncle Tom's Cabin*, of which the most famous episode is the escape of the slave Eliza across the ice of the frozen Ohio river, pursued (in the stage version, which was even more popular than the novel) by bloodhounds. North and South, the Whig party began to break up.

There was irony in this: preservation of the party had been one of Henry Clay's chief aims in bringing forward his proposals. Webster had accepted appointment as Fillmore's Secretary of State especially in order to rally the Whigs behind the Compromise, and used federal patronage ruthlessly to that end. But the Southern Whigs, who had fought so valiantly against the disunion forces in their section, were not forgiven: in the 1852 Presidential election the voters abandoned them for the Democrats. In Massachusetts the party split between the 'Conscience Whigs' (who leaned towards the abolitionists) and the 'Cotton Whigs' (who leaned towards the South). That too was electorally disastrous. So, for different reasons, was the nomination of General Winfield Scott for the Presidency in 1852. The South saw him as too much the puppet of Seward, and therefore of anti-slavery; Northern Protestants, full of resentment of the Irish refugees who were pouring into America to escape famine, and the Germans who were escaping political persecution, noticed that Scott had educated his daughters in a convent and refused to vote for him. Webster and Clay died in 1852: they had no successors as conservative statesmen whose personal authority was enough to unite their party in a national cause. The Whig débâcle was complete.

A new generation of sectional politicians was arising: of men, that is, who lacked a national following. Seward was one; Jefferson Davis (1808–89) of Mississippi, the spokesman of the South, was another. Webster's place in the Senate was filled by Charles Sumner (1811–74), a Massachusetts orator even more flowery and turgid than his predecessor, but of a very different political stripe. Sumner won the Senate seat only because of a split in the state Democratic party, which let in an alliance of Conscience Whigs and anti-slavery radicals. No one expected him to be re-elected, but meantime he became the voice of abolition in the Senate, as his friend Charles Francis Adams, latest of the family, was in the House: and a rancorous, insulting voice it was.

Posterity naturally sees in all this portents of civil war; but to contemporaries – to Stephen A. Douglas, for instance – the future did not seem so unpromising. Franklin Pierce, the new President, was a nonentity, but he was also a Democrat; and the Democrats controlled Congress. There was a coarseness in Douglas's nature, and an optimism bred by his intense ambition, which made him insensitive to the meaning of events, in spite of his great abilities (Seward once had to tell him that no man who used the word 'nigger' in public would ever be elected President). Yet it was in good faith that he now perpetrated a tremendous blunder.

The Compromise of 1850 had wrecked the Whig party and given the Democrats an unmanageable majority, largely composed of newcomers, in both houses of Congress – a majority which Pierce's weak leadership was unable to consolidate. Its Northern and Southern, free soil and slavery wings, were soon quarrelling bitterly over the spoils, and Douglas thought it his duty to try to unite them over some great measure. He fancied he knew the very thing. For years he had been pushing his 'Western Programme', a project to bind the East and West together by furthering settlement along the routes of emigration to Oregon and California, possibly by a homestead bill which would more or less make a present of the public domain to pioneer families; by establishing a transcontinental telegraph; and by one or more transcontinental railroads. Such a programme required the political organization of the lands between the Rockies and the river Missouri, across which pioneers were now pouring in ever-increasing numbers, many of them to settle in the valley of the river Platte. In fact these Platte settlers were beginning to harass Congress with demands for a territorial government, and were backed by the people of Missouri, Iowa and Illinois. Douglas had tried repeatedly to get Congress to act, but had always been defeated: the heart of the opposition coming from the Democratic Senators and Congressmen of the Southern states. Like any good politician, Douglas accepted that he would have to buy them off, and inquired as to the price. It did not seem too extortionate: the South was again hankering for a symbolic assertion of its equal rights within the Union. To get a bill through Congress all Douglas

needed to do was to include a provision applying the principles of the 1850
Compromise to the Nebraska Territory (as it was to be called). This would
theoretically permit slavery in the area; but popular sovereignty and the
facts of physical geography and population movement would ensure that
in practice it remained free soil.

There would be a mighty battle in Congress, of course, but that would
have the excellent effect of reuniting the Democrats; the West would
welcome the bill, especially after Douglas decided to propose the establishment of two new territories, Kansas and Nebraska, rather than just one; in
the end the South would have its symbol, the North would have the land,
the question of slavery extension would be settled for good (since there
would be no further territory into which the institution could, even in
theory, expand) and Douglas would be able to get on with the great work
of developing the West. Accordingly, in the winter of 1853–4 he presented
his bill to Congress.

He was bold and ingenious, and the Nebraska question had to be dealt
with somehow: it was becoming urgent. All the same, the bill had too
many inevitable enemies for real success to be possible; the dangers were
enormous, and all came to pass; in retrospect it is clear that Douglas should
have let the matter rest until a better season. The anti-slavery men denounced
the bill because it implicitly repealed the Missouri Compromise; the South
denounced it because it did not do so explicitly; and the Whigs, seeing a
chance to revive their own fortunes by splitting the Democrats, made all
the mischief they could. Since the key to passage still lay with the South,
Douglas conceded the explicit repeal of the Missouri Compromise, and
then was successful in pushing the bill through both houses of Congress.
Instead of the Democrats the Whigs split, irredeemably, on North–South
lines. Pierce signed the bill into law on 30 May 1854. So far so good. But
the South was not the only part of the country that was interested in symbolic
politics. The Missouri Compromise might have been superseded, might
be, as the Attorney-General thought, unconstitutional; nevertheless, to the
anti-slavery movement it had long stood as the one guarantee that 'the Slave
Power' might be checked, and the United States be held to its professions
of freedom and equality. The congressional abolitionists signed a manifesto
drafted by Senator Salmon P. Chase of Ohio which asserted that the
Nebraska bill was

part and parcel of an atrocious plot to exclude from a vast unoccupied region
immigrants from the Old World and free labourers from our own States, and
convert it into a dreary region of despotism, inhabited by masters and slaves.

They fought the bill relentlessly until it became law, and then carried the
battle to the country.

Douglas could overwhelm his opponents in Congress: out of doors it
was another matter. A hurricane of rage swept the North in what was

probably the most spontaneous outburst of popular indignation since the Stamp Act disturbances. Douglas had been too ingenious, like Grenville and Townshend; like Lord North with his Tea Act, he had passed a statute which had much to recommend it to practical men, but had overlooked the climate in which it would have to operate. All too many Northerners, even members of his own party, lacked his robust confidence that slavery could not spread, and that therefore the Kansas–Nebraska Act was a free soil measure. The outlook for the 1854 elections suddenly became alarming. Even Illinois was not safe. Douglas hurried back to his state to keep it in line, noting hostile demonstrations all along the way. 'I could travel from Boston to Chicago by the light of my own effigy,' he said. 'All along the Western Reserve of Ohio I could find my effigy upon every tree we passed.' In spite of his efforts, the elections went against his followers; and a dangerous opponent emerged. Abraham Lincoln, who had stuck to the trade of lawyer for five years, was provoked by the crisis to re-enter politics. Soon he was challenging Douglas for control of Illinois.

And the development predicted and feared since 1846 was coming about: a new, exclusively Northern political party was appearing. It would take a year or two to consolidate, but meantime, at Jackson, Michigan, in a grove of oak-trees, ten thousand anti-Nebraska citizens had met on 6 July 1854 and formed themselves into a Republican party – an example instantly followed in Massachusetts, Ohio, Wisconsin, Illinois and elsewhere. The party proved to be a powerful magnet: by 1856 it had absorbed most of the old Whigs, the old Free Soilers and the anti-Nebraska Democrats. It had, of course, no support in the South; for its guiding principle was of implacable opposition to any further expansion of slavery or concession to the 'slavocracy'. The Kansas–Nebraska Act, it said, was part of a plot to enable the slave-holders to control the government, to introduce Southern aristocracy to the democratic North, to burden the economy of the territories with the peculiar institution; at all costs the plot must be resisted. This frenzy began to alarm the South, which Calhoun had always been trying to unite in its own sectional party. The outlook for Douglas and those others who were trying to keep the Democratic party together was poor; and if the Democratic party failed, no other leaders, no other group had a chance of reconciling the sections, now that the Whigs had vanished. Even the churches had split: as early as 1845 the Methodists had broken into Northern and Southern wings, next year the Baptists did the same.

The rise of the Republicans was at first threatened by the unexpected emergence of a rival, the American party, nicknamed the Know-Nothings because of its origin as a secret society the members of which were supposed, to say, when challenged, 'I know nothing'. The Know-Nothings exploited the still-rising resentment of native Americans against the Irish and German influx. The foreign-born population went from 2,240,535 in 1850 to 3,096,753 in 1860; and its increase was mostly concentrated in the eastern ports of Boston, New York and Philadelphia. Inhabitants of those cities were alarmed, especially by the Irish, notoriously prone to be drunken and riotous; many conservative Whigs, led by former President Fillmore (who was the American candidate in 1856), who could not stomach Republican radicalism, joined the Know-Nothings; and so did many voters who thought the old parties corrupt and wanted a new reign of political virtue. The Know-Nothings did strikingly well in state and city elections in 1854; but they began to fade before 1856. They reeked too much of prejudice for many of the respectable. 'I am not a Know-Nothing,' said Lincoln. 'How could I be? How can anyone who abhors the oppression of Negroes be in favour of degrading classes of white men?' Much better to support the Republicans, who appropriated and discreetly rephrased Know-Nothing principles and put them in the party platform: the Republican party was to be the party of the Protestants and native-born until far into the next century. Furthermore, the inexperience of the Know-Nothing leaders told against them; they did not know what to do with electoral victory, while the Republicans, who inherited men and political machinery from the Northern Whigs, the Free Soilers and many Northern Democrats, showed themselves to be superbly skilful practitioners of the traditional arts of politics. They appropriated causes wherever it would do good: by 1860 they were not only the party of anti-slavery, free soil and Protestantism, but the party of temperance too (during one of their frequent public clashes, Lincoln gained kudos by ostentatiously refusing to drink whisky with Douglas, a famous toper). They showed themselves sympathetic to industry and business, and positively eager to steal Douglas's pet proposals of a transcontinental railroad and a homestead act for parcelling out the public domain in the West. Kansas–Nebraska, in short, had raised up a formidable enemy for Douglas, the Democrats and the South.

Nor were matters helped by a turn to violence. At times it seemed as if Boston was on the verge of another tea-party: the local view was that the abolitionists had been proved right by the South's 'treachery' over the Missouri Compromise, and consequently there was bitter resentment at the continuing enforcement of the Fugitive Slave Law: many Bostonians showed themselves ready to impede its operations, by any means, as their ancestors had been ready to impede the Tea Act. Massachusetts (not alone) passed a Personal Liberty Law which in effect (and quite unconstitutionally) nullified the Fugitive Slave Act, as South Carolina had once nullified the tariff. Wendell Phillips was always at hand to remind Bostonians of the cause. The Act had caused turbulence elsewhere; there were anti-slavery riots and a few slaves were rescued from recapture. But these demonstrations did not amount to much. Many found they could let off enough steam by writing letters to President Pierce addressing him as 'the chief slave-catcher of the United States'. Fighting began elsewhere.

Nobody had ever supposed that slavery could or would enter the Nebraska Territory, which under the 1854 Act stretched to the Canadian border. Kansas was a different matter. The anti-slavery North was quite sure that the point of the Slave Power's machinations was to seize that territory: 'Come on, then, gentlemen of the slave states,' said Senator Seward, 'since there is no escaping your challenge, I accept it in behalf of the cause of freedom. We will engage in competition for the virgin soil of Kansas . . .' This was not a challenge that the hotheads of the South were likely to ignore. Thus in a way the North created what it feared. The outcome was not what either side desired.

Thanks to the Kansas–Nebraska Act, the South was legally free to defy the likelihood that Kansas would remain free soil. If the slavery party could seize power in the territory, it might eventually be established as a new slave state, and as such send two more Senators and at least one Representative to Congress. The slave-holding counties of the state of Missouri, which bordered on Kansas, welcomed the chance, and in 1854 and 1855 sent settlers into the territory to exploit it. But they were overwhelmed by the spontaneous movement of free farmers from the Old North-West, from Kentucky and Tennessee: by 1860 the population of the territory was 107,000, much the greater part being free soil. Kansas had little attraction to slave-holders: they preferred Texas; and the climate and soil favoured such crops as maize and wheat (in the west, cattle) rather than anything slave-grown. Geography thus made Seward's challenge good: the anti-slavery movement contributed little in either funds or population, in spite of the foundation of something called the New England Emigrant Aid Society, and the fulminations of the Missourians, who thought they were being overwhelmed by a tide of Garrisonian abolitionists. Being part, still, of the turbulent West, they were disinclined to take defeat peaceably. So there followed years of intricate and violent conflict, in which the anti-slavery forces usually carried the day, but in which the pro-slavery party was supported by the government in Washington: for although Pierce had retired after one term, he had been succeeded by another Democrat, a tired old Jacksonian warhorse, James Buchanan (1791–1868), sometime Senator and Secretary of State, who only got his party's nomination because he came from Pennsylvania and it was essential to carry that state against the strong Republican challenge. He was completely dominated by the Southern Democrats in his Cabinet and in Congress.

The endless-seeming struggle (not until March 1861 was Kansas admitted to the Union as a free state) further embittered the broader conflict. In 1856 Charles Sumner made an abusive speech in the Senate on 'the Crime against Kansas' which enraged Representative Preston Brooks of South Carolina. He attacked Sumner with a stick on the Senate floor, so brutally as to endanger the Senator's life. News of the outrage against 'Bleeding Sumner' was followed by further bad news from 'Bleeding Kansas'. A pro-slavery crowd had invaded the town of Lawrence and destroyed much property. The crime was avenged by a fanatical abolitionist, John Brown (1800–1859), who murdered five pro-slavery men in May; two months later he had to fight for his life against a crowd seeking another instalment of revenge.

Civil war, it seemed, had broken out on the Western marches: the new President was scarcely strong enough to wring his hands. Lacking effective leadership, moderate men were at a loss; extremists on both sides gained ground accordingly, since it seemed they had best discerned the realities of the situation all along. The balance of power in the Democratic party tipped more and more to the South, as Northern Democrats deserted to the Republicans, a frankly Northern party: party loyalties were no longer an effective check on sectionalism. As events see-sawed, what depressed one side elevated the other; neither was ever left in tranquillity for long. The abolitionist contention, that so long as the sin of slavery continued, America could not hope for peace or liberty, began to seem fearfully plausible to some; so, to others, did the belief of the Southern 'fire-eaters' that so long as the South continued in the Union, slavery could not be safe. Both sides, without ever abating an instant their own self-righteousness, began to believe the threats and fear the anger of the other: double paranoia was hastening the patient's death. It was creditable to the judgement of Douglas and his dwindling following that they could see the unreality of all these alarums: but Douglas by his own recklessness had lost all power to control events.

The year 1857 brought another example of egregious meddling by otherwise sensible men. The Supreme Court, under the influence of the Chief Justice, Roger Taney of Maryland (1777–1864), declared that Congress had never possessed the constitutional right to pass or to enforce the Missouri Compromise. This provocation was especially pointless, because the Compromise was dead anyway, and the case in which the declaration was made (that of Dred Scott, a slave from Missouri who was claiming freedom through the courts – perhaps the only example of a slave taking a decisive part in the events that were leading to revolution) did not need this pronouncement to be settled. Taney seems to have supposed that the word of the Court would so impress the contending parties that they would, as it were, lay down their arms. He was deluded. He did not allow for the fact that he and four other justices of the seven-man Court were Southerners, which made it impossible for the North to believe in their disinterestedness; and his attempt to show that African-Americans could never be citizens, and that the Founding Fathers, whether in the Declaration of Independence (anti-slavery's favourite document) or the Constitution, meant to found a white man's republic, was offensive and untrue in itself, and couched in offensive language. The decision pleased the South, but the North simply regarded it as evidence that the slave conspiracy had subverted the Supreme Court. Tempers grew worse.

The year 1857 was also the year of a severe economic crisis. As so often before and since, the world market collapsed under the burden of its faulty organization. The North suffered badly. The South was unaffected, and made some provocative inferences. The 1850s were the great boom years of the ante-bellum period. Never had cotton-growing been so profitable. Large white mansions were built and paid for throughout the cotton kingdom; all the luxuries of the world seemed at the command of the great planters. Now the North was prostrated by a storm which passed them by. It made them more certain than ever that the industrial world could not do without the South's cheap and excellent product, on which, they thought, the prosperity both of England and the North depended. 'Cotton is King,' declared James Hammond, and would guarantee the wealth and independence of the South if it seceded: no one would dare make war on cotton.

Southern belief in cotton's supremacy was mistaken: planters could miscalculate like everybody else, and there was to be a cotton glut in 1861 which would help to defeat many calculations. But until then the South flourished and grew overbold, and in its persecution mania began to overreach itself. Douglas was the appointed victim.

What with the economic crisis and acute hostility to the South, with which he was identified, it seemed likely that he would fail to be re-elected Senator from Illinois in 1858. His opponent, Abraham Lincoln, staked everything on his free-soil platform, and the two men debated the issue up and down the state, in a legendary series of confrontations which gave Lincoln a national reputation. Douglas won the election for all that, a formidable achievement considering the odds, for which he seldom gets any credit. Certainly it did him no good with the Southern members of his party. Douglas vigorously opposed the attempt to foist a pro-slavery constitution on Kansas, and reiterated, in the debates, his conviction that slavery could not defy geography, so it was ridiculous to talk about spreading it. Southern extremists, who were now beginning to demand a Congressional law protecting their right (derived from the *Dred Scott* judgement) to carry slaves into every corner of the national territories – even into Oregon and Nebraska – resolved that, come what may, Douglas must not receive the Democratic nomination in 1860. Meantime the Republicans performed excellently in the state and Congressional elections of 1858; the Know-Nothings lost ground everywhere. Clearly, it would not take much for the 'Black Republicans', as the South called them, to win the Presidency; and if that happened, certain desperate souls swore – men such as Yancey of Alabama, Jefferson Davis of Mississippi – the South must secede from a Union dominated by anti-slavery.

Their argument was substantially fallacious. Abolitionist Republicans might threaten, but to abolish slavery peacefully would have required an amendment to the Constitution allowing the federal government to interfere in a matter which was otherwise reserved to the decision of the individual states. Such an amendment, requiring two-thirds majorities in both houses of Congress and a majority of three-quarters of the states' legislatures, could not possibly be passed over the resistance of the fifteen slave states, even if it was unanimously supported everywhere else, which was extremely unlikely. The Republicans repeatedly denied that they wanted to assail slavery directly, knowing the difficulty and unpopularity of the enterprise. They believed that if slavery were kept out of the territories it would begin to die;

apart from free soil, they wanted a Homestead Act, a transcontinental railroad and a protective tariff. The South was still opposed to all these schemes, not seeing any benefit to itself in them, and its entrenched position in Congress and the Democratic party made it unlikely that its opposition could be overcome. Even a man like Seward, who tended to run into exaggeration, was under no illusion that merely capturing the Presidency would give the Republicans all they wanted. It had never done much for the Whigs.

The slave-holders might have been reassured by these considerations, but perhaps their instinctive fears were wise. After all, their section had clearly lost ground to the North. There was now no hope of putting another Southerner in the White House: the choice would lie between a Republican and the renegade Douglas. Before long anti-slavery appointments to the Supreme Court would be made; the anti-slavery faction in Congress would steadily increase. Worse still, the non-slaveholding Southern whites – four-fifths of the total – might begin to listen to their Northern brethren, turn Republican, and challenge not only slavery, but the planter oligarchy which dominated their lives. In the states of the Deep South, the cotton South, where two-party politics did not exist and the slave-holders ran the Democracy, there were some disturbing signs of resentment and political activism. Perhaps there was something to be said for getting out of the Union peaceably, if it could be done, and setting up a new confederation explicitly committed to slavery for ever. But perhaps, in American conditions, the Constitution of the United States still offered the best guarantee of the slave-holders' interests, as their forefathers had done their best to make sure that it would. To renounce it was a gamble, but to cling to it might be to accept that in the not very distant future emancipation would be universal; or it might be to do no more than win a little time. The whole Atlantic world was turning against slavery. Proud and provincial, the slave-holders, or most of them, could not admit these possibilities except as a dreadful danger. Any steps to avoid them were justified, and by 1859 the only step which suggested itself was secession from the Union. But the planters still hesitated, and might have done so for years more, but for John Brown.

Since the Kansas affair, which had undeservedly won him a great reputation in abolitionist circles, the visionary had hit on a deadly plan. The slaves, he thought, might be induced to rebel against their masters if Northern sympathizers were at hand with weapons and suggestions. Brown therefore proposed to descend on some suitable spot in the South, launch a revolt and, as the slaves flocked to join him, organize them into an army. This army would retreat into the vastness of the southern Appalachians and become a permanent thorn in the side of the Slave Power. Eventually all the slaves would join, and the peculiar institution would be destroyed . . . It was a preposterous fantasy, well illustrating Brown's eccentricity, the abolitionists' ignorance of the South and their growing tolerance of bloodshed and treason if these might help the cause. Brown easily raised money and supplies from sympathizers in New England. On 16 October 1859 he and eighteen followers descended on the federal arsenal at Harper's Ferry on the upper Potomac, seized it, and issued a proclamation to the slaves.

Virginia snuffed out the threat without difficulty: Colonel Robert Edward Lee (1807–70) of the US army was at hand. Brown's handful was soon forced to surrender, and Brown himself was taken down to Charlestown, Virginia, tried and hanged. His last address from the dock made a great impression on Northern opinion, its only weakness being its untruthfulness:

I never had any design against the liberty of any person; nor any disposition to commit treason or incite slaves to rebel or make any general insurrection.

His last written message was more authentic:

I John Brown am now quite *certain* that the crimes of this *guilty land*: *will* never be purged *away*: but with Blood. I had *as I now think*: *vainly* flattered myself that without *very much* bloodshed; it might be done.

Brown's eloquence captivated New England. According to Wendell Phillips, Brown was 'the impersonation of God's order and God's law'. Abolitionist clergy welcomed the slave rebellion which, they thought, Brown's action would stimulate. Thoreau rejoiced that he was the saintly martyr's contemporary. The ravings of these lettered gentlemen drowned the numerous Northern voices which condemned Brown as a criminal. Lincoln thought he was justly hanged. The Republican party denounced his raid in its 1860 platform. A great anti-Brown meeting was held in Boston; to no avail. The impression made on the South was too deep. Here it was at last, the nightmare come true: the abolitionist appeal to the slaves to rebel, now naked and apparent, in spite of the endless disclaimers of Northern politicians, the doubts of Southern moderates. The fire-eaters instantly took command. Their programme was simple. Only a candidate pledged to the defence of slavery would be acceptable as the Democrats' nominee in 1860. That ruled out Douglas. If the Republican candidate won, the Southern states would leave the Union: they could not possibly be safe with a Brown sympathizer as President, and of course all black Republicans were Brownites at heart. Their tongues betrayed them. Had not Lincoln begun to proclaim that a house divided against itself could not stand? Had not Seward said there was an 'irrepressible conflict' between the sections? Now, in the light of Harper's Ferry, it was plain what they meant. They meant to win the conflict and unite the house by means of a slave uprising.

John Brown's raid thus marks the point of no return: it began the uncoiling of a terrible chain of events leading to rebellion and war. It seems a small, almost a ridiculous seed for such a harvest. And in fact Harper's Ferry, for all its significance, was the occasion, not the cause, of civil war. In the end, all the analyses come back to slavery. The commitment of the South to its peculiar institution not only entailed a persecution complex; it turned the section into a pseudo-nation. For more than a generation the South had been bringing its religion, culture, politics and trade into line. The same test was applied to everything, even to thought: was it consistent with slavery, did it build up the defences of a slave society? Matters came to such a pass that one planter, who was ready to treat his slaves kindly, even if it meant growing less cotton, ashamedly feared that he was 'near an abolitionist', so guilty did he feel about his heresy and so large a crime did the slightest variation from the line now seem in the South. It was this obsession which had destroyed the two-party system in the Deep South and given the fire-eaters a clear field in which to promote secession, and the idea of a new Southern nation. By 1859–60 this new Southern nationalism was merely looking for an excuse to break the Union: John Brown, and then Abraham Lincoln, did no more than provide it.

Even after Harper's Ferry, the few wise heads in the South urged restraint. Men like Sam Houston, the venerable founder of Texas, now its Governor for the last time, knew what the Union meant to the North and West; knew that there was an American patriotism quite as powerful as the Southern, and much longer established; and that it was backed by far greater resources. Some may even have glimpsed the significance of the cult of John Brown in the North. Thomas Bingham Bishop was the composer of a successful camp-meeting chorus, 'Gone to be a Soldier in the Army of the Lord'. On hearing of Brown's death, he quickly fitted some new words to the tune: 'John Brown's body lies a-mouldering in the grave . . .'. They proved ominously popular. The South paid little attention. It had its own song, 'Dixie' (written in 1859, paradoxically enough by a Northerner).[12]

The Democratic convention met in April 1860 and was a disaster. By a horrible fatality it was held in Charleston, the very capital of secessionist feeling, where they still remembered the Nullification Crisis. It was not a city where Northern and Western Democrats could feel happy: nor did they. Led by Yancey, the Southerners refused to hear of the nomination of Douglas: the Northerners would not abandon him. They had nothing to gain by doing so: a pro-slavery candidate could not carry any state outside the South. The Democratic cause had been weakenened by the Buchanan administration's record of incompetence and corruption: only Douglas might save it. The inducement to earn general contempt by sacrificing their principles was therefore small. Equally, the fire-eaters saw no reason to budge. Eventually the convention broke up. One fragment reassembled at

12 No one knows for sure why the South came to be known as Dixie. The most plausible theory, according to the *Concise Dictionary of American History* (New York, 1963), is that in French-speaking Louisiana, in the years immediately following the Louisiana Purchase, 'the word Dix [ten] was printed on the ten-dollar bank bills. Louisiana thus came to be known as Dix's Land; and, expanded to Dixie, the name spread to the whole South.' One of these ten-dollar bills is still displayed in a New Orleans bar.

Baltimore and nominated Douglas as the official Democratic candidate. The fire-eaters nominated John Breckinridge of Kentucky, Vice-President of the United States, who could almost pass for a moderate. The real Southern moderates, mostly remnants of the Whig party, rejected both names and nominated Bell of Tennessee, on a Constitutional Union ticket.

The Southern and Democratic vote being hopelessly split, the Republicans, without effort on their part, had the game in their hands. Their convention met in the rising metropolis of the North-West, Chicago. This proved fortunate for the local candidate. The nomination had been expected to go to Seward, but he was regarded as dangerously extreme on the slavery question and too sympathetic to Catholics and immigrants. The party managers were determined to do nothing to alienate any nervous person who had a vote. Accordingly they turned to the tall man with the high voice, in the shiny, rumpled black suit: Abraham Lincoln. He had made fewer enemies than Seward. He came from a key section, the North-West, and a key state, Illinois. In his debates with Douglas, and in various orations since, he had shown himself to be intelligent and eloquent; he was known to be honest (a nice contrast to the Buchananites); he could be built up as a popular candidate because he had been born in a log-cabin and had chopped wood for a living when young. No one suspected that he was a great man. To a professional, the only impressive thing about him was that somehow, in spite of losing two Senatorial elections, he had kept his dominant position in the Whig and Republican parties of Illinois. With judicious negotiations behind the scenes by his agents and uproarious clamour from the public galleries, which had been carefully packed with the local boy's supporters, the trick was done. 'The Railsplitter' was to be the next President of the United States.

Douglas fought a last, heroic, useless campaign. Lincoln won only 39 per cent of the popular vote, but he carried the majority of Northern and Western states with a plurality. He did not carry a single state in the South. When the news of his election reached Charleston, the process of secession was immediately set going.

In state after southern state conventions were summoned, bypassing the state assemblies and thus revolutionizing the state governments as the Committees of Correspondence had revolutionized the colonial governments eighty-five years previously. The loyalists struggled, but except in the Upper South they did so in vain. In December, South Carolina formally seceded from the United States, to be followed at once by Mississippi, Florida, Alabama, Georgia, Louisiana and Texas. These states next sent delegates to Montgomery, Alabama, to found a new inter-state government. Theoretically each seceding state could have become an independent country; but it seemed wiser to federate, as it has seemed wise to those earlier Founding Fathers of 1776: in adopting this course the Southerners showed how, in spite of everything, they were still intensely American. The Confederate States of America – usually known as the Confederacy – was announced to the world, in a document that was not quite as memorable as the Declaration of Independence, on 4 February 1861. Jefferson Davis of Mississippi was to be President. The CS Constitution was issued on 11 March: it strikingly resembled that of the US.

These events struck the North flat with amazement. The Union of the American States was such a profound commitment; the pride in the achievements of the American Revolution was so enormous; the belief in the promises of liberty, equality and property if America held together was so deep, that it seemed impossible that American citizens could really mean to destroy what the President-elect called 'the last, best hope of Earth'. The Republicans had never believed that the threat to secede was serious: they had dismissed it as an electioneering trick. Even after the event they could not quite take it in, and hoped against hope, indeed against reason, that the Unionist majority in the South would reassert itself as it had in the past. But now there was no Union majority in the South.

The winter months passed in a desperate frenzy of schemes to restore normality. Seward had one, so did Charles Francis Adams, so did Senator Crittenden (he came from Henry Clay's Kentucky and hoped to repeat Clay's triumphs). But the Senators and Representatives of the seceding states had withdrawn when their states went out, and the Northerners, finding the foe absent, seized the opportunity to pass a new, protectionist tariff, which would have outraged the cotton South had it still regarded itself as part of the Union. The Morrill Tariff (named after its chief planner) perhaps shows that subconsciously members of Congress knew that the secession was real, and aspired to be permanent.

The lapse in time between the election in early November and Lincoln's entry into office in March was unfortunate. Until then Buchanan remained President and had the duty of grappling with a crisis that threatened to shade from being a demonstration to being a rebellion to being a war. He proved as incapable as ever. Helplessly he allowed the secessionists to eliminate all Union presence from the Confederacy. The American government had always been such a loose, devolved, feeble affair that this was very easy: apart from the post and customs offices, there was little to remove save certain more or less unfinished or obsolete military and naval posts. The inland and most of the coastal ones fell immediately into Confederate hands; but at two points the Unionists could hold out – at Fort Pickens, off the Florida coast, and at Fort Sumter in Charleston harbour. This last quickly became the emotional focus of the crisis for both sides. The little fort lay right in the jaws of the Confederacy. It was temptingly weak, for it had been built for defence against a sea attack, not a land one, and it was both undermanned and ill-supplied. Its jaunty flag, fluttering the formerly sacred colours of the United States right under their noses, was a deep affront to the seceders, otherwise giddy with joy and confidence; while its presence at such a point was a matter of hope and reassurance to the North. Fort Pickens, which was much more defensible (it was to continue in US hands throughout the years following), was soon overlooked: attention was obsessively directed at Charleston.

Buchanan dithered, and would no doubt have gone on doing so – would even have allowed Fort Sumter to fall unresisting – but for the determination of his Attorney-General, Edwin Stanton (1814–69) of Ohio, appointed to replace a seceding Southerner. Arrogant, energetic, certain he was right, Stanton insisted that Sumter must be retained and if necessary be resupplied and reinforced. When Lincoln took the oath of office on 4 March the fort was still in United States hands; Virginia and the other states of the Upper South had still not left the Union; not a shot had been fired. Perhaps peace might still be preserved, but tension was rapidly mounting.

The Presidential oath commits him who takes it to preserve, protect and defend the Constitution, and with almost no exception all the Presidents, even the feeblest, have regarded it very seriously. Abraham Lincoln was the opposite of feeble, and on taking the oath he explained, in his first inaugural address, what he understood by it. 'The power confided to me,' he said, 'will be used to hold, occupy, and possess the property and places belonging to the government, and to collect the duties and imposts'; for his pledge to protect the government was registered in heaven. In this way a line was drawn, a warning was issued. But the rest of his speech was an attempt to show the South, in its own terms, that it was safe under a Republican administration and that therefore secession was unnecessary. Read today, what is most striking, next to Lincoln's desperate earnestness, is the way in which his very effort to be heard by the South reveals the gap between the two sides. Lincoln minimized that gap as best he could, say-ing it was no more than a dispute as to whether or not slavery should be extended; he pointed out that the Constitution was inviolate; he indicated that he would accept Crittenden's proposal to write a guarantee of slavery into the Constitution; he pledged the Republicans to leave slavery alone; he remarked, without a smile, that there was very little damage that any administration could do in four years, and he held up as a beacon to the South one of his deepest beliefs:

A majority held in restraint by constitutional checks and limitations, and always changing easily with deliberate changes of popular opinions and sentiments, is the only true sovereign of a free people. Whoever rejects it does, of necessity, fly to anarchy or despotism.

Surely the South would see this, and cease its rejection of him and of the majority which had made him President. At the very least, let it do nothing in a hurry. 'Nothing valuable can be lost by taking time.'

The speech did the orator credit, but it could not find its mark. For one thing Lincoln could not quite hide his feeling that secession was not only wrong but frivolous. For another, he offered the South nothing but the *status quo*, of which even the Crittenden Amendment was only a reinforcement.

He stuck to his refusal to countenance slavery expansion; and he did not recognize either the right to secede or the independence of the Confederacy. He did not say he would not fight, either: only that he would not assail the seceders. He did not lay bare all his thought: but behind his praise of the American system could be felt his commitment to human equality, his love of his country, his hatred of slavery. In essence, he did not offer the South the slightest reassurance. Even if he had, it is doubtful if the seceding states, buoyant in the excitement of their new Confederacy, would have paid any attention. They had finished with Uncle Sam.

For the next few weeks Lincoln was besieged by the mob of office-seekers that assailed every new President, and as a sensible party leader he devoted much time to them; but though they wearied him they did not distract him from the question of Sumter. He adopted Stanton's policy, but in his own fashion: he played for time. He hoped that, if it came to a showdown, he could keep the border states on his side. For this and other reasons he was determined not to fire the first shot; and he hoped against hope that no shots would be necessary. But he did not order the evacuation of Fort Sumter.

The matter was out of his hands. Many announcements were made by Southern leaders; many furtive negotiations were undertaken, some with the connivance of Seward, now Secretary of State. But since the Confederates had no intention of withdrawing the secession ordinances they had little choice, once it became clear that Lincoln had no intention of dropping the claims of the Union. A newborn nation, seething with bombastic pride, could not tolerate the impertinence of Sumter. General Beauregard received his orders; he mounted batteries against the fort, and on 12 April he opened his bombardment.

Mrs Chesnut and the other ladies of Charleston were appalled by the man-made thunder that crashed and reverberated incessantly through their town: they had never heard anything like it in their lives, and for a moment they glimpsed the nature of the abyss to which the slave states had been moving so recklessly for so long. In spite of the noise, no one was killed: Major Anderson, in command at the fort, was too skilful a soldier to let his men expose themselves. The fortifications were too good to be shattered immediately, but after a day and a night they could no longer be defended. Anderson asked for terms, which were granted; the stars and stripes were lowered, and the garrison marched out with the honours of war. War it was indeed; though how terrible was not yet clear.

15 The War About Slavery 1861–5

'Thus saith the Lord,' bold Moses said,
'Let my people go!
Or else I'll strike your first-born dead!
Let my people go!'
Go down Moses! 'Way down in Egypt's land:
Tell old Pharaoh, Let My People Go!

Contraband Hymn, 1861

If the attack on Fort Sumter settled that there would be a war, it also largely
determined what sort of a war it would be. Lincoln and the North never
hesitated in their response to the event: this was rebellion, and would
have to be suppressed. On 15 April the President issued a proclamation
announcing a blockade of all Southern ports and calling for a force of
75,000 volunteers to restore federal authority in the South. As a man who
believed in the permanence of the Union he could do no less. But to the
Upper South he seemed to be doing a great deal too much. The choice
before these states was indeed agonizing. Virginia, for example, had refused
to follow the example of the Cotton Kingdom because she did not see
Lincoln's election as any particular danger: she was well used to the ups
and downs of two-party politics and was, besides, deeply loyal to the Union
which she had done so much to create. But neither she nor any other of
the Southern states understood that term in Mr Lincoln's sense. For them
the states came first; the Union was a limited compact, as the old anti-
Federalists had taught, and the states retained their sovereignty, including
the right to secede if they saw fit. Above all, the Union was one of consent:
the essence of the Constitution and its checks and balances was that the
majority should not be able, legitimately, to coerce a minority. As the *North
Carolina Standard* had put it the previous autumn, 'a Constitutional Union
is the only one worth preserving . . . A Union of force, cemented and kept
together by force, and perhaps by blood, is not the Union of the Constitution.'

So Lincoln's proclamation was promptly followed by the secession of Virginia, Arkansas, Tennessee and North Carolina. Kentucky, Maryland and Missouri might have gone too, but the Unionist forces and the power of the federal government were just sufficient to keep them loyal. 'I hope to have God on my side, I must have Kentucky,' said Lincoln, for without that state the North risked being split in two, and Washington might be untenable. As it was, the second secession, vastly increasing the area and population of the Confederacy, made Lincoln's task nearly impossible.

Few great nations have been less ready in any way for war than were the Americans, North and South, in 1861. The military potential of both sides was enormous, or the struggle could never have dragged on for four years; but at the outset the means for realizing that potential were almost non-existent. True, the United States had founded an official military academy at West Point on the Hudson river in 1802. This institution had done so well that its graduates provided almost all the effective military leadership on either side during the Civil War, and did so from the start: Beauregard and Anderson were both West Pointers. Nor was it only their formal education which trained them: the men of the Academy had run the army during the decades of peace, had fought Indians and Mexicans in the occasional small war, and in some cases, such as that of George McClellan, who had been a railroad official, had gained further valuable experience in civilian life. As was quickly to be shown, in short, the professional American Officer Corps compared favourably in quality with any other in the world, except perhaps the Prussian.

But there were very few of these professionals, though there were more than peacetime America had been able to employ, at least as soldiers. To most of their countrymen titles like 'Colonel' and 'Major' were merely honorific, dealt out on the frontier even more lavishly than handles such as 'Judge' and 'Squire'. Soldiering meant parading in a fancy uniform on the Fourth of July and shirking militia training all the rest of the year. War, when it did not mean hunting down Indian villages, meant brilliant cavalry charges in red trousers, sweeping the paltry foe before you; it never lasted more than a few weeks. Morale, whether civilian or military, meant the confident assumption that nobody could beat an American, not even another American. As to problems of diplomacy, logistics, supply or finance, they were ignored, or at best dealt with by such slogans as 'Cotton is King'. Even the educated, even the politicians, knew little better. Abraham Lincoln was wise enough to see that he had everything to learn about his duties as Commander-in-Chief: he took to studying books on tactics and strategy in odd moments. Jefferson Davis was misguided enough to suppose that some fighting in the Mexican War and a term as Secretary of War in Pierce's Cabinet had taught him all he needed to know – taught him enough to teach his generals. In this vanity he was much the more representative of the two leaders.[1]

---

1 At least he had an inventive mind. As Secretary of War he had started a Camel Corps in the south-western deserts. He thought that howitzers mounted on camels' humps would be

The first months of the war were, therefore, chiefly shaped by the general unpreparedness. Perhaps the most important occurrences were the attempts by Lincoln and Davis to say what it was all about. In July Lincoln sent a message to Congress in which he began his long series of attempts to persuade his countrymen and the world that this was a war for democracy, a war to show whether a constitutional republic, 'a government of the people by the same people', could maintain its integrity against a rebellion. Jefferson Davis, in a message to the Confederate Congress, identified his cause with states' rights: with the right of a state to secede and the right of a minority to protect itself against a tyrannous majority. But even in such a solemn message, designed to put the best face on Southern actions, he was not able to conceal the connection between his political doctrines and slavery. The Northern majority was tyrannous, he said, because it actively opposed slavery, and so secession was practically justified as well as constitutionally proper. The truth was that 'states' rights' had evolved, as a creed, from the necessity to protect the peculiar institution. Virginia, for example, was not a cotton state, but she was a slave state, economically dependent on her relations with the other slave states, which purchased her surplus Negroes. If slavery was going to war, states' rights was a splendid excuse for Virginia to enlist on her customers' side. Not that it appeared that way to her people. Many of them – for example, Robert E. Lee – had freed their slaves; but when the war came they rallied to what was still their truest country. Lee, the favourite of General Winfield Scott, was offered the command of the United States army as well as that of seceding Virginia; he debated the matter with himself all night, before going with his state. But, like it or not, and he did not like it, he thereby committed himself – very effectively, as would soon be shown – to the military defence of slavery.

Slavery, then, was the central issue of the war from the start, though it was not at first convenient for Lincoln to say so. Not only was there far too much anti-black feeling in the North, there was the attitude of the loyal slave-holders of Kentucky and Maryland to consider (not that they were very sincerely loyal: many of them slipped off South to join the Confederates). He therefore laid enormous stress on the Union; it was for that he fought. As he was to say in August 1862, 'My paramount object in this struggle *is* to save the Union, and is *not* either to save or destroy Slavery.' It was to save the Union that, in the spring of 1861, thousands of young men flocked to Washington.

What did the Union mean to them? Curiously, this crucial question is seldom asked by American historians, and never answered satisfactorily. It is, to them, too obvious to bear thought. But non-Americans must consider it.

Many of the soldiers were no doubt unreflective types, content to accept

---

the very things for fighting Indians. Unfortunately, like so many bright ideas, this one proved impracticable. Camels and Americans conceived a profound dislike for each other.

words like 'Union', 'rebel' and 'nation' and act accordingly. But the intensely political quality of American life meant that for at least as many of these young citizens the matter had to be thrashed out in argument and private thought; their society forced them to be like Cromwell's russet-coated trooper, who knew what he fought for and loved what he knew.[2] Their leaders had to justify themselves to their followers, and the followers had to justify themselves to each other and to the folks back home. It was common practice to elect junior officers, as if a regiment were a township or a pioneer train. No wonder that the army was intensely politicized and that Lincoln had always to take its views into consideration. Eventually his pains were repaid: it was the army vote which re-elected him triumphantly in 1864, an explicit vindication of the Union cause.

Attachment to the Union had long been a commanding feeling, even before Andrew Jackson in 1830 proposed his famous toast: 'Our Federal Union – it must be preserved.' The rituals of American life fortified it, not only on the Fourth of July but in every schoolroom where, in that enlightened age, boys were taught the art of public speaking and practised the peroration of Daniel Webster's Second Reply to Hayne:

When my eyes shall be turned to behold, for the last time, the sun in heaven, may I not see him shining on the broken and dishonoured fragments of a once glorious Union; on States dissevered, discordant, belligerent; on a land rent with civil feuds, or drenched, it may be, in fraternal blood! Let their last feeble and lingering glance, rather, behold the gorgeous ensign of the republic . . . still full high advanced . . . bearing for its motto no such miserable interrogatory as, What is all this worth? Nor those other words of delusion and folly, Liberty first, and Union afterwards: but everywhere, spread over all in characters of living light, blazing on all its ample folds, as they float over the sea and over the land, and in every wind under the whole heavens, that other sentiment, dear to every true American heart – Liberty *and* Union, now and forever, one and inseparable!

The feeling was no doubt greatly reinforced by economic interests: as Stephen A. Douglas warned the South in 1860, 'You cannot sever this Union without severing every hope and prospect that a Western man has on this earth.' There were innumerable ways in which the various parts of the great republic had grown economically intertwined; even the South, even if there had not been a war, would have suffered grievously from its self-imposed exclusion from the markets and resources of the North; and then there was the plain geographical fact that, as Lincoln said in his first inaugural, 'physically speaking, we cannot separate'. The Americans were stuck with each other in one continent. Their religion, origins and political

---

2 The same process was at work on the other side. This was not another war between Roundheads and Cavaliers, but between two sorts of deadly Roundheads.

culture were much the same, their language was English. The Union seemed to be the merest expression of common sense and inevitability.

But these considerations have little to do with the passions of the Civil War. At the bottom of all American patriotism lay, and lies to the present day, the commitment to freedom – the favourite word, the favourite idea, the favourite boast. This freedom was a very concrete thing, the essential stuff of the American historical experience. The colonial and Revolutionary eras had been a continuous struggle to be free of England, in religion, politics, trade and everything else. In the nineteenth century, freedom meant the ability to go west, to run your own life, to make your own future, to worship your own God, to bring up your children in your own way, to speak your mind. The Declaration of Independence, the Constitution and eighty-odd years of political experience had not only reinforced, deepened and broadened the commitment to freedom, they had incarnated it in the United States, in a nation. It was not, perhaps, true that American freedom could not have survived the defeat of the North in the Civil War; but the great majority of Northerners, from Lincoln downwards, believed it to be true. Everything they valued in life seemed to be at risk with the Union. No wonder they fought.

It took them a long time to learn how. General Scott, the corpulent veteran of the War of 1812 and Mexico, had a strategic plan that he called the Anaconda, which was in many respects the same as that which eventually defeated the Confederacy: the rebels were to be attacked from all sides, from the sea, the West and the North, and squeezed to death. But the United States only had a tiny navy, so the decision to blockade the South created plenty of work for the Navy Secretary, Gideon Welles (1802–78), just as its interference with the regular course of North Atlantic trade would create plenty of work for Secretary of State Seward. Above all, an army had to be shaped out of the mass of green recruits provided by the state militias. Washington hummed with activity. Unfortunately this deluded the inexperienced press, politicians and parents of America into imagining that everything was in fair train to an early victory, and Lincoln, who was still over-optimistic himself, felt enormous pressure to launch an offensive to end matters briskly.

Appearances were never more deceptive. The South too was organizing. The Confederacy transferred its capital from Montgomery to Richmond, Virginia. Beauregard took command of the scratch army that was hastily assembling there. The fire-eater, Yancey, led a mission to Europe in search of diplomatic recognition of the new nation. But the North discounted all these signs of serious purpose. 'On to Richmond!' was the cry. Impatience mounted, and voices began to be heard impugning Scott's loyalty: after all, he was a Virginian. So at last the generals gave in. Scott being too old and fat to exercise field command himself, the job was given to Irvin McDowell, unluckiest of commanders. On 21 July, a boiling day, his raw levies attacked Beauregard's almost equally unripe troops in their strong position at

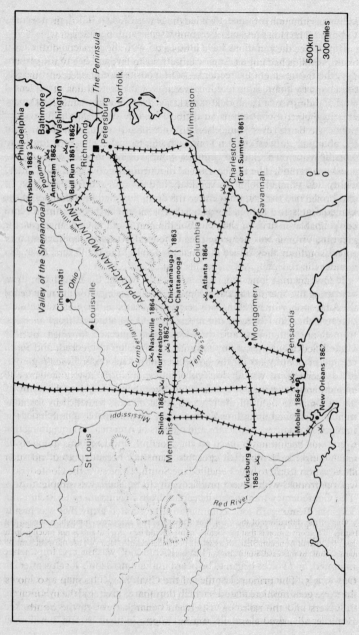

Philadelphia

Gettysburg 1863

Baltimore
Washington
Antietam 1862
Bull Run 1861, 1862

Potomac

Richmond

The Peninsula

Petersburg

Norfolk

Wilmington

Charleston
(Fort Sumter 1861)

Savannah

Columbia 1864

Atlanta 1864

Chickamauga 1863
Chattanooga

APPALACHIAN MOUNTAINS

Valley of the Shenandoah

Cincinnati

Ohio

Louisville

Cumberland

Nashville 1864
Murfreesboro
1862-3

Tennessee

Montgomery

Pensacola

Mobile 1864

New Orleans 1862

Shiloh 1862

Memphis

Mississippi

St Louis

Vicksburg
1863

Red River

500km
300miles

0   0

Manassas Junction, on a ridge above the little river of Bull Run in northern Virginia.[3] The ladies and gentlemen of Washington flocked out with picnic baskets to see the fun. For a time it was a question of who would run away first (the militia had improved very little, if at all, since George Washington's day), but the rebels gradually steadied. One of their commanders encouraged his troops by pointing to the next section of the line: 'Look at Jackson's men, standing like a stone wall!' – and thus a hero got his name. McDowell was not helped by the decision of the Pennsylvania militia to leave just before the battle: they had signed on for ninety days, and their time was up. Gradually it became clear that the North had been checked. Then, for no good reason (but it was so very hot and the experience was so very new) panic seized the Union troops. Instead of retiring a few miles in good order, which was all that veterans would have found necessary, they fled in abandoned terror all the way back to the bridges across the Potomac, which were soon choked by a roaring, hysterical mob. Had the Southern army been capable of swift movement, Washington could have been captured; as it was, Virginia was suddenly clear of federal troops, except for outposts on the southern bank of the Potomac. Several of the picnickers, failing to run away in time, fell into the hands of the Confederates.

This staggering blow began to sober the North. Lincoln, having got something like the measure of the problem, determined for the time being to ignore importunate back-seat drivers. He sent for General George B. McClellan (1826–85), who had just cleared the mountains of western Virginia of Confederates, and gave him a free hand to train what was now to be called the Army of the Potomac. General Scott retired, and more volunteers poured into Washington. Later on that winter Lincoln got rid of his Secretary of War, a machine politician from Pennsylvania who was more interested in the patronage of his office than in enabling the Army of the Potomac to fight effectively, and replaced him with Edwin Stanton, who soon showed himself to be one of the most valuable members of the Cabinet.

If it was beginning to dawn on the North that the war was going to be much longer and more disagreeable than had been expected, no such illumination seems to have benefited the South. To be sure, the Confederacy was confronted with a hard predicament. Its war aim was simple: to win

---

3 One of the difficulties of the Civil War is that the two sides gave different names to the battles. The convention is that the victor's name should be used, but this is not much help in cases like that of Antietam/Sharpsburg where both sides claimed victory. I use the most familiar names: thus, in this case, Bull Run, not Manassas.

Opposite: 5. The principal battles of the Civil War. The map also shows the three geographical features which dominated strategy: the mountains, the rivers and the railroads. Sherman's march through the South, for example, advanced along the railroad lines

from the North an acknowledgement of its independence. It had neither the power nor the wish to destroy the government of the United States (other than by seceding from it), nor did it have any designs on its territory. The difficulty was in choosing means to reach the goal. One route, much favoured beforehand, was that of 'King Cotton'. It was supposed that if Lancashire and its mills could not get any cotton, the British economy would totter, and to avoid a fall the British government would be forced to intervene, to recognize and guarantee the Confederacy, even at the price of war with the Union. So even before the Northern blockade could bite, an embargo was placed on the export of cotton in 1862. Lancashire began to feel the pinch, but its sufferings did little damage to British prosperity and never brought the British government anywhere near the point of intervention. In the end only Robert E. Lee's idea, of unrelenting brilliant battle, with the object of breaking the Northern will to go on fighting, offered any hope; but in the winter of 1861–2 the South did not adopt it. Instead she rested on her laurels, unwisely content already to have dealt the North a stinging rebuke.

Meantime the leaders of the North struggled with their own dilemmas. Tactics might for the moment be left to General McClellan, who was busily drilling his men at Washington and teaching them all the other elements of soldiering, from marksmanship to sanitation. Strategic choices might equally be postponed until the Army of the Potomac was ready to move. Still, they would eventually have to be faced; it would have to be decided whether to stick to the Anaconda plan or to attack one particular point; and when that was settled, enormous resources would have to be mustered for the gigantic effort required. How could Northern will be maintained in the long struggle to a remote victory?

True, by any conventional measure the North's military potential was so overwhelming that she should have been able to achieve a speedy victory. She was twice as populous as the South; she had command of the sea, thanks partly to Gideon Welles and partly to the fact that the South had no navy and no allies; her industrial strength was great and growing; her financial base was solid: Salmon P. Chase (1808–73), Secretary of the Treasury, was always able to borrow the money he needed to pay for the war (throughout which, it should be added, nineteenth-century Americans showed themselves nearly as reluctant to be taxed as had eighteenth-century ones). The war had come at a good moment in at least one respect: industrial techniques were now far enough advanced to enable the North to exploit her wealth in many valuable new ways. For example, it had just become possible to mass-produce boots and shoes. The soldiers complained that those they got seemed to be made of paper and rapidly fell to pieces; but without mass-production they would all too often have had to go barefoot, like so many Southern soldiers, or like so many soldiers throughout history. And what the North could not produce, she could purchase abroad: the first three years of the war, until Northern factories caught up with Northern demand, were a boom time for the gun-makers of Birmingham. But strong though the North was, her strength alone was not going to produce victory, least of all an early one. Skill was required, and skill was lacking; skill that only painful experience could teach. The great question therefore could not be shirked.

The behaviour of the Pennsylvania militia at Bull Run suggested that Union enthusiasm alone could not be depended on for the duration of a hard war. Americans were not schooled to the long haul (in the twentieth century 'Mr Dooley' would pithily characterize them as 'short-term crusaders'). War-weariness might diminish their fighting spirit to the point where the North would concede independence to the South rather than go on fighting. Today, with two world wars to enlighten us, we may guess that the danger was slighter than it seemed: nation-states, even when fighting in a bad cause under wicked leaders (for example, Germans under Hitler), give up only when all is lost. Yet Lincoln and his advisers can hardly be blamed for taking the problem seriously. And when, later in the war, they were confronted with draft riots, semi-treasonable peace movements and an endless stream of deserters, they must have felt that their anxiety was more than justified.

The cause of reunion, of restoring the *status quo*, was not enough. Lincoln had a semi-mystical belief that the future happiness of the world depended on a Northern victory, and voiced this idea more and more frequently. But it was too remote, too speculative a notion to fire many, especially as it was a long time before Lincoln's extraordinary personality began to inspire much respect in his fellow-citizens. The cause of anti-slavery lay much readier to hand; but it too had drawbacks – dangerous ones.

The abolitionists had been divided on the outbreak of war, as so often before. Garrison, who for years had urged the breaking of the covenant with Hell, as he called the Constitution because of its acceptance of slavery, welcomed the secession of the South; so did Wendell Phillips; and they were quite prepared to say so in public, whether on the speaker's platform or in the pages of the *Liberator*. Fortunately some sensible person warned them that if they did they would never be listened to in the North again. They stopped to think for once. The upshot was that they rallied to the Union cause, proclaiming that its victory was essential, for it would bring with it the destruction of slavery. This was the note that New England wanted to hear; this was the belief that sent the region's finest young men so eagerly to war. They, and their sympathizers in Europe, waited eagerly to hear Lincoln adopt it as the official creed of the Union. For more than a year they waited in vain.

Lincoln's difficulty was not a racialist qualm. His hatred of slavery was strong and deep, his attitude to black men one of straightforward friendliness, like his attitude to whites. To be sure, he shared some of the prejudices of his time; he doubted that it was possible for the two races to live in peace and equality together. He never supposed that this doubt justified the continuance of slavery. He wanted all men, everywhere, to be free. In the first period of the Civil War, however, he dared not touch the peculiar institution, as we have seen. The border states and Northern opinion had to be considered; and, ever conscious of his enormous responsibilities, Lincoln was disinclined to do anything that was not clearly necessary. So he took stern disciplinary measures against Northern generals who issued proclamations of slave emancipation in the areas of their commands, and bore the resultant abolitionist criticisms with his usual stoicism. At the same time he welcomed the abolition by Congress of slavery in the District of Columbia (when a Congressman, years before, he had drawn up a bill for that purpose himself) and the negotiation by Seward of a treaty with Great Britain in 1862 which at last effectively ended the Atlantic slave-trade. Nor did he demur when Congress passed first one and then another Confiscation Act, directed at rebel slave-holders.

Lincoln's caution gave little satisfaction to much Northern opinion, especially as it emerged that General McClellan was also cautious – exceedingly cautious, it seemed, lethargic. McClellan was overimpressed by his reasonable conviction that the South would be a very hard nut to crack. He clamoured incessantly for more time, more money and more training. The South, it seemed, was meanwhile making good her escape. The North's fretful anxiety was expressed in various trivial but revealing incidents, such as the hounding in the press of William Howard Russell, special correspondent of *The Times*, who made the mistake of writing too accurate a report of the Bull Run rout. He was eventually forced to go back to England.

Presently there was a major flare-up which was nearly disastrous. The Confederacy, dissatisfied with its diplomatic progress, or rather nonprogress (for both England and France, intimidated by the bellicose language of Secretary Seward, refused to recognize Southern independence), sent two new ministers to London and Paris: Messrs Mason and Slidell. These gentlemen slipped easily enough through the Northern blockade, but word of their presence in the area of his command soon reached Captain Wilkes of the US navy. He discovered that the two men had reached Cuba, and there boarded the British mail-steamer *Trent*, sailing for home. He stopped the vessel and relieved her of her two important passengers. He then sailed for Boston, where Mason and Slidell were confined in Fort Warren while Wilkes was given a public banquet and Northern opinion rejoiced. It was a blow against the South and a slap in the face for Great Britain, which had deeply disappointed the United States by her determined neutrality in the great struggle.

Today it is a little difficult to share the intensity of feeling which the *Trent* affair unleashed. Nowadays neutrals have learned to take the rough with the smooth and be thankful so long as they can stay at peace. Such a tame attitude was impossible to the subjects of Queen Victoria. Apart from the insult to the Union Jack, there was a widespread feeling that those coarse, vulgar, aggressive Yankees had behaved just as might have been predicted, just as they had behaved so often before: it was time to teach them a lesson. Mason and Slidell had relied on the protection of the British flag; they must be shown not to have done so in vain. On the other side of the Atlantic opinion was at first just as firm in praising Wilkes and wishing to retain his captives as prisoners of war. Fortunately neither Cabinet – neither Lincoln's nor Lord Palmerston's – wanted to let this trifle precipitate a ruinous war between Britain and America; after a decent interval, which allowed the North to have second thoughts, the two Southerners were released and continued their voyage to Europe (to their own deep disappointment: had their capture touched off an Anglo-American war the South's independence would probably have been assured).

Nothing more happened until the spring, when the war began at last to move into its major phase. As a preliminary the South tried to break the blockade with an ironclad vessel, the *Virginia* (formerly the USS *Merrimac*, a wooden ship that had fallen into rebel hands when the naval yard at Norfolk, Va., was captured). *Virginia* did great damage to federal shipping in Hampton Roads; but the next day, in the nick of time, the first Northern ironclad, the newly completed *Monitor,* appeared to give battle. The two strange monsters battered at each other for five hours, doing comparatively little damage; but in the end *Virginia* crept back to harbour and did not re-emerge. It was a momentous day in naval history, for it made the whole world's wooden fleets obsolete and set off a frantic hurry of shipbuilding and iron-cladding in Europe, and especially in Britain. Its chief consequence in the Civil War was that the federal government hastened on the production of more *Monitors,* so that the blockade was never broken. The South built four more ironclads, but lacked the industrial resources to do more; and none of them fought as successfully as had *Virginia.*

In the same spring of 1862 great events were happening in the West. In February an obscure West Point graduate, Brigadier-General Ulysses Simpson Grant (1822–85), thrust his forces up the Tennessee and Cumberland rivers and captured Forts Henry and Donelson, which were the strategic keys to the state of Tennessee. The Confederates were forced to evacuate it, and Grant pursued them across the state almost into Mississippi. But on 6 April they counter-attacked at Shiloh and nearly drove Grant and his army into the Tennessee river: only the arrival of reinforcements, and perhaps the death in battle of the Southern commander, Albert Sidney Johnston, saved the North. On 7 April it was Grant's turn to attack, and the Confederates had to withdraw into Mississippi. The casualties on both sides had been enormous (13,000 Northerners lost, 10,000 Southerners) in this, the first of the great butcheries which were to characterize the war; but in the end the Union held its ground, and the Confederacy had to reckon with having lost a great chunk of its territory. Soon afterwards a Union army and Union gunboats consolidated the gains of Shiloh and reconquered the Mississippi valley as far south as Memphis. And on 24

April Commodore David Farragut (1801–70) took New Orleans in one bold stroke: a feat, it will be remembered, that had been beyond the British.

After that nothing went right for the North for a long, long time.

By the spring of 1862 the Army of the Potomac was well-armed, clothed and otherwise equipped for war. McClellan had won the trust and affection of his troops, which he was never to lose (they appreciated his reluctance to throw their lives away). His insistence on thorough preparation and training had brought a semblance of much-needed professionalism to the North. But his caution, his procrastination, his reluctance to move finally exasperated the politicians (especially Stanton) beyond endurance. Lincoln had been able to overlook the impertinences which McClellan was silly enough to offer him, but he could not excuse the General's reckless refusal to consider political realities. Another great clamour for action was rising, especially among the President's own Republicans, and Lincoln could not resist their demands for ever in order to protect a general who, it seemed, was a poltroon and (it was whispered) a traitor, and who was certainly a Democrat. Finally, in April, McClellan was forced to move.

He had devised a most promising strategy that exploited the Union's command of the sea. He shipped his army down the Potomac to the coast of Virginia and landed it at the tip of the great peninsula where Jamestown had been settled and Yorktown had been besieged. Now, he hoped, it would see a third decisive event in American history. Certainly the capture of Richmond, which was what he hoped for, would have been a heavy blow to the South, though not so decisive as it proved at a much later stage of the war when the rest of the Confederacy had already fallen or been devastated. Protected on either flank by rivers (the James and the York), with a secure base behind him at Fort Monroe, he began to advance on a narrow front. Had he done so swiftly he would have won his crushing victory; as it was, he got closer to Richmond than any other federal general would do for nearly three years. But speed was something that McClellan could never achieve. The Southern defences were at first extremely weak, and a bold push could have overthrown them. It was not even tried. McClellan allowed himself to be deceived by a series of brilliant bluffs; he advanced at a snail's pace; and presently found that he had merely contrived to give the Confederates time to plan and organize effectively. Stonewall Jackson kept Lincoln and Stanton in quivering alarm for the safety of Washington, so that they denied McClellan troops he badly needed; meanwhile General Joe Johnston, a soldier as cautious as McClellan himself, conducted a masterly retreat. He backed away before the Union army while he gathered his strength, always retiring, never losing a man more than he had to. He brought McClellan within sight of Richmond spires, but his army was still intact.

Then he was wounded in a skirmish and had to hand over command to General Robert E. Lee.

Lee could have retreated as skilfully as Johnston, but that was not his style. He had a bold and restless spirit, and was especially gifted at taking his enemy by surprise and then hammering the surprise home. Besides, the time for retreat was past. He suddenly hit McClellan in his flank, and in the Seven Days' Battles (25 June–1 July) sent the Army of the Potomac reeling down to Harrison's Landing on the James river, desperate for a respite. Once more Virginia was secure, and once more the North had been humbled.

Lincoln and Stanton scraped together another army from the troops who had been held back from McClellan, and sent them against Lee under General Pope, who issued a threatening and boastful proclamation in the course of which he said that his headquarters would be in the saddle. Commenting that it was a better place for the hindquarters, Lee thrashed him soundly at the Second Battle of Bull Run (30 August 1862). Then he seized the initiative, at the same moment as General Braxton Bragg seized it for the Confederacy in the West. Lee's idea was to fight and win a battle in Pennsylvania: if he did so, and Bragg succeeded in conquering Kentucky, the blow to Northern morale would be colossal, coming as it would on top of months of defeat. Britain and France might well decide to recognize Southern independence. Washington might fall. In Stonewall Jackson he had found an ideal partner: a brilliant tactician and cavalry commander. It was worth the gamble, and, given the performance hitherto of the Northern generals, Lee probably thought the risk was slight. In the first week in September he crossed the upper course of the Potomac into Maryland and vanished into the hills. The next certain news that Washington had of him was that Stonewall Jackson had successfully attacked the great federal arsenal and depot at Harper's Ferry and carried off a mountain of booty.

Lincoln, meantime, had hastily recalled McClellan, presumably because, of all the available generals, he had been defeated least recently. McClellan quickly reorganized the Army of the Potomac and put some spirit into its disheartened soldiers, who were thoroughly glad to be once more under the command of Little Mac. Then he set off in pursuit of Lee. Whether, left to himself, he would have found him before Lee was ready cannot be known: by a stroke of pure good luck a copy of Lee's orders fell into his hands, and he was able to bring the Confederate General to battle at Antietam Creek in Maryland, just below the Pennsylvania border. 17 September proved to be the bloodiest day of the war: the Union army had to attack uphill and suffered terrible loss (12,000), but its greater numbers saved it from defeat and enabled it to inflict almost equal casualties on the Confederates. At the end of the battle Lee was left in possession of the field, but the Army of the Potomac was still in being, and the Confederate forces had suffered so horribly that there could be no question of continuing the campaign. Lee retreated into Virginia, where he heard that Bragg's offensive had also failed at the last minute. McClellan pursued him, but not vigorously enough to satisfy the President. On 7 November the General was dismissed, this time for good.

Six weeks previously, on 22 September, Lincoln had issued the Preliminary Emancipation Proclamation.

The President had been meditating some such step for months, for events were coming to point inexorably in the direction of a major assault on slavery.

Foremost was the consideration that slavery had caused the great rebellion. It had also poisoned political life for more than thirty years. The only way of making sure that it would never wreak such mischief again was to destroy it. Lincoln no longer had any doubt that it was a legitimate aim of the war to remove the cause of the war.

Then there was the question of morale, already mentioned. As the news of defeats poured in during that dreadful summer Northern spirits sank as much as Southern ones were lifted. Lee was right in thinking that it might not have taken much to break the Union will to go on fighting. But there was one element of Northern opinion that never faltered, that grew, in fact, more vigorous and vociferous: the abolitionists, who were steadily gaining ground in Congress, in the Republican party and in the country at large. Wendell Phillips, who before the war had at various times denounced Lincoln as 'that slave hound from Illinois' and as a huckster in politics, was still phrase-making at the President's expense, though he conceded that Lincoln was 'Kentucky honest'. Frederick Douglass called him 'the slow coach at Washington'. They were holding large and enthusiastic meetings. At the very least, it was unfortunate that they were dividing the North. Their energy could be immensely useful if harnessed to the Union cause by an emancipation decree. It might bring forth another surge of idealistic young recruits for New England's last crusade. They were badly needed, for the death-rate, as much from diseases caught in hospital as from wounds received on the battlefield, was appalling.

Emancipation might mitigate the manpower problem in another way as well. Ever since the war broke out the free blacks of the North had been trying to enlist. Intense race prejudice had usually rebuffed them, although one or two had succeeded in getting into uniform, like the runaway slave whose blood was the first shed for the Union: his head was cut open by a brickbat thrown by a pro-Confederate mob in Baltimore as his unit marched through the town on 18 April 1861. Then in August and September 1862, at New Orleans, General Ben Butler began to organize a regiment of free black volunteers, the 1st Louisiana Native Guards, which was mustered in on 27 September. There were tens of thousands more such men who might be enlisted, but they would not be likely to volunteer in any numbers if they felt that emancipation was not a Northern war-aim.

As a matter of fact no such doubt existed among the African-Americans, North or South, slave or free. To use the language of the day, Ethiopia was stirring. Four and a half million black Americans, who had never before been allowed much opportunity to shape their own destiny, were now taking a hand. In the North they thronged about the recruiting-offices, waiting for the call. In the South they preserved their usual calm appearance before their masters, but wherever Union armies drew near they ran away in enormous numbers. Soon every federal unit in the South was followed by a straggling crowd of escaped slaves. They had to be looked after, which was a nuisance; but they were also put to work, as cooks, drivers, navvies. It was not long before voices were heard suggesting that they might make soldiers.

Their legal status was highly uncertain. In the very earliest days of the war a Southern gentleman had actually crossed into federal lines at Fort Monroe in Virginia to claim the return of some of his runaway slaves. He had been firmly refused by Ben Butler (then commanding at that place) on the grounds that since slaves were property, they could rightfully be seized as contraband of war, even if they did the seizing themselves. This ingenious argument was thankfully adopted by Lincoln and the rest of the North: from then on the runaways were commonly spoken of as 'contrabands'. And as the war deepened in intensity, as both sides (but perhaps particularly the North) began to try deliberately to bring it home to each other by a policy of devastation and to deny each other necessary resources, Union soldiers began deliberately to encourage the slaves to desert the plantations. They could see how loss of the labour force would cripple the economy of the Confederacy, and therefore its capacity to make war; they could see what an accession of strength to themselves the four million slaves might be. Their racial attitudes probably did not much alter: some remained sympathetic to the blacks, some hostile, most indifferent; but they became abolitionists, of a very effective kind. By August 1862, some of them, at least, were welcoming the idea of enlisting 'the darkeys'.

There were some minor considerations present to Lincoln's mind: the fact that Maryland was now secure, and that Missouri and Kentucky were already so deeply divided that emancipation could hardly make things worse; the knowledge that foreign opinion, especially in England, would find it much easier to sympathize with the North if an explicit emancipation policy were adopted. But he was probably unaware of one major consideration, at least in all but its peripheral manifestations. Slavery was dying from the inside. The planters' revolution had already failed.

'Independence' and 'our domestic institutions' (slavery) – these were the twin themes that recurred in speech after speech, editorial after editorial, at the time of secession. War was accepted, eagerly in many cases, as the necessary price. In the high tide of the Confederacy before Antietam it was not yet thought seriously possible that the South might lose the war and her independence; but her domestic institution had already suffered debilitating blows.

Cotton production was plummeting, because of the embargo, and because of the blockade and the war (since food crops had to be grown instead). This had two weakening effects: it slashed the planters' income, and it unsettled their slaves. Worse still was the effect of the Confederacy and state governments' demands on Southern manpower, both black and white. The master went off to battle, the slave was carried away to work for the Confederate government as a blacksmith, factory hand, building labourer or a dozen other things, and the personal bond between the owner and his 'property' snapped for good. Worst of all was the direct effect of the war. It did not seem to matter whether a Union or a Confederate army crossed a plantation: either way the result was devastation, as crops were trampled down, stock was stolen, fences were destroyed. One Mississippi planter commented that there was no such thing as a friendly army in retreat. That was in 1864, but the ominous symptoms – weedy fields, empty slave quarters, half-wrecked buildings – had begun to appear long before. Many planters in areas of fighting sought to escape some, at least, of the ill-effects of war by retiring with their slaves deeper into the interior: many Southern roads were choked by lines of refugees trudging from one plantation to another; but this too was profoundly disruptive of slavery, and highly unprofitable. So the prosperity of the South, which slavery was supposed to guarantee and which in turn was essential to the continuance of slavery, was a thing of the past after only a year of war. Nor were there many symptoms of recovery. Here and there, the white men having gone to war, slaves turned recalcitrant. They worked shorter hours, or not at all, or only in response to pleadings – not the whip. True, slave labour was still plentiful and a huge economic asset to the Confederacy, since it implied long hours and little allowance for the weaknesses of sex or age; but the problem of controlling it, which had always been at the heart of the planters' concerns, was growing more and more intractable.

Seen in retrospect, against this background, the decision to issue an emancipation proclamation seems inevitable and easy. It was not so for Abraham Lincoln and his advisers. Under the Constitution the President had no right to meddle with private property in such a sweeping fashion except perhaps on the plea of the most extreme military necessity. More than that, an assault – any assault – on property – any property – was fundamentally antipathetic to the American tradition, which regarded property as sacred. Except perhaps for Salmon P. Chase no member of the Cabinet could lightly agree to what Gideon Welles, staring at the idea, called 'an arbitrary and despotic measure in the cause of freedom'. Lincoln might carry on with a high hand in other respects – suspending *habeas corpus*, for instance – but in this case, might he not at last be going altogether too far?

The matter was first broached to the Cabinet in July; by August all its members had agreed in principle, though some demurred as to the timing. Lincoln wanted to act at once; but Seward pointed out that it would be well to wait until there was a convincing Northern victory again. Otherwise the great deed would look like an appeal for help to the slaves, not a bringing of help to them. Lincoln accepted this suggestion in his own way. Silently he took an oath that if the Northern victory occurred, he would take it as a sign from God that his purposes were approved. Then came Antietam and Lee's retreat. He called the Cabinet together again and signed the Preliminary Emancipation Proclamation in front of them.

The text was anything but straightforward. Its guiding thought was the need to be secure from hampering legal counter-attack. So the rights of slave-holders in the loyal states, and even in those parts of the Confederacy which had been reconquered (chiefly Louisiana and the Sea Islands off the coast of South Carolina), were confirmed. And even in the disloyal areas the slaves would not be freed if their masters made peace by 1 January 1863. But if, by that date, the states designated should still be in rebellion, the slaves would be 'then, thenceforward, and forever free'.

Seward took the paper away to register and publish it. Later on that day there was a party at Chase's house. The full significance of what had been done began to sink in. Sombre statesmen who had spent their political lives reviling the Garrisonians or avoiding the opprobrious name now, in sheer lightness of heart, began to call each other abolitionists. A great shadow was lifting for ever.

The Emancipation Proclamation was, in the strictest possible sense of the word, revolutionary. If the policy it announced was carried through, an emancipation revolution, launched in answer to the planters' revolution, would fundamentally remake Southern society on a new principle. The Union cause would indeed become what Lincoln always claimed it was, the cause of democracy, of freedom, of equality; and all threat to the identity and sovereignty of the United States would be over. The work of the earlier Revolution would be completed. No wonder, if (as Lincoln now believed) it was God's will.

The South professed indifference: Lincoln's writ did not run in the Confederacy. Some hostile critics, especially British conservatives, professed to see in the Proclamation only an incitement to slave rebellion and murder. Some radicals were disappointed that he had given the rebel states three months' grace. On the whole the decision was hailed as it deserved. The slaves knew that 'Linkum' had done a great deed for them even if they could not read, and even though the Confederacy tried to suppress all reports of the Proclamation before it reached them. The news ran from mouth to mouth across Dixie by the rapid bush-telegraph that always so amazed the planter class, and was being exhaustively discussed in many slave quarters before the masters knew what had happened.

Yet the road to the final Proclamation was not quite straight. Lincoln liked to proceed by two steps forward, one step back, so as to make absolutely sure that his support was solid, indeed, clamorous; and he was never more careful than in this great matter. So on 1 December 1862 he put forward, not for the first time, proposals for gradual, compensated emancipation and for the colonization overseas of the freed blacks. He had several things in mind: among others, that only through Constitutional amendment could the Emancipation Proclamation be made permanent, and perhaps only gradual emancipation would be acceptable to Congress and the states. His central purpose was to test the waters; and, sure enough, they were stormy. But the wind blew strongest in one direction. The border states might chafe and petition against the Proclamation, but the radical Republicans in Congress vehemently demanded that he hold to it. Mrs Stowe came down to Washington to urge the same (he greeted her: 'so this is the little lady who made this big war'). The House of Representatives passed a resolution in support of the Proclamation. It was enough. On the afternoon of New Year's Day, 1863, Lincoln signed the final Emancipation Proclamation, confident that he could make it stick. At first his hand trembled so much that he had difficulty in writing. He had a superstitious pang, and then remembered that he had been shaking hands all morning with the crowd that had poured into the White House, according to custom, to wish him Happy New Year. He laughed, pulled himself together and wrote his name firmly.

In Boston two great public meetings were waiting for the news – one, mainly white, at the Music Hall, the other, mainly black, at Tremont Temple. When the news came by telegraph Frederick Douglass led the singing at the Temple; at the Music Hall the crowd shouted for Mrs Stowe, and before them all she bowed and wept for joy. The abolitionist crusade was vindicated, and the work of *Uncle Tom's Cabin* was achieved. An elderly planter in Kentucky thought the same. He called his slaves together, read out the Proclamation and told them that though it did not formally apply to them, he was sure their freedom was at hand, and advised them to make ready for it. In Washington a crowd of both races gathered outside the White House to cheer the President. The blacks said that if he would 'come out of that palace' they would hug him to death; that it was a time of times; that nothing like it would ever be seen again in this life.

Lincoln had done his duty; now the black people did theirs. They deserted the plantations in larger numbers than ever, at considerable risk, greatly weakening the Confederate military effort. The armies of the Union were correspondingly strengthened. Slaves and contrabands proved to be invaluable spies, guides and foragers for the advancing Northerners. Behind the Confederate lines the slaves eagerly succoured Union prisoners of war as best they could and helped them to escape in hundreds. 'If such kindness does not make one an abolitionist, he must have a heart of stone,' said one of these grateful fugitives, and another dedicated the book he wrote about his adventures 'to the Real Chivalry of the South' – the blacks who had helped him and the others. Nor was that all. Whether as soldiers or hired labourers, Negroes laid miles and miles of military roads; dug innumerable rifle-pits, raised forts, felled forests. They built bridges, drained marshes, filled sandbags, unloaded vessels, threw up entrenchments, dragged cannon to the front. They humped cotton bales abandoned by Southern planters down to the Mississippi levees, where they could be shipped to Union headquarters – demeaning work, since it seemed like a reversion to slavery. They stood on guard duty for endless tedious hours. And more and more they were allowed to fight. The first black regiment to be raised, the 54th Massachusetts, was nearly wiped out in a valiant but unsuccessful attack on Fort Wagner, the key to the seaward defences of Charleston, in 1863. The *New York Times* called this battle the blacks' Bunker Hill, for though they lost the fight, it proved their commitment to the Union cause and their excellent quality as soldiers. The black garrison of Fort Pillow on the Mississippi was actually wiped out in the following year, by Southern soldiers who would not accept their surrender – an infamous action which excited widespread passionate condemnation in the North. The Battle of Milliken's Bend (1863) was won by black troops, who later figured in large numbers and with conspicuous gallantry in Grant's great Virginian campaign and in the Battle of Nashville. By the end, Negroes had furnished 178,975 soldiers, organized in 166 regiments, to the Union army – one-eighth of its entire strength. They had provided a quarter of the sailors in the Union navy. They had successfully insisted on being treated, in the all-important matter of pay, as the equals of white soldiers, and had convinced Northern opinion that they deserved it. They had won fourteen Congressional Medals of Honour, the highest military decoration. In the end the Emancipation Proclamation had justified all the hopes placed on it.

Meanwhile there was still a war to be fought, little progress was being made, and it would be some time before the effect of emancipation would be felt. The western armies were held up at Vicksburg, a strongpoint on the Mississippi which denied the Union control of the river and thereby prevented it from splitting the Confederacy into two. In December the Army of the Potomac, commanded by the well-intentioned but not very clever General Burnside, launched an attack across the river Rappahannock at Fredericksburg, against an unconquerable Southern position. Lee beat back the Unionists easily, in his most convincing if not his most elegant victory. Northern casualties (12,500 dead or wounded) were as bad as those at Antietam. At the New Year a long-drawn-out, bloody and inconclusive battle was fought at Murfreesboro in central Tennessee. When it was over the Confederates, under Braxton Bragg, retreated eastwards, but the Federals were too exhausted to pursue them and stayed where they were for another six months. Again the casualties had been appallingly numerous: 13,000 Federals, 10,000 Confederates.

The military character of the Civil War was now clear. It was the first industrialized conflict. This meant, among other things, that it was technically feasible to arm, supply and reinforce enormous armies continuously and move them rapidly to any battlefield. Had it not been for the railways the South might have made good her independence. Instead, the existence of 22,000 miles of railway in the North meant that soldiers and supplies could be moved easily from one end of the country to the other, if necessary. Thus the South's advantage of interior lines of communication was neutralized, and her comparative shortage of railway mileage (9,000 miles) became a major strategic weakness. Still worse was the fact that she did not have the resources to maintain her roadbeds, rails and engines adequately. In this and many other ways the Confederacy suffered crucially from under-industrialization: its only important manufacturing plant was the Tredegar Ironworks at Richmond, whereas the North had innumerable works of the kind. All the devotion, energy and more than Yankee ingenuity which Southern inventors gave to the Cause, and which Southern soldiers applied to the capture of material from the North, could not make good the fearful gap. But both sides operated on a scale hitherto unknown anywhere.

Hence the colossal scale of Civil War battles. These proved to be fearfully debilitating. After two years of war the volunteer spirit began to flag, and both North and South had to resort to conscription, which caused bad trouble, especially in the North. The aftermath of the Battle of Gettysburg was marred by an outbreak of ferocious anti-conscription riots in New York, which quickly turned into anti-black riots, in which a black children's orphanage was burned down and several blacks were lynched; hundreds of whites died. Inflation, caused by the vast borrowings of the federal government, galloped away: prices had increased by 99 per cent by the end of the war. A vociferous minority of Peace Democrats, nicknamed 'Copperheads' (after a common poisonous snake), indulged in an opposition which was nearly, and occasionally quite, treasonable. War-weariness, and resentment of the administration's bad luck and incompetence, were expressed at the polls: the Republicans did badly in the 1862 Congressional elections (though they did not lose control of the houses) and might expect to do worse in the Presidential election of 1864 unless they had won the war by then. Three Confederate ships, *Florida*, *Alabama* and *Shenandoah*, built surreptitiously in England, ravaged the unarmed maritime commerce of the North; since they could not carry their prizes home through the blockade, they burned them on the high seas. Their activities deeply embittered Northern opinion against Britain, which had blunderingly allowed the raiders to escape from Birkenhead; at times it looked as if there might yet be a third Anglo-American war.

Lincoln's burdens were crushing, and visibly aged him; those of Jefferson Davis were worse. The Southern President had his weaknesses (of which a poor judgement of men was probably the worst), but he was the best man available for his almost impossible job, of creating a nation state and fighting for its life simultaneously. He met obstruction and heartbreaking difficulties at every turn. The blockade, steadily tightening, prevented the importation of goods from Europe in any quantity, and such blockade-runners as there were (they made enormous fortunes) tended to import items, such as hats and dresses from Paris, with an eye to their own profit rather than to the military needs of the Confederacy. Anyway, the South had few resources with which to pay for imports. The idiotic King Cotton policy meant that when cotton could have been got to Europe and there exchanged for arms, it had been withheld, in order to intimidate the Europeans (who discovered, much to their own surprise, that they could at a pinch manage without Southern cotton, using Indian instead); then it had been burned, to keep it out of the Yankees' clutches and to forestall those unpatriotic planters who might have been tempted to defy the embargo; finally the cotton-fields had largely been turned over to food crops from which to feed the armies. The South was able to raise a certain amount of money on the London and Paris exchanges on the security of future cotton crops, but nothing like enough to buy all it needed.

As if this was not enough, Davis had also to struggle with the inadequacies of the South's political structure. States' rights had been the slogan under which the South seceded; states' rights were enshrined in the new Confederate Constitution; for states' rights the South would, it seemed, commit suicide. All too frequently Davis had to struggle bitterly with state Governors (Joe Brown of Georgia and Zebulon Vance of North Carolina): at first over matters of principle, such as conscription and the suspension of *habeas corpus*; in the end over desperately needed military supplies. He was not helped by his Vice-President, Alexander Stephens of Georgia, who denounced him as 'weak and vacillating, timid, petulant, peevish, obstinate, but not firm', or by a Cabinet that consisted largely of mediocrities. He was not even able to evolve a system of priorities for the allocation of such supplies as there were. The western and eastern theatres were left to scramble against each other for men and munitions; the eastern theatre, being that of Richmond, Virginia and Robert E. Lee, tended to get the lion's share, although the war would eventually be won and lost in the West. Davis was partly to blame for this: he never saw, until it was far too late, the need for a supreme military commander; he thought he could do it all himself. The one person in a position to make him see sense in time was Lee, but Lee himself thought and fought rather as a Virginian than as a Southerner: he too seems not to have understood the importance of the West and the imperative need for devising an overall strategy. The contrast with another Virginian general is instructive: he was in some respects the Confederacy's George Washington, but he lacked Washington's comprehensive grasp of politics and war.

Yet at least he could see that the South was growing weaker and weaker: she could not afford to depend solely on the hope that Northern war-weariness would increase, unassisted, to such an extent that Lincoln would give up the struggle; she might give up first herself. So Lee once more turned to the offensive. In the late spring of 1863 he began to move North again.

Essentially his plan was the same as that which had so nearly succeeded in the previous year. Seasoned by all its campaigning under its incomparable commanders, the army of Northern Virginia was at this point as fine a force, in terms of fighting quality, as any that the world has seen. Lee could depend on his soldiers implicitly, as he could on Stonewall Jackson, as he could, he thought, on the doltish command of the Army of the Potomac. Richmond strained every nerve to supply him adequately. He set out to invade Pennsylvania. If he succeeded, the fright given to Northern civilians would alone be well worthwhile: it might induce them to withdraw troops from the West, where it was beginning to look as if Vicksburg might fall at last. He might, in addition, capture Washington and thereby win the war: for surely, after such a fear, Britain and France would recognize the Confederacy. To do all this, to be sure, it would be necessary to destroy the Army of the Potomac, which in spite of all the batterings he had administered to it he had never yet quite contrived; but Lee had not earned his reputation by pessimism. He set to work.

First it was necessary to protect Richmond against another Northern offensive, which was launched in April. This Lee did by the victory of Chancellorsville on 2 May 1863. In dense forest – the untouched wilderness of central Virginia – it proved easy enough to bewilder and outflank the invader. Lee even dared to break the old rule and divide his army in the presence of the enemy, so that he could attack from two sides at once. The outcome entirely justified him: the Army of the Potomac had to retreat, after sustaining heavy losses, and Mr Lincoln began to look about for yet another new commander (the loser at Chancellorsville was General Hooker). Yet perhaps the Confederate loss was the heavier: Stonewall, returning from a moonlit reconnaissance, was shot by one of his own sentries. He took a day or two to die, lingering in delirium. His last words were: 'Let us cross the river and rest in the cool of the trees.' But his comrades had a long hot road to go: he crossed the river alone.

Lee crossed, not Jordan, but the Potomac. He feinted as brilliantly as ever: the North was first puzzled, then terrified. In Washington all was confusion: at length command of the resistance was given to General George Meade (1815–72), a West Pointer of little prominence (the appointment was so unlikely that when Meade was roused from sleep to receive it he thought the messenger had come to arrest him). The Army of the Potomac hurried after Lee, who now burst out of the Maryland hills into the broad valleys of central Pennsylvania, just west of the state capital, Harrisburg, and the great alluvial plain: fat farmlands, hitherto untouched by war.

But Lee did not have quite the complete control of his army that he had enjoyed in Stonewall's time. His cavalry commander, Jeb Stuart, was by no means so reliable, and perhaps the gracious Lee was incapable of being sufficiently firm with him. At any rate, at this crucial moment, Jeb Stuart was away on a raid, and Lee had no knowledge of the whereabouts of the enemy, except that he was somewhere on his flank. Then on 1 July they blundered into each other at the small town of Gettysburg. Longstreet, commander of Lee's first corps, dislodged the Federals from the town easily enough, but at the price of driving them southwards into an admirable defensive position along a fish-hook shaped ridge. It was Fredericksburg reversed; not Lee's sort of battle. He said afterwards that it was all his fault, but beforehand his clear judgement was that manoeuvring was impossible (because the Yankees would simply watch their opportunity and then hit him in the flank) and so was retreat. So he resolved on the same tactics that had decimated poor General Burnside's men seven months before: a series of frontal attacks uphill.

The result was the most terrible battle of the war, a struggle which went on for two days, producing frightful casualties (23,000 killed, wounded or missing for the North, about the same for the South). The Confederate soldiers performed prodigies of valour, but at last could do no more. The final attack failed; Lee ordered a retreat. It was made more dismal by pouring rain, but perhaps that, and the exhaustion of the Northern army, preserved Lee from total destruction. Once more he got away with a saving remnant across the Potomac; and once more Abraham Lincoln, who had felt that he had his enemy in his grasp at last, soundly berated his victorious general for too sluggish a pursuit. Yet overall he could afford to rejoice: the South would never again be able to launch such an offensive, and on 4 July, Independence Day, the day after Gettysburg, Grant took Vicksburg. Lincoln proudly announced that 'the Father of Waters flows once more unvexed to the sea'. Even the outbreak of the New York draft riots could not destroy the meaning of the two great victories. The strategic initiative had passed to the North for good, and the South's doom was sure, so long as the Union's will held firm.

It was time, and more than time, to consider what to do when the Union had achieved its final victory. True, that process, thanks to Robert E. Lee, was going to take eighteen months more, and there was going to be at least one agonizing moment when it looked as if all might be lost; but no one knew this in the summer of 1863. And for months Congress had been steadily growing more assertive on the question of the post-war settlement. If one wants to pick a moment as the opening of the Reconstruction tragedy, the fall of Vicksburg will do as well as any other.

Lincoln's policy during the war had two clearly distinct but overlapping phases. In the first, his task was to find the means of winning and to convince his fellow-citizens that victory was worth its cost. In the second, he had to prepare a peace.

By the autumn of 1863 he had substantially completed his first task. So he accepted an invitation to deliver a few suitable words at the dedication of a cemetery for the fallen at Gettysburg. The main address of the day was delivered by an elegantly fluent windbag, who gave a speech full of clichés that lasted two hours. Lincoln's lasted barely two minutes. Yet very soon this little Gettysburg Address was being quoted and applauded everywhere; for in it Lincoln at last achieved the perfect distillation of what he had been trying to teach his people since, in his inaugural address, he had first put the case for majority government.

Fourscore and seven years ago [he began] our fathers brought forth on this continent, a new nation, conceived in Liberty, and dedicated to the proposition that all men are created equal.

Now we are engaged in a great civil war, testing whether that nation or any nation so conceived and so dedicated, can long endure. We are met on a great battle-field of that war. We have come to dedicate a portion of that field, as a final resting place for those who here gave their lives that that nation might live. It is altogether fitting and proper that we should do this.

But, in a larger sense, we can not dedicate – we can not consecrate – we can not hallow – this ground. The brave men, living and dead, who struggled here, have consecrated it, far above our poor power to add or detract. The world will little note, nor long remember what we say here, but it can never forget what they did here. It is for us the living, rather, to be dedicated here to the unfinished work which they who fought here have thus far so nobly advanced. It is rather for us to be here dedicated to the great task remaining before us – that from these honoured dead we take increased devotion to that cause for which they gave the last full measure of devotion – that we here highly resolve that these dead shall not have died in vain – that this nation, under God, shall have a new birth of freedom – and that government of the people, by the people, for the people, shall not perish from the earth.

For Lincoln's original audience the importance of the address was that it summed up their deepest beliefs, which, whatever their validity (the twentieth century has shown up a certain element of presumption in them, as well as their essential correctness), were neither cheap nor silly. In their name, summoned by Lincoln's sober language, they could continue to fight in stern Puritan hopefulness.

For Lincoln the important point was probably the single phrase 'all men are created equal' (lifted from the Declaration of Independence). For him, by now, the causes of Union and of emancipation were one. The casualty lists were continually lengthening, and the deaths from diseases contracted in the appalling hospitals were double the number of those in battle. As Lincoln contemplated the horrible suffering, he wondered, ever more anxiously, what sins of omission or commission he and his countrymen had committed to deserve this chastening at God's hands – the God in whom, before the war, he had almost ceased to believe; and he resolved that in the making of the peace, the remaking of the Union, those sins would not be repeated.

The deepest sin, of course, the root of the whole matter, was slavery, but that was well on the way to final extinction. The Emancipation Proclamation was doing its work. As a wartime measure it could not permanently outlaw slavery, even though it freed the slaves; but already proposals were being brought forward for an amendment to the Constitution, ending the peculiar institution for ever. More pressing were the intimately related problems of what to do with the former slaves, and what to do with the rebels.

Lincoln, determined to avoid those faults of arrogance and rigidity which had played so large a part in bringing about the Civil War, early decided on his course. The blacks would have to trust to the wisdom and mercy of their former masters; this might not be a bad fate if the South was shown wisdom and mercy by the federal government. Lincoln demonstrated what he meant in his plans for the reconstruction of Louisiana, the first Southern state to fall back entirely into Union hands. Let 10 per cent of the state's voters take the oath of loyalty to the Union and renounce slavery, and they could set up a new government, which would be readmitted to the Union on the old terms. Lincoln's only reservation was that certain categories of rebel – functionaries of the 'so-called' Confederate government, for example, or men who had resigned US military or naval commissions – would be excluded; otherwise pardon would be available to all who took the loyalty oath.

Lincoln can have had few illusions about the difficulty of what he was undertaking, and was as flexibly ready as ever to try something else if this scheme failed; but underneath the magnanimity and caution which were such leading traits of his character lay a flint-like self-assurance. Against all odds, he was successfully guiding the Union towards victory; he would also guide it towards peace, and a just future. The difficulties quite failed to daunt him.

Yet they were formidable, and on one of them his enterprise must, I think, have foundered. The Southern whites were obdurate. They were of no mind, it proved, to show wisdom and mercy to the blacks. Had Lincoln lived he would have been faced by such tokens of resistance as the infamous Black Codes,[4] and thus have been forced to take the road of radical reconstruction. To suppose that he would not have done so is to mistake the nature of his relationship with the Republican party, of which he was after all the leader; and to forget that he was, and knew himself to be, the Great Emancipator. He had incurred grave responsibilities for the welfare of the former slaves; he was not the man to shirk them.

In his lifetime it was resistance from the other side, from these same radical Republicans, which seemed likeliest to thwart his generous projects. The stronghold of these men was Congress, which they had dominated since the Southern withdrawal in 1861. The radicals did not share either Lincoln's magnanimity or his self-confidence, and some of them wanted another presidential candidate in 1864: one more extreme in his views and more subservient to Congress. They did not trust the Southern planters, and thought that far more obstacles should be placed in their way, lest they regain control of the states and both oppress the freedmen and challenge the Republican ascendancy in Congress. They felt further that a reconstruction plan should have some explicit provisions for safeguarding the interests of the blacks, though at this stage neither they nor the President were willing to do more than toy with the idea of Negro suffrage. They were appalled by actual events in Louisiana (General Banks, Lincoln's agent there, showed himself much too co-operative with the planters). All through the spring

4 See below, pp. 352–3.

and summer of 1864 the dispute raged. Eventually the radicals pushed the so-called Wade–Davis bill through Congress: it embodied some of their own stringent ideas, for example by requiring 50 per cent of the white male citizens to take an 'ironclad' loyalty oath before a state might recover its powers. Lincoln vetoed it, since it would have tied his hands. The radicals were enraged. They were convinced that the war had been caused solely by the machinations of the planters (not true Americans, in their view, but aristocrats and Tories) and they were determined to break the oligarchy's power once for all. They were reinforced in their determination by many of the allies that the Republican party's success had won for it. They were the supporters of protective tariffs, of transcontinental railways, men who had done well out of the war and meant to do well out of the peace, and the thousands upon thousands of office-holders. All of these feared what a vengeful, unreformed, politically adroit South might achieve if allowed back into the Union on anything but the stiffest terms. After all, the South had usually dominated the federal government before the war. She must never do so again.

At times all these disputes seemed premature. The blockade was tightening daily on the southern coastlines; no hope now of rescue for the Confederacy from Europe. In eastern Tennessee the South had thrown away the victory of Chickamauga (19–20 September 1863) when the Union Army of the Cumberland had come within an inch of total destruction; failure to follow through had given Washington time to hurry in reinforcements, by road, river and (most spectacularly) railroad, and to put the whole operation under the command of Ulysses S. Grant. On 24–25 November the Union took its revenge, and in the Battle of Chattanooga expelled the Confederacy from Tennessee. The next step would be to break through the mountain barrier into central Georgia, but Grant would not take it in person: Lincoln, at last acknowledging his outstanding talents, plucked him away from the West to make him overall commander of the Union armies with the rank of lieutenant-general (the first soldier since Washington to hold that rank). His brilliant second-in-command, William Tecumseh Sherman (1820–91), was left to complete the Western campaigns. But it was long indeed before these victories and dispositions produced their promised fruit.

Grant left Meade in command of the Army of the Potomac, but himself settled the strategic and tactical plans of campaign for dealing with Lee. He marched his men south in May 1864, disappearing with them into the thick green woods of Virginia, like so many Northern generals before him, and like them came to grief. In a series of battles (the Wilderness, 5–6 May; Spotsylvania Court House, 8–19 May; Cold Harbor, 3–11 June) he and Lee inflicted frightful punishment on each other's armies: Union casualties were 55,000, Confederate, 40,000; and at the end of it Grant had neither destroyed the Army of Northern Virginia (his essential objective) nor taken Richmond. Instead he found himself laying siege to the Confederate capital from the south and east; while Lee's army, though grievously reduced, was securely entrenched on his front, with the vital railway lines that brought in supplies from the interior of the South quite out of reach. And Northern opinion shuddered at the length of Grant's 'butcher's bill'.

Other Union generals had despaired when confronted with lesser difficulties; but Grant never despaired, and Lincoln backed him steadily, even when he was at fault. He had neglected the Shenandoah valley, down which so many surprise Confederate attacks had driven so often in the past; now Lee mounted one more. He sent General Jubal Early on a spectacular raid against Washington, followed by another into Pennsylvania, which produced panic in the federal capital and greatly damaged Lincoln's chances of re-election. Grant retaliated by sending one of his most competent and pitiless generals, Phil Sheridan (1831–88), to devastate the valley, which was not only Early's base but also one of Lee's chief sources of supply. After he had finished Sheridan commented that if a crow now wanted to cross the valley he would have to carry rations. And though Lee and his men survived in their entrenchments at Petersburg, a few miles south of Richmond, they were also trapped. If Grant kept up the pressure, their defeat could only be a matter of time.

Yet once again the outlook for the Union in the late summer was as gloomy as it had been cheerful in the spring. A swelling chorus of discontent spoke of failing Northern morale. The Copperheads were more active and vociferous than ever. The Presidential election being at hand, the Democrats drafted an election platform which in effect conceded independence to the Confederacy, for it demanded an immediate armistice and made no mention of slavery. They nominated General McClellan for the Presidency: he accepted the nomination but rejected the platform. Nevertheless, a McClellan victory would probably mean victory for the platform too, since it would be read, probably correctly, as a popular repudiation of the war as well as of the war-making President; and at the end of August it seemed very likely to Lincoln that McClellan would win.

Then came the news that on 1 September Sherman had taken Atlanta, Georgia. His campaign had lasted all summer. He had fought his way down from the mountains to the edge of the Georgian plain only in the teeth of an intensely skilful retreat by Joe Johnston, who had kept his army effective and in being every inch of the way, and on the whole inflicted more damage than he had received. But Johnston's Fabian tactics were deeply resented by Jefferson Davis, for they were allowing the Yankees to get at the untouched heart of the Confederacy. When Sherman reached the outskirts of Atlanta the President lost patience and replaced Johnston by General John B. Hood, who had been intriguing against his commander for months. It was a fatal choice. Hood had some virtues, but common sense was not one of them. To save Atlanta he launched a series of vigorous attacks which only weakened his army. He was able to delay the inevitable for a few weeks more, but at the end of August had to abandon the place after destroying his supply dumps there. This loss was serious enough on its own, for Atlanta was a centre of communications and of the South's infant industrial production. What was worse, its fall gave just that fillip to Northern morale which was needed. Abraham Lincoln was re-elected by a landslide. Worst of all, Georgia was laid open to Sherman's army.

He waited for some time, considering what to do. His line of communication with his base at Chattanooga and Nashville was already dangerously long and was threatened by Confederate cavalry raiders under the brilliant leader Bedford Forrest. To move forward through hostile country and protect his communications at the same time was, Sherman decided, beyond his strength. To stay where he was, in Atlanta, was to condemn himself to impotence. Boldly, he decided to cut loose from his base and march through Georgia to the Atlantic, living off the country. He knew that the South was so weakened that he would be unlikely to meet any very formidable resistance; but he had insight enough to see that there was another, crueller, stronger reason for such a campaign. If he cut a trail of scorched earth through the Southern heartland it would be a fatal blow to Confederate strength and morale. The rebels would discover their total impotence and accept that their defeat was certain. Before long they would surrender. He resolved to 'make Georgia howl'. As soon as Lincoln was safely re-elected, Sherman disappeared. Burning everything of military value in Atlanta so that it would be of no use to the enemy, he marched off to the sea.

He had the easiest possible passage. Hood knew as well as Sherman that he could offer no effective resistance to the march; but he thought he might counter it by striking at Sherman's base at Nashville. If he succeeded there, he said boastfully, he would march on Ohio. This decision would have had little to recommend it, even if Sherman had left Nashville undefended, since he clearly thought he was now independent of his communications: if he was right, the loss of the city would make little difference to him. But Nashville was far from undefended. Hood staked one of the last two Southern armies there, and lost his gamble: he was utterly defeated by General George H. Thomas (1816–70), a Unionist Virginian who had never before had quite such a splendid opportunity to show what he could do. His demonstration now was absolutely convincing. As Bruce Catton says, at the Battle of Nashville (15–16 December 1864), 'for the one and only time in all the war, a Confederate army [was] totally routed on the field of battle'.[5] Next month Hood was relieved at his own request, and the fragments of his army were sent to do what little they could against the triumphant Sherman.

That commander had reached the sea and taken Savannah, as a Christmas present for Abraham Lincoln, on 21 December. His month of invisibility had stirred considerable anxiety in the North, but it had been a strategic triumph. Behind him lay a swath, some fifty miles wide by 250 miles long, of burned-out mansions, liberated slaves, devastated fields, wrecked railway

5 Bruce Catton, *The Penguin Book of the American Civil War* (Harmondsworth, 1966), p. 258.

lines and despairing white civilians. He had also picked the country clean of livestock and provisions. Georgia was finished. Now it was South Carolina's turn: at last the proud Palmetto state, which had been the heart and centre of the rebellion, would receive her punishment. The trail of destruction turned north; and Sherman continued to display his mastery of war. He outwitted his opponents (Johnston and Beauregard were only two of the generals now gathered against him) as well as outfighting them; he bypassed Charleston, which fell all the same, and seized the state capital, Columbia, on 17 February 1865. That night half the town burned to the ground, in fires that were lit accidentally-on-purpose by drunken, vengeful Northern soldiers (Sherman got the blame, though it was quite untrue that, as alleged, he had ordered the arson). As spring began the army turned towards North Carolina and Virginia, to rendezvous with Grant at Richmond.

Before it got there, however, the war was over.

On 31 March Grant launched his long-prepared offensive against Lee's lines at Petersburg.[6] Lee was now so weakened that he could offer no effective resistance. By this time even his devoted soldiers were despairing. There were so few of them left, and under Grant's inexorable pressure of men and guns they had to stretch their lines ever thinner. They were dressed in rags, barefoot, underfed and dangerously short of ammunition. And what was there left to fight for? The Cause was petering out in bitter squabbles between the political leaders, each blaming anyone but himself for the débâcle. It was, said the soldiers, 'a rich man's war and a poor man's fight'. It had taken them a long time to realize it; and the rich men had already lost not only the war, but the thing for which they had launched it. In the North, thanks in large part to strong pressure by the administration, Congress had finally passed the Thirteenth Amendment, outlawing slavery for ever, and sent it to the states for ratification. In the South, Jefferson Davis, as a last desperate measure to raise new manpower, had induced the Confederate Congress to give freedom to any slave who enlisted in the army. Slavery was dead, and the Confederacy almost so. And now Sheridan turned Lee's flank, while Grant destroyed his centre. On 2 April Richmond had to be evacuated. Jefferson Davis and the government fled south-west; Lee began a desperate march to the west, hoping to get beyond the Federal pursuit so that he could turn south and link up with Joe Johnston.

The President of the states so soon to be re-united was waiting for the finish behind the federal lines. He could not quite believe that he was witnessing it. Only a month earlier, as he took the oath of office for the second time, he had seemed oppressed with the idea that all might still be far from over.

---

6 He had waited so long chiefly so that the hampering mud of winter could dry. In this respect as in many others conditions during the sieges of Petersburg and Richmond were much like those which were to prevail on the Western Front fifty years later.

Fondly do we hope, fervently do we pray, that this mighty scourge of war may speedily pass away. Yet, if God wills that it continue until all the wealth piled by the bondsman's two hundred and fifty years of unrequited toil shall be sunk, and until every drop of blood drawn with the lash shall be paid by another drawn with the sword, as was said three thousand years ago, so still it must be said, 'The judgements of the Lord are true and righteous altogether.'

Now it seemed that the Lord had at last relented. Peace was at hand, slavery was dead, a Freedmen's Bureau had just been set up to help the former bondsmen, and the Union was about to be restored. To realize all this, and to demonstrate it too, Lincoln went to visit fallen Richmond on 4 April. He landed at the waterside almost unattended, and was instantly recognized and surrounded by a huge, happy crowd of rejoicing blacks, anxious to hail the Messiah come to free his children from their bondage, anxious to look at last on the spring of life, they said, after years in the desert without water; or rather, anxious no more: 'I know I am free,' cried one woman, 'for I have seen Father Abraham and felt him.' They burst into a hymn:

Oh, all ye people clap your hands,
    And with triumphant voices sing;
No force the mighty power withstands
    Of God the universal King.

It was a long time before Lincoln was able to walk through the crowd to the Confederate White House and sit in Jefferson Davis's chair. When he went back to his ship he was escorted by a troop of black cavalry. Perhaps by then he and all the people of Richmond believed in the great victory.

Meanwhile Robert E. Lee was finding it impossible to stage an organized retreat. So complete was the collapse of the Confederacy that supplies could not be got to the soldiers: some went four days without rations. Desertions multiplied: for months now they had been so numerous that he had not been able to spare troops to bring back the runaways. Now men simply fell out on the road west. Grant's pursuing army found something new: rifles abandoned at the roadside.

Grant was behind; Sheridan, in front. One more battle might be glorious, but would end in annihilation. Instead of ordering a useless sacrifice, Lee decided to surrender. On 9 April 1865 he met Grant at Appomattox Court House, a country crossroads in the forest, and handed over his sword.

It was one of the great symbolic moments of American history. Grant, to his annoyance and subsequent embarrassment, by accident had no clean uniform to put on; so it was in his usual scruffy attire that he received Lee, resplendent in grey coat and soft leather. They quickly agreed on terms. Lee did not want a guerrilla resistance, which would have poisoned the American future indefinitely. Grant wanted to ease the return of the rebels to citizenship as much as possible. The Southern soldiers were to lay down their arms and disperse to their homes; Lee's request that they might keep their horses to help in the spring ploughing was acceded to, and Grant (living up to his name) gave them an issue of rations. Above all, he gave his word that all the members of that army, from Lee downwards, would be left alone by federal authority so long as they kept to the terms of their parole. Grant knew that he was acting as the President would wish. Nothing must be done to add to the bitterness of defeat; all means must be tried to reconcile the Southerners to being Americans again.

A few weeks more, and Joe Johnston and everyone else had surrendered. The last hostilities of the war, curiously, took place in the North Pacific, where Union and Confederate fishing vessels fought each other until at last the great news reached them. By July the Civil War was entirely over. Roughly 359,000 Union soldiers, 258,000 Confederates, had died either on the battlefield or in military hospitals, which means that it was and is the bloodiest war in American history in terms of absolute numbers as well as in the proportion of casualties to the population. It left indelible traces on the American consciousness. It is very understandable that the soldiers of both sides hurried home and tried to put it behind them. The Union army held a great victory parade in Washington before dispersing. Jefferson Davis began an irksome captivity in Fort Monroe. Abraham Lincoln was assassinated.

16 Reconstruction 1865–77

We have the right to treat them as we would any other provinces that we might conquer.

> US Representative Thaddeus Stevens, January 1863

What's the use of being free if you don't own enough land to be buried in?

> Freedman to Whitelaw Reid, 1865

Our main and fundamental objective is the MAINTENANCE OF THE SUPREMACY OF THE WHITE RACE in this Republic. History and Physiology teach us that we belong to a race which nature has endowed with an evident superiority over all other races, and that the Maker, in thus elevating us above the common standard of human creation, has intended to give us over inferior races a dominion from which no human laws can permanently derogate.

> Official charge to new recruits to the Ku Klux Klan, 1867

On the evening of Good Friday, 1865 (14 April), four years after Fort Sumter fell and barely a week after Appomattox, Lincoln went to the theatre. He had invited Grant to go with him, but the General said that he had to return to the army (his real reason for refusing was that his wife had quarrelled with Mrs Lincoln). The play was a favourite comedy of the time, *Our American Cousin*, so attractive that the bodyguard slipped away from the door of the President's box to watch it himself. The opportunity was seized by John Wilkes Booth, an indifferent actor and a Southern sympathizer, half-crazed with vanity, who for weeks had been organizing a murderous conspiracy. He entered the box, shot Lincoln through the head and jumped down to the stage. One of the spurs that he was foolishly wearing caught in the decorative bunting, so that he fell in such a way as to break his left leg, but he still had sufficient strength and self-control to yell out

'*Sic semper tyrannis!*'[1] before making his escape through the wings and the stage door of the theatre. At the same time one of his associates attacked Seward, who was at home recuperating in bed from a carriage accident. The Secretary of State suffered serious injuries, but eventually recovered. The President was taken to a little house across the street from the theatre, where he lingered unconscious for some hours. Death came at 7.22 in the morning of 15 April. Stanton, watching at his bedside, set the seal on his passing: 'Now he belongs to the ages,' he said.

There was an explosion of grief and rage in the North. Lincoln was given the greatest funeral in the history of the United States. Booth was hunted down and killed while resisting arrest. His fellow-assassins were caught, tried and sentenced – in most cases, to death. Nothing could repair the loss. It was not just that Lincoln was a good and great man. His talents had seldom been needed more. The problems of peace would have perplexed even him; his successor was to make them much worse. With Lincoln died the remote chance of a good peace. Booth condemned the South to generations of squalid backwardness and the races in America to a long, unhappy struggle which is not over yet. Some such outcome might well have occurred even if Lincoln had lived; he never pretended to be a miracle-worker; but his prestige, his wisdom, his political guile, would surely have shortened America's racial agony or mitigated its intensity.

It took a little time for the full measure of the loss to be realized. Lincoln was succeeded in the White House by Andrew Johnson of Tennessee (1808–75), his Vice-President. The Republicans rallied to the new man; some even thought he might prove a stronger President than Lincoln. He had an excellent record: he had been the only Senator from the South to stick to the Union in 1861, and he had governed his native state from 1862 to 1865, gaining good marks for the strict manner in which he tried to purge Tennessee of rebel sympathizers (though close observers might have noticed a needless truculence in his behaviour). Disillusion was slow in coming: the war party was very reluctant to break with its chief, even after his pugnacity and contrariness had been demonstrated again and again, even after they noticed that 'the faces in the ante-chamber of the President look very much as they would if a Democratic administration were in power'. In the end he precipitated one of the biggest political rows in American history. It is an exciting and not very edifying story; it must be told; but its somewhat superficial dramatics shall not be allowed to obscure the underlying difficulty which had the country in its grip. The North had won a mighty victory. How could it make that victory actual and permanent? How, so to speak, could it cash in its chips? How could it prove, to itself and to the future, that the mighty effort had been worthwhile?

True, the Union had been saved. Never again would the South

---

1 'Thus always to tyrants': the motto of the state of Virginia. Another version is that he shouted 'The South shall be free!'

contemplate secession or rebellion; even the ancient shibboleths of nullification and states' rights had lost much of their magic. But the North had long ago persuaded itself that it was fighting for something greater and nobler than even the Union: for democracy; for liberty and equality; for the last, best hope of earth. The multitudinous ghosts of the Union dead insistently demanded that this commitment be honoured; so did the living: all the former soldiers and their families. The opportunity seemed promising, for the South was prostrate and passive, curious, perhaps even hopeful, for a moment, so complete was her defeat and ruin. A Northern visitor reported, 'In North and South Carolina, Georgia, and Florida, we found this state of feeling universally prevalent. The people wanted civil government and a settlement. They asked no terms, made no conditions. They were defeated and helpless – they submitted. Would the victor be pleased to tell them what was to be done?' And then, there were the African-Americans – the free Negroes of the North, the freed slaves of the South.

In the last analysis, they were what it was all about. The Union could not have been saved without the help of the blacks. The great experiment in liberty and equality might go forward; but it would have little meaning if the whites alone profited from it. The North had won; but the victory would be hollow if the ex-Confederates renewed their system of racial oppression and, on that foundation, once more challenged the dearest interests and beliefs of their fellow-citizens. Lincoln and the rest had surely not died in vain; but it might seem so if justice was not done to the former bondsmen. And should not the South be disciplined? Was it not a just punishment, as well as prudent, to compel her to abandon her old ways?

Besides, the Negroes demanded it. There were four and a half million of them; they were a force to be reckoned with. It was not only that their leaders, such as Frederick Douglass, were articulate and energetic, nor that they had many powerful white friends among the old abolitionists. The rank and file could justly claim that they had won their freedom through their own efforts, once the opportunity had arrived. Douglass had always believed that 'once let the black man get upon his person the brass letters, *US*; let him get an eagle on his button, and a musket on his shoulder and bullets in his pocket, and there is no power on earth which can deny that he has earned the right to citizenship in the United States'. It seemed self-evident to many by 1865. Lincoln had said as much in his last public speech. Now was the time to make good that citizenship throughout the country.

Such was the view of the victorious North. Otherwise, she asked little of the South. The debts incurred by the Confederacy and the individual seceding states must be repudiated, of course, and Jefferson Davis was kept in prison for two years; but he was not hanged, and would have been let out sooner – might never have been imprisoned – but for the murder of Lincoln. Otherwise, it was as if the dignified behaviour of Grant and Lee at Appomattox had infected everybody. Lee himself went home and lived out his last few years in honourable retirement; the other Confederate leaders were also allowed to go in peace. In short, the South having clearly given up secession as a bad job, fair treatment of the Negro was to be both the sufficient symbol of Northern victory, the generally accepted proof that the right side had actually won, and the single real concession exacted from the losers. And there was room for adjustment even on this point. No one, in the spring of 1865, was quite clear how far to go in conceding equal rights to blacks. The North had a long tradition of racial prejudice, particularly in the matter of employment, which the events of the war had done much to weaken but had certainly not destroyed. In several Northern states, for example, Negroes were still forbidden to vote. The situation was delicate, dangerous and volatile; but it also contained a great opportunity. A statesman of Lincoln's dexterity might possibly have snatched from it a settlement of the great difficulty which would have been tolerable to North and South, blacks and whites, alike; in which case the whole later history of America would have been wonderfully different. But Andrew Johnson was not a dextrous man.

His personal position was difficult. He had been a Jacksonian Democrat all his life, though his pride in his own unaided rise from illiterate poverty to eminence, and in the beliefs and character which had made it possible, always meant more to him than party principles or identifications. His true party was that of Andrew Johnson, and he had always defended it vigorously (often by attack) against the great planters of Tennessee, both as a champion of the poor whites from whom he came and as a staunch Unionist. Lincoln had chosen him as his Vice-Presidential candidate partly because, as a Democrat from a border state, he might enhance the Union ticket's appeal in the hard-fought election of 1864. With such a record Johnson, unsurprisingly, did not feel at home with the great men and professionals of the Republican party. Even if he had, he would not have taken their advice. He was an incorrigible loner, slightly less flexible than granite. He took decisions in a hurry and refused to alter them.

In some ways he was like the next American President to face impeachment. Andrew Johnson and Richard Nixon were both outsiders in Washington and in party politics; both were egotistical, given to self-pity and to maudlin insistence on their humble origins: Johnson was capable of breaking off an important speech to recall fondly that when he was a tailor the coats he made were always good fits, while Nixon tended to drivel about his poor and saintly mother. There were differences, of course – for one thing, Johnson had a much higher standard of personal political conduct than Nixon – but the essential similarity was that neither understood the principles, loyalties and psychologies of normal American politicians. It was on this ground that Lincoln had been supreme; a party politician to his fingertips, he had always known when to stand firm and when to yield, and how, throughout, to win, retain and increase the trust and affection of the men he dealt with. Johnson and Nixon could only see men who disagreed with them as personal enemies, and attributed the worst motives to them. Johnson was even capable of hinting in a public speech that Republican leaders such as Thaddeus Stevens and Charles Sumner were plotting to assassinate him.[2] Perhaps the moral is that the American political and constitutional system can stand a lot, but it cannot work if the President is neurotically intransigent, for its operating principle is give and take; compromise and moderation.

Blind to these considerations, President Johnson lost no time in laying down the principles on which he meant to proceed, and he stuck to them unyieldingly thereafter. The disastrous results of his policy never made him doubt its correctness; others were always to blame; and the last words he ever spoke in a public speech were 'God save the Constitution' – as if he in his time had not been one of the worst dangers that the Constitution faced. The sacred text, as he understood it, was his lodestar. His exposition of the points at issue in 1865 demonstrated his regional origin, and also how little he understood the significance of the great struggle that had just occurred. Within very broad limits, he said, the Constitution respected states' rights. Once a rebel state accepted those limits, it had put itself in harmony with the law and the nation again and could not be denied re-admission to Congress. Defeat in war proved that the South was wrong in attempting secession; the Confederate debt was therefore illegal and had to be repudiated; the Thirteenth Amendment outlawing slavery was now a part of the Constitution, which the Southern states must explicitly acknowledge. That done, no more could rightfully be demanded of them; nor might Congress legislate on matters affecting their interests while their Representatives and Senators were absent. In practice this meant that the future of the Southern blacks could not be settled until after the white South had regained most of its old political rights and privileges. Johnson never admitted this in so many words; but his actions all tended in that direction. The fact was that as a poor white Southerner himself his feelings towards blacks were, at best, mixed.

He meant to exclude Congress from any part in the process of reconstruction. In this he was following precedent: Lincoln had always done his utmost to keep control of really important political measures, as when he vetoed the Wade–Davis bill. The Emancipation Proclamation itself had been in part a successful bid to pre-empt Congressional action. To begin with, Johnson had a free hand: the thirty-ninth Congress would not assemble before December 1865 unless the President called it into special session, which he had no intention of doing. Much might be achieved in the interval; the more so as the Republicans still expected that they would be able to work with the President. 'While we can hardly approve of all the acts of

---

2 To be fair, it must be mentioned that the wilder Republicans tried to prove that Johnson had been a party to Lincoln's murder. Both sides were base and foolish; but that hardly excuses Johnson. Folly in the President of the United States is rightly regarded as a more serious, less normal matter than folly in Congressmen.

government we must try to keep out of the ranks of the opposition,' Thaddeus Stevens, a veteran Republican troublemaker, told Charles Sumner in the summer. Johnson saw a chance to settle the whole question of reconstruction (or 'restoration', as he preferred to call it). Accordingly, the ex-rebel states were instructed to elect conventions to draw up new state constitutions, which would next be ratified by the voters and under which elections to Congress could be held in the autumn. Johnson had been disappointed to find that he could not hang Jeff Davis; he had been slow to issue pardons to leading rebels; then suddenly he started issuing pardons by the hundred, more to escape embarrassment, it seemed, than for any other reason. Soon it was plain that, armed with their pardons, former Confederate leaders were re-entering politics in force, and after the autumn elections would completely dominate the new Johnson-inspired Southern state governments.

Even that might not have mattered (though it alarmed many Northerners) had the restored South shown greater discretion. In the event she showed as little understanding of the dam-Yankees as ever. Johnson had let it be understood that he spoke for the North as authoritatively as had his predecessor; and the South was all too willing to believe him. The conventions did as he suggested (he would have regarded it as unconstitutional to give orders to states, even to recently rebellious ones), though very ungraciously: they rescinded the secession ordinances, repudiated the Confederate debts and ratified the Thirteenth Amendment. Johnson's silence on all other questions was a hint not lost on them. They began to settle the Negro question in their own fashion. The moment when they might have acquiesced in Northern plans vanished.

It was scarcely surprising. Southern bitterness ran deep. Defeat was educative to the extent that it induced Southerners to become Americans again (by the twentieth century they would be among the most noisily patriotic of all groups) and persuaded many of them that the section would have to make a serious effort to industrialize: in this way a 'New South' might arise. It would be long before anyone would accept that the whole secessionist adventure might have been morally wrong, socially unwise, politically misconceived. Southern women, particularly, remained ferociously loyal to 'the Cause'. Mourning and commemoration were to be major preoccupations for several generations to come: soon war-memorials appeared in every important Southern town, usually in the form of a statue of a boy in grey, his heroic young face staring resolutely northwards. The Yankees were not forgiven; their protégés, the freedmen, were not accepted. Slavery was dead, but slavery was what the Africans were meant for, and something as near as possible to slavery was what they were going to get. The South might have been defeated in war, but her resources for racial oppression were by no means exhausted.

This response, which gradually crystallized during the late summer and autumn of 1865, had two principal expressions.

One was violent. Very soon the freedmen and their friends found themselves attacked and threatened; but the climax did not come for a year or two, although the Ku Klux Klan was actually founded at Pulaski, Tennessee, on Christmas Eve, 1865. Even so, the struggle between Congress and President over the future of the South from the start took place against a background of brutal conflict. The low points, no doubt, were the race riots in Memphis at the end of April 1866, when forty-six blacks were killed, and the massacre of 30 July in the same year at New Orleans, when approximately forty people were killed and 160 wounded (mostly blacks) by the police force, acting under the orders of the city's mayor. (Ten policemen were 'wounded slightly'.) But every day there were lesser incidents: a man shot, or a woman strung up by her thumbs.

The South's second weapon was not lawlessness, but the law. No sooner were the Johnsonian legislatures elected than they began to pass the so-called 'Black Codes': statutes which, far from conferring on the freedmen the right to vote, denied them all but the most rudimentary civil rights and liberties. Provisions varied somewhat from state to state, but on the whole it is true to say that the codes, while at last recognizing the legality of black marriages (though not to white persons), while conferring on blacks the right to sue and be sued in the courts, even to testify against whites, and the right to hold property, and while recognizing their right to be paid wages, in every other respect tried to maintain the slavery laws. For instance, freedmen were required to hire themselves out by the year, and were denied the right either to strike or to leave their employment. Slavery was thus to become an annually renewed institution. Any black found unemployed or travelling without an employer's sanction would be arrested, fined for vagrancy and turned over to whatever white employer desired his services. (Immediately after the end of the war the former slaves had exercised one of the unfamiliar privileges of freedom by leaving the plantations in droves, chiefly, no doubt, to seek out relations and friends from whom they had been separated by the internal slave-trade, but also from sheer joy at being able to travel and from curiosity to see the world.) Schooling was one of the most passionately cherished ambitions of the ex-slaves, yet no provisions were made for black education. The Louisiana code went into considerable detail about the free labourer's life, quite in the style of slavery times:

Bad work shall not be allowed. Failing to obey reasonable orders, neglect of duty, and leaving home without permission will be deemed disobedience; impudence, swearing, or indecent language to or in the presence of the employer, his family, or agent, or quarrelling and fighting with one another, shall be deemed disobedience. For any disobedience a fine of one dollar shall be imposed.

The Mississippi code imposed swingeing fines on anyone wicked enough to entice a labourer away from his contracted employer with promises of better pay or conditions. All codes forbade freedmen the use of weapons of any kind. So much for the Northern crusade for human equality. As a leading Northern liberal, Carl Schurz, remarked, the codes embodied the idea that although individual whites could no longer have property in individual blacks, 'the blacks at large belong to the whites at large'.

It is doubtful if the Southerners fully realized what an affront these codes would seem: they were more impressed by the differences from slavery than the freedmen and Northerners could be. Even Andrew Johnson realized that they had gone too far: at any rate he did not object when the military commanders in the South nullified the codes. He would have been wiser to take the lead in opposition, but presumably he felt that the states, however unwise, were acting within their constitutional rights. So he said nothing: it was not for him to interfere. It was left to Congress to express the boiling indignation of the North, which that institution, as soon as it assembled, proceeded to do. It denounced the South and set up a joint committee of the two houses to propose a programme of congressional reconstruction. Crucially, it also provided that until such a programme had been worked out, none of the Southern Representatives and Senators chosen under the Johnson-sanctioned constitutions would be allowed to take their seats; for the legality and desirability of those very constitutions was one of the key matters at issue, and the entry of former rebels into Congress would grievously impede, if not entirely frustrate, the Republican programme. This action was, as a matter of fact, perfectly legal under the Constitution,[3] and was the North's last weapon (Andrew Johnson had thrown away all the others); but the President denounced it as unconstitutional, and continued to do so to the bitter last.

The intrigues of the winter and spring of 1865–6 need not be described. It is enough to record that the huge Republican majority in Congress settled upon three measures. First, a Fourteenth Amendment to the Constitution, which, among a tangle of provisions for excluding ex-Confederate leaders from politics and repudiating the Confederate debt, did establish, in law at least, the right of all citizens of the United States to equal protection of the laws, and defined a US citizen (it had never been done before) in such a way as to include all African-Americans. Henceforth anyone was a citizen who was 'born or naturalized in the United States, and subject to the jurisdiction thereof'. The *Dred Scott* decision was thus at last repealed. Second, an extension of the life and powers of the Freedmen's Bureau, the institution which, under the shelter of the army, was doing what it could to ease the transition from slavery to freedom for the Southern blacks. Third, a civil rights law which explicitly stated what was implicit in the Fourteenth Amendment: that citizen rights were to be enjoyed by all persons born in the United States, not subject to any foreign power, 'of every race and colour, without reference to any previous condition of slavery or involuntary

3 'Each House shall be the Judge of the Elections, Returns, and Qualifications of its own Members . . .' (Art. I, sec. 4).

servitude'. Johnson vetoed both the Acts, which were later re-passed by the necessary two-thirds majority in each house. He could not veto the Amendment, though he could and did denounce it at the same time as he transmitted it, in obedience to the law, to the state legislatures (which quickly ratified it). There was by now a total breach between him and the party which had put him into office. Congressional elections were at hand. Both sides prepared for a decisive struggle: perhaps the bitterest of the kind yet known.

It was for long customary for historians and others to talk as if the issue had lain between the President and the Republican radicals alone. The facts were more complicated, as everyone knew at the time. Johnson's intransigence had united the Republican party, driving it in mere self-defence to support radical courses in a manner which was inconceivable in Lincoln's day. The political leaders, the party organizers, the party press, even many of the army commanders – all who had supported the Union cause, in fact, except for Seward and his small surviving following, and the curmudgeon Gideon Welles – had been forced to abandon the President. To do otherwise would have been to give up the commitments of a lifetime, and even the spoilsmen felt the thrilling, unfamiliar call of principle. When they denounced the President's policy, they were dismissed, and gloried in the fact. 'I aimed to do my duty,' said one postmaster, 'but all the Post Offices in Illinois could not buy me to the support of A. Johnson.' Nor was Johnson without allies, though they did him little good. The Northern Democrats saw a chance to recover from their wartime errors, such as the Copperhead platform of 1864 which had contributed to their destruction on election day. The quicker the South was restored to Congress, they thought, the sooner the old ascendancy of the Democrats in national politics would be revived. So they brought their Copperhead notions up to date and eagerly offered their support to Andrew Johnson, proposing to settle the reconstruction question by giving the ex-Confederates a free hand in the South. And waiting in the wings were those same ex-Confederates, though one planter declared that they did not really support the President: 'They prefer him, doubtless, to the so called Radicals, but in their hearts they hate him. They cling with an undying hope to the wretched rebel cause and desire to manifest their hatred for everything which does not immortalize that.'[4]

Johnson tried in vain to find a middle way between these opposites. He staked everything on rallying the people at large to support their President – vainly, because the prestige of Lincoln's office had now shifted to Lincoln's party. The President made matters even worse for himself by his so-called 'swing around the circle'. This was an immense speaking-tour he undertook

4 B. F. Moore to Lewis Thompson, 3 September 1866. Quoted in Roark, *Masters Without Slaves*, p. 185. The writer later became a Republican, so perhaps his views should not be accepted quite unquestioningly.

in September 1866 through the Northern and Western states. He carried a
cortège of generals and Cabinet officers with him, who had to listen in
frozen embarrassment as their leader repeated the same speech over and
over again, railing at his enemies with undignified ferocity. He began to be
heckled savagely in a way that frequently made it impossible for him to be
heard. Johnson had been a very successful stump-speaker in Tennessee,
where that art had been prized ever since the days of Andrew Jackson; but
now he had lost his touch, or it was not what 1866 and the North required.
His experience at Indianapolis was typical:

Fellow citizens – (*cries for Grant*). It is not my intention – (*cries of 'Stop', 'Go on'*)
to make a long speech. If you give me your attention for five minutes – (*'Go on,'*
'Stop,' 'No, no, we want nothing to do with traitors,' 'Grant, Grant,' 'Johnson,' groans).
I would like to say to this crowd here tonight – (*'Shut up! We don't want to hear*
from you, Johnson! Grant! Johnson! Grant! Grant!')

The President gave up and retired from the balcony. At St Louis he
compared himself to Jesus Christ and shouted 'hang Thad Stevens!' as if
he meant it. At Cleveland he rounded on a heckler, throwing grammar and
coherence to the winds:

. . . those men – such a one as insulted me to-night – you may say, has ceased to
be a man, and in ceasing to be a man shrunk into the denomination of a reptile,
and having so shrunken, as an honest man, I tread on him. I came here to-night
not to criminate or recriminate, but when provoked my nature is not to advance
but to defend, and when encroached upon, I care not from what quarter it comes,
it will find resistance, and resistance at the threshold.

It was a despondent and defeated party which eventually returned to
Washington, leaving the field to the demagogues on the other side, who
were proving themselves expert at 'waving the bloody shirt', as it was called
– that is, at asserting that the opposition was in collusion with criminals and
rebels and insulting the sufferings of the glorious dead.[5]

The election was decisive: the Republicans overwhelmed Johnsonians
and Democrats alike and were now free to push through whatever legislation they liked. Johnson would veto everything, of course, and did; but
there was little difficulty in overriding his vetoes. To be sure, the President
retained an ample power to annoy, and it was this that eventually led to his
impeachment. He insisted on dismissing Edwin Stanton; Congress was
equally intent on keeping this last ally in the executive; eventually, after a
chain of discreditable events, which included an episode when Stanton

5 The phrase arose from an incident during the impeachment of Andrew Johnson, when Ben
Butler, leading for the prosecution, produced a nightshirt stained with what was said to be the
blood of a carpetbagger from Ohio who had been flogged by whites in Mississippi.

barricaded himself in the War Department and sustained a siege, the Republicans finally lost their temper and instituted impeachment proceedings, which if successful would have cast the President out of office. The business lasted from March to May 1868 and was abandoned after the prosecution failed, four times, to get the necessary two-thirds majority in the Senate. It was soon realized that the failure of the impeachment was the best thing that could have happened, for there was not a shred of evidence that Johnson had engaged in the 'Treason, Bribery, or other high Crimes and Misdemeanours' which the Constitution lays down as grounds for impeachment.[6] Had Johnson been ejected, it would have been for nakedly political reasons, and the whole basis of the Constitutional system would have been overthrown: the principle of co-existent, mutually independent powers; of checks and balances; of laws, not men. Instead, America would at least temporarily have got a Parliamentary government without really wanting or planning to; and Congress could not have been made fit to exercise supreme power under such arrangements without radical Constitutional amendments which could probably not have been agreed. In short, a successful impeachment would have badly weakened the federal government for years, if not for decades; the unsuccessful one did damage enough. At least it had the one good result that for the next hundred years all Presidents took warning from Andrew Johnson's example and did not try Congress too far. For the rest of the nineteenth century the Presidents were indeed almost weakly deferential in their dealings with the legislature: though this was by no means so clearly a good thing.

The problems posed by having such a man as Johnson in the White House were better solved by going round him, as Congress did by overriding his vetoes, or as Seward did when he negotiated the purchase of the Russian colony of Alaska by the United States in 1867, and cajoled the Senate into approving the treaty; best of all, by replacing him through the normal processes, which happened when Ulysses S. Grant was elected to the Presidency on the Republican ticket in 1868. Grant, who had been so great a general, was to prove as poor a President in his way as Johnson had been in his; but at least the Congressional majority no longer had to worry about executive sabotage; it could concentrate undisturbed on the problem of the South and the blacks.

So the Republicans concentrated; and in the end they were defeated, as was inevitable. It is important to understand why, since the difficulties they struggled with were to perplex many generations of Americans after them, almost to the present day.

The blame can scarcely be laid at their door. They did the best they could in the circumstances, and if they occasionally made mistakes, lacked understanding or gave up from pure weariness, these are universal human traits, which characterize successful as well as failed undertakings. Perhaps

6 Art. II, sec. 4.

their programme was too backward-looking to be altogether realistic. They hoped to make over the South in the image of the ante-bellum North, with a few little improvements such as black suffrage. The South was to be industrialized, her plantation agriculture was to be transformed into a system of family farms, her towns were to grow, above all she was to develop a two-party system in which a chastened Democratic party would compete with a revived Whig party strengthened by its association with the victorious party of the North, and embodying, as the Republicans had in Lincoln's pre-war Illinois, the aspirations of small farmers, craftsmen and businessmen. In this way the political and social legacy of the slave-holding aristocracy would be destroyed, and the federal government would be controlled, indefinitely, by the Republican party, for to its ascendancy in the North and the West would be added its strength in the South.

This vision did not take account of the speed and extent to which the North herself was changing; worse, it did not take account of the fashion and degree in which the South had changed. Perhaps it was just as well. Too much insight might have led to premature hopelessness. And Radical Reconstruction was pre-eminently one of those things which it is better to have begun and failed in than not to have attempted at all.

The central difficulty was that the South was faced with a fundamental economic problem. The disappearance of slavery had left a void in all Southern institutions, it necessitated the remodelling of society in all its aspects, but just as the peculiar institution had in origin been primarily an economic system, so, on its death, the prime task was to replace its role as the determinant of investment, of the distribution of capital and income, of consumption and of labour organization. In the long run there was very little that Northerners, either collectively or individually, could do to affect the outcome of this process: necessarily, it would be settled by the interplay of impersonal economic forces and the wishes of the Southerners, black and white.

At first the initiative lay with the blacks. The fall of the Confederacy accelerated all those tendencies which had been emerging previously: suddenly the freedmen seized control of their own destiny. They exhibited their new-found strength in ways that astonished and deeply offended their former masters. On one plantation they refused to allow the mistress into the house, instead dancing round her singing 'I's free as a frog, Hallelujah!' More significant, in the long run, was their consensus on the future. They were prepared, after the initial period of dislocation, to come home and work in the cotton-fields again; but the terms were changed. They hoped to get ownership of the land, or enough of it at least to support them in independence (the slogan of the time was 'forty acres and a mule', which were supposedly to be provided by the federal government); they were intensely eager to educate themselves; and they were determined to reject any form of labour organization which seemed to resurrect slavery. In particular, they wanted cash wages, freedom to come and go, an end to the field-gang system and a limited working day. Like most socio-political programmes, this was only achieved in part; but modern economic historians have laid great emphasis on the importance of what was achieved.[7] Suddenly the labour force of the South was working only nine or ten hours a day (the usual stint of labourers elsewhere in the United States) instead of from dawn to dusk, as under slavery. The labour supply, in other words, dropped by nearly a third. So, in consequence, did the production of the crops on which the prosperity of the ante-bellum South had depended – above all, cotton. Furthermore, the world price of cotton, which had touched dizzy heights during the war, rapidly returned to its previous level, and then fell below it, as other regions – India, Egypt – began to compete with the South. Even before the Civil War cotton prices had had a long-term tendency to fall: the planters had been able to maintain and increase their incomes only by growing and marketing more and more cotton, a feat which in turn had only been possible because slavery and the internal slave-trade ensured a large, docile and (above all) cheap work-force that could be rapidly deployed as new cotton lands were opened up. It was this aspect of the plantation system to which emancipation dealt the final, irreversible blow. It meant that planters faced a permanent slump in their income, in addition to the vagaries of the weather and the burden of federal taxation. Never again would cotton pay for the old magnificent way of life. Besides, the plantation system was now not only unprofitable, but in other respects pointless. The freedmen flatly refused to work in line under the threat of the driver's whip. The air was thick with denunciation of black laziness, but the freedmen were unmoved. They were not going to work, for others, longer or harder than they saw fit. They had had enough of that in the past.

All plantation societies exhibited this phenomenon after emancipation: they all tended to lapse into subsistence economies, to produce, that is, not for the market but for the immediate needs of the workers. It happened in the British West Indies. It need not have happened in the South had the blacks been given the land and training they desired: they were capable of working extremely hard for themselves, as they had proved on the plant-ations in South Carolina and Mississippi that had been handed over to them during the war. Now they hoped for further distribution. Had this occurred, not only would Southern blacks have been in a position to preserve and exercise the political, social and legal rights which the North was so anxious to grant them, they might also have largely restored Southern agricultural productivity. Thaddeus Stevens was anxious to give them land. But his proposal went too far for the era. The connection between economic independence and political strength was not clearly seen (though it had been one of Thomas Jefferson's axioms); the radicals did not want to alienate

7 Above all, Roger L. Ransom and Richard Sutch, *One Kind of Freedom: The Economic Consequences of Emancipation* (Cambridge, 1977).

their conservative allies, whether in the North or the South; and besides there were grave practical difficulties. Under the Southern Homestead Act of 1866, for instance, land was actually made available for distribution among the freedmen, but it was of poor quality and the offer was not taken up. To get decent land for them would have infuriated the envious poor whites as well as the rich. Besides, the legal position was far from clear. The Confiscation Acts had been wartime measures: how could legal proceedings under them be justified now that peace had been restored, when no other proceedings – no treason trials, for example – were being taken against the former rebels, when indeed the President was issuing all those pardons? Johnson had directed the return to their first owners of the Mississippi and South Carolina plantations which the freedmen had been working.[8] It would have been infinitely difficult and disagreeable to take them back again, or to make seizures anywhere else; and the South was already seething over the activities of the agents of the US Treasury, who were going here and there confiscating the planters' last marketable asset, their cotton bales, in settlement of unpaid taxes. It is not surprising that Stevens's proposals were never taken up; but it was disastrous for the future of the blacks, all the same, and for the South as a whole. The prospects for Southern farming would have been at best precarious, whatever the system of landholding or the distribution of land between the races; but at least a more democratic arrangement, something nearer to what the Republicans envisaged, would have spread the deficits and surpluses more evenly, and by increasing the number of people with money to spend might even have stimulated some measure of that economic growth for which, as it turned out, the South had to wait until the twentieth century.

The radical programme, then, was crippled from its start; yet the Republicans seemed to hold every trump. First and foremost was the power of Congress to legislate. This power was most usefully employed when yet another amendment, the Fifteenth, was added to the Constitution: it ordained that 'the right of citizens of the United States to vote shall not be denied or abridged by the United States or by any State on account of race, colour, or previous condition of servitude', a measure not altogether acceptable even to all Northern opinion, but the state legislatures ratified it and it became part of the Constitution in March 1870. Congress also used its power to sweep away the Johnsonian governments in the South. The Military Reconstruction Act of 2 March 1867 divided the South[9] into five military districts, each to be governed by a general of the US army. These

---

8 Though as it happened the Mississippi plantation that had formerly belonged to Jefferson Davis and his brother (a highly enlightened slave-holder) were to be worked by freedmen-proprietors for nearly twenty years more.

9 Except for Tennessee, which, thanks to the exertions of its Republican-appointed Governor, was deemed fit to re-enter the Union as early as 1866. The paradoxical result was that white supremacists recaptured power in Tennessee sooner than in any other state of the Confederacy.

generals had the duty of enrolling all qualified voters (in effect, all adult males, except those classes of ex-Confederates excluded by the terms of the Fourteenth Amendment), of calling together constitutional conventions which would set up new, acceptable state governments and of presiding over the first elections under these arrangements. Then, when the new governments had ratified the Fourteenth Amendment and Congress had approved the new constitutions, the reconstructed states would be at last re-admitted to the federal legislature and the military regimes could fade away. This measure went pretty far, and was effective. Opposition to it was ferocious, and discovered certain loopholes and weaknesses; but they were promptly made good by supplementary legislation. By 1870 the process was complete to the Republicans' satisfaction, and every Southern state was once more represented in Congress.

The second great asset of the reconstructionists was the blacks. This showed itself in various ways. It quickly became clear, for example, that the new governments, which were chiefly manned by whites who had been Unionists during the war, would not be able to sustain themselves at elections without the help of black voters. So a vigorous programme of political education was undertaken, the object of which was to teach the former slaves how to vote and, especially, how to vote Republican. It would be a mistake to see this as a one-way process, a matter of 'calling on Africa'. The eagerness of the ex-slaves to make good their freedom was immense, and they did everything they could to support the new regimes, supplying a high proportion of the political personnel. The fact that they could do so quite capably was in itself enough to refute the assertions of the white supremacists, although these, who had no intention of being refuted, preferred to emphasize the inevitable failures rather than the successes. The successes are better worth remembering today. A surprising diversity of African-American leaders emerged. One of them was an Old Etonian; another was a former slave who had learned to read by spying through the window of a white school next to his place of work. Now they provided members of the state conventions and legislatures; US Representatives; and even two US Senators – Hiram Revels and the ex-slave Blanche K. Bruce, both from Mississippi.[10] No black was elected to the Governorship of a state, but Jonathan J. Wright, originally a Pennsylvania lawyer, sat on the Supreme Court of South Carolina, and there were several Lieutenant-Governors. Through these men the African-Americans served notice on an unresponsive white America that they would no longer be passive members of the community.

However, the Republican leadership in the South during Reconstruction was never predominantly black, and would have failed immediately if

10 Revels, who sat in 1870–71, and Bruce, who sat for a full term (1875–81), were the only African-Americans to sit in the Senate before the election of Edward Brooke of Massachusetts in 1966.

it had been. The radicals were also able to call on the energies and abilities of the two groups known respectively as scalawags – that is, Southerners who were ready to break ranks and co-operate with Reconstruction – and carpetbaggers – outsiders from the North who came to Dixie after the war. No two groups have been more maligned in American history, precisely because Reconstruction could not have gone so far as it did without them. Some among them were undoubtedly opportunist rogues of the kind who fanned out over the whole of America after the war, looking for profit and not being too scrupulous as to how they got it. Even the rogues, it might be argued, served a purpose, bringing a breath of fresh air – their brains and energy – into an area that was much in need of such refreshment; and most of the Reconstructionists were decent and valuable citizens. Some were native white Southerners who had learned the lessons of the war and were anxious to apply them: to give the South not only the industrial and financial structure she had lacked, and to make good the fearful material destruction, but also to set up a political, educational and social system like that to which, quite as much as to her wealth, the North owed her victory – to which, indeed, she largely owed her wealth. Many of the carpetbaggers were Union soldiers who had discovered the South during the war and liked the country (much as their descendants discovered California during the Second World War and went back there as soon as they could). Now they came to settle, drawn by an ancient American lure; for, partly as a result of the war, but more because of slavery, much of the South, compared to neighbouring states, was still a wilderness: in other words, a fresh frontier for pioneers to conquer. Behind these aspirant farmers, as on the westward march, came the great capitalists and industrialists, looking for ways of realizing the mineral wealth of the South – the coal of the mountains, the oil of Louisiana, the iron of Alabama.

Finally, there were the institutional auxiliaries of the federal and state governments: the churches (operating through the American Missionary Association); the army; the state militias, which were raised after the army had shrunk to its normal size and returned to its normal job of hunting Indians; the Union League, the nearest thing there was to a full-time Republican party organization; and, above all, the Freedmen's Bureau (officially known as the Bureau of Refugees, Freedmen, and Abandoned Lands). The Bureau was set up by Congress just before the end of the war; during the immediate post-war period it did heroic work in feeding the freedmen, in organizing hospitals and schools for them, and in supervising the terms under which they were hired as free labourers.

Overall, this was a formidable array of weapons, and it was not wholly ineffective. The new state constitutions did effectively overhaul Southern government, sweeping away the indirect elections of South Carolina, for example, by which in the ante-bellum period the choice of all the highest state officials had been kept in the hands of the planter oligarchs. Property qualifications for voting and office-holding were abolished for ever; the first systems of public education were set up, for whites as well as for blacks, that the South had ever known;[11] imprisonment for debt was abolished; state orphanages and lunatic asylums were set up; and a framework of law was provided, modelled on those of the Northern states, within which capitalist corporations could function safely – a major departure for the land of Jefferson and Andrew Jackson. All these important and valuable innovations survived the years of controversy without difficulty, and did something towards the modernization of the South. Even the stimulus to black education, largely the work of the church groups, was not wholly lost in the years ahead; such distinguished universities as Atlanta, Howard (at Washington, DC; named after the head of the Freedmen's Bureau, General Oliver O. Howard) and Fisk date from this period. The great amendments remained part of the Constitution. But there the credit side of the ledger stops.

For the question of reconstruction would not ultimately be settled by reason, common sense, good intentions and Congressional enactment. Even the freedmen were not necessary to a settlement, though they had more at stake than anyone else: they were too few, as the slaves had been too few, for their own good. Like the anti-slavery struggle, like the Civil War itself, this was a fight that would be settled by time, will and physical force; but now the greater strength was on the wrong side.

Time alone would have been enough to defeat the North, had it not had to struggle against the folly and impatience of the white South as well. Most Americans find it hard to keep up a quarrel. They are a friendly, outgoing people; they like to be liked; the slightest show of goodwill and they forget their strongest grievances. To judge by their behaviour, the Northerners were never very vindictive to the Southerners: they could not imagine, for instance, treating fellow-Americans as the Russians treated the Poles after the unsuccessful rising of 1863. They were disconcerted by the relentless hostility that the defeated South displayed: by the insults offered to their soldiers by Southern ladies, the steely refusal of Southern politicians to compromise. 'At a distance I felt a great sympathy for the people here: now that I am here and know how the pulse of the people beat, I have lost a great portion of my sympathy,' one young Northerner wrote to his friend, a future President, in 1865.[12] Bewilderment changed to rage as the Black Codes were passed, as violence mounted, as Mississippi refused to ratify the Thirteenth Amendment because, forsooth, it gave Congress power to enforce the abolition of slavery, and as Louisiana repudiated the Constitution

11 The North had begun to provide free public schooling in the thirties and forties. In this respect, as in so many others, the ante-bellum South had undoubtedly been backward; but it will set things in proper proportion if we note that the system of state education was only just beginning in England at this very time. The Forster Education Act became law in 1870. However, it should also be recorded that the state of Mississippi did not introduce public education for any race until 1919.

12 James Atkins to James Garfield, 7 December 1865. McKitrick, *Andrew Johnson*, p. 37.

which Lincoln had defended so earnestly against radical critics, on the grounds that it was 'the creature of fraud, violence and corruption'.[13] 'We tell the white men of Mississippi that the men of the North will convert the State of Mississippi into a frog pond before they will allow such laws to disgrace one foot of soil in which the bones of our soldiers sleep and over which the flag of freedom waves,' said the *Chicago Tribune* in December 1865. Fine words: but the North could not keep it up. Not all the bad behaviour of the South could ultimately overcome the wish to bury the old dispute, to be magnanimous to a fallen foe, to forget an intractable problem and turn to the rich challenges of the new era of industrialism that was opening. The bloody shirt could not forever distract attention from the excitements of life in the new cities, in the new West, the new factories, the new farms, the new professions, the new pleasures (baseball had suddenly become a national obsession). The attention of the North to affairs below the Mason–Dixon line slackened, and so it became easy to believe the propaganda which said that the reconstructed governments were all insufferably corrupt and incompetent, that the white supremacists knew what was best for blacks, that the radical Republicans were mere twisted fanatics. Besides, time killed off the radical leaders, and they had no successors. The Republican party did not repudiate its old programme (it was far too useful at election times) and indeed continued for another twenty years, though ineffectively, to try to protect the hard-won black right to vote; the Civil War veterans who rapidly came to dominate the party did not forget the cause for which they had fought; but the passion died, or shifted to other issues. Politics was no longer a crusade, but much more a matter of day-to-day business: it was convenient for Presidents, Senators and Congressmen, few of whom would have made convincing crusaders, to seek the co-operation of the Southern leaders rather than their destruction. Besides, the Democratic party in the North soon abandoned the racism which it had embraced so fervently during and immediately after the war, and was prepared to compete for black votes; in return it seemed only fair that the Republicans should compete for white supremacist votes, or at least not stimulate the Southern racists into vigorous action against them. This sort of attitude was made easier by the persistence of race prejudice in the North. As an effective political force it was broken by the war and reconstruction; Northerners were now much more concerned to hate the Irish and the other European immigrants flooding in upon them, rather than the blacks, of whom they saw few; but still, there was no love of the black to make it impossible to forget his injuries. In fact one of the reasons why the North saw so few blacks was that they were not allowed to compete for good Northern jobs. They were excluded from the rising labour unions, and so from the factories, except as strike-breakers recruited by the factory-owners, which did not increase their popularity. By the mid-seventies, in

13 W. E. B. Du Bois, *Black Reconstruction in America* (London, 1966), pp. 454–5.

short, the African-American was seen, at best, as a bore and a nuisance. There was no political risk for anyone in abandoning him.

Southern attitudes were not ductile like Northern ones. The reason was simple enough: too much was at stake. For the North, the Civil War had been primarily a defensive enterprise, which had ended by greatly strengthening the American Union – indeed, by superseding the term: ever since, Americans have tended to talk of 'the nation', an even more cohesive idea. For the South, the war had meant the Emancipation Revolution, which had shattered society and all its structures. For the North, 'reconstruction', that curiously dry term, meant primarily the political task of reintroducing the defeated states to full participation in politics on tolerable terms. For the South, it meant rebuilding society from the foundations. The task was too important to be either postponed or left to other hands. Decisions taken after Appomattox would settle the fate of the South for the foreseeable future; no wonder there was a bitter competition to have the preponderant influence in their making, and bitter argument as to what they should be.

Two fundamental facts conditioned everything that happened. The first was that the South was not united. Apart from the division between the races and between ex-Confederates and Republicans (whether scalawags or carpetbaggers), there was the continuing division between the classes. It is hardly possible to overstate the bitterness felt, in those parts of the South where the yeomen farmers or poor whites predominated, against the planter class, immediately after the war. A traveller in northern Alabama reported:

They are ignorant and vindictive, live in poor huts, drink much, and all use tobacco and snuff; they want to organize and receive recognition by the United States government in order to get revenge – really want to be bushwhackers supported by the Federal government; they 'wish to have the power to hang, shoot, and destroy in retaliation for the wrongs they have endured'; they hate the 'big nigger holders', whom they accuse of bringing on the war and who, they are afraid, would get into power again; they are the 'refugee', poor white element of low character, shiftless, with no ambition.

That was in 1865. Three years later the Republicans of Georgia thought these class attitudes still strong enough to be worth appealing to at election time:

Be a man! Let the slave-holding aristocracy no longer rule you. Vote for a constitution which educates your children free of charge; relieves the poor debtor from his rich creditor; allows a liberal homestead for your families; and more and more than all, places you on a level with those who used to boast that for every slave they were entitled to three-fifths of a vote in congressional representation. Ponder this well before you vote.

The Republicans were perfectly right in thinking that these divisions were of permanent importance; but they boded no good for the future of Southern society.

The second decisive fact about the South was the fashion in which the economic question was settled. We have seen how quickly the freedmen's hopes were blighted. The planter class, though disgraced, bankrupt, disfranchised and unpopular, kept the land. Some individuals, of course, went down to economic defeat. Others rose, the class survived. The strategy was not at first clear. Strenuous efforts were made, of which the Black Codes were part, to restore the old plantation system, but after some years it was clear that without slavery this was impossible: the ex-slaves simply would not co-operate. So the great estates were divided up into family farms and let out to tenants, black and white. Thus a version of the Republican hope for the South was realized: a caricature of Northern homesteading.

The new pattern of Southern agriculture was dominated by debt. Many of the planters had mortgaged their lands to raise desperately needed capital, or just to get their hands on some cash again, after they had seen all the profits of slavery vanish into the Confederate war-effort. Since their new tenants had even less in the way of cash or capital they were obliged to borrow from the landlords in order to get started, and in consequence had to pay debt-charges as well as rent. The system that emerged was that known as sharecropping: a somewhat primitive economic form, since it turned essentially on transactions in kind, not money. Tenants agreed to farm the land; in return they were given a share of the crops they raised. Some brought tools or a mule to their new life and were therefore allowed to keep a relatively high proportion of the crop; but most depended entirely on their landlords for seed, tools, ploughs, mules (to draw the ploughs) and, eventually, food, since it paid the landlord to compel his tenants to get their supplies at his own country store rather than to allow them to raise corn and pigs themselves. Food production in the South after the Civil War was about 50 per cent less than it had been before: the region ceased to be self-supporting in that item. The corollary was that the production of cotton was greatly increased.

On a long view of the South's best interests, this was worse than absurd, as many people pointed out at the time. Monoculture puts a country, or a region, too much at the mercy of the market, the weather and tradition (since to grow the same thing everywhere all the time discourages useful innovation: for example, cotton-picking was not mechanized until after the Second World War). Cotton, furthermore, depleted the soil, so that farmers had to add the price of fertilizer to their other costs. But stark structural realities gave the South no choice. The producers were all debtors; their creditors demanded collateral for their loans; the only collateral that all knew and trusted was cotton. Not surprisingly, the only men to do well out of this system were the merchants. These were usually no more than owners of the little country stores that began to speckle the Southern countryside.

They were the only sources for the necessities of life; among those necessities was credit, which they were ready to extend on easy terms; but the return they exacted was absolute control of what the farmers grew, when and how. They lent the money, placed high prices on the goods they sold, took the cotton and with the proceeds bought themselves into the planter class. Before long the South was as hierarchically organized as ever. Once more a dominant class monopolized the economic surplus. The only difference was that, because of the shortage of labour and the depressed price of cotton, the surplus was smaller than it had been under slavery.

Debt-slavery, or peonage, became the rule for most of the poor farmers of the South, white and black, as it was for the peasants of Latin America. It was made worse in bad years, when the price of the crop did not equal the outstanding debt; and good years seldom did much to improve matters, especially since many landlords were expert at cheating their tenants when it came to settling accounts. So the entire labouring class of the South sank into hopelessness, ill-clothed, ill-fed (the deficiency disease, pellagra, became very common), illiterate (the freedmen's zeal for schooling fell off noticeably as it became clear that education would not necessarily lead to a better way of life). It was the worst possible basis for social progress. The despair of the South was expressed sometimes in a turn to rhapsodic religion; sometimes in savage race conflict (lynching, rare in the ante-bellum South, became all too usual); all too rarely, and never effectively, in politics, which was based, as before the war, on the determination of the planting class to maintain its rule.

This was not a matter of naked self-interest. The planters were still honestly convinced of their superior fitness. Blacks they saw as idle, thieving and stupid: the shock of being deserted, on the day of Jubilo, by their most trusted servants had left a residue of enormous bitterness. They had absolutely no intention of sharing political power with them. 'This is a white man's government . . .' – the expression runs through thousands of speeches, articles and letters of the time. Everything which challenged this axiom was to be resisted; particularly the policies of the federal government.

Even this was not so purely selfish a calculation as it may seem. The basic principle of American democracy, the principle, indeed, for which the North had fought, was that the majority must rule; and Republican policies after the war seemed set to deny the application of that principle to the former rebel states. White Southerners were not allowed to choose their representatives freely; enormous numbers of them were not even allowed to vote, after the 1867 Act came into operation. The chief instruments of this tyranny (as it was seen) were the blacks. Therefore their leaders must be defeated and they themselves reduced once more to subservience – to serfdom, if not slavery. This programme had the added advantage that it was one round which all Southern whites could unite, thereby overcoming the unhappy class antagonisms which might otherwise have come to threaten planter control.

Finally, there was physical force. Secure in their renewed sense of right-eousness, it was too much to expect that the hot-tempered and impetuous white Southerners should wait for power to revert to their hands after 1867 by the slow lapse of time and the mechanics of free elections alone. Four years of war and rebellion had weakened inhibitions and scruples which had never been very strong in Dixie anyway. The South had been a violent region before the Civil War and had a long tradition, going back to the colonial era, of what was known as 'regulation':[14] of vigilantism; of taking the law into your own hands. This tradition was now savagely reactivated.

The Ku Klux Klan began as one of those jolly secret societies of which so many Americans at all times have been so fond (even the Union League had its ritual of secret signs and passwords). 'Ku Klux' is a fanciful corruption of the Greek *kuklos*, or drinking-bowl, which indicates both that the founders were men of some education and that their purposes were not very sinister. Perhaps at first it only seemed a good joke to dress up in white hoods and sheets and ride about the country at night frightening the freedmen. But the Klan changed its spots very rapidly. By 1867 its brutal techniques were well known and were coming into wide use in the South; and its objects were clear. It wanted to restore Democratic control of the Southern states by preventing blacks from voting; it wanted to drive them from such landholdings as they had been able to acquire and occupy; it wanted further to intimidate them so that they would never again make any attempt to assert themselves. The Klan was measurably successful in all three respects.

For five years its members rode out in their robes and masks, whipping, burning, murdering or making lurid threats to do so. The Klan, and similar organizations such as the Knights of the White Camelia which sprang up in its wake, was in some respects rather like a guerrilla movement or the Provisional IRA: not only in its hit-and-run tactics, but in the fact that citizens were unwilling or afraid to collaborate with the authorities in suppressing it; but it knew better than to attack the army of occupation, official buildings or the institutions of government. It left the Northern schoolteachers who had come south to instruct the ex-slaves to the cold shoulders of the Confederate women; unless the teacher happened to be male, in which case he might be beaten up or otherwise made to feel unwelcome: 'Dear Bro:' (wrote one of them), 'We are in trouble. Five men disguised in a Satanic garb, on the night of the 26th inst, dragged me from my bed and bore me roughly in double quick time 1½ miles to a thicket, whipped me unmercifully and left me to die. They demanded of me that I should cease "teaching niggers" and leave in ten days, or be treated worse . . . I am not able to sit up yet. I shall never recover from all my injuries . . .' The black and the scalawag might expect no mercy at all. The Klan also particularly resented the Freedmen's Bureau, for its officials, at least until 1868, tried to protect the freedmen by supervising labour contracts and

14 See above, p. 153.

hauling their oppressors into special courts for correction.[15] For the Klan never lost sight of its objective of driving the freedmen down into peonage, down towards the mudsill, down to be a permanently subordinate rural proletariat. 'I noticed that just about the time they [the blacks] got done laying by their crops, the Ku-Klux would be brought in and they would be run off so that they [the owners of the land] could take their crops,' said an observer in Georgia in 1871.

The Klan's atrocities were in some measure counter-productive. They were heaven-sent propaganda material for the radicals, and kept up the zeal of the North when it would otherwise have flagged. Seeing this, the respectables of the South made haste to disavow the night-riders, though many had been among them (even Robert E. Lee gave the Klan his blessing, though he cautiously refused to be its Imperial Wizard). By 1873 the Klan had ceased to ride: other methods were found for 'redeeming' the South from the Republicans and their allies. But its work long survived it. Southern opinion fastened on what it took to be the glamour, the courage, the patriotism of the 'night hawks', and thereafter violent extremism was legitimized in Southern politics (as the Fenians legitimized violence in contemporary Ireland). Liberals, moderates and conservatives from then on could always be outflanked if they showed any disposition to co-operate with the blacks: the tradition of the Klan could be invoked, none would dare to denounce it and a few good lynchings would restore the *status quo*. In this way the frontier and Revolutionary tradition of the people's justice was finally perverted.

The Southern leadership also adopted methods that were slightly more subtle than the Klan's. It tried to undermine the North's belief in its cause by filling the air with denunciations of the Freedmen's Bureau (which succumbed to its enemies in 1872) and the corruption of the Reconstruction governments. In actuality these governments were no worse than any others in one of the most exuberantly dishonest political eras in American history, and much better than some; but they were vulnerable, for example in the matter of state debts, which had soared to unmanageable heights. This was largely because, in their eagerness to rebuild the South, the governments, with the approval of the voters, had done all they could to induce capitalists to renew and extend the railroads:[16] with such success that by 1877 the total mileage of track in the South had risen from just over 9,000 to nearly 14,000. Still it made good copy for critics. The 'Redeemers' also tried, with some

15 The Bureau also made sure that freedmen who signed contracts stuck to them; indeed, it had the reputation of being the only authority which could make the ex-slaves work. This aspect of the Bureau shows how limited was its vision, for the contracts it enforced were only marginally better than the ones it disallowed, and both unduly restricted the African-American's freedom as a working man. The blacks were willing enough to work hard – for themselves, or for those, like the Bureau, that they trusted.
16 When the people of Arkansas were asked to vote on some railway proposals, they were not vexed with tedious detail. The ballots were simply marked 'For Railroads' and 'Against Railroads'. The Ayes had it.

success, to persuade the freedmen that they were better friends to them than the strangers from outside Dixie, and made promises which some of them meant to keep. They organized vigorously and campaigned furiously, with the predictable result. One by one the Southern states were redeemed for the Democrats and white supremacy. By 1876 Republican governments survived only in Louisiana and South Carolina, and there only by virtue of military occupation. Resentment against these relics was rising to a dangerous pitch. Violence was endemic in Louisiana, and in South Carolina former Confederate General Wade Hampton was posing as the state's Garibaldi, at the head of his own private army of Redshirts.

'Corruption is the fashion,' said one Southern Governor. The Redeemers were helped by the fact that the Grant administration, blatantly incompetent and dishonest, split the Republican party. An alliance of Democrats and 'Liberal Republicans' fought the election of 1872 on what was in effect a Copperhead platform, and although Grant survived the challenge, the episode proved that two-party politics was back for good, and that in a close race the South might well prove the decisive factor. Then in 1873 came one of the great crashes which punctuated the business cycle every twenty years or so; it was followed by a prolonged depression, for which the administration got the blame. The Democrats, denouncing Republican corruption and overspending, won the Congressional election of 1874 and seemed well placed to win the Presidential election of 1876 on a traditional anti-big-business Jacksonian platform; for the Republicans had been exceedingly lavish in their attentions to the great corporations, especially the railroads. If the Democrats won the Presidency the South could be sure that Reconstruction would be at an end: the last garrisons would be withdrawn, and the last carpetbag governments would fall. In the event it was a close-run thing: votes were stolen on both sides, but if the popular vote had been honestly counted the Democratic candidate, Samuel Tilden of New York, last surviving member of the Albany Regency, would have been elected President with a majority of about twenty electoral votes.

The Republicans, however, refused to let power slip from their hands so easily. The carpetbag governments in Louisiana and South Carolina announced that Rutherford B. Hayes (1822–93), the Republican candidate, had carried those states and was therefore elected President by a margin of one electoral vote. It was the most outrageous piece of election-rigging in American history (which is saying something) and for a moment it looked as if it might precipitate a renewal of civil war. The Northern Democrats, after sixteen years in opposition, were ready to use any means to regain the power that was rightfully theirs – or so they threatened.

The Southern Democrats were, uncharacteristically, more cautious. In the first place, Reconstruction was dead. Even if Hayes became President he would have to abandon the carpetbaggers or face the certainty of another rebellion: there was no longer any significant support for them anywhere. Sure of white supremacy, then, the Southerners were free to consider what they would do with it; and the answer seemed clear. The South was still in a ruinous condition; she needed all the investment she could obtain to restore the economy and enter the industrial age at last; her support would go therefore to the party most likely to satisfy these needs by, for instance, voting money to repair the broken levees of the Mississippi, or by making land grants for building another transcontinental railroad through Texas, New Mexico, Arizona Territory and California – the so-called 'Southern' route. The homeland of Andrew Jackson abandoned his creed and turned for salvation to the doctrine of 'internal improvements of a national character' and federal assistance originally promulgated by Alexander Hamilton, John Quincy Adams and Henry Clay. (Many former Southern Whigs were active in this apostasy, and the ruling group in Virginia actually called itself the Conservative party.)

The Northern Democrats were loyal to the ancient faith. The national revulsion against Grantism had been the power behind their renewed political success; they refused to make any concessions to their allies. The Republicans were less restrained. They absolved themselves of their recent sins by deciding that Hayes was to be a reforming President; he and his associates were delighted by the prospect (which proved to be illusory) of reviving the Whigs in the South; they had no ideological objection to internal improvements; and the Presidency was at stake. It would be unsafe to let the country fall into the hands of the vengeful Democrats. So they promised the South home rule, and railroads, and political patronage. In return the Redeemers promised to treat the African-Americans well, and organized to make sure that Congress would not overturn the electoral college's decision (their agreement was crucial because, though the Republicans controlled the Senate, the Democrats controlled the House). So Hayes was inaugurated as President in March 1877 (jokes about 'Rutherfraud' and 'His Fraudulency' immediately began to circulate); and soon afterwards the Redeemers took over – not only in the state capitols, for Hayes kept most of his promises, and many a good Republican was dislodged from his postmastership to make way for a Democrat chosen by the new masters of the South.

So the great quarrel of the Civil War and the emancipation crusade finally flickered out in a shabby, undercover bargain of which the best that can be said is that it was legal and averted violence. As such it was welcomed with a universal roar of relief, which showed how deeply ordinary people had dreaded another war – a war which among other things would have made the much-vaunted republic look discreditably like its less successful neighbours south of the border. Now the nation could turn to new things. The old politicians died or retired; the bloody shirt became a less and less effective gimmick; the former rebels vaunted their patriotism. No doubt they did know best, as they claimed, about black–white relations. The once-radical *New York Tribune* editorialized that 'after ample opportunity to develop their own latent capacities' the blacks had only proved that 'as a race they are idle, ignorant, and vicious'.

Necessarily the African-Americans were the losers by this settlement. The planter-merchant class was already back in the saddle economically; the Compromise of 1877 (as some historians call it) guaranteed the restoration of its political power; not surprisingly, the rest of the nineteenth century saw a steady decline in the blacks' social position. For although the divisions among Southern whites were many and bitter they were always patched over, in the end, in favour of a united attack on the blacks. Thus, the alliance between the Redeemers (that is, the old planter class) and the ordinary farmers, which had won back Southern control of the Southern states, soon broke down, for the Redeemers, perhaps mindful of their promises to President Hayes, showed themselves suspiciously respectful of blacks' rights, in return getting their votes in elections, and unduly conservative in their approach to public finance and economic problems. Before long a series of revolts broke their power (and with it any hope of an effective Whig or Republican party in most of the South); the rednecks[17] seized control and, finding that the South's difficulties were as intractable as ever, blamed them on the blacks. The aristocrats, who dreaded an alliance between poor blacks and poor whites, welcomed this development. Rabblerousing and black-baiting became the standard expedients of all Southern politicians anxious about re-election, and resulted in the notorious Jim Crow laws (nobody knows exactly why they were so-called) by which blacks were rigidly excluded from voting, through such devices as the grandfather clause, the white primary and the poll-tax;[18] from all but the poorest and most servile occupations; from the best residential areas of Southern towns; from the schools and universities which white people attended; from white hotels and restaurants. Even trains and (later) motor-buses were segregated. By 1900 white supremacy had developed such a complex and formidable social system that the chief African-American leader of the day, Booker T. Washington, gained his reputation by forcefully advising his people to exploit it by accepting it. He reasoned that African-Americans could make no political progress until they had made economic progress; that they could be said to make economic progress only in so far as they gained control of their own economic lives; and that the only way they could do this was with the help, or at any rate the acquiescence, of the white power

17 So-called because, unlike the gentry, the Southern poor farmers had to work in the open all day long, with the savage sun beating down on their fair Anglo-Saxon necks. There was very little Mediterranean immigration to the South.
18 The poll-tax was a payment which citizens had to make before they were allowed to vote. It excluded the poorest, among them almost all the blacks, from the exercise of their Fifteenth Amendment rights, but since many poor whites were thereby disfranchised a 'grandfather clause' was inserted in half a dozen Southern state constitutions permitting the poor to vote if their immediate ancestors had done so in 1867. No blacks qualified under this clause. The white primary laid down that only whites could vote in the Democratic party primaries, because the party was a voluntary body and not covered by the Fifteenth; but in the post-bellum 'Solid South' the primaries were the real election, so the effect was to make a black citizen's vote useless, even if he were allowed to cast it at the general election.

structure. As first head of the Tuskegee Institute in Alabama from 1881 onwards he manifested apparent lack of interest in civil and political rights and a passionate concern with vocational training for blacks. He flattered the racists (who did not see, or did not believe, that his ultimate goal was integration and equality) and so won their acceptance, respect and aid. Unfortunately the vocational training he purveyed was better adapted to the old, rural America than to the urban America into which the blacks were beginning to move (a tendency he deplored), so it is far from clear to what extent his strategy succeeded, and really assisted African-American economic emancipation.

The consequences of 1877 for Southern whites were also dismal. Under-urbanized, under-capitalized, her soil exhausted by poor husbandry, her major crop increasingly devastated, from 1892 onwards, by the boll weevil, the agrarian South became more than ever a land of nostalgia for the glorious ante-bellum days, a land of introversion and provincialism, a land, it seemed, without hope; a land paying a tragic price for tragic miscalculations. The waste of human potential was the worst thing about it all. An economic and educational system devised principally to keep things as they were, and the blacks unprivileged, was unable to do much for its white citizens either. Southern blacks were the only Americans with worse prospects than Southern whites (except for the Indians). Some industrial development there was, most noticeably at Birmingham, Alabama; but not enough. The great capitalists had little taste for the risks entailed by investment in a region with such poor prospects and such an unskilled labour force; the Republicans, who on the whole dominated the national government until 1913, had little interest in a region that after 1877 always voted Democratic.

Reconstruction, then, failed to save the South from herself, and the African-American from the South. It did have a dramatic success in another direction. The Fourteenth and Fifteenth Amendments were to be dead letters in Dixie, but they put solid ground beneath the blacks in the North. They were few in number compared to those in the South, though increasing; but their importance is not to be measured in numbers. Their existence, and their organization, meant that in parts of America the principle of human equality was still acknowledged, if not very willingly or, too often, socially (*de facto* segregation in the North would for long be nearly as pervasive as *de jure* segregation in the South), then at least politically: blacks could vote and trade their votes for benefits, like other Americans. Furthermore, these Northern, urban blacks were pioneers of the great adaptation, from country to city, that the twentieth century would bring; forerunners. Their success was as much the outcome of the Emancipation Revolution, of the application of the beliefs of the Age of Equality, as the death of slavery itself. And what the Reconstruction Amendments had done for them, they would one day – a century later – begin to do for the blacks of the South.

In that sense, then, Reconstruction was a victory. But it was a victory too long in coming; and, as this chapter has demonstrated, there are other reasons why, for Americans, a sour taste of failure and disappointment will always hang about the epoch. Not until the mid-twentieth century were many of their historians to find any good to say of it.

BOOK FOUR

The Age of Gold

Little of all we value here
Wakes on the morn of its hundredth year
Without both feeling and looking queer.
In fact, there's nothing that keeps its youth,
So far as I know, but a tree and truth.

Oliver Wendell Holmes

An imbalance between rich and poor is the oldest and most fatal ailment
of republics.

Plutarch

17 The Billion-Dollar Country
1865–1900

When the charge was made during the campaign of 1891 that the Fifty-first Congress was a Billion-Dollar Congress, the complete reply, the best in kind ever evoked, was that this is a Billion-Dollar Country.

Thomas Reed, 1892

To the west, to the west, to the land of the free
Where mighty Missouri rolls down to the sea;
Where a man is a man if he's willing to toil,
And the humblest may gather the fruits of the soil.
Where children are blessings and he who hath most
Has aid for his fortune and riches to boast.
Where the young may exult and the aged be at rest
Away, far away, to the land of the west.

Nineteenth-century English song[1]

The America which fought the Civil War was still in many crucial respects the America which fought the Revolution. The great majority of the population was Protestant, and of English, Welsh, Scottish or Irish descent. It had an outlook that may be summed up crudely as republican, middle-class and respectable. Above all it was rural, in origins, residence, outlook and occupation: the 1860 census classified five out of every six Americans as rural dwellers.[2] All this was to change dramatically between Appomattox and the First World War. The Jeffersonian republic of farmers, from being an aspiration, became a memory. In its place, instead of a plain, dignified,

---

[1] The child Samuel Gompers (see Chapter 18) sang this song with great fervour in his cigar-factory in London; it helped turn his mind to the idea of emigration to America, as it had earlier turned the thoughts of Andrew Carnegie's father.

[2] The definitions used in the census until the mid-twentieth century mean that even this figure is an understatement, the definition of 'urban' covering a great many places that were no more than villages in the countryside.

provincial society, clinging to the edge of a continent yet gazing eagerly westward, there entered the twentieth century a continental nation, hugely rich and productive, populous, harshly urbanized, heavily industrialized, infinitely various in its ethnic origins, its religions, languages and cultures, transformed into the first fully modern society by its rapidly evolving technology; and yet still, for good and bad, recognizably the country of George Washington who founded it and Abraham Lincoln who rescued it. It was not so much a matter of continuity as of physical identity. Societies, after all, are made up of human beings, and little changes more than the human body between the cradle and maturity. Yet the human personality seems to be pretty constant through all bodily changes. It may be an illusion, but if so it is a permanent one.

The chief reason for this transformation was the Industrial Revolution. This epoch was given its name in France, where it was first noticed that the guillotine was not the only machine which could profoundly alter human history; but it began in England and Scotland in the eighteenth century. The cultural conditions which made it possible in the mother country were equally present in the still very English America of the post-Revolutionary era. A delight in ingenious inventions and a shrewd sense of how to make money by them was, for instance, at least as common in New as in Old England; and in fact it was not long before the Americans outstripped Britain, and the Yankee inventor became proverbial for his ingenuity. It was as significant that a New Englander invented the improved cotton gin as that the South was transformed by it. Even as early as the War of the Revolution a hopeful engineer had demonstrated a practicable steamboat to George Washington, and before the Battle of New Orleans, thanks to the genius of Robert Fulton, such boats were already common on the Mississippi and its navigable tributaries. By 1846 Cunard had established the first transatlantic steamship line. In 1844 Samuel Morse set up, between Washington and Baltimore, the first electric telegraph, and flashed along the wire the message: 'What has God wrought?' In 1854, at a great industrial exhibition in Paris, an American threshing machine was exhibited which beat all comers: it could thresh 740 litres of wheat in half an hour, which was not only better than six men (60 litres) but better than its nearest competitor, an English machine, which could thresh 410 litres in the time. Although the steam railway was an entirely British invention, the speed and completeness of its application to North American conditions was uniquely astounding. The first American railroad was the Baltimore & Ohio, opened in 1830. By the time Fort Sumter fell there were 31,256 miles of railroad track in the United States. Soon after the Civil War, Thomas A. Edison got busy improving the telephone, inventing the phonograph (or gramophone in British English) and perfecting the electric light bulb.

The Industrial Revolution, which still continues, has been the most important development in human society since men took to farming: its consequences have been so multifarious as to defy summary. Yet some aspects of its initial impact on America must be listed, beginning with its effect on communications.

Steamboats, telegraph, railroads: all had the effect of bringing American producers closer to their customers and making it easier for them to discover and penetrate new markets. In this matter, as in every other of the first era of industrialism, the railroads were of transcendent importance. It was their success in binding the North-East to the North-West which largely created the alignment that was victorious in the Civil War; perhaps the least of their achievements. It is scarcely too much to say that they underlay every new development, whether in politics, economics, culture or religion, in the middle and later years of the nineteenth century. In the West, the promise of the road was so great (for it would make sending goods to market cheap and easy, and in turn would bring all the refinements of the city, not to mention good factory-made farming implements, itinerant lecturers, revivalist preachers and more settlers) that intense competition grew up between the speculators of different regions and the boosters of different towns (at an earlier date, along the Mississippi, the competition had been for the privilege of becoming a regular stopping-place for steamboats). Links to the rising metropolitan centres being now so important, many a town was made or ruined by the decisions of the great railroads. Buffalo Bill founded a town he called Rome, in Nebraska, which he was sure would make his fortune; unhappily the Kansas Pacific Railroad founded Fort Hays, a mile or two away; seeing which way the wind blew, the inhabitants of Rome unbuilt their city in three days, carting everything off to the rival town. Soon Cody himself had to settle there. This was long before the days of the Wild West show; when that concern was at its height Buffalo Bill was able to enlist the help of another railroad to give another town which he founded – Cody, Wyoming – a flying send-off.

Perhaps the boldest exploitation of the new transport system was devised by the cowboys of Texas. The removal of the Indians and the destruction of the buffalo opened the Great Plains, covered as they were by the deep rich sea of buffalo grass, for grazing by cattle. Vast herds of longhorns rapidly spread, watched over by cowboys employing techniques learned largely from the Mexicans. After the Civil War cattle fetched huge prices in the North-West, where Chicago was beginning its long career as chief slaughterhouse to the world. The transcontinental railroad had reached western Missouri. The Texans decided to drive their cattle 1,500 miles to the railhead. The Long Drive was launched in 1866, and after some initial teething trouble was a wild success. Cow towns in Kansas, notably Abilene[3] and Dodge City, boomed overnight, and during the season when the cattle reached town displayed all the vigour, vice and violence of mining camps. The Chisholm and Western Trails along which the cattle moved became as legendary as the Oregon Trail. But all good things come to an end,

3 Not to be confused with Abilene, Texas.

especially in pioneering country. After ten years it was clear that the Drive could not last much longer, in the first place because Kansas was filling up with farmers who refused to abide the risk that their own cows might be infected by diseased Texan cattle. Besides, it was no longer necessary for the cows to go to the railroad: the railroad was willing to go to the cows, even though they grazed as widely as the buffalo had done, on the ranges of Nebraska, Montana, Dakota Territory, Colorado and Wyoming as well as in Texas and Kansas. For a brief moment the cowboy was king of the West. His reign was brought to an end by overgrazing, the coming of sheep and fenced farms, and the ruinously cold winters of 1885–6 and 1886–7; while it lasted, in spite of the stirring picture the cowboy made, sitting relaxed in the saddle of his trusty pony, it was created and sustained by the railroad, just as it was the railroad which made possible the profits of the supplanters.

Yet the impact of industry on the West was as nothing compared to its impact on the East. The staples of American economic life, since the seventeenth century, had been agriculture and commerce. It had been the lure of profit to be made by supplying the coastal towns of America, and even communities overseas, which had from the first induced American farmers to grow for the market, and not make do with what they could raise for themselves and their families. It had been the availability of surplus produce – grain, tobacco, timber, fish, cotton – which had made it possible for the ports to grow rich by exporting and importing. This symbiosis of farm and town was reproduced, on a gigantic scale, in the nineteenth century, so much so that cities like Cincinnati, St Louis and Chicago owed their rise to their function as entrepots, as river or lake ports. The railroads intensified this pattern without, it might appear, much altering it: if it was now much more important to have a railroad station than a riverside, nevertheless all the important cities managed to maintain their position or enhance it in this way if only because they were already so big as to seem tempting customers (all those potential passengers, and all the goods which they needed or desired!) to the railroads. But in fact there was one great difference, and it was crucial. The railroad was man-made. This did not mean, merely, that large numbers of workers were needed to survey its course, lay its roadbed and its rails, and maintain both, though the economic impact of the fact was not slight: by 1890 there were 166,703 miles of railroad (and more to come) and a single railroad corporation might have as many as 36,000 employees. This was different only in quantity, not quality, from conditions created by canal or highway building. The essential distinction lay in the fact that the rails had to be manufactured out of iron and, soon, steel. Engines, wagons and carriages had to be constructed and maintained in engineering workshops. Coal to heat engine boilers had to be dug and shipped. To sum up, the long, long years of railway building created and sustained hundreds of thousands of new jobs; new coal and iron mines; new coking plants (for the manufacture of steel); new iron and steelworks; new towns, which were also new markets; new skills; and new forms of financial and industrial organization. This was the epitome of the true Industrial Revolution. It was this which began to turn the Americans into a nation of town-dwellers, and then city-dwellers; it was this which, by the demands it created, stimulated the amazing growth in production and wealth that, before the end of the century, had entirely outstripped anything the Old World could show; it was this which began an entirely new class-structure; it was this which finally freed the United States from its dependence on overseas trade by generating a self-sustaining, continental economy. And so modern America was born.

The foundations for this achievement were laid well before the Civil War. The concentration of industrial labour in factories was as essential a part of the revolution as technology, and although its arrival was less conspicuous than that of the railroad and took longer than the improvement of communications to make itself fully felt, it got to America at much the same time. By the 1830s the processes that went to the making of cotton thread and cotton cloth, everywhere the first industry to be modernized, had been concentrated in mills in new towns on the rivers of New England – towns like Lowell, Massachusetts, whose original workers were Puritan girls fresh from the farms. For a time these girls were famous, both for the new tasks they performed with the spinning and weaving machines and for the enlightened way in which they improved their education in their leisure hours. It was no wonder that they sought work in the mills, for it was becoming harder and harder to make a living on New England farms, as the products of the region's stony soil felt the competition of the new, Western lands now coming into production; and the wages in the cotton factories were quite high. But New England was competing in the world market, especially in the free-trade thirties, forties and fifties, when the South kept the tariff low; before very long working conditions deteriorated, wages fell and the New England girls were driven out of the mills by the competition of immigrants, who by working longer hours for less pay could help the manufacturers sell their products somewhat more cheaply and thus defeat the competition of the Lancashire mills.

Of equal importance to an industrial revolution is the availability of capital for investment. On this point Andrew Carnegie (1835–1919), the steel magnate, perhaps said the last word: 'It is astounding the amount of working capital you must have in a great concern. It is far more than the cost of the works.' To launch such a concern it was first necessary to accumulate sufficient funds, whether by saving or borrowing or selling, to buy a site, build a factory (or ironworks, or steel foundry, or shipyard), hire and train and pay workers, buy raw material, advertise for customers and ensure that your manufactures could be delivered. Initially it would be desirable to have cash in hand, after all this, to pay for new machines and to set against the depreciation of old ones: later on, and of course the sooner the better, the profits of the concern would have to cover this cost. It would also be as well to have something in hand in case the market suddenly collapsed as, in nineteenth-century conditions, it would be certain to do at some stage. These were the ideal circumstances. In reality, they were seldom or never attained. The manufacturer had to borrow to set up his plant and borrow to keep it going, which added interest charges to all his other overheads. Capital was thus of crucial importance at every stage of industrial life, and the capitalist was the great man of the age. Only the man whose resources were large enough to ride out the periodical storms, whether as a lender or as a manufacturer, could be sure of avoiding all the woes of early industrialism, whether bankruptcy, unemployment or takeover. There were few such men in nineteenth-century America, and the prestige of those who did emerge was consequently enormous. So was their wealth and their power.

The importance of capital in the early Industrial Revolution was so great and so obvious everywhere that it gave rise to several new social and economic theories, of which the most famous is Marxism. It also gave rise to the term 'capitalism', and this was by no means so acceptable a development. As commonly used, the term is at once too vague and too precise. Too precise, because it emphasizes one element in the rise of the modern industrial economy and subordinates all others in a way which ignores so many facts as to be positively question-begging; too vague, because of its use in political argument. For too many people it has become an all-purpose explanation of everything that has occurred in the past few hundred years; a swear-word to label all they dislike about the past. For too many others, 'capitalism' has come to seem the fine flower of human history, the only begetter and guarantor of freedom, progress and civilization. For them, capitalism is a perfected system which ought never to have been tampered with in the slightest degree, and ought now to be restored as carefully as if it were a vintage motor-car.

To the historian of the United States neither of these views makes sense. Even though the USA rapidly became the greatest capitalist country, its capitalist age – the epoch, that is, in which private capital was indeed the dominant force – was conspicuously short, lasting only from the end of the Civil War to 1929. Only during that period, which raced to apply modern techniques to the largely untouched resources of North America, was the need for massive capital investment so urgent and so difficult to satisfy adequately that the appetites of the capitalists, the money men, prevailed over all other social forces. In that age, laws and legal processes were altered, reinterpreted, perverted or ignored; the interests of working men and women were trampled upon; the appeal to the greed, foresight or gambler's instinct of the wealthy led to innumerable shady operations; the principles of political economy were reinvented, and the interests of the consumer, the ultimate customer, were for long ignored. But by the second decade of the twentieth century the problem of capital accumulation had been solved: the work of the previous sixty years bore fruit in the ceaseless generation of new funds for investment. If progress and prosperity were to be maintained other considerations had to be allowed due weight; what neglect of them could lead to was demonstrated in the Great Crash of 1929 and the long depression that followed, which proved that the great capitalists had been allowed to rule the roost unchecked for a little too long. So ever since 1933 capital has been allowed to be only one of many powers struggling to preserve and extend their interests.

Yet its predominance in what may be called the Age of Gold (after its favourite metal)[4] cannot sanely be denied. It was precisely this predominance which marked off the period from the years before and after it. To be sure, the foundations had been a long time a-laying. Capital had been of essential importance in the very opening of America, from the Virginia Company onwards, and the first American multi-millionaire, John Jacob Astor, had made his pile in the fur-trade long before 1834 (when, seeing that the fashion for beaver hats had been superseded by one for silk, he sold out). But for long the problem of securing funds for investment was almost crippling. The success of the Erie Canal touched off the canal boom, but, like the Erie, it had to be supported by state securities. It was the faith and credit of Pennsylvania which encouraged British speculators to invest $35,000,000 in that state's internal improvements. The British lost the lot in the crash of 1839 and the ensuing depression: in 1842 Pennsylvania repudiated her debts. Various morals were drawn from this affair. Europeans concluded that American securities, even federal ones (bonds, that is, backed by the credit of the United States), were worthless; and it was long before they invested in America again. The Americans concluded that it was madness to risk the good name of their political system, and perhaps its very existence, by letting their state and municipal governments undertake industrial and commercial developments which private enterprise could handle. Roads, canals, railways and telegraph lines were still enormously desirable, but the risks of creating them must in future be borne by individual citizens. This implied that to the same citizens would belong the profits. Astor would not be the last millionaire or even, for long, the richest.

Private capital proved equal to the responsibilities and opportunities thus given to it. It grew rapidly between 1839 and 1861. Individuals might meet disaster in the periodic panics, depressions and recessions which punctuated its upward course, but the business class as a whole prospered mightily. The Civil War brought it ascendancy.

Like so much about the Civil War this was unplanned and unforeseen. The Republicans thought of themselves as the party of the working man

4 Mark Twain, America's greatest writer, attached the label 'the Gilded Age' to the earlier part of the period; a happy thought, as it touched on the new rich's taste in interior decoration as well as their leaf-thin respectability and the corruption of the politics of this meretricious time. To apply the label to the whole period 1865–1929 would be seriously misleading; and faith in the importance of the gold standard eventually became such a cardinal tenet of the capitalists that my variant seems preferable. An attractive, alternative would be the Age of the Railroad, except that the roads' decline began well before 1929.

and, especially, the farmer. Lincoln spoke for them when, in his first inaugural, he affirmed that

labour is prior to and independent of capital. Capital is only the fruit of labour and could never have existed if labour had not first existed. Labour is the superior of capital and deserves much the higher consideration.

Businessmen themselves were so far from expecting to do well out of the war that they deplored the prospect of hostilities and did all they could to avert them. The mayor of New York, thinking of his city's huge investment in the South and the cotton trade, even proposed that New York too should secede from the Union. The South had clamorously noticed and denounced the rise of Northern capital for the previous thirty years; one of the most plausible (though in fact fallacious) arguments for secession was that Dixie was in thrall to New York and Boston; but she certainly did not expect that her bid for independence would bring about exactly what she most feared: not only emancipation for the slaves, but hegemony for Wall Street.

Yet secession cleared the way for the Republicans' economic programme as nothing else could have done. Revenue tariffs, raised to help pay for the war, quickly had protective elements grafted onto them, elements which were never to be entirely removed during the next seventy years, which were rather to be added to and intensified. So American manufacturers were henceforward to have a privileged place in the American market, to the discomfiture of their foreign competitors. Businessmen were also to get most of the profit from the measures which the war Congress passed to aid Western development and cement ocean-to-ocean unity. The 1862 Homestead Act was supposed to help pioneer farmers by giving them homesteads (farms) of 160 acres each out of the public domain in the West, provided only that they cultivated the land for five years. Unfortunately for such pioneers the act also allowed them to buy the land cheaply, if they were able, for $1.25 an acre, after only six months' cultivation. This enabled land speculators to lay their hands on vast areas of the best land for what were, to them, trivial sums: they simply hired agents to masquerade as real farmers. Settlers had to buy their land from the speculators, at inflated prices. But so it had ever been on the frontier. The Acts setting up the Central Pacific and Union Pacific Railroads (1862) and the Northern Pacific Railroad (1864) were novelties of spectacular importance. For one thing these, with Chase's National Currency Acts of 1863 and 1864, which awarded national charters to certain banks, were the first incorporations performed by the federal government since 1816, when the Second Bank of the United States was incorporated. Thirty years of Jacksonian rhetoric against monopolies and monsters were thus discarded. For another, Congress thereby found its way round the ban on any new government-sponsored business enterprise. Transcontinental railroads were held to be of the utmost national importance, but even they could not justify the mortgaging of the national credit (an exceedingly wise principle, in view of the immensely erratic economic performance of these railroads when at last they were in operation). Instead, Congress tempted investors by making lavish grants of land along the lines of the proposed roads. Funds raised by selling such land, or by borrowing against the security it provided, were supposed to pay for laying the tracks. The whole operation of carrying the rails across the continent was so risky, so difficult (the golden spike at Promontory Point, Utah, which linked the Union Pacific rails going west with the Central Pacific ones going east was not driven until 1869), that the enterprise might have had to wait for many years more without the land grants. Nevertheless, those grants (131,000,000 acres in all) were another immense boon to speculators, making the West the province of New York, as a Senator from Wisconsin complained at the time; and they added vastly to the resources of Wall Street and the other financial centres of the East, centres already much strengthened by the wartime banking acts, which gave the big banks enormous advantages over smaller or newer ones. Only the big banks could service the national debt which the war was rapidly increasing, and they exacted a high reward for doing so.

The war does not seem to have accelerated economic growth; if anything, it was a plateau between the giddy expansion of the fifties and the post-war boom. Indeed at first it seemed as if business forebodings would come true and the war be a check to prosperity. It took Northern industry many months to adapt to the needs of the army and the navy, and meantime it had lost its market in the South. But soon the United States industrial machine showed its capacity as a wartime producer for the first time. Profits were enormous, even allowing for wartime inflation, in part because wages did not rise nearly so rapidly as prices. Nor was the war allowed to interfere with the plans of certain individuals. The new resource, petroleum, had been produced commercially at Oil Creek, Pennsylvania, for the first time in 1859; the young John D. Rockefeller soon afterwards took his first step towards empire by merging five refineries. The war ended in a victory which seemed as much a vindication of American industrialism as of American nationalism; and the process of conversion from war to peace proved a new stimulus to business, as the federal government settled its contracts and as returning veterans looked for goods on which to spend their pay, their savings and their pensions: in this way some $700,000,000 was pumped into the economy. The boom continued until 1873. Andrew Carnegie, a railroad man, who was already making $50,000 a year at the war's end, was now drawn to steel as irresistibly as Rockefeller to oil: first the Bessemer and then the open-hearth processes were making the metal a plentiful and cheap commodity for the first time in history. The railroads, which had earlier sustained the demand for iron, were still building frantic- ally, and now stimulated steel; steel-making in turn stimulated demand for coke. When Carnegie of Pittsburgh joined forces with Henry Clay Frick, who controlled the processing of coke in Pennsylvania and the fields where the right sort of coal could be mined, another great industrial empire began to take shape. The headlong expansion of the American population (thirty-one million in 1860, fifty million in 1880, sixty-three million in 1890) bred an equally headlong expansion and proliferation of demand. It seemed that nothing could fail. All that was necessary was to exploit the resources of the continent to the utmost, and there was a rapidly burgeoning class of geologists, engineers and other technicians to show how to do it.

In the long run such greedy calculations would be amply justified; meantime difficulties arose. Purchasing power was increasing at a great rate, no doubt, but there were still too many people – poor, pinched or simply parsimonious by tradition – who could not be customers for the industrialists' wares. The great firms of mail-order catalogues (Montgomery Ward, Sears Roebuck) carried the good news of cheap, diversified products far and wide, to isolated farms, small towns and Southern plantations (or what was left of them); the railroads made it easy to fill orders from these catalogues rapidly; but still demand did not quite keep up with production. American capitalism was not organized to adjust to such a condition. Competition was the fiercely affirmed law of its life. Everyone with a little money plunged into the market, hoping to get richer quickly by finding a business which would crush its rivals; towns, as we have seen, competed for the favours of the railroads; inventors rushed to the patent office with their new devices and then hurried to find capitalists to manufacture and sell them; eager adventurers, like the notorious Jay Gould, looked ceaselessly for opportunities to make money by outsmarting other manipulators of the stock exchanges; politicians exacted enormous favours, for themselves and their constituencies, from the businessmen, especially the railroad kings (who complained about it bitterly), in return for charters and subsidies and rights to mine for minerals on public lands. The fact that there was never enough capital for all the projects that were launched ought to have ensured investors an ample return on their money, and those who managed to hold on to their investments and did not fall victim to the many fraudulent prospectuses that circulated, not to mention other, even less honest practices that were common, eventually reaped their reward. But it took time, and the limited though ever-expanding market for industrial goods, services and processes, coupled with the shortage of capital, inevitably created tensions and contradictions. The search for funds meant that investors were regularly promised far higher returns than a company could earn for years to come. This tended to reduce the soundest concerns to the condition of speculative gambles, and, far worse, to produce permanent instability on the stock markets, where only rogues like Gould or his associate Jim Fisk could thrive.

The uncertainties of the economy were such that no one quite knew when, from being a winner, he might suddenly plunge into loss. Thus, the federal government tried steadily, in the decade after the Civil War, to return to its old modest scale and get out of the business of economic management; the culmination of this trend came in 1875 when an Act was passed undertaking to make the paper currency, the 'greenbacks' (originally issued to finance the Civil War), convertible into gold on 1 January 1879. This anti-inflationary measure no doubt played its part in bringing on the depression that persisted, with ups and downs, for twenty years. At any rate many people of the time thought so, and found their business calculations thrown out. Or there was the panic of 1873, which broke out when the great financier Jay Cooke, who had marketed the government's loans during the war, suddenly went bankrupt. He brought down thousands with him in his fall. Even the richest were not safe: Cornelius Vanderbilt, 'the Commodore', lost an immense amount of money – it would have crippled anyone else – in his unsuccessful attempt to buy control of the Erie Railroad in 1868. He was beaten by the machinations of the men he was trying to dislodge from management, Gould, Fisk and David Drew: they issued more than $50,000,000 worth of 'watered' stock[5] and thereby kept control of a majority of Erie shares; but this device increased the indebtedness of the railroad by nearly 400 per cent, for the money raised by selling watered stock, though no doubt useful to the sellers, did not equal the nominal value of the shares or the returns that the purchasers exacted, and above all was not necessary for building up the railroad itself (not that Gould would ever do anything so quaint as to invest a penny, if he could help it, in engines, rails, safety devices or stations).[6] In these circumstances it is not surprising that railroads frequently crashed (Erie went bankrupt in 1893) for their earnings could not meet their debt charges. Not even the greatest escaped: in 1893, besides the Erie, the bankrupts included the Northern Pacific, the Union Pacific and the Atchison, Topeka & Santa Fe. The managers rather relished such disasters, which freed them to run trains instead of paying shareholders, but it was hard luck on the shareholders just the same.

The great game of capitalism had a hundred other hazards which regularly claimed their victims. In any single case it might not matter much, except to the individual loser and his dependants; but unfortunately, as the industrial economy grew ever larger, involving the destinies of more and more people, its financial structure grew ever more entangled, so that one man's failure

5 Originally, stocks in companies were sold only in quantities sufficient to raise as much capital as a corporation needed to get started, or to expand its activities. This kept the load of debt to a tolerable size. Then managers began to dilute, or 'water', these original share issues by issuing fresh ones, whose yield was not necessary for running the business, either simply to enrich themselves with the proceeds or to swamp the holdings of their rivals in a sea of shares, as Gould and Fisk swamped Vanderbilt, or both. Such operations not only burdened a corporation with unnecessary debt, they also damaged its standing on the stock exchanges and, if on a large enough scale, undermined public faith in all shares. On the other hand, Vanderbilt always maintained that there was nothing wrong in issuing stock so long as a corporation's profits made it possible to pay dividends: it was the only way of distributing and releasing capital that would otherwise have remained locked up in the corporation's treasury.
6 Jay Gould did not go entirely unpunished for being America's most celebrated scoundrel. He was excluded from respectable society in New York and was twice beaten up by victims of his operations. He took his revenge by manipulating the stock market against their interests. He died in 1892, worth $77,000,000.

(say, Cooke's) might lead to a run on his bank, which in turn would call in its loans, which meant pressure applied to other businessmen, possibly a downturn in economic activity, possibly a panic, if a big enough business were involved – Cooke's again: so that suddenly dividends might be cut or suspended, factories closed, banks broken, and a downward spiral might begin, ending who knew where. Stricter state or federal laws might have helped to contain some of these ill-effects, but such laws were not on offer: apart from the universal creed that government should mind its own business, no one in his senses would have committed the management of American industry in any measure to the notoriously venal politicians of the period. No, if the economy was to be put on on a stable, predictable course, so that America's great prospects could be realized steadily and harmoniously, the businessmen would have to do it themselves.

The businessmen were not wholly unsuited to the task. Perhaps no generation of Americans has ever received such a bad press as the so-called 'Robber Barons'. In part this was simply because of their utter charmlessness. Their virtues – courage, ingenuity, strength of will and in many cases a gloomy personal rectitude – were themselves unattractive, and their vices – their greed, their selfishness, their philistinism, their almost complete lack of scruple where business was concerned – were thoroughly repulsive. Of them all only Jim Fisk, who perhaps expiated his sins by being murdered in a quarrel about a woman, and Andrew Carnegie, the ebullient, idealistic salesman of steel, seem to have had any human warmth; and Carnegie's behaviour during the Homestead strike and lockout[7] was markedly less straightforward than that of his partner Frick, who had never pretended, in Carnegie's fashion, to be the friend of his workers, and at least made it plain from the start of the episode that he expected the workers to go back on his terms or not at all. Frick, with some reason, felt betrayed by Carnegie, and the two men parted company; years later, when Carnegie tried to effect a reconciliation, Frick told the go-between, 'You can say to Andrew Carnegie that I will meet him in hell (where we are both going) but not before.' Like other multimillionaires, notably Pierpont Morgan, Frick spent much of his money on works of art, and left his elegant grey New York mansion and its incomparable contents to be a museum. Visitors can admire one of the finest personal collections of European art ever made; but the house itself, for all its grace, is somehow cold and morose. It seems to be haunted by the empty spirit of its builder, who sat alone in it, year after year, chewing his gold. Carnegie, who remarked that the man who died rich died disgraced, poured out his stupendous wealth on libraries, concert halls, schools, swimming-baths, teachers' pensions. Rockefeller died rich, but appears to have given away as much as he kept, to institutions such as the University of Chicago. A devout Baptist, he never seems to have had any doubts about his social utility. 'I saw a marvellous future for our country, and I wanted

7 See below, p. 420.

to participate in the work of making our country great. I had an ambition to build,' he explained, in extreme old age. The long years in which his great creation, Standard Oil, was denounced as the worst of monopolies left him unruffled, although he hired a public relations man to proclaim his virtues to the public.

Nevertheless, the issue ought not to be posed in terms of personalities. The question is one of social function. Matthew Josephson asserted that the nineteenth-century capitalists were socially evil because, like the medieval robber barons, they battened by force on the labour of others without contributing anything in return.[8] This is a defensible view. Even before the Civil War it was clear that there was a sharp distinction between the men who invented and organized and worked the industrial system and those who financed it. The first sort were interested in making things, the second in making money. The incessant plundering that disgraced the history of the railroads after the Civil War cannot be justified on economic grounds. Nothing can be said for Jay Gould, who got richer and richer while leaving a trail of devastation behind him in the form of bankrupt railroads, unemployed workmen, unfinished lines. Yet Gould was the almost inevitable price that America paid for her system of economic freedom. So long as the question of capital accumulation was all-important, and so long as government was kept at bay, the only source of funds was Wall Street, where stocks and bonds were trafficked in; and since the world is full of greedy scoundrels, some of them were certain to appear in that favourable environment. It is idle to say that things would have been different under socialism. For one thing, there is nothing in the history of real or self-styled socialist states to indicate that scoundrels are less common or successful in such regimes than under capitalism, and not much to suggest that socialist economics are more efficient than capitalist ones; for another, socialism, in any form, was not a choice which nineteenth-century America was in a position to make. The circumstances and the traditions of the country worked decisively against it. The only alternative economic system which was presented was slavery; and as we have seen, it had been rejected. Liberal capitalism was not going to start dismantling itself in the moment of its victory. It ignored its critics for a generation.

Instead many of the best and brightest of their time went into business, confident that they were furthering civilization and their country's best interests by so doing. Nor were they wholly wrong. It was they who undertook the job of bringing order out of the chaos that America's exuberant industrial growth had created.

Gradually *consolidation* and *co-operation* became terms with some of the magic of *competition* itself. Tired of the business of building parallel lines to steal each other's traffic, and issuing watered stock, and designing attractively cut-price railroad rate schedules in the interest of cutting each other's

8 Matthew Josephson, *The Robber Barons* (New York, 1934).

throats, and the occasional spectacular crash, the railroads began to work together. By the end of the century the greater part of America's track mileage was tied up in half a dozen systems, which were thus able to impose a certain uniformity and stability on their operations. Even greater advances were made by Rockefeller and Standard Oil. Like other businessmen, the oil men first tried the so-called 'pool' arrangement, by which, unofficially, the various companies agreed to divide their market equitably between themselves on a pre-arranged basis: extra profits, should they accrue to any one company, would be distributed among all the pool members. Unfortunately it turned out that the members could not resist stealing marches on one another: they kept their word only so long as it was immediately advantageous to do so, and there was no legal remedy against recreants. 'We can stand a great deal of cheating better than competition,' said a participant in a railroad pool; but in the end cheating, and the tangle of arrangements needed to try to circumvent it, always broke the pools down. So the Rockefeller lawyers came up with the idea of the 'trust', giving a new meaning to an ancient word. Under the trust arrangement holders of stock in the various oil companies handed over their shares to Rockefeller and his associates, acting as a board of trustees; in return they got trust certificates, which paid dividends but gave no power. The trustees made all the decisions. So successful was this arrangement for a time that by 1898 the Standard trust refined 83.7 per cent of all oil produced in the United States, and produced 33.5 per cent of it. The example was an inspiration to other industries, and trusts proliferated in such businesses as electricity and meat-packing.

Andrew Carnegie took a different line. He preferred informal arrangements which left him with absolute personal control of his organization; but he was such a brilliant industrial leader that even without pools and trusts he was able to advance steadily towards the dominance of the steel industry. He was especially skilful at inducing customers to prefer his steel to that of his competitors; he inspired his workers to toil ever harder, yet cut them down ruthlessly when they dared to press for higher wages than he thought desirable. He was not as quick at adopting important technical innovations as he liked to pretend ('Pioneering don't pay' was one of his maxims) but he always did so in time to undersell his competitors. By the end of the century it was clear that Carnegie was excellently placed to destroy all the other large steel-producers in the country, a fate that could only have been averted, if at all, by a fearful battle of price-cutting and stock-market manipulation which would have had frightful consequences far beyond the steel and coal industries. Carnegie made the first moves, and Wall Street trembled; there was immense relief when it was discovered that the magnate had decided to retire and devote himself to philanthropy, if he could get a good price for his company. The banker John Pierpont Morgan bought him out for $480,000,000: he subsequently gave away $325,000,000 in various good causes. Meanwhile Morgan merged the

Carnegie Steel Corporation with various lesser steel companies, and the result was the first billion-dollar trust, US Steel ('Big Steel'), which has dominated its field from its foundation in 1901 to the present day.

This episode was the final signal that the industrial world had entered upon a new phase, that of finance capitalism. By the 1890s, and especially after the panic of 1893, which threatened universal ruin, the money men were determined to get control, and were in a position to do so. They were no longer dependent for business and funds on London: the growth of American industry in the previous twenty years had generated enormous profits which were at the sole disposal of New York. Only they could help companies through difficult times when there were too few customers and too many creditors, and the chastened industrial managers were eager to accept their help and leadership. In return for their assistance the New York banks usually exacted drastic reorganization, heavy fees and seats on the board for themselves or their representatives. The leader in this movement was the House of Morgan, which stood, then as now, at the corner of Wall Street and Broad Street, next door to the New York Stock Exchange. Morgan's was the centre of American capitalism in more than mere geographical position. Between 1893 and 1913 (the year of his death) its chief was behind all the moves to stabilize operations and promote mergers in the railroads, in shipping, in the new electricity industry, in the telegraph, in telephones, as well as in steel. J. P. Morgan was the spider in a vast web of interlocking directorships (741 of them in 112 corporations), and as during the same period Standard Oil was steadily extending its influence, by the end of the first decade of the twentieth century it was almost the case that all the leading American capitalists were associates either of Morgan or of Rockefeller. The rationalization of industrialism by private capital might be said to have been very successfully completed.

The Morgans and the Rockefellers thought so. But neither at the time nor subsequently were their achievements unquestioned. In the first place it is far from clear that the larger and larger corporations, trusts and holding companies that emerged from their machinations were any more efficient than the smaller concerns which they superseded. They conferred more power on their masters, and more money; but in their actual economic functioning, in the basic business of production, there was little or no visible gain from giantism. A superficial case might be made for Rockefeller: he had a genius for cutting production costs, which certainly increased Standard Oil's profits and may even have lowered the price of petroleum to the consumer. But he owed his unique position and immense wealth not to his flair for thrift but to his perception that the oil producers were at the mercy of the refineries and the shippers: after he got his dominating position in both by single-mindedly pursuing control of the refining process, he was able to dictate terms to the owners of the oil wells, whose product had to be processed and shipped to market before it could earn them a penny, and also to the railroads, which could not afford to lose Rockefeller's custom.

It was powerful business, but it is hard to see what the gain was to the economy from Rockefeller's monopoly. His critics thought he was simply taxing the oil industry for his private benefit. Morgan was worse, for he did not always succeed. Thus in the first years of the twentieth century he put together a syndicate to beat the British and monopolize the transatlantic passenger steamship business, but was soon defeated: as a banker he did not know enough about shipping. He and his associates thought as money men protecting or forwarding their investments, not as creators of new wealth. In short, the power of the finance capitalists may have acted as something of a brake on America's development.

And financial crises continued to occur. Economic historians still differ as to the cause; but whatever it was – whether the unwise greed of speculators, the inherent contradictions of free enterprise, over-production, under-consumption, monetary profligacy or such frequent accidents as war and bad harvests – it was and is plain that the great trusts were impotent to control it. Too many railroads lay outside Morgan's grasp, too many oil wells outside Rockefeller's (especially after the great Texan field opened in 1901 with the first gusher at Spindletop). In all other areas the over-capitalized giants, which had lavishly issued watered stock in generous anticipation of future earnings (US Steel was launched on the greatest flood of 'water' thus far seen), found themselves still dangerously exposed to the competition of smaller concerns; and if one of the giants should ever crash the repercussions for the American, indeed for the world, economy would be appalling. For the United States was by 1900, thanks less to its big businessmen than to its active population and vast resources, the world's leading industrial nation. It produced more coal and pig-iron, and manufactured more raw cotton, than its nearest competitor, Great Britain; produced more iron ore and steel than Germany; more gold than Australia, and nearly as much silver as Mexico; more tobacco and cotton than India, and more wheat than Russia. Britain had a much larger merchant fleet, Russia had far more sheep and produced somewhat more petroleum; but even in these departments America's achievement was increasingly formidable – her production of crude oil, for instance, more than doubled between 1899 and 1909. Every year, in short, increased the giant's pre-eminence. America was still a debtor nation, borrowing more than she lent; but her enterprises were generating ever-mounting quantities of money that were beginning to find their way into investments overseas. The day was not far off when, as the saying goes, if Wall Street sneezed, the rest of the world would catch a cold. And Wall Street had not discovered how to stop itself sneezing.

From another point of view the triumph of the trusts seemed not so much inefficient or irrelevant as immoral. The bigger business grew, the larger were the bribes it could offer to national and local politicians, the greater was the pressure it could bring on the voters, in such a way as to undermine the democratic principles on which the United States was based. Others noticed the appalling conditions of labour throughout industrial and urban America, and asked why employers never had money to spare to improve them, though there always seemed to be funds in hand for re-investment or for Wall Street battles. Others again looked at the rising class-consciousness and class-hostility that industrialism bred, at the tensions provoked by the immigrant workers imported in large numbers to operate the economic machine, at the hideous industrial towns, at the shacks and rookeries of the New York slums, and asked if things would not be better managed if the trusts were disciplined. Others reasoned that whatever excuse for themselves the trusts might make, there was clearly something wrong with America, and it would be folly to rest content with business civilization as it stood: even if big business was not the cause of everything that had gone wrong, it was at least as certainly not the cure.

America had changed, was still changing, was moving into ever stranger waters. The fact spread a deepening malaise ever more widely in the national consciousness as the nineteenth century wore to its end. The old self-confident spirit was never very far away, perhaps: it was manifested with great exuberance in Chicago at the 'World Columbian Exposition' of 1893, which was visited by twenty-eight million people, who marvelled at this celebration of America; but the Exposition was also marked by a meeting of the American Historical Association at which the young Frederick Jackson Turner read a paper arguing, in part, that since the 1890 census had shown that every part of the continental United States had now been organized, most of it already into states, the 'frontier' was closed and a new epoch was at hand. American institutions, formed in more propitious conditions, would be severely tested. The paper had a colossal influence, for all sorts of reasons, among them the fact that his audience was all too ready to be convinced. Other voices had been uttering similar warnings for years. In 1883 the prophet of the single tax reform, Henry George, had pointed with alarm to the filling-up of the West and the continued influx of immigrants: 'What, in a few years more, are we to do for a dumping-ground? Will it make our difficulty the less that our human garbage can vote?' In 1886 the *North American Review* announced, quite wrongly, that 'the public domain of the United States is now exhausted'. Americans knew, before Turner told them, that their country had radically altered, and they did not much like it. The census of 1890 had also shown that the foreign-born element in the population now numbered over nine million (the total US population in that year was sixty-three million) and although as a percentage of the whole this was not much of an increase on the pre-Civil War figure (14 per cent instead of 13 per cent) it was easy to feel dangerously swamped by the incomers, especially as they tended to concentrate conspicuously in a few urban centres. Not only that: the composition of the immigration was changing rapidly. By 1890, when 445,680 Europeans were admitted, fully 25 per cent were from eastern or southern Europe: were Catholics, Greek Orthodox or Jews; Italians, Greeks, Hungarians or Slavs. Numbers and proportions of this 'new immigration' were going to go on rising steadily for the next two decades and more.

American history has been largely the story of migrations. That of the hundred years or so between the Battle of Waterloo and the outbreak of the First World War must certainly be reckoned the largest peaceful migration in recorded history; probably the largest of any kind, ever. It is reckoned that some thirty-five million persons entered the United States during that period, not to mention the large numbers who were also moving to such places as Argentina and Australia. Historians may come to discern that in the twentieth and later centuries this movement was dwarfed when Africa, Asia and South America began to send out their peoples; but if so they will be observing a pattern, of a whole continent in motion, that was first laid down in nineteenth-century Europe. Only the French seemed to be substantially immune to the virus. Otherwise, all caught it, and all travelled. English, Irish, Welsh, Scots, Germans, Scandinavians, Spaniards, Italians, Poles, Greeks, Jews, Portuguese, Dutch, Hungarians, Czechs, Croats, Slovenes, Serbs, Slovaks, Ukrainians, Lithuanians, Russians, Basques. There were general and particular causes.

As regards the general causes, the rise in population meant that more and more people were trying to earn their living on the same amount of land; inevitably some were squeezed off it. The increasing cost of the huge armies and navies, with their need for up-to-date equipment, that every great European power maintained, implied heavier and heavier taxes which many found difficult or impossible to pay, and mass conscription, which quite as many naturally wanted to avoid. The opening up of new, superbly productive lands in the United States, Canada, Australia, New Zealand and the Ukraine, coupled with the availability of steamers and steam trains to distribute their produce, meant that European peasants could not compete effectively in the world market: they would always be undersold, especially as the victory of free trade was casting down the old mercantilist barriers everywhere. Steam was important in other ways too. It became a comparatively quick and easy matter to cross land and sea, and to get news from distant parts. The invention of the electric telegraph also speeded up the diffusion of news, especially after a cable was successfully laid across the Atlantic in 1866. New printing and paper-making machines and a rapidly spreading literacy made large-circulation newspapers possible for the first time. In short, horizons widened, even for the stay-at-home. Most important of all, the dislocations in society brought about by the French Revolution, the Industrial Revolution and the various wars and tumults of nineteenth-century Europe shattered the old ways. New states came into being, old ones disappeared, frontiers were recast, the laws of land-tenure were radically altered, internal customs barriers and feudal dues both disappeared, payment in money replaced payment in kind, new industries stimulated new wants and destroyed the self-sufficiency of peasant households and the saleability of peasant products. The basic structure of rural Europe was transformed. Bad times pushed, good times pulled (American factories were usually clamouring for workers): small wonder that the peoples moved. It was a necessary phase in their development, which roughly followed a standard pattern everywhere. The Industrial Revolution would first make itself felt as a disturbing force, driving people off their farms and into emigration, or factories, or both. Then it slowed down the increase in the birth-rate, it raised the standard of living, it created new employment on a large scale. Consequently emigration fell off. By the end of the century the British and the Germans were no longer the leading nations among the migrants: their industrialization had reached maturity. Their place was taken by the comparatively backward Poles and Italians.

Particular reasons were just as important as these general ones. For example: between 1845 and 1848 Ireland suffered the terrible potato famine. A million people died of starvation or disease, a million more emigrated (1846–51). Matters were little better when the Great Famine was over: it was followed by lesser ones, and the basic weaknesses of the Irish economy made the outlook hopeless anyway. Mass emigration was a natural resort, at first to America, then, in the twentieth century, increasingly, to England and Scotland (a fact regularly and unfortunately overlooked by most Irish-Americans today, who seem to think that they are Ireland's only overseas representatives). Emigration was encouraged, in the Irish case as in many others, by letters sent home and by remittances of money. The first adventurers thus helped to pay the expenses of their successors.

Political reasons could sometimes drive Europeans across the Atlantic. In 1848 some thousands of Germans fled the failure of the liberal revolution of that year (but many thousands more emigrated for purely economic reasons). Pogroms in Tsarist Russia later brought large numbers of Jews to America. The collapse of the Kingdom of the Two Sicilies in 1860 destroyed the economy of southern Italy by exposing it to competition from the north: hence, in due course, the arrival of the Sicilians and Neapolitans. Swedes and Norwegians abandoned the struggle of farming in their cold and narrow fields, and once more set out for Vinland the Good. European and American commerce began to stir up the ancient societies of the East: so Japanese and Chinese began to settle in California and Hawaii.[9]

If such external stimuli faltered, American enterprise was more than willing to fill the gap. The high cost of labour had been a constant in American history since the first settlements; now, as the Industrial Revolution made itself felt, the need for workers was greater than ever. The supply of native white Americans was too small to meet the demand: while times were good on the family farm, as they were on the whole until the 1880s, or while there

9 Hawaii was slowly drawn into the economic network of the United States in the later nineteenth century. It was annexed in 1898 and became a state of the Union in 1959. Asiatic emigration to the islands was facilitated by the demographic collapse of the native Hawaiians under the impact of Asian and European diseases.

was new land to be taken up in the West, the drift out of agriculture (which was becoming a permanent feature of American, as of all industrialized, society) would not be large enough to fill the factories. Theoretically the shortfall might have been made up by emigration, both black and white, from the South; but the sharecropping system and the dreadful interlockings of a society based on racial rivalry tied Southerners of both colours to their blighted homeland, and anyway Northern workers would soon have made trouble if large numbers of blacks had been brought among them. So employers looked for the hands they needed in Europe, whether skilled, like Cornish miners, or unskilled, like Irish navvies. Then, the transcontinental railroads badly needed settlers on their Western land grants, as well as labourers: they could not make regular profits until the lands their tracks crossed were regularly producing crops that needed carrying to market. Soon every port in Europe knew the activities of American shipping lines and their agents, competing with each other to offer advantageous terms to possible emigrants. They stuck up posters, they advertised in the press, they patiently answered inquiries, and they shepherded their clients from their native villages, by train, to the dockside, and then made sure that they were safely stowed in the steerage.

Steerage was never a particularly pleasant experience. In the days of sail it was appalling. Apart from the frequent scandals, of captains who went to sea with inadequate supplies or who sought to make dishonest profits either by overcharging their passengers for what they fed them or by simply not feeding them enough (sometimes people actually starved to death), or of brutal crews, or of owners who sent out unseaworthy vessels (the Irish had particularly horrible experiences in these 'coffin-ships' at the time of the famine, when they could not afford to be choosy), or of shipping brokers, who chartered whatever vessels they could find, however rotten, and then touted for emigrants until they could crowd in no more (these were known as 'paper ships'), there were the inevitable uncertainties of the weather – the crossing was supposed to last no more than six weeks, but it might take more than three months – and the appalling living conditions, scarcely changed from the days of the *Mayflower*. There was very little room, so there was no privacy; hygiene was minimal; all the passengers were seasick over each other; there was no ventilation. According to Herman Melville, the author of *Moby Dick*, steerage smelt exactly like and as strong as a cesspool. Because of the danger of fire in wooden ships, cooking was difficult or impossible; such food as there was was hard to store or preserve, hence the custom of taking along live animals, which added to the general dirt, stink and unhealthiness; everything got damp and nothing could be got really dry. It is not surprising that the mortality figures at times recalled those of the old slave ships. On one voyage 108 German passengers died out of a total of 544. In 1853 the *Washington*, a New York vessel specially built for the migrant traffic, lost ninety-four passengers from cholera on one voyage.

The coming of iron and steam made a vast difference. To be sure, steerage was still invariably uncomfortable and, for many, actively unpleasant. Sea-sickness was still nearly universal, and since many people were still crammed into open bunks it was still impossible to get away from the sight, sound and stench of each other's distress. Many other evils were as little amended. But at least the voyage would now last only a short and certain period (failing really violent storms); the journey from north-western Europe now seldom lasted more than twelve days. The passengers contrived to enjoy themselves, singing folk-songs and dancing on deck. Mortality dropped: in 1880, for example, when 457,257 immigrants landed in America, only 269 died at sea. As time went on other conditions began to improve. The great steam lines – Cunard, White Star, Hamburg-Amerika and so on – competed with each other for the traffic. Industrial employers subsidized them, as an inducement to carry plenty of steerage passengers; in rivalry for the money, they began to pamper the migrants (as no doubt their directors put it to themselves). By the eve of the First World War, when the traffic was at its height, conditions on the bottom deck were quite tolerable. Even tablecloths made an appearance. This was just as well, for it eased the transition from the migrant business to tourism which followed the war, as America closed her doors to poor Europeans and Europe opened hers to prosperous Americans.

Famous photographs still show us the bewilderment of the arrivals at New York: peasant women grasping small children with their right hands, huge bundles with their left; men in black hats and vast moustaches looking wary; immigration officials looking weary. Various fates awaited the travellers. Proportionately few of them went to settle the public lands in the West, for they mostly lacked the skills needed to hack homesteads out of the wilderness. Instead, when they could, the farmers among them bought already cleared land from restless Americans who, having used up the soil and caring nothing for husbandry, were all too ready to move on. The only exception to this came about in Wisconsin and Minnesota. These states were largely settled after the Homestead Act came into operation, and not even prudent Scandinavians could resist the lure of free land. So they made their way to that region and took it over: Vinland at last.

The boldest immigrants might take one of the special trains to California. These were subsidized, like the liners, the object being to get able-bodied young men to the mines and wharves of the West as quickly as possible. Conditions compared favourably with those in steerage, but otherwise there was not much to be said for them. Families, even those which took the trains, seldom got much further than Chicago or Milwaukee, which became the great German stronghold of the prairie states, as Cincinnati was of the Middle West. And although the immigrants were conspicuous in the great surge of the internal American movement which was carrying the centre of population ever further westward[10] their chief cities remained Boston and

10 This notional point crossed the Mississippi for the first time in 1981.

New York, where they first landed. Of the two New York grew the faster. It had so much to offer, employment above all, for its great age had dawned, the era when it was the real capital of the United States. Its harbour attracted the ships, its excellent canal and rail connections with the interior made it the inevitable middle man for all who wanted to import or export. Even before the Civil War the South had sent much of its cotton to New York for re-export to Old or New England; after the war every region did the same with its own produce, whether foodstuffs, other raw materials or manufactured goods. From New York they flowed out to the Atlantic and, more and more, across the continent. Orders for articles of every kind flowed in upon the city and were filled by its innumerable manufacturing establishments. For New York was the country's greatest industrial city as well as its greatest port and financial centre. Factories were uncommon: instead, a myriad of little workshops supplied the consumers' needs, for example, in the matter of shirts and dresses. Much of the work could be and was done at home, in the slums. These now developed with extraordinary speed on both the east and west sides of Manhattan Island, as the city built up as far as Central Park (prudently reserved and planned by Frederick Law Olmsted, an abolitionist turned landscape architect: without him the site would have been built over like everywhere else on that expensive lump of rock) and then passed it into the fields of Harlem. Every empty tenement room was a vessel waiting to be filled with cheap labour; none had to wait long. Housing conditions in New York soon became a scandal; so were working conditions, and they were often identical. In boom times an immigrant family, or at least its female and youthful members, would sit round the table throughout the day and much of the night, cutting out, stitching, lace-making, fine-sewing, in bad light and worse air. In slump times they might not be so fortunate, and a stream of returning migrants would fill the steerage from West to East. But the westward stream was always the larger.

Beginning life in the New World was appallingly difficult. Immigrants arriving at New York had first to run the gauntlet of the officials at the great reception centres of Castle Garden and, later, Ellis Island, where they would be medically examined, have their nationality and names recorded (often with hilarious inaccuracy) and have to prove that they were neither going to take jobs which American workers might fill nor become charges on the public from lack of funds. Since these last two requirements were contradictory, it is perhaps surprising that in a normal year 80 per cent of the immigrants got through without much difficulty. Then they would have to shake off the horde of dockside sharks waiting to take advantage of their inexperience by seizing their baggage and exacting a fee, and taking them to filthy lodging-houses, for a further fee, where they would be grossly over-charged until their money ran out, when they would be thrown into the street, perhaps ending up in the pauper refuge maintained for their reception. Those were luckiest who were met at the docks by friends and relations who could shepherd them through the difficulties of learning English and finding a job and a home. After non-English-speaking nationalities had established themselves in large numbers they set up efficient reception networks. A young Jew arriving from a Russian *stetl*, or ghetto, might thus be accommodated in a boarding-house run by a Jewish matriarch who, if she did not consider him good enough to marry one of her daughters, could at least pass him on to a town or neighbourhood where he could get employment. But if these resources failed and the travellers were nevertheless to escape the clutches of the many scoundrels who wanted to exploit them, their likeliest resort would be to the local politicians. These too were exploiters; but they were not so much interested in an immigrant's money as in the vote which they would shortly enable him to cast. In return for that valuable possession there was little that they would not and nothing that they could not do.

This was not only the age of the rising cities; it was the great age of the city machines, as they were called. Some, like the Democratic organization in New York, Tammany Hall, founded in 1789, had fairly respectable origins; others grew up in response to conditions, or in emulation of St Tammany.[11] By the 1870s all, without exception, were the scandal and the glory of their time. The immigrants played an essential part in their development. To understand how and why requires a glance at the forces which brought about the development of the machines.

It was a new stage in the politics of patronage. No longer was the politician's job simply that of manipulating the spoils system to reward party workers and of working the state and national governments to further or defend the interests of a particular place, state, region or big economic interest. Now the great railroad companies needed land grants. Other industrial concerns needed charters of incorporation (which would give them the privileges belonging, in English law, to limited liability companies) and, sometimes, the assistance of the state militia in suppressing violent strikes. The new cities needed all sorts of facilities: street lighting, sewers, police, roads, bridges, harbour works, prisons, schools, housing, parks, hospitals. It was inevitable that these interests should look to politics for their appeasement; and inevitable that the politicians, ever anxious to make themselves useful, for a price, should do what they could to oblige. The late nineteenth and the early twentieth centuries together amounted to a period in which various experiments were tried to see what was the best way of satisfying the demands of the American people on their political system. Bossism was the first of these experiments.

11 Tammany was a Delaware chieftain who, traditionally, was among those who welcomed William Penn to America in 1682. During the eighteenth century the memory of this friendly Indian was kept green and he was posthumously endowed with the combined powers of Hercules, Aesculapius and Alfred the Great. During the Revolution 'St Tammany' societies were founded in opposition to the pro-British societies of St George. Tammany became the chosen patron saint of the Revolutionary army.

The machine was firmly based on the city district known as the ward – was, in fact, little more than an alliance of wards. A ward boss maintained his ascendancy in his neighbourhood by methods that would have been recognized by Sam Adams of the North End of Boston. George Washington Plunkitt, a luminary of Tammany Hall, explained it all at the beginning of the twentieth century:

I know every man, woman, and child in the Fifteenth District, except them that's been born this summer – and I know some of them too. I know what they like and what they don't like, what they are strong at and what they are weak in, and I reach them by approachin' at the right side.

For instance, here's how I gather in the young men. I hear of a young feller that's proud of his voice, thinks that he can sing fine. I ask him to come around to Washington Hall and join our Glee Club. He comes and sings, and he's a follower of Plunkitt for life. Another young feller gains a reputation as a base-ball player in a vacant lot. I bring him into our base-ball club. That fixes him. You'll find him workin' for my ticket at the polls next election day . . . I rope them all in by givin' them opportunities to show themselves off. I don't trouble them with political arguments. I just study human nature and act accordin'.

A competent city boss expected his precinct captains and ward-heelers to be as assiduous and knowledgeable as himself. He and his men did their utmost to look after the immigrants and to hurry along their citizenship papers. When these last came through, the machine had secured itself another little band of faithful voters. As Plunkitt remarked, 'The poor are the most grateful people in the world, and, let me tell you, they have more friends in their neighbourhoods than the rich have in theirs.' At ward level the machine operated more like an enormous family or a tribe than anything else. Plunkitt, for example, was always the first at the scene of a fire (devastating blazes continued to be a feature of American city life, as in colonial times), making sure that the victims had shelter, clothes, and a little money to see them through the emergency. (It might of course have been better if the city government, which Tammany Hall usually controlled, had done something to reduce the risk of fire in the slums instead of accepting pay-offs from landlords to wink at breaches in the regulations.) In summer huge picnics would be organized to take the neighbourhood kids out of town to a little fresh air and green grass. Trouble with the courts would bring the bosses into action again, to interpret where necessary, explain, and generally fix things (including, if need be, the judge – but he was probably a creature of the machine anyway). In winter the bosses made sure that there was always some fuel, and perhaps a Christmas turkey, for the deserving (that is, the party faithful). Men who were sacked were reinstated, the unemployed were found jobs, often on the city payroll. In return all that was asked was zeal on election day. 'Vote early and often' was the cry. Boss Butler of St Louis was occasionally known to call out to his men, in full hearing of the police at the voting-station, 'Are there any more repeaters out here that want to vote again?'

This system was wonderfully adapted to the needs, and even more to the experience, of the immigrants. They came from a world where the state was little more than a distant instrument of oppression which taxed them heavily, punished them brutally, took away their sons for years at a time as conscripts and gave them little or nothing in return. In such a world the only reliance was on family and neighbours. They came to America, and, lo!, things operated in much the same way as at home. Family, neighbours and, in times of unusual difficulty, a local chieftain to rely on and obey. No wonder that they settled in rapidly. The Irish did it best. They brought with them a literate knowledge of English, substantial experience of electoral politics (largely learned in Daniel O'Connell's great campaigns of the 1820s and 1830s), a spontaneous clannishness and a useful strain of Catholicism. They had long looked up to their priests as leaders; the habit continued in America, the more so as the priests still had political objectives, especially the fostering of a system of parish schools where good Irish children could study, untainted by the godlessness and Protestantism of the free public schools which were almost universally available in late-nineteenth-century America. Since there were always more children than Catholic schools for them it was frequently necessary to do battle with public authorities to try to modify the public schools' curricula. So priests and bosses were both anxious to organize and sustain a solid Catholic-Irish voting bloc, and worked together. It is no wonder that the Irish very soon came to dominate the city organizations. 'The Irish was born to rule,' said Plunkitt vain-gloriously, and compared their performance in New York favourably (and justly) with that of the native Americans in Philadelphia, where wholesale plunder of the public treasury ('boodling') was the order of the day. The only drawback was that as they prospered the Irish tended to move out of the city centre to the more salubrious suburbs that were springing up everywhere. This dispersion of the faithful was a sore point to the bosses. They began to make it a condition of holding a job under the machine (policeman, fireman, street-sweeper, clerk) that the holder should stay in his first place of residence and continue to vote there.

But this was a puny check on a great movement. The vast wandering of the peoples, the insatiable quest for betterment, which brought Jews from the Pripet Marshes to New York and Chicago, and took American farmers from New York to the Pacific Coast, where they met Chinese from Fukien and Kwantung come to work as navvies on the railroads, was not to be balked. The cities now developed what one wise commentator has called the Tenement Trail:[12] it was shorter in miles than the Oregon Trail or the Long Drive, but it took years or decades to get from its beginning to its

12 Samuel Lubell, *The Future of American Politics* (New York, Doubleday Anchor edn, 1956), pp. 65–71.

end. A family which started in a squalid one-room apartment on the Lower East Side would gradually promote itself to better accommodation as its savings and income mounted, until eventually it could cross the rivers into the boroughs of the Bronx, Queens and Brooklyn. The places it left behind were never empty: other families, intent on making as good, followed closely behind. The process goes on today, which explains why the poorer parts of New York, once solidly Irish, Jewish or Italian, are now just as solidly black or Puerto Rican. The big city still holds out its promise of improvement, though unfortunately, nowadays, the promise seems to be more than a little delusive.

But in the nineteenth century the promise was kept, and not only in New York. Most of the immigrants had left home in hopes of bettering themselves, and their letters home were full of proud claims that they had done so: 'We have now a comfortable dwelling and two acres of ground planted with potatoes, Indian corn, melons, etc. I have two hogs, one ewe and a lamb; cows in the spring were as high as 33 dollars, but no doubt I shall have one in the fall' (an Englishman writing from New Hampshire, 1821); 'We can eat our beefsteaks or ham every morning with our breakfast' (a Welshman, 1846); 'A breakfast here consists of chicken, mutton, beef, or pork, warm or cold wheat bread, butter, white cheese, eggs, or small pancakes, the best coffee, tea, cream and sugar' (a Norwegian woman, writing from Wisconsin, 1847); 'I am exceedingly well pleased at coming to this land of plenty. On arrival I purchased 120 acres of land at $5 [£1] an acre . . . You must bear in mind that I have purchased the land out, and it is to me and mine an "estate for ever", without a landlord, an agent or tax-gatherer to trouble me. I would advise all my friends to quit Ireland – the country most dear to me; as long as they remain in it they will be in bondage and misery' (an Irishman, Wisconsin, 1849);[13] 'I had planned last Christmas that I would spend this Christmas in Sweden – but when I gave more thought to the matter, what can one do in Sweden but work for sour bread and salt herring?' (a Swede, 1896).

Of course, not all were pleased. 'O, that I had never seen this land, but had remained in Germany, apprenticed to a humble country craftsman!' lamented a Jewish pedlar in 1842. 'From what I understand,' wrote an Ulsterman to his sister in 1787, 'David will be for coming here and I will say nothing in such a case between you but that I am confident you will have time enough to repent it if you come.' Another such, a century later, a clerk reduced to casual manual labour, was entirely disillusioned: 'Any person who can live at home at all had better stay there, for in this country I can neither see comfort nor pleasure . . . of course people writing home won't tell the truth but will give glowing accounts of everything; don't

13 I wonder how long it was before this settler discovered that in fact he had not escaped the tax-gatherer, a common enough figure on the frontier, who at times seemed a heavy burden to farmers.

believe a word of it.' Some were homesick, more failed to prosper; perhaps a third of the entire number went back to Europe. Towards the end of the period 1815–1914, 'birds of passage' appeared – individual workers, especially Italians, who went to America each spring when jobs were easiest to come by and returned home for the winter. But two-thirds of the total number of entrants stayed in the United States for good.

They were not entirely welcome, and got less so as time went on. The immigration came in three great tides, each stronger than the last. The first rose in the 1830s and 1840s to a high-water mark in 1854, when 427,833 new arrivals were recorded; the second, starting in the seventies, rose to a height of 788,992 in 1882;[14] the third brought in an average of one million immigrants a year in the decade before First World War. These tides were roughly connected with the push-and-pull of the American and European economies, as well as with purely political factors, such as the policy of the Russian Tsars towards the Jews. There was a long American tradition of welcome to these incomers: the fact that every white American was the descendant of migrants does not seem to have mattered very much; the belief that the United States was a haven of liberty to the persecuted did. At other times businessmen loved to calculate how much a skilled immigrant was worth to the American economy (and indeed the amount was substantial: during the later nineteenth century it was reckoned that one factory worker in three was an immigrant). Finally, in times of prosperity and self-confidence, such as those which immediately followed the Civil War or immediately preceded the First World War, it was hard to think that the immigrants, the numerical proportion of whom in the population remained constant, were a very dangerous threat, if they were a threat at all: 'let 'em all come' was the attitude. But against these views were others, equally indigenous; and they too, like the immigration, had their three tides of potency: in the early 1850s, in the eighties and early nineties, and in the First World War and its aftermath.

The first significant eruption of nativism, as hostility to immigrants is called, occurred in the early 1850s, as has already been described.[15] It was expressed largely in terms of the no-Popery tradition, which was enjoying its last significant triumph in England at the same period.[16] Know-Nothingism subsided as the Irish immigration, against which it was chiefly directed, fell away, and as the all-absorbing problem of slavery came to dominate politics again. The next upsurge of nativism came during the slackest years of the

14 These figures, though precise, are not entirely accurate. Whether they err in counting up or counting down is not clear from *The Statistical History of the United States*, where I found them. Thus, arrivals at the land borders of the United States were not properly counted before 1904; while after 1867 no attempt was made to exclude from the reckoning citizens of the United States returning to their country.

15 See above, pp. 303–4.

16 In 1850 the Pope established a system of dioceses in England for the first time since the Reformation, and created Nicholas Wiseman Cardinal and Archbishop of Westminster. This so-called 'papal aggression' provoked a storm of anti-Catholic feeling in England.

late-nineteenth-century depression. Protestantism was no longer such a dominant force in American society, nor were the Irish regarded with quite so much enmity; so it is not surprising that hostility was now largely expressed in economic and political terms. A series of violent clashes between largely immigrant workers and the capitalist class – a railroad strike and riots of 1877, the Haymarket affair in Chicago in 1886,[17] the Homestead strike of 1892, when an immigrant socialist nearly succeeded in murdering Henry Frick, another railroad strike in 1894 – made it seem that all too many immigrants were now violent revolutionaries, intent on stirring up class conflict and destroying the American political and social system. Native Americans might have been less alarmed by all this had they not begun to be aware of the emergence of grave social problems connected with industrialism and urbanization, and of the glaring disparity between the enormous wealth of the Astors, Vanderbilts, Morgans, Carnegies, Fricks and Rockefellers and the miserable living conditions of so many workers. With the return of good times after 1896 this movement also passed.

In due time, however, it was succeeded by another, the most formidable, and eventually the most effective, of them all. The roots of this movement were as usual to be found in social anxiety, and the policy which its supporters wanted Congress to adopt was one of immigration restriction; but the nature of the anxiety was now more various than ever before, and the justification of the policy was for the first time racialist. The labour unions, now organized in the American Federation of Labor, feared the immigrants as competitors for their jobs and as tending, by their willingness to work for low wages, to keep the income of the industrial workers low. The conservative patricians of New England, prosperous persons of English descent, resented their loss of political power to the Irish and Italians, and were prepared to exploit any form of social discontent to regain power in the cities, or at least to lose no more of it. In the South it was feared that immigrants did not have the correct racial attitudes: five Italians were lynched, in Tallulah, Louisiana, for associating on equal terms with blacks; in Georgia, in 1914, Leo Frank, a Jewish factory owner who had been convicted, on the flimsiest evidence, of murdering one of his woman employees, was taken from jail and hanged by a hysterical mob. Old-style anti-Catholicism supported a journal called *The Menace*, which concentrated on the popish plot. Growing international anxiety, which fed on the half-conscious perception that in the world of modern technology America was no longer invulnerable to foreign aggression, coupled with a long tradition of hostility to Asians, led in California to outbreaks of severe hostility to Japanese immigrants, just as the earlier movement had produced the Chinese Exclusion Act of 1882 and its successors, which forbade all Chinese immigration. This ominous conjunction of forces generated an equally ominous ideology. A library of books like Madison Grant's *The Passing of the Great Race* (1916) warned the Americans

17 See below, p. 419.

that they could not safely continue to admit members of inferior races to their country, and asserted that all races were inferior to the glorious Nordic race, whether they were Alpine, Mediterranean, Jewish, black or Oriental. Congress responded to political pressure by setting up an Immigration Commission, chaired by one William P. Dillingham, to investigate the immigrants and make recommendations. The resultant Dillingham Report was published in 1911; it consisted of forty-two volumes of tendentiously organized data tending to draw a distinction between the 'old' immigrants from the West and North of Europe and the 'new' immigration from the South: naturally it found that the new immigrants were deeply unsuited to life in the free, Protestant, Nordic American republic. In this way official support was given to the ever-more-popular farrago of racist nonsense that was then masquerading as anthropology.

It is rather too easy to condemn the nativists for their panic and their prejudices, which were in the end to work so much mischief, playing a part in bringing about the war with Japan and in excluding European political refugees during the 1930s when they had never needed help more. It should be borne in mind that the great nineteenth-century migration was, in modern terms, a very odd affair. No country today can or will permit the perpetual, unregulated incursion of foreign millions; yet such permissiveness was normal then, as the empty places of earth had to be filled. Timid, absurd and nasty though the nativists were, their attitudes foreshadowed those which, one way or another, necessarily shape governmental policies today, when the world is no longer empty. Mass migration nevertheless continues: politics, war, economics, technology make it inevitable – as inevitable as resistance to it. Today's struggle, in every nation, is to try to find a just balance between these forces. Nowhere is the achievement of such a balance more likely and unlikely than in the United States, with its traditions of rejection and welcome, its poverty and its wealth, its space and its crowd. Today its people grapple with the problems of new Mexican, Puerto Rican, Cuban and South-East Asian immigration, not to mention the migration of blacks from the South to the Northern cities. It is not for a historian to predict the outcome, but the spectacle of present difficulties makes it easier to have sympathy and respect for the achievements, whatever their limitations, of earlier generations of Americans.

The thirty-five millions were, after all, absorbed. It is now fashionable to denigrate the image of the melting-pot, made popular by a play of that name (written by an English Jew, Israel Zangwill) that had a long run in New York in 1909; for although the descendants of the immigrants have been thoroughly Americanized in many ways, not least in language, politics and manners, they have not lost, nor, by their fellow-citizens, been allowed to lose, their sense of apartness: ethnic groups are perhaps more fundamental to the structure of American society than economic ones, and show every sign of equal permanence. In short, not everything was melted in the pot. But a lot was, and the process happened remarkably swiftly. Already by the beginning of the twentieth century (with some assistance from the great capitalists, still concerned about their labour supply) the immigrants had become sufficiently integrated into American society to form a powerful voting block. Presidential candidates courted them at election time; Presidents vetoed bills which sought to apply a literacy test to new arrivals. The old tradition of more or less free entry (except for the Chinese) was successfully defended until the First World War. The effectiveness of the defence shows how thoroughly and intelligently the immigrants had learned the trick of American politics; the fact that it was possible at all is surely notable evidence of the essential liberalism of American political institutions.

Yet it would be a struggle to maintain them. The immigrants came to a country where social evolution had always proceeded very rapidly, under an incessant series of new stimuli: the Revolution, the opening of the West, the Civil War, industrialism, immigration itself. The ground was never still: America had institutionalized the earthquake. In no other respect was it more clearly the first of modern nations. The transformation proceeded at such speed, with such leaps and bounds, and so entirely regardless of the capacity of society to absorb and profit from it, that it is not surprising that there were repeated crises of adjustment, or that many ordinary Americans found the whole thing too much to be borne. The immigrant question was not the only one to agitate them during the Age of Gold; nor even, as the next two chapters will show, the most distressing.

18 Congressional Government
and its Critics 1869–96

Public office is a public trust.

Grover Cleveland

We voted with our party no matter where it went.
We voted with our party till we haven't got a cent.

Populist song, 1890

The federal government did nothing to check and little to modify the most
notable tendencies of post-bellum American society, whether good or bad.
It would have been futile to oppose the energies which were making America
over, and undemocratic too, since the great majority of the people shared
the outlook and values of the new capitalists. What is perhaps surprising is
the extent to which the politicians were able to make themselves useful
in the new age without noticeably altering their old procedures and institutions. No amendment to the Constitution was passed between 1870 and
1913, and the Reconstruction amendments were ignored or re-interpreted
as much as possible, so that they might not stand in the way of a return to
the old system. The Civil War could not be forgotten, but at times it seemed
as if there were a conspiracy to pretend that it had not happened. Slavery
had polarized and dramatized pre-Civil War politics. Its extinction made
the pretence all the easier to sustain. For the slavery issue had cut across
all party and institutional lines, had sharply limited the possibility of compromise between sections, states and individuals, and in the end, by bringing
on a revolutionary war, had profoundly altered the relations of the executive
with the legislature and the judiciary, and of the national government with
the states. Now the war was over, slavery was dead and the work of Abraham
Lincoln was quickly undone. At times it seemed as if the politicians were
trying to undo the work of Andrew Jackson too.

Never before or since has the Presidency counted for so little as it did in
the last three decades of the nineteenth century. Undistinguished Presidents

followed one another (Grant, Hayes, Garfield, Arthur, Cleveland, Harrison and again Cleveland) without making much of a mark. The hero of Vicksburg and Appomattox was at a loss in the White House. It was never shown that he himself was dishonest, but members of his family certainly took every possible advantage of his position to enrich themselves, and members of his administration, at every level, including his private secretary, were thoroughly corrupt. The most noticeable thing about Grant's successor, President Hayes (apart from the circumstances of his election), was that his wife, 'Lemonade Lucy', refused to serve any alcoholic drinks in the White House. The most noticeable thing about President Garfield was that he was shot by Charles J. Guiteau, a disappointed office-seeker. His Vice-President and successor, Chester A. Arthur, a veteran spoilsman, pleasantly surprised everyone by his dignified performance as President, but that was all. And so it went on for more than twenty years.

Never before or since have the great barons of Congress loomed so large. The ascendancy over the government which the struggle with Andrew Johnson had given them was not lightly relinquished, nor was the control of the spoils system, although in 1883 public opinion, aroused by the murder of Garfield, compelled the passage of the Pendleton Act, the first attempt to reform the civil service by introducing competitive exams to be taken by candidates for places in the bureaucracy. The Speaker of the House of Representatives, an autocrat in that chamber, bulked larger in political life, most of the time, than any President. Senators like Roscoe Conkling of New York and James G. Blaine of Maine exploited their influence with entire selfishness, caring about nothing but their own desires and ambitions. To them, business corporations existed to subsidize politicians; politics was simply the means to bully businessmen; either way, the faction leaders – 'Half-Breeds' or 'Stalwarts' in the slang of the time – got richer. It was small wonder that politics stank in the nostrils of the fastidious; or that one chapter in the classical work on America in this period is entitled 'Why the Best Men Do Not Go into Politics'.[1]

Never has the two-party system been more rigid or more triumphant or more entirely a battle for office between the Ins and the Outs. There were still deep divisions within the nation, of course, and more were developing, but they were not of a kind to keep practical men from the 'wheeling and dealing', the realistic division of the spoils, the fixing of elections and the hoodwinking of voters which were to them the very stuff of politics. Never have the states been left more entirely to their own devices.

The result was a caricature of the Jeffersonian system. The federal government once more accepted strict limitations, and the principles of republicanism were proclaimed from every stump; but the spirit – greedy, selfish and short-sighted – was everything that Jefferson would have deplored. And since the age saw the collapse of every social structure which the Jeffersonians

1 See James Bryce, *The American Commonwealth* (first published in 1888).

had held dear, it was peculiar that Jeffersonian political shibboleths should still be affirmed.

Various explanations might be offered for this paradox of an old politics and a new society. Some would argue that it was a tribute to the wisdom of the Founding Fathers, whose Constitution was sufficiently flexible to contain the revolutionary forces of the Age of Gold without too much creaking. Others might as plausibly argue that the same story proved the essential weakness of the Constitutional political system; having shown itself impotent to end slavery peacefully, it was now equally incapable of ordering the industrialization of America humanely. Others again would point to the frightful shocks which the system had endured since 1852. Apart from the central horror, of Americans killing each other in battle, one President had been murdered, another impeached; three great political parties had split (the Whigs in 1852, the Democrats in 1860, the Republicans in 1872) and one, the Whigs, had vanished entirely. Federalism had proved impotent to contain the sectional conflict, and the Union itself had nearly succumbed. Small wonder that when eventually the dust settled there was a determined effort to restore what all thought of as normality. The Supreme Court led the way. It had suffered grievously in its authority during the war, when, for example, Lincoln had defied its fiat and suspended the writ of *habeas corpus*. From the moment the war was over the Court did all it could, by the direction and detail of its decisions, to cut down the growth of constitutional innovations and to restore its own authority and the autonomous power of the states, even if it meant watering down the effect of the Fourteenth and Fifteenth Amendments. The *Dred Scott* decision, with its severe restrictions on the power of the federal government, could not actually be revived, but the Court went further in that direction than would have seemed imaginable at the height of Radical Reconstruction, and the country acquiesced. It was a later generation, recovering from a later war, which invented the awful word 'normalcy', but the craving for a quiet life after the storm was the same in 1877 as in 1920.

It ought also to be borne in mind that although the changes brought about by the Industrial Revolution were rapid and profound, they were not as yet so widespread as to engulf the whole of America, or anything like it. Most native Americans had been born in the countryside, indeed most of them still lived there. A political system which had been designed to suit a republic of farmers was therefore not so out of date as it might seem. Besides, to the precise extent that it reflected what was becoming a past distribution of power, it was unlikely to change: rural politicians had the usual professional fondness for gerrymanders and were not willing to sacrifice any of the advantages the old system gave them, whatever the injustice. Not for a very long time indeed, not until 1962, would the courts be ready to impose the rule of absolute equality between voters on all elections, state, municipal and national. Until then the rural interests would be over-represented in Congress and the other chambers of power, and they took every care to keep it that way.

The most important consideration was probably the sheer intractability of the case. Perhaps the political system needed wholesale reform (women were claiming the right to vote); but no one ever had leisure to ponder the problem and make comprehensive suggestions. There was always a new election coming up, or a new distribution of the spoils to be undertaken in the wake of an electoral victory. The political system had been carried on even during the war, when a third of the states were out of the Union and a large portion of the main opposition party was tainted with treason. Office-holders and candidates had entangled themselves in commitments which could not be evaded in peace. Sudden emergencies, such as the crash of 1873, demanded all one's attention. Reform, if it was to come, would have to come piecemeal, and was slow on the road because of the mere complexity of life. The case is not unusual.

Meantime it could be said that the old system was not doing too badly by the country. There were some frightful scandals, to be sure. In 1869 Jay Gould and Jim Fisk took advantage of President Grant's gullibility to try to corner the gold supply, an operation which, to succeed, required the co-operation of the US Treasury. Since the project would wreck the money market, such co-operation could be got only by bribery; fortunately at the last moment the administration realized what was happening and, by selling gold in enormous quantities, broke the price and the Gould–Fisk 'corner'. The affair created a great stir; it was the first in a series of episodes which eventually discredited Grant and the Republican Congress of which he had made himself the obedient servant. The Democrats carried the House of Representatives in the election of 1874 and, as we have seen, made an almost successful bid for the Presidency in 1876; but they were not very convincing embodiments of the reforming principle. Their chief objection to the extravagance and alleged corruption of the Reconstruction governments in the South was that the freedmen were the chief beneficiaries; elsewhere their aim was to get a hand in the game themselves. Samuel Tilden, their candidate, had fought Tammany Hall a few years before, when it was dominated by the notorious boss Tweed, whose depredations cost New York city $100 million or more; but after all Tweed (who died in jail in 1878) was a Democrat too. It became generally accepted that the morals of politicians of either party were a joke. 'If a Congressman is a hog, what is a Senator?' inquired Henry Adams cynically (this latest twig on the old tree was too fastidious, or perhaps just too curmudgeonly, to be a politician, so he became a wit and a historian instead). In another saying of the age, an honest man (voter or politician) was defined as one who, when bought, stays bought. Some wag, defending the Pennsylvania state legislature against its enemies, said that it was the finest body of men that money could buy. The millionaires took the hint: until at least the turn of the century the state government was owned by Carnegie (steel), Frick (coal), Rockefeller (oil) and the Pennsylvania Railroad, which united their interests. Henry Demarest Lloyd said that

Standard Oil could do anything with the Pennsylvania legislature except refine it.

Yet it would be wrong to imagine that all the politicians and millionaires either were, or saw themselves as being, mere rogues. The capitalists were well aware of the enormous profits they might make, but they knew also that they ran enormous risks. They remembered the great Railway Mania in England in the forties, which had wiped out the savings of a generation. They competed mercilessly with each other, for in the totally unregulated market of the day the slightest trace of scruple was a weakness, laying you open to lethal attack, as Commodore Vanderbilt had found in his struggle with Jay Gould. The operation of laying railroads across America was on a vastly larger scale than anything ever attempted in Europe: no one could say when, if ever, it would show a profit. To succeed in the task, or at any rate to get a guarantee against failure, the capitalists needed the assistance of Congress. And if, to get adequate land grants, it proved necessary to bribe Congressmen, why not? The Congressmen and Senators themselves had seen to it that bribery was the only way of doing business with them. Frequently they would introduce bills so bothersome to business that they would be offered handsome sums to withdraw them. The money would be accepted, since obtaining it was the only point of the enterprise, and the bill would be dropped. This technique was known as 'the Strike'. Others would call it extortion.

Naturally the politicians did not take a severe view of themselves. Their patriotism was indisputable; many Congressmen had fought in the Civil War or had played their part as war Governors, Senators or Congressmen. If not exactly godly men, they were at least thorough Protestants. They believed in the glorious future of their country, and said so at every opportunity. They had never pretended to be disinterested; they were in politics to make a living and, if possible, get rich: it was the American way, and only while such benefits seemed likely would enough able recruits be found to fill the innumerable posts which the federal system created. Above all they were loyal to their parties and the principles which these stood for. To the outsider the differences between the parties might seem to be more geographical than ideological, and party principles might not seem to be worth all the emphasis that was placed on them; but to Republicans and Democrats these were all serious matters. They might indeed have argued that it was precisely the fusion between geography and political principles that gave the parties their value. A Republican from Pennsylvania, for example, with his strong commitment to protective tariffs and free enterprise, was obviously the man to represent a state whose prosperity depended, or at least was thought by the majority of its voters to depend, on just these arrangements. If he showed any sign of weakening in his support of them he could and would be quickly replaced. The minority interests of the state would equally readily turn to the Democrats, with their long-standing commitment to freer trade. Other issues, such as bribery and corruption, were of secondary importance to the voters, and everyone knew it.

It was just this genial acceptance of human weakness and greed which alienated the Mugwumps. They were one of the first groups of citizens to make their dissent matter. They were named by their opponents, who could not take seriously fine-drawn ladies and gentlemen who believed that politics, in America at any rate, ought to be something nobler than the arts of shabby compromise and raiding the public purse. The typical Mugwump was a member in good standing of the middle class, a citizen of the old Anglo-American stock, and (except in New York, where opposition to Tammany Hall cut across party divisions) a Republican: probably one of the former Liberal Republicans, who opposed Grant's re-election in 1872, possibly a former abolitionist, although the abolitionist temperament was usually too radical to be satisfied with any form of conventional politics, and after the death of slavery found, in many cases, new causes, either in the rising labour movement, of which Wendell Phillips became a powerful supporter, or in that for women's suffrage (a transition brilliantly depicted by Henry James in his novel *The Bostonians*, in 1886). As their enemies quickly realized, the Mugwumps' essential weakness was not their dislike of getting their own hands dirty, but their inability to recognize that others might have good reasons for being less squeamish. For instance, the city government of Philadelphia was notoriously corrupt: the ruling Republicans saw and seized all the opportunities for graft that new municipal necessities entailed. In 1841 a Gas Trust had been set up to bring coal gas, for light and heating, to Philadelphia. The Trust had been deliberately set up to be legally safe from political interference; but those who had designed it had not realized what would happen when one of the trustees was himself a politician. James McManes, an Irish immigrant, used his position on the Gas Trust to become the Boss of Philadelphia. He controlled the Public Buildings Commission, he controlled the schools and, sheltered by the legal immunity of the Gas Trust, he was able to conceal his financial dealings from the inquisitive. Soon thousands of workmen were dependent on McManes for their jobs, and of course voted as he told them on election day. Many, indeed, were expected to do more: they had to subscribe to the boss's campaign chest and work on their neighbours to get them to the polls (where, because the secret ballot had not yet been introduced, it was easy to make sure that they did the right thing, the more so as the police were under McManes's control too). Favoured contractors paid large sums to the politicians who employed them to lay gas-pipes or build schools, and recouped themselves out of charges to consumers and to the city authorities. Philadelphia's debt soared; when the respectable protested they found that gas was unaccountably slow in arriving in their neighbourhoods; and it was much the same with street paving, street lighting, public transport and sewage disposal. It was necessary to build a new City Hall; but perhaps it was not necessary to use the most expensive materials on the most magnificent scale (its tower is taller than the Great Pyramid and St Peter's in the Vatican), the cost of which (met by the taxpayers) of course included a cut for politicians. It was calculated that the Gas Ring had stolen some $8 million. So it is not surprising that the Democrats, proclaiming themselves as the party of reform, swept the city elections in 1876. Once in power they started cutting down on public works expenditure, which earned them the gratitude of the Mugwumps; but as they thereby also threw large numbers of manual labourers out of work the voters as a whole were less pleased and soon brought the Republicans back to power. Not until the early eighties was a typical Mugwump alliance of dissident Republicans and Democrats able to break the Gas Ring and give Philadelphia some semblance of efficient, honest government; and even that achievement was limited. According to James Bryce, it was but substituting a state boss for a city one.[2]

The true Mugwump never learned the obvious lesson from such stories: that somehow or other the poorer classes must be provided for, if only because they had votes. Political bosses might be, and often were, cold-hearted, coarse, narrow, greedy men, with no undue respect for the law; but they did have the priceless virtue of looking after their own people. 'I think that there's got to be in every ward a guy that any bloke can go to when he's in trouble and get help – not justice and the law, but help, no matter what he's done.'[3] Such was the philosophy of the bosses. Their whole influence depended on their helpfulness and reliability. If they made promises they kept them (which is partly why so many notorious scoundrels were known as 'Honest John' or 'Honest Bill') and in return they could depend on carrying a large and faithful following to the polls. To the beauty of all this the Mugwumps were blind; which explains why Plunkitt called them 'morning glories': they never discovered a means of keeping their followers true until the afternoon, even though they occasionally swept state or city elections after especially noisome scandals came to light. They never posed a serious threat to the practical politicians at any level, nation, state or city; and though their desertion helped to defeat the Republican Presidential candidate, James G. Blaine, in 1884 ('Blaine! Blaine! James G. Blaine! The continental liar from the state of Maine . . . !') he owed his narrow defeat at least as much to the indiscretion of a clerical supporter, who announced to all the world, in the candidate's unprotesting presence, that the Democrats were the party of 'Rum, Romanism and Rebellion!'. Nothing could have been better calculated to rally the opposition, and the Democratic candidate, Grover Cleveland, was elected President by a majority of 29,000 votes. Blaine was unlucky, and did not, perhaps, fully deserve the constant obloquy that was heaped on him by Democrats, party rivals and political cartoonists; but his defeat gave every good Mugwump deep satisfaction, which was just as well, for Mugwumpery never did so well again.

2 Bryce, *American Commonwealth*, Part V, Chapter 79.
3 Quoted by Oscar Handlin, *The Uprooted* (Boston, paperback edn, 1973), p. 190.

Yet it would be a mistake simply to dismiss the Mugwumps as a parcel of snobs. Their criticism of late-nineteenth-century politics was based on unrealistic moral absolutes; but so is the Bill of Rights. They were, in fact, the spokesmen of the American conscience in their time; and given the intensity of the politics of conscience in America – the tradition of the Puritans, the tradition of the Revolution, the tradition of the abolitionists and the Union cause, all fused with American nationalism into the self-righteous belief that the United States was the 'last, best hope of earth', as Abraham Lincoln had called it in his high-priest vein – it is not surprising that the Mugwumps, if they had little power, had a great deal of influence. President Cleveland, for example, a slow, solid, honest man who came to the White House without much in the way of a programme, gradually adopted many of the Mugwumps' pet notions, identifying himself with such principles as further civil service reform and economy in government; and over the years he made himself the rallying-point of all those Democrats in New York state who were opposed to Tammany. Another Mugwump victory was the widespread, and eventually universal, adoption of the secret or 'Australian' ballot, which thirty-three states had introduced by 1892. Previously polling-stations had all too often, and not only in Philadelphia, been scenes of the most flagrant violence and bribery; the secret ballot forced the machines to be more discreet in their operations and overall greatly increased the purity of elections. Finally, Mugwumpery was to benefit from the fact that this was the great creative era of American education. A system of free public schools was spreading across the country, where children were taught to idolize the stars and stripes and other tenets of good citizenship; old universities, such as Harvard and Princeton, were being reformed, new, innovative ones (such as Johns Hopkins, in Baltimore) were being founded; in all of them the young were taught Mugwump principles, a blend of idealism, nationalism, middle-class morality and personal ambition that was to leave its deep mark on the next epoch of American history. Eventually the great machines were to pay a ruinous price for ignoring the claim of conscience in American politics. The agents by whom it was presented were to some extent self-serving and self-deceiving. That did not help the machines.

Meantime it seemed as if an effective challenge to the *status quo* was much more likely to come from one or other of the groups outside the consensus. Not from the blacks, to be sure: they were steadily losing ground to the Southern segregationists, and were not yet numerous enough in the North to exercise any counter-leverage through their votes in that section, where public opinion was abandoning their cause in favour of reconciliation with the Southern whites. The Supreme Court, going through its dimmest intellectual period, found barely plausible constitutional arguments for upholding the racist legislation of the Southern states (only Mr Justice John M. Harlan upheld the Court's honour by recording vigorous dissents from the majority rulings) and in the decision of *Plessy* v. *Ferguson* (1896) adopted the principle of 'separate but equal' accommodations put forward as a justification by the state of Louisiana for segregation of railway carriages. The Court explicitly stated that state governments would have fulfilled their educational obligations to the citizens if they operated 'separate but equal' schools. This doctrine was damaging in several ways. By allowing school segregation, a practice based solely on racial hostility and contempt, the Court was legitimizing the said hostility and contempt, was endorsing the view that black was inferior to white. It was also entering into a conspiracy to deny adequate education to the blacks, because the Southern states had no intention of giving blacks equal facilities, even if they were separate, and the Court had no intention of inquiring whether they had done so or not. At the beginning of the twentieth century the Southern states spent more than twice as much money per head on the education of white children as they did on that of blacks. (The precise proportion was $4.92 to $2.21.) The courts were carefully uninterested in such information, and the phrase 'the equal protection of the laws' in the Fourteenth Amendment was reduced almost to meaninglessness. Finally, *Plessy* v. *Ferguson* damaged the education of Southern white children, not only because the school system reflected the worst prejudices of their parents, but because the cost of running two parallel systems, even if one was done on the cheap, was so high that neither could have enough spent on it.

Treated with ever-increasing rigour in the South, thrust into menial work in the North and, which was worse, treated as if they were invisible – their deprivation a problem which their white fellow-citizens refused to notice – the Negroes turned in on themselves. They followed Booker T. Washington. Their churches throve. And once more a solace was found in music. The spirituals were giving birth to the blues; in the bars and brothels of New Orleans and other Southern cities the movement was beginning that would soon give the world ragtime and jazz.

Another group which was largely excluded from the enjoyments of American society at this period was the new industrial working class. The difficulty in this case was intricate and peculiar. Nothing in the dominant political tradition allowed for the emergence of such a class. Even as late as the eighties there were still many who perceived their society only in terms of a contrast with aristocratic Europe: the United States was a working man's country in the sense that everyone there had to labour to achieve fortune and respect; capital was simply a special form of labour. Immigrant intellectuals and workers who dismissed this view as sophistry, and said instead that America was developing a class structure based on divisions of labour, wealth and ownership, exactly like the European model, simply confirmed the old-fashioned in their view, for these new arrivals were patently subversive, probably socialist, and anyway not to be trusted. Besides, had not Mr Jefferson denounced European cities and their large, propertyless populations as sinks of evil – precisely the sort of thing that must never be allowed to pollute America? It was woefully true that in spite of the best efforts of the right-minded, cities had arisen, but since they were sordidly un-American nothing need be done about them. Most of their inhabitants were foreign, anyway.

Such were the liberal attitudes of all too many Americans of the old stock. They did not attract the workers, who by slow and painful stages had to train themselves in appropriate techniques for safeguarding their interests in the new age. Strikes were nothing new, and there had been attempts to organize working men's parties as long ago as the 1830s; but it was only after the Civil War that a significant labour movement arose. Even then its progress was slow, irregular and uncertain, and must seem especially so to British eyes.

It is true that American workers were usually, in some important respects, better-off than their European fellows. Their wages were higher, their food was better; so was their clothing; so, frequently, was their shelter. And the American economy grew so rapidly in the period between the Civil War and the First World War, whether in population, production or consumption, that the demand for labour was buoyant, on the whole. In the late nineteenth century the deflation that followed the crash of 1873, coupled with rigidity of wages, which continued to be paid at traditional levels, meant that the workers' real income steadily improved for about twenty years. As against these advantages must be set the diseases (smallpox, diphtheria, typhoid) which repeatedly swept the slums and factory districts; the appalling neglect of safety precautions in all the major industries; the total absence of any state-assisted insurance schemes against injury, old age or premature death; the determination of employers to get their labour as cheap as possible, which meant, in practice, the common use of under-paid women and under-age children; and general indifference to the problems of unemployment, for it was still the universal belief that in America there was always work, and the chance of bettering himself, for any willing man. A more subtle grievance was the slow degeneration of the working man's status: as new wealth produced new classes the labourers felt that they were losing the dignity and influence, if not the power, which they had formerly enjoyed as equal American democrats. All these problems were real enough and grave enough to make the emergence of a strong union movement likely, and as time went on other problems were added to them. But the unions never, from beginning to end of the Age of Gold, came near to realizing their potential.

The root reason was the extreme heterogeneity of the American work-force. It was divided, like the British, into an 'aristocracy' of skilled crafts-men and a mass of comparatively unskilled hands. But it was also divided by several American peculiarities: for example, sectionalism. In the East, where conditions had long been settled and the Industrial Revolution had brought, as well as its factories, mills and foundries, European ideas of class-consciousness, job identification and joint action might thrive, but in the West the old, undifferentiated America still flourished. There, a man might move easily from job to job – might be a miner one year and a farmer the next; and his relations with his employers were likely to be as informal, occasionally as violent, as any other social relation on the frontier. There could be little common ground between such a man and a steelworker in Pittsburgh. Westerners wanted to form broad alliances of the discontented to agitate for general improvement; Eastern workers were much more interested in evolving exclusive working-class organizations to concentrate on working-class wrongs. Then, there was racial prejudice. North and South, the black was universally snubbed and slighted. He was certainly not welcomed by the emergent craft unions. No wonder, then, that he had no objection to being used as a strike-breaker when the opportunity arose. The white workers had never shown any solidarity with him: why should he show any with them? The immigrants in many cases felt the same. Those of them, particularly, who belonged to the 'new immigration' – Poles, Jews, Italians, etc. – had little experience of industrial labour, and none of the English language. They received, at best, a cool welcome from the labour aristocracy. So they too let themselves be used as strike-breakers by big business and accepted wage-rates that undercut union demands; and even when, in due course, they understood the need for unionization, they tended to form their own unions and in some cases to monopolize certain trades. This did nothing to help the cause and spirit of working-class unity.[4]

It should also be borne in mind that the industrial working class never formed a majority of the American population. For most of the nineteenth century the farmers were the majority; and even when that ceased to be true, the numerical ascendancy passed, not to the blue-collar workers, but to the vast amorphous group that must, I suppose, be called the middle class.

Organized labour thus operated from a weak basis, as was amply demonstrated, again and again, during the post-reconstruction years. Attempts to wrest some concessions from the mine-owners in western Pennsylvania through a secret society, mostly Irish, known as the Molly Maguires, failed when ten of the leaders were hanged for murder and conspiracy in 1876. The evidence against them was provided by an undercover agent employed by Pinkerton's Detective Agency, a sinister body which got its start during the Civil War and subsequently became the industrialists' secret police, furnishing spies, gunmen and strike-breakers on demand. (The Pinkerton tradition was to prove all too durable, and was influential in the founding conception of the Federal Bureau of Investigation, set up in 1908.) The year 1877 was one of great railroad strikes, which culminated in ferocious

---

4 It suited the employers excellently. A steel man wrote in 1875: 'We must be careful of what class of men we collect. We must steer clear of the West, where men are accustomed to infernal high wages. We must steer clear as far as we can of Englishmen who are great sticklers for high wages, small production and strikes. My experience has shown that Germans and Irish, Swedes and what I denominate "Buckwheats" – young American country boys, judiciously mixed, make the most effective and tractable force you can find.' Quoted in Henry Pelling, *American Labour* (Chicago and London, 1960), p. 76.

riots in Pittsburgh that lasted for three days, caused twenty-six deaths and did $5,000,000 worth of damage to property. The workers were totally defeated and turned away from the union idea in search of allies. They gave support to the Greenback party, which had come into being in protest against the return to the gold standard and was popular in frontier regions which now, as so often in the past – in colonial Massachusetts, in Jacksonian Tennessee – hoped to find economic salvation in an inflated paper currency: in this case, the Civil War paper dollars, or 'greenbacks'. But the proposed remedy was too remote from the real problems of both farmers and workers to serve for long as the basis for an effective movement, and although the Greenback party won over a million votes in the Congressional elections of 1878, it fell to pieces almost immediately when the Hayes administration in January 1879 announced that greenbacks would henceforward be convertible at face value into gold. It would no longer be of any advantage to borrow gold and repay in paper.

Much more promising was the association known as the Order of the Knights of Labor, which rose rapidly to fame in the early eighties. As it evolved under the guidance of its Grand Master Workman, Terence V. Powderly (1849–1924), the Order was an attempt to solve the new problems of social relations in accordance with traditional American notions, side-stepping both unionism and socialism. Originally it borrowed a good many organizational features from the Freemasons, which got it into trouble with the Roman Catholic church. Powderly, himself a Catholic, induced the Knights to drop their secrecy and most of their ritual, which he must have found difficult, for Americans love dressing up and mumbo-jumbo, as the success of certain fraternal and charitable organizations such as the Shriners have amply demonstrated in the twentieth century. His reward was a rapid growth in membership, based on two sorts of local assembly: the 'trade assembly', which was in all essentials a union, and the 'mixed assembly', which almost anyone could join, even small employers. Dues were high and gave the central body, run by Powderly, considerable leverage, since it would be up to the executive to decide which undertakings to back with its treasury. In principle this formula might have worked well: the Order could switch tactics according to opportunity, and by inducing farmers and city-dwellers, skilled and unskilled workers, socialists and small businessmen to co-operate might eventually mount a serious challenge to the ruling alliance of big business, the old political parties and Southern oligarchs. Unfortunately the difficulties were immense, for the hostilities between the various components of the Order were deep and bitter; and Powderly was not the man to overcome them. He was a poor administrator and insufficiently flexible. He was deeply opposed to strikes as weapons, preferring the boycott, although in many cases, particularly in the industrial East, it could not be applied effectively. For a few years the Knights were successful, and their membership swelled to a peak of more than 700,000 in the summer of 1886. But 1886 was the year of trial for Powderly and the

Knights, and they failed the test. The chief cry of the working men was now for the eight-hour day; strikes and public meetings were held all over the country to secure this concession, and some dramatic clashes with authority occurred, the most famous being the Haymarket meeting in Chicago on 4 May, when some unidentified idiot or *agent provocateur* threw a bomb which killed a policeman and wounded others. (Only the day before, during a fight between strikers and strike-breakers at the McCormick Reaper factory, the police had killed two workers.) The police rioted, inflicting bloody injuries on everyone they could catch. The leaders of the workers' movement in Chicago were arrested. It was never convincingly shown that these men had anything to do with the bomb (several of them were certainly innocent) but they were socialists and (with one exception) foreign-born. That was enough for the police, the courts and many business leaders. In due course, though scarcely according to due process, four of the prisoners were hanged. The strike action in support of the eight-hour day planned for the month of May failed; similar strikes on the railroads and in the meat-packing industry also failed. Powderly could do nothing in all this but wring his hands: he dissociated himself from the martyrs of the Haymarket, not wishing the Knights of Labor to get a name for anarchism, and he tried to stop the meat-packers' strike. All this disgusted the workers. A revival of trade-unionism proper was taking place, for during the eighties a mild economic recovery, which had helped to swell the membership of the Knights (by bringing their dues within more people's reach), had also stimulated efforts to create an American organization on the lines of the British Trades Union Congress. Some attempts were made to work out a demarcation agreement with the Knights of Labor, but the chance was muffed, partly because of Powderly's inefficiency, partly because of bitter feelings lower down the hierarchy on both sides. The failure of the Knights to provide effective leadership in the crisis finished the possibility of collaboration. In December 1886 a 'Trades Congress' was held at Columbus, Ohio, where the American Federation of Labor was launched. Before very long the Knights of Labor went into a sharp decline; Powderly was dethroned in 1893; then the socialists were expelled; by 1900 the Order was little more than a memory.

The AFL, on the other hand, became a permanent feature of the American scene. It owed this somewhat limited achievement above all to able and realistic leadership, which was supplied for nearly forty years by Samuel Gompers (1850–1924), its first president. Gompers, of Dutch–Jewish parentage, grew up in England, emigrating to America at the age of thirteen. His strength was that he understood perfectly the grievances, aspirations and limitations of the craft-workers, of whom he was one. He modelled the AFL accordingly. He worked in a cigar-factory in New York. It was a room in a tenement, airless, filthy, smelly, with a constant risk of tuberculosis (called the cigar-maker's disease); the sort of sweatshop that was then known as a buckeye. But it was a place where workers could talk, shape each other's views and discover leaders. Before long Gompers was the head of the cigar-makers' union, and in 1886 he became the first president of the AFL. Most of his members, like himself, had come to America on a quest for personal betterment, and a union, or a league of unions, was only an instrument to further that quest: it carried no implications of class-consciousness, or solidarity, or socialism, or indeed any particular programme. The important point was by one means or another to safeguard and if possible to better your standard of living; to get a larger slice of the great American cake. Strikes were allowable, if directed pragmatically to the achievement of a precise goal: for Gompers, indeed, one of the merits of the AFL was that it would increase the funds available to strikers by giving them a national war-chest to draw on and make strike-breaking more difficult; but it was an equally good idea to get what you wanted by collaboration with the bosses. Gompers, rather like Booker T. Washington, hoped to get concessions from the employers in return for organizing and disciplining the American workforce. In return for (say) the eight-hour day, the AFL would guarantee that there would be no trouble on the factory floor, no strikes or commotions, until the next contract had to be negotiated. (Unfortunately all too few employers saw the advantage of this: the majority continued to harry unionism for all it was worth and then wondered why their workforce was hard to control.) As to ideology, all Gompers had to offer was what came to be known as 'voluntarism'. This meant that unions ought to operate as mere friendly societies, looking voluntarily after their own members in sickness and old age: compulsory insurance, imposed and organized by the state, was a socialistic, un-American idea. Nor did Gompers believe in a highly centralized, high dues system such as the Knights of Labor had been. Local unions must be allowed the greatest possible autonomy. The AFL's dues were only 3 cents a year.

This extremely restricted programme was worthless to the unskilled or the unemployed, and even some skilled workers would get very little out of it: when Carnegie and Frick set out to crush the steelworkers' union in the strike and lockout at the Homestead works in Pittsburgh in 1892, there was not much that Gompers could do, while strikers fought a pitched battle with Pinkerton men, and blacklegs were poured into the works, and Frick was stabbed by a foreign-born anarchist from New York, and the strike was broken, and Carnegie cabled that life was worth living again, and Rockefeller (who believed in 'obedient servants and good masters') sent his congratulations. As a result the steel industry was to all intents and purposes de-unionized for the next forty-five years. Given the immense strength of the great capitalists in the late nineteenth century, it is perhaps likely that any more ambitious organization than the AFL would have come to grief, like the Knights of Labor. In 1893–4 Eugene Victor Debs (1855–1926), perhaps the most attractive figure ever thrown up by the American labour movement, founded just such a militant, all-inclusive big union for the railroad workers; but he was defeated by the combination of hard times

(1893 saw one of the most serious crashes in American economic history, followed by an intensified depression), the hostility of the railroad craft unions (or brotherhoods), the unity of the employers – who knew a dangerous enemy when they saw one – and the intervention of the federal government. Members of Debs's American Railway Union went on strike at the works of the Pullman Palace Car Company; the ARU instituted a boycott of Pullman cars and trains hauling them; the US Attorney-General, employing a new legal device, the so-called 'labour injunction', accused them of acting in restraint of trade and of impeding the free circulation of the mails, and sent troops against them; the strike and the boycott collapsed and Debs served six months in prison. That was the end of the ARU, though not of Debs, or American socialism (he was converted to that doctrine in prison), or of the idea of 'One Big Union'. Yet Gompers and the AFL survived in rather better shape, and the sluggish conservatism of 'Big Labor' in the twentieth century owes a lot to the Gompers tradition, which explains, for instance, why the AFL had only three presidents in its first ninety-three years (ignoring John McBride, who dislodged Gompers for one year in 1894), each of whom died in office,[5] of extreme old age, while the AFL grew arthritic around him. Perhaps, if Gompers had set a livelier precedent, the AFL might not be so decrepit today and might have achieved more during its earliest years.

As it was, it lay low; and the only serious challenge mounted to the Congressional and business oligarchs in these years was thereby so isolated that its failure was almost inevitable.

This challenge came from the West in these, the years when the pioneer saga was ending. There was still a great deal of public land to be taken up. Oklahoma was not opened to settlement (that is, stolen from the Indians) until 1890; even after that last border had been crossed, after the mob of waiting cowboys and farmers had heard the starting gun and raced across the line to claim the choicest pieces of the former Indian Territory, there was still an immense acreage waiting to be claimed for exploitation. But on the whole the eighties were a decade when it was generally recognized that the new country was filling. In future Americans would have to make do with the place they were in, or retreat. Sometimes they took the second alternative: one of the more poignant symbols of the time was the stream of prairie schooners heading east, not west as they always had done before. Those who chose not to admit defeat could no longer steer for the sunset with the same certainty of finding the happy valley across the ranges, although individuals might and did choose still to seek their fortune in California or Oregon or, when the Klondike Gold Rush started, in Alaska or the Yukon. The happy valley had already been claimed. As a rule, obstinate farmers would now have to find a new way out of their difficulties.

---

5 Actually, George Meany (president 1952–79) resigned two months before his death; but this exception most definitely proves the rule. Meany was eighty-five when he died.

Their difficulties were very great. Once the Indians and the buffalo had been cleared away there had been a rush to occupy the High Plains: the Missouri Plateau, the Dakota Territory, central and western Kansas and Nebraska, western Texas. Settlers (some of old American stock, some immigrants fresh from Europe – Scandinavians, Germans, Hungarians, Poles) had been energetically encouraged by the transcontinental railroads.[6] Others, white and black, fled from Southern tenancy as it closed round them: they scrawled 'Gone to Texas' (or just 'GTT') on their cabin doors and left for the still largely empty vastness of that state. During the seventies the great railroad land grants were rapidly distributed, at minimal prices, to eager pioneers, and the remaining public lands were also gobbled up, under the Homestead Act, with amazing speed. Times looked good. The Great American Desert had, it seemed, been finally proved mythical: rainfall was abundant, harvests were good and were easily marketed, credit was easy. Everywhere between the Canadian border and the Rio Grande, between the Rockies and the valley of the Missouri, towns mushroomed, farms blossomed. What did it matter if, in order to survive your first year, you not only had to live in a hut made out of turf cut from the prairie (a sod cabin), but had to borrow freely in order to pay for your stock, your seed, your fencing (barbed wire, made in Chicago, was just coming in), your farm machinery? Here in his buggy came the friendly agent of the friendly mortgage company, eager to lend you all you required at a very moderate rate of interest. What did it matter if the only cash crops you had a chance to sell profitably were wheat and corn? The point was, they would most certainly be profitable. Next year's harvests would pay all debts – no doubt about it, for the golden future of the Far West was clear – so clear that Eastern capital was hurrying to invest. Savings were abundant in places like Boston, New York and Philadelphia in those years, and in their hinterlands, too, and mortgages on Western lands were favourite investments.[7] This was also the time when the cattle kings and beef barons were at their height. They imported good English stock, to improve the American breed. The railroads carried the cows to the stockyards at Kansas City and Chicago, where the animals were slaughtered and then put into tins by the Philip D. Armour company or its rivals. Many Easterners preferred cows even to farms, and eagerly invested in the range.

Then came the winter of 1886–7, and the first disaster struck. The cattle died in their hundreds of thousands. Thoroughbred English strains lacked the toughness of the little longhorns; they perished in the vast snowdrifts that piled up against the barbed wire. A late spring found the range a desert again. The cattle kings were ruined.

6 See above, p. 396.
7 A visitor to Vermont, noticing that state's barren hills, asked what crops were grown there. 'Why, can't you see the western mortgages?' was the answer. By 1890 there were as many mortgages as families in Kansas and four other Western states.

Worse was to come. The plains were entering a cycle of dry years. In 1887 came a summer of drought: the harvest failed in Kansas. In the next ten years it failed most of the time over most of the Western states. It suddenly dawned on the Easterners that the West was not such a golden investment after all. The supply of credit dried up. The high hopes of the recent past were dead. Pioneers who, a few years back, had set out with the proud motto, 'Kansas or Bust!' now turned back, their wagons scrawled with the sad announcement, 'In God We Trusted, in Kansas We Busted.' Some of them could not even move back, for their wagons, like their oxen, their furniture and all their other movables, like their land itself, were mortgaged. Foreclosures became devastatingly common. Nor were the farmers weighed down by personal debts only. In happier times it had seemed merely sensible to give the new towns in the new states every modern convenience – street lighting, trams, handsome public buildings. In the good times the pioneers had blithely voted the taxes to pay for these toys. Now the times were bad, but the taxes had to be paid just the same. To cap it all the price of wheat was falling with every year that passed. The crop's value went down by 30 per cent between 1880 and 1890, and fell further thereafter; in 1894, after the panic of the previous year, it hit its lowest point in American history – 49 cents the bushel (in 1870 it had been $1.05). Down with wheat went the farmers' income.

It is not in human nature, or at least not in American human nature, to accept the blame for such calamities or to shrug them off as the work of inscrutable Fate. The farmers' wounds were in large part self-inflicted, and they ought to have known better. There had been flush times on many an earlier frontier (in Alabama, for example, after the Battle of New Orleans) and they had always ended disastrously. The optimism of the American farmer, which had made him a hero, had also made him something of a sucker, who believed his own boosting as well as the promises of the speculators who had real estate to dispose of. He was engaged in an extremely risky business, struggling with the ever-unsteady and uncontrollable variables of the weather, technology and the market, on a basis of inadequate capital, insufficient knowledge and poor communications: it was not Eastern capitalists, after all, who put 4,000 miles of land and sea between the Plains farmer and his ultimate consumers in Europe. But no such admissions, even had they been of a mind to make them, would have been of any help or comfort to the farmers of the West. Instead they looked round for something to blame against which they could take action; and they fixed, inevitably, on the railroads, and, less inevitably, on the new social, economic and political system which the railroads represented.

The problems of American agriculture were beyond the powers of American railways to cause or cure; but angry men and women could not see that, and besides it was notorious that the railroads were ill-run and had grave problems of their own. The battle of half a dozen men for control of the Western routes – Harriman, Huntington, Stanford, Villard and the inevitable Gould – was scarcely over, while at the same time the roads further east were engaged in a ceaseless, ruthless competition with each other. They used every means at their disposal to achieve a victory, however small. No one of importance was neglected. If he was a Congressman, businessman, state official, newspaper editor or anything else influential, he was given a free pass to travel where he liked: this practice got so out of hand that in the end it was said that everyone could travel free on the railroads except those who could not afford the fares. Big shippers were given special terms – 'rebates' – to encourage them to use particular lines; as time went on they got into the way (Standard Oil was particularly firm about this) of insisting on rebates as a condition of using a line at all. Shippers from East to West were given better terms than shippers from West to East. Secret rates were charged to favoured customers. And meantime the railroad network was not even rationally planned. Thousands of miles of roads were built every year, but more with an eye to the war between the giants than to the economic needs of the United States. The war was so widespread and so devastating that the roads, in spite of their enormous capital assets and colossal turnover, tottered constantly on the brink of ruin: in 1880 20 per cent of the mileage in America was controlled by bankrupt roads, and in the next six years foreign investors lost $600,000,000 through the general mismanagement.

The Western farmers had little sympathy for foreign capitalists, whom they regarded as no less villainous than American ones. The real burden of this appalling operation fell, they argued, on their shoulders. It was not merely that they were discriminated against, paying unduly high rates so that the railroads could recoup their losses on free passes and rebates.[8] It was not even that they felt that middlemen were absorbing too much of the profit that was earned by the sale of wheat: the grower could not earn enough to pay his way, let alone pay his debts, but the railroads, the bankers, the processors and merchants of America's farm products, these all grew rich on the traffic. It was not that the farmer was frequently cheated, high-grade grain being classified as inferior and paid for as such; or even that there were seasonal fluctuations in the value of the dollar, so that it was worth less when the farmer had to sell his harvest, more when he had to buy his supplies. All these were real grievances, sharpened by the persistent drought. To the farmer they amounted to proof of a last grievance, greater than all the others of which it was, nevertheless, only the sum. Clearly there was a conspiracy against American agriculture. A monster was arising in the East, a monster of industry, high finance, commerce, urbanization; it

8 In justice to the railroads it must be recorded that the rates they charged were not really extortionate, and fell throughout the period. The real crime of the financiers who manipulated and mismanaged the roads was that they neglected all considerations of safety, maintenance and technical efficiency in their struggle to keep afloat. The farmers, however, got little or no benefit from the decline in railroad charges: other middlemen took up the slack, as it were, and the farmers continued to pay through their noses for getting their crops to market.

threatened everything the traditional American farmer believed in, from the old-time religion to the equality of all citizens in a democracy – 'government of the people, by the people, for the people' – a phrase their spokesmen were never tired of quoting. As the hard times deepened in the late eighties they roused themselves for battle.

Their initial instrument was the so-called Farmers' Alliance. This was not so much an organization as a loose confederation of organizations ('suballiances'), each in its way concerned with bettering the farmers' lot. Originating in Texas, the Alliance grew very rapidly in the later eighties and undertook many useful tasks, such as organizing co-operative purchasing and marketing, lobbying Congress, sending round lecturers to advise on better husbandry and modern farm machinery, and laying on such entertainments as picnics, barbecues and conventions in the wicked towns which the virtuous farmers and their wives had a natural desire to visit. The chief importance of the Alliance, however, lay in its ability to draw the farmers of all America together. In particular it was important as a means of developing contacts between the West and the South.

Conditions in the South were rather worse than they were in Kansas, but they were also very similar. The South and the Plains were given over to monoculture (cotton and wheat); the South had been thrust back to something like the frontier stage by the Civil War and the collapse of slavery, the West was still largely at that stage; family farms had become the standard economic institution in both regions; and, above all, the farmers in both were burdened by debts and interest charges in a period when money was getting dearer and dearer. Wheat and cotton prices alike nearly halved between 1860 and 1890.[9] About the only thing which separated South and West was that they had fought on different sides in the Civil War; and even that came to matter less and less, in large part because conditions in western Texas (which had been part of the Confederacy) were so similar, in climate, crops and social structure, to those in the rest of the High Plains. It is not surprising that the sections came together in the Farmers' Alliance.

Nor is it surprising that the members of the Alliance began to seek redress in politics. Disgruntled Americans had never been content, when feeling unduly poor, to rely on sweet reason and mere social or economic action. Sam Adams's father had fought for paper money and a land bank in colonial Massachusetts; a debtor party had swept Kentucky in 1819;[10] not to mention that there had been a strong element of debtor resentment behind the American Revolution, the rise of two-party politics and the great Southern rebellion. Thanks to Appomattox, the precedent of Jefferson Davis was now as obsolete as those of Daniel Shays and the Whisky Rebellion, but more recent examples could be found. When the federal government returned to

9 In rounded figures: 1860, wheat $1.50 per bushel, cotton 15 cents per pound; 1890, wheat 87 cents per bushel, cotton 8 cents per pound.
10 See above, p. 270.

the gold standard there had sprung up the Greenback party, as we have seen, to agitate for the return of non-convertible paper dollars. The Greenback movement had coincided with the beginnings of a widespread agitation for alcoholic prohibition: in 1880, when the Greenbackers fought a Presidential election for the last time, the Prohibition party fought one for the first time (and is at it still). Eight years later the great national parties seemed as much out of touch as before: Democrats and Republicans battling over the tariff and competing to get their hands on the spoils. To the members of the Farmers' Alliance it seemed only sense to start a new movement, which should bring their case forcefully before the American people. All over the West and South in 1888 farmer parties (calling themselves Independents, or People's parties) contested the state elections and in many places did surprisingly well, though at the Presidential level everything went on as usual: a Republican, Benjamin Harrison (1833–1901), grandson of William Henry Harrison, replaced a Democrat, Grover Cleveland, in the White House. In the years that followed irresistible pressure built up among the discontented to repeat the experiment on a national scale, in the hope of founding a great new political party which should sweep either the Democrats or the Republicans or both into the oblivion which had earlier swallowed the Federalists and the Whigs.

Not all the farmers agreed that this was the sensible thing to do. For one thing, not all the farmers were unsuccessful: for example, dairy farming in Wisconsin, Illinois and Indiana was highly profitable, and the dairy farmers were too strong and well-organized to be victims of the monopolists. In the South, where the Democratic party enjoyed a virtual monopoly of power, office and electoral success, Ben Tillman of South Carolina argued that the proper course was to take over the Democratic party from within. He demonstrated his case by capturing his own state in this fashion and holding its Governorship for four years, after which he was elected US Senator – an office he held until his death in 1918. But Tillman did not do very much with the power that he wrested from the 'Redeemer' oligarchy;[11] and anyway the problems that obsessed the farmers could not be solved within the borders of one state alone, or even within the borders of both sections. They would have to be tackled nationally, and the national leadership of both the old parties was quite unresponsive to the new movement. So conferences and conventions were held during 1891 and 1892, culminating in the great convention at Omaha, Nebraska, in July 1892, when the newly formed People's party nominated General James Weaver, late of the Army of the Potomac, for President of the United States. His running mate was Major James Field, late of the Army of Northern Virginia. Weaver was a good candidate: an able speaker, an upright and diligent man who had served

---

11 By this time the Redeemers were also sometimes known as 'Bourbons' because, like the French royal family after 1814, they were thought to have learned nothing and forgotten nothing. No doubt they were also fond of Bourbon whisky.

three terms in Congress as a Greenbacker and had been the Greenback Presidential candidate in 1880. The ticket received 1,029,846 votes, as compared with 5,555,426 for the successful Democrats and 5,182,690 for the Republicans: a good beginning. But the real strength of the People's party lay in its platform and in the enthusiasm of its supporters; these were the forces which were to make a deep mark on American history.

The Omaha platform remains an impressive document even today. It opened with a stirring preamble written by Ignatius Donnelly of Minnesota, which set forth the Populist attitude as clearly as possible:

We meet in the midst of a nation brought to the verge of moral, political, and material ruin. Corruption dominates the ballot-box, the legislatures, the Congress, and even touches the ermine of the bench[12]. . . The newspapers are largely subsidized or muzzled; public opinion silenced; business prostrated; our homes covered with mortgages; labour impoverished; and the land concentrating in the hands of the capitalists. The urban workmen are denied the right of organization for self-protection; imported pauperized labour beats down their wages; a hireling standing army, unrecognized by our laws, is established to shoot them down,[13] and they are rapidly degenerating into European conditions. The fruits of the toil of millions are boldly stolen to build up colossal fortunes for a few, unprecedented in the history of mankind; and the possessors of these, in turn, despise the republic and endanger liberty. From the same prolific womb of governmental injustice we breed the two great classes – tramps and millionaires.

There followed a long list of the changes favoured by the Populists: 'a national currency, safe, sound and flexible'; 'the sub-treasury plan of the Farmers' Alliance, or some better system' (this was a plea for help to the farmers with the financing of their labours); 'the free and unlimited coinage of silver'; 'a graduated income tax'; a postal savings bank; 'all land now held by railroads and other corporations in excess of their actual needs, and all lands now owned by aliens, should be reclaimed by the government and held by actual settlers only'; the nationalization of the railroads, the telegraph and the telephone systems; 'the unperverted Australian or secret ballot system'; 'the further restriction of undesirable immigration'; a shortening of the working day; the disbanding of the Pinkertons; 'the legislative system known as the initiative and referendum'; Presidents and Vice-Presidents to be elected for one term only, and Senators to be directly chosen by the people. An earlier endorsement of votes for women was dropped from the programme and a tactful endorsement of 'fair and liberal pensions to ex-Union soldiers and sailors' was included – in American politics there has never been any advantage in opposing veterans' benefits.

What is impressive about the Omaha platform is how much ground it

12 This is rhetoric: American judges do not wear ermine, only seemly black gowns.
13 An allusion to the Pinkertons.

covers. For good or bad (the plank about immigrants can hardly be called liberal) it drew up the agenda on which reformers were to operate for the next twenty years. This was in large part the work of the miscellaneous reformers who rallied to the Populist standard in the eighties; but it speaks very well for the intelligence and public spirit of the farmers that they should enthusiastically lend themselves to a programme which read like rank revolutionism in the conditions of 1892. They were not just a selfish single interest, lobbying for more money. They wanted to redeem the soul of America.

This became ever clearer as the great crusade went on. Nothing like it had been seen since 1840. A succession of remarkable orators suddenly strode the land. There was 'Sockless Jerry Simpson', who got his nickname because he taunted an opponent with wearing silk stockings and himself was said to wear no socks at all. There was 'Pitchfork Ben' Tillman, already mentioned. There was Tom Watson of Georgia, and General Weaver himself. The most remarkable portent was perhaps Mrs Mary Lease of Kansas. The People's party had shirked the duty of furthering women's suffrage, but it had nevertheless produced the first really effective and important woman politician. Mrs Lease was of Irish birth, appearance and temperament; she had a scorching tongue and abounding energy; it was she who told the farmers to raise less corn and more hell, which became the slogan of the movement. 'The people are at bay,' she cried. 'Let the bloodhounds of money who have dogged us thus far beware!' She became a political power in her own right; she and her associates, by giving voice to the anxieties and preoccupations of millions, changed the course of American history, though at the price of personal failure.

They were helped in their battle by the turn of events. Honest, obstinate Grover Cleveland had scarcely taken office again when the panic of 1893 erupted. It was followed by a depression which lasted for four years. Today, the causes do not seem very mysterious. As usual, the unregulated capitalist cycle had led to over-expansion – that is, businessmen had bought and built more than they could pay for – which was necessarily followed by a sudden contraction as individuals, banks and companies found themselves in difficulties for money. Even in 1893 there were some radical groups who saw the downturn in these terms. But there are fashions in economics as in everything else, and in the last years of the nineteenth century far too many Americans, as it happened, were obsessed with the currency question and, whether they were radical or conservative, interpreted everything that occurred in terms of gold and silver. The first consequence of this obsession was the destruction of President Cleveland.

Cleveland had become President originally because of his reputation for total honesty in a corrupt age; and during his first term he had demonstrated that the reputation was well deserved. He had struggled against the grosser forms of patronage, against the Congressional habit of ladling out pensions to all who could make a case, however bogus, that they had earned them by their sufferings for the Union in the Civil War, and against the chaotic way in which Congress settled the tariff. The Democrats were supposed to be the low-tariff party, the Republicans the protectionists; but whenever the subject came up for debate all party consistency was thrown to the winds in the scramble for special treatment. Every state, and therefore every Congressional delegation, was split between protectionists and free-traders; individual Senators and Congressmen voted as they thought would best please their constituencies. No rational tariff was possible in the circumstances, and, as Cleveland saw, the result was oppressive to consumers and helpful only to monopolists. But when he came out in open opposition to the excessively high tariff he only injured himself. All the special interests turned against him, and in 1888, although he increased his popular vote and popular majority, he only won a minority in the electoral college.

His stand on the tariff seemed to be vindicated when the Republicans pushed through the notorious McKinley Tariff of 1890 (named after its architect, the Republican Chairman of the House Ways and Means Committee) which blatantly favoured the special interests; indignation about this was no doubt one of the reasons why Cleveland was elected in 1892. The day after he took office panic broke out on Wall Street.

As always in such crises, the word went out that business confidence must be restored (it would have been considered wild socialism to suggest that what needed restoring was public confidence in business). Cleveland, like some other conservative statesmen at other times and places, sacrificed everything to achieve this end, and failed. Businessmen continued timid; that is, they would not invest because they did not see much chance of profit and because many of them were bankrupt; the economy did not revive. Instead the mystic message came to Wall Street that all would be well if Cleveland defended the gold standard; that is, if he maintained the ability of the US Treasury to pay its bills in gold, rather than silver or paper money; and he believed what he heard, believed it a great deal too fervently. There was not much room for ideas in Cleveland's massive head, but when one had battered its way in it could never be dislodged. Cleveland became the leading 'gold-bug'. He called Congress into special session to repeal the Sherman Silver Purchase Act of 1890, which had put a certain amount of the white metal into circulation as coins; and after a bruising political battle the Act was revoked, to the great disgust of the Western and Southern wings of the Democratic party, which were hearing mystic messages of their own about the importance of 'free silver'. The economy did not revive. Cleveland tried to lower the tariff, but another frightful Congressional scrimmage (some 600 amendments were proposed to the administration bill) resulted in a tariff very little different from the Republican one that it replaced, except that it included provisions for a federal income tax. This tax was promptly declared unconstitutional by the Supreme Court (Mr Justice Harlan again dissenting), less on legal grounds than because of the political prejudices of an exceedingly reactionary bench. The economy did not revive. A drain of gold from the Treasury continued, faith in the credit of the US government began to weaken and in desperation Cleveland called in J. P. Morgan. The government issued four bond issues, to be paid for in gold, between 1894 and 1896; Morgan marketed them on Wall Street (for a consideration); at great cost, enough gold was raised to meet the government's obligations. Then new gold discoveries in the Klondike and South Africa vastly increased the supply of the precious metal, and the gold standard was safe until 1929. The economy did not revive – at least not during Cleveland's administration.

The political consequences of this story were of profound importance. Given the primitive administrative machinery which was all that the administration had to work with, the economic convictions of the President and the attitudes of the bankers on Wall Street (where further disruptive panic would have followed any unorthodox move on Cleveland's part) and in the City of London, it is difficult to see how the bond issues could have been avoided. To Western and Southern Democrats, however, they were merely proof that Cleveland had betrayed them. Then, the gold-bug administration showed itself stonily indifferent to the sufferings of ordinary Americans in the depression. A wave of strikes swept across the country in 1894 in an attempt to deter employers from laying off their workers. The Cleveland administration's sole contributions to the crisis were the invention of the labour injunction and the dispatch of federal troops to break the railroad strike in Chicago, overriding both the Constitution and the protests of the Governor of Illinois, John Peter Altgeld. The Congressional elections in the autumn were disastrous for the Democrats, and although the Populists also lost ground, their ideas did not: both main parties by now contained large numbers of Populist fellow-travellers.

The People's party, in fact, had a great opportunity before it. Discontent was now as vigorous and vocal in the East and in the cities as in the West and South; socialist ideas were gaining ground, many of which were similar or identical to Populist proposals. A serious bid for the support of industrial labour would have met many obstacles – not least the caution of Samuel Gompers – but might have won extraordinary rewards. Unfortunately the metallic obsession proved even more ruinous to the progressives than to the conservatives.

Behind the cry of 'free silver' lay the all-too-concrete interests of the miners and mine-owners of the Rockies. If gold was for the time being too scarce, silver was too plentiful: its producers were desperate to keep its price up. They were well able to finance a propagandist campaign which could appeal to the inflationist traditions of the frontier. The original Populists were, as a matter of fact, really advanced thinkers on the currency question, looking forward to the day when what their opponents disdainfully called 'fiat money' – greenbacks – would replace the fetish of metal, and government could regulate the amount of money in circulation simply by the issue of paper backed only by its own credit – the system that is now universal.

(The system breeds its own difficulties, not least a permanent inflationary tendency which no one living today is likely to regard lightly, but at least it is an improvement on a money supply randomly determined by the amount of precious metal that happens to be available at any one moment.) However, they were forced on to the defensive and then swept aside by the mania for silver which swept the West and South during the mid-nineties. The rest of the Populist programme came under fire: what votes were in it? Said General Weaver, 'I shall favour going before the people in 1896 with the money question alone, unencumbered with any other contention whatsoever.' Unfortunately silver as an issue had no appeal to the industrial workers whatever – rather the reverse, for the gold-bugs told them again and again that industry would be ruined unless the threat to dilute the currency with silver coins was beaten back. What the workers wanted was work, and an end to the labour injunction; questions to which the silverites were deaf. So the Presidential election of 1896 turned into a grand battle between the sections: between East and West, North and South; between the new urban industrial society and the old agrarian world. It settled, in a sense, the future identity of the Democratic and Republican parties; it eliminated the People's party for ever; and it was economically entirely irrelevant, though it turned entirely on questions of economics.

The Republican campaign was dominated not by the candidate, William McKinley (1843–1901), another worthy mediocrity, but by his puppet-master, Marcus Alonso Hanna (1837–1904), a successful businessman who was also a politician with flair. Hanna knew better than to believe all the panic-mongering that was going on among the influential, but he took care to encourage it, for it would help his candidate. He exacted unprecedentedly large contributions from big business (Standard Oil and the House of Morgan were made to hand over a quarter of a million dollars each) and spent lavishly, while carefully coaching his man as to how to behave. McKinley waged the classical 'front-porch' campaign, staying sedately at home in Ohio, where he received an endless flow of delegations. They addressed him in speeches previously arranged, and sometimes written, by the candidate's advisers, and received suitable replies. Meanwhile a flying squad of Republican orators went up and down the land, lecturing insistently on the importance of the gold standard. (Republicans who believed in silver had walked out of the nominating convention and now worked for the opposition.)

The Democrats convened at Chicago sure of nothing but that Cleveland and all his works must be repudiated (as a result there was a secession of gold-bugs). The platform, written largely by Altgeld, reads for the most part like a re-orchestration of the Omaha platform. The Populists, or rather Populism, had captured the Democratic party. The victory was confirmed when William Jennings Bryan of Nebraska (1860–1925) was nominated for the Presidency.

Bryan was the perfection of an American type. His undeniable abilities were always endangered, and eventually swamped, by his conditioning. A son of the West, he believed with equal passion in America and in the Bible, as interpreted by the most literal-minded Protestants. America stood for the prospect of human betterment; the Bible promised that the prospect would be realized. In his old age he would make himself pitifully ridiculous by launching a campaign against Darwinism, believing that Darwin contradicted Christ and that without a supernatural assurance human hopes could not be fulfilled. 'Evolution, by denying the need or possibility of spiritual regeneration, discourages all reforms, for reform is always based upon the regeneration of the individual.' So he ended as the counsel for the prosecution in the celebrated 'monkey trial' of 1925 in Dayton, Tennessee, when a young schoolmaster was prosecuted for teaching Darwinism, in breach of an anti-evolutionist state law. But there was a greater consistency between the old Bryan and the young than the sophisticated realized. All his life he spoke for the plain people of rural America, now holding up the prospect of reform, now rebuking the backsliding times, as occasion demanded. In 1896 he captivated the Democratic convention with a speech that was both heavily Biblical in language and the purest distillation of Western silver Populism:

You come to us and tell us that the great cities are in favour of the gold standard; we reply that the great cities rest upon our broad and fertile prairies. Burn down your cities and leave our farms, and your cities will spring up again as if by magic; but destroy our farms and the grass will grow in the streets of every city in the country . . . If they say bimetallism is good, but that we cannot have it until other nations help us, we reply, that instead of having a gold standard because England has, we will restore bimetallism, and then let England have bimetallism because the United States has it. If they dare to come out in the open field and defend the gold standard as a good thing, we will fight them to the uttermost. Having behind us the producing masses of this nation and the world, supported by the commercial interests, the labouring interests and the toilers everywhere, we will answer their demand for a gold standard by saying to them: You shall not press down upon the brow of labour this crown of thorns, you shall not crucify mankind upon a cross of gold.

The importance of this speech, with its declaration of holy war against the rich and mighty, and its invocation of the sacred names of Jefferson and Jackson, was that, together with Bryan's subsequent campaign, it recommitted the Democratic party to its original principles. There would still be rich, conservative Democrats in the decades to come, even conservative Democratic Presidential candidates, but just as Hanna had bound the Republicans to the wealthy, so Bryan had bound the Democrats once more to the poor and weak – an action that was to keep his party out of power for sixteen years, but in the end proved to be of immense benefit to it. And it should not be forgotten that it was Populism, as well as the silver agitation, that made this departure not merely possible, but almost inevitable.

Meantime Bryan carried his battle to the people. No front porch for him: 'the Boy Orator from the Platte'[14] travelled 18,000 miles, made 600 speeches and was heard by an estimated five million people. It was a method of campaigning that had a bigger future than McKinley's. He did not always convince those he heard: his single-minded concentration on silver did nothing for him in the East, where, on election day, he failed to carry a single state. But it was Gospel to the West. The excitement was so tremendous that, years later, Vachel Lindsay was inspired to write one of the few great political poems in the English language by his memories of 'Bryan, Bryan, Bryan, Bryan':

. . . It was eighteen ninety-six, and I was just sixteen
And Altgeld ruled in Springfield, Illinois,
When there came from the sunset Nebraska's shout of joy:
In a coat like a deacon, in a black Stetson hat
He scourged the elephant plutocrats
With barbed wire from the Platte.
The scales dipped from their mighty eyes.
They saw that summer's noon
A tribe of wonders coming
To a marching tune.
Oh, the longhorns from Texas,
The jay hawks from Kansas,
The plop-eyed bugaroo and giant giassicus,
The varmint, chipmunk, bugaboo,
The horned-toad, prairie-dog and ballyhoo,
From all the newborn states arow,
Bidding the eagles of the west fly on,
Bidding the eagles of the west fly on . . .[15]

All to no avail. Bryan polled 6,502,925 popular votes and carried twenty-two states with 176 electoral votes, but McKinley beat him by 600,000 popular votes and carried twenty-three states with 271 electoral votes. The Republicans captured both houses of Congress, of which they were to keep control until 1910. The People's party, having endorsed Bryan, now melted fairly rapidly into the Democratic party. (This meant, among other things, that the one-party South was stronger than ever, and the plight of the Southern blacks worse.) Cleveland went into dignified retirement as another conservative President settled into the White House.

---

14 Bryan, at thirty-six, was only a boy in the political world; but it is worth pointing out that he was two years younger than Theodore Roosevelt, four years younger than Woodrow Wilson, neither of whom, in 1896, had a national reputation.
15 Vachel Lindsay, *Collected Poems* (New York, 1937 edn), pp. 97–8.

And then, for no reason that anyone could well understand, the economy revived. Business boomed, farmers found they could at last afford to re-paint their barns, the nightmare of the hard times melted away, Americans got back their self-confidence, and a period of great prosperity, with politics to match, began.

19 The Progressive Adventure 1897–1914

The most successful politician is he who says what everybody is thinking most often and in the loudest voice.

Theodore Roosevelt

Prosperous or not, self-confident or not, the Unite States had reached a point, in the closing years of the nineteenth century, when radical improvements in its political, social and economic arrangements were so plainly necessary that they were actually attempted, and therefore may be called inevitable. Women and men, young and middle-aged, rich, poor and in-between, West, South and North, all acknowledged the necessity and had some hand in shaping the improvements. It was an epoch very much to the American taste, for it seemed a proof that faith in progress, and particularly in the potential for progress in America, was justified. The word 'progressive' had long been a favourite in common speech, as foreign observers such as Rudyard Kipling had already noticed;[1] now it became attached to a political party, a movement, an era. It remains a curiously empty word, but historians will never be able to do without it. And after all due reservations have been made it would be churlish to deny that the United States did in many respects move forward during the period before the First World War – did begin to tackle a good many serious problems intelligently. It is a moderately encouraging story.

Yet America crossed the watershed between the nineteenth and twentieth centuries – in a sense, between the past and our present – in battle, like Britain. There was a warning in this, but it was not noticed. The 'progressive era' began with gunfire in Manila Bay and ended with gunfire in the North

---

1 See Rudyard Kipling, *Captains Courageous* (London, uniform edn, 1899), pp. 84, 120, 191 and, especially, 87: 'I tell you, Harve, there ain't money in Gloucester 'ud hire me to ship on a reg'lar trawler. It may be progressive, but, barrin' that, it's the putterin'est, slimjammest business top of earth.'

Atlantic. Had the Americans understood the meaning of the first event they might have been less astounded by the second, or even have averted it altogether. As it was, they devoted themselves, all but a few of them (Andrew Carnegie was the most conspicuous exception, with his Endowment for International Peace), to their usual pursuits, and the darkest forces at work, which were pushing the whole world to disaster, went unnoticed, unanalysed, unchecked. Almost all Americans continued to think of themselves as probably better than other peoples, and certainly much safer. The progressive generation was quite unaware that, in the twentieth century, war would be the almost constant guide of the national destiny – strengthening, warping, encouraging, perverting all projects. Progressives would owe to warfare some of their most spectacular victories and some of their most shameful defeats. By failing to take it into sufficient account they would come several times to the very brink of destruction. It is a matter for painful speculation how much happier our age might have been had they been wiser.

Historians still argue about the origins of the Spanish–American War of 1898. It was the first foreign war since the Mexican, which had ended fifty years previously. The two conflicts were in some respects strikingly alike – short, successful, aggressive, muddled affairs; both were crowned by territorial aggrandizement and left legacies of conflict. But it is the long gap between them which really needs consideration; and it needs to be asked whether the ending of that period of peace (if we disregard the Civil War and the Indian wars for a moment) was accidental or was significant of a profound change in America's outlook and position.

Geography, historical circumstance and political tradition intersect to condition all nations, and the United States in the nineteenth century was no exception. The world was so large, the oceans so wide and their own continent so vast and empty it was impossible for the Americans to be much concerned with foreign affairs. Furthermore, it was a settled assumption of British foreign policy, from the Treaty of Ghent onwards, that a war with the United States was always likely to be more trouble than it was worth; and while America was at peace with the British Empire (its greatest neighbour) it was buffered against interference from other quarters. The British and the Americans might have their tiffs, for there was always plenty to dispute about; but they were at one in the view classically expressed in the Monroe Doctrine, that the New World was to be preserved against the ambitions of the other great powers. The profits of trade and industrialization from Canada to the Falkland Islands were to be reserved to the English-speaking world; and although the competition between its two principal components, as they built up their ascendancy in the Caribbean and further south, was intense, it never led them to break with each other and so let in the rival pretensions of the Spanish, the French or the Germans. There was, in fact, a partnership between Britain and the United States; but it was so informal, and punctuated by so many rows, that most Americans never detected it. Their notion of Anglo-American relations remained that which had emerged from the Revolution, been strengthened by the War of 1812, and been strengthened again by the Civil War: John Bull was an obsolete bully, but Uncle Sam could handle him. Their notion of war was shaped rather by the experience of killing Indians than by Gettysburg or the Wilderness. Their notion of diplomacy was that it was the preserve of upper-class stuffed shirts who cost the country too much money (though the American foreign service was and is kept pitiably short of funds by Congress). Geographical isolation and strategic security turned the Americans in upon themselves. The conflicts that mattered were their domestic ones. Occasionally these might have diplomatic repercussions, as witness the deep embarrassment caused to the federal government by the anti-Chinese, and later the anti-Japanese, outbursts of feeling in California, which led to the passage of much racist legislation; but that was unusual. On the whole, foreign affairs were noticed only as topics for Fourth of July addresses, or campaign speeches, when it was thought desirable to let the eagle scream a little. Then American statesmen were happy to congratulate their constituents on the immeasurable superiority of their free, republican and democratic institutions; happy to denounce the aristocratic corruption of the Old World; happy to throw in allusions to those favourite shibboleths, Washington's Farewell Address, the Monroe Doctrine and (after 1900) the Open Door. The chances were high that neither these orators nor their audiences had given anything that could be dignified with the name of thought to the implications of these time-worn slogans; but then neither they nor their audiences set much value on thought applied to foreign relations. What they wanted was rhetoric.

Not that Americans were uninterested in the rest of the world. For one thing, it persisted in the habit of sending large numbers of its inhabitants to settle in the United States. For another, as the descendants of the immigrants grew up and prospered, the resultant ethnic communities – Irish-Americans, German-Americans, Italian-Americans and so on – organized themselves into lobbies to influence national policies in favour of their ancestral countries; and whether by exporting dollars to their relations (like the Italians and Slavs) or guns (like the Irish) they profoundly affected the history of those countries. Then, prosperous Americans liked to travel on the fast, luxurious liners that the development of iron and steam technology made possible; enterprising businessmen sought out new fields for profit; missionaries tried to convert the heathen. Perhaps this last was the most characteristic trait: there was a missionary of some kind in almost every American breast. For this people cherished two somewhat inconsistent beliefs: that they were special, indeed unique, and it was vain for lesser breeds to emulate them; and that nevertheless the American way of life was the only model worth emulating and ought to be exported as widely and rapidly as possible. They were benevolent, whether they were trying to save Europe from itself by making it sign a pledge against war, as if it were strong drink (before 1914), or trying to mitigate war's cruellest effects (afterwards). But they were dangerously naïve. They did not really understand foreigners and therefore did not understand themselves in relation to foreigners, which was worse still. The dangers of this naïvety were reinforced by the political system. The various waves of nativism, imperialism and, after the First World War, isolationism always found politicians democratically ready to co-operate and thus win votes; brought to the fore, also, many politicians who knew no better than their constituents.

This did not matter much during most of the nineteenth century. The shield of the Royal Navy (maintained by Great Britain, at her own expense and for her own purposes), America's real remoteness across the oceans and the salutary display of strength and purpose that was the Civil War combined to keep the United States as free from undesirable foreign entanglements as the Founding Fathers wished. But the world was changing. Expanding America, borne on the wings of industrial technology, was beginning to meet similar expansive forces, sustained by the same inventions. The scramble for Africa in the 1880s did not involve the United States, which was occupied in swallowing the last of the American West and was beginning also to take an interest in the Pacific; but the scramble for Asia, which occured in the nineties, concerned it deeply. The American people were as eager as any European nation to bring progress to China in the same way as the British had brought it to India: by trade, by preaching, by teaching, if necessary by gunfire. They took a proprietorial attitude to Japan: had it not been an American sailor, Commodore Matthew Perry, who between 1852 and 1854 had forced that country to open commercial and diplomatic relations with the rest of the world? So the events of the nineties filled them with alarm: the Sino-Japanese War of 1895, the acquisition by the European powers of several key Chinese ports, the extension of extraterritorial rights even in ports which they did not own, what seemed to be the ever-strengthening British hegemony (the Chinese customs were administered by the British), finally the Boxer Rebellion in 1900, which the United States actively helped to crush. Even while the legations in Peking were under siege, John Hay, McKinley's Secretary of State, circulated a note to the powers stating that in future the United States wanted 'China's territorial and administrative entity' to be preserved and wanted all parts of China to be equally open to all nations for trade. This was the Open Door. In its mixture of high-mindedness, low attention to the main chance (Hay, like many of his contemporaries, thought that the China trade was much more lucrative, and more open to American capture, than was really the case) and total inattention to the actualities of power, it was a characteristic American diplomatic initiative of the pre-Pearl Harbor type. Like the Monroe Doctrine, it had better luck than it deserved. None of the other powers felt itself strong enough to make a grab for sole rule in China (though that too would change in due course); so all were happy to acquiesce in Hay's suggestion. China would remain formally independent; in reality she would be exposed to simultaneous robbery from all quarters. Only the robbers would not try to swipe each other's loot.

Properly understood, these events not only showed that the forces which were carrying America into the imperialist phase of her history were at work in other countries too, which was by itself enough to make the world a more dangerous place for the United States; they also showed that the strength of the British Empire was beginning to decline. Britain's nineteenth-century pre-eminence had various causes; perhaps the most important was simply that she was the first industrialized nation. Now that other countries were successfully copying her, indeed in many respects surpassing her, it would be more and more difficult – eventually, impossible – for her to hold on to the extraordinary position and possessions that she had won in the world. To begin with she had to admit to herself that she could not annex China, or even keep that country as part of her exclusive informal Empire. She was beginning to wane, by inches. This meant that America could no longer rely on the Royal Navy as an automatic guarantee against alien interference. In 1903, preoccupied with the rising threat from imperial Germany, Britain withdrew her Caribbean squadron, glad to think that the United States would take her place. Yet this development was perhaps the most ominous of all, for it implied that, to protect her interests, America would now have to take a much more leading, active part in diplomacy, and would have to build up her armed forces to a far greater extent, than had been customary for nearly a hundred years. The only alternative was to think and behave like a third-rate power, eventually to be treated like one and in the end, perhaps, to become one. And although two generations of Americans were to agonize over the choice in the first decades of the twentieth century, there could be no doubt, given the country's proud and energetic temper, which way it would eventually be settled.

For one thing, the United States, as has been shown, was in the grip of forces, above all galloping industrialism and urbanization, which were making play with all the advanced countries. An upsurge of passionate nationalism marked the last twenty years of the nineteenth century and the first fourteen of the twentieth in all the leading European countries and Japan. As the headlong pace of modern development showed no sign of slackening – rather the reverse – the peoples and their rulers clung to each other for reassurance and cemented their union with hatred, fear and contempt of foreigners. In the deepest sense, none of the great powers took foreign policy any more seriously than the United States: they used it as a weapon in internal politics, never considering seriously that it might fatally wound the hands which wielded it. And so the world went on to disaster.

It should therefore be clear that the United States was running out of time in the nineties; but the peace could undoubtedly have been preserved for many years more but for a string of secondary causes. To be sure, these secondary causes were themselves products, or perhaps by-products, of the great underlying determinants of the age: nationalism, economic ambition, social tensions, political obsolescence. But they were not in themselves very formidable. Better management could have faced them down quite easily.

Businessmen were zealous to export, since they feared (prematurely) that the domestic market was saturated. American farmers were looking for a protected market overseas where they need not fear foreign competition and so could dump the results of what they were told was their propensity to over-produce. Many of the new urban newspapers, struggling to build their circulations ever higher, were quite unscrupulous in their attitudes. There had been trouble in Cuba for years, as the inhabitants carried on a never victorious, never defeated revolt against their Spanish rulers, who were anxious not to give up their country's last colony in the New World. Cuba, only ninety miles from the coast of Florida, naturally interested American readers, who were regularly regaled with more or less false stories of Spanish tyranny. The rogue newspaper publisher, William Randolph Hearst, sent the artist and reporter Frederic Remington to Havana with instructions to report and draw the atrocities and the war. Remington wired back that there were no atrocities and no war and that he was coming home. Hearst told him to stay where he was: 'You furnish the pictures and I'll furnish the war.' Hearst could not afford to be scrupulous: he had a private war of his own on his hands, a circulation war with another newspaper publisher, Joseph Pulitzer, who was eventually to redeem his name by founding a School of Journalism at Columbia University, New York, and also the Pulitzer prizes – given annually to what is taken to be the best piece of journalism, and to the best specimens of theatrical, historical and fictional writing. Hearst reasoned that he could defeat Pulitzer only if there was a war, for nothing else sells newspapers so well. He got his way. A United States battleship, the *Maine*, on a courtesy visit to Havana, blew up in harbour on 15 February 1898, killing most of the crew. The explosion was almost certainly an accident, but Hearst thought otherwise. 'Remember the *Maine!*' screamed his papers, announcing that the episode was the result of a fiendish Spanish plot. Clamour for action mounted appallingly. As usual, there was an election due: President McKinley felt he had no alternative. After much prayerful wrestling he did the weak thing and declared war on Spain.

It was a short, businesslike affair. Fine new American warships crushed the Spanish effortlessly. The Royal Navy observed a benevolent neutrality in the Atlantic. In the Pacific, Commodore George Dewey sank or disabled the pathetic squadron of cruisers and gunboats that the Spanish mustered against him, and seized Manila in the Philippines. In the Caribbean an expeditionary force landed in Cuba and inflicted a tactical defeat upon a Spanish force at the Battle of San Juan Hill (1 July 1898). It was a cowboys-and-Indians affair, rather absurdly making a national hero of Lieutenant-Colonel Theodore Roosevelt, second-in-command of a body of volunteer cavalry known as the Rough Riders, no doubt named after the performers in Buffalo Bill's Wild West show. The battle led to a stalemate on land, and the American army began to rot away from disease; but at sea another crushing American victory soon followed, the Battle of Santiago Bay (3 July). Santiago surrendered on 17 July, and that was the end of the Spanish Empire in the Americas. In the subsequent peace treaty (signed at Paris) Spain granted independence to Cuba, and the United States took Puerto Rico, Guam and the Philippines to be colonies of her own. It was as neat a piece of piracy as the Mexican War; and as in the past the US government salved its conscience by making a cash payment to the defeated enemy. The war's only consequence of real value was an investigation by the US army which established the nature of yellow fever and thus led to its elimination, at least in mainland America. It was also not without importance that the war enabled McKinley to begin the modernization of the government offices in Washington which was long overdue. He found the War Department asleep, and left it awake.

For a time, the Americans were proud to have joined the ranks of the overtly imperialist powers. It was as if they had yet to discover that life is a serious business. They received the compliments of the arch-imperialist himself (Kipling) in the notorious verses, *The White Man's Burden*:

Take up the White Man's burden –
  Send forth the best ye breed –
Go bind your sons to exile
  To serve your captives' need;
To wait in heavy harness,
  On fluttered folk and wild –
Your new-caught, sullen peoples,
  Half-devil and half-child.

Understandably, the new-caught Filipinos did not see it like that. American missionaries comforted themselves for the seizure of the Philippines with the thought that the natives could now be converted to Christianity: it was disconcerting to discover that they were Christians already, having long ago been forcibly converted to Catholicism by Spain. In fact the Filipinos, like the contemporary Japanese, felt themselves ready for modern nationhood and saw in the Spanish–American War a wonderful opportunity to win their independence, which their leader Emilio Aguinaldo proclaimed immediately after the Battle of Manila. When they discovered that the United States proposed to substitute its rule for Spain's they took up arms and fought so well that it was three years and more before they too were defeated. The shameful, though not unprecedented, sight of Uncle Sam behaving like George III roused widespread opposition within America, led by Bryan, who again ran for the Presidency against McKinley in 1900; but he lost as decidedly as he had done in 1896. McKinley had not been so sure of victory as to omit all useful precautions, however: he had taken

Theodore Roosevelt (now Governor of New York) onto his ticket as Vice-Presidential candidate. The problem of the Philippines remained, even though Bryan and Aguinaldo were both crushed. The islands were valueless as markets and expensive to defend, being 6,000 miles from the American mainland; but the rise of Japan to ascendancy in the eastern Pacific after the Russo-Japanese War (1904–5) meant that their defence could not be ignored. Before long everyone, even Theodore Roosevelt (who had been influential in bringing about their annexation), agreed that the Philippines were an expensive nuisance and their conquest had been a mistake.

Yet the imperialist instinct was by no means exhausted. The Caribbean had long been an area of great appeal to American expansionists, and the events of the Spanish War had vastly strengthened their ambitions. The latest Treaty of Paris had given the United States an official protectorate of Cuba. The difficulties of strategy during a war in two oceans reinforced the arguments for a trans-isthmian canal through Nicaragua or Panama, at the same time as the conquest of yellow fever made the scheme at last practicable (the French had made a great effort to dig a canal in the eighties, but their workmen had been wiped out by the disease). Britain's withdrawal from the Caribbean and the American annexation of Puerto Rico further involved the United States in the Caribbean; and always the pressure of trade and investment drove it to look southward. The first quarter of the twentieth century was to see intervention in Latin America on an unprecedented scale: armies entered Mexico, the US Marines sustained or overthrew governments in the islands, American business interests came to dominate the economy of the Caribbean and in dubious circumstances the United States dug a canal through the isthmus of Panama (1904–14). In an age of accelerating competition between the nation-states America was coming to play a conspicuous part, as greedy and short-sighted as the rest; and never thought to ask where, unless restrained, this sort of behaviour would lead.

For the prime concern of the American people, as so often before and since, was their own domestic life. Imperial wars might be exciting to read about, but real life happened on the sidewalks of home. Besides, a change was at hand. The long political stagnation that had followed the Civil War epoch was coming to an end: a great alliance for reform was emerging, and would dominate public life for the next two decades. It gave the voters much more to talk about than foreign affairs and imperial responsibilities.

Probably at no time in a democratic society are change, improvement, even reform, quite absent: conservative governments have to adjust to the changing demands of time as well as radical ones. But epochs which generate reform over a wide span of life and years do not arise from such piecemeal impulses. They occur when a society is confident and efficient enough to contemplate large-scale innovation unafraid, and when there is a consensus among its rulers and shapers that such innovation is desirable. A consensus of this sort emerged rapidly in the first years of the twentieth century, until by the beginning of the second decade it seemed that all Americans were now reformers.

The preconditions for a reforming movement were amply present. The upturn of the business cycle enabled Americans rapidly to put behind them all painful memories of 1893 and 1894. At the time it seemed to be a justification of the gold-bugs, for the United States was now committed to the gold standard (a commitment made matrimonial, so to speak, by the Gold Standard Act of 1900), and even of the protectionists, for the tariff was raised yet again in 1897. Closer analysis would have shown that, if anything, the inflationist ideas of the Greenbackers were the ones that had been vindicated. Large numbers of banknotes had been put into circulation in the mid-nineties, and gold coin had suddenly become so common as seriously to mitigate the deflationary effects of making only one kind of currency, and that in a precious metal, the basis of trade. Money was becoming cheaper again, which was hard luck on industrial wage-earners, whose wages stayed the same, but excellent news for primary producers, above all for farmers. The farmers had another bit of luck when atrocious harvests in Europe in 1897 created a voracious demand for the bumper crops of America. Wheat poured out and gold poured in, and all the middlemen, as well as the agriculturalists, benefited. Trade revived in the West. Meanwhile times were so good in Europe that the local factories could not meet the demand: American producers were stimulated to supply the deficiency. For a brief moment, as Britain faltered under the strain of the second Boer War, more capital flowed out of America than flowed in – an unprecedented state of affairs, but one of only short duration, for the time being. British and European investors noticed how well American firms were doing and began to buy their securities in large quantities. Before long a stock-market boom was under way. The percentage of workers unemployed went down steadily, halving between 1897 and 1914; industrial production of all kinds went up. Immigration rose from 216,397 in 1897 to 1,218,480 in 1914 – the last being the second highest figure in the whole of American history. Immigrants do not come in such numbers to a stagnant or unprosperous country.

It is clear, then, that in spite of occasional hiccups (above all, the panic of 1907) these were good years for the US economy, and so presumably for the American people. The second inference is not quite so soundly based as the first, to be sure, and there are plenty of indications that prosperity was not equally diffused among the classes, ethnic groups and sections. Prices to the consumer went up faster than wages, after keeping behind them for twenty-five years; the gap between the incomes and property of the rich and the poor widened; some trades did better than others; the South continued to lag far behind the rest of the country; all these things created tension. But the national growth (the Gross National Product, which went from $14,600,000,000 in 1897 to $38,600,000,000 in 1914) nevertheless made itself felt universally, even among the poorest: it was in this period that the blacks of the South started their Great Migration to the North, attracted, like Europeans, by the work and wages now available there. With the single exception of Florida all the states of the South lost black population during this period, and all the states of the North and West gained it. If only by increasing variety of experience and employment, these were promising years for the African-American. The number of lynchings began to decline.

With such solid ground under their feet it is not surprising that the Americans entered a creative, recreative and even more than usually energetic phase. Their faith in their country and its destiny now assumed an almost triumphal aspect. Not that their faith had ever been seriously shaken. Even at the height of the Populist movement or the depths of the nineties depression, the chief concern of the discontented had been to make America live up to her promise, not to remould her according to alien lights. Still, there had been a defensiveness about Americanism, understandable enough in the circumstances – a defensiveness exemplified by the resurgence of nativism. Now both defensiveness and nativism melted away (not for ever). Not that America was now supposed to be without faults. No doubt there has always been a tension in American minds between the idea that the city has been set upon a hill because it is already perfect and the idea that it has been set up in order to become perfect; in practice the former notion prevails in times of insecurity, so that any suggestions for change, and those who make the suggestions, are regarded with suspicion, while the other prevails in times of self-confidence. So it was at the dawn of the twentieth century. An amazingly wide range of citizens saw possibilities of improvement in their country and worked together to bring it about. Scorn of the dead past, co-existing happily with automatic reverence for George Washington and Abraham Lincoln, was built into every American soul, and there was a competitive eagerness to make the most convincing claim to the future. Everyone with serious business in hand now claimed to be furthering progress (quite like the boosters of new towns and railroads). Eventually the word and its adjective were captured by Robert La Follette (1855– 1925) and Theodore Roosevelt, who between them were responsible for launching a new political party, called the Progressive, in 1912; the platform of that party is still the best document to turn to initially for an understanding of the so-called Progressive Era. It was rather short to be called an era on any time-scale longer than that of American history; yet it was full of fluctuations and mutations, and even the Progressive platform tells only part of the story. Many battles had been won and lost before the document was drafted, and much was to happen after it had been forgotten which nevertheless made significant modifications to the meaning of the word 'progressive'.

At the beginning of the period, when McKinley was safely installed in the White House and gold was becoming plentiful again, the most important component of the idea of progress in America was probably that provided, somewhat paradoxically, by big business. A generation of industrialism had left its mark in all sorts of ways; one was a common belief in the efficiency of business and desire to emulate its techniques. Andrew Carnegie, the leading expounder of the businessman's creed (in 1900 he published a book entitled *The Gospel of Wealth*), seems to have held that the methods by which he had made himself a multimillionaire so many times over would have similarly wonderful results if applied to the fields of humanitarianism and international relations. There was nothing strange about the first assumption. It was widely shared. Charitable foundations, endowed with vast amounts of capital to be spent for a variety of worthy ends – perhaps predominantly educational and medical – now became permanent features of the American scene: corporations for philanthropy. The excursions into international relations were rather more eccentric. Henry Ford, the genius who showed how mass-production, assembly-line methods could make a car a cheap product, available to the millions, eventually brought himself and philanthropic diplomacy into ridicule when he sent his Peace Ship to Europe during the First World War with instructions to her cargo of do-gooders to bring back peace by Christmas. The instructions proved to be inapplicable. Before that, however, Carnegie had played a large part in bringing together the conferences which, in 1899 and 1907, set up the International Court of Arbitration at the Hague, forerunner of the World Court and the post-1945 International Court of Justice.

Business progressivism, then, was neither entirely unidealistic nor wholly ineffective. But it was chiefly concerned with the sphere that businessmen knew best. Having secured a gold currency the bankers, industrialists and merchants felt free to progress towards their other objectives. There were two schools of thought as to what these should be. One held on to the faith in competition and contested the ascendancy of the great trusts; the other held that the time had come to secure past gains and keep open the possibility of new ones by co-operation – in other words, by building up the trusts still more. The second school was on the whole victorious during the progressive period, although the first had its successes too. Undeniably it expressed what may be termed either new prudence or new timidity among the very rich.

There was still something of the old buccaneering spirit about. In 1907, during the panic of that year, J. P. Morgan got possession of the Tennessee Iron and Coal Company for US Steel. By this move US Steel extended its dominance into the South and greatly increased its assets, for the Tennessee Company was to prove an extremely profitable investment.[2] Morgan's activities in this matter were highly adroit and, it appears, none too scrupulous: for example, he seems to have lied extensively to the President of the United States about the transaction, and thereby avoided a possible brush with the Sherman Anti-Trust Act (passed in 1890) of the kind which

2 And in the 1980s was US Steel's only hope of recovery from the combined curse of shrinking markets, outdated plants and incompetent management.

had wrecked one of his earlier combinations, the Northern Securities Company[3], in 1902. But on the whole Morgan was now a conservative, cautious influence. He had come to understand well the fragility of his great combinations. US Steel, the biggest of them all, failed to pay a dividend in 1903. If it made a habit of this the investors who had bought its watered stock might sell out, the price of steel shares might tumble and the great merger come unstuck. This in turn would bring steel prices down, and the financial structure of the United States, which was deeply involved with the steel industry, would be at risk again. In the event, after a few uncertain years, US Steel settled down as one of the best-paying stocks on the market; a 'blue chip'; one of the most reassuringly solid things in the business world. But Morgan and its other masters feared that there might yet be a resurgence of price wars and price-cutting. Wherever the great banker looked he seemed to see signs of weakness. Only his excellent business connections in Europe had enabled him to check the panic of 1893. Since then he had been able to introduce a certain measure of stability into selected industries – railroads, for example; but not enough. Industry was still burdened with the need to earn sufficient income to pay off the watered stock that had been issued so lavishly in more sanguine times; Morgan's own operations had added vastly to the quantity. The nub of the matter was this: if the great trusts could not earn enough income to meet any demand that they repay the capital, as well as the interest of the various debts they had incurred in launching themselves, they would continue to be at the mercy of any downturn in the business cycle; any serious recession would plunge them into difficulties, which in turn would involve the banks and foreign investors who were the chief sources of their risk capital and short-term borrowings. In an unregulated stock market they were also vulnerable to raids by speculators of the Jay Gould type, who might for purposes of their own try to drive down the value of their shares. They were vulnerable to their smaller competitors. If Bethlehem Steel began regularly to out-earn US Steel, for instance, the latter would soon feel the pinch. Yet the collapse of 'Big Steel' would not only ruin the industry and all connected with it (including, perhaps, the House of Morgan); it might start a chain reaction (I permit myself an anachronism) which in the end might bring about the collapse of capitalist America, and perhaps of Europe too. Morgan, in short, had begun to envisage the possibility of just the sort of general crisis that was to occur in 1929; and as he built up his astonishing collection of art, assembled in his travels about England, France and Italy, where greedy dealers placed the treasures of libraries and palaces in front of his glassy eye and huge red nose, he turned over various remedies in his mind. Gradually it became clear to him that safety could lie only in a partnership between American business and the American government. Similar conclusions forced themselves on the other leading capitalists; and they began

---

3 See below, p. 451.

a slow quest to set up such a partnership. They drew up an agenda: American capitalism had a long way to go in the development of the institutions necessary to keep the show on the road. Among other things, a major reform of banking was necessary. The consequence was that big business made itself felt at every stage in the progressive story, and not by any means as a purely reactionary force.

All the same, it would be a mistake to suppose that business, however profoundly it had shaped and now coloured the day-to-day operations of American life, was the key to progressivism. Nor could the industrial working class, however active, muster the power necessary to dominate the epoch. That privilege belonged to the new middle class.

This class had emerged as, numerically, the chief beneficiary of the great transformation of American society. America's rapid development under the impact of industrialism and urbanization implied an equally rapidly developing need for professional services. The need for a new order was generally felt, and implied the recruitment and training of new men, and new women, to administer it. Society was now rich enough to pay for their services. Hence in the last decades of the nineteenth century there was a mushroom growth among the professions. Doctors and lawyers, of course; but also engineers, dentists, professors, journalists, social workers, architects. This was the age of the expert: he was given a free hand, and at times a respect, such as he has seldom enjoyed since. Business itself went professional: one of the heroes of the age was Frederick W. Taylor, prophet of 'scientific management' and the inventor of time-and-motion study; the Harvard Business School was founded in 1908. Each new technical marvel – the telephone, the phonograph, the motor-car, the aeroplane (the Wright brothers made the first powered flights of a heavier-than-air machine in 1903) – increased the faith that there was a sound technical answer to every problem, even to the problem of government. When a devastating hurricane and flood wrecked the port of Galveston, Texas, in 1901, the local businessmen proclaimed the regular authorities incompetent to handle the task of reconstruction and handed the city's government over to a commission of experts – a pattern that was to be widely followed in the next few years.

This may stand very well for what was happening generally. The new class, conscious of its power and numbers and rather too confident in its ability, was anxious to get hold of American society and remake it according to plan. All round were problems that needed solving – crime, disease, bad housing, drunkenness, political corruption – and the new class thought it knew what to do about them. It was still very American in its outlook, very traditional: just as the experts themselves had taken advantage of a society open to the talents to rise, so they wanted their disadvantaged fellow-citizens to rise also; and the democratic individualistic ideology made it seem perfectly legitimate to bid for political power, that is, for votes: to go down into that arena was simply to carry out one's civic duty. Motives did not need to be examined too closely, since they were self-evidently virtuous.

What was new, and important at least to the experts, was the tool-kit they brought to their tasks: their improved spanners, so to speak. It was in the spirit of Edison, the most representative figure of the age, that the new middle class set out to apply their spanners to such various contraptions as the trusts, the state and city machines of the old political parties, and the new urban wastelands. Behind the zeal of these technocrats lay an older tradition, betrayed in the word they used to describe the philanthropic centres they established in the slums, 'settlements': to them the cities were wildernesses, the inhabitants alien savages and the new settlers were bringers both of superior techniques and superior ideas, like the settlers of old – like the Puritans who sailed to Massachusetts with guns and Bibles.

It is thus possible to see in the very approach of these progressives certain limitations, a certain inexperience, which were likely to impede their quest. The most serious difficulty, however, lay elsewhere, in the composition and structure of this new class.

For one thing, it was not wholly new. The trans-Mississippi West might be only half-tamed, the big cities might be as raw as mining towns, but the progressives themselves were not. They were mostly of old American stock, brought up on the old pieties, which their new expertise only veneered. It is astonishing, for instance, how many of them believed in the prohibition of alcoholic drink: in totally forbidding, that is, its manufacture, sale and purchase. Many were also passionately anti-socialist, anti-immigrant and anti-working class. True, they were also anti-big business, and fought many doughty battles against such concerns as the Southern Pacific Railroad, which at the beginning of the twentieth century ruled California as its private fief and was eventually forced, by California progressives, to retreat. But the progressives were too conservative in their instincts, too parochial in their outlook, ever to propose, let alone carry out, fundamental changes in the American system. The boldest thought which they evolved was Herbert Croly's suggestion, in *The Promise of American Life*,[4] that the aims of Thomas Jefferson could now best be achieved by the means of Alexander Hamilton – centralized national institutions and a co-operation between business and government. Had Mr Jefferson lived to encounter this remarkable proposition, he would no doubt have expostulated that this distinction between ends and means was false; and there were plenty of living Jeffersonians to repudiate Croly's thesis. But the trouble was that although Croly was not very radical, no one had anything better to propose, so the progressive movement continually threatened to run out of ideas or, worse still, to lapse into reaction; for there is not much of a step between fighting the innovations of big business and fighting all innovations whatever. Three times were the progressives saved, nationally, from sterility: in 1912, by the split in the Republican party; in 1915, by President Woodrow Wilson's

4 Published in 1909, this book explained Theodore Roosevelt's career to himself. It is intelligent, well informed and almost unreadable.

need to launch a new programme to secure his re-election; in 1917, by the entry of the United States into the First World War. But none of these things did much for progressivism at a local level, and they did not save it for long nationally.

Still, it cannot be denied that the progressives were an impressive generation, as intelligent, high-minded, energetic and good-hearted as any in American history. If their achievements were limited and flawed, they were real; they greatly assisted the adaptation of America to the requirements of modern government; and they laid the foundations, intellectual, personal, ideological – even organizational – of that liberalism which, after 1933, was to become one of the chief creative forces in American politics and society. This is not small praise.

The event which launched the progressive adventure was the murder of President McKinley in 1901, by Leon Czolgosz, a lunatic of the Booth and Guiteau type. Poor McKinley was an even more innocent victim than Lincoln and Garfield: he incurred his fate only because he was head of state at a time when a small number of adolescent revolutionaries had decided that the assassination of heads of state was the right way to bring in the millennium. They killed the President of France, the King of Italy, the Empress of Austria and McKinley. His death horrified the respectable, for he was succeeded by his Vice-President – 'that damned cowboy' as Mark Hanna called him. McKinley had been the embodiment of party regularity; Roosevelt, though he had always been a loyal party man, as befitted a professional politician (the Rough Riders episode had been a mere interlude in his career), was unpredictable, for he was energetic, brilliantly intelligent and young (at forty-three, the youngest man ever to assume the Presidency). He had got to be Vice-President in part because, as Governor of New York, he had created such difficulties for the corrupt Republican bosses in that state that they had insisted on kicking him upstairs. Now that he had risen rather higher than they had wanted they were understandably apprehensive.

Roosevelt was indeed a portent. He was the ablest man to sit in the White House since Lincoln; the most vigorous since Jackson (whom in some ways he resembled); the most bookish since John Quincy Adams. His short-sighted eyes, blinking through pince-nez, might give the idea of a scholar, and he had much of the necessary aptitude, being the author of several solid works of history, including one best-seller, *The Winning of the West*, which did its bit to fix the popular legend of America to scholarly foundations. But the robust and philistine society in which Roosevelt grew up had little time for mere intellectuals, as many fine minds, such as Henry James[5] and Henry Adams, were to complain, and Roosevelt was by nature

5 Theodore Roosevelt on America's greatest novelist: 'a very despicable creature, no matter how well equipped with all the minor virtues and graces, literary, artistic, and social'; a 'miserable little snob'. Roosevelt could not forgive James for settling in England; he blushed to think that he was once an American, and thanked heaven when James became 'an avowedly British novelist'.

too violently self-assertive to be content with the fairly gentle rivalries of academic life. He was still a child when he took the decision to turn himself into a man of action. By dogged exercise he built up his skinny, sickly frame. All his life he eagerly followed whatever pursuit seemed likely to prove his manliness. He boxed, he wrestled, he swam, he carried a revolver with him wherever he went, even into states where it was illegal, even when he was President, which dismayed law-abiding persons such as the President of Harvard. At various times he was a rancher, a big-game hunter in Africa, an explorer in South America, a soldier in the Spanish–American War (he accounted for his decision to volunteer by saying that he wanted to have to explain to his children why he had fought, not why he hadn't). The bitterest disappointment of his life was that he was not allowed to fight in the First World War: he never forgave President Wilson for stopping him. His neurotic compulsion to flex his muscles explains several of the odder episodes in his public career and makes him in some respects an unattractive figure. But on the whole his contemporaries shared his values, and as they expected politics and politicians to be entertaining if possible they revelled in his incessant showing-off and in his pungent gift of speech: as for example when he compared investigative journalists to Bunyan's man with a muck-rake, and thus gave a new word to the language.[6] At all moments between McKinley's death and his own, eighteen years later, he was probably the best-loved man in America.

Although the intricacies of his individuality are fascinating and almost endless, in the last resort he is best understood in conventional terms. Like Disraeli, another flamboyant performer, he had more substance than his show suggested, and the substance was of a fairly normal kind (he could not have gone so far otherwise). He was intensely ambitious, and he knew that it would be unwise to trust to his luck and brilliance alone, so he served a long apprenticeship in the routine politics of New York Republicanism, an apprenticeship which taught him all he needed to know about party politics and gave him a solid grounding in the art of administration too ('the bulk of government is not legislation but administration,' as he remarked in later years). He wanted to be President, but he had no programme of Presidential action: he relied on circumstances to show him what needed to be done. Above all, he was content with the goals that the American political system suggested. Not for him dictatorial or Messianic fantasies. He did not even defy tradition to the extent of running for a third term in 1908. He stridently asserted the excellence of being American; he was awed by the glory of being President; and he believed, as a Christian gentleman with a comfortable unearned income, that he owed it to his countrymen to

6 Journalists now wear the term *muckraker* as a badge of honour, but Roosevelt meant to be thoroughly insulting. Bunyan's muckraker was content to rake to himself 'the Straws, the small Sticks, and Dust of the Floor', blind to the celestial crown that was offered him (*Pilgrim's Progress*, Part 2). Roosevelt, like many politicians since, wished that journalists were less fond of exploring the seamy side of politics.

do something in their service. At bottom he was perfectly safe, from the Hanna point of view; only he brought a flair to politics which was new. Between his insurgent appearance and 'regular' reality it is no wonder that he was able to work the political system beautifully.

His first care was to secure his nomination for the Presidency, as Republican candidate in his own right, in the 1904 election; his next, to win that election (which he did, triumphantly: he gained 336 electoral votes and had a majority of 2.5 million over the Democratic candidate). But the interest of his first term as President scarcely lies in these predictable manoeuvres. Roosevelt knew, as well as any other party-political pro, how the patronage system could be exploited by a sitting President to look after his personal interests; there really is no more to be said. It was in other ways that he showed himself to be a President of a new kind, or rather, of an old kind revived.

He kept his ear cocked to catch the cries and shifts of public opinion (an assiduously cultivated relationship with newspaper reporters helped). Thus, the first crisis of his administration was the anthracite coal strike of 1902. It was not much different from any of the other major strikes which had dotted the history of the previous twenty-five years, but Roosevelt sensed that since on the whole people sympathized with the miners, who worked in dreadful conditions for miserable pay, he could help himself by helping them. So he intervened dramatically, sending federal troops to the mine districts of western Pennsylvania, ostensibly to protect the mine-owners' property but really to see fair play for the miners, and summoning both sides to Washington, where he helped them to come to an agreement which gave the strikers much of what they wanted. The contrast with Cleveland's behaviour during the Pullman strike could not have been more marked. Roosevelt's prestige soared, and was further helped by the Northern Securities case, which occurred at about the same time. J. P. Morgan, in his usual fashion, had negotiated an agreement between the competing railroad barons of the far North-West, one which bid fair to eliminate wasteful competition between the lines in that region. A holding company, Northern Securities, was set up to carry out the arrangements. To Morgan's astonishment Roosevelt challenged the bargain in the name of the Sherman Anti-Trust Act, which had previously been used effectively only against labour unions. The President forced the dissolution of the new company. His action made little economic sense, but the unpopularity of big business was such that this sort of 'trust-busting' action gained Roosevelt further increments of enthusiastic support. He helped himself again by beginning work at last on the trans-isthmian canal. A squalid intrigue, from the disgraceful details of which most Americans were happy to avert their eyes, engineered a revolt in Colombia which gave birth to a new country, Panama; which then agreed that the United States might build the canal through its territory on spectacularly favourable terms: the USA was allowed to create a colony from sea to sea, the Canal Zone, through the middle of the new republic. Roosevelt got the credit for actually starting what had been talked of for so long, and nobody minded that in the process he had proclaimed the Roosevelt corollary to the Monroe Doctrine: he asserted that the United States had a right to do what it liked to, with or in Latin American countries, so long as it could plead its own interests or an ill-defined duty to police the western hemisphere on behalf of the civilized world. Roosevelt clothed this imperial arrogance in stately words for public consumption; in private he revealed his attitude more sincerely when he talked irritably of his wish to spank those wretched little republics.

These various decisive actions were not lost on intelligent observers. The President of Princeton University, Dr Woodrow Wilson, who had made his academic reputation twenty years earlier with a book on what he called Congressional government, now began to feel that he had underrated the modern Presidency. He wrote a new book, *Constitutional Government in the United States* (1908), in which he remarked of the President that

He can dominate his party by being spokesman for the real sentiment and purpose of the country, by giving direction to opinion, by giving the country at once the information and the statements of policy which will enable it to form its judgements alike of parties and of men . . . Let him once win the admiration and confidence of the country, and no other single force can withstand him, no combination of forces will easily overpower him. His position takes the imagination of the country. He is the representative of no constituency, but of the whole people. When he speaks in his true character, he speaks for no special interest. If he rightly interpret the national thought and boldly insist upon it, he is irresistible; and the country never feels the zest of action so much as when its President is of such insight and calibre . . . A President whom it trusts can not only lead it, but form it to his own views.

No such bold claims for the Presidency had been heard since the days of Andrew Jackson; yet they did but lay bare the significance of Theodore Roosevelt's leadership, unveiling the role which all ambitious twentieth-century Presidents would seek to play, and the scope which existed for playing it. Wilson's words were indeed prophetic, and some of the prophet's friends began to feel that he ought to be given his turn at the job he described. The analysis was clearer about Roosevelt than he had so far been about himself. But it contained a trap, for it outlined a programme for modern Presidents which was tempting yet, as many of them have found out (including Wilson himself), extraordinarily difficult to realize. And in 1908 the vision was perhaps premature, for Congress was still there, and still, apparently, as much in command of the government as ever. Like the President, its members sensed that rewards were now to be won by gratifying the taste for reform, and they did not mean to let Roosevelt monopolize them.

The railroad problem, for example, had become intolerable to almost everyone, and Congress at last began to tackle it seriously, passing the ineffective Elkins Act against rebates in 1903 and the Hepburn Act of 1906, which gave the Interstate Commerce Commission broad powers to fix maximum and minimum railroad rates, extended its jurisdiction to cover the Pullman and other sleeping-car companies, empowered it to inspect the accounts of railroad companies and made its orders binding until a court had reviewed them (and afterwards, if the court sustained the commission). This act was a characteristic triumph of the Progressive Era. Travellers were tired of paying high fares for places on unsafe trains (railroad accidents were not so frequent or so spectacular as steamboat explosions in the old days, but there were far too many of them). Western farmers felt as bitter as ever about their innumerable grievances. Other shippers, such as oil and coal companies, disliked the chaos of rates brought about by totally free competition. The railroads themselves disliked the system under which they operated. They did not want to give rebates to extortionate giants like Standard Oil (which Theodore Roosevelt liked to denounce, thereby helping to make Rockefeller's trust the universal whipping boy of the age). They disliked having to undercut each other in the quest for traffic, for even if undercutting ruined a rival, it often came near to ruining the undercutter too. They did not even much appreciate their unpopularity, which was, they felt, undeserved. The late William H. Vanderbilt, the Commodore's son, had got into fearful trouble in 1883 for saying 'the public be damned!' (he was forced to sell all his railroad shares to Morgan), but had he not been right? Why should the railroads provide unprofitable lines and trains which the public would not pay for? No doubt their safety record was appalling (and railroad men disliked getting killed or maimed as much as anyone else) but how, given the competitive world, could the lines earn enough money to service their debts, pay their shareholders, maintain their equipment, pay their workers' wages *and* improve safety? They felt they were being ruined by undercutting, rebates and free passes.

In short, there was pressure from all sides to reform the conditions in which the railroads operated, and the Hepburn Act was Congress's response. After a long and bitter debate in the Senate the Act was passed by a majority of seventy-one to three. It had sailed through the House easily, and finally been approved there by a vote of 346 to seven.

This law and the manner of its passage was characteristic of all the important legislation of the Progressive Era. As its lopsided majorities should suggest, it was generally acceptable, a compilation of compromises, rather than radical. It had only needed months of struggle for passage because the reformers initially wanted more than they could get; because the irreconcilable conservatives, though few, were good fighters; and, above all, because the railroads, though in principle in favour of reform, disliked in practice the concessions that reform required of them, especially the degree to which they lost independence to the ICC. The Act, as passed, was full of loopholes, some of which would be closed by later laws. It was a useful and important beginning, that was all. But the ballyhoo which surrounded it convinced everyone that something wonderful had occurred. Had not the President stumped the country in support of the bill for months? He had, and whipped up a storm of public concern. He had worked hard to persuade Congress in other ways, cultivating Democrats and Republicans with fine impartiality, using the patronage freely, and knowing just when to stand firm, just when to offer a compromise. Those Congressional majorities suggest that his labours were somewhat unnecessary and that he did not altogether deserve the credit for the measure which he greedily appropriated. Some sort of bill was due. But the episode served to bolster the growing myth of Presidential power, and thereby to strengthen real Presidential influence. Soon Roosevelt would be gruffly defending himself against charges of executive usurpation, just like Andrew Jackson before him.

Similar observations might be made, in all respects, of the other big laws of the Roosevelt years. All of them did something to increase the regulatory powers of the federal government; most of them were of more help to the consumer and the industrialist than to the industrial worker; none of them was very radical, and all of them passed Congress by huge majorities. Next to the Hepburn Act, and passed in the same year, came the Meat Inspection Act and the Pure Food and Drug Act. Both benefited from the enormous uproar created by the publication of *The Jungle*, a novel by Upton Sinclair, the most famous of the muckrakers, who exposed the miserable condition of the workers in the Chicago stockyards and the grossly insanitary conditions in which meat was slaughtered and canned for sale there. Sinclair was more interested in the workers than in poisoned meat, but as he said, 'I aimed at the public's heart and by accident I hit it in the stomach.' Americans did not appreciate being sold poisoned food, and let their Congressmen know; Theodore Roosevelt himself was appalled, especially as official reports came in to confirm Sinclair's findings; the largest firms of meat-packers, whose chief interest was in the export of meat to Europe, where strict sanitary regulations were enforced, were delighted at the prospect of disciplining the multitude of their smaller competitors – something they had been trying to do for decades. So the Meat Inspection Act went easily through Congress. It laid down rules for the sanitary operation of slaughterhouses and canning factories, and set up a federal inspectorate to enforce them – another accretion of power to Washington. The Pure Food and Drug Act, the pet project of Dr Harvey Wiley of the Department of Agriculture, forbade the sale of adulterated products in inter-state commerce, and gave Wiley, as head of a new bureau of food and drug inspection, power to make sure the law was obeyed (but when it seemed that the bureau was going to ban saccharine, which Roosevelt took in his coffee, the obstreperous chemist was soon cut down to size). This Act, too, was supported by the big boys of American commerce, and opposed, naturally on high grounds of principle, by their smaller, weaker rivals, who made a good living out of selling worthless or even dangerous patent medicines (such as Lydia Pinkham's famous all-purpose cure) and tainted whisky. It too got a large Congressional majority.

The year 1906 was the *annus mirabilis* of Republican progressivism. The President was well satisfied with Congress, and he himself towered over the national scene. Not only had he sponsored much useful legislation; not only did he conduct the day-to-day business of government, its administration, with businesslike skill; not only did he, very occasionally and very warily, initiate a prosecution under the Sherman Act; he was awarded the Nobel Peace Prize for his part in helping Russia and Japan to end their war with each other by the Treaty of Portsmouth, New Hampshire, in 1905. It was an optimistic time: everywhere serious reformers began to pluck up their hopes. Perhaps their moment was come at last.

If so, it seemed that they would have to find a fresh leader. By the end of his second term Roosevelt had shot dozens of bears; he had called a conservation conference at the White House in 1908 to publicize the need to husband America's physical resources; he had shown off America's fine new navy by sending it off to sail round the world; and he had co-operated with Morgan to overcome the panic of 1907 that had momentarily threatened progressive prosperity. These and his other achievements did not satisfy him, but he had given his word, all too flatly and publicly, on the night of his election in 1905: he would not seek a third term, dearly though he would have liked to keep his job, for he was only just fifty and felt as energetic as ever. At least he could, like Andrew Jackson again, choose his successor: William Howard Taft, who, thanks to Roosevelt's warm backing, easily defeated Bryan's last bid for the Presidency in 1908. His patron tactfully took himself off to Africa to slaughter animals, confident that he had left the country and the Republican party in good hands. He did not return for more than a year, and by the time he did so a great political storm was brewing.

Taft was an enormously fat man and had proved invaluable to Roosevelt in the various administrative posts he had occupied, such as Secretary of War. Apart from that he was noted for his legal learning, an attribute which would eventually carry him to the Chief Justiceship of the United States (1921–30) – the only ex-President ever to sit in the Supreme Court. At first he found it difficult to realize he was President, so much had Roosevelt dominated the office; and he does not seem to have expected to achieve very much: 'this is a very humdrum administration' he once remarked, not without satisfaction. But he was not yet an iron-bound reactionary, though he became one in his old age; in a sense he too was a progressive; he had a lawyer's sense of duty and initiated far more anti-trust prosecutions than Roosevelt had done: it was he who broke up the Standard Oil Company, forcing it to dissolve into thirty-four separate organizations (John D. Rockefeller kept his large stake in all of them). But he was not a creative politician; not the man to take the lead and master events, or even his party; and it soon became clear that this ability to lead was just what was essential.

For the Republican party had been too successful. Its steady run
of electoral victories had attracted to it a most heterogeneous range of
supporters, and even before Roosevelt's retirement they had begun to
quarrel among themselves. There was the tariff, a subject which Roosevelt
had prudently left alone. The hard core of the Republicans in Congress
were as stoutly protectionist as ever; but many Senators and Congressmen,
perhaps especially those from the Mid-West, felt that since the United
States was now so prosperous and so clearly stronger than all its competitors, the time had come to lower the tariff somewhat and give American
consumers the blessing of a lower cost of living. Andrew Carnegie said
the same. The Democrats had always reasoned in this way. There was an
almighty row in Congress, which Taft was unable to mediate successfully.
Instead he took sides with the high-tariff men of the East, led by Senator
Aldrich of Rhode Island and the Speaker, Joe Cannon of Illinois, who in
this matter went against his own section. For the tariff of 1909 raised the
rates on imported manufactured goods while lowering those on the raw
materials produced in the Mid-West. This 'eastern-made bill to protect
eastern products' was described by Taft in a speech in Minnesota as 'the
best bill that the Republican party ever passed'. Mid-Western Republicans
felt betrayed.

Their indignation was strengthened by two other quarrels. Congress was
now receiving recruits who had succeeded in politics by taking the liberal
route in state and city affairs, often in the teeth of their local Republican
machines. Men such as Senator Robert La Follette of Wisconsin, and
Congressmen George Norris of Nebraska and Jonathan Dolliver of Iowa,
brought with them to Congress the habits of insurgents (as they were soon
to be named) and chafed against the rigid rule of the regular party leadership,
which they saw as the mere tool of big business. They hoped, by overthrowing Speaker Cannon, to help clear the way for reforms, especially of
the tariff, which they favoured; and at first it seemed that they would have
Taft's assistance. But the President eventually decided that Cannon was
more of a help to him than a hindrance: a calculation that was soon
exposed as faulty, for the Speaker did little to accommodate Taft's views
on legislation, while the insurgents, with Democratic help, succeeded in
stripping him of many of the powers which Speakers had enjoyed over the
House of Representatives ever since the days of Henry Clay. In the long
run this weakening of the Speaker greatly helped Congressional conservatives, since his power fell into the hands of the chairmen of the various
committees who, being chosen by seniority, tended to be old and stick-in-
the-mud, when not downright reactionary; but it seemed a victory for
progressivism at the time; and Taft had been on the wrong side of the fight.

Still more damaging was a breach that opened between Taft and Roosevelt. This was occasioned by Gifford Pinchot, the head of the US Forest
Service, who in Roosevelt's day had earned great applause by introducing
strict measures of conservation (a word he claimed to have invented) in the

national domain. Pinchot was one of the first to perceive that America's resources of timber and minerals would not last for ever, and he led a very successful campaign to curb the traditional energy with which Western entrepreneurs had exploited the new country. Almost 150 million acres were added to the government reserves of forty-five million acres, which did not make the Roosevelt administration particularly popular in the land-greedy Far West. Taft appointed a Western man, Richard A. Ballinger, formerly mayor of Seattle, to be Secretary of the Interior: he and Pinchot soon fell out. Pinchot behaved badly, and Taft supported the secretary against him, eventually dismissing the forester in January 1910. Pinchot rushed over to Europe to seek the aid of Theodore Roosevelt, who returned to America in June; Taft stuck to Ballinger; and before long 'the Colonel' (as he was universally known), who never got used to being an ex-President, had persuaded himself that in 1912 it would be his duty to the cause of progress to try to take the Republican nomination and the Presidency away from the man to whom he had given them.

From a purely party point of view, he had some justification. The Republicans were splitting dramatically, and the insurgent wing (now beginning to describe itself as 'progressive') was getting stronger and stronger. Taft had made himself unacceptable to what was now the most dynamic element in his party. And Republican disarray was proving a huge tonic to the Democrats. Taft tried to purge the insurgents in the primary elections of 1910; he failed; the insurgents carried state after state; and in the general Congressional and gubernatorial elections of the autumn the Democrats swept to victory in every section except the Pacific West (where the progressive Republicans scored a smashing victory in California, defeating the Old Guard and the Southern Pacific Railroad simultaneously). Even before election day Roosevelt was convinced that some radical steps were necessary. He read Herbert Croly, he began to preach what he called 'the New Nationalism' (a popularization of Croly's ideas) and he went on a huge speaking tour in a vain effort to hold the Republicans together and stave off their defeat.

The sequel may be briefly sketched. The insurgents gathered round Senator La Follette to form the Progressive Republican League, with the avowed aim of denying Taft renomination in 1912. Their original candidate was to be La Follette, but before very long 'the Colonel', having suffered one too many affronts at the hands of the administration, threw his hat into the ring and took the League away from its founder. He then moved against Taft. His instrument was the new institution of the primary election. One of the chief concerns of progressives was to rescue politics from the undue influence of the great capitalists, and the politicians, seeing a chance to reassert their own independence, had in many states lent themselves to the cause. The result was the adoption of various measures, the most important of which were the direct election of Senators, which became part of the US Constitution in 1913; the referendum; the recall; and the primary election.

The referendum idea permitted any proposal to be laid before a state's voters, provided that enough of them had petitioned the legislature to have it put on the ballot; the recall election was a device by which an unsatisfactory politician might be forced to face the voters again before his normal term ran out. Though widely adopted in state constitutions, particularly in the West, neither procedure found its way into national politics or the national Constitution. The recall election, in particular, proved rather futile: it was a sort of modernized form of impeachment and, like impeachment, was too cumbersome to be effective. There have been next to no successful recalls in modern times. The primary idea was much more successful. Instead of a party's candidates being selected in private, by party bosses or any other unrepresentative group, they would now be chosen by the registered voters of that party. There might be primary elections for state offices, or for federal ones (Senatorships and seats in the House of Representatives). There might be primary elections for the Presidency. Not all states had (or have) adopted the system (and it has never been incorporated in the Constitution) but there were enough for Roosevelt to make a great showing in 1912. He swept triumphantly through them all, and arrived at the Republican convention in Chicago announcing that 'We stand at Armageddon and we battle for the Lord.' Nobody quite knew what this stirring message meant, but it was certainly memorable. However, it did not guarantee success. Taft, using his patronage as President to the utmost and benefiting from the support of the bosses, retained the support of a majority of the delegates, and was renominated.

Roosevelt had always prided himself on his 'regularity'. Not for him the nice conscience and the finicky disloyalty of a Mugwump. But his blood was up. He and his followers walked out of the convention as soon as the control of the Taft managers was made apparent, and on 6 August met as the Progressive party. 'The Colonel' was the candidate; Hiram Johnson, the Governor of California, was the Vice-Presidential candidate; the bull moose challenged the Republican elephant and the Democratic donkey as the party symbol; the party platform, embodying the New Nationalism, was one of comprehensive radicalism, promising such things as votes for women, the prohibition of child labour and the eight-hour day. It denounced 'the unholy alliance between corrupt business and corrupt politics', the labour injunction and convict labour, and demanded a national system of social insurance. It endorsed labour unions. All this might have alarmed the mighty, except that it was notorious that the funds for the new party were largely supplied by the House of Morgan and that a senior Morgan partner, George Perkins, had had a leading hand in drafting the platform – which is why it also contained a pledge for banking and currency reform. It remained the most remarkable thing of its kind since the 1892 Populist platform. It was also notable for the fact that, unlike the Populist platform, its concerns were overwhelmingly industrial and urban. America had changed profoundly in twenty years.

However, it had not changed so much that an entirely new party, suddenly appearing from within the Republicans, could brush aside both the old parties at once. The Democrats held fast, and could now make a fairly convincing case for themselves as a progressive party. There was the Bryanite tradition: its leader accepted that he could never again be nominated, but his ex-Populist followers were still numerous and vigorous. There was the strong commitment of the Democratic city machines to first- and second-generation immigrants, and to Catholics. Overlapping substantially with this group was organized labour. The workers had had a thin time of it since 1896. A string of court decisions had weakened the AFL, and as many important strikes had been defeated. Worst of all, in California in 1910 desperate union men had dynamited the *Los Angeles Times* building, which had been erected by non-union labour: twenty lives had been lost in the explosion, and there had been a nationwide reaction of anger and alarm. Plainly, the unions needed all the friends they could get, and ever since 1908 Gompers had skilfully led them to look chiefly in the direction of the Democrats. This had not been acceptable to the more radical wing of the labour movement, which turned rather to Debs and the Socialist party; but the radicals were an inconsiderable force. Their union movement, the Industrial Workers of the World (IWW, or 'Wobblies'), was no sort of threat to the AFL because of its incessant splits and quarrels. Even the strongly pro-labour platform of the Progressives did not lure the majority of workers away from the Democrats. That party was also helped by its control of the House of Representatives after the 1910 election. It set up the so-called Pujo Committee (named after its chairman, Pujo of Louisiana) to investigate the 'money trust' – in other words, J. P. Morgan, who was discovering, to his vast surprise, that most of his fellow-citizens regarded him as one of the problems of capitalism, instead of part of the solution (in 1911 Taft brought suit against US Steel under the Sherman Act). Morgan did not testify before Pujo at any length until after the 1912 election, but the mere existence of the committee seemed to confirm the Democrats' commitment to reform. The impression was rubbed in by the man they nominated for the Presidency, Governor Wilson of New Jersey.

Wilson had all the right credentials. Initially a Cleveland Democrat, he had been moving leftward for ten years or so. He had acquired national fame as a reforming President of Princeton. In 1910 he accepted the Democratic nomination for the governorship of New Jersey. Winning election, he had shown himself to be a strong reforming leader: he had broken with the bosses who had nominated him, and that in itself was enough to commend him to the progressives, who were nearly as strong a force among the Democrats as they had become among the Republicans. There was an eloquence, an elevation in Wilson's speeches that stirred men's hearts. He was the man; as candidate he held the Democracy together, preaching of a 'New Freedom' (against the New Nationalism) in terms that were reassuringly old-fashioned: 'As to the monopolies, which Mr Roosevelt proposes to legalize and to welcome, I know that they are so many cars of juggernaut, and I do not look forward with pleasure to the time when the juggernauts are licensed and driven by commissioners of the United States.' 'If America is not to have free enterprise, then she can have freedom of no sort whatever.' He ran against finance capitalism like Jackson running against the Bank of the United States. (His inaugural address, too, was to sound very Jacksonian.) Taft, who soon despaired of re-election, stayed in the race just to spoil things for Roosevelt; and in due course Wilson was elected President with 6,296,547 votes to Roosevelt's 4,118,571. Poor fat Taft was a dismal third, with 3,484,956 votes; and Eugene V. Debs, the Socialist candidate for the fourth (but not the last) time, surprised everybody by more than doubling his 1908 vote to 900,672. The Democrats captured both houses of Congress. For a moment it seemed that everyone was a progressive. The reforming tide was at its peak.

Woodrow Wilson was perhaps luckier in the moment of his first election than any President since Andrew Jackson. Not a cloud was in the sky; his party colleagues in Congress were eager to respond to his wishes; the country was expectant; and twelve years of progressive turmoil had established a fairly comprehensive agenda for action, if the President chose to adopt it. It was a great opportunity which a quietist such as Taft might have deliberately forgone; but Wilson was an activist.

His personality embodied many of the sources of the progressive impulse. For one thing, he was an educated professional. He had no private means, but his family had been able to send him to Princeton, to law school in Virginia and to Johns Hopkins University in Baltimore, where he attended the graduate seminar in history – the first of its kind in America. As President of Princeton he had shown himself to be a better educational reformer than he was a scholar; but he always knew himself to be a politician and orator by temperament. He had imbibed from his father, a distinguished Presbyterian minister, the tendency to do-goodism and to over-confident idealism which was so marked a feature of the era. He was intensely ambitious, and excited by the thought of getting power into his hands; perhaps he was tempted to think, like Lincoln, that the best thing about the American political system was the scope it offered for men like himself to rise to the top. As events were to show, he was also like Lincoln in having an instinct for great issues; there was a prophetic touch in him and, as events were to show, a deep emotionalism: the sorrows of the world were real to him. Persons near at hand were perhaps less so. He was courteous enough, but he was a poor judge of character, rather too disdainful of less able or upright mortals, and, in the end, with his thin frame, false teeth and professorial eyeglasses, definitely not one of the boys. His eloquence, vision, sincerity and intelligence could dazzle, charm and fascinate the most unlikely mortals, even hard-bitten party bosses, who did not at once realize what a ruthless and realistic politician he was; but he was difficult to love. Some found him easy to hate, notably Theodore Roosevelt, whom he had defeated, and Roosevelt's closest political ally, Senator Henry Cabot Lodge of Massachusetts. He relied more on intuition, when it came to decision making, than on logic, and was absolutely stubborn in defending his intuitive conclusions. He demanded unquestioning loyalty from his family, friends, colleagues and subordinates; those who opposed him too persistently he regarded as personal enemies. Women were attracted to him.

In 1913 such a man, determined to leave a great mark on history, could not fail. He was helped by the fact that although he had made his career in the North he had been born and bred in Georgia and the Carolinas; as he once said, 'the South is the only place where nothing ever has to be explained to me'. The Democrats in Congress, dominated by Southerners, were naturally anxious to help the first President from Dixie since Andrew Johnson. Their new-found ascendancy had one evil consequence: Southern practices of racial discrimination, which the Republicans had hitherto kept at bay, now entered the federal government, where Jim Crow would prevail for the next twenty years and more. Wilson seems scarcely to have noticed, or to have noticed that he was disappointing the numerous blacks who had voted for him. He was much too busy pushing through the Underwood tariff, which fulfilled an old Democratic dream by lowering the schedules significantly for the first time since the Civil War; the Clayton Act, which strengthened the anti-trust laws; and the Federal Reserve System, which went some way to fill the gap in America's financial institutions resulting from the absence of a central bank. He developed new techniques of leadership, or perhaps it should rather be said that he revived old ones. Realizing, as befitted the author of *Congressional Government*, that it was essential to collaborate with Congress, he spent long hours on the Hill, cajoling and reasoning with Congressmen and Senators; and he revived the practice, discontinued since the time of Thomas Jefferson (who was no orator), of reading his messages to Congress in person, especially the annual State of the Union addresses. It worked wonderfully well. Even when the economy slid into a recession in 1914, leading to the loss of many Democratic seats in Congress (and to the slaughter of the Progressive party which thereafter, abandoned by Theodore Roosevelt, more or less ceased to count), he was able, by appropriating several leading ideas of Roosevelt's New Nationalism – by accepting, above all, that the powers and activities of the federal government must be increased and therefore feeling free to propose further legislation, for instance, a law forbidding child labour in factories and sweatshops – to find new work for the legislature and enhanced authority for himself. By the elections of 1916 he had compiled the most impressive record of legislation proposed and passed of any President since George Washington, and in so doing had confirmed the insights of Herbert Croly. Wilson, with the great liberal lawyer Louis D. Brandeis at his elbow, might orate of the New Freedom and the delights of small-scale government as well as small-scale business; in fact the spirit of Alexander Hamilton was more potent. Wilson's actions strengthened the capitalist order by reforming it; they increased the functions and size of the federal bureaucracy; and they gave added power and authority to the Presidency. In a word, whether he admitted it to himself or not, Wilson's mission was the same as Theodore Roosevelt's: it was to give the United States an economic and political government adequate to the demands of the modern world, and the nostrums of the venerated Jefferson seemed to be of very little use to him in the task.

Yet, even if we concede that his goal was the right one, it cannot be said that he really attained it. By comparison with the past, even the recent past, his achievements were impressive; measured against what needed to be done, they were almost trivial. The story of the Federal Reserve Act illustrates the point to admiration.

The panic of 1907 may in retrospect be seen as the turning-point of the Age of Gold. For a week in October a team of New York bankers, led by Pierpont Morgan, struggled heroically against a crisis which threatened to bring down the whole American financial and economic structure; and they prevailed. But it had been a close-run thing, and victory would probably have eluded them had it not been for Morgan's unique personal authority (at one moment he locked a couple of dozen of America's richest men into his library on Madison Avenue and then forced them to pledge their millions to the salvation of Wall Street). As he himself remarked later, it was not healthy that economic security should rely so much on one man. But the panic also demonstrated, to those with eyes to see, three even more important points.

First, it had been brought on by an all-too-familiar combination of speculative greed and dishonest or incompetent financial management. In other words, the conditions which had led to panics in the past – in 1837, for instance, or 1873 – were not correcting themselves as American capitalism matured: they were getting worse.

Second, the general economic effect of panics and crashes was getting greater all the time. Even though the 1907 panic was quickly brought under control and then halted in its course, it plunged America into depression for the next year, and the smooth and rapid growth of the years since 1897 was not renewed, even after confidence was restored. Prosperity was at best patchy and uncertain until the outbreak of the First World War.

Finally, it was apparent that the only agency big enough to control events in future was the federal government. The Secretary of the Treasury had come to Morgan's aid in 1907 with deposits of thirty-five million dollars from the federal surplus, which was fortunately just then a healthy one; on another occasion a much larger operation might be necessary, since the government's obligation to protect American prosperity was now acknowledged. Clearly it would be better if another crisis could be prevented by a steady application of government policy; *ad hoc* contrivances like those adopted in 1907 were not enough; in short, a federal law was necessary – perhaps more than one.

This was the reason for the Federal Reserve Act. It was the first episode in the process by which Washington has since become the determining factor in the US economy; but it was a very modest first step. The problem which the business world saw as a result of 1907 was the unsatisfactory state of the currency. Even allowing for the increased production of gold and the fantastic profitability of the American economy, there was simply not enough money available to the national banks for use in emergency – such an emergency as that in 1907 when the failure of two leading finance houses, for lack of ready cash, nearly brought the whole structure of finance capitalism tumbling. New forms of credit would have to be devised, and they would have to be backed by the federal government, precisely as Alexander Hamilton had argued when he founded the First Bank of the United States.

Popular hostility to Wall Street was so deep, and the dissensions among the bankers themselves were so sharp, that it proved impossible to get a new bank law through Congress under either Roosevelt or Taft; but it soon became one of the Wilson administration's chief projects, and was duly achieved in the autumn of 1913. The Bank of the United States was not revived: the ghost of Andrew Jackson was still powerful enough to prevent it; but an effective substitute was devised, acceptable both to Wall Street and to the present leaders of Jackson's party – Woodrow Wilson and William Jennings Bryan (now Wilson's Secretary of State). The reserve system reflected political and geographical realities by being a federation of twelve districts or regions, the two most important being those centred on New York and Chicago; but it was directed from Washington by a Federal Reserve Board, consisting of the Secretary of the Treasury, the Comptroller of the Currency and five other members, all appointed by the President. (This arrangement was not particularly welcome to the bankers, who would rather have appointed the board themselves; but Wilson saw no reason for allowing the poachers to elect the gamekeepers.) The Board was and is substantially independent of the President, but by placing its headquarters in Washington and by controlling appointments to it the authors of the Act (Congressman Carter Glass of Virginia chief among them) made sure that it would be a national body, with a strong sense of its political obligations as well as its commercial ones. In return for conceding this measure of political interference the capitalists got a flexible and dependable currency administered by the equivalent of a central bank. The conditions of 1907 therefore ought not to recur.

Nor did they. But no two financial crises have exactly the same occasions: the Federal Reserve Act of 1913 tackled only one sort of weakness and left the United States vulnerable to a dozen others. Nothing was done to bring the stock exchanges under control or to regulate the flow of funds in and out of the country. No one (except the handful of American Socialists) saw the necessity of regulating wages and profits so that consumer spending power could grow with the economy and wealth be dispersed widely, instead of concentrating in the hands of a comparatively small group of irresponsible millionaires. Above all, nobody saw that even as a banking reform the Act did not go far enough. It was, after all, the New York bankers who had so grossly over-capitalized so many enterprises that even the gigantic earnings of American industrialism might prove to be insufficient to pay the interest due to all the savers who had bought stocks and bonds. Nothing was done to strengthen the tens of thousands of small state banks, where a large part of the nation's capital was deposited. These conditions were signs of trouble for the future. And the Reserve Board, even though appointed by the President, soon fell under the dominance of Wall Street and remained thus enthralled until 1929. The gamekeepers surrendered to the poachers. Greed, dishonesty and folly had as large a scope for their operations as ever.

Reservations of this kind apply to most of Wilson's other reforms. The Underwood tariff (1913), for instance, was a serious move in the direction of free trade, but the sudden outbreak of the First World War made it nugatory almost as soon as it came into operation. In twenty years' time Franklin Roosevelt would have to reform the tariff all over again.

In other respects too the times were less propitious for great achievement at the federal level than they seemed. It is anyway arguable that the energy of the progressive middle class was most effectively expended at state and city level, where, for example, able young women like Frances Perkins – horrified at the Triangle fire of 1911, when 146 young women died in a New York sweatshop disaster – could make themselves felt by lobbying successfully for a state law to prevent such a thing happening again. In city after city, state after state, the revolt against the corrupt and by now intolerably inefficient old machines swept reform administrations into power (such as those of 'Golden Rule' Jones in Toledo, Ohio, or E. H. Crump, later to be a notorious boss himself, in Memphis, Tennessee). Some good was achieved. But Washington lacked the money, the expertise and the authority to be of much help in these local efforts. It did not even do much to advance such a cause as women's suffrage: the breakthrough came in the West, where between 1910 and 1914 nine states gave the vote to women. This proved a significant lever: the suffragists organized against the Democrats in those states in the 1914 election, since the majority party had not endorsed the Anthony Amendment to the US Constitution;[7] fewer Democrats than had been expected were returned to Congress, which frightened the party leaders so much that they instantly converted to support of the Amendment. In the 1916 election both main parties said they were in favour of women's suffrage, disagreeing only about the means to achieve it; in 1917 New York state gave women the vote, after an effective campaign

---

7 The Anthony Amendment was named after its author, Susan B. Anthony (1820–1906), sometime abolitionist and temperance reformer, who became the most effective American suffragist of the nineteenth century. Modelled on the Fifteenth Amendment, it states simply that 'The right of citizens of the United States to vote shall not be denied or abridged by the United States or by any States on account of sex. The Congress shall have power to enforce this article by appropriate legislation.'

by the leading suffragist, Carrie Catt. It was clearly only a matter of time before the Anthony Amendment was passed, and in fact (helped by the patriotic contribution women made to victory in the world war) it became part of the Constitution in 1920, in good time for the elections of that year. It was one of the most triumphant and characteristic victories of the progressive years, being a cause behind which East and West, working and middle classes, town and country, had eventually been able to unite; and perhaps most of all in that it was a reform brought about from below. The national politicians, including the President, had been little more than the playthings of a great tide.

Two other issues illustrate the same point, and a further one, that although adjustment to a new age was necessary, many Americans were most unwilling to adjust. This was especially so in the rural areas of the West and South. There, even as the triumph of progressivism vindicated the Populists, much of whose programme the new movement realized, the energies that had inspired Populism turned sour. Progressivism owed its success to the combined forces of half a dozen groups; but that did not redeem the new cities in the eyes of the farmers. They remembered the words of Bryan; they remembered his defeats; they could hardly take Roosevelt and Wilson to themselves in the same way, and they felt America slipping out of their hands. The country must be redeemed and purified. At the very least the wicked lure of alcohol must be rooted out. This Bible Belt zeal received reinforcement from two unlikely sources. First, many urban progressives had been born on farms in the Mid-West and shared rural intolerance and provincialisms: when they discovered that the working classes in the cities were untrustworthy, frequently wanting more than the middle classes were prepared to concede, they too fell back on proposals which might restore order. Secondly, many businessmen and social workers were well aware that drunkenness was a real problem, entailing, among other things, much loss of working time and much violence in the home. They lent their support to temperance proposals, overlooking the point that temperance could often be the stalking horse for prohibition. By 1914 the anti-drink crusade was much nearer to victory than anyone suspected, though it would take a war to carry it to its goal. Even had they known as much the progressives might not have worried. They were still naïve in a great many respects, and found it possible to dream that prohibitionists might be right and that a teetotal America might be possible and desirable; a clean bright place giving an example of sober virtue to the human race.

Similar tensions lurked behind the rising tide of anti-immigrant feeling. Nativism had a long history behind it; and it ebbed as often as it flowed. But each time the tide turned, it turned from a higher point on the beach. Anti-Catholicism, racism and anti-radicalism were its three main expressions; but the fact that they were invariably stimulated by trouble shows that what really underlay nativism was anxiety about the future and the need to find a scapegoat. Thus there was an upsurge of nativism in

1914, when a recession began; and in the troubled years after 1918 the golden door was to be slammed shut, in an attempt to assuage anxiety.

But what is most noticeable, if the campaign for women's suffrage, that for prohibition and that for immigrant restriction are compared, is that all three could pose as reform movements and at the same time make use of conservative arguments: for example, that women would purify the soul of America and recall her to better things. In this way they were able to win a strikingly wide range of support; and they resembled all the other great progressive causes. Was the progressive mission one to redeem America, and make her once more the small-town, small-farm, just, Protestant and republican Utopia she had surely been, if not in your own childhood, then in your grandparents' time? Or was it a mission to bring in the golden age of the future, when everyone would vote in pristine equality and machinery would solve all ills? No one could say; yet it was a crucial choice, and the failure to make it perhaps best explains what was eventually to go wrong. Of what use was it for business to propose, Presidents to dispose and Congress to legislate, if the wishes and opinions of those who were to administer the results were to fluctuate wildly from decade to decade, almost at times from year to year? Neither reform nor reaction could be sure of durable achievements, and, caught between past and future, too many men of goodwill would find their aspirations destroyed. The progressive mission eventually petered out because the pretence could no longer be sustained that all necessary reforms could be supported by everybody. Woodrow Wilson himself was eventually to discover, the hard way, that ideals divide as well as unite. In retrospect progressivism seems little more than a rehearsal, during which, in sunny times, the Americans learned the techniques they would need in the stormy age to come.

20 The Education of Woodrow Wilson 1914–21

It would be the irony of fate if my administration had to deal chiefly with foreign affairs.

Woodrow Wilson, 1913

The headlong development described in the last three chapters had one result which the American people expected and, in their boastings, anticipated, but which they were not really prepared for and certainly did not understand: it turned the United States into a great power; indeed set it fairly on the road to becoming the greatest power in the world. At the same time the rise of modern industrialism meant that many other nations were also expanding. Sooner or later their ambitions were certain to collide, and that, in a world not yet sobered by experience, made war very likely. Willy-nilly, America would be part of this painful process, and the history of the world would eventually turn on how she responded to it. Yet it would be a long time before she understood and accepted her destiny – if she ever entirely has.

Thus the outbreak of the First World War in 1914 took most Americans completely by surprise. In a wiser world it would not have done so. The increase of international tension during the previous twenty years had been palpable to anyone with eyes to see. But most citizens of the United States had been cheerfully unaware of danger, and it exploded upon them like a thunderclap. With horror and fascination they read newspapers telling of the rape of Belgium, the invasion of France, the battle of the Marne and the consolidation of the Western Front in the long, parallel systems of trenches. They felt pity for the combatants and their victims, especially the women and children of Belgium; most of all they felt relief that they themselves were not involved and, they thought, never would be. 'Peace-loving citizens of this country will now rise up,' said the *Chicago Herald*, 'and tender a hearty vote of thanks to Columbus for having discovered America.' The *Wabash Plain Dealer* 'never appreciated so keenly as now the foresight exercised by our forefathers in emigrating from Europe'. The

President issued a Proclamation of Neutrality on 4 August that was widely welcomed; and then they all settled down to wait out the conflict.

Yet the United States would be lucky indeed to remain at peace. Once more a naval war was being waged in the Atlantic and in all the coastal waters of Europe. Such conditions had shaped American history dramatically in the past: in 1781, in 1798 and in 1812. The USA had nearly come to blows with Britain and France during the Civil War, on account of the blockade. Now that Britain and Germany were in a death-grapple on the high seas there was all too much reason to fear that the United States would be dragged in. This is so clear in retrospect that it suggests a further reflection: that in its own interests the United States ought long before to have tipped its weight into the balance of power. Had Germany confronted an alliance between Britain, France and America, she might have been deterred from going to war.

Unfortunately there was never the slightest possibility that such an alliance, or any informal substitute, could be arranged. A century of peace with Europe (nobody counted the Spanish–American War) had given the United States a false sense of security; and the popular view of international relations had been shaped chiefly by the stern warnings of George Washington and Thomas Jefferson. 'No entangling alliances' was a watchword all too easily learned. Theodore Roosevelt, driven, perhaps, more by his native restlessness than by any deep insight, had made a few gestures against this tradition, for example by sending representatives to the Algeciras Conference on the future of Morocco in 1906; and he had won the Nobel Peace Prize. The citizens were proud of him, but their attitudes were otherwise unaffected: basically they believed that the United States did not need a foreign policy. Anyway, they were at this period more interested in Asia and Latin America than in the place where the real trouble was building up, Europe. President Taft tried (rather unsuccessfully) to extend American influence in China, where traders and missionaries alike saw a fair field for their labours, especially after the Chinese Revolution of 1911; President Wilson was for long deeply concerned with the Mexican Revolution, which also broke out in 1911. It lured him into a thoroughly misguided intervention, from which Mexican–American relations were not to recover for years. In pursuit of what was largely a personal vendetta against the transient dictator of Mexico, General Huerta (Wilson said 'I am going to teach the South American republics to elect good men'), he sent a detachment of US Marines to occupy the port of Veracruz. In 1916 he sent General John J. Pershing across the frontier at the head of a punitive expedition after the Mexican revolutionary leader, Pancho Villa, sacked the town of Columbus, New Mexico. No one has dared invade the United States since; but the Mexicans, however bitterly divided on other issues, were at one in resenting Wilson's high-handedness. The citizens of the United States were largely oblivious of all this. The Open Door and the Monroe Doctrine: sheltered by these slogans, Americans who thought about foreign affairs at all hoped to be left alone to develop their own spheres of influence, in China and south of the Rio Grande, while the other powers developed theirs elsewhere.

In 1914 Woodrow Wilson was nearly as much a victim of these fallacies and this wishful thinking as the most near-sighted of his fellow-citizens. His own background (unlike that of many American academics) was profoundly Anglophile. England was the only foreign country he knew at all well (in his pre-Presidential days he liked to go for bicycling holidays in the Lake District) and was the source of many of his favourite political doctrines. He modelled himself on Mr Gladstone, his greatest hero. He believed all the stories[1] (some of them true) which were being circulated about German atrocities in Belgium, and was naturally sorry for France. He allowed his administration to co-operate closely with Britain in solving the cotton problem, which was causing bitter anti-British feeling in the South: for the British blockade cut off Southern trade with customers in Central Europe, just when there was a bumper crop to be shifted. Cotton prices collapsed, falling by as much as 50 per cent.[2] Once they were aware of the problem the British, who were desperately anxious not to alienate America (they had reason), guaranteed that cotton would not fall in price below eight cents a pound. But Wilson's conviction was that America could, and therefore should, remain neutral; and to facilitate this policy he tried to suppress all unneutral impulses in himself and everybody else. He stopped listening to atrocity stories and advised his countrymen to be neutral in thought as well as in action. This was rather more than most Americans could manage, but they liked his attitude.

Wilson soon found that it was little help in the problems he actually faced. For example, Britain had had the sense to reform her army in the years before 1914, but had given insufficient attention to the means of arming it adequately. She had no chemical industry to speak of (she imported her dyes and drugs largely from Germany) and therefore could not manufacture explosives in the vast quantities now necessary. Frantic efforts were made to correct this state of affairs, but meantime Britain had to turn to the only other source of supply, the United States. Orders started pouring in, to the joy of American manufacturers, who would otherwise have been struggling with an economic recession, the more so as the Royal Navy imposed a tight blockade on European waters, and all American exports to Germany began

1 These stories had an immense impact on American opinion, although many were almost ostentatiously false. For instance, a woman in San Francisco told her friends that she had actually seen Belgian children whose hands had been cut off by the Huns. She admitted later, 'Of course, I hadn't, but it was true, and that was the only way I could convince them.'

2 This incident makes an ironical counterpoint to the Lancashire cotton famine during the Civil War, when English workers patiently endured mass unemployment until the victory of democracy ended the Northern blockade and Southern cotton could flow to market once more. Officially, the people of the cotton South may have believed that in 1914 Britain was fighting for democratic civilization; but they were disinclined to endure any inconvenience on that account.

to fall off rapidly. Voices were raised to say that this wartime munitions trade (America also manufactured small arms for the Allies) was un-neutral because it helped one side rather than both. The voices grew louder and more anxious when the British, having rapidly exhausted their supplies of cash, sought to borrow money on Wall Street. The bankers asked the President if they might lend, and he reluctantly gave his permission. He was impressed by the argument of Secretary of State Bryan, that 'money is the worst of all contrabands because it commands everything else'. But if it was un-neutral to give Britain the means to carry on the war, it was un-neutral to refuse to do so.

This was, perhaps, the crucial moment when the truth made itself felt that real neutrality was impossible for a country so powerful as America had now become: she was bound to take sides, because whatever she did would affect the course of the war. To deny Britain and France their loans would be to deny them the means, not just of victory, but of survival. To help them was to injure Germany and Austria-Hungary (empires from which millions of Americans, or their families, had emigrated, and with which they preserved close ties). The United States had to choose. This was too horrible a fact to face, for it implied a certain responsibility for the fate of Europe and a remote but real risk of war. So Wilson did not face it. He took refuge in legalisms: the Allied request was legitimate under international law, and the Central Powers too were welcome to shop in the United States if they could get past the blockade. America was not responsible for the doings of the British. All very true, and beside the point. The United States had given decisive help to the Allies, and in due course would have to pay for it. The choice had been made, the decision taken. It was probably the inevitable one. In the first place, the public conscience of the American people, as expressed in the press and politicians' speeches, could not decently have stood by without protest if Wilson handed over Britain, France and Russia to the dictates of Belgium's ravisher. The Germans did not seem so beastly under the Kaiser as they later did under Hitler, but their genius for making themselves unpopular was already very effective. Second, the bonds linking Britain and America were now stronger than they had been since the Revolution. This was partly the result of patient work by British diplomatists, who had long ago seen that American friendship was indispensable if British power was to be preserved. Chiefly it arose from the basic dispositions of history, as laid down long ago by the founders of the old British Empire. The thirteen colonies might have thrown off British sovereignty (with French help), and the American republic might, ever since, have been slowly emancipating itself from economic, social and cultural tutelage; but the language remained, the religion, the political values, the commercial and financial ties. Nor were these static links: they were dynamic forces, driving the two societies to evolve in the same direction. They had been doing so for more than a century. By 1914 Britain and America were more alike than they had ever been before, both in organization, outlook and experience.[3] The fact that the leaders of progressive America, educated, middle-class ladies and gentlemen, had been in the habit of exchanging ideas and information with their British counterparts for years was also not without importance. In the last analysis it has to be recognized that it would have taken a mighty effort of will, a herculean application of cold intelligence, a deliberate jettisoning of tradition, decency and friendship, and a readiness to face an almighty storm of protest from the Anglophiles, to bring Woodrow Wilson to the point of abandoning Britain in order to make sure of peace. Since he preferred to evade the issue, heroism was out of the question, and the pro-Allied choice was made fairly easily. To the extent that he recognized what he was doing, he could comfort himself with the thought that nothing was certain. He saved Britain; he might yet induce the belligerents to negotiate; surely America would not need to fight. For Germany could not possibly want to make such a formidable addition to the roll of her enemies: she already had work enough.

Unfortunately for herself and for America, Germany did not see matters in this light. She could not be expected to sympathize very keenly with the American dilemma. After all, the British were threatening her with starvation. It was the Germans' business to break the blockade if they could and do everything in their power to impede Anglo-American trade. Their best, indeed their only weapons were submarines. Of these they had few to start with (Admiral Tirpitz had not favoured them before the war), but those few achieved such spectacular results in terms of ships sunk and cargoes lost that they became immensely popular with both the German public and the high command. Nor was the German navy very concerned about its choice of targets. Any ship which carried assistance to the Allies seemed to be fair game. On 7 May 1915 a submarine off the west coast of Ireland saw a great vessel looming towards her through the morning mists. The commander launched his torpedo, and the Cunard liner *Lusitania* went to the bottom, carrying with her her cargo, including a quantity of munitions, and 1,198 souls, including 128 Americans.

American opinion was appalled. It was true that the Germans had warned travellers against sailing in *Lusitania*, but no one had taken them seriously: to sink an unarmed passenger vessel of such marginal military importance had seemed to be a barbarism to which no civilized nation would descend. The Americans knew better now, and in the outrage voices began to be heard (among them that of Theodore Roosevelt) demanding war.

There was no chance of Wilson listening, but even so his new dilemma was exceedingly painful. He was still convinced, as a good nineteenth-century liberal, that international law forbade a belligerent to wage war at the expense of civilians and neutrals, or to interfere in any way with a neutral's legitimate commerce (the question of whether *Lusitania*'s cargo of arms and munitions

---

3 Even in such a matter as immigration, Britain now resembled America. For instance, there had been an enormous inflow of Irish and Jews during the nineteenth century.

was legitimate commerce was brushed aside as unimportant). To acquiesce in German practices was to make a cowardly retreat in the face of a criminal bully. Yet to make effective protests risked war, a war for which America was in every sense unprepared.

Wilson decided to take the risk. He tried to damp down the bellicosity of his countrymen, such as it was, by a speech in which he said that 'there is such a thing as a man being too proud to fight'; but he sent vigorous notes of protest to Berlin – so vigorous that Bryan, fearing they might touch off war, resigned, to become leader of the peace movement. And indeed Wilson's line was difficult to defend. He would hold the Germans strictly accountable, he said, for any further loss of American passengers, even on armed British vessels. In the language of diplomacy this was to threaten Germany with a breach of diplomatic relations and possible war, an outcome which might well seem disproportionate to the interests at stake.

Had the breach occurred in 1915 or 1916 Wilson could not have hoped to carry a united country to war with him – if indeed he could have got a declaration of war out of Congress. Yet to have climbed down after such pronouncements would have destroyed him politically. Luckily for him the Germans saved him from his own bad logic. They saw no point in alienating the Americans while the submarines were not yet in a position to deliver a knockout blow to the British; and accordingly they agreed to abide by Wilson's demands. After the spring of 1916 the submarine campaign was suspended.

Wilson showed his sense of relief at this narrow escape by taking vigorous steps to ensure that he would never again be caught in such a trap. He was learning. In America he launched what he called the 'Preparedness' campaign, winning Congressional approval for an immense programme of shipbuilding which would give the United States a navy second to none with which to protect its maritime interests. The idea was that this would deter Germany from further provocation. Abroad, he set out seriously to discover a means of ending the war and thus of saving America from all possibility of being sucked into it. He sent a trusted personal emissary, Edward House, to sound out the governments of the warring powers, and exerted himself to display his neutrality. He did this chiefly by quarrelling with the Allies, especially Great Britain.

The British command of the sea was nearly absolute, and so much resented by the Americans that they began to talk of 'navalism' as a sin of the same order as German militarism: 'freedom of the seas' was a potent cry. The British strictly forbade neutrals to trade with Germany and Austria; neighbours of the Central Powers, such as Holland and Denmark, were forbidden to import anything by sea which might find its way across their frontiers (as a result the war was a period of acute hardship for these little countries). American vessels trading across the Atlantic were regularly stopped and searched by British ships; contraband goods were confiscated. A black list was compiled of firms guilty or suspected of trading with

Germany, whose shipments were therefore liable to instant seizure. The mails were intercepted and censored. As the war went on the British, nicely judging the American temper, slowly increased the pressure. Woodrow Wilson protested in vain. By the summer of 1916 he admitted that he was 'about at the end of my patience with Great Britain and the Allies'. On top of everything else, Britain's savage repression of the Easter Rising in Dublin had done almost as much damage to her moral standing in the eyes of the American public as the attack on Belgium had done to that of Germany. Wilson's resolution to commit the full strength of the United States to the search for peace grew: it was plainer and plainer that the war was a major hurt to American interests, whether the country was a belligerent or not.

Before any decisive new departure could be undertaken there was a Presidential election to be held. Wilson had done his best to prepare for it by appropriating the more tempting items in his enemies' domestic programmes; but somewhat to his surprise, somewhat to his dismay, the winning issue turned out to be the slogan 'He Kept Us Out Of The War'. The mood of the country, understandably enough, was overwhelmingly pacific. Wilson privately doubted his ability to live up to the slogan: he knew that the decision really lay with Germany, which might at any minute resume submarine warfare. But he had of course no objection to winning the peace vote, and was narrowly re-elected, receiving 277 electoral votes to the 254 given to his Republican opponent, Charles Evans Hughes (the Progressive party was dissolving).

That matter out of the way, Wilson set earnestly to work as a peace-maker. On 18 December he sent identical diplomatic notes to the belligerents asking them to state their war-aims. He hoped that, if they could be induced to do this, they might also be induced to accept America as a mediator in the search for a compromise peace. So they might have done, had their quest for victory been all it seemed: had both sides believed what they proclaimed, that they were only fighting in self-defence. Unfortunately the belligerents had war-aims they could not decently avow. Germany, for example, wanted the Belgian Congo, and the reduction of Belgium herself to satellite status; while the Allies had their own plans for carving up Turkey and destroying for good the strength of the Central Powers. They were fighting for conquest; besides, any compromise peace in 1916 or 1917 must have been a thinly disguised German victory, for Belgium and northern France were still occupied: if Allied blood was no longer to be shed, then Allied diplomacy would have had to make many concessions to get this territory evacuated. Yet Britain and France felt themselves far from defeated. It is not surprising, therefore, that Wilson's *démarche* was received with dismay in London and Paris, and that the only question it raised in the minds of the Allied governments was how it might be painlessly frustrated.

A similar reaction might have been expected from the Germans: if they defined their war-aims in terms acceptable to American opinion, they would be throwing away the fruits of their victories; if they replied frankly, they would discredit themselves. Best to reply evasively. But it so happened that Wilson's intervention coincided with a fateful change in German policy. Tirpitz had now built up a large submarine fleet; Tsarist Russia was plainly on the brink of defeat; the time had come, the high command determined, for an all-out effort against Britain. Before it was taken, however, the diplomatists were allowed one last attempt at negotiation. Accordingly Bethmann-Hollweg, the German Chancellor, returned a surprisingly conciliatory answer to Wilson's note, and the President for some weeks was able to sun himself in the illusion that a compromise peace was possible. He was so pleased with the German attitude that he began to put heavy pressure on the British, going so far as to order that no more loans should be made to them, since they seemed uncooperative.

For the Allies it was perhaps the most dangerous moment of the war and, had the Germans had the wit to see it, it might have been decisive. But Hindenburg and Ludendorff were bent on settling matters their own way – by blood and iron. At a conference at Pless Castle in eastern Prussia it was decided, over the anguished protests of Bethmann-Hollweg, to re-open the submarine offensive. It was assumed that this would bring America into the war but that, the generals thought, did not matter. Before US strength could be brought to bear, the Russians would have been forced to make peace and the U-boat campaign would have starved Britain into asking for terms. The decision was taken in early January 1917 – at the very time that Wilson was assuring House that 'there will be no war'.

It was a bold scheme, which almost succeeded. But the Germans had overreached themselves. The British convoy system blunted the submarine offensive. Russia was totally defeated, but the terms that Germany exacted were so unbearably harsh that an army had to be kept in the East to enforce them; consequently the great Western offensive, when it came (in March 1918), was not sufficiently overwhelming, and the Anglo-French front held. Worse yet, the Americans were indeed forced into war by the consequences of the Pless decision, and this fact guaranteed German defeat.

The announcement that Germany was resorting to unrestricted submarine warfare (that is to say, that all Allied or neutral vessels on the Atlantic would be torpedoed without warning, whatever their mission) abruptly awoke Wilson from his dream that the belligerents would accept his proposals for 'peace without victors'. This was no unplanned *Trent* affair, no 'calculated outrage' from 'any little German lieutenant' such as Wilson had feared. It was an attempt by the imperial German government to drive all American shipping off the high seas, in order to starve a people into surrender. To acquiesce in this murderous humiliation was unthinkable; but Wilson shrank from the obvious alternative. The German note was received on 31 January 1917; three days later Wilson broke off diplomatic relations. News of sunken shipping began to come in; but still the President did not go to war.

His instincts were profoundly pacific. He had been a child in the South during Civil War and Reconstruction: he knew, as no other President has known, what the costs of war might be. Among them he could reckon soldiers dead or mutilated and families wrecked by the loss of their 'boys', as he always thought and spoke of them (he had no sons, but he had taught young males for years at Princeton, who always stayed the same age while he got older). He knew how war could defeat the hopes of those who entered upon it and warp the course of social and political development: he foresaw the end of the New Freedom in war fever. In a war, a united America must win, of course; but she might be transformed for the worse. Even the diplomatic price would be high: the tradition of more than a century would be abandoned when the United States consented to embroil itself in the quarrels of Europe.

The sinkings went on. The British gave Wilson the text of a German cable which they had intercepted and decoded. It was from Alfred Zimmermann, Under Foreign Secretary, and was so monumentally provocative that it deserves to be extensively quoted:

Berlin, January 19, 1917. On the first of February we intend to begin submarine warfare unrestricted. In spite of this it is our intention to keep neutral the United States of America. If this attempt is not successful we propose an alliance on the following basis with Mexico: that we shall make war together and together make peace. We shall give general financial support, and it is understood that Mexico is to reconquer the lost territory in New Mexico, Texas, and Arizona . . . Please call to the attention of the President of Mexico that the employment of ruthless submarine warfare now promises to compel England to make peace in a few months.

Wilson published the text of this interesting document; Zimmermann, to the astonishment of the government in Washington, admitted that it was genuine; and the American people were left to contemplate what seemed to them a monstrous plot against their national integrity. The point about 'ruthless submarine warfare' reminded them of their losses at sea and of the Germans' reputation for frightfulness. The sorry state of Mexican–American relations lent an air of reality to Zimmermann's scheme which it did not deserve, for Mexico showed no interest. At last the people knew their own mind. Wilson asked Congress to approve the arming of merchantmen; when a little group of Senators filibustered the proposal to death, he authorized the measure under an ancient Act of 1797, relic of an earlier international crisis. The Russian Revolution of March overthrew the Tsardom, thus making the Allied cause more attractive to democratic Americans. The President bowed to necessity, and on 2 April 1917 went before a joint session of Congress to ask for a declaration that a state of war existed between Germany and the United States. He got what he wanted by a nearly unanimous vote in the small hours of Good Friday. It fell on 6 April that year: for the third time the cruellest month thrust the American people into a major war.

In his address to Congress Wilson set the country on a new course. He did not mention the Zimmermann telegram, perhaps because he thought so foolish a plot to be unworthy of serious notice, but he reviewed the question of unrestricted submarine warfare at length, making the point that, if America wanted to preserve her property and, especially, the lives of her citizens, she must either submit to German bullying or retaliate with war: 'armed neutrality, it now appears, is impracticable'. America would not, could not, submit: she would defend her rights and the hitherto sacrosanct principles of civilized maritime warfare. So far, it was a prescription for war on the Atlantic. But Wilson had convinced himself, and now tried to convince his hearers, that Germany's conduct showed that her government could not safely be allowed to co-exist with democratic nations. 'We are glad, now that we see the facts with no veil of false pretence about them, to fight thus for the ultimate peace of the world and for the liberation of its peoples, the German peoples included . . . The world must be made safe for democracy.'[4] So he proposed all help to the Allies, and the raising of a huge American army, initially of half a million men. And he ended by painting a glorious vision of what might be achieved:

It is a fearful thing to lead this great peaceful people into war, into the most terrible and disastrous of all wars, civilization itself seeming to be in the balance. But the right is more precious than peace, and we shall fight for the things which we have always carried nearest our hearts – for democracy, for the right of those who submit to authority to have a voice in their own Governments, for the rights and liberties of small nations, for a universal dominion of right by such a concert of free peoples as shall bring peace and safety to all nations and make the world itself at last free.

He was rewarded with tumultuous cheers, led by the Chief Justice of the United States. It did not comfort him. 'My message today was a message of death for our young men,' he said afterwards, in a moment of Lincolnian insight. 'How strange it seems to applaud that.'

Wilson's address carried a substantially united America into war; but he risked a great deal. If his promises of universal peace and democracy could not be kept, disappointment might be as bitter as hopes in 1917 were high. It is worth asking why the promises were made. In part, the answer must be that Wilson had been convinced by the outbreak and conduct of the war that, in Norman Angell's famous phrase, there was a state of international anarchy, and that, until it was remedied, the world could not be safe either for democracy or for the American people. He had already, in the previous year, announced himself ready to abandon the isolationist tradition if, by signing a treaty or forming an alliance, America could help to bring into

---

4 I have always liked G. K. Chesterton's melancholy comment: 'The world cannot be made safe for democracy, it is a dangerous trade.'

being and to sustain 'a concert of free peoples' – a league of nations, that is, such as was becoming the popular remedy for the ills of the world. In 1917 he took advantage of the need to declare war to commit his country firmly to this policy.

But there was more to it than that. There was the matter of national tradition. Jefferson and Lincoln had dedicated the Revolution and the Civil War to the cause of humanity; Wilson would do the same with his war. Finally, he was under a compulsion common to all modern societies. The British, for instance, believed (or the civilians did) that they were fighting a war to end war. Mere national self-defence, let alone the lure of conquest, was no longer cause enough. The best that can be said for Wilson as he declared a war for democracy, an ideological war, is that any other man in his place would have had to offer such a justification for his actions, and that few others could so eloquently have articulated one so noble and so plausible.

Having committed themselves, the Americans began to work with their usual enormous energy. Their view was that having entered the war they had better do all they could to bring it to an early end. Their fleet, in conjunction with the Royal Navy, rid the Atlantic of the submarine menace. General Pershing set to work to raise and train an army for Europe. President Wilson, bypassing the regular Cabinet, appointed talented outsiders, businessmen of proved capacity working for a dollar a year, to oversee the war effort. Bernard Baruch, a Wall Street financier, headed the War Industries Board: in effect he was economic dictator, controlling the whole vast field of American manufacturing in the interest of the war-effort. Herbert Hoover, who had made a fortune as a mining engineer and earned international fame by his work to relieve the starving people of Belgium and occupied France, was made Food Administrator: he boosted American farm production to unheard-of heights and tripled exports to the Allied countries, which might otherwise have failed from hunger. The American Federation of Labor pledged its support to the war-effort and was eventually rewarded by a huge increase of numbers and influence. The standard rate of income tax was raised to 6 per cent, while a surtax of up to 77 per cent was imposed on incomes of more than a million dollars a year. The railroads were nationalized for the duration of the war; fuel use was as strictly regulated as industrial production; labour relations were supervised by the administration. For the second time the US government showed what it could do in a crisis.

Less happy were some other expressions of the wartime spirit. Hostility to the Germans was so intense that it led to a campaign of persecution against the whole German-American community, which was supposed to consist largely of traitors and spies, although the President had expressed his confidence in its patriotism. Unfortunately he had at the same time remarked that 'a few' might be disloyal, and had promised that disloyalty would be dealt with 'with a firm hand of stern repression'. That was excuse enough. German music, German literature, German philosophy and the German language were all denounced; German books were removed from libraries, German-language newspapers were suppressed and German-American citizens were vindictively hounded. At least this hostility gave the other 'hyphenated Americans' a welcome breathing-space (during the period of neutrality they had been much attacked); and hatred of the Kaiser blotted out hatred of the Pope. But the radical and pacifist opposition to the war which soon announced itself was stigmatized as pro-German and persecuted accordingly. When the October Revolution brought the Bolsheviks to power and they made peace with Germany they were immediately tagged as agents of Prussian imperialism, and so were their sympathizers: 105 Wobblies were sent to prison for impeding the war-effort. Eugene V. Debs, bitterly opposed to what he thought was a bloody war of the plutocracies, appalled by the campaign against freedom of speech which had shut down the socialist as well as the German-language press, and determined to demonstrate what was happening to the Constitutional guarantee of free speech, made a speech denouncing the war and was sent to prison for 'wilfully and knowingly' trying to obstruct the operation of the Conscription Act. To make sure that such wickedness would never go unpunished the administration pushed through an Espionage Act and a Sedition Act. Wilson did not seem to remember the outrage that an earlier Sedition Act had caused; or to care about the illiberal consequences of the new one. No one who weakened support for 'the boys' in uniform deserved any mercy. Debs was to stay in prison until Wilson left office.

Brewers, it was discovered, were commonly of German origin; King George of England had given up alcohol to help the cause; and anyway the manufacturers of beer and whisky used up corn which might otherwise have been sent to feed the Allies. It was a heaven-sent chance for the prohibitionists. They whipped up hostility to the brewing interests, and by banging the patriotic drum induced Congress not only to pass a law enforcing prohibition while the war lasted, but actually to pass a Constitutional amendment (the Eighteenth) forbidding the export, import, 'manufacture, sale, or transportation of intoxicating liquors', for ever. The patriotic cry was so noisy that no effective opposition could be organized, and the amendment became law on 29 January 1919, to come into effect a year later. This reform was to cause great trouble in the future, but in the long run it proved less important than the other wartime amendment, the Nineteenth, which at last gave all American women the vote and became law on 26 August 1920.

Immigration from Europe was cut off at the same time that a huge market for unskilled labour arose in the North. The opportunity was seized by the African–Americans, who now began to leave the South in large numbers to fill the war-built factories. This great migration stimulated hostility in the North among white workers facing this new competition. There was a race riot at East St Louis, Illinois, on 2 July 1917, in which some thirty-nine blacks and nine whites were killed. Two months later, at Houston, Texas, black soldiers were provoked into an uprising in which seventeen whites were killed, for which outrage thirteen blacks were later hanged and forty-one sent to prison for life. Lynching revived in the South on such a scale and with such special horror (burning to death was quite common) that President Wilson was at last moved to denounce it: 'We are at the moment fighting lawless passions. Germany has outlawed herself . . . and has made lynchers of her armies. Lynchers emulate her disgraceful conduct.' But it did no good. Some 454 persons were lynched between 1918 and 1927, 416 being blacks, and forty-two being burned.

The actual fighting of the war went well. All the German calculations proved faulty. Britain did not surrender, nor was she starved (though it was a near thing). The great spring offensive of 1918 failed: its last thrust was decisively checked in the Second Battle of the Marne (15–18 July), in which American troops played an honourable part and Pershing showed himself to be a highly competent commander. Marshal Foch ordered a counter-attack, and the long-awaited Allied advance began. By September more than a million American troops were engaged, and in the Battle of the Argonne (26 September–11 November) they inflicted one of the great defeats on the Germans which soon brought an end to the war. But even more important to that end was their mere presence on the field, which proved that the Allies now had inexhaustible manpower reserves while the Germans no longer had any.

Meanwhile, from the moment that the struggle began, Woodrow Wilson, delegating his administrative duties with great skill, devoted most of his thought to the problem of ending it decently and giving the world new hope, as he had promised. He had no doubt of his countrymen's support; the difficulty, he supposed, would lie in imposing America's will (really, his own) on Europe. He manoeuvred to overcome this impediment with all the skill that he had shown in the earlier rough-houses of New Jersey and Washington politics.

Wilson was to be much maligned, especially by J. M. Keynes, and most of the criticisms were unfair. Yet one of Keynes's observations went to the heart of the matter. At his core, this son of the manse was a Presbyterian preacher still. Profoundly sensitive to words and ideas, expert at using them, ambitious, yet moved, in the end, by moral visions as by nothing else, Wilson seems never to have lost his feeling that eloquence would finally govern the world: as if Lincoln's second inaugural had prevailed over Booth's bullet. It was to prove his last illusion; during the war it was his strength. He reflected on the causes of the conflict, and on proposals to end it and prevent its recurrence; in the fullness of time he laid out his conclusions in a series of orations, the first of which contained the famous Fourteen Points that gave their name to the whole series.

Heir to both North and South, Wilson combined Jefferson Davis's faith in the letter of the law with Abraham Lincoln's earnest moralism. Both traits emerged in his grand strategy for the peace. He saw that the international law in which he had believed so deeply and which he had tried so hard to enforce between 1914 and 1917 was a fiction; force, fear and ambition ruled the world. For remedy he turned, as we have seen, to the English liberals' idea of a League of Peace, or of Nations, which, committed to liberal principles, would resolve international disputes by legal processes – if necessary, by legal sanctions – instead of by the brutal means of war. The League Covenant (which he drew up himself) would replace international anarchy as the Constitution of the United States had replaced the quarrelsome independence of the former colonies. It was a noble dream, but it clearly exhibited Wilson's residual naïvety. It had the same weakness as the old idea of the Social Contract, from which in part it derived: it depended on the goodwill of the nations to work, though it was the absence of international goodwill that made it necessary. If goodwill existed, it would not be needed. It was an ideal to work for, not a means to an end. It was not sufficient to realize Wilson's hopes, nor have succeeding generations brought it much closer; yet they have clung to the ideal, for without it the long-term prospects of mankind are black. Wilson's reputation has risen or fallen with men's attachment to the idea of a league of peace and their belief in its practicability.

His other proposals were much more down-to-earth and so roused much more opposition. The second of the Fourteen Points was an assertion, against Great Britain, of the freedom of the seas, a last relic of the doctrines of America's neutrality: 'Absolute freedom of navigation upon the seas, outside territorial waters, alike in peace and in war, except as the seas may be closed in whole or in part by international action for the enforcement of international covenants.' It was inconsistent of Wilson to advocate this doctrine, for at the very time of its delivery the United States, that former champion of neutral rights, was harrying neutral commerce assiduously; it was also unwise, for it opened a rift with Britain; but the pride and pocket of America had been too badly hurt by the blockade for this opportunity for a slap at 'navalism' to be forgone. For the rest, the Fourteen Points denounced secret treaties and insisted on the old nineteenth-century mixture of nationalism and liberal institutions: self-determination and democracy. Adopt these panaceas, link them with a League of Nations and secure peace for all time. Such was Wilson's message to his allies and his enemies.

The details of the Fourteen Points (and of the various 'principles', 'particulars' and 'declarations' which he added to them in public addresses before the armistice) were to be greatly modified at the peace conference; but it was the attitudes underlying them which first created trouble. British politicians were comparatively sympathetic, but they rejected 'freedom of the seas' and continued to believe, as always, in the principle of the balance of power (which, according to Wilson, was a great game, immoral and 'now forever discredited'). The French were total unbelievers in the utility or effectiveness of such pronouncements: as always, they stuck to *realpolitik*.

The Germans, while they were winning, had no use for such sentimental aspirations; they believed only in force. The Russians were by now out of the war; their new Bolshevik rulers could see nothing in the Fourteen Points but a conscious challenge to their own programme for the world – and they were quite right.

But it is the peculiar genius of American statesmen to combine lofty visions with effective politics. Underlying Wilson's preaching was the hard fact that the Allies were increasingly dependent on American strength; they had at least to pretend to take the Points seriously, and their publication in January 1918, bringing the hope that there was a way in which this terrible experience of war could be put behind mankind for ever, made Wilson for a moment supremely popular with the peoples of Europe. Merely as an ideologue, he could not be ignored, since he was also President of the United States. When the German front began to crumble, it was to him that the enemy turned. They hoped to get better terms than they would get from France and Britain; probably they hoped to split the alliance. They offered to surrender on the basis of the Fourteen Points. To their surprise they found Wilson a hard bargainer. He exacted a German revolution (so they overthrew the Kaiser); the evacuation of all occupied territory; the laying-down of arms; acceptance of the Fourteen Points and the President's subsequent addresses. There were objections to many of the American conditions from both the Allies and the enemy, but Wilson held firm and, thanks to the undrained strength of the United States, was able to impose his will. British, French and Germans, politicians and generals, were forced into line; and on 11 November 1918 an armistice took place. The Great War was over (though many little wars, its offspring, continued to rage) and Woodrow Wilson deserved much of the credit for ending it. It was a great moment – the real high point of his career – and was greeted with wild joy, and tears, and dancing in the streets in all the cities of the West.

Years later someone asked Lloyd George why he had not retired at this supreme hour, with his credit intact. He answered that it had been impossible, looking down from the balcony of Buckingham Palace on the rejoicing crowds, not to believe that he could still do the people service. It may be that similar feelings clouded the vision of Wilson and Clemenceau. Yet forces were now set in motion that would end in the destruction, not only of these three great men, but of their great achievements, victory and peace. As Wilson stood highest, he fell the farthest.

Almost since the beginning of the war he had aspired to use American power to bring about a just and secure peace through the application of democratic principles. Now his moment had come. He determined to go to Paris as head of the American delegation to the peace conference.

This decision, given Wilson's character and ambitions, was inevitable. The task of peacemaking was too delicate and too important to be left to anyone else; it is impossible to name a substitute who could have performed more effectively than Wilson. All the same, his participation had some most unfortunate consequences. In the end it wrecked his health and thus his hopes; from the beginning it weakened his political position. He stayed in Europe, with one brief interruption, for over six months, and during that time lost control of the American government. He never regained it, and the painfully difficult process of adjusting American society to the return of peace had to be carried out without the guidance or even, it seemed, the notice of the President. Neither Congress nor the mediocre Cabinet could fill the gap; and thus the leaderless country went through a crisis which finally brought about a profound reaction against Wilson and all he stood for. Progressivism had had a very long run, anyway; a reaction was due; but Wilson's abdication of so much of his responsibility made it more violent than was necessary. The seeds of much future trouble, then, were sown by this action of the President.

At much the same time he made two bad mistakes. The Congressional elections had been held as usual in the autumn of 1918;[5] and Wilson, who had suffered much from the refractory behaviour of the outgoing Congress, tried hard to secure a more amenable successor. It was the sort of task that Lloyd George and Clemenceau carried out easily enough; but it defeated Wilson. He published a statement asking the voters to return a Democratic majority, so that he might continue to be 'your unembarrassed spokesman at home and abroad'. The President was driven into this blunder by the campaign the Republicans were waging against his foreign policy and conduct of the war: just as he was beginning negotiations with the Germans, the opposition leaders began to howl for 'unconditional surrender' (Theodore Roosevelt was especially vicious), and they were campaigning widely against the third of the Fourteen Points, which advocated universal free trade. Wilson warned that a Democratic defeat would be interpreted in Europe as a repudiation of his leadership. All the same, he would have done better to be silent, for it was already clear that the Democrats would probably lose; by coming out for the defeated side the President exposed his prestige to a sharp deflation. Worse, he thus put an end to the wartime truce which had previously kept the Republicans under some sort of restraint. They had not been very scrupulous in observing the truce, but they had on the whole given the President the support he needed, while a faction of his own Democratic party, the Southern, Bryanite, pacifist section, had frequently deserted him in Congressional votes. And it was widely believed by voters in the North and West, chafing at the same time under wartime price controls and wartime inflation, that the Democratic South had made unreasonable profits out of the sale of cotton, the price of which, unlike that of wheat, was unregulated. This belief greatly helped the Republicans on election day, and Wilson's attack enabled them to associate him with his unpopular party and denounce all his policies. It would have been wiser for the President

---

5 It is notable that none of their wars has ever been allowed to prevent the Americans from holding elections.

to issue a 'coupon' endorsing all those members of Congress, whether Republican or Democratic, who had supported him during the war. As it was, he alienated the Republicans without gaining anything, for as expected the Democrats lost heavily, in large part because their constituents knew that they had obstructed the war effort.

Even then Wilson might have redeemed his defeat by taking chosen Republicans into his confidence and counsel, thereby gaining their support: by appointing former President Taft, or former Secretary of State Root, to the Paris delegation, for example. He did nothing of the kind: the only Republican he took to Paris was of no political weight. Wilson's enemies (now led by Senator Henry Cabot Lodge: Theodore Roosevelt died that winter) girded their loins for his return. He would have to bring back a very good treaty indeed to defeat them.

The task proved to be beyond his powers. In Paris, Wilson learned, slowly and painfully, just how limited are goodwill, intelligence and hard work when unsupported by more material forces. He arrived in Europe and made a triumphal tour through France, England and Italy. Soldiers cheered, children presented him with bouquets, peasants dressed up in their traditional costumes for him, George V brought out the gold dinner service at Buckingham Palace, the Milanese showered him with violets and mimosa and serenaded him with a band which he was kind enough to conduct for a few bars himself. But the acclamations of the peoples were of no help in the conference rooms. Rather the reverse: they deluded Wilson about his strength. Thus on one occasion he appealed to the Italians for support against their own leaders and was resoundingly rebuffed. This humiliation did not strengthen his hand in the negotiations. And the war was over. America was no longer in a commanding position. Her soldiers were streaming homewards across the Atlantic in hundreds of thousands (he had passed a shipload of them on his way out of New York harbour): their going symbolized the weakening of the President's position. No longer could he compel European realities to bend to his will. He would have to compromise, as if he were a politician and not the Messiah.

He found the process painful and exhausting, but also instructive and challenging. The myth, so mischievously propagated by J. M. Keynes, that Wilson was the stupid victim of the guile of George and the obstinacy of Clemenceau, has no truth to it (Clemenceau, indeed, recorded that, next to General Pershing, Wilson was the most obstinate man he had ever met). To Wilson's mind the overriding interest of the world, and therefore of the United States, lay in the creation of the League of Nations. He put this item on the conference agenda and made sure that the League Covenant was written inextricably into the peace treaty. In spite of subsequent arguments and rearrangements, this achievement endured, surviving even the defection of the United States. The League functioned as an instrument of international co-operation and pacification, on the whole quite impressively, throughout the 1920s. Wilson was also able to redraw the map of Europe, substantially according to the great principle of national self-determination that his speeches had proclaimed. Soon ten new or resurrected states (such as Poland, Czechoslovakia and Finland) joined the community of nations: it was Wilson who had secured the recognition of their independence, and through the exertions of his Food Administrator, Hoover, rescued their populations from starvation. Winston Churchill calculated that the Versailles Treaty left less than 3 per cent of the European peoples under foreign rule. Even Germany remained united and independent, and lost only a handful of outlying provinces.[6] Wilson would have added that all remaining difficulties could, should and would be referred to the League, there to be settled according to the dictates of democratic law and justice. In spite of much buffeting, the Franco-Anglo-American entente emerged in one piece from the negotiations. All in all it was a mighty achievement, substantially warranting Wilson's belief that it secured the future peace of the world. It would also act, he thought, as a bulwark against the extremes of Left and Right – of the Bolsheviks and those who were soon to be known as fascists. He had paid a price for it; but the politician and idealist in him agreed in thinking that it was not too high. Compromise and concession were after all of the essence of democracy, whether it was seen as an ideal or as a mode of practical politics.

Nevertheless the concessions he had made had been enormous, and many of them deeply affronted elements of American opinion. Britain, for example, who owed her survival in the war to her success in using the Royal Navy to starve her enemy while preventing him from starving her, forced the abandonment of 'freedom of the seas', Clemenceau concurring ('with freedom of the seas, war would cease to be war'). Japan, who had taken all Germany's Pacific colonies north of the Equator (Japan's ally, Great Britain, taking everything south of that line), insisted on helping herself to Germany's Chinese possession, Shantung, and although American diplomacy eventually succeeded in dislodging her, Woodrow Wilson had to accept the *fait accompli* for the time being, although it was a flat contradiction of self-determination in a part of the world in which many Americans were extremely interested. The French, the British and the British Dominions took over the German Empire in Africa and elsewhere, and immense stretches of the former Ottoman Empire in the Middle East; the nature of the transaction was delicately disguised by the pretence that the imperialist powers were merely exercising 'mandates' under the League of Nations, and Wilson thankfully accepted the fiction (it was a perversion of one of his own pet ideas); but not all Americans could be depended on to do so, for their anti-colonial tradition was still vigorous. Furthermore, Wilson had let himself be inveigled into taking part in the disastrous attempt by Britain and France to crush the Bolsheviks by supporting the White Russians. The

6 The importance of this fact, from the German point of view, may be understood by comparing it with the situation that emerged from the Second World War.

Americans were never very deeply involved and soon withdrew; but the whole affair did look very much like an entanglement in those distant quarrels of no concern to the United States which Washington and Jefferson had warned against so earnestly.

Overshadowing everything was the question of Germany. That country had surrendered on the express promise of a magnanimous peace; the sort of 'peace without victors' which Wilson had recommended in January 1917. The idea of such a peace had warm and wide support in both Britain and America: it did not take a genius to see that a vindictive settlement might breed another war.[7] Wilson's advisers in Paris were deeply committed to leniency. The President owed his towering prestige in large part to his association with such ideas. To his admirers it seemed inconceivable that he would put his name to such a treaty as that of Versailles: one which exacted formidable compensation from the Germans under humiliating conditions (the treaty which the Germans had to sign contained a formal assertion that Germany was guilty of starting the war). Yet he did so, and his reputation has never quite recovered. Much later it was to be argued that Germany could well afford the reparations that were exacted from her; but at the time informed opinion thought otherwise (Keynes put the case with the utmost brilliance in his *Economic Consequences of the Peace*); the Germans themselves thought they were being deliberately reduced to beggary (the more so, as the Allied blockade continued for months after the armistice, in spite of American protests); the vindictive nature of the terms was plain to see, and so was the risk, thus created, of another war.

It was Clemenceau's doing. Presiding at the conference, with grey gloves and weary eyes, he displayed all the characteristic virtues and vices of French diplomacy: above all, its brilliant short-sightedness. Clemenceau's only concern was to prevent another German invasion of France; he was indifferent to what happened outside Europe and not even very concerned with the Russian Revolution: he disliked the Bolsheviks, of course, because they had repudiated the Tsarist loans to which hundreds of thousands of French investors had subscribed before the war, and because he had always fought the Socialists, and because a left-wing fanatic wounded him in an assassination attempt during the negotiations; but his attitude was essentially one of 'bored acquiescence'[8] – it did not occur to him that France might one day need a strong and friendly Russia, just as she had before 1914. Still less did he see the wisdom of, if possible, making friends with the late enemy. So his actions created the very disaster he sought to avoid. He did not particularly trust the British or the Americans (as a matter of fact, he trusted nobody very much) and would have liked even more radical measures for weakening and disarming Germany than he got: for instance,

---

7 Though it should be noted that there was another school of thought which demanded the stiffest possible terms to punish Germany for her crimes.
8 J. Hampden Jackson, *Clemenceau and the Third Republic* (London, 1946), p. 215.

the establishment of an independent buffer state in the Rhineland. But since neither Britain nor the United States would agree to this, he heaped what chains he could on the defeated foe and gladly accepted the offer of an Anglo-American guarantee against another invasion from the east. It was a fatal, perhaps a fated, mistake: the offer was soon withdrawn, and the Germans bitterly resented their chains. *Realpolitik* had overreached itself, not for the first time: a generous peace could not have lasted a much shorter time than did the actual 'Carthaginian' peace of Versailles, and it would not have alienated British and American opinion.

In face of French obstinacy, there was little that Wilson could do on the central issue. He secured the acceptance of the League of Nations and comforted himself with the reflection that the reparations provisions were so absurd as to be unenforceable: they would soon be compromised.[9] Meanwhile he had to be content to instil a little moderation and realism into British and French claims, which originally added up to $320,000,000,000. Finding himself forced to acquiesce in Clemenceau's policy, he, characteristically, took it over. By the time that Lloyd George (much too late) awoke to the dangers that the treaty was creating, Wilson and Clemenceau had formed a working partnership, which seems to have given great satisfaction to both of them. They made no concessions to Lloyd George, and Wilson indulged his Presbyterian zeal by exacting strict terms from the fallen foe. It was at this time that he offered Clemenceau his military guarantee, though he should have known that no treaty embodying it was likely to pass the US Senate. It was probably Wilson's hope that, by playing the balance of power game which he had formerly repudiated, he could avert another war, since his own game had been abandoned. Certainly it is unlikely that Germany would again have attacked in the West if she had been confronted with a solid Anglo-Franco-American alliance. (Unfortunately the combined effect of a horrible war and an unpopular treaty meant that no such alliance was to be possible.) If this was indeed Wilson's calculation, it shows better than anything how much he had learned in the school of reality since 1914.

Too much: he had got far ahead of his countrymen. Henry Cabot Lodge and the other Republican intractables in the Senate had been busy taking soundings since the winter, and had settled on a list of conditions which they could insist on attaching to the treaty in return for ratifying it (since the passage of a treaty requires a two-thirds majority of the Senate). Most of these conditions related to the League and were reckoned acceptable by the Allies, whose prime concern was to secure American co-operation on any terms. But it is clear, from the course of the controversy, that underlying

9 This actually happened. The Reparations Commission fixed the sum due at $66,000,000,000; in 1921 it was reduced to $44,000,000,000; in the end Germany (who repudiated her liabilities during the Depression) paid no more than $5,000,000,000 or so. Allowing for inflation, and the vastly greater destruction of the later war, this compares very reasonably with the $1,000,000,000 which France had to pay Germany as indemnity for the Franco-Prussian War.

the dispute about the League lay another, about America's place in the world. The terms of the treaty, League or no League, were too clear and painful a challenge to preconceptions to go unquestioned. Liberal intellectuals such as the journalist Walter Lippmann, who had actually drafted many of the Fourteen Points, read their Keynes and repudiated Versailles. Men like Herbert Hoover, who had experienced the horrors of war and its aftermath at first hand and laboured mightily to relieve it, were so sickened by European folly and ingratitude (already the United States was being called 'Uncle Shylock' because it insisted on repayment of war loans) that they wanted to turn their backs on the continent for ever. The hundreds of thousands of American men who had fought in Europe had hated the experience and were resolved never to repeat it. Lodge and the nationalists feared that the League and the treaty would fatally hamper America's ability to go her own way: for instance, they said, the Monroe Doctrine was incompatible with the Covenant. Provincial pacifists shrank in horror, as Wilson had once done, from the pollution of the Old World: as Wilson had once hoped, so they hoped, to save mankind by preachment. Above all, there was a general return to the maxims of the past. Americans were still isolationists at heart; the unpleasant experiment of 1917 had never been intended to be a prelude to permanent involvement in the affairs of the world, and its results changed few minds on this point. Against these forces, what had the President to offer? Only his eloquence and devotion; his diminishing prestige; and the unsatisfactory document that had been all he could squeeze out of intractable circumstances in Paris.

What followed his return in June 1919 was one of the great American tragedies; but it was of more significance in the story of Woodrow Wilson, perhaps, than in the history of the United States. Worn out by his labours; appalled at what might flow from the repudiation of his handiwork; filled with a prophet's vision and also, unfortunately, with the vanity of Jonah, he refused all compromise. The Senate must take its medicine, he said; when House (now fallen quite out of favour) advised him to be as conciliatory in Washington as he had been in Paris, he replied, 'One can never get anything in this life that is worth while without fighting for it.' When the Senate baulked, he set out on a great speaking tour through the West, to rally the people to him: together they would overcome Senator Lodge. His case, we have seen, was by no means watertight; yet his eloquence was never greater. He defended the treaty with a passion worthy of a better cause – a passion that made it impossible to present its humble virtues, such as they were, in the coolly convincing light they deserved – and foretold, all too accurately, what would happen if Americans were to drop the burden of international responsibility which they had so recently assumed. The choice, he assured them again and again, trying to press home the lessons of his own education, lay between peace with the treaty, faults and all, or war without it. But it was all to no purpose. He suffered complete nervous prostration at Pueblo, Colorado; was hurried home to Washington;

and there suffered a massive stroke. It did not kill him, to his misfortune; but it incapacitated him for government, and turned his native obstinacy and assurance to granite. The forces mounting against him were insuperable, but he would not bend, though the German-Americans (seven million of them) thought the treaty was unjust to Germany, and the Irish-Americans resented its failure to secure self-determination for Ireland, and the haters of the British Empire, who were noisy if not especially numerous, damned the League because Britain, her colonies and the dominions would between them have six votes in it. Compromise of some kind was essential to save the treaty, but from his sick-bed Wilson refused it implacably; his will hurled the Democrats into unsuccessful battle against the Republicans; and when the Lodge amendments were passed, he forced his supporters to vote against the entire document. Lodge and his irreconcilables voted against it too, and thus it was Wilson himself, in collaboration, as it were, with his bitterest enemies, who made America take the first steps back down the isolationist path. The point is worth rubbing in: in spite of the fervour of the opponents, there was almost certainly a majority in the United States in 1919–20 for some sort of treaty, some sort of League; neither the people nor the politicians were, for the most part, yet ready to abandon their responsibilities; but after the final defeat of the treaty in the Senate, in March 1920, that was rapidly to change.

The rest of the Wilson administration was a complete failure. The summer of 1919 had been marked by more race-riots, including an appalling outbreak at Chicago in which thirty-eight people were killed and 537 injured. The country was in a wild mood of fear and reaction: after some bomb outrages, culminating in an attack on the House of Morgan on Wall Street – attacks which were presumably the work of the sort of crazed, conceited fanatics who have done so much harm since – the fear of Bolsheviks swept the country as the fear of German spies had done two years previously. It was urged on by the Attorney-General, Mitchell Palmer, himself the victim of an attempted assassination: but he was moved less by vengefulness than by his hope that the Red Scare would launch a successful Palmer-for-President boom. He arrested a thousand anarchists and socialists, and deported many of them to Russia. Five members were expelled from the New York state legislature because they were socialists. Strikes were ruthlessly broken by industrialists determined to regain control of the economic process which the war had compelled them partly to yield. Wartime boom was followed by post-war slump as orders for munitions, uniforms and rations ceased. The inflation which the war had brought did not cease: prices, which had risen by 62 per cent between 1914 and 1918, rose by 40 per cent between 1918 and 1920. The loans to the Allies ceased in 1920, which meant that the Europeans could no longer buy American exports: consequently US overseas trade was halved. In the South a new Ku Klux Klan began to arise, as vicious as the old and intent on attacking Jews and Catholics as well as blacks. The Chicago White Sox threw the World Series, the baseball championships, in return for a bribe (they were promptly nicknamed the Black Sox). The police went on strike in Boston, and there was a general strike in Seattle. Meanwhile Wilson lay inert in the White House, doing nothing, saying nothing. The American people prepared his last repudiation.

The year 1920 was to be one of Republican victory, one in which the successful candidate must reflect the people's desire for humdrum normality. So the Grand Old Party nominated Senator Warren Gamaliel Harding of Ohio, an amiable nonentity whose chief contribution to the Presidential campaign was the revolting neologism 'normalcy', which well signified the synthetic tranquillity in which his countrymen hoped to smother their anxieties. His running mate was the Governor of Massachusetts, Calvin Coolidge. Against this pair the Democrats sent James Cox, the Governor of Ohio, who, out of respect for Wilson, made the question of the League the centre of his campaign. He and his fellow-candidate, the former Assistant Secretary of the Navy, Franklin Delano Roosevelt of New York, a distant cousin of Theodore, made as good a fight as they could; but it was useless. Harding swept to one of the biggest electoral victories in American history.

In March 1921, Woodrow Wilson wearily retired. He was to outlive his successor, and his countrymen did not quite forget him. From time to time he croaked out a warning. But America was dancing to a different tune. The gayest years of the Age of Gold were beginning.

21 Irresponsibility 1921–33

Keep away from bootleg hootch
When you're on a spree
Take good care of yourself, you belong to me . . .
Steer clear of frozen ponds (ooh! ooh!)
Peroxide blondes (ooh! ooh!)
Stocks and bonds (ooh! ooh!)
You'll get a pain, ruin your bank-roll . . .

Popular song, 'Button Up Your Overcoat'

Free association yields one image as the key to the twenties: the canyons of New York city in a storm of paper – whether ticker tape filling the air as it was chucked in countless uncoiling reels from office windows to greet the return of Lindbergh from his solo flight to Paris in 1927, or the deep litter thrown to the floor of the New York Stock Exchange in the disastrous days of the Great Crash two years later. The image is apt. For not only were the great parades up Broadway and Fifth Avenue the typical carnival of the decade (Lindbergh was not the only celebrity to be welcomed to Manhattan, though he was the most fervently worshipped); not only was the Crash the event which has dominated our view of the twenties ever since it happened. The great walls of the canyons themselves tell us something. This was the decade of the triumphant skyscrapers, the decade which launched the Empire State Building (1,248 feet) and Rockefeller Center – for which the unlucky thirties had to pay. New York had conquered: the symbol of American life was no longer to be a log cabin or a family farm, it was to be a gigantic cigar. In 1925 Harold Ross from Colorado launched the greatest of all American magazines, inevitably named the *New Yorker*, with the express mission of startling the staid, such as 'the old lady from Dubuque'. Harlem, not yet called a ghetto, exploded in jazz and poetry, and white folk flocked uptown to enjoy what the newly citified black folk were creating. As the golden years of Tin Pan Alley opened (they would last until the coming of rock) Rodgers and Hart gave the world their first big hit, *Manhattan*. Urban America had triumphed: 'the twenties' were to be cele-brated on the sidewalks of New York (the song of that name was Al Smith's anthem). Just as American football is pre-eminently the television game, best watched from a deep chair in front of the box, a can of iced beer in your hand, so baseball was the game of the city in the days when you actually had to go to the stadium to see it played. The greatest sports hero of the decade was 'Babe' Ruth, the star of the New York Yankees, the Bambino, the Sultan of Swat, who hit sixty home runs in one year, 1928 – a record that stood until 1961; George Herman Ruth, who was bigger than Dempsey the boxer, than Tilden the tennis player, than Jones the golfer. Ruth, who once killed a fan by hitting a homer (the fan, in his excitement, had a heart-attack), was an entirely urban figure. The mimic battles of sport were the fitting preoccupation of the twenties, a time in which the quest for 'normalcy', the belief in the possibility of happiness and a good time, led great numbers of people, perhaps especially the young, who now had money to spend in large amounts for the first time (and so the world of pop was born), to turn their backs on the struggle of work and politics as much as possible and to seek salvation in the ephemeral. It was foolish – it was fun. 'What Lincoln said in '62' suddenly seemed boring. So everybody Charlestoned. At the Republican convention in 1920 the bands played a song called *Mr Zip, Zip, Zip* instead of *John Brown's Body*. The last veterans of the Civil War shuffled offstage; their successors, the veterans of the First World War, wanted to forget their own experiences in a hurry.

Beneath all the froth life went on much as usual; but the legend of the twenties did not arise out of nothing: it is still the best route to the truth about the times.

It is impossible to pinpoint the moment at which 'the twenties' began: legendary epochs elude the tidy historian. Certainly, the new day was at hand when President Harding took office. The amazing disparity between the job and the man has the right twenties flavour: it was an era of contradic-tions. Harding was not intelligent or firm or hard-working enough to be a successful President. His other personal weaknesses hardly mattered. True, he committed adultery in a coat-cupboard at the White House because he was too afraid of his wife to take his mistress to more comfortable quarters; but then several Presidents since have had their sexual difficulties and improprieties. True, he was rather too fond of giving government posts to poker-playing cronies whose honesty turned out to be inadequate; but Harry Truman was to do somewhat the same. True, his oratory stunned the mind:

Progress is not proclamation nor palaver. It is not pretence nor play on prejudice. It is not the perturbation of a people passion-wrought, nor a promise proposed . . .[1]

---

1 It is only fair to add that Harding toned down his alliteration markedly after he became President: he was upset by the merciless ridicule it had brought on him from people like the journalist H. L. Mencken.

but real eloquence has seldom distinguished the modern Presidency. And Harding had his good points. His admirers thought he looked like George Washington. He was magnanimous, for example letting Eugene Debs out of the jail into which Woodrow Wilson had thrust him. He was determined to do his best to live up to the Presidency, hoping to be, not the greatest President (he knew himself too well for that), but the best-loved. Partly by good luck, partly because of his anxious respect for men who were abler than he, he put together an administration which, if it contained too many rogues and too many millionaires (the New York *World*, a liberal newspaper, guessed that the Cabinet altogether was worth $600,000,000), also contained three really able men, who were to give the period much of its character: Andrew Mellon, Charles Evans Hughes and Herbert Hoover.

Andrew Mellon, the second richest man in America, was Secretary of the Treasury. His fortune had initially been built upon the exploitation of the new metal, aluminium, but his family also controlled the Gulf Oil corporation. No appointment could have been more reassuring to Old Guard Republicans. Mellon came from Pennsylvania and his outlook was entirely predictable. He believed in a high tariff, low taxation, the greatest freedom to get and spend wealth, and in having a friendly government at Washington to back up big business leadership when necessary. He had no time for labour unions, no interest in farmers, no concern for consumers. As to the business cycle, he was a fatalist, regarding booms and slumps as natural phenomena which it was a waste of effort to try to control. He was personally honest, by the standards of the business class, but unhappily those standards were rather lax. He presided at the Treasury throughout the twenties – indeed until 1932. So he became an obvious target for the wrath of all those who blamed the Republican administrations of the twenties for the Great Depression.

Something can be said for Mellon, all the same. He was not the greatest Secretary of the Treasury since Hamilton that his admirers loved to call him; indeed, his failure to mitigate the Depression must always count as a crime. He was callous and complacent. But his failure to foresee the Depression is scarcely surprising or even very culpable: nobody else foresaw it either, and today's historians, who still cannot agree on exactly what caused it, are hardly in a position to blame Mellon and the other statesmen. If hindsight fails, how could foresight have succeeded? According to his lights, Mellon did very well by the American economy.

He was deeply conservative, but then so were the President and Senate that appointed him. The chief measure of the Harding Congress was the replacement of the Underwood tariff by the Fordney–McCumber tariff of 1922, which imposed the highest rates known until then in American history. It was an act of almost conscious atavism – back to the days of McKinley and Aldrich! (Harding had got the Presidential nomination largely because he seemed to be a new McKinley.) Mellon, even had he been a liberal, would have had to accept the tariff as a constraint on his actions. Another constraint was the revulsion against the active government of the Wilson era: it would have been impossible to get many new programmes through Congress, even had Mellon been disposed to try; nobody yet dreamed of setting up a welfare state. In the circumstances, Mellon's policies were probably the best that could have been implemented. The high tariff soon produced a vast budgetary surplus; Mellon therefore felt able to reduce taxation sharply every year. The rich, naturally, were the chief beneficiaries, but then, as events were soon to make all too plain, American prosperity was heavily dependent on their willingness and ability to spend, and tax cuts encouraged them to do so. Mellon's remissions, which went on right through the decade, seemed like so many votes of confidence in the business civilization and were appreciated accordingly. They regularly released new spending-power into the market. This was a far better use for the money than allowing it to pile up in the Treasury.

Andrew Mellon thus played a part in stimulating the economic buoyancy which was so marked a feature of the twenties. The plain facts of life in America were still more exhilarating. Thanks to Henry Ford, the motor-car had come into its own. The Model T was the best-selling automobile until 1926, but Ford's methods were being copied and surpassed by his competitors, above all by the giant General Motors, which did not subscribe to the great man's celebrated dictum, 'You can have any colour you like, so long as it's black,' or to any other of his conservative business attitudes. GM's innovations lay rather in the fields of organization and marketing than in technology, where Henry Ford's strength lay; but it was precisely in those fields that the crucial advances were now to be made, so, willy-nilly, the Ford company had to emulate General Motors if it wanted to remain one of the industry's leaders. In 1927 Tin Lizzie was retired, and after fourteen months of mysterious preparation her successor, the Model A, was unveiled to the world and became for a year America's best-selling car. But in the gap the newly formed Chrysler Corporation had seen and seized an opportunity to launch its own cheap, popular model, the Plymouth, with huge success. Those two years, in short, saw the emergence of the motor industry in the form it has since retained: at the top the great monopolistic corporations, General Motors, Ford and Chrysler; at a respectful distance, a cluster of much smaller firms, competing for what was left of the market after the monopolies had finished with it.

This was no bad prospect in the twenties, for the market seemed to be infinitely buoyant. The assembly line made cars wonderfully cheap; wages rose fairly steadily from 1917 onwards, registering a gain, in real terms, of 26 per cent between 1920 and 1929; credit was available on the cheapest terms (Ford and GM did all they could to encourage sales by setting up organizations whose sole purpose was to facilitate hire-purchase – or instalment buying, as it is called in America); the irresistible appeal of the car to the consumer, which needs no explanation, did the rest. The result was a multifarious transformation of American life which is not over yet. The economic impact alone was striking enough. The mass market for cars pushed the auto-makers into the front line of American businesses. By 1929 the industry was the largest in the country, employing nearly half a million workers, and Detroit was America's fourth largest city. US Steel, the pre-war giant of the corporations, was hopelessly dwarfed by the Big Three. The demand for petroleum products made the oil companies ever larger, more profitable and more powerful. Demand for the materials which went to the making of automobiles – steel, glass, rubber, paint, for instance – soared, stimulating these industries too, and stimulating rapid technological innovation, for the car itself was changing yearly. It needed good roads to drive on: road-builders and the producers of concrete profited. A whole new profession, that of car-dealer (whether of used or new vehicles), sprang up. And still the sales rose. In 1920, 1,905,500 cars were produced; in 1929, 4,455,100 – a figure not to be surpassed until 1949. By 1929, 26,704,800 automobiles, trucks and buses were in registered ownership. It was reckoned proudly that the whole population of the United States could, in theory, be fitted at one moment into existing motor-vehicles.

Yet perhaps the social results were even more impressive than the economic and, in the long run, more important. The car began to break down the ancient sharp division between town and country. The movement perhaps began with the prosperous urban middle class, anxious for a holiday from New York: they were delighted to discover the rest of their country. After one lengthy motor journey a gentleman with the wonderfully pretentious name of Frederic F. Van De Water reported that 'we had lived on Manhattan Island so long that we had come to consider all America suspicious, hostile, abrupt, insolent . . . New York and all it signifies, while geographically of the nation, are no more intrinsically America than a monocle is part of the optic system.' He and people like him began a movement that would eventually cover America with motels and wayside restaurants serving drinks, hot meals and Howard Johnson's celebrated multiplicity of ice creams. But the cheap car enabled the working class also to travel, for pleasure, or in search of work. Even poor rural people, it turned out, could own cars, and when they did so many of them used the freedom thus attained to depart – to the West, or to the cities; and thus one more of the great migrations of American history began. Even more important, perhaps, was the impact of the car on daily life. It came into use for all sorts of short trips – to work or to the shops – which had previously been made by trolley-car or urban railway. It made a whole new pattern of living possible: vast suburbs began to spread over the land, to the great profit of the building industry. No longer did you have to live in comparatively cramped quarters near the railroad station. Nor did you have to take your annual holiday at one of the traditional, crowded resorts near home. Instead you could speed over the hills and far away, where planners like Robert Moses of New York state had prepared parks and beaches for you: a new function for government. Even Congress, though in its most conservative years, was ready to take a hand: under the Federal Highway Act of 1921 federal funds paid for 50 per cent of the new trunk highways.

The carefree motorist, in short, was not only the symbol of the twenties: he was its central driving force. For ill as well as good: he brought traffic jams as well as mobility, and as early as 1925, 25,000 people were killed by cars in one year – 17,500 of them pedestrians.

There were yet other ways in which the consumer stimulated American industry to new feats: the popularity of the cinema, for instance, produced a whole new giant business as Hollywood took wing; radio was a magic word for gamblers on the stock market; the demand for alcohol was actually increased by prohibition and put millions of dollars into the pockets of bootleggers, rum-runners and outright gangsters (most notably, Al Capone of Chicago); and the very rich lived in a whirl of parties, yachts, furs and cosmetics (at least according to the legend fostered by Scott Fitzgerald in the decade's representative novel, *The Great Gatsby*). The near-absolute exclusion of European goods acted as a short-term boost to American industry. It is no wonder that Mr Mellon presided over an epoch of prosperity or that he got the credit for creating it. People are naturally inclined to be generous when times are good.

His formidable colleague, Secretary of State Charles Evans Hughes (Theodore Roosevelt had described him as 'the bearded iceberg'), presided over an epoch of lasting peace, or so his countrymen hoped. Hughes, former Governor of New York, former Presidential nominee, future Chief Justice of the United States, represented what was left of progressive Republicanism; in foreign policy he belonged to the nationalistic school of Henry Cabot Lodge, which had no objection to a vigorous foreign policy provided that it was untrammelled by alliances and the League. But, as he very quickly discovered, the Americans, having shaken off Woodrow Wilson and the yoke of internationalism, were disinclined to assume that of nationalism. The last tide of idealism, which had seemed to carry a majority to support some sort of League as recently as 1920, had ebbed very fast: on reflection, the returned soldiers and their families wanted no more action of any kind which implied the possibility, however remote, that the dreadful experience of the war might be repeated. They could only be interested in proposals to diminish, not to increase, their diplomatic responsibilities; even the World Court at The Hague came to seem to them a dangerous institution; at any rate Hughes and his successors could never induce Congress to allow American membership. So it is not very surprising that the greatest achievement of Hughes's term in office was the Washington Naval Conference of 1921–2. This was indeed a welcome enterprise. Ever since the end of the war the rival empires, British, American and Japanese, had found themselves caught up in a naval race in the Pacific. Each had vulnerable possessions to protect (in the American case, the Philippines, the Hawaiian islands and

Guam), none wanted another war, but so far none had thought of a means of averting it. Pressure for some sort of conference mounted during Harding's first year in office, and when finally one opened at Washington on 12 November 1921, Hughes took the lead. The results were spectacular. The naval race ended, the United States, Britain and Japan agreeing to scrap large parts of their navies. They agreed to respect each other's imperial holdings in the Pacific; not to add to their fortifications, naval bases and coastal defences there; and to settle disputes peacefully; nine Powers recognized the principle of the Open Door; and Japan, in an ecstasy of co-operation, evacuated Shantung and Siberia.

It was a remarkable and promising achievement, and had it been followed up the Pacific War of 1941–5 might never have occurred. Unfortunately the next step towards a permanent pacification of the East required economic concessions by the United States. The high tariff excluded the Japanese from the only market to which they could have exported profitably; their failure to export meant that they were unable to import essential raw materials; the net result was a prolonged depression, which slowly but surely turned Japan towards the mixture of authoritarianism at home and imperialist war abroad which was to prove so catastrophic for the world. This disaster, like every other, was unforeseen by American statesmen; but even if it had been, there was nothing they could do; Congress and its constituents remained obstinately attached to the Fordney–McCumber tariff.

The diplomatic, or rather the undiplomatic, disposition of the American people was also illustrated by another important development in the early twenties. Ever since the Dillingham Report the forces which were making for immigration restriction had been gathering strength. Organized labour had struggled, on the whole successfully, to maintain the wage-levels reached during the war and to improve them: it feared the continued importation of cheap labour from overseas. During the war general suspicion of the foreign-born had increased ('hyphenated Americans' were assumed to have a divided loyalty) and the Red Scare afterwards had not helped. What may be called the cultural panic of the post-war period expressed itself, as was natural, in noisier and noisier assertions of American superiority and in a dread of foreign infiltration. The great industrialists no longer believed that they needed an immigrant labour supply: there were enough unemployed native workers for their purposes. The hyphenated Americans themselves had not yet attained their full political strength. The result was a series of illiberal acts: the Immigration Act of 1917 (passed over Woodrow Wilson's veto); the Quota Act of 1921 (a stopgap measure); and the Johnson–Reed Act of 1924. The intricacies of these laws need not be detailed: the Johnson–Reed Act was so ill-devised that it took five years to come into operation and gave conscientious bureaucrats infinite trouble as long as it lasted. The general effect can be easily summarized: mass immigration was ended (the annual average went down from 862,514 in the 1907–14 period to no more than 150,000[2] – all that was allowed under the 1924 arrangements) and discrimination against suspect nationalities was built into the system. Immigration from the so-called Asiatic Barred Zone – China, Japan, Indo-China, Afghanistan, Arabia, the East Indies – was stopped almost entirely;[3] and immigration from everywhere but Northern and Western Europe was made exceedingly difficult, by the expedient of allotting four-fifths of the permitted admissions to persons from that area. The spirit in which the Golden Door was slammed shut was lucidly expressed by Senator Albert Johnson, of Washington state, a sponsor of the 1924 Act, who explained that 'the foreign-born flood' was a threat to the happiness of individual Americans and to American institutions and liberties.

It is no wonder, therefore, that the myth of the melting pot has been discredited. It is no wonder that Americans everywhere are insisting that their land no longer shall offer free and unrestricted asylum to the rest of the world ... The United States is our land. If it was not the land of our fathers, at least it may be, and it should be, the land of our children. We intend to maintain it so.

Of course neither Senator Johnson nor anyone else foresaw the tragic consequences that this Act would begin to have nine years later. He was simply enjoying himself, in the ancient fashion of Congress, giving his prejudices the force of law.

He was answered indirectly some years later from the dock, when Bartolomeo Vanzetti heard that his appeals for a fresh trial had been finally rejected, and that he and his fellow-defendant, Nicola Sacco, were to be executed. They had been arrested in 1920, at the height of the Red Scare, and later found guilty of murdering and robbing a postmaster in South Braintree, Massachusetts. Superficially the case was ordinary enough, even down to the fact that the evidence against Vanzetti and Sacco was far from conclusive;[4] but it became famous, became indeed the American equivalent of the Dreyfus Affair, because the defendants were anarchists, draft-evaders and immigrants; because the judge showed extreme prejudice against them, even to the length of boasting afterwards of what he had done to 'those anarchist bastards'; and because the friends and associates of Vanzetti and Sacco skilfully alerted the Left throughout the world to what seemed to be a monstrous perversion of justice, all too typical of America in the twenties. Crowds swarmed threateningly outside the US embassy in Rome, there was a general strike in Montevideo and an attempt to bomb the US consulate in Lisbon. A bomb actually did go off inside the American ambassador's house in Paris, and, tragically, another exploded during a

---

2 The real average was some hundreds higher, because of a contradiction (typical of its muddles) within the 1924 system itself.
3 It was this provision of the Act that led Japan to declare a day of national mourning when it became law.
4 But it now seems clear that Nicola Sacco was indeed guilty.

large demonstration in favour of Vanzetti and Sacco in Paris, killing twenty people. These events alerted opinion in America itself, where the original trial had been little noticed: the liberal intelligentsia mobilized with a vigour and enthusiasm that it had not shown since Woodrow Wilson sailed for France. Money was collected, speeches were made, articles published, demonstrations were held outside Boston State House (where the police threw many of the demonstrators into jail) and outside the prison where the victims languished. All in vain: the Governor of Massachusetts appointed a committee of the utmost respectability to advise him on the question of pardon or a fresh trial (the men had by now been in prison for seven years), and the committee, headed by the President of Harvard, found that, although the judge had disgraced himself, the defendants were guilty as charged. So on 9 April 1927 they were told that they were to be executed. Vanzetti's last statement was as movingly dignified as all his words and deeds throughout the affair, perhaps the more so because his English was slightly imperfect:

I not only am not guilty of these crimes, but I never commit a crime in my life, – I have never steal and I have never kill and I have never spilt blood . . . I would not wish to a dog or to a snake, to the most low and misfortunate creature on the earth – I would not wish to any of them what I have had to suffer for things that I am not guilty of. But my conviction is that I have suffered for things that I am guilty of. I am suffering because I am a radical and indeed I am a radical; I have suffered because I was an Italian, and indeed I am an Italian; I have suffered more for my family and for my beloved than for myself; but I am so convinced to be right that if you could execute me two times, and if I could be reborn two other times, I would live again to do what I have done already.

He and Sacco were electrocuted (that cruellest form of execution) on 23 August. Perhaps it would have been some consolation to them had they known that their case had provoked the first serious rebellion against the narrowness and conservatism of the post-war Republican ascendancy, and that the energies it had released, the alliances it had forged, were not to disappear afterwards, but were to go on to other struggles, and eventually to victory.

The execution of Sacco and Vanzetti touched off further riots in London, Paris, Germany and elsewhere. But the episode was no more than a transient embarrassment to American foreign policy. The permanent difficulties were domestic. The Harding and Coolidge administrations were aware of the need for some sort of co-operation with the European powers, but they had to move with the utmost caution, for fear of alarming Congressional isolationists, such as Senator Borah of Idaho, well-nicknamed a 'Son of the Wild Jackass'. Though Borah could never be got to believe it, isolation in the strict sense of the word was impossible. The United States, now the world's creditor, had too many overseas interests to protect. There was the question of war-debts. The Americans wanted to be paid; their former allies

– Britain, France, Italy, Belgium (the new Soviet Union repudiated imperial Russia's obligations) – felt that this insistence was ungracious: if America had given treasure to the common cause, so had they, and oceans of blood as well. The trouble was that Americans in the twenties no longer accepted that they had been right to make common cause with the Europeans. These then argued that they could pay their debts only if they were allowed either to collect handsome reparations from Germany or to export goods to the American market (thereby earning dollars with which to meet their obligations). The magnanimous Americans were against reparations (why be beastly to the Germans?), but the debts were another matter: as President Coolidge remarked, 'They hired the money, didn't they? Let them pay it!' And of course there could be no question of modifying the prohibitive tariff. It was the same old brick wall. So the ex-Allies negotiated what settlements they could with Washington. Congress set up a War Debts Commission which was dominated by the Secretaries of State, the Treasury, and Commerce (Hughes, Mellon and Hoover) and showed itself as reasonable as possible within the bounds laid down by the legislature. Meanwhile many Americans, and American financial institutions, were hurrying to invest in Germany as she recovered from the devastation of the war and its aftermath. The money soon went from Germany to her former enemies, as reparations; and then found its way back to the United States as payment of war-debt. It was a neat and symmetrical system, fine as long as it lasted, but it was irrelevant to the real problems of the international trading system, and indeed by distracting attention from them made them worse. Once more the provincial prejudices of the provincial assembly of a provincial nation were laying up a great store of trouble for the future.

Hampered though they were, the statesmen did their best. Hughes stage-managed the Naval Conference; poor President Harding decided to take America into the World Court. He was still immensely popular; like Woodrow Wilson he decided to carry his cause to the people, and in the summer of 1923 set out on a speaking-tour through the West. He was following a bad example. The tour was too much for a man in Harding's state of health (he had a weak heart); even a holiday in Alaska proved too exhausting, and there was no sign that the people were any readier to come to the rescue of the World Court than they had been to come to the rescue of the League of Nations. Deeply depressed, by this, and his illness, and his knowledge that scandals were about to erupt, Harding reached San Francisco, where he suddenly died on 2 August 1923, to the consternation of his countrymen. As his funeral train crossed the country on its way back to Washington they turned out to register their sorrow and love as they had never done since the death of Lincoln.

Then the scandals came out. There was Charlie Forbes, the cheery creature whom Harding had put in charge of the new Veterans Administration. The VA provided medical care, pensions and other benefits for old soldiers: it provided ample opportunities for graft, which Forbes had seized. There was Albert B. Fall, the Secretary of the Interior. He had been unanimously confirmed, without a hearing, when his nomination was brought to the Senate; for he was then a Senator himself, from New Mexico. Fall had been indiscreet in accepting loans from a man who was trying to lease Teapot Dome, a hill in Wyoming under which there was supposed to be an oil field, from the Department of the Interior; but what ruined him were the lies he told about the indiscretion, which made everything seem so much worse than it had really been. There was Harry Daugherty, the Attorney-General, Harding's political manager, who seemed to have traded his political influence for cash.[5] Many smaller offenders were exposed, some of whom were driven to suicide. Harding's reputation plummeted and did not begin to recover until the 1970s.

It looked for a moment as if the Republican hold on power was loosening. The post-war recession had profoundly injured American farmers, cutting exports by half and driving down agricultural prices. The 1922 elections had been good for progressives, bad for Old Guard Republicans. Now there were the Harding scandals. Fortunately for the party, the new President, like Gerald Ford fifty years later, was just what the situation required. Calvin Coolidge was a man of flinty personal integrity. Furthermore he advertised himself brilliantly without appearing to do so. At the time of Harding's death he was holidaying at his father's farm in Vermont, where he had been born and raised. The news that he was now President reached him with some difficulty, as the house was twelve miles from the nearest telegraph station. When a messenger at last arrived, in the middle of the night, Coolidge got up, dressed, and was sworn in by his father, a Notary Public, in the living room, by the light of an oil-lamp. Never was old-fashioned Yankee austerity, Yankee thrift, Yankee character, more conspicuously displayed; never (from the point of view of party managers) more usefully. Coolidge began as he meant to go on.

He had perhaps the most fascinatingly intricate character of any President since that other hero of Massachusetts, John Adams. There is always another story to learn about 'Silent Cal';[6] but his historical importance lies in two facts. First, he was a veteran politician, as much so as Harding had been, yet clean and strong-willed as Harding was not. Consequently it was easy enough for him, moving with deliberate speed, to reform the administration in time for the 1924 election, which the Republicans won handily, since the great boom of the twenties was now well under way, the Democrats were

5 Nobody has ever doubted that Daugherty was a crook of some sort, but he covered his tracks very astutely and was acquitted at his trial (probably through bribing a juryman). Mrs Harding destroyed six-sevenths of her husband's papers. So it is not surprising that even Harding's accomplished biographer, Francis Russell, has been unable to establish the truth.
6 Perhaps the most appealing is the one about the lady who found herself next to him at dinner. 'Mr President, I have bet my friend that I can make you say more than three words.' 'You lose.' And there was the reporter who asked him about a sermon he had just been hearing. 'The minister preached on sin.' 'What did he say?' 'He was against it.'

hopelessly split (between wets and drys, conservatives and progressives, friends and foes of the Ku Klux Klan) and a third party, the Progressives,[7] took the field, their candidate being old Senator La Follette, fighting his last campaign. Coolidge got 15,718,211 votes; the Democrats, 8,385,283; the Progressives, 4,831,289. Second, Coolidge was not only a quietist by temperament and conviction, but a traditional Republican of the truest stripe. He venerated wealth and Andrew Mellon. As President, he thought it was his duty to mind the store while the Republicans ran the country as they saw fit. He intervened in the economic process only to veto the proposals of more active men in Congress.

He was almost equally supine in foreign affairs, with much more excuse. The isolationist mood had deepened and strengthened; the internationalists were chasing after moonbeams, such as the outlawry of war. Coolidge himself was no isolationist; he never renounced the Wilsonian principles that he had avowed when Governor of Massachusetts, in 1919, in Wilson's presence. Under his administration the quiet work of re-integrating the United States in the world diplomatic community went on; negotiations, in which the leading part was played by Charles E. Dawes, first Director of the Budget,[8] gradually reduced the reparations question to manageable dimensions. In countless small ways the United States moved forwards, until it was in effect an unofficial member of the League. But the constraints on really effective American diplomacy remained as rigid as ever. What they were was well demonstrated by the story of the Kellogg–Briand Pact. This tragic farce began in the spring of 1927, when the French Prime Minister, Aristide Briand, called publicly for a treaty outlawing war between France and the United States. Briand knew, of course, that such a treaty would be nothing but a sentimental gesture (there was not the remotest likelihood of the two countries going to war, so the treaty would avert nothing), but like all French statesmen he was haunted by the knowledge of France's military weakness and by fear of a revived Germany. He hoped that a sentimental gesture might be the first step towards a revival of the Franco-American alliance. The Americans, of course, also saw this possibility, as a trap. Coolidge and Frank B. Kellogg, who had succeeded Hughes as Secretary of State in 1925, had no intention of being destroyed as Wilson and Harding had been destroyed. So they countered Briand's appeal by asking for a multilateral treaty, by which *all* the civilized powers would renounce war as an instrument of policy. This suggestion was immensely popular with all the fools who thought that peace could be maintained without effort or expense, and there were many such in every

7 Its only link with the Bull Moose party was its name.
8 The establishment of the Bureau of the Budget (now the Office of Management and the Budget) was the most lasting achievement of the Harding administration. It meant that for the first time the President was able to control the expenditure plans of the government. No longer did the departments go straight to Congress; everything now had to be channelled through the White House. It was a very important accretion of Presidential power.

nation. Their governments trooped obediently to the conference table and on 27 August 1928, at Paris, all the major belligerents of the Second World War except the Soviet Union signed the Kellogg–Briand Pact (officially known as the Pact of Paris) renouncing war – and the Soviet Union adhered immediately after the meeting. Its absence from Paris had been through no wish of its own. Once more America was responsible. Since the USSR refused to acknowledge the Tsarist debt, the USA refused to acknowledge the USSR as a legitimate government, and had not let it send emissaries to Paris for fear this might be construed as recognition through the back door. It was a curious way to treat one of the great powers; but then, thanks to the Kellogg–Briand Pact, the United States would never need allies again.

Meanwhile the years of 'Coolidge Prosperity' rolled onwards. It was a happy, hopeful epoch, and in retrospect it is sadly clear that it would not have taken very much wisdom to realize its promise. The most controversial aspect of American life at the time was undoubtedly prohibition. The great experiment had got into dreadful difficulties almost at once. Congress never made funds available to pay for an adequate number of enforcement officers: wisely, because the number would have had to be astronomical. As a result the temptation was irresistible to smuggle booze into the United States by land and sea; to manufacture it in the privacy of one's own cellar; to run speakeasies (illegal saloons) where it could be sold at extortionate prices, or bootlegging businesses (criminal grocers) which brought it and the same extortionate prices to the private citizen's doorstep. It was all especially tempting to the thriving mobs of New York and Chicago. Professional, organized crime, in fact, grew so profitable, thanks to the Eighteenth Amendment, that it has been big business ever since: when prohibition ended it took up illegal gambling, drug-smuggling, prostitution and general extortion instead. The price of official righteousness comes high. In the case of prohibition, $2,000,000,000 worth of business was simply transferred from brewers and bar-keepers to bootleggers and gangsters, who worked in close co-operation with the policemen and politicians they corrupted. Blackmail, protection rackets and gangland murders became all too common, and no one was punished. In New York city, out of 6,902 cases involving breaches of the Volstead Act (the law, passed in 1919, which was supposed to enforce the Eighteenth Amendment), 6,074 were dismissed for 'insufficient evidence' and 400 were never even tried. Out of 514 persons arrested in gambling raids in 1926 and 1927 only five were held for trial.

No wonder, then, that prohibition was once more a matter of controversy in Coolidge's time: 'wets' emerged to do battle with the 'drys'. Yet today it seems less important than the newly revealed capacity of the American economy to grow through the invention and manufacture of consumer goods (washing-machines were making their first appearance); or than the experiments in modern government which were being made in some of the states, above all in New York, where the remarkable Al Smith (1873–1944), an honest man sprung from Tammany Hall, was Governor, and was gathering round him a generation of equally remarkable younger men and women – Harry Hopkins, Frances Perkins, Robert Moses, Franklin Delano Roosevelt – who were to become widely known elsewhere before very long.[9] Even the South began to show signs of life. The new Klan, which in 1924 seemed to be sweeping all before it, was soon discovered to be hollow: beyond its talent for terrorizing Jews, Catholics and blacks in rural parts it had little to offer but scandals of greed, corruption and sexual hypocrisy. By 1926 it had passed its peak, and the way was cleared for several portents of change, the most vivid of which was young Huey Long of Louisiana (1893 – 1935), who was elected Governor of that state in 1928 and proceeded to turn it upside down.

Long's initial strength was as a spokesman for the bitter grievances of Southern white farmers. For the prosperity of the twenties – this was perhaps its crucial weakness – by no means encompassed all Americans, and those whom it excluded were hard put to it indeed. The wartime boom in cotton collapsed in 1920; next year the boll weevil wiped out 30 per cent of the crop; two bumper years in the mid-twenties simply destroyed the price of cotton again. Meanwhile, the New England textile industry collapsed under competition from mills in the South, where labour costs, because of the general poverty, were low: bankruptcies were commonplace, and in ten years (1923 – 33) the workforce employed in the industry shrank from 190,000 to less than 100,000.

Some industrial workers had their difficulties; but the farming population – still nearly one-third of the whole nation in 1920 – was the largest group of victims. Its produce came off the land in ever-increasing abundance; but the domestic market was saturated, and the high tariffs prevented foreigners from earning the dollars they needed for buying American crops. Besides, the United States was not the only country with a food surplus. Canada, Australia, even (in that pre-collectivist period) Russia were effective competitors. The Republican administrations did not believe in direct assistance to farmers, and when an aid bill was passed by Congress Coolidge vetoed it. Actually, the McNary–Haugen Bill (as it was called) offered only illusory help, but to the farmers this was 1896 all over again. Good weather continued; they could not agree among themselves to restrict the acreage they planted (or at least they could not abide by their agreements) so bumper harvests continued too, prices continued low and their desperation increased. For the first time in American history the farm population began to shrink. It was approximately 1,500,000 smaller in 1930 than it had been in 1920, and was now only a quarter of the total population. Hundreds of thousands of

9 Though it could be argued that an even more characteristic figure of the period was Mayor Jimmy Walker of New York, a corrupt, engaging scamp, whose rule was chiefly notable for His Honour's taste for pretty girls, and for the affability with which he greeted distinguished visitors to the city, such as Lindbergh. Another notable mayor was Big Bill Thompson of Chicago, famous for incompetence, collusion with Al Capone, and for threatening to poke King George V on the snoot should His Majesty ever come to the Windy City.

farmers and their families had left the land for the cities for good. In so far as the land was over-populated (for the tractor was making agriculture less labour-intensive) this may have been, in the long run, a healthy development: but it was not a joyous migration.

Yet enough voters were doing well in 1928 to make Coolidge's re-election a certainty if he wanted it. He did not. 'I do not choose to run,' he said, with characteristic precision, and when it became certain that he meant it the Republicans turned inevitably to the third giant of the Harding Cabinet. Herbert Hoover had bulked large in American imaginations ever since his heroic labours during and after the First World War. As Secretary of Commerce he had vastly extended the importance of his department, and accelerated the modernization of American industry, thereby further accelerating prosperity. He had recently refreshed his humanitarian reputation by once again organizing a successful relief programme when the Mississippi broke its banks in 1927, devastating an immense area. The Republican party regulars disliked him for his shyness, coldness and disdain for politicians, but they needed him. He was the most popular Republican, the only man certain to beat the most popular Democrat, Al Smith.

The race between these two men was in one sense the race between the past and the future: between a man born on a farm, who stood for the old, predominantly rural, Protestant America, which believed in self-help above all other social virtues, and a man born in the city, who stood for immigrants and Americans of immigrant stock, a Catholic, someone who understood the new, complex demands that politicians have to meet in modern society. Yet, in another perspective, both were moderns, for Hoover had proved himself a highly capable administrator and had enormous attractions, as 'the Great Engineer', for the professional middle class; and in another, both were primitive, for Smith, like Hoover, had risen from extreme poverty and believed in the old American values of hard work, thrift and personal honesty which had always guided him and, he thought, made his success possible. Tragically, both men were to show themselves unequal to the challenges ahead.

The election demonstrated that many parts of the country were still bitterly suspicious of city politicians, wets and Catholics. The Protestant clergy flung itself into the fray as never before. One Baptist preacher, the Reverend Mordecai F. Ham, told his congregation, 'If you vote for Al Smith you're voting against Christ and you'll all be damned.' When Smith toured the South-West, fiery crosses, the symbol of the Klan, blazed in the fields, and for the first time since Reconstruction a Republican Presidential candidate carried several ex-Confederate states (Texas, Virginia, North Carolina and Florida, and Tennessee, which had gone for Harding in 1920). But what above all defeated Smith was prosperity. Hoover spoke of the permanent elimination of poverty being at hand; he clearly meant it, he was energetic, able, full of plans; he talked of two cars in every garage. People believed him and voted accordingly. It was worse than 1916, when they voted for the man who had kept them out of war.

Already the forces which were to destroy Coolidge prosperity were at work. Indeed, the first signs of trouble came as early as 1926, when the sale of new housing began to slacken. This had various causes, among them the collapse of a land-boom in Florida, where thousands of sun-hungry Northerners had been hoaxed into buying pieces of swamp, miles from the sea, in the belief that they were getting valuable properties near the beach in a paradise of sand, sunlight and gentle sea-breezes. The exposure of some spectacular frauds, the collapse of the Florida railroad system and a couple of hurricanes opened their eyes and set back the development of Miami by twenty-five years. 'The world's greatest poker game', as some cynic had dubbed the boom, was over. A more serious cause of the housing slowdown was the fact that the market was becoming saturated, like the market for farm products. Of course there were still tens of millions of Americans who needed better housing than they were ever likely to get, but they had no money. By 1926 those who had money had usually already obtained their houses or mortgages; and though new buyers came on to the market every year, they were not numerous enough to sustain the boom. This mattered, because the building trade is labour- and materials-intensive. To put up a house requires many pairs of hands at every stage, from manufacturing the bricks or cutting the timber to putting in the plumbing; and every house that is built is a small stimulus to half a dozen industries – not to mention that the occupants will add to the band of prosperous consumers, since wants increase with house-ownership. A faltering, then, in the building industry was a bad signal. Others followed. By the late summer of 1929 demand had slackened so much that all the major indices of industrial production were turning down – warnings of impending layoffs and reduced dividends, if of nothing worse.

Such ebbs in commerce are wholly natural and indeed predictable. In other circumstances their impact and duration can be minimal. Unfortunately, in the late twenties, two other factors made the impact of this particular turndown catastrophic. The first has already been touched on. The Mellon–Coolidge–Hoover philosophy of government and economics forbade the federal government to take any preventive action, and indeed had largely deprived it of any instruments of action, even had it wanted to do something. A modern government can usually stimulate demand by reducing taxation; but Mellon had already reduced taxation so much that there was little further to be done in that line. He could have pressed Congress to lower the tariff, which might have stimulated demand by lowering prices, since cheap European goods could then have entered the American market and forced their American competitors to cut their rates (though that in turn would probably have entailed lower wages and dividends); with the dollars thus obtained the Europeans would have bought American goods, or paid their American debts, and so assisted the American

economy. But it is in the highest degree unlikely that Congress, still dominated by protectionists, as events were soon to prove, would have agreed
to such a policy, and anyway Mellon never dreamed of proposing it. Finally,
the federal government could have acted as governments have done so often
since, and by an extensive programme of public expenditure maintained
employment and stimulated demand. Unfortunately such a policy was as
yet unthinkable. The long Jeffersonian tradition forbade the American
government to use its power in that way. Government revenues, it was
believed, ought properly to be devoted to extinguishing the national debt,
and Mellon was a very proper man. Under his management the debt shrank
from $24 billion or thereabouts in 1920 to some $16 billion in 1930.

So if a damaging recession was to be avoided the private sector would
have to act. Unfortunately it was wholly inadequate for such a role. It acted,
indeed, but everything it did turned a minor fluctuation into a catastrophe.
The worst crisis of American capitalism was at hand.

As we have seen, some of the great industrialists understood the importance of a comparatively high wage-level and a comparatively low price
level to keep the economy healthy. Inconsistently, they also believed in the
prohibitively high tariff; nor did they object to the golden tide of virtually
untaxed dividends which Mellon's policies poured into their coffers and
those of their shareholders. Their profits were huge: they ploughed back
the bulk of them into new factories, new production techniques, new
jobs – which last did something to mitigate the effect of their bigoted
anti-unionism. They would not see that the doubling of the average annual
earnings of the workforce between 1914 and 1923, a gain of 19 per cent in
real terms, and the gain of 13 per cent in real terms between 1923 and 1928,
was the true source of their new wealth; they did all they could to prevent
organized labour from pushing up wages still more. Membership of the
AFL declined from just over four million in 1920 to less than three million
in 1929. But the crisis cannot really be laid at the door of the manufacturers.
Even a stronger union movement or a somewhat more enlightened
wages policy could hardly have beaten back the storm. It is to the financial wing of the system that we must turn in order to understand what
happened.

'The business of America is business,' said Calvin Coolidge in one of
those aphorisms which ensured that the words of Silent Cal would be
remembered far longer than those of more talkative politicians. Unfortunately Americans did not understand their business very well – certainly
not in the 1920s. The generation of the first J. P. Morgan, as we have seen,
knew enough of their weakness to set up the Federal Reserve System; but
this measure was not in itself sufficient, it was no more than a first step;
and so little did post-war American financiers understand this that they
actually did all they could to weaken the FRS – rather like an otherwise
unarmed soldier throwing away his rifle before a battle. This was characteristic. At every stage the story displays the devastating consequences

of a bland unawareness of economic and political essentials. But perhaps nothing is more shocking than the complacent acceptance of a national financial structure which its manipulators should have known was fundamentally unsound. Thus, the banking system, in spite of the FRS, was still pretty much the ramshackle affair that Andrew Jackson's depredations had made it. The vast wealth of cash and credit which the American industrial machine, the greatest in the world, generated so abundantly was dissipated into thousands upon thousands of small, amateurishly managed, largely unsupervised banks and brokerage houses, instead of being used to strengthen the central banks so that they could, in time of trouble, come to the rescue of their weaker partners. Every state had a separate family of banks, and the members of each family were essentially isolated, living from hand to mouth, unable to help each other or, too often, themselves. Even in the palmy days of Coolidge prosperity there were over 600 bank failures a year: in other words, every year an appreciable portion of America's earnings and savings went down the drain. Nor were there effective means for ensuring that bankers or stockbrokers were honest. All too many of them were not; and all too many were idiots.

The high financiers were not much better. If a single moment may be selected as the beginning of the downward journey, it is that of the Dawes Agreement. In itself this was an admirable measure, and it rightly earned its architect nomination as Coolidge's Vice-President in 1924. It rescued Germany from the abyss into which the reparations controversy, the great inflation of 1923 and the French occupation of the Rhineland had plunged her. It was an act of the highest statesmanship in the best American tradition. But it was not, it could not be, a signal that the German economy was now entirely re-established: at best the patient was beginning a slow and painful convalescence. The financiers of New York saw things differently. They were of the stock which had formerly looked for bonanzas in Eastern canals, in Western ranches, and from goldmines in the Rockies. Part of the Dawes Plan was an international loan to Germany. Wall Street subscribed heavily, and did not stop there. It invested some $3,900,000,000 in loans to Germany – to states, municipalities and private borrowers – in the next five years, with absurdly little consideration (in spite of warnings) of whether it would ever get a decent return on its money. For one thing, the money was in large part not its own, but that of Americans looking for somewhere to put their savings: Wall Street got its profit out of fees for services rendered. It brought borrowers and lenders together, and encouraged them. In this spirit it discovered a Bavarian village which needed $125,000 to build a swimming-pool. By the time the financiers had finished, it had borrowed three million. In the short run this sort of thing seemed justified. A hectic flush of prosperity spread over Germany; an entente was negotiated between France, Britain and their late enemy; reparations, and the war-debts payments which depended on them, flowed smoothly at last. Meanwhile American industry was largely left to look for its financing to its own resources; fortunately its profits were so huge that this was no problem.

Germany was not the only unsound foreign field for investment in these years, though it was the most important. Some $8,500,000,000 in all went abroad, not all of it unwisely. But eventually it dawned on Wall Street that there was more money to be made at home, and the bankers diverted their attention and their funds from Germany to the United States. This had a bad effect on Germany: it was like cutting off a patient's blood transfusion. It was to be even more devastating for America.

In 1927 the economy seemed to be on a very solid footing. The boom was in some ways smaller than its predecessors. Percentages of profits, of numbers employed, had been higher in earlier times; money had been cheaper. But this is one of those cases where percentages are misleading. The fact is that the sheer quantity of wealth had never been so great, so tempting. The economy was expanding; there were vast sums to be earned by the middlemen who organized the expansion. Unhappily for themselves the New York financiers had let much of this business slip through their fingers. To recapture it they had to go into the stock market: to use their enormous capital reserves not to assist the launching of new enterprise, the refinancing of old, the development of successful undertakings – that could come later – but to regain control from the usurpers of Detroit, San Francisco and Chicago. New York began to buy; and the price of shares began to soar.

It had been rising ever since the end of the post-war depression, for indeed there was a great deal to be said for spending your more or less untaxed savings on stocks and shares which, in those sunny years, would yield every year a higher dividend (reflecting the boom in production), which would also be largely untaxed (good Mr Mellon). But the injection of Wall Street's huge resources into the market set off an upward rush. The bankers wanted shares: they bought them, paid and looked for more. As the months went on, lesser mortals were drawn in. It looked so simple. To judge from recent performance, you only had to spend a hundred dollars today to become rich tomorrow as the high interest rolled in. Even the dullest, safest stocks were paying 12 per cent by the end of 1928: an excellent rate of return, better than you might get by putting your firm's working capital into further production. Not only that, the price of shares themselves was going up. It was irresistible. No work, no skill were required; there was no chance (it seemed) of losing. The middle class took the plunge. By the late summer of 1929 there were approximately nine million individual investors in the market.[10]

It was a heaven-sent opportunity for swindlers. Some were merely incompetent bankers or stockbrokers who thought they understood economics:

---

10 The population of the United States was estimated at about 122 million. Most of the nine million investors owned only small pieces of the action. But they bought all they could: for which they and their dependants (who have never been counted) would in due course suffer acutely.

in good faith they advised their ignorant but greedy clients to buy – to buy almost anything; they did so themselves; the less scrupulous of them helped themselves surreptitiously to their clients' money, or dipped into the funds of the institutions they headed, to further their schemes. Bigger men, often previously respectable men, launched new corporations with alluring titles (the American Founders Group, the Shenandoah Corporation, the Blue Ridge Corporation) and misleading prospectuses: they thus parted many a fool from his money. The biggest sharks of all – Ivar Kreuger, the Swedish match-king, Samuel Insull, the English-born electricity wizard (in his youth a protégé of Thomas Edison) – raised colossal sums on the market to further their ever more colossal ambitions. They thus got a reputation for genius: by the end the very size of Insull's operations (which he himself no longer understood) seemed to be proof that money was safe, if invested with him. In 1932 he was to flee the country to avoid embezzlement charges. Self-styled experts in the financial press (read more and more widely, with uncomprehending awe) advised as confidently and rashly as stockbrokers, and were as often self-deceived. Prices began to gallop. The silent, hidden battle for ownership of the goose which laid the golden eggs continued: almost unnoticed, she started to lay rather fewer.

This was how matters stood at the moment of Herbert Hoover's inauguration in March 1929. The vast stock-market bubble was still swelling, and the few cool heads in America understood perfectly well that it would burst, as all previous bubbles had burst since the days of the South Sea Company. But they were afraid to incur the dreadful odium of pricking it. Indeed, the outgoing President had announced that in his opinion share-prices were low. A friend asked incredulously if he really thought this. Coolidge replied that in his Yankee opinion anyone who speculated on the stock market was a fool; but as President of the United States and head of the Republican party it was his duty to tell his followers what they wanted to hear. The Federal Reserve Board made a last timid attempt to discourage the gamblers by raising the rate charged for their bank loans by 1 per cent, and by suggesting that anyway FRS banks ought not to lend their clients money for stock-market operations. Unfortunately Charles E. Mitchell, head of the National City Bank and a director of the Federal Reserve bank in New York, the chief component of the system, was deeply involved in the speculation: he used every ounce of power and influence at his command, and forced the Board to eat its words. This was the last effective exercise of the control which for fifty years Wall Street had wielded over public financial policy – and it was utterly disastrous.

For, thus encouraged, the boom roared on. Shares were now changing hands at prices which no dividends would ever be large enough to justify. You bought a share only in order to sell it at a profit; you bought it 'on margin' (with credit, that is, not cash); you assumed that there would always be another sucker. Yet by the late summer warehouses were choked with unsold goods, and factories were therefore beginning to diminish their output. It dawned on some of the shareholders in September that it might be prudent to sell their shares. At least one of the big professionals decided that the time had come to be a bear: to try for profit by selling short, thereby bringing the market down, and buying at the lower price thus produced. The Dow Jones average began to decline.

At first the suckers did not notice, or, if they did, assumed that the price rise would soon resume. It did not; and through September and October the snowball of sellers grew. There came a day – 23 October 1929 – when, suddenly, it seemed that everybody was selling: over six million shares changed hands, and prices slumped. The next day was remembered as 'Black Thursday': the wave of selling continued, a record-breaking 12.9 million shares changed hands, and only the intervention of a bankers' consortium led by the House of Morgan stopped the price of shares collapsing completely. But already thousands of small investors were ruined, as were some stockbrokers (at least one of these tried to commit suicide at the end of the day's trading). Things were calmer on Friday and Saturday; and President Hoover, like Coolidge before him, felt it his duty to issue a reassuring statement. 'The fundamental business of the country,' he said, 'that is production and distribution of commodities, is on a sound and prosperous basis.' Unfortunately this remark carried with it the connotation that perhaps, though the fundamental business was sound, the stock market was not. Sunday was the day of rest; on Monday the slide began again. Nine million shares were traded; by the end of the day the price of shares had gone down by $14,000,000,000 altogether since the middle of the previous week. The selling had been sharpest at the end of the trading day. Next day, 'Black Tuesday', collapse was total: 650,000 shares in US Steel, bluest of 'blue chips', the most respectable of 'securities', were dumped on the market in the first three minutes. The New York Stock Exchange reacted like a zoo where all the animals had gone mad. The superintendant later recalled how the brokers 'roared like a lot of lions and tigers. They hollered and screamed, they clawed at one another's collars.' And they sold and sold and sold. Radio collapsed, General Electric collapsed, Tinker Roller Bearing and Anaconda Copper collapsed. It was as if the whole fabric of modern, business, industrial America was unravelling. Montgomery Ward, the great mail-order firm, collapsed. The bankers' consortium of the week before was quite unable to stem the torrent. Woolworth collapsed. Men rushed screaming from the floor into the street: 'I'm sold out! Sold out! Out!' Trinity Church on Wall Street was packed with desperate men of all creeds in search of comfort. By the time the exchange closed at 3 p.m. 16,383,700 shares had been sold at a loss of $10,000,000,000 – 'twice the amount of currency in circulation in the entire country at the time'.[11] And, simul-

---

11 This quotation, and almost all the other details in this paragraph, have been gratefully lifted from Gordon Thomas and Max Morgan-Witts, *The Day the Bubble Burst* (London, 1979), pp. 373–84.

taneously, panic had been wrecking all the other stock exchanges – in San Francisco, Los Angeles, Chicago. A great part of a generation's savings had been wiped out. The rest were to go in the long slow slide that went on until 1932, when US Steel, which had stood at $262 a share in 1929, stood at $22; General Motors at $8; Montgomery Ward at $4. Coolidge prosperity had come to a brutal end.

For if the market for industrial products had been slackening in the summer, when cash and credit seemed to be in limitless supply, it could only come almost to a halt when, suddenly, there was no money, or, at least, there was a great shortage of it. The consequences were devastating. Money is the lubricant of trade: that, indeed, is its only function. It comes in many forms, but basically in two, currency and credit. The stock-market crash destroyed credit: nobody trusted banks or brokerage houses any more; nobody would lend against the security of stocks and shares. Consequently there was a desperate scramble for currency on the part of all those who needed money to keep themselves and their businesses afloat, for wages still had to be paid, bank loans serviced, raw materials acquired, bills, of all kinds, settled – and no creditor was now willing, or indeed could long afford, to wait for payment. All plans for industrial expansion had to be abandoned. Middle-class consumers suddenly had to retrench, or worse: for all too many of them had bought shares on margin and were now called on for cash. Often they could only raise it by selling their possessions for what they could get – the wife's fur-coat, the family car, the house itself – and the cumulative effect of such forced sales of course helped to reduce prices and therefore earnings and profits. Even worse off were people with mortgages: these were usually short-term affairs, but before the crash it had been easy enough to re-finance them. Now, suddenly, it was almost impossible, and there was an epidemic of foreclosures. The housing industry slumped. Even those who still had money in the bank, few debts and good salaries, were affected by the panic and paused in their outlays. It became difficult for firms and corporations, whose shares were sliding down, to borrow the money they needed just to keep their businesses going: bankers were now hesitant, all the more so as many of them were themselves in deep trouble, having thrown away vast sums in stock-market speculation. Soon, as a result of this contraction in trade, factories began to lay off their workers, who thus turned, in an instant, from contributors to the national income to charges upon it. Unemployment, which according to the federal bureau of labour statistics stood at 1.5 million in 1929, was up to at least 3.25 million by March 1930. And soon the factories began to close down altogether.

Hoover saw the peril and acted to avert it. During the rest of his Presidential term, in fact, he was to act incessantly, doing more than any previous President had done in any previous economic crisis. His bad luck was that what he did was never enough, so that he seemed to be doing nothing, and his personality prevented him from doing more. This devoted man in the end trod the same Via Dolorosa as his great hero Woodrow Wilson.

Meantime he sent for the leaders of the business community and persuaded them to give undertakings not to lower wages or lay off workers. He was convinced that with a little time and patience the bad corner could be turned and renewed prosperity be found beyond it. He believed it and said so, very often, very publicly: for it was part of a President's duty to restore confidence, since only confidence would persuade frightened capitalists, large and small, to start investing or producing again. He was joined by a reassuring chorus of Cabinet officers, businessmen ('Just grin,' said the head of US Steel, 'keep working') and patriotic citizens. For a moment in early 1930 it seemed as if the magic was succeeding. Then the second great blow fell on the American economy. Once more the chickens came home to roost, the bad effects of faulty statesmanship made themselves felt, Hoover's prognostications were falsified and his reputation began to collapse.

For the rest of the world was feeling the effect of the American disaster. It is important to remember that, throughout the twenties, the United States had been the only one of all the industrial nations to seem solidly prosperous. All the others were walking wounded, victims of the dislocations brought about by the First World War, except Russia and Germany, which were stretcher cases. Above all, the United States had been the only important source of investment capital and the only source of the money needed to pay reparations and war-debts. The flood of dollars had been drying up before the crash, diverted as it was to the home market and the stock exchanges; now it was reduced to less than a trickle, and before very long the economies which it had floated were wrecked.

This development took more than a year to make itself fully felt, however; meantime Congress pushed the economic thought (if that is the word) of the twenties to its ultimate absurdity: during 1930 a new American tariff, the Smoot–Hawley, was promulgated. It carried protection to heights even beyond those of the Fordney–McCumber tariff. Presumably the rationale was that since American industry had (allegedly) needed protection in the days of its strength, it needed still more now that it was weak. But the schedule of duties was not compiled in any systematic or scientific way. Instead there was the usual brawl of logrollers in Congress as Republicans and Democrats, Senators and Congressmen, farm representatives and spokesmen for industrial states, competed and bargained and engineered to help the special interests they favoured; just as if the times were normal.

The White House was quite unable to influence the process. A thousand economists signed a petition begging the President to veto the tariff bill; instead he signed it into law – perhaps the most unaccountable action of Hoover's career, for it was read as a confession that he had entirely lost control of economic policy. It signalled to everyone with money to use or lose that there was no hope of rational and effective leadership from the United States. It was the rejection of the Versailles Treaty all over again.

The nations turned in despair to each save herself. As the economists had expected, the Smoot–Hawley tariff was the last blow to world trade. America's trading partners[12] instantly raised tariff barriers against her, in revenge and self-protection; now there could be no hope of re-stimulating American production by foreign demand, for their governments would not allow the foreigners to buy American. Nor could there be any question of re-stimulating foreign production by American demand. World commodity prices continued their headlong descent, to the great injury of primary producers such as Australia, Brazil, Argentina – and the growers of wheat and cotton in the United States. More: though it would be untrue to say that the tariff barriers caused the Second World War, the destruction of the world trading community removed an obstacle to the coming of that war. Japan, for instance, despairing of any assistance from the West, turned decisively to the politics of imperialism and autocracy. In 1931 she invaded Manchuria, in quest of raw materials and markets. The old mercantilists would have approved; their successors wrung their hands. The League of Nations could only pass impotent resolutions; Hoover told his Secretary of State, Henry L. Stimson, that he would take any measures to resist Japanese aggression, so long as they did not involve the use of force. The bankruptcy of American foreign policy was thus fully exhibited for the first, but not the last, time.

Meanwhile no economic recovery occurred. A gigantic new oil field was discovered in eastern Texas, which produced in such abundance that the price of oil collapsed to a few cents a barrel; the industry suffered accordingly. In 1930 there was a drought east of the Rockies which brought particular devastation to the South. In Kentucky, where the coal-mines had already been forced to close, relief workers found families sleeping huddled on the floor together, having sold their beds and stoves cheap to buy a little food. (Next year, there would be violence in the coal-fields.) In the autumn elections the Democrats took control of the House of Representatives and came within one seat of controlling the Senate.

Next, in the spring of 1931, the strain on Europe became critical, and the European governments were unable to agree on measures to deal with it. The great bank of central Europe, Kredit Anstalt, failed, like so many others in that dismal season; it was followed by the collapse of the German banking system, and then the Bank of England came under the fatal pressure, for it had underwritten both the Kredit Anstalt and the German banks. To save herself, Britain went off the gold standard in September, in effect abandoning her traditional role as the world's banker. Hoover had launched a moratorium on international debts in the summer, but though this had slightly lightened the pressure on the European economies, it was not enough. It became clear that among all the other frightful consequences of

---

12 'Trading partner' is a post-1945 cliché. The phrase was not in use during the twenties and thirties, because American businessmen were blind to the truth it expresses.

the débâcle would be the inability of the United States to collect either the principal or the interest of the loans it had made, either the public war-loans to the Allies or the myriad of private loans made so merrily during the twenties to Europe and Latin America. When the French Prime Minister proposed, in December 1932, to pay the next instalment of debt to America, his government was immediately voted out of office. Business confidence weakened still further. Perhaps it did not matter very much, economically, whether the debts were paid or not; but the American public was determined to get its money if it could, and the collapse of its chances was one more black mark against Herbert Hoover's management.

There was still as little sign of recovery at home as abroad. That glory of the twenties, the automobile, on which so much depended, had outlived its popularity, or rather the ability of the masses of Americans to pay for it. Sales of new cars slumped, from just under 4.5 million in 1929 to just over a million in 1932. All other industrial products failed similarly. The pressure on the employers was soon too great to be resisted; and certainly they were not inspired to resist by the gloomy, unreassuring reassurances of poor, reserved, chilly, heavy Herbert Hoover. His proclamations of hope and courage were now received with total scepticism: as early as 1930 a leading Republican Senator was driven to speculate that there must be some concerted effort on foot to use the stock market as a method of discrediting the administration. 'Every time an Administration official gives out an optimistic statement about business conditions, the market immediately drops.' So it is not surprising that the industrialists soon forgot their undertakings and began, reluctantly, to cut wages and hours and to give their workers the sack. Soon the only rising curve in the statistics was that of unemployment.

It was five million at the end of 1930, nine million at the end of 1931, thirteen million at the end of 1932. The raw figures do not begin to convey the horrors that now suddenly entered American lives. The physical consequences of this general worklessness were bad enough. The prosperity of the twenties had never been as universal as its boosters proclaimed, nor its level as high. Still, more Americans than ever before had earned enough money to taste some of the luxuries and comforts of life, as well as to take the necessities for granted. Now, in their millions, they found themselves stripped of everything – jobs, possessions, housing – often unable to find a night's shelter for their families, or enough to eat. In Youngstown, Ohio, unemployed men went to the municipal incinerator to keep warm and slept at night on the piles of garbage there; in Chicago the garbage was picked over for food by desperate women, competing with flies and maggots. Starvation was a real threat, malnutrition a daily fact of life, in the greatest food-producing country in the world. The food was not even dear: the collapse in world prices had seen to that, and farm incomes (which had benefited little from the boom) had fallen by more than half. But precisely because prices were so low, it would pay nobody to shift harvests to market. In Oregon sheep were slaughtered and left to the buzzards because farmers could afford neither to feed them nor to ship them. Wheat in Montana was left to rot in the fields. In Philadelphia, meanwhile, one family lived off dandelions.

As bad as the hunger, weariness and cold (gas and electricity companies could not for ever overlook unpayable bills, though they were often surprisingly patient) were the humiliation and despair. The descent came by stages: the loss of one job; the search for another in the same line; the search, growing frantic, for work in any line; the first appearance at the bread-line, where, astonishingly, you met dozens of other honest men who had kept the rules, worked hard and were now as low as the professional bums. It was work you wanted, not charity; but you were forced to plead desperately for charity. Often you did not get it, for there was not enough to go round.

The bitter truth was that American society was hopelessly ill-organized to cope with such an emergency. The assumption had always been that on the whole the thrifty and diligent would never know real want; private charity was a duty, which would look after the unfortunate; the riffraff could be left to look after themselves. This assumption had been out of date since the Civil War; but it had never been so ruthlessly tested before. Private charity soon began to run out of funds. By 1932 the Red Cross could grant only 75 cents a week to each impoverished family. Public authorities were helpless, for the greatest need was in the cities, and the cities, so long the object of rural suspicion, were prevented by law from tackling the problem of relief by such measures as fresh taxation or public works without the consent of the state governments; and it was long before that consent was forthcoming. For it seemed to all too many businessmen and state legislators that to admit the size and permanence of the relief problem by trying to do something about it would undermine still further that mysterious quality, 'confidence', without which there could be no recovery. So the unemployed were left largely to their own devices: whether selling apples on the sidewalks (but there was a glut of apples as well as of sellers), or offering to shine shoes, or, in the case of hundreds of thousands of adolescents, taking to the roads and railroads as tramps.

Clearly the problem of relief was too big for any agency except the federal government. From every quarter the clamour began to rise for Washington to tackle the problem directly, instead of leaving it to the thousand and one local organs of government. If Hoover, as it seemed, could not give work to the people, let him give them bread.

He refused to do anything of the kind. There were horrible ironies here. None of those who knew him best doubted his compassion. He was toiling desperately, eighteen hours a day, to mend matters: greying, putting on weight, his hands trembling, his voice hoarse, his eyes red with exhaustion.[13]

13 This describes Hoover best in the autumn of 1932, at the end of the gruelling election campaign of that year; but he got into that state only because of three years of ceaseless overwork.

In 1919 Keynes had described him as having the air of a weary Titan; what would he have said of him in 1932? Yet Hoover, who had first earned his great reputation by organizing the feeding of the starving children of war-time Europe, now set his face against Americans who, if they were not yet starving, in all too many cases soon might be.

Hoover had not grown inhumane. But he had always been an ideo-logist, who believed in what he called American individualism: in the social arrangements which had made it possible for a poor Iowa farm boy to be-come, first, a millionaire by his own efforts, and then President of the United States. The system which had made such an achievement possible must not be tampered with in any circumstances; it must be vigorously defended, whether against monopoly capitalists (Hoover retained many of the attitudes of a pre-war Progressive) or the Kaiser's armies, or the Bolsheviks, or, now, the economically and politically ignorant who wanted the state to take on responsibilities which, in the American system, belonged exclusively to the individual. He was being asked to abandon the convictions of a lifetime, and he could not do it. In that he showed his unfitness for his position (as had George III). 'Time makes ancient good uncouth.' What America needed was a leader who could accept this truth. Hoover could not. He clung to what, until then, most men had deemed to be the essence of America. Even the agonies of the Depression could not shake him: if the will was there, organized private charity could deal with them, as he himself had dealt with the agonies of Belgium. If the state made itself responsible for seeing that men had work, food, shelter – made the direct pursuit of happiness its business – then everything that made the United States unique and glorious would be betrayed. The mission of the federal government was to get the productive machine operating again without destroying the moral fibre of the citizens.

All this seemed beside the point to the unemployed. And Hoover was inconsistent. He allowed, indeed encouraged, the states and the cities to organize relief; he set up a Reconstruction Finance Corporation to assist businesses in trouble by making them loans; he came to the rescue of farm animals whose owners could no longer pay for their feed. Why then would he do nothing for the mass of his fellow-countrymen? Hoover had an answer, but by the election of 1932 the people were no longer listening to him. He had become a joke in bad taste. The shanty towns that sprang up round the great cities, where impoverished families sought shelter, were known as 'Hoovervilles'. The newspapers they slept beneath were 'Hoover blankets'. He was seen as stony, unimaginative, hard-hearted, inert. These impressions were reinforced by the affair of the Bonus Marchers. These were unemployed First World War veterans, who had been promised 'bonus' payments in 1945, cash presents to see them through their old age; now they demanded payment in advance, since old age could hardly be worse than what was already happening to them; and they marched on Washington to demand their due. Hoover hid in his office and refused their petition, seeing it as no more than an unusually spectacular raid on the Treasury. Eventually he ordered the army to disperse them from the little Hooverville they had established not far from the White House. The army Chief of Staff, General Douglas MacArthur, a flamboyant egoist on a white horse, made a bad affair worse by driving off the veterans with tanks, guns and tear-gas, giving them no chance to leave quietly. The public was revolted by the business, and if Hoover had not already lost the coming election, he did so then.

Meanwhile the economy continued to spin down the deflationary spiral. Even crime and vice felt the cold wind: in 1933 the New York police estimated that the number of speakeasies in the city had fallen from a high of 32,000 to only 9,000. The scandals of the palmy days began to be uncovered. The 'match-king', Ivar Kreuger, committed suicide in March 1932, just before the full extent of his swindling was revealed; Insull's electricity empire crashed at much the same time. Senate investigators began to publish the full extent of the frauds and malpractices that Wall Street had tolerated while the going was good.

In their despair and disgust the Americans did not abandon their ancient political system; rather they gave it one more chance. They turned from the Republicans not to the Socialists but to the Democrats. Franklin Roosevelt, the Governor of New York, secured his party's Presidential nomination after a sharp struggle. He showed a dramatic flair for smashing obsolete traditions by flying to Chicago[14] to accept the nomination in person. 'I pledge you, I pledge myself, to a new deal for the American people,' he told the delegates. Thereafter he ran a dazzling campaign, defeating Hoover by 22,815,539 votes to 15,759,930; Hoover carried only six states. But it would be four months before the new President could take office, and meanwhile the attrition of the business system went on. Confidence was still a corpse, and under the impact of previous disasters a still worse one began to draw near. Bank failures, we have seen, had been endemic during the twenties. They were vastly more numerous during the Depression: as many as 2,298 banks broke in 1931, for instance; but the really worrying thing was that every year brought down bigger banks than the year before. No recovery measures could be effectively taken by Hoover now; he had been repudiated; and Roosevelt refused to lend the outgoing President his authority – he could not afford to tie himself to that sinking ship. So when the third acute crisis of the Depression struck, there was no one to resist it. Suddenly the bank depositors (private and commercial) discovered that they had lost all faith, not so much in the national banking system as a whole (though they would have had good reason) as in the particular banks where they had put their money. For money was performing an unnerving vanishing trick: there were two-thirds less of it than there had been in 1929. Withdrawals soared; still more banks broke; the governors of the various

14 He did not travel again in a plane until the Second World War.

states began to declare 'bank holidays' – in other words, they shut the banks and froze the deposits. This new panic erupted in mid-February 1933. During the next two weeks bank holidays became nearly universal. On 4 March, Inauguration Day, the last hold-outs gave way, and the banks in Chicago and New York refused to open for business. In that ghastly moment it seemed as if the entire economic structure which so many generations had laboured to rear and improve had collapsed for ever. It was with dread in their hearts, and not very much hope, that people waited to hear what the new President would say, and to see what he would do.

BOOK FIVE

The Superpower

Oh yes, I know the faults and the other side,
The lyncher's rope, the bought justice, the wasted land,
The scale on the leaf, the borers in the corn,
The finks with their clubs, the grey sky of relief,
All the long shame of our hearts and the long disunion.
I am merely remarking – as a country, we try.
As a country, I think we try.

Stephen Vincent Benét, 1940

We have got to understand that all our lives the danger, the uncertainty, the need for alertness, for effort, for discipline will be upon us. This is new to us. It will be hard for us.

Dean Acheson, 1946

22 The Era of Franklin Roosevelt
1933–8

It's a big holiday ev'rywhere
For the Jones family has a brand-new heir
He's the joy heaven-sent, and they proudly present
  Mr Franklin D. Roosevelt Jones!

When he grows up he never will stray
With a name like the one that he's got today.
As he walks down the street folks will say, Pleased to meet
  Mr Franklin D. Roosevelt Jones!

Popular song, 1939

Washington, DC, 4 March 1933. A cold, windy day. A cripple took the Presidential oath and then addressed America.

This is pre-eminently the time to speak the truth, the whole truth, frankly and boldly. Nor need we shrink from honestly facing conditions in our country today. This great nation will endure as it has endured, will revive and will prosper.

So first of all let me assert my firm belief that the only thing we have to fear is fear itself – nameless, unreasoning, unjustified terror which paralyses needed efforts to convert retreat into advance.

His stern voice rang out, both to those present at the Capitol and to tens of millions listening anxiously to their radios:

Our greatest primary task is to put people to work. This is no unsolvable problem if we face it wisely and courageously.

It can be accomplished in part by direct recruiting by the government itself, treating the task as we would treat the emergency of a war, but at the same time, through this employment, accomplishing greatly needed projects to stimulate and reorganize the use of our natural resources.

It was one of the turning-points of American history. In a few minutes Roosevelt did what had so wearyingly eluded Hoover for four years: he gave back to his countrymen their hope and their energy. By the end of the week half a million grateful letters had poured into the White House – first waters of a flood that was never to dry up. Rhetoric was and is the curse of American politics; but here for once were words that meant something – words that became deeds.

For the trust reposed in me I will return the courage and the devotion that befit the time. I can do no less . . . We do not distrust the future of democracy. The people of the United States have not failed. In their need they have registered a mandate that they want direct, vigorous action. They have asked for discipline and direction under leadership. They have made me the present instrument of their wishes. In the spirit of the gift I take it.

To most Americans the disaster of the Depression had come as an earth-quake, without warning destroying their old lives so totally that they lost all their self-confidence. Their lives and their country were suddenly, it seemed, equally and entirely beyond their helping: they were lost in a dark wood. Now came a guide whom they trusted. Ultimately that trust was what saved them, for it was a renewed trust in themselves. The first achievement of the New Deal (as, following the phrase in Roosevelt's acceptance speech, his administration was to be universally known) was this restoration of faith; and the first question that needs to be answered is, how could Roosevelt manage it?

He had been born (in 1882) to privilege, to the richer branch of an old Dutch gentry family of New York state. His mother, Sara Delano, came from a similar clan, of Huguenot origin. He was a pampered only child; as a young man he led the life of an easygoing aristocrat both at Harvard, where he picked up no more than a smattering of erudition, and later as a not very diligent lawyer in New York city. His first remarkable act was to marry Eleanor Roosevelt, his distant cousin, Theodore's niece, who was as extraordinary a woman, it turned out, as he was a man. He soon turned to politics but, perhaps surprisingly, stuck to the Democratic party, to which his own branch of the family had always belonged. His charm, energy, shrewdness and tall good looks carried him easily up the ladder, from state Senator (1910), to Assistant Secretary of the Navy in the Wilson administration, to Vice-Presidential candidate in 1920. Then disaster struck: in 1921 he contracted poliomyelitis and lost the use of his legs. Although he recovered sufficiently to be able to stand for short periods in iron leg braces, it was always to be agony for him. His real quality began to show. Doughtily supported by his wife, he refused to surrender to his illness, somehow keeping his political career going. By standing in for him on every possible occasion, Mrs Roosevelt became a political figure in her own right. Gradually he re-established himself as an effective member of the New

York Democracy. He made the nominating speech for Al Smith at the convention of 1924, and Smith picked him to be his successor as gubernatorial candidate in 1928. He won his election by a narrow margin just as Smith went heavily down to defeat in the Presidential race, failing to carry his own state. No doubt this encouraged Roosevelt to strike out as his own man; at any rate he soon established himself as an independent force. He responded effectively enough to the Crash and the Depression to win re-election in 1930 by a huge margin. He took vigorous action to assist the towns and cities of the state in furnishing relief to the unemployed, and his Temporary Relief Administration (TERA) may be mentioned as the first of all his alphabetical agencies. He became the favourite for the Democratic Presidential nomination in 1932; the sequel has already been told.

The man who spoke to the American people in 1933, then, having overcome fearful blows in his own life (not only polio: he had fallen deeply in love with his wife's secretary in 1918, and given her up for various good reasons; but he was to be lonely ever after), was well qualified to tell them that they were not and could not be defeated. But what inspired them was more than grit. It was more than his gallantry and charm, of which he made no use on 4 March. At bottom, Franklin Roosevelt was a man of power and vision. He was a master politician, who took command with absolute authority: he knew, like the elder Pitt, that he could save the country and that no one else could. His strength and ability went along with a profound, creative desire to shape America for a better future: his administration was to pursue reform as well as recovery. On Inauguration Day his hearers sensed above all his inner certainty and his deep sympathy with their plight.

Those closer to FDR (as they referred to him) discovered that he was better able to respond to people in numbers, at a distance, than to the needs of intimates. Like many a man who is totally committed to his career – in Roosevelt's case it might for once be truer to say wedded to his destiny – he was highly egoistic. At close quarters he could be evasive, cold, occasionally brutal, if others grew too demanding. If they kept their place he could be boundlessly patient and generous;[1] but who can always know his place? Many paid in the end a very high price for the privilege of working for FDR. Yet so intoxicating was his leadership that few seem to have regretted it. Like Eleanor Roosevelt, they felt it was enough to have served his great purposes. (She herself did so by endless travelling, public appearances, letter-writing, journalism, all in order to keep the people in touch with their President, and the President in touch with the people.) Louis Howe, Roosevelt's closest adviser for more than twenty years, remarked, as he lay

---

1 A good example of his patience was the question of the White House cook. A favourite of Mrs Roosevelt, she did not believe in pampering her employers. The President only made occasional brief expostulations; and the food continued filthy throughout his four administrations.

dying, 'I have been as close to Franklin Roosevelt as a valet, and he is still a hero to me.' America got the benefit of this devotion.

The new President's first actions were governed by the need to build on the inspiration of the inaugural speech. He called the new Congress into special session at once. The most urgent problem was the rescue of the banks. A radical measure might have been difficult to get through Congress with any speed; worse, it would have done nothing to restore confidence – on the contrary, it would have deeply alarmed the propertied classes. So Roosevelt simply took over the conservative proposals of the Hoover administration. His own men collaborated with their predecessors, and in five days a banking bill was ready: it was rushed through Congress in under eight hours. Meantime the President had held the fort by proclaiming a national banking holiday. This way of announcing that the banks were not going to re-open just yet tickled the American sense of humour: spirits began to rise, in spite of the inconvenience. They rose still further eight days after the inauguration, when on a Sunday evening the President gave the first of his famous Fireside Chats on the radio. In these broadcasts Roosevelt, who had a strong actor's instinct, projected himself with astonishing success into the homes of America, aiming always to sound like a friend of the family talking at the fireside. But the performances were always best when the lines were good. On this first occasion he was able to announce that the banks in the twelve Federal Reserve cities would re-open the next day, and thanks to his Emergency Banking Act would be safe. The people listened to that warm voice and believed: the next day bank deposits exceeded withdrawals.

A characteristic piece of New Deal legislation, the Banking Act was a conservative measure that yet reformed the ramshackle US banking system: many weak banks were not allowed to re-open, while solvent ones were backed explicitly by the federal government, which took on greatly increased powers to govern the whole system. The act can therefore count as the first of the New Deal reform measures. The same cannot be said of Roosevelt's second initiative, on 10 March, when he sent a message to Congress demanding a wholesale slashing of civil service salaries and veterans' benefits. No Congress would normally look at a proposal so damaging to so many well-organized voters; but in the crisis atmosphere this deflationary conservative measure was hurried through like the banking bill, though by no means so unanimously: ninety Democrats opposed it. Again, Roosevelt's purpose was to rally the ranks: by showing his willingness to save money he hoped to encourage the rich to spend it. One industrialist at least responded by urging his employees to go out and buy something – anything: 'President Roosevelt has done his part: now you do something.' For a few precious weeks Roosevelt had the confidence of the business community, even winning the endorsement of the House of Morgan. It was enough: by June the threat of total economic collapse had disappeared.

He had not been elected President to save the bankers, all the same; and at this very time the so-called Pecora Committee (named after its special attorney) was conducting a ruthless investigation, on behalf of Congress, into the seamy side of American high finance. The current J. P. Morgan might toploftily say he approved of Roosevelt: he cowered before Pecora. Besides, Roosevelt meant to be an effective reformer as well as a redeemer. Before long he recommended to Congress a securities bill for regulating Wall Street: it became law on 27 May. It provided that full information must be made available to the public whenever new securities were issued, and that directors who issued misleading prospectuses were liable to prosecution as criminals. That was bad enough from the point of view of the Wall Street speculators and manipulators; worse came a year later with the Act setting up the Securities and Exchange Commission, a body which had the duty and power to oversee the stock exchanges of the nation and punish wrongdoers. It was headed by Joseph P. Kennedy, a notable millionaire speculator, and proved highly effective. Before long it was an axiom on Wall Street that the administration was anti-business, though it was really only against dishonest and incompetent business.

Meantime, in 1933, the torrent of legislation rolled on, Congress being overwhelmingly eager to pass whatever laws the President and his team of brilliant young advisers (many of them were professors, which led to the term 'the Brain Trust') saw fit to recommend. On 31 March the Civilian Conservation Corps was established. This expressed, better perhaps than anything else he ever did, Roosevelt's compassion for the unfortunate. It took a quarter of a million unemployed young men and set them, under quasi-military discipline, to carrying out a gigantic programme of reafforestation, dam-building, marsh-draining, thus hitting three targets simultaneously: the land was reclaimed, so were the boys (they were given schooling as well as work), and their small wages went to the help of their families. The veteran problem, which had proved so fatal to Hoover, was also solved in this way. A second expedition of unemployed veterans descended on Washington; they were warmly received, notably by Mrs Roosevelt, who kept them supplied with cups of coffee, and soon enlisted in the CCC.

To continue the work of cheering everybody up, the President remarked that it was a good time for a beer, and in advance of the Twenty-First Amendment, which abolished prohibition by repealing the Eighteenth, he had the Volstead Act changed to permit the manufacture of beer and light wine again.[2]

Nor did Roosevelt lose sight of other claims. A sweeping Agricultural Adjustment Act, which gave the federal government wide new powers to help the farmers, was ready for his signature by 12 May; and before that, on 19 April, he had taken the United States off the gold standard. His Director of the Budget thought that it was the end of Western civilization; but

2 The Twenty-First Amendment became law on 5 December 1933.

Roosevelt hoped that this inflationary measure would not only counteract his earlier cuts, but do something to counter the terrible deflationary effects of the Depression which were still all too evident. The New Deal also came to the rescue of mortgaged farmers and city-dwellers by taking steps to prevent foreclosures, then dreadfully common: the federal government, in essence, underwrote both the lenders and the borrowers. And on the same day as the Agricultural Adjustment Act the Federal Emergency Relief Act was signed, which swept away Hooverism and recognized the national government's duty to come directly to the rescue of the unemployed with a federal dole: 500 million dollars was made available for distribution through state and municipal agencies.

So far so good; but the President's hand was now being forced, for the first but not for the last time. The unemployed were getting help; now those still working, on short hours and for reduced wages, and their employers, who had almost forgotten what it was to make a profit, clamoured for assistance, to such effect that the Senate in early April passed a bill that Roosevelt thought was unconstitutional and unwise. He substituted a measure of his own, the National Industrial Recovery Act (NIRA), which suspended the anti-trust laws in return for certain concessions by big business, of which the two most important were that the workers might freely organize themselves into unions, and that a federal bureau, the National Recovery Administration (NRA), might lay down and enforce codes of conduct for each separate industry. The NRA was to have a short and stormy career, but the transformation it launched in American industrial relations was to be permanent, one of the New Deal's most solid achievements.

Other important laws came thick and fast. A cherished dream of the liberals during the twenties, especially of the veteran old Progressive Senator George Norris of Nebraska, had been the scheme to use the federally owned dams at Muscle Shoals on the Tennessee river to generate cheap electrical power for the people of the Tennessee Valley. This project had been bitterly opposed by the electricity companies, and conservatives in Congress had tried to sell off the dams (which had been built to generate power for the production of nitrate for explosives during the First World War) to private concerns. Norris had been able to stop that, and now his dream came true. The Tennessee Valley Act set up the Tennessee Valley Authority as the first publicly owned electricity organization in the country. It was rank socialism, but no one seemed to care: the TVA created thousands of jobs as it built more dams and constructed power-lines; as a secondary activity it trained the farmers of the Valley in conservationist agricultural techniques; and its electricity not only began to reach hundreds of thousands of poor homes which would otherwise have had to do without refrigerators, electric stoves and electric light, but tempted industrialists to set up plants in what until then had been one of the most under-industrialized regions of the country.

The Glass–Steagall Banking Act, which consolidated the achievement of the spring emergency measure and added the exceedingly important provision of a federal guarantee for bank deposits, and the Farm Credit Act, which consolidated the farm mortgage rescue, with NIRA, were passed by Congress on the hundredth and last day (16 June) of its session; the whole hectic period since the inauguration therefore became known as the Hundred Days. A legend of Napoleonic defeat was thus transformed into one of Rooseveltian victory.

It was, indeed, astonishing how far America had come. Never before had there been such an orgy of law-making, never before had so bold an attempt been made to adjust the country to new times. But the work was only beginning. The pace of that first spring was never again to be equalled, but a great transformation was under way. The demands made on the American people were not to slacken significantly until the eve of the Second World War. For the men and women round Roosevelt (Frances Perkins, the Secretary of Labor, was the first woman to become a Cabinet officer) were not content to pass emergency measures and then let the federal government sink back into the dignified indolence of the late nineteenth century. The Coolidge era was over for ever. Former Wilsonians, former Progressives, they each had one or more long-cherished reforms to push, now that they had the power and now that the temper of the country was so obviously propitious. They saw their opportunity, as Boss Plunkitt would have said, and they took it. They were no morning glories, but able, experienced, hard-driving professionals.

They were more single-minded than their chief, whose priorities were somewhat different. While happy to maintain the momentum of the Hundred Days and happy in bringing, first hope, then achievement, to the country, Roosevelt based his strategy on his perpetual preoccupation with leadership. During the first years of his Presidency his aspiration was to be the generally supported leader of all the people. The vision of national unity, which has shimmered before the eyes of so many great democratic politicians (the obvious British example being Lloyd George), shimmered before FDR. In some respects his instincts were profoundly conservative. He was a countryman, for example, who often found it difficult to realize the needs of the modern city-dweller; and his economic opinions were in many cases far from forward-looking. Thus, it is hard for the present generation, after a lifetime of inflation, to understand the passion and conviction with which men of Roosevelt's day believed in the scientific necessity of balancing the national budget in order to avoid what was, in the thirties, an absolutely minimal risk of inflation.[3] Their minds were

---

3 To be sure, under Presidents Carter and Reagan the ideal of a balanced budget would once more be held up to reverence, in spite or because of the stupendous deficit which continued to grow under both men. FDR never in his wildest nightmares could have supposed that budgets might repeatedly be unbalanced by more than $100 billion. In the 1990s, Congress and President Clinton made strenuous and fairly successful efforts to balance the budget again, at least in the short term. They were helped by a surge of great prosperity. Whether this rectitude will last for long remains to be seen (1999).

governed by abstractions, instead of their own concrete experience (besides, Henry Morgenthau, Roosevelt's Secretary of the Treasury, was not really adequate to his job, though he had able assistants). Roosevelt was a committed anti-inflationist, so much so that in the end he sacrificed the New Deal to his principles. He believed in American capitalism as much as he believed in American democracy, and he hoped for the co-operation of the business class, in part because he was rescuing it from disaster and in part because, like Hoover, he thought, not wrongly, that without business support and confidence the economy could not make a complete recovery. Besides, he was temperamentally averse to harsh choices, which might limit his freedom of action. So he played down the Democratic party, in 1934 refusing even to go to its traditional beanfeast on Jefferson's birthday, and as long as he could he played down his reformer's role too.

In many respects this lofty pose of being above the battle paid him handsomely, making it easier for former Progressives and Republicans to desert to his standard. But essentially the aspiration was misconceived and it broke down on the stubborn facts of the situation. Only lavish government spending could pull the United States out of its downward deflationary spiral, and such spending inevitably made a balanced budget impossible. This alienated the conservatives. Furthermore, the New Deal programmes necessitated taxation increases (especially if the President was to keep alive his hopes of one day achieving solvency) and some of that increase (very little in practice) had to come out of the pockets of the rich. They did not like it, any more than they liked government-imposed reform of the economy they were used to ruling. From early 1934 onwards the alienation of the old business community – the magnates of New York, Philadelphia and Chicago (businessmen further west were less upset) – grew deep and bitter, until the rich alluded to the President only as 'that man in the White House'. At the same time Roosevelt slowly learned to abandon his aspirations and to come out as the champion of the people against the 'economic royalists'. By 1936 the lines were sharply drawn – more sharply, perhaps, than in any other election in American history – and the Republicans, identified as the party of Wall Street, were swept to what seemed to be eternal oblivion.

Other choices could not be made so easily, or if they were, were made badly. The most conspicuous example of the latter mistake was the sabotage of the London Economic Conference immediately after the Hundred Days had ended. This conference was a legacy of Herbert Hoover's conviction that the root of the Depression lay in international trade relations. He had summoned the conference to put things right. It was unlikely to achieve any great success, since economic nationalism was rapidly gaining ground everywhere as a result of the slump; but its failure was disastrous. On 4 July 1933 Roosevelt rejected his emissaries' attempts to achieve some sort of stabilization of the world currencies, on the grounds that this might interfere with his efforts to tempt businessmen to reinvest by pushing up prices in the United States. In the narrowest terms of economic advantage, he had a case; but he overlooked America's obligation, as the world's leading industrial and financial power – a power, furthermore, which was largely to blame for the catastrophe – to do something to help the weaker trading nations; and he was totally blind to the consideration that this was a chance – the last, as it turned out – for a significant measure of international cooperation to rescue the world economy and thus avert the new world war which, as we have seen, was already beginning to grow out of the Depression. The most disturbing comment on his action was made by Hjalmar Schacht, the Nazis' financier: he praised Roosevelt for being an economic nationalist like Hitler and Mussolini. By 1934 Roosevelt had begun to see that he had gone too far, and pushed a Trade Agreements Act through Congress, which enabled him to revise tariffs freely. A major source of domestic political strife was thus at last removed, but otherwise the Act led to very little. The New Deal never developed a coherent trade policy, and in that respect one of the chief causes of the Depression remained virtually untouched.

On the whole Roosevelt did better when he fudged the issues. There was profound disagreement among Americans as to exactly what the situation required, and what, indeed, the laws of the Hundred Days meant or implied. To the business community the battle had been won when public confidence in the future of the economy had been restored. Even though the more far-sighted among the millionaires, such as Joseph Kennedy, saw that the task would not be complete without some measure of banking and financial reform, most businessmen thought the job had been finished by the summer of 1933: the economy had plainly begun its long slow crawl up from the abyss. To the progressive reformers, as we have seen, the emergency was a priceless opportunity to put into effect reforms which had been waiting for their hour since 1917. A handful of more radical temperaments – many of them university graduates – were allured by the possibility of total political transformation, and drifted into the Communist party, or towards the Trotskyites. Probably the majority of Americans believed that the all-important task was that of getting work again; they showed themselves willing to try almost any panacea that was offered as an end to unemployment, and they judged politicians strictly by the state of the labour market; except for the farmers, who judged them by their traditional criteria – agricultural prices, the state of farm mortgages, the farm standard of living and the independence or otherwise of the small farmer. Clearly the President could not hope to satisfy all these groups all the time; but Roosevelt's political genius was displayed in the brilliance by which he kept so many on his side for so long.

His chief instruments were the so-called alphabetical agencies. Such bodies had existed for decades. Their original was the Federal Trade Commission of 1887; since that date their establishment had become a traditional response to problems; but never had so many been set up in such a short period. They were uncountable. NRA, RFC, AAA ('the Triple A'), PWA and WPA are the most important examples. It will be convenient to examine them one by one, thus displaying the personalities of the New Deal, their achievements, their failures and, not least, their incessant rivalries and feuds, and in this way convey some sense of what the Rooseveltian transformation amounted to.

The National Industrial Recovery Act appropriated $3,300,000,000 for public works (a traditional method of relieving unemployment and economic stagnation which had enjoyed remarkable success under, for example, Napoleon III of France in the nineteenth century); and in its opening section set as ambitious a range of targets as could well be devised:

A national emergency productive of widespread unemployment and disorganization of industry, which burdens interstate and foreign commerce, affects the public welfare, and undermines the standards of living of the American people, is hereby declared to exist. It is hereby declared to be the policy of Congress to remove obstructions to the free flow of interstate and foreign commerce which tend to diminish the amount thereof; and to provide for the general welfare by promoting the organization of industry for the purpose of co-operative action among trade groups, to induce and maintain unified action of labour and management under adequate governmental sanctions and supervision, to eliminate unfair competitive practices, to promote the fullest possible utilization of the present productive capacity of industries, to avoid undue restriction of production (except as may be temporarily required), to increase the consumption of industrial and agricultural products by increasing purchasing power, to reduce and relieve unemployment, to improve standards of labor and otherwise to rehabilitate industry and to conserve natural resources.

Something for everyone. The key words are probably 'co-operative' and 'unified'. They reflect Roosevelt's early hope that he could lead a united country along the path of recovery. Big firms and little firms would co-exist without the ruthless trade wars of the past, the undercutting and the overselling and general social recklessness which had ruined the American economy; capital and labour would be reconciled in a common programme; town and country would harmonize their interests and ambitions, and the resources of the continent would be husbanded for the future. Congress delegated large powers to the President to see that it all came about. This vision (which has something in common with the rhetoric of Mussolinian Italy) represented one version of America's destiny, and had long appealed to one sort of Progressive. It implied forceful political leadership, supplied either directly by a Roosevelt in the White House or by a Morgan pulling strings in Wall Street. It implied planning; it implied the suspension of the Sherman Act and the legitimation of some form of working-class organization – the AFL or a wider grouping. It corresponded to one of the deepest, most characteristic wishes of patriotic citizens, that their cherished democracy should show itself capable of disinterested, vigorous, single-minded action in a crisis. Unfortunately, aspirations are not enough. The

NIRA programme was too vast, put together in too much of a hurry, and it ran counter to too many political and economic realities for any success to be more than partial and temporary.

The chosen head of the National Recovery Administration (NRA) was General Hugh Johnson, a veteran of the Wilson administration's organization for the First World War (he had worked under Bernard Baruch on the War Industries Board). A torrent of a man, with a wild tongue and a weakness for drink, he incarnated the will to succeed, to transcend the feuds and pettinesses of everyday life in one vast national effort to end the Depression – for America, a crisis so much worse than the war had been. He was a champion booster, and at first swept all before him. He gave the NRA a symbol, the Blue Eagle,[4] which was displayed on flags, buildings, letterheads, newspapers – wherever Americans identified themselves with his programme. He held huge parades of NRA participants, the largest of which, a quarter of a million strong and watched by a million and a half, choked the streets of New York from morning until long after nightfall on 13 September 1933. It was twenties hoopla turned to useful purposes; the chief participating dignitary was no longer the corrupt gladhander Jimmy Walker (who, following exposure, had been induced to take a permanent holiday) but Governor Herbert Lehman, the rightful heir, at state level, of Al Smith and FDR himself. Like a frantic entrepreneur, Johnson flew from city to city in an army plane, rounding up pledges and promises; his agency negotiated codes of conduct for the great industries of America, and the manufacturers undertook to observe them. In short, the practices of industrial capitalism were to be reformed, 'unfair' competition was to be eliminated, making it possible to maintain prices or even to increase them; and businessmen, stimulated by the renewed prospects of profit which this offered, would begin to invest again. They would be able to pay wages and open factories once more, and the ordinary American, at present on the dole, would become a consuming, producing citizen again.[5] Workers would be guaranteed a minimum wage and the forty-hour week, and under Section 7(a) of the NIRA, in return for letting capital have a free hand in ordering its side of business, would have the right of collective bargaining and the right of organizing freely. Company unions were thus undermined; the brutal strike-breaking practices of the recent past were outlawed. The AFL leadership did not see, or did not like, this opportunity; but John L. Lewis of the United Mineworkers did, and his energetic and astonishingly successful

4 Considering that the bald eagle is the American national emblem, and that 'blue' is the demotic synonym for 'sad, weary, melancholy', the symbol was grievously apt for 1933 in a way that General Johnson cannot have intended.

5 It is important to realize that this side of the NRA programme was essentially one of cartelization: the world was to be made safe and agreeable for big business; the tendency towards oligopoly was to have the protection of the law. This was what Morgan and the other great capitalists had wanted before the First World War: the NRA was the realization of their dream. Unfortunately, as so often happens, the dream, once realized, began to show its weaknesses.

efforts to promote unions in the major industries soon brought about a decisive split in the ranks of organized labour.

Yet it all proved a bubble. In the first place, Roosevelt, for reasons good and bad, detached the public works programme authorized by the NIRA from Johnson's agency and handed it over to his Secretary of the Interior, Harold Ickes, a former Bull Mooser. Ickes, a man of prickly, indeed spiny integrity (he loved to think of himself as a 'curmudgeon'), turned the Public Works Administration (PWA) into a great creative agency; the American landscape owes more to him, in the way of bridges, highways, dams and public buildings generally, than to any other individual in history, and scarcely a penny was lost in the traditional way of corruption. But neither Ickes nor the President had yet understood the capacity of a public works programme to stimulate the economy; so the PWA did no more than keep the construction industry alive, whereas, thanks to the multiplier effect, it might have been the engine of a real recovery; while Johnson, who did grasp this point, was left to cajole industry into good behaviour without either carrot or stick to make it keep its promises.

At first, mesmerized by Johnson's enthusiasm, or the general euphoria at having an activist government at last, or by the willingness to try any port in a storm, or by the suspension of the Sherman Act, or by all these things together, the industrialists co-operated. The best-known, earliest and most successful of the codes was that for the cotton textile industry, which among other things ended the scandal of child labour in the cotton-mills and thereby prompted Roosevelt to remark, 'That makes me personally happier than any other one thing which I have been connected with since I came to Washington.'[6] The coal code eliminated child labour in the mines, equalized wages and introduced a thirty-five-hour week. But it was easier to get codes agreed than to secure compliance with them, especially since, fearing that the whole NIRA was unconstitutional (he had good reason, as events were to show), Johnson did not dare to use the draconian powers it gave him lest he be challenged in the courts. And the commitment to minimum wages, maximum hours and regulated prices, loudly proclaimed by the administration, not only implied that businessmen might have to accept increased costs without the compensation of increased profits, but went counter to the policy of reactivating American industry by conciliating its owners. There were some astonishing victories: Henry Ford, for instance, who refused to subscribe to the automobile code, nevertheless observed its wages and hours provisions; but they could not compensate for the discontent which began to engulf the NRA from all sides, nor, above all, for the fact that the economy showed few signs of immediate, complete recovery.

---

6 Characteristically, the employers impudently tried to persuade the NRA that the minimum wage provisions of the cotton textile code made a banning of child labour unnecessary. It was this sort of thing that drove Clarence Darrow to declare after an NRA conference that he had not realized before how much the rich loved the poor.

The NRA became, unfairly, the scapegoat for this failure, although it created no fewer than two million jobs. Nor could it fight back effectively: it was too riddled with contradictions,[7] reflecting the confused economic thought at the very heart of the New Deal, where a dozen different advisers with a dozen different points of view (all of them at least partially valid) struggled to win the President's backing. As 1933 wore into 1934 controversy grew ever noisier and more vigorous. Personal antagonisms at the top did not help, nor did the widespread feeling that the NIRA gave altogether too much power to the government in Washington to regulate American lives and businesses: old Carter Glass actually accused it of transplanting Hitlerism to every corner of the nation. In September 1934, Hugh Johnson resigned and the agency was reorganized; but it was too late. The case of *Schechter Poultry Corporation* v. *United States* was already finding its way through the courts, and on 27 May 1935, the New Deal's 'Black Monday', a unanimous Supreme Court declared the NRA unconstitutional, on two grounds. The lesser was that the industrial code that was being challenged regulated the trade in kosher fowls in the New York area (it was alleged that the Schechter Corporation had violated various provisions of the code eighteen times) and as such was an interference in intra-state trade: the commerce clause of the Constitution[8] did not give Congress or the President the right so to interfere. The press and the radio seized on the fact that one of Schechter's alleged offences was the sale of 'an unfit chicken' to a butcher: so posterity knows this landmark decision as 'the sick chicken case'. The nickname is not altogether unfair, for certainly the NRA codes had become tinged with absurdity: before Roosevelt put a stop to it, diligent bureaucrats had come up with a Dog Food code and a Shoulder Pad code and a Burlesque Theatrical (strip-tease) code. This was added *prima facie* evidence of the sort of unconstitutional abuse and extension of power which the Court condemned; though it is only fair to add that its reliance on a restrictive interpretation of the commerce clause caused a storm of criticism at the time, which has not yet altogether abated.

However, the decisive argument in the opinion, which Chief Justice Hughes[9] himself drafted and delivered, lay in its opening pages. The government had argued that the codes, and the NIRA generally, were justified by the need to fight the Depression. Hughes did not condescend to ask whether the fate of the national economy really depended on what happened to an unfit chicken. Instead he took the argument seriously. 'Extraordinary conditions,' he allowed, 'may call for extraordinary remedies. But ... Extraordinary conditions do not create or enlarge constitutional power.

7 For instance, the NIRA explicitly declared war on monopolies; but friends and critics within and without the NRA could never decide whether on balance the agency was more of a help or a hindrance to monopolists.

8 Art. 1. sec. 8: 'The Congress shall have Power ... To regulate Commerce with foreign Nations, and among the several States, and with the Indian Tribes.'

9 Hughes, the former Secretary of State, was Chief Justice from 1930 to 1941.

The Constitution established a national government with powers deemed to be adequate, as they have proved to be both in war and peace; but these powers of the national government are limited by the constitutional grants.' And he had no difficulty in showing, indeed his style suggests that he took considerable intellectual pleasure in showing, that the grants of power made by Congress to the President in the codes provision of the NIRA were far beyond the limits imposed by the Constitution, amounting to 'an unconstitutional delegation of legislative power' – for they enabled the President to make what laws he liked for the regulation of any economic activity whatever. His case was unanswerable.

'Black Monday' was seen as a mortal blow to the New Deal. It proved to be nothing of the sort. Most of the useful parts of the NIRA, Title I (Title II, which set up the PWA, was unaffected), were soon re-enacted, with greater care for the letter of the law, and survived all challenge, and Roosevelt was soon producing fresh bursts of valid legislation. The role and power of Washington in the national life continued to grow. But the Supreme Court had sharply reminded Roosevelt of his own self-proclaimed mission, to show that the resources of democracy were not exhausted and that the American Constitution was equal to the demands made of it. That mission could hardly be achieved by violating the Constitution. Roosevelt learned his lesson, and we may be thankful for it. The whole episode shows, not only how far he was from being a revolutionary, but how solid were the constraints on his actions. 'Extraordinary conditions do not create or enlarge constitutional power': so long as Americans were determined to stick to that maxim and to the values it implies, no President – not even one so popular as Roosevelt, in a crisis so deep as the Depression – could govern alone; and as for becoming a dictator (the constant complaint of FDR's enemies), it was impossible.

Section 7(a) was rescued by the Wagner Act, named after its chief architect, Senator Robert Wagner of New York, which was signed by the President on 5 July 1935. The National Labor Relations Act (its official title) strengthened and extended the rights gained by the unions under the NIRA and gave John Lewis his second wind. His leadership of the miners in the twenties had not been very successful: following a great strike in 1922, in which some twenty strike-breakers were killed but nothing else was achieved, he had had to watch his influence decline and the membership of his union slump while the industry decayed under the triple weight of over-production, over-manning and under-investment. The Depression made everything far worse: by 1933 membership of the UMW was down to 150,000, and Lewis feared that communist organizations might succeed in their challenge to his leadership. But 7(a) gave him his chance. The word went out (not only to the miners) that 'President Roosevelt wants you to join the union' (which was going rather beyond the facts, for in this as in other matters Roosevelt started from a more conservative position than was always recognized) and soon Lewis had a revived membership of 500,000, thanks largely to his vigorous recruiting. He then embarked on a serious attempt to get the AFL to abandon its traditions and organize industrial unions. The Wagner Act gave him invaluable help. Three months after it was passed the AFL held its annual conference at Atlantic City. Opposed to Lewis were the heirs of Gompers, the leaders of the old craft unions. With him were such figures as David Dubinsky of the International Ladies Garment Workers Union[10] and Sidney Hillman of the Amalgamated Clothing Workers. There was a frightful row; at one stage Lewis got involved in a fight with another union leader, and three weeks later he and his friends founded the Committee for Industrial Organization (after 1938, the Congress of Industrial Organizations) which set up as a rival of the AFL. The CIO successfully unionized the automobile and steel industries, and greatly expanded union membership elsewhere. Stimulated by this competition, the AFL recovered its former vigour and expanded likewise. By 1938 there were some nine million union members in the national workforce. There had been fewer than three million in 1933. These unionists became some of the most dependable supporters of Roosevelt, the New Deal and the Democratic party.

The NRA was a premature experiment in a fully planned economy conducted with inadequate tools. Its failure epitomized the collapse of the New Deal's attempt to co-operate with business. The history of the Triple A epitomizes its happier relations with another special interest group, the farmers of America. The reason for this comparative success was simple: since the palmy days of the slave power the American political system had repeatedly demonstrated its ability to accommodate interest groups; this indeed was one of the things it did best, and at root the farmers' problems had grown so intolerable because of the unusual refusal of politicians in the business-dominated twenties to take them seriously. When the Depression converted the Democratic party to the principle of federal aid to the unlucky, and the New Deal took office, the farmers got back their 'clout' at Washington and the usual logrolling politics of the US Congress did the rest.[11]

It is important not to lose sight of essentials. These were the tragic years of American agriculture. The long slow slide downhill of the twenties had ended devastatingly in the Depression, like a disease suddenly entering its terminal phase. The high tariffs of the twenties and the effectiveness of

10 A charming and characteristic incident of the New Deal years was the musical revue *Pins and Needles*, created and staged by members of the ILGWU. It had a long run on Broadway; no one was allowed to stay in the cast for more than a few weeks, and eventually a special performance of the show was mounted at the White House for President Roosevelt. The hit song was 'One Big Union for Two'.

11 'Clout': a slang word in American politics, deriving particularly from Irish-American circles in Chicago. It originally meant corrupt influence at City Hall. Thus one might say of a bootlegger, 'He won't be charged – he has too much clout.' Nowadays it just means political power or influence. 'Logrolling': help me to roll my log and I'll help you roll yours. Thus, in the thirties, urban representatives voted for farm bills, and farming representatives voted for urban reforms.

foreign competition had cut the farmers off from their traditional foreign markets: customers who could not sell to the United States could not buy from it. The Depression destroyed the domestic market. Purchasing power in the cities collapsed, and the effects worked back through the chain of textile factories, meat-processors and vegetable-canners to the primary producers. Farm income fell by two-thirds between 1929 and 1932.[12] Even worse, whereas the price of all farm products dropped by more than 50 per cent, the price of the products the farmer had to buy, for living and working (clothes and footwear, for instance), went down only by a third. Among the grim implications of these figures was the collapse of the rural credit system: dozens of small country banks broke, and with them fell both their debtors and their creditors. The remaining banks, desperate to survive, foreclosed their mortgages on farms as soon as payments ceased. Farmers stopped buying anything from the great mail-order houses and dropped their insurance policies. Their ruin thus increased the difficulties of urban capitalists. It was clear that farm prices would be driven even lower if agricultural output continued as high as ever, but no individual farmer dared risk a further loss of income by curtailing his planting and reaping: all voluntary schemes for reducing production failed. So the crisis spread and deepened: nowhere was the Depression more of a calamity than in rural America.

Despair erupted in violence that might have become revolutionary: these were men of the stock of '76. In the summer and autumn of 1932 there were demonstrations throughout the farm belt. In the spring of 1933 there were renewed outbursts, especially in Iowa, then as now the heart of American farm country, where an organization called the Farm Holiday Association took the lead. Attempts were made to stop the movement of produce to market, and thus, by creating a shortage, to force up prices. They did not succeed. More effective were interruptions of mortgage foreclosures. In the most spectacular of these incidents a crowd of Iowa farmers, masked with blue handkerchiefs, interrupted foreclosure proceedings in a courthouse, threatened to lynch the judge, dragged him outside, put one end of a rope round his neck and the other over a limb of a tree, and then, after half-throttling him, making him say his prayers, throwing dirt at him, and yet, in spite of all, failing to intimidate him, gave up the enterprise, merely stripping off his trousers and smearing him with axle grease. It could have been worse, and in other countries unquestionably would have been; but the episode seemed a shocking warning in America.

So no wonder the Roosevelt administration lost no time in tackling the farm problem. The Secretary of Agriculture, Henry A. Wallace of Iowa, was an old hand: his father had been Secretary in Harding's Cabinet, whose efforts to help the farms had been regularly frustrated by the opposition of

12 The average net income per farm went from $945 in 1929 to $304 in 1932. The realized net income of all farmers went from $6,274,000 to $1,922,000.

Herbert Hoover. The younger Wallace had abandoned the Republicans in disgust in 1928. Now he could put his lifetime's devotion to scientific agriculture and the farmers' cause to good account. The Agricultural Adjustment Administration was his instrument. It was to be even more riven by feuds between radicals and conservatives than the NRA, but it enjoyed far more consistent political support; and the shape it gave to American agriculture has lasted to the present day.

That shape was in large measure predetermined. In the first place, all agreed that the central problem was the frightful disparity between industrial and agricultural prices. According to the enabling Act the Triple A was set up precisely to deal with this problem. The farmers' favourite remedy was dumping: that is, the purchase of the agricultural surplus at a good price by the government and its disposal overseas for whatever it would fetch. Wallace and his more radical associates, such as the Assistant Secretary, Rexford Tugwell (one of the Brain Trusters), were against this practice, since it was highly injurious to America's trading relations with other countries; they held off as long as they could; but by the end of the thirties the perpetual surplus of American agriculture was forcing them, in spite of their convictions, to dump, if only because storage was getting to be frighteningly expensive. During most of the New Deal, nevertheless, this last resort was forestalled by more novel devices. Of these the most spectacular was the curtailment of production that was undertaken in the first months of the Roosevelt administration. Industry, it was reasoned, cut back when demand fell off: agriculture must do the same. American traditions were still too strong for the New Dealers to allow themselves to resort to compulsion (though at the time the farmers would probably have welcomed it); instead they bought the farmers' acquiescence. The proceeds of a special tax on processing (canning meat, milling grain and so on) were used to compensate generously farmers who agreed to plough up their cotton crops, or restrict their acreage of wheat planting or slaughter their baby pigs. Ten million acres of cotton that might have made shirts and dresses were dug under; six million piglets were murdered prematurely, and although some of the meat was used by the government to supplement the diet of the urban unemployed, nine-tenths of it was inedible. There was an immense outcry from the public. Wallace was disgusted. 'To hear them talk,' he said, 'you would have thought that pigs were raised for pets.'

Nevertheless the public had a point, as Wallace well knew. The destruction of food and fibre, in a world where so many (even in normal times) went hungry and naked, was an obscenity; and Wallace was aware that it was the fault of the 'profit system', as he and the President termed it, that the abundance of America could not be distributed to the needy of, say, China, or even of the USA. Only wholesale socialization of the American economy – in a word, revolution, peaceable or otherwise – might begin to remedy the evil; and there was all too much reason to doubt that even revolution could do the trick (it had failed spectacularly in the USSR). So the starving

Chinese would have to fend for themselves, while Americans solved the problem of abundance by destroying the abundance, as one observer put it. They were startlingly successful. The emergency measures of 1933 did something; then in 1934 and 1935 came dust-storms. The Great Plains had entered the dry phase of the climatic cycle once more; there was a prolonged drought; exhausted and neglected by the greedy methods of traditional farming, the soil of western Kansas, Oklahoma, the Texan panhandle and eastern Colorado blew away on the gales. Eventually it darkened the skies over Washington, DC, stained the winter snows of New England red and fell upon ships 300 miles out on the Atlantic. Tens of thousands of farming families were ruined and took their hopeless way west, pathetic caricatures of the pioneers, to charity camps in California. The price of farm products began to rise, falteringly at first, from their low point in 1932, and had nearly doubled by 1937; and those farmers who weathered the storms began to prosper again, assisted by a flood of new programmes out of Washington – conservation programmes, electrification programmes, resettlement programmes. A divided Supreme Court, in one of the worst decisions in its history, struck down the original Agricultural Act in January 1936 (*US* v. *Butler et al.*), but the essential parts were quickly re-enacted (it was election year) under the guise of a soil conservation law, and in 1938 the farm programme was put on a permanent footing by a new AAA. Washington, having literally set its hand to the plough, would not look back.

This became the secret of the farmers' strength. During the decades of neglect they had been, though still so large a part of the population, not voiceless, but ineffective in national politics. Now they could always be sure of a hearing, and a respectful one too, for neither the White House nor a Democratic Congress, in which Senators and Representatives from the cotton South held dominating positions, was going to alienate so large a block of citizens (roughly 25 per cent of the population) by withdrawing favours to which they had got used. Especially not since the activities of the AAA taught the farmers, far better than the Populists had ever managed, how to unite and organize. Under the AAA it was the farmers, meeting and voting, who decided how many acres should be taken out of production every year and supervised each other to make sure that the reduction actually occurred. All the other programmes were administered in the same manner. By the end of the thirties the farmers were no longer the desperate clients of Washington: they gave terms to the bureaucracy. Once more vast surpluses built up (in federally paid-for granaries); only now they threatened not the farmer, but the national government, with financial disaster. Henry Wallace was landed with the responsibility; he was nearly at his wits' end as to how to discharge it when he was elevated to the Vice-Presidency, and then war, which brought an insatiable need for all supplies, came to the rescue, and the American surplus began to reach the starving world at last.

The fact that the New Deal was less in command of events than it seemed was well illustrated by another aspect of the farm programmes. The farmers who took the lead in the administration of the AAA were not the worst-hit victims of the Depression: not the sharecroppers of the South, the tenants of the Middle West, the hired hands everywhere, the illiterate, the black, the ignorant, the smallholders trying to live off pocket-handkerchief holdings, owners of exhausted land, or young men and women forced to stay on the land because there was no work in the cities.[13] Apart from every other obstacle in their way they were often too ill-fed to have enough energy to stand up for themselves in meetings at the end of a hard day's work. So the big commercial farmers and, in the South, the landlords carried all before them, greatly helped by the fact that AAA subsidies were paid, as it were, to acres, not individuals: the bigger the farm, therefore, the more money the farmer received from the government. With abundant collusion from within Congress and the Department of Agriculture they strengthened their position more ruthlessly and determinedly than big business did under NRA, and with far more permanent success. The reforming followers of Tugwell within the administration, the organizations of poorer farmers outside it, made no great headway against them; and the ebb of the Depression diminished such sense of social solidarity as had been induced in 1932. In short, the renewed prosperity benefited the strong farmer; the weak suffered much as before; and after 1941 (when the factory boom of the Second World War opened up the job market again) the movement from the land to the cities resumed. It was probably an economically necessary process; but the human and political gains to America would have been enormous if the movement could have been regulated with intelligence and compassion, instead of being left, in the old way, to the brutally impersonal operations of 'the profit system', which were only marginally braked by the commitment of the New Deal and succeeding administrations to maintain the existing farm population *in situ*. Agriculture Secretaries came and went and made the same pledges to uphold the small family farm (anything was better than the effort and conflict involved in thinking out a new policy); but the number of such farms went on shrinking, and nobody did much for the displaced.

That things might have been happier was demonstrated by the third major enterprise of the New Deal, the great relief operation.

It is almost impossible to give a coherent account of the evolution of the Roosevelt programme for poor relief. Critics of FDR's administrative methods (they were and are numerous) can point in scorn to the fact that the programme changed its form almost yearly – in early days, more than yearly. The Federal Emergency Relief Administration was largely replaced by the Civil Works Administration, which then gave way to FERA again;

13 Those who can stomach a grossly enriched prose will find a powerful account of three poor farming families in James Agee's *Let Us Now Praise Famous Men*, first published in 1941, superbly illustrated by Walker Evans's noble photographs.

then came the period of consolidation under the Works Progress Administration, which was cut back in 1937 and re-expanded in 1938; and all the time the incessant rivalries of the New Deal, in this case predominantly between Harold Ickes and Harry Hopkins,[14] meant that there were always at least two major relief organizations: for whatever else might come and go, the PWA went on until the outbreak of the Second World War, though Roosevelt at one stage thought he had abolished it.

This is not a tidy picture; but the Depression was not a tidy phenomenon, and it could not be effectively fought by the tidy methods of an Ickes. Nothing in Roosevelt's career mattered more to him, ultimately, than the task of rescuing the millions of innocent victims of the great storm and of transforming American attitudes to them. Indeed, though it was long before he fully recognized it, one of his chief historical tasks was the foundation of the American welfare state. For this great undertaking he had, in Harry Hopkins, a man in whom 'the purity of St Francis of Assisi combined with the sharp shrewdness of a race-track tout',[15] the perfect instrument. Hopkins was as loose in his methods as Ickes was tight. Working on a tiny salary, from a dim little office, with an exiguous if devoted staff, by methods that might have been designed to appal the Bureau of the Budget (if so they certainly succeeded), he yet spent his way through more money than any other single New Dealer, transformed the lives of more Americans, revolutionized attitudes to unemployment, and incidentally did more than any man next to the President himself to make over the Democratic party. He destroyed his health in the process, otherwise the President might have picked him as his own successor. He was widely regarded as Roosevelt's evil genius, but this former social worker from Iowa, with his selfless passion for the public service and his fondness for Keats and horse-racing, rendered, in peace as in war, 'a service to his country which will never even vaguely be appreciated'[16] because it was, literally, incalculable.

No one has ever reckoned with certainty the number of unemployed on Inauguration Day, 1933: estimates vary from twelve to sixteen million – say, a quarter of the labour force. All classes were haunted by the spectres of hunger, waste, despair and something, perhaps, even worse: said the mayor of Toledo, Ohio, in 1932: 'I have seen thousands of these defeated, discouraged, hopeless men and women, cringing and fawning as they come to ask for public aid. It is a spectacle of national degeneration.' It was time to do something. After the passage of the Federal Emergency Relief Act, Roosevelt summoned Harry Hopkins, who had worked for him in a similar

14 Harold Ickes always believed that Hopkins gave his chief agency a name (Works Progress Administration) with initials confusingly like those of the PWA so that he could get credit with the public for Ickes's achievements; Hopkins's biographer, who details the battle between the two men, does not dismiss the idea (Robert E. Sherwood, *The White House Papers of Harry L. Hopkins*, London, 1948, Vol. i, p. 71).

15 Sherwood, *Hopkins*, Vol. i, p. 49.

16 General George Marshall on Hopkins's wartime activities.

job in New York, to be its administrator. Hopkins set out to spend the Act's $500,000,000 in a hurry.

The importance of his activities in the end lay less in what he did than in what he began. Hopkins himself had no illusions. In 1936 he commented, 'we have never given adequate relief,' and in January 1937[17] Roosevelt expressed his essential agreement, announcing, in his second inaugural, that he saw 'one-third of a nation ill-housed, ill-clad, ill-nourished'. There was not even a regular federal relief programme: FERA payments went to the states and the cities, to supplement their resources, not direct to the needy. But the great point was to have reversed the legacy of Herbert Hoover. When in the summer of 1935 Roosevelt again demonstrated his political mastery (which had seemed to be waning after the Supreme Court's action in destroying the NRA) by launching a second Hundred Days of 'must' legislation, the Social Security Act (which had been making a slow progress through Congress since January) was the heart of it. Riddled with anomalies and exceptions, this act was nevertheless the foundation stone of the future. It began to extend to Americans the sort of protection against the distresses of old age and poverty that the Germans and British had long enjoyed. It was financed entirely, and from the economic point of view unwisely, by contributions: by taxes levied on the employers and by deductions from the wages of the employed. This was to have some harmful results in the near future, but Roosevelt was clear about the political importance of the arrangement. 'We put those payroll contributions there,' he said, 'so as to give the contributors a legal, moral, and political right to collect their pensions and their unemployment benefits. With those taxes in there, no damn politician can ever scrap my social security programme.'[18] There was to be no retreat to Hooverism; and later administrations would take care of some of the weaknesses of the original act. (So they did: the system was extended, under Truman and Eisenhower, to another twenty million workers; Lyndon Johnson augmented it with a system of medical insurance.)

The Social Security Act was for the future. While the Depression lasted, there had to be relief; and the Depression lasted throughout the New Deal. Hopkins and Ickes achieved wonders, within the limits restraining them. Ickes, wearing his hat as Secretary of the Interior, rescued the Indians. In 1934 he put through the Indian Reorganization Act, which not only stopped the depredations described in Chapter 5 of this book, but actually made provision to buy land and present it to the tribes. It recognized tribal

17 One of the smaller but useful reforms of the New Deal was to move the date of the Presidential inauguration back two months, from March to January. Never again would there be a long interregnum such as the two which nearly destroyed America, in 1860–61 and 1932–3.
18 FDR's thesis was to be vindicated in the 1980s, when largely because of actuarial miscalculations (people living longer than expected) the insurance system was nearly bankrupt. Even so conservative a President as Ronald Reagan dared not solve the problem by reducing pensions.

authority, encouraged the adoption of modern forms of tribal government and did something for Indian education. By the time that enemies of the red man won national power again, after the Second World War, the Indians had recovered so far that they were able to beat off the attackers and begin the slow rise which, with many setbacks, has characterized their history ever since. This was one of the most complete, characteristic and heart-warming successes of the reforming New Deal.

Wearing his hat as head of PWA, Ickes did the lion's share of the building, while Hopkins did the boondoggling. This derisive, unfair, but convenient term came into use among the enemies of the New Deal to describe make-work jobs – the example always used was leaf-raking – for which 'reliefers' (another term of the time which has happily lapsed) were paid wages. Actually, this reflected Hopkins's perfectly sound principle that the souls of the reliefers must be saved as well as their bodies. Proud and individualistic Americans found going on the dole a horribly humiliating experience. It involved a means test; it was a confession of failure; once it was accepted it tended (many thought) to become narcotic: its recipients lost the will, the hope to seek work again. This last point was dubious, for most of the reliefers jumped at the chance of earning. Hopkins saw to it that they got that chance. He set them to building roads, schools, playgrounds, sports fields; unemployed teachers were paid to keep the schools open in the countryside and to hold adult classes in the cities; streams were dredged, bridges built, handicraft courses were set up and students were put through college. FERA's Division of Rural Rehabilitation gave or lent money to farmers with which to buy seed, fertilizer, livestock and tools and so keep off the relief rolls. Some of Hopkins's other ideas were magnificently imaginative. Acting on the excellent principle that 'they've got to eat just like other people', he made work for writers and artists, which is why so many American post-offices are now adorned with rather awful mural paintings, and why so many book-collectors still hunt for the Federal Writers American Guides, a set of volumes on states, cities and territories which, collectively, remains one of the best introductions to America that there is. The monument which even more perfectly expresses the spirit of the New Deal is Timberline Lodge high on Mount Hood in Oregon. It seemed pure boondoggle at the time; nobody foresaw its successful future as a ski-lodge. It is built round a Cyclopean chimney on the edge of the snow slopes, gazing over the smoky forests, every giant stone of it telling of the love and skill of the men who built it. In the spirit of medieval craftsmen they carved small wooden statues of birds and animals, and set them on the newel posts of the Lodge's many stairs. Those statues have since been worn almost into shapelessness by the touch of thousands of hands, but there they stay, as reminders. Timberline is a true American cathedral; and photographs of its joyous opening and dedication by President Roosevelt still adorn it.

Not the most brilliant boondoggling, however, could rescue the American industrial economy; nor could the Triple A; the NRA failed. Wall Street bankers were too frightened, too selfish and, as the Crash had proved, too incompetent (when not too dishonest) to take on the responsibility. In the spring of 1933 J. P. Morgan Jr showed how unworthy he was to be his father's heir by refusing to use the resources of the House of Morgan to rescue a single, much smaller New York bank: dull and timid, he was determined to leave the entire banking problem to Washington. All the same, he and his like still commanded vast power, even if they now used it only to obstruct, and throughout the summer a savage if silent struggle went on between them and the administration. Ultimately victory went to the New Deal, because so many of the banks were still insolvent and would never be able to re-open without the assistance of the federal government. In this way New York lost its ultimate control over the American economy. The administration's agency for exercising its new power was one it had inherited from Herbert Hoover, the Reconstruction Finance Corporation; but under Roosevelt it was utterly transformed. Hoover had envisaged the RFC as an agency for lending money to financial institutions which were in difficulties; he had not realized that their chief difficulty, in most cases, was their load of debt, which RFC would only make heavier; and he vetoed an attempt to enlarge the Corporation's functions. Roosevelt, on coming to power, gave the RFC to Jesse Jones, an energetic Texan businessman with the drive and optimism of his state: a stark contrast to the cautious Easterners who ran the corporation under Hoover. Jones's first task was to get control of the banks and then rescue them, whether they liked it or not (mostly they didn't), on his terms. This involved using the vast funds at the RFC's disposal ($500 million in money, $1,500 million in government-guaranteed, tax-free bonds) to buy shares in the banks. Jones did this on such a scale that by 1935 the RFC was America's largest financial institution, the banks' banker, a super-bank, owning about one-fifth of the total banking stock in the country. As such it was in an excellent position to direct investment policy, and Jones saw to it that banking services were made available where, from the national point of view, they would do most good – for instance, in communities that had been without banks until then. Jones's expansionist, inflationary outlook was just what the situation required, and he must be given a large part of the credit for the substantial recovery that was under way by the time Roosevelt ran for re-election. Not that his position as a state-financed, government-backed super-banker could be indefinitely tolerated in a system still committed to free capitalist enterprise: Franklin Roosevelt, who liked to think of himself as the successor of Andrew Jackson, had no mandate to re-create The Monster. So once the banking system was operating smoothly again, the RFC stopped buying bank shares, and its role as the organizer of capitalism reverted to a reformed Federal Reserve System, reorganized by the Banking Act of 1935. But the RFC had plenty more commitments to keep it busy. Through its Commodity Credit Corporation it financed the operations of the Triple A.

Through the Export–Import Bank it tried to revive foreign trade. Through the Electric Home and Farm Authority it stimulated the market for electricity, of which the TVA was becoming a major supplier. In co-operation with the Federal Housing Administration it helped real-estate dealers find customers and first-time house-buyers find mortgages. In short, all the other New Deal agencies discovered, to their delight, that the RFC with its revolving fund (for its investments brought in substantial dividends) was a bottomless source of cash which was always on tap and did not have to be filtered through Congress. Congress might have objected to this state of affairs – it was supposed to control the purse-strings, after all – except that Jesse Jones was always very helpful in financing projects for particular Senators and Congressmen in their states and districts. No wonder that the RFC became FDR's favourite political instrument; no wonder it outlasted all the other New Deal agencies (it was not dismantled until 1953). In retrospect its importance lies less in the size of the power it wielded over the American economy, great though that was, than in the new role in which it displayed the federal government – a role which had been foreshadowed in the First World War; but now it was peacetime. The RFC was the new governor of the economic machine, and the master of the RFC was the President of the United States.

Roosevelt's re-election in 1936 was the most certain thing since George Washington's. To be sure, he had long been under attack from the Left for not doing enough (his most vehement critic on that side being Senator Huey Long, until his assassination in September 1935) and on the Right for doing too much. The *Literary Digest*, a distinguished magazine, conducted a poll by telephone and predicted that Roosevelt would lose. It had not noticed that 67 per cent of American households still lacked telephones, though their members had votes. In reality, nothing could weaken the President's hold on the American people. He had accustomed them to look to him for ideas, leadership and help; and although the Depression still persisted, it was much mitigated. The New Deal policies had created six million jobs, softened the sharp edges of unemployment as an experience and laid the foundations for a better future; done all this, besides, with good humour and palpable goodwill that were immensely endearing. 'Mr Roosevelt is the only man we ever had in the White House who would understand that my boss is a son-of-a-bitch,' said one working man. Others who thronged to his campaign meetings and parades shouted out remarks like 'He saved my home,' 'He gave me a job.' 'I would be without a roof over my head if it hadn't been for the government loan. God bless Mr Roosevelt and the Democratic party who saved thousands of poor people all over this country from starvation,' wrote a farmer. 'Your work saved our humble little home from the Trust Deed sharks and are we a happy couple in our little home, and listen too, the Real Estate Business is now over 100 per cent better than in 1932, life is 1,000 per cent better since you took Charge of our United States.' That was a former life-long Republican Californian real-estate broker, writing to his President.[19] The blacks, who had been harder-hit than any other section of the population by the Depression, turned away from the party of Lincoln to the party of Roosevelt, for he was helping them too. With such friends, there was no need to count the enemy, but somebody did so all the same. At the election Roosevelt carried every state except Maine and Vermont; he got 27,751,612 popular votes, while his opponent, Governor Alfred Landon of Kansas, got 16,681,913 votes – a respectable testimony to the stubbornness of American party loyalties, but not much more. For the fourth election running the Democrats increased their numbers in Congress; for the first time since 1894 there were fewer than a hundred Republican Congressmen; and there were only sixteen Republican Senators. The *Literary Digest* went out of business.

Roosevelt's position, at the beginning of his second term, was to all appearances unassailable. He had vindicated American democracy in a darkening world, rescued 'the profit system' and brought succour to the millions of his desperate fellow-citizens. For this achievement he had been lifted to a pinnacle from which nothing could cast him down. But he had no intention of merely basking in his glory. There was much work still to be done for America, and he intended to do it.

The business leaders were not going to help him. Having brought the United States so close to shipwreck they very naturally felt that as soon as the new pilot had steered them off the rocks they ought to be given the helm again. Roosevelt's refusal to make way for them, or even to take their advice, they took as an insult (it was certainly a vote of no confidence). They were muddled with outworn slogans that preached the wickedness of strong government, the virtues of 'free enterprise'. Besides, 'that man in the White House' had put up their taxes and supported the labour unions. With few exceptions, they broke with him entirely, except when they needed help from Jesse Jones.

Reluctantly, Roosevelt had accepted their enmity. Now he meant to be a leader of a different sort. Perhaps he could still hear the cheers that had greeted him at the Democratic convention in 1936 when he had shouted that 'I should like to have it said of my first Administration that in it the forces of selfishness and of lust for power met their match . . . I should like to have it said of my second Administration that in it these forces met their master.' Superb in his own political skill, and properly confident in the creativity and devotion of his New Dealers, nothing can have seemed beyond his power.

Yet, as he should have known, it was still necessary to tread warily. True, he had wrought some astonishing transformations in the previous four years; but he had not appointed a single Supreme Court Justice; the Republican party, though so weak in Congress and with only a handful of governorships to its name, was scotched, not killed (subsequent decades have shown

19 For these voices of the people, see Leuchtenburg, *Franklin D. Roosevelt*, pp. 189 and 193.

it to be unkillable); most significant of all, he had not yet made over the Democratic party. No doubt that body, including many of its Senators and Congressmen, owed him a lot; no doubt its votes had come largely from the new supporters he had won to it; but the actual full-time party workers and representatives were still much what they had always been. Beneath the surface unanimity and the cheer of the victory parties lurked the old divisions which had wrecked Woodrow Wilson. They were now to come near to wrecking Franklin Roosevelt.

In the rashest moment of his career he decided to attack the Supreme Court first of all his enemies. To understand his decision we must remember that the Court had tried him severely and had been setting itself more and more inflexibly against reforming statutes, whether state or federal, since 1921, when former President Taft had been made Chief Justice. He told his brethren that he had been appointed to reverse a few decisions, and for the next ten years led them down an ever darker track of reaction, inflex- ibility and pedantry, ostensibly to protect the Constitution from bolshevism, but really to protect Taft's own economic and political prejudices. His retirement and death were the signals for a vigorous political outcry: before Hughes could be appointed as his successor the progressives in the Senate denounced the recent record of the Court (it had taken to disallowing acts of Congress with an abandon never displayed before); and Hoover's original nominee to fill another vacancy on the bench was rejected. But these warnings went for nothing. Under Hughes, the Court majority continued on the same reactionary course, in spite of the protests of three of the ablest Justices, Brandeis, Stone and Cardozo. In these circumstances a clash with the New Deal was inevitable, not only because New Deal statutes were often so badly drawn up as to be of questionable constitutionality (as we have seen, the decision in the sick chicken case was unanimous), but because the whole thrust of New Deal policy was directed against the political philosophy which the Court majority held sacred. Mr Justice Sutherland, for one, was not impressed by arguments that an economic crisis demanded a reinterpretation of the Constitution: he had lived through economic crises before. The Constitution must be preserved and respected in bad times as in good.

Roosevelt did not disagree with this truism; but he did not take the same view of what the Constitution was as the aged judges did, and he grew more and more restive with the principle, indiscreetly laid down by Charles Evans Hughes in his youth, that the Constitution was what the judges say it is. Black Monday was bad enough; but it was followed by the disastrous session of 1936, when in succession the Court invalidated the AAA; an Act regulating prices and working conditions in coal-mining; and a New York state law setting a minimum wage for women workers. Significantly, none of these decisions was unanimous: it seemed that six old men were wantonly intent on carving the heart out of a political programme overwhelmingly supported by the people of the United States. Even the Wagner Act and the new Agriculture Act seemed to be in danger. In the circumstances it is not surprising that the President decided to safeguard the New Deal against judicial counter-revolution before bringing forward anymore new proposals.

His mistake was not to consult Congressional Democratic leaders first (indeed, he consulted nobody worth mentioning). He should have known better. In the first place, it is extremely difficult, as several Presidents have found, to weaken formally any of the co-equal branches of the federal government. They are entrenched, not just in the Constitution, but in the habits, if not always the affections, of the sovereign American people: it is difficult, indeed probably impossible, to rally enough support for long enough to win the day in an assault upon them. To make such a constitution work, then, it is necessary for its principal instruments to show respect and restraint towards each other. The Court majority, to be sure, had been showing little respect for the Presidency and Congress, but the way to defeat it was not by behaving in the same fashion. Tampering with the Constitution is the sin of witchcraft in American life; any President (or for that matter any judge, or any member of Congress) who can be plausibly accused of the offence may expect to find his support melting mysteriously away from day to day. And Roosevelt was blatantly trying to tamper with the Constitution by packing the Court: the plan he suddenly unveiled on 5 February 1937 proposed the appointment of extra Justices up to the number of six, if those Justices over the age of seventy did not 'voluntarily' retire. The excuse for this proposal was that the Court needed to be made more efficient. Many of Roosevelt's most ardent supporters in other matters were deeply unhappy about the scheme; for one thing, the senior Justice, Louis Brandeis (then aged eighty), was one of the President's staunchest allies. It seemed ungrateful to imply that he was no longer up to his job.

Even more important, in practical terms, was the reaction of the conservatives among the Democrats. These men on the whole represented the main traditions of the party as it had existed between the Civil War and 1913. They were in many cases elderly; and, crucially, many of them were Southerners. Like their counterparts in the Republican party and elsewhere, they had been ready to accept the measures of the early New Deal, if only because of the general emergency, and because of the predominantly rural nature of their constituencies – constituencies which had been greatly aided by the AAA and its related agencies. They had not liked subsequent developments nearly so well, above all Roosevelt's ever-deepening commitment to the wishes of organized labour. John L. Lewis's campaign to destroy the resistance of heavy industry to a unionized workforce was bad enough in itself; but the New Deal's commitment to raising wages and cutting working hours was worse. Taken together these tendencies directly threatened the continuance of the South as a region of unorganized, badly paid labour, where restrictions on hours, and expensive provisions for worker safety, were minimal. Besides, many of the workers there were black. If the CIO could unionize the South it would not only reduce the attractiveness of that region to business investors looking for low labour costs; it would begin to destroy the edifice of white supremacy, for you cannot give a man the power to organize and protect himself economically without giving him the power to do so politically (and vice versa). The Southerners regarded Roosevelt's popularity among labour and blacks with the gravest misgivings. They feared for their future power in the Democratic party. Assuming that FDR would not try to succeed himself in 1940, it was important that the party should not swing so far in the liberal direction as to be irrecoverable in that year. The Supreme Court issue was perfect as an excuse for rebellion: it enabled the conservatives, most respectably, to cry halt. Besides, most Southern Senators were constitutional lawyers at heart, like their forerunner Calhoun. They were sincerely affronted when sacrilegious hands were laid on the ark. They abandoned their leader. 'Boys, here's where I cash in my chips,' said one of them.

The resultant battle dragged on until the autumn. It was made ludicrous at an early stage, when the Supreme Court reversed itself by approving the Wagner Act. Mr Justice Roberts and the Chief Justice himself had at last understood the danger to the Court of constantly challenging the Presidency, Congress and the voters, and adopted the doctrines of judicial caution which Stone and Brandeis had been vainly urging upon them for years. One of the reactionary Justices gave up the battle and retired, to be replaced by a stalwart Southern liberal, Hugo Black of Alabama. Chief Justice Hughes issued a paper showing that Roosevelt's allegations that the Court was overworked and inefficient were wide of the mark. There the dispute should have ended, but Roosevelt was grimly determined on victory and struggled on until it became clear that Congress was never going to support him. He then had to acknowledge the first and most devastating defeat of his Presidency.

Matters were made worse by economic events. The men closest to the President at that moment – Henry Morgenthau, the Secretary of the Treasury, for example – were orthodox financiers and economists who had managed to convince themselves, in the middle of a just barely convalescent economy, that the United States was in serious danger of inflation and that it was therefore essential to balance the federal budget at last. They persuaded their chief, and he began to run down the spending programmes, at just the moment when the new social security taxes were anyway taking large amounts of purchasing power out of the market. The result should have been foreseen: the industrial recovery was cut off suddenly, factories once more began to close and the number of unemployed leaped upwards. By Christmas two million more workers had lost their jobs. Republicans began to talk of 'the Roosevelt depression'. After bitter and prolonged debates within the administration the spending programmes were revived, and Roosevelt tried to push through new measures. But he had lost too much authority in the Court battle; the continuing aggressiveness of the CIO alarmed many middle-class citizens, which in turn affected their representatives; very little of the new legislation was passed, though a Fair Labour Standards act, introducing the forty-hour week, did get through. The rest of the Congressional session was wasted in futile wrangling.

Roosevelt grew more and more annoyed, and eventually, in the summer of 1938, decided to try to purge the Democratic party of mutineers. He toured the country, asking Democratic voters in that year's primary elections to reject such enemies as Senator George of Georgia or Senator 'Cotton Ed' Smith of South Carolina. But he had not prepared the ground sufficiently, and it is always hazardous for a President to intervene in local battles, as was proved when George and Smith were triumphantly re-nominated; and to make matters worse, in the autumn election the Republican party, profiting from the recession, staged an effective come-back, taking eight Senate seats and no less than eighty-one House seats from the Democrats. The latter still had a majority in both houses, as Roosevelt took some comfort in pointing out, but their liberal wing had been seriously weakened. Congress was now dominated by conservatives, all too many of whom believed, or professed to believe, that Roosevelt was aiming at a dictatorship, which made it their bounden duty to resist everything he proposed. In two years' time, they fondly supposed, he would retire, and with any luck a conservative would succeed him – either one of the new Republican stars or a right-wing Democrat. The disasters of the past eighteen months had left their mark on the administration. The New Dealers were showing signs of that curious sterile fatigue which so often overtakes reforming governments at the end of their time (comparable cases are the Wilson administration in 1919 and 1920, the Attlee government of 1950–51). Harry Hopkins's health had collapsed; Eleanor Roosevelt wanted Franklin to retire in 1941, in spite of the talk about a third term that was already being floated. All in all, it seemed that the New Deal was at an end.

Radicals could mourn; but their works remained, enormous and irrevers-ible. Later critics have blamed the New Deal for not going further, faster: it is always so easy to demand the impossible, and so tempting to play down the importance of starting something. FDR and his team had started a lot, and as he himself said after the 1938 elections, 'It takes a long, long time to bring the past up to the present.' Rather than comparing the New Deal to Utopia, it is better to bring out its actual achievements. Of these unques-tionably the most important was the preservation of American democracy, the American Constitution and American capitalism. Men are so governed, in their perceptions as in everything else, by abstractions that it was difficult or impossible for many of Roosevelt's critics to see this; they thought of him and spoke of him as if he were a cat of the same stripe as Hitler, Mussolini or Stalin; but nowadays the truth is plain and he must be placed along with Washington and Lincoln, as a shaper, preserver and defender of the American Constitution and political system. His task entailed adaptation and sacrifice, and hence aroused fierce opposition. But in the end he prevailed, even in defeat: for if the Supreme Court reminded him, forcibly, of the limits of his own power, he taught the Court itself an even more salutary lesson – not to stand in the way of necessary change – and so equipped it for its important role in modern American democracy. In his relations with Congress he showed what could be done, on what a scale, when executive and legislature were in partnership; he proved, as Theodore Roosevelt and Woodrow Wilson had suggested by their careers, that in the twentieth century it was necessary for the Presidency to take the lead, and Congress to accept the role of junior partner, as much in fashioning the laws as in administering them; but his relations with Congress after 1937 also showed that at times the President must content himself with piecemeal achievements – indeed, that has been the normal state of affairs ever since. He also accustomed Congress, and the country, to the necessary activism of modern government, so that the stream of statutes, which seemed so astonishing in the Hundred Days, has become the norm of Congressional life (though few of the laws passed have anything like the importance of the first New Deal legislation). He thus enabled the American government to assume the responsibility of safeguarding the welfare of the American people in a sense far more radical than that envisaged by the Founding Fathers, but not in a fashion inconsistent with what they most valued – republican government. As a side-effect of all this, the federal bureaucracy grew, and Washington became a great city at last. More important, by his gallantry, energy, eloquence and warmth of heart, he not only transformed the prestige of his office but galvanized an entire generation with faith in their country, their leader and their political system. In this way he laid the foundations for the achievements of the next generation: the impetus he gave to politics would not be exhausted for another thirty years. Thanks to Franklin Roosevelt, in short, six years (1933 to 1938) transformed America from a country which had been laid low by troubles which its own incompetence had brought on it, and which it was quite unable to cope with, to a country, as it proved, superbly equipped to meet the worst shocks that the modern world could hurl at it.

It was enough.

23 The Reluctant Giant
1933-45

> Some indeed still hold to the now somewhat obvious delusion that we
> of the United States can safely permit the United States to become a
> lone island, a lone island in a world dominated by the philosophy of
> force. Such an island may be the dream of those who still talk and vote
> as isolationists. Such an island represented to me and to the overwhelming
> majority of Americans today a helpless nightmare, the helpless nightmare
> of a people without freedom. Yes, the nightmare of a people lodged in
> prison, handcuffed, hungry and fed through the bars from day to day
> by the contemptuous, unpitying masters of other continents.

> Franklin D. Roosevelt, Charlottesville Address, 10 June 1940

Diplomacy is perhaps the most difficult of the political arts, and the theory
was once widely held that democracies were especially bad at it. It is
undeniable that the United States, during the first 160-odd years of its
independence, all too often showed itself to be diplomatically inept. There
were some well-earned triumphs, but on the whole the record is dismal.
This is especially true of the period between the two world wars, when the
results of incompetence were calamitous for all mankind. They should have
been avoided. Winston Churchill always insisted that the Second World
War need not have happened. Determined police action at an early stage
could and should have been taken to stop Hitler. It is more difficult to see
how war between Japan and the West could have been avoided, but even
so it cannot positively be said that preventive action would have failed. It
was never tried. And the war came.

Blame for this state of affairs must rest in large part on the statesmen
who let it come about or (in the case of Germany and Japan) actively
encouraged it; but the most important lesson of the period – perhaps the
only one worth learning – will be overlooked if the matter is left there. The
fact is that the leaders of the Western democracies partly shared the delusions
of their countrymen, and were in any case shackled by them. Very few

politicians saw the nature of the world's predicament as clearly as Churchill, and even he might have been less perceptive if he had been in office during the thirties instead of in opposition. Even he, even if he had retained his clarity of vision, would have found it extremely difficult to induce the British, let alone other nations, to act against Hitler in time. Public opinion throughout the West had learned many lessons from the First World War, almost all of them wrong. It clung to its errors with passionate determination. The errors were not all of the same stripe. Some people favoured pacifism, others an Anglo-German *rapprochement*, others distrusted their government too deeply to collaborate with it until the anarchists, socialists or communists had remodelled it. All were chasing shadows. Yet the moral is not that they were uniquely silly or misguided. In their opinionated bewilderment and their reluctance to commit themselves to action they strongly resembled their descendants. The decade of the thirties remains supremely worth study for that reason. For, as the history of the United States was to show, though a lot was learned, correctly this time, in the immediately following years, the underlying difficulties of conducting a wise diplomacy in a democracy were not removed, and in the sixties they reasserted themselves with appalling results. If they are not to do so yet again, with perhaps the worst result of all, they must at least be faced, and their history be studied.

World peace was already in great danger when Franklin Roosevelt took office. Adolf Hitler had become German Chancellor just over a month previously, and Japan was continuing her conquest of Manchuria. It is clear that Roosevelt hoped to redeem this state of affairs, and he never gave up trying. He was influenced by the example of both Theodore Roosevelt and Woodrow Wilson, and he had a deep personal revulsion from the horrors of modern warfare, which he had seen on a visit to the Western Front in 1918. In an election speech in 1936, he said:

I have seen blood running from the wounded. I have seen men coughing out their gassed lungs. I have seen the dead in the mud. I have seen cities destroyed. I have seen two hundred limping, exhausted men come out of line – the survivors of a regiment of one thousand that went forward forty-eight hours before. I have seen children starving. I have seen the agony of mothers and wives. I hate war.

In this he spoke perfectly for his fellow-citizens, and his speech was acclaimed. At the same time his sense of himself as a man of destiny made his duties as Commander-in-Chief attractive to him rather than otherwise. He wanted to take the lead in a vigorous search for world peace, but failing that he was happy to look after America's defences. He devoted a good deal of highly successful effort to his 'Good Neighbor' policy: to safeguarding America's rear by cultivating good relations with Canada and Latin America. The United States withdrew its troops from Haiti, which they had been occupying since 1914; it renounced the notorious Platt Amendment, which gave it the right to intervene at will in Cuba; it began the long process of dismantling its unilateral control over the Panama Canal; and it renounced the right of unilateral intervention anywhere in the western hemisphere. Theodore Roosevelt would not have approved of his cousin's activities, but the Latin Americans did: FDR became stupendously popular south of the Rio Grande, which was a good thing for his country during the Second World War. As a former naval person he was happy to build up the US navy to the modest degree allowed by the Washington Naval Treaty, using PWA funds to do so; but he had to take care, for when in 1936 he presented the largest peacetime naval budget in American history the pacifists made a loud and vigorous, though unsuccessful, protest. He neglected the army. He was happy to let his Secretary of State, Cordell Hull, ride his hobby-horse of free trade, once the collapse of the London Economic Conference had made the exercise futile. The world's central problem, the policies of the aggressor nations, remained untouched.

Institutional reasons partly determined this. Foreign policy and its execution were still the more or less exclusive prerogative of the State Department: the White House had not yet sprouted its modern jungle of auxiliary offices, such as the National Security Council, to supplement, duplicate or, in some administrations, supersede State; the Pentagon was a thing of the future; so was the Central Intelligence Agency. And during the first five years of his Presidency Roosevelt had little time for foreign affairs. So his interventions in the field were almost inescapably impulsive, ill-informed, ill-thought-out and transitory. On the whole it is surprising that they were no worse. This was in part due to Roosevelt's own concern and intelligence, in part to his effective collaboration with the State Department team. But between them FDR and his advisers shaped one of the feeblest eras of American diplomacy.

Hull was a Congressional veteran who had drafted the first income tax law under the Sixteenth Amendment in 1913, had led the 'dry' faction at the 1932 Democratic convention (he came from the godly state of Tennessee) and was picked for his post in the same way as Vice-Presidents are. He had been an outstanding supporter of Roosevelt-for-President among the Southern Democrats; he had been a life-long campaigner for the good old Democratic cause of lower tariffs; and he had useful links with his former colleagues in the Senate. He was an able and tenacious negotiator when given the chance; a dignified figure, who was prepared to stick stubbornly to his view if he thought it correct, but nevertheless always showed a becoming deference to his chief. He entirely lacked the vision and energy which might have helped Roosevelt to face reality himself and induce his countrymen to do likewise. As the long train of disaster unrolled, Cordell Hull could always find a reason for not doing anything this time. On the other hand he was always prepared to say something, especially if he saw a chance to lecture unreceptive ears (Japanese for choice) on the sanctity of treaties, the importance of the peaceful resolution of international disputes and the glories of free trade. Otherwise his chief skill was that of ousting his rivals from the President's councils, and even there he usually took his time. Nor were his deficiencies made good by his officials. True, American ambassadors were often perceptive – Dodd at Berlin, Messersmith at Vienna, Grew at Tokyo, all sent wise and frequent warnings – but it was not convenient to pay them any attention. Instead (for instance) Hull publicly disowned Hugh Johnson when in 1934 the General said that events in Germany (he was thinking of the Jews) made him sick – 'not figuratively, but physically and very actively sick'. So little did Hull share this feeling that he rejected every opportunity to rescue Hitler's victims: between 1933 and 1941 some 75,000 German Jews only were allowed into the United States, although even under the restrictive arrangements of the 1924 Immigration Act something like 180,000 might have come. In this matter, as in too much else, Hull and the State Department's responses were timid, unimaginative and legalistic.

This might have mattered less if Roosevelt had seen his way to being more imaginative himself; but he too was constrained by a circumscribed vision. Even as late as the 1940 elections he seems to have thought that America might contrive to stay at peace without handing victory in the Second World War to Hitler; and there is no reason to question the solidity of his earlier commitment to the base policy of peace at any price. Furthermore, as he showed again and again during the thirties, he would not allow foreign policy considerations of any kind to interfere with his domestic programme. The Italian invasion of Ethiopia; the Spanish Civil War; the German occupation of Austria and Czechoslovakia – in every one of these crises Roosevelt felt himself unable to take any effective action because of possible adverse repercussions in Congress. He loathed the turn the world was taking, but did not feel he could do anything about it.

To judge from the response of Congress and the people to the deepening crisis, he was right in his assessment. Between 1933 and 1935, when comparatively little was happening, he was allowed a fairly free hand; but after the outbreak of the Ethiopian War and Hitler's announcement of German re-armament, he was put on a very short rein by various Neutrality Acts. For the American people did not see the rise of fascism as a signal for action; rather they took fright and did all they could to stay out of trouble. Their state of mind is commonly spoken of as isolationist, but this label, though convenient and emotionally accurate, obscures the point that at least two tendencies were at work. One was unilateralism: the conviction that America must remain a free agent, as she had been ever since her treaty with France was ended during the French Revolution. Unilateralism took no account of the technological and economic changes which had made physical isolation impossible and permanent collaboration with friendly nations essential. It was strongly nationalistic and well entrenched in the Senate. It was a convenient rationale, not just for the widespread dislike and distrust of foreigners, those benighted creatures who did not enjoy the benefit of American institutions, but for the steadily increasing resentment, in Congress and among conservatives generally, of the steadily increasing power of the Presidency. It was easy enough to argue that unless Roosevelt was closely watched he might drag America into a war so that he could, as war leader, gratify his well-known dictatorial tendencies and overthrow American democracy. Nonsense, of course; but nonsense which all the enemies of that man in the White House found it very easy to accept. Most of the more contemptible manifestations of isolationism grew from this root.

The other tendency was pacifism, a more honourable but no less foolish persuasion. It had given the world the Kellogg–Briand Pact in the twenties; its proponents were incapable of acknowledging that conditions in the thirties demanded a different sort of response. The Depression took its toll. Domestic economic problems seemed more pressing, more real, than any foreign scare, and diminished confidence that America had answers for the world's difficulties. Above all there was the memory of the trenches. Modern war was horrible, and getting more so. Every bomb dropped by the Japanese on China, or by the fascists on Guernica, was one more argument for steering clear of it; the pacifist mentality found it too painful, as well as too humiliating, to admit that America might no longer have the power to do so. There is something moving about the way in which these citizens and their representatives, whether in Congress or in such bodies as the Women's International League for Peace and Freedom, laboured for peace, not out of weakness or cowardice, but because it was a value they cherished. Their pacifism contrasts finely with the war-mania of imperial Japan or Hitlerite Germany. But it was no less self-defeating, for by weakening America it made an attack upon her more likely, not less.

All isolationist tendencies were strengthened by the inquest which Congress and revisionist historians conducted on the First World War during the thirties. The conclusion was reached that America had been dragged into it solely by the wiles of financiers who had invested in an Allied victory. The invasion of Belgium, the sinking of the *Lusitania*, unrestricted submarine warfare, the Zimmermann telegram, were all discounted; and Woodrow Wilson's belief that the Allied cause, being that of democracy and legality, must also be that of America, was derided or ignored, like his beliefs that only through international organization could further war be averted, and that the world was now so closely knit that the United States could not stand aloof any more, even if it wanted to. Wilson's reputation has probably never stood lower than in the thirties (the increasing futility of the League of Nations did not help it); and among the consequences were the Neutrality Acts of 1935, 1936 and 1937. The last of these made earlier, temporary arrangements permanent. Among the actions it outlawed were the sale of arms or loan of funds to belligerents, the arming of American merchant vessels and sailing on belligerent ones. Belligerents wishing to buy non-contraband goods must pay for delivery and ship them themselves – the so-called 'cash and carry' provisions. Above all the President was given no freedom of choice. When war broke out he was required to invoke the Act, and he was not allowed to discriminate between aggressor and victim: neither might receive armaments from the United States. It is not surprising that the *New York Herald-Tribune* said that the act should have been called 'an act to preserve the United States from intervention in the War of 1914–18'. Roosevelt, with the battle over the Supreme Court on his hands, did not wish to make more trouble for himself by vetoing the law, so he signed it, an action he bitterly regretted a year or two later. The chief consequence was that the conduct of American diplomacy, already difficult enough, became nearly impossible: only the outbreak of war in 1939 made repeal possible, and even then it was a slow and piecemeal business. Meanwhile Roosevelt had more or less lost control of foreign policy. He did not even try very hard to induce Congress to relax the immigration laws to admit Jewish refugees, for the opposition to any such liberalization was blindly, cruelly obstinate. A widespread, erroneous impression was that the faltering economy, of which mass unemployment seemed to be so permanent a feature, could not stand the strain of an influx of penniless refugees; and uglier forces were at work. Anti-semitism was active and vocal, finding expression in such demagogues as the 'radio priest', Charles Coughlin, and the professional rabble-rouser, Gerald L. K. Smith, and in such organizations as the German-American Bund, which was lavishly supported by Hitler. As a result of all this America, at the time of the Munich crisis, was impotent. All Roosevelt could do was bombard the Europeans with messages urging them to make peace on just and liberal principles – messages which Hitler ostentatiously ridiculed and which unconsciously bore out an earlier remark of Neville Chamberlain's: 'It is always best and safest to count on nothing from the Americans but words.'

The worst consequence was that when war broke out American neutrality positively favoured the Nazis, since it was not they who needed to procure ships, planes, guns and other military supplies from the United States. Roosevelt had foreseen this, but his efforts to enlighten Congress were for long entirely in vain. The chairman of the Senate Foreign Relations Committee was Key Pittman of Nevada, who cared for nothing but the silver lobby: among his other disqualifications for the post was his habit of drinking himself into a stupor. Senator Borah of Idaho was still active: when, in August 1939, Roosevelt told him that war in Europe was imminent, he blandly contradicted the President. His own sources, he said, were better than the State Department's, and assured him that there was not going to be a war.

The best that can be said for the Americans is that they were no more foolish than the British, and were infinitely less so than the Germans or the Japanese or J. V. Stalin. Nor should it be forgotten that one of the minor constraints on Roosevelt was the attitude of the other democratic governments. Whenever he proposed a course of action the British were certain to find it too risky. Not the least shocking consequence of Chamberlain's appeasement policy was that it kept the British at arms' length from the Americans. Roosevelt's offers of help were coolly declined, and he was reduced to watching while a policy in which he did not believe failed utterly.

Even so late as 1940 only 7.7 per cent of all Americans were ready to enter the war;[1] in May 1941, according to a Gallup poll, 79 per cent of the people were still opposed to a voluntary entry, though by then most of them expected to be forced in. But too much should not be made of this state of mind; as the shrewd German ambassador had observed previously, if the Americans were frightened enough they might change from isolationists to interventionists in one jump. Nor was that all. As the circumstances which had driven Woodrow Wilson to go to war reappeared, worse than ever, Wilsonian ideology came to life again. Roosevelt, for instance, had been an isolationist perforce throughout the first six years of his Presidency; but after Munich he changed his stance decisively. The world had come right to the brink of war and been saved only by the sacrifice of Czechoslovakia. A month later Hitler unleashed a furious terror against the German Jews. They were beaten up by Nazi thugs, their property was looted, they were stripped of their civil rights: tyranny let loose an obscene madness. 'I myself could scarcely believe that such things could occur in a twentieth-century civilization,' said Roosevelt. Peace, democracy and justice were in danger while Hitler ruled, and the President began to plan accordingly. Suppose the Nazis began to meddle in Latin America? FDR renewed his courtship of the southern republics, and began the long job of expanding, training and equipping the armed forces of the United States, lest Hitler try to come in by the back door. He still had to move warily, because of isolationist opinion, and by September 1939 was not visibly in a much stronger position, either internationally or politically, than he had been a year before; but in fact the gathering of America's strength had begun, and was not to be reversed.

Hitler's brutality and recklessness were bringing about a great change in American opinion. People were beginning to realize that he would never stop while there was a frontier to cross or a statesman to double cross. Ambassador Messersmith held that the logic of the dictator's career would drive him on to fight the world, so the United States should resist him at once, while it could still have some allies. Cordell Hull and other good Wilsonians who had pinned their faith on international law were outraged and frightened chiefly by Hitler's lies, by his contempt for treaties and all the machinery of conciliation. If they were not yet ready to relinquish the dream of peace, they, and soon most other intelligent Americans, with their profound commitment to democracy and the idea of progress, found the

---

1 A. Russell Buchanan, *The United States and World War II* (New York, 1964), Vol. i, p. 14. It is not perhaps surprising that so many Americans shivered on the brink once they saw that they had reached it, and Buchanan makes the excellent point that American entry would not have helped very much at that particular date.

prospect of a world in which such a creature as Hitler was dominant so revolting that even if he had been no sort of threat to their more material interest they would still have felt it necessary to thwart and defeat him if they could. For the interests of great nations, and of that humanity of which great nations are only a part, cannot be reduced to the calculations of a balance-sheet – though some of the great corporations, which had kept Mussolini supplied with oil during the Ethiopian War and which went on trading profitably with the Nazis to the very eve of war, in the teeth of their government's protests, seemed to think otherwise. Standard Oil, New Jersey, actually formed a cartel with IG Farben, the great Nazi petrochemical company, and refused to develop 100-octane aviation fuel for the US army because that institution, fussily, would not let it share the secrets of its research with Farben.

Other Americans were still unconvinced. The isolationists kept up a loud chorus of denunciation and formed the America First Committee to make sure that the 'mistake' of 1917 was not repeated. America First had an amazing range of supporters, from proto-Nazis to socialists – even to the Communist party, which vigorously opposed all American involvement in the 'imperialist' war from the time of the Nazi–Soviet Pact (August 1939) to Hitler's invasion of the Soviet Union (June 1941). Apart from such cynical or merely deluded elements the America Firsters all seem to have believed that the war was just another power struggle, Hitler's victory in which, though no doubt deplorable, would not seriously affect America; that intervention in the war, on the other hand, would infallibly destroy American democracy, wreck its economy, bring about a totalitarian government, lead to persecution of the Jews, the German-Americans and the Italian-Americans, or, alternatively, to a Jewish dictatorship, or to communism, or to millions dead, or anyway, to rationing; and that it was impossible that Hitler would or could attack the impregnable United States, shielded by its oceans and its huge military strength (the possibility of attack from Japan was never mentioned). In other words, the frightful consequences that the internationalists expected from further appeasement would come, the isolationists believed, from intervention in any form; and they resisted all the measures of the administration for dealing with the emergency, though they never succeeded in stopping them. They simply did not believe that, in the words they attributed to Franklin Roosevelt (not very inaccurately, in spite of his denials), America's frontier was on the Rhine.

The President was undeterred. When, in the spring of 1940, Hitler let loose the *blitzkrieg* and the nations of Western Europe went down before him like ninepins (Denmark, Norway, Holland, Belgium, France), Roosevelt's policy became one of all aid to the Allies short of war. The Republicans, convening in Philadelphia, nominated Wendell Willkie for the Presidency. Willkie was of German descent and had been a leading opponent of the New Deal throughout the thirties: as head of a huge electricity company he had been particularly opposed to the TVA. The nomination of such a man, and the dominance of isolationists in the Republican party, seem to have decided Roosevelt to defy tradition and seek a third term in office. Willkie himself, a renegade Democrat, turned out to be both an international-ist and comparatively liberal domestically; he had an appealing personality, and in Roosevelt's opinion was the strongest candidate the Republicans could have chosen. So it was necessary for the Democrats to field their own strongest man, and there could be no doubt who that was: 'WE WANT ROOSEVELT!' roared the galleries at the Democratic convention in Chicago. FDR had been talking wistfully for a year and more of the charms of retirement, but he did not propose to leave the field to his enemies and the enemies of the New Deal, whether within or without the Democratic party. The 1940 election thus became a referendum on the Roosevelt years. The President ensured that by choosing Henry Wallace, the most liberal member of his Cabinet, as his running-mate. He had grown weary of the antics of 'Cactus Jack' Garner, who had exploited the Vice-Presidency to become the unofficial leader of the opposition in the Senate; by forcing Wallace on a very reluctant convention he showed that, whatever might be the case in Congress, he was master of the Democratic party nationally, and his were the policies it would have to support. Foreign policy was not neglected. Although in his speeches Roosevelt stressed his commitment to peace (one statement, 'Your boys are not going to be sent into any foreign wars,' was to come back to plague him), in his actions he showed himself the staunch friend of Britain, now fighting desperately for her life, and the resolute enemy of Hitler. As the election campaign began he traded fifty old destroyers for military bases in British possessions in the western hemisphere, by-passing Congress (and thereby provoking new cries of 'dictatorship!' from the isolationists, and from Irish-Americans such as Senator Walsh of Massa-chusetts, who blindly hated Britain); and as it roared to its climax he signed the Selective Service Act, which conscripted young men in peacetime, an unheard-of breach with tradition. Willkie denounced him as a warmonger, accused him (rather inconsistently) of having neglected America's defences, and pointed out that the Depression had not been ended by eight years of the New Deal; but he was answered by events. The new defence programmes created a huge industrial demand (Roosevelt had called for the building of 50,000 planes a year); suddenly, at last, there was work again for everybody, and every front page of every newspaper in the country could not help reporting every day the efforts that the administration was making to improve America's security. America First was answered by the bipartisan Committee to Defend America by Aiding the Allies, and Roosevelt took two Republicans into his Cabinet: Henry L. Stimson as Secretary of War and Frank Knox, who had been Landon's Vice-Presidential candidate, as Secretary of the Navy. The landslide was not quite on the scale of 1932 and 1936; FDR's popular vote held steady, but the Republicans gained heavily, so that his majority was no more than five million (out of fifty million voting), but he carried thirty-eight states. Meantime the staunch resistance of the British people and the heroism of the Royal Air Force had dealt Hitler his first defeat. In October he called off his invasion plan (Operation Sea Lion) until the spring. It was never renewed.

Britain was still far from secure. The Battle of Britain might have been won, but the Battle of the Atlantic was intensifying. Vessels were being sunk far faster than British shipyards could replace them. Just as bad, money was running out: very soon Britain would be unable to pay for the supplies she needed. Roosevelt's response was threefold. He educated the American public in some of his most dramatic speeches. At stake in this war, he said, were the four essential freedoms, of speech, of religion, from want and from fear; America must become the arsenal of democracy. He greatly increased US naval activity in the Atlantic, most of which he in effect annexed. He pushed the so-called Lend-Lease Act through Congress in the first months of 1941. It would be wrong to beggar Britain while aiding her, he explained; he wanted to 'get away from the dollar sign' (he remembered the damage that war-debts had done to Anglo-American relations after 1920); he intended to say to Britain, 'We will give you the guns and ships that you need, provided that when the war is over you will return to us in kind the guns and ships that we have loaned you;' in a press conference he compared the idea to lending a neighbour a garden hose to put out a fire. It was a pious fraud: the hose was never likely to be returned. The important thing about the Lend-Lease Act was that it authorized the President to give what military aid he liked to whom he liked 'in the interest of national defence'. A few months earlier he had set up an Office of Production Management to shift American industry from peacetime production to military production as much as was necessary. These two actions were even more significant than they seemed at the time. They not only conferred enormous new economic and political power on the Presidency; they began the transformation of Woodrow Wilson's 'great, peaceful people' into the world's first superpower, with all that that entailed. And Britain survived.

By May 1941, Roosevelt seems to have become convinced that the United States would enter the war sooner or later; but he refused to fire the first shot, so important was it to bring a united nation to battle. Britain was left alone to fight aggression in the West. China in the East was given somewhat niggardly Lend-Lease aid; partly because of competing claims on American production, partly because Roosevelt was still hoping against hope to preserve peace of some sort in the Pacific so that all efforts could be concentrated on the Atlantic theatre. American pilots were allowed to volunteer for service with Chiang Kai-shek, however, in Colonel Claire Chennault's so-called 'Flying Tigers' group.

America gave Hitler every provocation during this period; but he did not take the bait. It was his only show of prudence, if that is what it was: it seems likelier that his crazy dream of omnipotence (a common criminal fantasy) debarred him from recognizing that a war against the United States would almost certainly end in defeat. Whatever the case, he evaded serious discussion of the matter. He was not really interested in the degenerate democracy. Besides, he had a penchant for taking risks, and it had previously served him well. Britain was the only enemy still in the field against him, and she did not look very formidable. He did not worry much about war against Russia, either, for on 22 June 1941 he invaded her, although the campaign in the West was still undecided. His flair would see him through.

None the less, he was not above an attempt to keep the United States busy outside his sphere. The Japanese and German governments had engaged in a mutually distrustful flirtation for years, the high points being the signature of an Anti-Comintern Pact in 1936 and of a Tripartite Alliance in 1940 (Italy being the third signatory). Neither party was clear what this association would achieve, but both hoped that something would turn up. At one point Hitler thought he had found a useful ally for his attack on Russia: only the Japanese thereupon signed a neutrality treaty with Moscow. The Japanese, with rather more reason, thought that Germany might be of use by keeping the Western powers in check. Reckoning in this fashion they lured each other down the path to their common destruction, and America to her meeting with destiny in the Pacific.

In some respects the question of Asia's future was more revolutionary than that of the future of Europe. In the 1930s the collapse of the Versailles system was certainly endangering the world, and the activities of Hitler and Stalin were poisoning civilization; but in Asia an even mightier rope of events was being twisted. The impact of modern industrialism on the East had been shattering. In the previous century, for example, steamboats and railways had destroyed the structure and gravely wounded the culture of that ancient China which had always previously survived and absorbed barbarian incursions, however violent. The result had been a period of complete Western hegemony, in which Britain, France, Germany, Russia and the United States had all acquired Eastern empires – Britain, as usual, taking the lion's share: India, Burma, Malaya, Hong Kong, part of Borneo and a predominant position in China which her statesmen were too canny to try to turn into formal rule. In the palmy days of Edward VII it had looked as if it would all go on for ever. Europeans despised Asiatics both racially and culturally; the strength of the great empires seemed unchallengeable, except by each other. When in 1911 a revolution broke out in China it only seemed to make that country weaker than ever: after the First World War she was little more than the geographical expression one historian has called her.[2] That did not stop the Versailles powers pledging themselves to preserve China's territorial integrity and independence: they wished to continue to plunder the helpless giant without getting in each other's way.

But the old system was already doomed. Britain, France and Holland were, after 1918, over-stretched: they lacked the resources to defend themselves and their empires at the same time. And Japan, an Asian power, had

2 R. W. Van Alstyne, *The United States and East Asia* (London, 1971), p. 111.

with astonishing speed learned everything the West had to teach, and was very well placed to apply the lessons. Japan, her rulers decided, had a mission, like other civilized states: she would be the leader of a resurrected Asia. A new empire would be carved out, superseding all the old ones, in which grateful, disciplined Koreans, Manchurians, Chinese, Filipinos, Indonesians – even, perhaps, Indians – would learn the arts of civilization from the new master race. Japanese exports, which were unable to cross such barriers as the American tariff, would instead monopolize a huge market created by conquest. Dominance in the East Indies and Malaya would ensure supplies of oil and rubber, and thus make Japan self-sufficient in raw materials at last.

Such was Japan's imperial dream. In retrospect it is easy enough to see that it was preposterous. Left to herself, Japan might have been able to maintain her position in the East a little longer than proved possible for the European powers; but the inexorable resurrection of China would have defeated yellow imperialism in the end as it defeated white. In fact the dream had been broken before Pearl Harbor. For though the Chinese were fighting a civil war (between the Kuomintang and the communists) as well as the Japanese, the latter's military enterprise was, by 1939, getting nowhere. Supplies were still reaching both Chiang Kai-shek and Mao Tse-tung; there was no sign that the 'Chinese Incident' (as mealy-mouthed Tokyo called it) was coming to an end; the strain on Japanese society was deepening. But the events of the thirties had at least demonstrated, for all with eyes to see, that the days of the white man's ascendancy were over. Europeans now traded with China only on Japanese sufferance; and their colonies in Hong Kong, Indo-China, Malaya and the islands survived only while the Japanese spared them.

These developments created enormous difficulties for America. She might, in theory, have acquiesced in the Japanese adventure and traded with the new empire until it foundered. But this would have been to conspire with an aggressor nation against the people of China; would have been to frankly condone imperialism; would have led to a quarrel with Japan's rivals and America's friends, the European democracies, which were also, by an unfortunate chance, the only important European imperialists (Portugal did not count, and Germany had lost her colonies after the First World War); and would have brought on a ceaseless storm of protest and denunciation from the American businessmen and missionaries who still hoped to exploit China themselves. Besides, the United States had colonies in the Pacific (the Philippines, Guam, Hawaii) which, thanks to the Washington Naval Conference of 1921–2, were inadequately defended. Now that Japan was the predominant naval power in the western Pacific she could pick off America's possessions at any time. The possibility did not make Washington feel any more kindly towards her.

Yet the intense pacifism of the inter-war years stopped America from attempting any resolute and effective preventive action. The Chinese were helped, but only enough to irritate the Japanese, not enough for victory (for one thing, the Americans were backing the wrong horse, and sent all their aid to the corrupt and lethargic Kuomintang instead of to the communists). When, in December 1937, an American warship, the USS *Panay*, was bombed on the river Yangtse, the United States protested, but no more. Protest became a habit. Then, very late in the day, America began gradually to deny Japan access to the raw materials she needed to carry on her war – as much because the United States needed the materials itself as because they would be used by the Japanese against China, and possibly against the French, Dutch and British Empires. By the summer of 1941 an American embargo was denying Japan oil, iron and rubber.

It was at this point that the cross-purposes of the two countries took a tragic turn. Going somewhat beyond the President's intentions, American diplomats made it a cardinal point that Japan must cease her war of aggression and would get no supplies until she did; but they offered her no positive inducements to behave. Perhaps there were none to offer. China was an irremovable stumbling-block. The United States could not recognize Japanese hegemony in North China, or the Japanese conquest of Manchuria, or even, it seemed at times, the conquest of Korea (which Japan had ruled since 1905): apart from anything else, any such recognition would have been patently inconsistent with American objections to Hitler's empire-building. It was too late to adopt a policy of free trade, admitting Japanese exports and sending raw materials in return: the Japanese armed forces would never have accepted it as an adequate reason for getting out of China. The embargo, in short, was the very least the Americans could do to mark their serious displeasure with the Chinese Incident; but by hampering the Japanese in their war it affronted what they defined as one of their most vital interests, a point not properly understood in the State Department.

A similar blindness afflicted the Japanese. They wanted a free hand to get on with their unjust war against China; and for that purpose they laid claim to the supplies from Malaya and the Dutch East Indies which were sustaining British's battle for survival against Hitler. This was a vital interest of the West, and in common prudence Japan should have respected it (just as, in common prudence, the British should have taken greater pains either to avert or to resist a Japanese attack). But the wilder elements were in control in Tokyo. Hitler's assault on Russia meant that for a long time Japan would not need to worry about the intentions of the USSR. Her northern flank secure at last, she could safely plunge southwards. Emperor Hirohito could do no more than voice his doubts; the naval command had swallowed its own; the politicians, tamed by the ever-present threat of assassination by the military, did as they were told; on 16 October General Tojo was summoned to form a new Cabinet. Plans were laid for war with Britain and the United States. The Japanese did not suppose that they could successfully invade America, but they did believe that by swift action they could establish an impregnable defensive zone in the western Pacific, and that crushing blows in the East would convince the American people that there was nothing to be gained from obstructing Japan any longer. In the utmost secrecy Admiral Yamamoto prepared his strike force, believing, as he did, that 'we will have no hope of winning unless the US fleet in Hawaiian waters is destroyed'.

Washington expected an attack of some kind. Throughout 1941 negotiations had been proceeding, but neither side made offers which the other felt able to accept. Roosevelt, desperately anxious to concentrate on the European and Atlantic war, which would be even harder to win if war broke out in the Pacific, did his utmost to postpone a final breach, in the hope that if he delayed long enough the Japanese might decide to stay at peace after all; and he was reluctant to fire the first shot in any theatre. Japan was nearly as hesitant. On the Emperor's orders Tojo made a last peace offer, for militarism, despotism and fanaticism co-existed in Japanese minds with a powerful interest in Western civilization and an especial fascination with America. After all, it had been Commodore Matthew Perry, USN, who had forced open the sealed islands to Western trade, techniques and ideas. 285,000 Japanese were settled in Hawaii and California. Relations between the two countries had been increasingly close for nearly a hundred years – always excepting the vital realm of trade; and even there Japan had taken nearly two billion dollars worth of American exports during the thirties. Respect for American strength was almost equal to Japanese readiness to defy it if necessary. The US government found the Japanese offers of immediate evacuation of Indo-China and eventual withdrawal from China inadequate, for they depended on the resumption of American exports of strategic goods to Japan and the abandonment of the Philippines: in effect, acceptance of Japanese hegemony in the Far East. Hull rejected them contemptuously and put forward his own counter-proposals, which Japan could not and was not expected to accept.

So war was more or less inevitable, and on 7 December 1941, thanks to the brilliance of their cryptographers in cracking Axis codes, the Americans were able to decipher and read the Japanese government's latest orders to its envoys in Washington before the envoys themselves could do so. These orders showed that something was going to happen immediately. All the signs were that the Japanese were preparing an attack to the south; the army and navy staff, unconvinced by General MacArthur's belief that he could successfully defend his command, the Philippines, thought that the enemy would strike first there; accordingly the Chief of Staff, General George C. Marshall, flashed a warning to MacArthur. But as a matter of routine, the warning, that the Japanese were planning some sort of surprise attack at 1 p.m., Washington time, was also sent to other American forces, such as the ships of the Pacific Fleet in their base at Pearl Harbor in the Hawaiian island of Oahu.

A farcical series of accidents now supervened. December the seventh was a Sunday, when (as the Japanese well knew) by long tradition the

American services in peacetime took life easily, so much so that their telegraphic network closed down for the day and even General Marshall could not reactivate it in time. The warning could not be telephoned, as that might reveal to the Japanese that their code had been broken. In the circumstances it was thought best to send the message by the commercial network, Western Union. Unfortunately, although Marshall's telegram reached Honolulu with twenty-seven minutes to spare, the only means of getting it to naval headquarters was by entrusting it to a messenger boy on a bicycle. He did not prove speedy enough.

Other warnings had been ignored or misinterpreted. A Japanese midget submarine had been detected and sunk near the entrance to Pearl Harbor at quarter to seven that morning; nobody realized what she portended. Temporary radar stations had been installed at the base, and two keen young soldiers were practising on one of them. At two minutes past seven they detected aircraft approaching from the north and reported accordingly to their superior officer; unfortunately he assumed that they were American planes and did nothing (unless the legend is true that he arrested the soldiers for playing with radar sets out of hours). Everyone else at Pearl Harbor was in a weekend mood. Edgar Rice Burroughs (the creator of Tarzan), who had for some time been worried about the general lack of preparedness, was taking the air outside his house on a height in Honolulu from which he could see the tranquil ships of the Pacific fleet drawn up in shining rows. At 7.55 he was pleased to note the beginning of what he took to be a spectacularly realistic battle practice.

For Yamamoto had successfully gathered his forces to a point in the empty, un-isled seas of the north Pacific, 275 miles or so from Pearl Harbor. Torpedo bombers, dive bombers, high-level bombers, fighters – 360 planes in all – left the decks of his carriers, stormed down over Oahu and for nearly two hours hammered the arrogant Anglo-Saxons. Three battleships were sunk (*West Virginia, Arizona, California*), one capsized (*Oklahoma*), others were severely damaged, and many smaller craft were either damaged or sunk; 120 planes were destroyed;[3] 2,403 Americans (mostly sailors) were killed. The Japanese lost only twenty-nine planes and three midget submarines. At a quarter to three the messenger boy, who had sensibly kept out of the way during the battle, delivered his telegram. At 3.45 p.m., six hours after the Japanese force had withdrawn, the general commanding in Oahu ordered a blackout.

President Roosevelt called it all 'a day that will live in infamy', and so it is remembered. It was also one of history's most spectacular misjudgements. In the first place, the Japanese hit the wrong targets. Most of the ships could be and were made serviceable again; had the bombers attacked the oil

---

3 Not long before, Washington had sent word both to Pearl Harbor and to Clark Field in the Philippines urging alertness against saboteurs. Accordingly the planes on the ground were crowded wing tip to wing tip, which made them excellent targets, though not for saboteurs.

tanks and other onshore facilities, the effect of their raid might have been felt much longer. Second, although the aircraft carrier was already known to be the key to naval success in modern warfare, Yamamoto had attacked Pearl Harbor at a moment when all the carriers of the Pacific fleet were absent. Third, the fleet posed no immediate threat to Japan: it could have done nothing to impede her simultaneous swoop upon the Philippines, Singapore and the East Indies, and might as well have been left alone, if only to save supplies. Fourth and finally, nothing, not even the attack on Fort Sumter, has ever aroused the American people to wrath like this episode. The isolationism and pacifism of so many, the hesitations of so many more, were swept aside by this unprovoked attack of an aggressor power (for the Americans stuck stubbornly to the view that they had done nothing wrong in opposing Japanese incursions into Manchuria and China). 'Lick the hell out of them,' advised one isolationist Senator. He spoke for the country. America First dissolved overnight. It became the settled purpose of the mightiest nation in the world to destroy the Japanese Empire root, trunk, branch and twig. Three days after Pearl Harbor, Hitler, after some last-minute hesitation, honoured his promise to his ally by declaring war on the United States, thus clearing the last obstacle from Roosevelt's way. 'We are going to win,' said the President in a Fireside Chat, 'and we are going to win the peace that follows.' The new crusade to make the world safe for democracy could now officially be launched.

To us it is known as the Second World War. It is such a huge and familiar subject that a certain amount of omission is desirable and possible. For the purposes of this history it is necessary only to isolate the significance of the war for the American people, in terms of their experiences, achievements and hopes.

The war achieved what the New Deal had so falteringly attempted. The need to produce ships, planes, tanks, guns, bullets and bombs did what the need to rescue the unemployed could not. Roosevelt announced that the time for 'Doctor New Deal' was over; now it was the time for 'Doctor Win-the-War'; but the distinction was largely false. For the war brought its own new deal – a deal based on very different values and calculations from the peacetime one, but perhaps all the more effective for that. The democratic, capitalist nation of abundance suddenly began to show what it could do when put to it, and surprised even itself.

It was another period of migration. In four years twenty million Americans moved house as the needs of the wartime economy dictated; twelve million more left home to join the armed forces. Of all the states and regions California was the greatest gainer, for it was there that the shipbuilding and aerospace industries expanded most rapidly, and many of the millions who passed through the Golden State on their way to the Pacific war liked the climate so much that they promised themselves to return for good when the war was over. Perhaps this sort of alteration in the outlook of individual

Americans was the most important of the immediate social consequences of the war. The men in uniform who served overseas had a doubly revolutionary experience, especially if they saw action; but even the stay-at-homes did not stay at home. The United States became a nation of transients again; the structure of the economy became fluid, obeying new forces which would soon transform it almost out of recognition (especially when, after victory, freedom of consumer choice was restored and the production of automobiles was resumed); soon social, political and cultural patterns would alter in response.

The war replaced the Depression with a boom to dwarf the twenties. Like all booms it was unevenly experienced: thirty-five states actually lost population during the war, as their inhabitants went off, either to join the armed forces or to find war-work; half a million small businesses failed, because they could not get essential supplies, which were mopped up by the war industries; the demand for farm produce soared, but emigration from rural areas created a severe labour shortage which led to an amendment of the Selective Service Act: farm workers were no longer to be liable to conscription while they stayed on the farm. The production of bricks slumped, reflecting the fact that wartime housing, factory and office-building used materials that could be produced more cheaply and be more quickly erected. But the production of raw steel increased by roughly 20 per cent between 1940 and 1945; that of rayon and acetate yarn by 55 per cent; that of fuel oils by 44 per cent; that of wheat flour by 27 per cent. Only 560 locomotives were manufactured in 1940; in 1945, 3,213 were – the largest number since 1923. Prices went up by 28 per cent in the same period, which was good news for manufacturers; but it was not particularly bad news for the workers, whose average annual earnings increased, in real terms, by 40 per cent.

Indeed, these were good years for labour, and crowned the achievements of the New Deal. The power and influence of the unions reached their brief zenith. Total membership rose from 8,944,000 in 1940 to 14,796,000 in 1945, the increase being fairly equally shared between the AFL and the CIO. It was the unions more than anyone else that found the money and the campaign workers for Roosevelt's fourth Presidential campaign in 1944; and FDR, who drew great comfort from his rapport with the workers of America, was happy to bear their interests in mind: besides, he needed their co-operation for the war-effort. But the very strength of the unions, and their success in extending organization to industries and plants from which they had formerly been kept out, aroused their enemies. Much was made of the strikes that occurred, and it was true that, after falling in 1942 and 1943, the number of work stoppages rose rapidly in 1944 and 1945; but the impressive thing about this set of statistics is that in terms of working days lost, or duration of stoppages, the war years showed really substantial reductions, warranting Roosevelt's observation that the common cold did more than strikes to delay the invasion of Germany. Working men were as eager as anyone else to help the war-effort. But the conservatives were sufficiently alarmed and sufficiently powerful to put the Smith–Connolly Act through Congress in 1944, the first of many attempted interferences with the right to strike.

The impact of the war on African-Americans will be discussed in Chapter 25: suffice to say here that it was complex and far-reaching, and occasionally involved disgraceful violence. However, the worst episode of racial oppression to dishonour the American cause during the war involved not the African- but the Japanese-Americans. In 1940 about 129,000 of these lived on the West Coast, chiefly in California. First-generation Japanese (known among themselves as the Issei) were debarred by law from obtaining US citizenship, but their children, the Nisei, having been born in the United States, were automatically citizens and were beginning to bring forth a third generation, the Sansei. They were a blameless people, hard-working and peaceable, farmers and market gardeners for the most part. They had always suffered from the racial hostility of the white Californians, and after Pearl Harbor this burst into flame. The Nisei, it was contended, simply because of their race, were not to be trusted; they were probably all Japanese spies, and if a Japanese army ever landed would no doubt flock to join it (in actuality, 33,000 Japanese-Americans joined the US army, and their units were the most-decorated in American history). Feeling grew so intense that President Roosevelt, callously calculating that such action would help Californian morale, ordered the removal of the Issei and the Nisei to what he unblushingly called 'concentration camps' in Wyoming, Colorado, Arkansas and the Californian deserts. A strong resemblance to Indian removal and the Trail of Tears emerged when the Japanese-Americans' land was seized as soon as the owners had been rounded up. Except for Attorney-General Biddle, who protested at the blatant unconstitutionality of the policy, none of the men or institutions of American government come out of this story well: not Roosevelt, or the Governor of California, Earl Warren, or the US Supreme Court, which initially upheld the deportation and did not repudiate it until 1944. The last of the Nisei were not allowed to return to their homes, or what was left of them, until 1946.

About the only agreeable thing to record of this episode is that as a result of the abandonment and destruction of the Japanese farms and gardens the price of fresh fruit and vegetables soared on the West Coast, leading to bitter complaints from the white citizenry.

Yet such discreditable episodes must not be allowed to obscure the main point, which is the enormous energy and ability displayed by the American people in their pursuit of victory. It was a great creative, innovative period. The evolution of the federal government was sharply accelerated. The alphabet agencies of the New Deal were superseded or outnumbered by the bodies brought into being by the war: for example, the Supply Priorities and Allocation Board; the War Production Board; the War Manpower Commission; the National War Labor Board; the Office of Defense, Health and Welfare; the Office of Price Administration; the Office of Production Management; the War Shipping Administration; the Office of War Mobilization; the Office of Scientific Research and Development; the Federal Public Housing Authority; the Office of Defense Transportation; the War Food Administration. The RFC took on a new importance as it played a central part in organizing American finance and industry for war purposes through such subordinate bodies as the War Insurance Corporation, the Defense Plant Corporation, the Defense Supplies Corporation and the Rubber Reserve Corporation. Of course a great many of these agencies would be abolished after 1945; but meantime they broke down resistance to 'big government' in many quarters (especially conservative ones) which the New Deal had never been able to reach, at any rate since the collapse of the NRA. In part this resulted from a fundamental decision which Roosevelt took early in the war. He did not dismiss his New Dealers; indeed many of them, notably Harry Hopkins, Jesse Jones and Henry Morgenthau, gave distinguished service during the war; so did Mrs Roosevelt; but the Commander-in-Chief did not propose to rely exclusively on their abilities. In effect, he created a coalition government – a government which coalesced not simply Democrats and Republicans, but New Dealers and big business-men, members of the executive and members of Congress. He tried to enlist the services of Alfred Landon, the 1936 Republican Presidential candidate; he succeeded in enlisting those of Wendell Willkie. Businessmen were found who could organize the war industries (which included such novelties as the large-scale manufacture of penicillin). Above all, the Congressional leaders were brought into the centre of power. It was inevitable: both before and after Pearl Harbor, Roosevelt had a vast agenda of tricky, war-related business to get through Congress. Besides, everybody remembered what a nuisance Congress had been to Abraham Lincoln and Woodrow Wilson: it must not happen again. So gestures of reconciliation were made from both sides, and accepted. On the whole all went well. True, the conservative Republicans and Democrats who had dominated Congress since the 1938 elections used their new-found power to cut down some of the New Deal agencies, especially those which helped the poor: WPA, CCC, the Farm Security Administration; but it is hard to see those agencies surviving the outbreak of war and return of prosperity anyway; and on the whole the conservatives gave good service. Their role was well symbolized by James Byrnes, a racist reactionary of South Carolina, formerly a justice of the US Supreme Court, and before that a Senator: Roosevelt made him head of the Office of War Mobilization, with headquarters in the White House. Byrnes performed competently enough his important job, which consisted largely of persuading all the great home-front agencies to work smoothly together; but even though he was known unofficially as 'the Assistant President' the future lay elsewhere, with Senator Harry S. Truman of Missouri, chairman of the Senate Committee to Investigate the National Defense Programme. Truman, though he came from a Border state with strong Southern sympathies, had always been a loyal Roosevelt Democrat; he carried out his wartime job, of checking wasteful expenditure as much as possible, with conspicuous efficiency and good sense; it was said that he saved the country $15,000,000,000; and he earned gratitude in important quarters by accepting advice that he ought not to look into the use being made of certain huge appropriations which, voted by an ignorant Congress on the vaguest terms, were secretly being employed to build the first nuclear weapons.

Yet had he pursued his investigation at Oak Ridge, Tennessee, at Hanford, Washington, and at Los Alamos, New Mexico, he would not only have discovered the biggest threat to man's future ever yet evolved, indeed the force which was going to dominate that future; he would not only have found out where $2,000,000,000 of public money went; he would have seen the perfect microcosm of how the United States made war, and what the social and economic impact of its efforts would be. It was the colossal industrial power and skill of America that enabled her to do what none of the other belligerents could contrive: to build practicable atomic weapons in time for use in the war. She thereby created a whole new industry that by 1950 would be the biggest in the country. It entailed the uprooting of 45,000 workmen to build Hanford, and as many to build Oak Ridge – to create new cities in the wilderness. It entailed the use of material resources on the largest scale: at one moment General Groves, the head of the Manhattan Project, as it was code-named, indented for more copper than was to be had in the whole United States. It exploited the achievements of the New Deal: power generated by the great dams of the TVA system was put to use at Oak Ridge. It created boom conditions (for instance in the uranium industry) and foreshadowed a new wave of general prosperity. Life at the great laboratories parodied, echoed or foretold conditions elsewhere during the war and during the Cold War which followed it. Security was extremely tight for the civilians involved in the Project, whether scientists who built the bombs or workmen who built facilities for they knew not what;[4] General Groves kept them all under strict quasi-military discipline. Within the confines, there was a certain democratic camaraderie and a distant approximation to social equality, arising not merely from the traditions of the scientific profession but also from the fact that housing was provided, in standard units, by the federal government, and there was little to spend money on, so that pay differentials could not create significant stratification. And in the innermost circle of the scientists a crushing sense of their awesome responsibilities to the race and to the future began to grow.

4 It was also farcically inefficient. Thanks to the skill of the Allied intelligence services, no word of the nuclear project and its progress ever got to the Nazis; but the Russians, who were equally or more the object of suspicion for men like Groves, early realized that something big was going on and took highly effective steps to find out what.

Elsewhere even a strictly rationed, wartime America gave an impression of renewed energy, hope and confidence, while the deployment of her prodigious strength began rapidly to change the configuration of world politics. Before long both Germany and Japan had reason to regret their rashness in challenging Uncle Sam. Churchill's reaction to the news of Pearl Harbor had been simple: 'So we have won after all!' This meant many things at various stages of the war. Early in 1942 it meant, perhaps crucially, overwhelming material aid to Britain and Russia in their struggle. The US navy and air force could now be used without restraint to safeguard supplies on their way to Britain and Murmansk; in both cases, as Churchill and Stalin were to acknowledge, the result, which probably could not have been achieved by any other means, was that the German attack now began to break, East, West and South, on invincible walls. In the Pacific, the Japanese at first carried all before them: the Philippines fell, and General MacArthur, after leading a heroic defence of his base at Corregidor outside Manila, was forced to flee to Australia. (He was under orders to take up the supreme command of America's land forces in the Pacific theatre.) The men he left behind had to surrender, and were atrociously treated by their conquerors. Not only the Philippines, but the East Indies, Thailand, Malaya, Singapore and Burma fell to the Japanese; they threatened Australia; they stood on the borders of India. But they were on the brink, not just of the greatest naval war in their history or in the history of the US navy, but of the greatest naval war in the history of the world: a war which they lacked the resources either to win or, contrary to their cherished hopes, to sustain for more than a few years. Admiral Chester Nimitz was now in command of the whole Pacific Ocean area. When the Japanese tried to continue their advance down New Guinea and into the Solomon Islands, they were checked by Nimitz at the Battle of the Coral Sea (7–8 May 1942); their advance in the central Pacific was arrested at the Battle of Midway (3–4 June), where operational command was brilliantly exercised by Admiral Raymond Spruance. The Battle of the Coral Sea saved Australia; that of Midway saved the Hawaiian Islands; together they stopped the Japanese advance in the Pacific for good. Both battles exemplified something new in naval warfare: for the first time all the fighting involved planes; the ships of the two fleets never saw each other. Midway was a fitting first instalment of revenge for Pearl Harbor: it was a battle deliberately sought by Admiral Yamamoto, and American skill at naval warfare showed itself superior to his. After Midway nothing lay before the Japanese for three years but hard fighting and irreversible retreat, inch by inch, to their own shores, there to await final defeat.

First, however, America had to save the rest of the world. The matter of supplies was absolutely crucial: without them there could be no assurance that Britain and Russia would hold out. At one moment it seemed as if the Battle of the Atlantic had been lost at last, for the Germans were sinking Allied ships of all kinds faster than they were replaced. By the end of

November 1942 the U-boats had destroyed eight million tons of shipping, while the Allies had only been able to launch approximately six million. Gradually, however, as sailors and airmen gained experience, and as the huge American industrial machine swung into action (soon it would be delivering ships at the rate of more than one a day to the impatient navy), the Allies got the upper hand; the Battle of the Atlantic was won, though not ended, by the summer of 1943. Thenceforward supplies and troops could move eastward in comparative safety.

There remained the problem of Hitler, as apparently secure in his continental fortress as the Japanese seemed secure in their 'Greater East Asia Co-Prosperity Sphere'. Roosevelt and his advisers had made a strategic decision, months before Pearl Harbor, in conjunction with the British, to undertake the defeat of Germany before that of Japan. The President had to resist strong countervailing pressures at various moments during the war, but he never reversed this priority. For it had become his settled conviction that Nazi Germany posed a far worse long-term threat than did imperial Japan. Hitler in his madder moments may have deluded himself that all he wanted was a long period of peace during which he could cram Berlin with hideous palaces; his enemies knew him better. Like such forerunners as Alexander, Caesar and Napoleon, he was too restless ever to stop short of victory, death or total defeat. A world in which he had established a permanent dominion over Europe, Russia and the Middle East would not for long have been one in which the United States could peacefully enjoy life, liberty and the pursuit of happiness. Rather, a profoundly divided, economically faltering democracy would have confronted a triumphant German empire based on slavery; and sooner or later there would have been a war, possibly, for the Americans, a losing one. Such were Roosevelt's thoughts; they still seem plausible; and they implied the absolute necessity of getting to grips with Nazism as soon as possible, and of eventually uprooting it and all other forms of fascism from European soil. Doubtful at first, Americans soon came to welcome the assistance of communist Russia in this noble and necessary mission, and frequently girded at the apparent reluctance of the British to hurry forward with the attempt to re-open a second front in France to relieve the pressure on the Soviet Union. They were also for long so eager to obtain Russian aid against Japan that they were ready to pay a high price for the prospect of it. But although Japan was the worst-hated enemy and killed or wounded great numbers of American soldiers, sailors and airmen, she could never rationally be seen as posing a permanent threat to the survival of the United States and Western democracy in the way that Hitler's Germany did. Japan could certainly be defeated, as the Coral Sea and Midway had proved; the only question was how long it would take. To believe in the defeat of Hitler took, in 1942, rather more of a leap of faith.

Russian resistance was doing him frightful, possibly mortal, damage; but it was clearly essential to engage him elsewhere, for without some relief of pressure the Soviet Union might yet crack, and unless American soldiers were promptly set to fighting Germans, the country might lose interest in the Atlantic theatre and insist on giving priority to the war in the Pacific. For it was not only on the West Coast that Americans thought of the war as one of vengeance against Japan above all else; and in a people's war it may be that the followers, as much as the leaders, will decide what it is all about. Europe's claims to priority were not invariably and universally self-evident. American Jews could be content to know that they were fighting for the survival of their race and religion as well as for their own lives and happiness. A great many of their fellow-citizens were happy to go to the rescue of beleaguered Britain, whose resolute stand in 1940 had been much admired. Few, it is to be presumed, shared General MacArthur's passionate personal commitment to liberate the Philippines; much more representative was the case of Willie and Joe, who had joined the National Guard in peacetime for 'meals, clothes and a couple of bucks for Saturday drilling',[5] and then suddenly found that their division was mobilized and that they were full-time soldiers at $21 per month. Such soldiers, and their families at home, needed a lead, in strategy as well as ideals; and Roosevelt also had to consider those Americans who, as one journalist put it, 'want the United States to win so long as England loses. Some people want the United States to win so long as Russia loses. And some people want the United States to win so long as Roosevelt loses.' At the very least it was necessary to keep them all entertained.

So the British and American high commands, now working in double harness as the Combined Chiefs of Staff, evolved and executed (with much unhappy bickering) a triumphantly successful strategy. An American expeditionary force, commanded by General Dwight D. Eisenhower (soon to be universally known as 'Ike'), landed in North Africa and helped the British to clear it of Germans (1942–3); then Sicily and Italy were invaded, drawing off fifty or so divisions from the Russian front; then, when a great armada had been assembled and the Germans, it was hoped, had been sufficiently weakened and distracted in both East and South, the Western Allies at last invaded the continent, on D-Day, 6 June 1944. The Germans fought on tenaciously and occasionally brilliantly, but they were under too much pressure: as in 1914–18, but now against infinitely higher odds, they proved unable to sustain a two-front war. The Americans, British and French, under the supreme command of Eisenhower, pushed east; the Russians pushed west; German cities, industries and oil supplies were obliterated under a hurricane of bombs; at last, when even Hitler could see that the end was near, the Nazi dictator committed suicide, and soon

5 Bill Mauldin, 'A Rare Reunion with Willie and Joe'; see *International Herald-Tribune*, 8 June 1978. The National Guard is the federal militia. Bill Mauldin is one of America's ablest cartoonists; his G Is, Willie and Joe, are his most celebrated creations: he and they went through the war together.

afterwards the remains of the German forces surrendered unconditionally, in May 1945.

The war against Japan had not stood still meanwhile; in fact it had made wonderfully rapid progress. Nimitz and MacArthur had begun their counter-attack in New Guinea as early as July 1942: they had reconquered much of the enormous island by January 1943, and during the same time dogged heroism had captured the little island of Guadalcanal, thus giving a name of glory to America's military annals and opening a crack in the defence perimeter of the Japanese Empire. More than that: these campaigns taught the Americans the necessary techniques for their task. At the heart of them lay the idea of 'island-hopping'. Whereas the Japanese hoped to wage a war of defensive attrition, in which, by disputing every inch of ground, they might wear down their opponents, the Americans imposed a war of selective attack: they bypassed islands and bases of secondary importance and concentrated overwhelming force against those few points that they really had to capture. MacArthur's variant on this was 'leapfrogging': he simply bypassed strong Japanese points altogether, leaving them, as it was said, to wither on the vine while he seized weak points in their rear at comparatively light cost in American casualties. The Japanese fought with extraordinary heroism and tenacity, but in vain. Air power was the crucial factor: the Americans, thanks to their immense industrial superiority, were able to overwhelm their enemy with the production of planes and bombs, sinking his ships, destroying his fighters, flattening his defences on the ground. The US navy won victories large and small: for example, the Bismarck Sea (March 1943), the Philippine Sea (June 1944) and Leyte Gulf (October 1944); the army and the Marine Corps (which particularly distinguished itself in the capture of Iwo Jima in February and March 1945) finished the job. On 1 April 1945, MacArthur returned to the Philippines, as he had promised. The next island to be captured would be Okinawa, in the Ryuku chain; beyond lay Japan herself.

By the early summer of 1945, then, the war in Europe was over, and the war in the East was nearly as good as won; but long before then a new set of problems was beginning to perplex American policy: problems which were to prove much more intractable than those of the war had been. The United States had shown itself more than capable of dealing with its enemies; but the question of how to handle its friends now began to seem too much for it, for it was bound up with the question of how, after such an experience, the Americans envisaged their country's future place in the world.

Pearl Harbor had taught the Americans several useful lessons: that they ought anyway to look to their defences; that other nations could not be trusted to leave them alone; and that, if they wanted a stable, peaceful world order in which American values could make their way to universal acceptance while the American economy flourished, they would have to work for it. It was the old Wilsonian proposition, and the Americans (feeling, among other things, rather guilty about their rejection of the prophet in

1919–20) enthusiastically adopted the old Wilsonian programme: collective security and an international organization to keep the peace. America must always be ready to act effectively in concert with other free and peace-loving peoples to protect the good order of the world, which victory in the war was going to establish. In the years after 1945 a few solemn and eminent noodles like Senator Robert Taft (son of the twenty-sixth President) would try, in a half-hearted way, to revive the old isolationist verities; but they never made much headway. In future the crucial debate would be between schools of internationalists. This was all to the good; but although the Americans plumed themselves on their new-found strength and righteous purpose, and on having at last accepted Wilson's teaching, they overlooked the point that this teaching was no longer entirely adequate to the world's problems, if it ever had been. Many were as blind as ever to certain new and old and important lessons.

Their President and natural spokesman was not among them. Roosevelt has been called a 'renegade Wilsonian'.[6] This is rather unfair: FDR never wavered in his commitment to Wilson's vision of a green and peaceful world, and the manner in which the two men exercised their leadership in war was very similar. But Roosevelt had despaired of the original Wilsonian mechanisms for achieving universal peace and freedom (he dismissed the League of Nations as 'nothing more than a debating society and a poor one at that') and, more significantly, saw promise in the very principles and techniques which Wilson had renounced. If he did not actually favour secret treaties, he certainly believed in Great Power hegemony. After the war, he thought, responsibility for the happiness of the world would lie with those he called 'the Four Policemen' – the United States, the Soviet Union, Britain and China. He once went so far as to tell Molotov, the Soviet Foreign Minister, that all other countries should be disarmed. And he never wavered in his belief that agreement and co-operation between the Four Policemen were essential. That was why he was prepared to go to such lengths in wooing Stalin; and in spite of bursts of irritation at Russian boorishness he never gave up, even at the very end of his life. The Yalta agreements, negotiated with Stalin and Churchill in February 1945, were the high point of his policy and the achievement by which it should be judged.

The doctrine of the Four Policemen shows that Roosevelt had, as he claimed, made a thoughtful study of Woodrow Wilson's failure. The Versailles settlement had collapsed not, chiefly, because of its injustices, but because the victors of 1918 had lost the will to support it and each other. Roosevelt was determined to avoid this mistake. Unfortunately he overlooked the fact that, in statesmanship, too great a preoccupation to avoid the errors of the past makes it likely that you will fall into the errors of the present. Roosevelt's policy was ultimately at the mercy of forces somewhat

6 Daniel Yergin, *Shattered Peace: The Origins of the Cold War and the National Security State* (Harmondsworth, Penguin edn, 1980), p. 44.

outside his control, and it is perhaps the truest criticism that can be made of them that he did not take enough precautions to influence or combat these forces.

His first difficulty was with the American people. In the winter of 1940–41 he had talked, not of the Four Policemen, but of the Four Freedoms.[7] In August 1941, he and Churchill, meeting at Placentia Bay in Newfoundland, drew up and issued what they called the Atlantic Charter, setting out their war-aims. Their Charter lacked something of the vigour and precision of the Fourteen Points, but it committed the United Nations[8] to self-determination, democratic self-government, free trade, universal peace and universal disarmament. Excellent objects: perhaps they will be attained one day. Roosevelt did not say how they could be, and carefully excluded any mention of the League of Nations or any similar body from the document (the British had wanted one inserted). All in vain: in the next few years the American people convinced themselves that the 'wider and permanent system of general security' which the Charter mentioned must be a reformed League of Nations; and Roosevelt had to acquiesce in the idea. Characteristically, he wove his own idea of the Four Policemen together with the popular programme of a reformed League, so that the United Nations Organization, as it eventually emerged, consisted of the Security Council, where, it was thought, the great powers, each with its veto, would make the decisions that mattered, in concert, and a debating society, the General Assembly. A contradiction, then, was built into the very structure of the UN, last of the alphabet agencies, that did not promise well for its future, and arose from the contradictions and self-deceptions of American policy. A less airy approach might at the very least have spared the world something of the slow disillusionment with the new organization that has deepened with every decade since its foundation, as tragic an occurrence as the betrayal of 1919, so great were the hopes and energies that have thereby been brought to nothing.

Roosevelt liked to think that he was a more realistic statesman than Wilson, but the gulf between aspirations and actuality in his Four Freedoms speech is larger than anything in Wilson's utterances. Thus he promised 'a world-wide reduction of armaments to such a point and in such a thorough fashion that no nation will be in a position to commit an act of physical aggression against any neighbor – anywhere in the world. This is no vision of a distant millennium. It is a definite basis for a kind of world attainable in our own time and generation . . .' While his words raised hopes, his

---

7 See above, p. 560.
8 This phrase originated because Roosevelt did not want all the political trouble that would follow an attempt to negotiate an Anglo-American treaty of alliance and have it ratified by the Senate; so the term 'the Allies' could not be used accurately (though historians may write of 'the allies', since that is what they were). 'The United Nations' had a splendid ring, and need not, being a mere phrase, be submitted to Congress. It was one of Roosevelt's all-too-many, all-too-neat methods of circumventing the Constitution in wartime.

actions ensured their disappointment. It followed, also, that he could not teach the Americans the *realpolitik* he was practising: it would have shocked them too much. It might even have revived isolationism, for the Four Policemen arrangement was strikingly like an entangling alliance. Many Americans might have objected to a proposal that they should constantly patrol and discipline the wayward globe. So Roosevelt kept his own counsel and spoke of the association with Britain and the Soviet Union as a league of right-minded, democratic peoples. This, too, was unfortunate. Not only was it a travesty of the already notorious facts about Stalinism, it initiated the tradition by which Presidents in the next few decades came to think that foreign policy is too serious a matter to entrust to the people – hence a long story of deception and disaster.

The other pillars of the projected Rooseveltian peace were almost equally rickety. Nobody could object to the proposed Atlantic Utopia, but a great many people outside America were likely to have serious objections to any particular proposals for its realization. The British, for instance, had good reason to baulk at the principle of universal free trade, since their economic recovery in the thirties had largely been brought about by protection and imperial preference. They accepted the American programme only because the United States was so strong and they needed its help so much. They were somewhat rueful about the Bretton Woods agreement of 1944. This set up a new framework for international financial and economic relations; a world monetary system pegged to the dollar and governed, in the last resort, by the US Treasury. It was the last heavy financial sacrifice required of the British in the name of allied victory, and very heavy it was, providing a safety net for the British economy (through the International Monetary Fund) which was to prove invaluable in the coming decades, but at the same time saddling Britain with unduly heavy financial burdens that hindered her financial recovery. Yet Bretton Woods was a civilized arrangement, to which Britain freely consented, that had been properly and reasonably negotiated. There could be no guarantee that the United States would always behave so well. For the ghost of mercantilism walked again. It was an ancient tradition of American business that it could look to the federal and state governments for assistance when required; and now that the stricken world needed American capital as never before the pressures were naturally enormous to extend this tradition of usefulness into the foreign field. The combination of expansionist American free enterprise and the immense strength of the US government would be irresistible; and it might well lead the American people into all sorts of dangerous, undesirable or plain unjust dealings with other countries. 'The world must be made safe for the American profit system' was not a slogan that the world itself would find self-evidently just.

Then there were the French. President Roosevelt and the leader of Free France, General de Gaulle, were temperamentally quite incompatible, and de Gaulle's total intractability – necessary, he thought, if France was to regain her place among the nations – infuriated the Americans almost beyond reason. There are few funnier photographs in political history than those of the Casablanca Conference in January 1943, which show the Allied leaders trying to appear united after Roosevelt had knocked some French heads together. FDR looks furious, de Gaulle looks majestically aloof and Churchill looks as deeply miserable as anyone must have been who was a genuine friend of both sides. Then, the Chinese: it was clearer and clearer that the Kuomintang was a most dangerous associate, being corrupt, incompetent and bottomlessly selfish; but dared America try to collaborate with the communists? Were they really just the agrarian reformers that some alleged? In any case there would be the devil to pay with certain elements in the United States if Washington ditched Chiang in favour of Mao. Even if all these questions were settled satisfactorily, the question of Germany and Japan would remain. What on earth was to be done with them after victory? Henry Morgenthau put forward the suggestion that Germany should be de-industrialized; but this would have been so palpably a disaster for the whole European economy that the idea, tempting though it was to haters of the Hun, was quietly dropped. As for Japan, Roosevelt at the Casablanca Conference had called for the unconditional surrender of all the Axis powers: but did this really mean that the Japanese would not be allowed to surrender if they insisted on keeping their Emperor? Nobody knew.

Then, the United States was stoutly anti-colonial. Winston Churchill repeatedly spoke, acted and wrote in the spirit of his famous remark that he was not going to preside over the dissolution of the British Empire. This disquieted the Americans more than was necessary, for Churchill's imperial views were far from representative of his countrymen's; but it was hard to be sure of that while the old man bulked so large in the world's affairs. All too many American policy-makers, including at times the President, were inclined to suspect foul imperialist calculations behind every strategic proposal that the British put forward: for the long tradition of Anglophobia survived the war. But even if, as proved to be the case, the British were willing to give up their Empire and their armaments there was no reason to suppose that Stalin would give up his.

There it was: the central problem of American foreign relations had become the question of how to live with the Soviet Union. Secretive, suspicious, tricky, the Russians had been made almost besottedly anxious about the security of their frontiers by the dreadful trauma of invasion in 1941. They did not pretend to believe in collective security *à la* Wilson: it had proved too elusive and unhelpful in the thirties. Instead they wanted to consolidate their power by traditional means: rectified frontiers, annexations, client states. If the West would accept these ambitions, so much the better. If not, too bad. In this spirit the Russians had seized the Baltic states in the days of the Nazi–Soviet Pact, had annexed part of Finland after the Russo-Finnish War of 1939–40, and now proposed to give Poland a large chunk of eastern Germany in compensation for the loss of an equally large piece of territory to the Soviet Union. Many were the voices raised in the West to say that Stalin should instead be compelled to disgorge. He should be forced to accept the new world order, the *pax americana*, and set up Western-style democracies in Eastern Europe.

This was not Roosevelt's way. He knew that it was mere sentimentalism, given the actual balance of forces, to talk as if the United States could or would impose its policies on the USSR in matters of vital interest to the latter. He said repeatedly that America would never fight Russia just for the liberties of Eastern Europeans (one seems to hear distant echoes of Neville Chamberlain's remark about Czechoslovakia: 'a far-off country of which we know nothing'). Instead he favoured friendly persuasion. He hoped, by constantly exhibiting frank, warm and honest collaboration to the Russians, to induce them to modify the full rigour of their policy and to persuade the Poles, Lithuanians and others to accept the fact of Russian hegemony. In this way the Eastern European question would be settled amicably and satisfactorily to American opinion, and then what would there be left to quarrel about? Surely not Germany. FDR's attitude to this last topic was so cavalier that Washington still lacked an agreed German policy in April 1945, weeks only before the end of the war in Europe.

Unfortunately certain realities made the Rooseveltian view of Russo-American relations ultimately untenable. First, the United States had several objects in view – the defeat of Japan, universal democracy, a new international organization, free trade, Soviet–American friendship, for example – while the Russians had only one, or one, at any rate, which took precedence of everything else: national security. Roosevelt, trained in the give-and-take politics of American democracy and believing too fondly in the possibility of establishing comradely relationships with 'Joe', thought that there was great scope for flexibility and compromise in East–West dealings. The Russians did not. Nothing which touched on the defence of their frontiers was open to negotiation, and unfortunately, as tends to be the case in such matters, almost everything came to be seen as touching that defence. Besides, they did not trust the West: even as late as March 1945, Stalin accused England and America of planning a separate peace with Hitler. There is no particular sense in looking for rational explanations of this distrust. Advanced paranoia is by definition morbidly sensitive. Stalin, a monster of practised treachery, who had killed so many of his closest associates and therefore lived in an atmosphere of perpetual suspicion and fear, was quite incapable of believing that the leaders of the West meant to act honourably by him. (For the same reason there could be no question of allowing the peoples of Eastern Europe to settle their own destiny, or of allowing any freedom to the Russians themselves.) Instead he put the worst construction on every blunder. Roosevelt, for instance, very unwisely promised him a second front, that is to say a landing of Anglo-American troops in occupied Europe, in 1942 – a landing which, if successful, would take some of the pressure off the Soviet armies. D-Day was in the event postponed for two years. Stalin was mightily annoyed. Yet the military reasons for the delay were compelling. In 1942 an Allied landing in France would almost certainly have failed even to establish a bridgehead and great numbers of British lives would have been sacrificed uselessly. A premature attempt in 1943 might have been equally unsuccessful, and as costly to the Americans as to the British. Unsuccessful attempts would hardly have given any serious relief to the Russians. Stalin, therefore, was in effect demanding a useless holocaust, like the ones he offered up himself, of kulaks, old Bolsheviks and soldiers in the Second World War. The Western high command is not to be blamed for refusing his demands. Yet the refusal did nothing for Allied relations.

At bottom, however, the difficulty transcended personalities – even Stalin's. As a matter of fact, the dictator did from time to time show himself ready to make concessions to the American point of view and to behave with personal graciousness. Presumably he set a certain value on the possibility of post-war co-operation with America, if only because he might thereby get aid in rebuilding his shattered country. But the price that the Americans set on their friendship was in the last analysis higher than he was prepared to pay, and there was very little that any American President could do to lower it.

No one has ever plausibly accused the American people of doing things by halves. The emergence of Hitler as a national enemy and his attack on the Soviet Union had changed attitudes to the Russians to a staggering and unhealthy degree. American volatility was displayed flagrantly. Whereas, as late as 1939, most citizens (if opinion polls may be believed) would, if forced to choose, have picked fascism rather than communism, since communism waged war on private property, by 1942 the majority found no words too kind for Stalin and his system. The switch was made easier by the comfortable delusion, assiduously propagated, that the USSR had abandoned communism. 'Marxian thinking in Soviet Russia,' said the *New York Times* in April 1944, 'is out. The capitalist system, better described as the competitive system, is back.' That granted, the architect of the Gulag archipelago, many of whose crimes had long been public knowledge, could be eulogized as 'the man who saved the civilized world'. 'A child,' it was said, 'would like to sit in his lap and a dog would sidle up to him.' The NKVD was 'a national police similar to the FBI' and the Russians, 'one hell of a people', were remarkably like the Americans. Communism was like Christianity, being based on the brotherhood of man; and as Douglas MacArthur commented (quite accurately) from Corregidor in 1942, 'The hopes of civilization rest on the worthy banners of the courageous Red Army.' Hollywood leaped onto the bandwagon by issuing a tedious, fellow-travelling movie, *Mission to Moscow*, which one day would get its makers into a lot of trouble.

So Roosevelt had reason to think that a permanent alignment between

Moscow and Washington would be popular and, therefore, practicable. But the very vivacity of pro-Russian feeling carried a warning: the pendulum might swing just as fast in the opposite direction. And there were plenty of people willing to push it. The Russian experts in the State Department were anti-Soviet to a man. The Catholic church and the Polish-Americans both had good reasons for deeply distrusting Stalin. Formerly isolationist Senators were now ready to agree, however reluctantly, that Woodrow Wilson had been right all along; this meant that they now upheld his policies with the rigidity and obstinacy with which they had formerly opposed them. They accepted the Atlantic Charter programme; they supported the proposed United Nations Organization; and they were ready to support all the other military and economic arrangements which might tend to the defeat of Germany and Japan. These were large and genuine concessions. Unfortunately, they were not large enough to cover Stalin's Eastern European policies; and conservatives still had a deep distrust of FDR. They eyed him suspiciously. So did Stalin. Between the two sides, his policy began to collapse.

The risk had always been there. In March 1943, as he held forth on the post-war world, he had seemed to a witness, the British Foreign Secretary, Anthony Eden, to be 'a conjuror, skilfully juggling with balls of dynamite'. Perhaps he could have continued to juggle. Certainly the peoples of the West thought so. Everything seemed to be going so well in the spring of 1945. As the Russian armies closed in on Berlin, the British and the Americans crossed the Rhine (7 March). Iwo Jima was declared secure on 16 March. The Yalta Conference had been a great success, reaffirming the Atlantic Charter and promising Poland a broadly based democratic government. Soon a general conference of the United Nations would meet in San Francisco to set up the successor to the League of Nations. It seemed that victory and a just settlement were at hand. Then in mid-April, that fated period in American history (13 April, Fort Sumter; 15 April, Lincoln's death; 19 April, Lexington), on the twelfth, Franklin Roosevelt suddenly died.

The shock to the world was immense. Signs of his collapsing health had been visible since before the 1944 election, but few had realized what they portended, and nobody expected his disappearance so soon. American soldiers in China wept like children. In beleaguered Berlin Goebbels and Hitler superstitiously hoped that the event was a heavenly sign that the tide had turned in their favour. Elsewhere the world mourned, and wondered anxiously what the future held without the strong man's guiding hand. In the United States it was above all the poor who lamented their friend's passing. As the funeral train passed through Georgia, where the death occurred, black women fell on their knees in sorrowful reverence, acting for their country.

Tributes poured in. Roosevelt's services in peace and war had been gigantic. He had given his country a modern governmental structure, taught it to take up its international responsibilities and led it to universal triumph. He had palpable faults and committed frequent blunders, but probably no other man of his time could have performed as well, let alone better.

The ill-effects of his going made themselves felt at once. In the long run it was perhaps a good thing that power now passed to a younger, more vigorous man, and Roosevelt had chosen the right successor. Henry Wallace had impressed only his most faithful followers as Vice-President during the third term, so he was put aside in favour of Harry Truman when in 1944 Roosevelt, believing that his continuance in office was still necessary for his country, ran yet again (and won yet again). The energy and intelligence of the man from Missouri made themselves felt from the moment he became President, but he came totally unprepared, either by training or knowledge, for the conduct of foreign relations, which were then at a crucial turn. The result was that for more than a year American foreign policy was wavering, inconsistent, unpredictable; and the chance of a permanent understanding with Russia was thrown away.

Probably it had never been a real chance. Probably, whatever the West did, said or thought, Stalin would have been satisfied only with establishing satellite communist tyrannies throughout Eastern Europe, in the name of national security; and there was no way in which such an outcome of their efforts for the liberation of Europe could have been made acceptable to Americans, to those, at any rate, who concerned themselves with foreign affairs. To suggest that there was room for compromise on the point was to risk being denounced as an appeaser: the memory of Munich was repeatedly going to distort Western policy in the next thirty years. Besides, the Soviet view that American democratic affirmations merely expressed a will to dominate the world was not altogether groundless: as the British discovered at Bretton Woods, the Americans were unalterably convinced that what was good for American capitalism was good for the world. Some Americans were as enthusiastically ideological and missionary-minded as the Russians. Americanism is a crusading faith, anxious to liberate the peoples, to expose and confound their enemies, and forestall any ideology or revolution which threatens the continuance, or even just the convenience, of the liberal, capitalist, individualist system. Americans regarded all communists and communist states as subversive of peace and freedom: they did not accept that Marxist communism did not necessarily entail an aggressive foreign policy – communist rulers being free, in principle, to wait passively (or fairly so) while the fruit of revolution ripened spontaneously on the capitalist tree. They attributed to the Soviet leaders something of their own energy, conviction and determination. In return, Stalin may have attributed to the Americans something of his own implacable distrustfulness, and neither he nor his successors could see the world except in terms of an irrepressible conflict between capitalism and communism. All in all, these were not attitudes that made for peaceful partnership.

So conference followed conference, each less successful than the last; no peace settlement in Europe was ever agreed; new spheres of influence were claimed and appropriated by East and West, new crises erupted, and before very long a new arms race was developing. It was a melancholy outcome of the great anti-fascist struggle, and a confirmation of two of history's more dismal lessons: that grand alliances rarely survive the shock of victory, and that great powers usually behave as rivals rather than as partners.

24 Cold War Abroad and at Home 1945–61

Geography explains the policies of all the Powers.

Napoleon

By 1948 what became known as the Cold War dominated diplomacy.[1] Thenceforward all countries made their calculations, whether economic, military or political, from the basic assumption that the USA and the USSR were now enemies and might at any moment start to fight.

That the two superpowers (as they would come to be called) did *not* turn to battle for the solution of their difficulties is perhaps the most encouraging fact of modern times. Common sense had something to do with it. Just as Britain, Germany and France had at last learned, by very bitter experience, that the pleasures of war against each other were not remotely worth their cost, so the rulers of both the Soviet Union and the United States felt, in 1945 and 1946, that the last thing they wanted for their war-weary countries was another global conflict. Russia, indeed, was nearly prostrate, though American statesmen somehow could not believe it, or at least take it into account. She had lost twenty million lives and untold physical assets in the war. America, by contrast, was abounding: her total gross national product had gone up by 35 per cent since 1941. This prosperity, as well as the memory of nearly four years of grim warfare, made her people exceedingly reluctant to think about future battles, and her soldiers were anxious to put past battles behind them; they insisted on as rapid a demobilization as possible. By the autumn of 1946 all the enormous citizen forces which had won the war had been disbanded: it was the pattern of 1865 and 1919 all over again. This time the Americans were not isolationists: they had learnt that lesson very thoroughly. But they were inclined to put more trust in the

---

1 The origin of the phrase 'Cold War' is uncertain. The journalist Walter Lippman has perhaps the best claim to its invention.

efficacy of the United Nations and their own palpable goodwill than was realistic.

There was another reason for the good conduct of the powers. The war had not ended with a whimper. On 6 August 1945 an atomic bomb had been dropped on the Japanese city of Hiroshima, killing 70,000 people, injuring 51,000 and destroying more than 70,000 buildings. Three days later another bomb was dropped on Nagasaki, killing nearly 40,000 people and injuring 25,000. On 14 August the Japanese government surrendered.

No Presidential decision in history has been more disputed than the decision to drop the bomb. Yet to President Truman at the time it seemed a straightforward matter (Harry Truman's weakness was that he liked making decisions and tended to see them all as straightforward matters). The Japanese had been retreating steadily across the Pacific, but had defended each of their island strongholds with appalling tenacity, inflicting fearful losses on the Americans. The mere certainty of ultimate defeat was not allowed to demoralize a warrior people. The latest manifestation of their will to damage their foe was the coming of the suicide pilots, specially trained men who turned themselves and their planes into bombs, plunging down from the sky onto American ships with terrible effectiveness. It seemed all too certain to the US high command that there would be an equally stubborn resistance to any invasion of the Japanese archipelago, and that, without such an invasion of Japan proper, the war would never end. Casualties would probably be immense. When, therefore, the first experimental atomic bomb was successfully exploded at Alamogordo, New Mexico, on 16 July 1945, the Chiefs of Staff instantly began to make plans for using it against Japan. Some of the scientists who had made the bomb thought it would be a better idea to use the weapon in a demonstration to convince the Japanese that they had better surrender; but no one could suggest how such a demonstration could be arranged, or how it could be made convincing: the desert at Alamogordo looked much the same after the test explosion as it had before. Whereas, to use the bomb against military targets in Japan would surely bring about a rapid surrender, which everyone deeply desired.

All the same, had Truman fully grasped what he was doing, he might have hesitated. Even as it was, when ordering the bombing he laid down that 'military objectives and soldiers and sailors are the target and not women and children.' Unhappily he overlooked or refused to face the fact that the only worthwhile military objectives left were cities containing women and children, who therefore experienced what he rightly called 'the most terrible bomb in the history of the world' at both Hiroshima and Nagasaki. His ineffective squeamishness is rather puzzling: large-scale destruction of cities and civilians had been a characteristic tactic of the Second World War from its beginning, and the fire-raids on Tokyo (9 March 1945) were at least as horrible as the atomic attacks. To judge from his diary, Truman was in awe of the new weapon, but not enough to do any good. He did not know about the long-lasting effects of nuclear radiation; even if he had it might not have made very much difference, so joyful was he at the idea of ending the war at a stroke. Nevertheless it was exceedingly unfortunate that no one rightly calculated the long-term military, diplomatic and social consequences of Hiroshima. That event proved that the possible results of applied research in modern warfare were limitless. It soon became evident that the very existence of the human race, and perhaps of all terrestrial life, was at risk; no nation wishing to protect its independence, it seemed, could be sure of doing so for long unless it possessed atomic weapons or had for its ally an atomically armed country.[2] Nor was the art of making atomic weapons beyond discovery by non-Westerners. The operations of various atomic spies may have shortened the period of America's monopoly of nuclear arms, but it was not going to be a long one anyway, contrary to what almost all Americans were led to believe. The Soviet Union soon equipped itself with bombs of its own, and a great arms race was under way, one which continued for forty years and which dominated history in a way without parallel in the past.

For it turned out that there were few limitations to the ingenuity of American and Soviet scientists in devising weapons of horror. The rulers of each country, determined not to be vulnerable to blackmail ('Do as I say or I'll nuke you!'), poured out money and resources of all kinds upon their research establishments, and diplomacy was never able to catch up: prospects for agreed disarmament always lagged behind the latest devices. So the arsenals of terror filled up to bursting point, and the world grew steadily more dangerous, especially as lesser powers began to equip themselves atomically. Britain and France developed small but expensive nuclear armouries in order to convince themselves that they were still great powers; China armed later, in order to safeguard the balance of power in Asia; later still, other countries began to toy with the idea of atoms. The necessary technology grew cheaper and cheaper, more and more generally available; the moral sense dulled. The prospects of the nations darkened. Against these considerations can only be set the fact that so great was the fear of nuclear war that governments with the power to wage it behaved with great circumspection; crises which in earlier ages would almost certainly have brought on armed conflict were resolved peaceably; the uneasy restraint of the immediate post-war years persisted. It was a frail guarantee of the human future; but it held.

These developments foreclosed many choices for the Americans. Never again would they be able to rely, as they always had, on the wide oceans to keep them reasonably safe from attack, the less so as missile weaponry (another technological legacy of the Second World War) developed rapidly. Unless they felt they could trust Stalin and his successors not to abuse their

---

2 Subsequent history has shown that national independence is less at the mercy of atomic powers than was thought in 1945, when they seemed all-sufficient.

opportunities (few Americans after 1948 were inclined to run that risk) they would have to maintain their alliances and their armed forces and continue in the arms race they had begun. Negotiated disarmament would probably remain a desirable but very distant goal. Never again could American diplomacy be idle; the responsibilities of great power burdened the country inescapably.

As a result the position of the army, navy and air force in American life changed permanently. Traditionally, the armed forces had never counted for much in peacetime, either with the politicians or the public. Now, as alarm about the Soviet Union mounted, so did the leverage of the generals and admirals. They quickly grasped that the best way of increasing the defence budget, and hence their own influence, was by sounding the alarm of war. They struck up alliances with industrialists (especially aircraft manufacturers) who were eager for orders. They quarrelled bitterly among themselves about the allocation of funds: navy against air force, both against the army. In 1948 the Director of the Budget commented that 'the idea of turning over custody of atomic bombs to these competing, jealous, insubordinate services, fighting for position with each other, is a terrible prospect.' But no Budget Director, no Secretary of Defense, no President, was ever able to discipline them for long: they had too many friends and clients.

The purely economic effects of the arms race were equally striking. For a quarter of a century (until the Nixon administration) a conscript army was maintained, much of it abroad, in such places as West Germany, Japan and South Korea. Great fleets patrolled the seas, the planes of the Strategic Air Command were constantly in the air, even after the rise of rocketry made them obsolescent, billions of dollars were spent on maintaining all these forces, on arming them and on developing new weapons for them. These expenditures remade the industrial map of the United States. Weapons research created new employment in a manner that left the memory of New Deal experiments in public expenditure far behind. Defence establishments of all kinds were allocated to regions which private enterprise might have left to stagnate: for example, the committees of Congress being usually dominated by elderly veterans of the Democratic South, their states and districts got the larger part of the federal largesse that was now flowing. Georgia, Texas and Florida began to bloom under a rain of dollars. Vast areas of New Mexico and Arizona were set aside for weapons testing. Where defence went, other industries and private investments followed: soon the economic gap between the South and the rest of the Union, which had endured since the Civil War, began to close, and the South-West became the most rapidly growing part of the country (South and South-West together were eventually known by a new name, 'the Sun Belt'). California was the chief beneficiary of this new movement. Rich in good land, in oil, in minerals, and with a marvellous climate, it became the leader in the new high-technology industries. By 1960 it was outstripping New York and becoming the most populous state in the Union.

Yet even this result of the atomic bomb was not wholly good, for it created vast new interests which were conservative in outlook and, being based on arms expenditure, essentially militaristic. This was a quite unprecedented element in American society. Even if true peace returned there would be resistance in the Sun Belt to cuts in spending for defence; dollar-minded patriotism would see every move to achieve an understanding with America's foreign rivals as dangerous trifling with the country's safety; the prosperous clients of the warfare state would develop a certain indifference to the distresses of other parts of the country; and though the immense wealth generated would make life amazingly comfortable for most of the citizens, and would be spent lavishly on public enterprises, so that California, for example, was soon crowded with notable universities growing rich on contracts with the US Defense Department, and possessed the most generous welfare arrangements in the world, nevertheless the distribution of wealth was still highly unequal. There were vast areas of indifferent housing in Los Angeles, increasingly inhabited by poor blacks. The middle classes, for all their public spirit, achieved a culture that was at best shallow and at worst vulgarly corrupting. The Golden State had always been a haven for exotic religions. In the new era many of them became mass affairs, peddling doubtful comforts to the gullible. These new cults had none of the grim frontier strength of primitive Mormonism; they were tailored, rather, to a consumer society with a taste for cheap salvation.

In the 1940s none of this could be foreseen. America stood almost alone in a ruined world. Her good luck was indeed astonishing, and later events become a little more comprehensible if we assume that, consciously or not, many Americans felt uneasy, or even guilty, about being so uniquely lucky. Of course they told themselves and everybody else that their success was the reward of virtue. Henry Luce, the publisher of *Time*, *Life* and *Fortune* magazines, had complacently proclaimed the opening of 'the American century' while the war was still being fought. The 'American Way of Life' (another cliché of the period) was vindicated with every bottle of Coca-Cola sold. Nevertheless, Americans were often intensely apprehensive about the future. Meantime the post-war depression which everyone had expected did not occur. Millions of veterans returning from the war were only anxious to settle down and raise families. Their demands for housing, medical care, college education, cars, washing-machines and well-paid employment were transmitted to the federal government through the American Legion, the Veterans' Administration and other such bodies; Washington showed itself anxious to oblige by making large funds available, and thus a huge consumer boom was stimulated.[3] It was assisted by the fact that during the war the

---

3 There is a certain irony in the fact that the number of returning veterans roughly equalled the number of the unemployed in 1932. This statistic sufficiently suggests what might have been the result had the policy-makers of the thirties seriously tried to spend their way out of the Depression.

Office of Price Administration had largely succeeded in holding down prices while wages rose and went into savings, for there were then few goods available for consumer purchase. Now, as industry returned to peacetime production and began to pour out goods, it was discovered that the masses had the money to buy them. Nor did the good times cease (though they occasionally faltered) when the impetus of demobilization was exhausted: between 1947 and 1960 personal disposable income went up, in real terms, by 17 per cent, while the population increased from 141 million to 181 million. A steadily expanding market, a steadily improving standard of living for all and only trifling inflation seemed to be the new law of nature. Encouraged by the prospect of an endless boom, moneylenders grew amazingly confident. By the mid-fifties they were regularly lending former GIs the entire purchase price of houses, and most cars were bought on credit – $100 down and three years to pay. All this stimulated the boom still more. American prosperity became the wonder of the world. In the mid-forties, while Europe starved and (in the winter of 1947) froze; while revolution marched across China, which had not known peace for over thirty years; while the British Empire in India came to an end amid great bloodshed; while Stalin prepared to consolidate his new empire in Eastern Europe by the tried methods of police terror; and while dictatorships rose and fell as usual in Latin America, the citizens of the United States began to enjoy a generally diffused well-being which eclipsed even the experiences of the mid-twenties.

Yet the rest of the world could not be allowed to go hang. The American people and government had seen what that led to and were determined to shoulder their responsibilities – rather too determined, it emerged.

Matters were most nearly straightforward in the Far East, except (a large exception) for the Chinese puzzle. Since the United States had undoubtedly played much the greatest part against Japan, it felt free to exclude all its allies from any part in the post-war settlement. The Japanese, who had never been conquered before, showed themselves willing to adopt the ways of their conquerors, so General MacArthur, who had received their surrender, set out to teach them democracy. Surprisingly, given the General's autocratic temperament, the experiment turned out excellently. MacArthur had a deep understanding of what the historical moment required of his country and repudiated the imperialist tradition. America would lose a golden opportunity, he said, if she used her immense new influence 'in an imperialistic manner, or for the sole purpose of commercial advantage . . . but if our influence and our strength are expressed in terms of essential liberalism, we shall have the friendship and the co-operation of the Asiatic peoples far into the future'. Time would eventually destroy these hopes; but meanwhile MacArthur ruled with huge success. He comported himself very much as a new Shogun (the Mikado Hirohito had kept his title but been shorn of his divinity and political power) and at his command the Japanese set about turning themselves into democrats and rebuilding their shattered country. They were startlingly successful in both respects, to the gratification of the Americans. Reconciliation was hastened by the triumph of the communists in China in 1949, an event equally displeasing to the Japanese and the United States, and by the outbreak of the Korean War in 1950. A formal peace treaty was negotiated, and signed in September 1951, at the same time as one committing the Americans to undertake the defence of Japan against any foe, since the Japanese were forbidden to have any armed forces themselves.

No such happy outcome could be expected in Europe, if only because Germany was now divided into two parts. This was a quite unintended result of the war, and came about because Russia and her allies found it impossible to agree on the government of the defeated country. It was possible to set up a tribunal at Nuremberg which tried and sentenced the surviving Nazi leaders; all other matters were divisive. Stalin was determined to eliminate all possibility of a repetition of the 1941 attack on Russia and to squeeze the utmost in reparations out of the Germans. Unfortunately the reparations policy, unacceptable to Western statesmen on economic grounds (they clearly remembered what trouble reparations had caused between the wars), soon became indistinguishable from one of wholesale plunder; and Soviet security seemed to demand the permanent subjugation of Germany and the establishment by brutal means of communist governments, backed by the Red Army, everywhere else. In Central Europe only Czechoslovakia held out for a time; in South-Eastern Europe, only Greece – and there a civil war was raging between the government and communist guerrillas.

Policy-makers in Washington watched these developments with growing indignation. The truculent diplomatic conduct of the Soviet government did nothing to better international relations. Molotov would soon become notorious for always saying '*nyet*' to any Western proposal, and in this way a Russian word entered the English language. President Truman stated privately that he was tired of 'babying the Soviets'. And the surest friends of the United States were deeply alarmed, in the late forties, by Soviet conduct. The British did not fear a communist *coup d'état* in their own country, but the consequences of a communist takeover in Italy, France and West Germany would have been most unpleasant to them, for Europe would thus have been united under the hegemony of a single aggressive power – the thing which British policy had worked and fought so hard for so long to prevent. To French democrats the issue was even more pressing. Having just endured the horrors of one occupation and one sort of collaboration they were unwilling to risk another which was likely to be more permanent. France's Communist party was notoriously subservient to Moscow: it could not be trusted to respect either French liberties or French diplomatic interests. Italy, a former enemy, might not have won a hearing, even though there were millions of Italian-Americans in the United States, but for the existence of the papacy. Pius XII had never seen fit to take the lead in opposition to Nazism or fascism; but he exerted his authority and influence to the full in opposing Stalinist communism. Poland, the most Catholic country in northern Europe, had been swallowed up: Italy must not go the same way.

All these fears found expression in Winston Churchill's celebrated speech at Fulton, Missouri, on 5 March 1946, which announced to the world, and to President Truman (who was sitting on the platform behind him and had read the address beforehand), that 'from Stettin in the Baltic to Trieste in the Adriatic, an iron curtain has descended across the continent'. Russia, through the agency of Communist parties and fifth columnists everywhere, was trying to destroy Christian civilization. She must be resisted by a permanent alliance of the staunch English-speaking peoples – the United States, Great Britain and the British Commonwealth.[4] This bellicose message was not well received in all quarters, but it chimed in very well with the contingencies of American domestic politics.

The Republican party had now been excluded from national power for nearly fourteen years. It could not regain the Presidency before 1948, but meantime there were the Congressional elections of 1946 to look forward to. Working in the Republicans' favour were the inevitable reaction against the party of the war which had toppled Churchill in Britain and the long-flowing conservative tide which had set in in 1938. But they needed a cry, or thought they did, and the slogans of anti-communism were just the right sort of thing. They were familiar, from the days of the Red Scare; Stalin's actions made them plausible; and the Yalta agreements, which had been presented as such a triumph of Soviet–American friendship, such a proof of the special understanding between FDR and Uncle Joe, made the Democrats vulnerable. For it was becoming gospel on the Right that at Yalta vital national interests had been given away, either in treachery or folly.

In the event, the Republicans did extremely well, regaining control of both houses of Congress for the first time since 1930. It is doubtful if their general victory owed much to the anti-communist cry: the process of adjustment from war to peace was proving painful, price controls had been lifted and as a result the cost of living was galloping upwards; but here and there were signs of how the wind was setting. In California a returning serviceman, Richard Milhous Nixon (1913–94), was elected to the House of Representatives, having waged an unscrupulous campaign insinuating that his opponent was a secret communist. He was not unique.

The Truman administration had to take account of these signs. It was entering on a very difficult period. The outstanding figure in the government was now General Marshall, Army Chief of Staff throughout the war, recently

4 This affirmation of Anglo-American unity was not unconnected with the fact that Britain was just then trying to win Congressional approval for a loan of $3,750,000,000. After the Fulton speech it went through easily on a tide of anti-communist feeling.

returned from an unsuccessful mission to China, where he had hoped to reconcile Chiang Kai-shek to Mao Tse-tung and bring peace to that unhappy country. In January 1947 he had been appointed Secretary of State. His chief assistant was Dean Acheson, an able lawyer of long Washington experience. President Truman himself was proving to be, as Acheson later called him, 'the captain with the mighty heart'. All three were men of compassion, courage and (within the limits of their humanity) wisdom. Europe was foundering in the throes of the worst winter in living memory. If the victory over Hitler was to be worth anything, the peoples of that continent must first be rescued from starvation, and next put on the road to a renewal of strength and hope. Otherwise the whole of society might collapse for good, or again succumb to dictatorship. And if the rich, well-fed, well-organized Americans stood by and simply watched disaster happen, they would never be forgiven, nor deserve to be. A programme of economic aid must be devised; but how was a discredited Democratic administration, which everyone expected to be defeated in the next Presidential election, to get such a programme through the Republican Congress?

The answer was, by a series of delicate strokes. Truman first asked Congress for a grant of $350 million for the prevention of starvation. Then, in March, Britain having stated that she could no longer bear the burden of propping up the Greek and Turkish governments against the threat of Soviet-backed communist insurgency or economic collapse (it being as much as the British could do to keep themselves warm for a few hours each day), the President appeared before a joint session of Congress to say that 'it must be the policy of the United States to support free peoples who are resisting attempted subjugation by armed minorities or by outside pressures' (what later became known as the Truman Doctrine) and to ask for Congressional authorization for aid to Greece and Turkey in the form of money, trained personnel, commodities, supplies and equipment. Senator Taft warned in vain against this renewed abandonment of isolationism: Senator Vandenberg of Michigan, a somewhat vacuous Republican whom the Roosevelt and Truman administrations had been cultivating for years, came out in support of the proposals, which became law in May. But help to Greece and Turkey left Western Europe still prostrate. General Marshall, returning from a fruitless visit to Moscow, had seen for himself the vast desolation. The health of the American economy needed a healthy Europe for mutual trade. It was now the unanimous view of the administration that the Soviet Union was bent on expansion at all costs, and meant cunningly to exploit the opportunity to carry communism as far as the English Channel. Such fiendish plots must be checked. So on 5 June 1947 General Marshall made a celebrated speech at Harvard. 'Our policy is directed against hunger, poverty, desperation and chaos,' he said. 'Its purpose should be the revival of a working economy in the world so as to permit the emergence of political and social conditions in which free institutions can exist.' He invited proposals from Europe, promising a generous response. The fish rose to the bait – non-communist Europe expressed enthusiastic interest and deep appreciation, and soon had put together a programme to present to the United States which set the recovery campaign off to a good start and meant that, when all ended happily, the programme would be known forever by Marshall's name. Senator Vandenberg rallied to the flag again. Dean Acheson, who had temporarily left the administration, led a Citizens' Committee for the Marshall Plan, which by dint of endless speechifying up and down the country mustered widespread support for the programme. Acheson was greatly helped by Stalin's refusal to take part, or to allow his East European puppet governments to take part either; and in February 1948 the Communists seized power in Czechoslovakia. These developments made the administration's insistence that the Marshall Plan was an anti-communist measure, and an urgent one too, all the more convincing, and unhappily most Americans – at any rate, most Republicans – were more impressed by anti-communist arguments than by suggestions that it might not be altogether moral to leave America's recent allies to starve to death, or even that it might not be economically prudent to do nothing to rescue the world economy, now more prostrated than it had been during the Depression. So it would have been a grave embarrassment had the Soviet Union joined the programme; it did nothing of the kind, the plan was voted through Congress by comfortable majorities, and in the end $13,000,000,000 was made available to fund it. Presently a vast flood of American goods poured eastwards, and the rebuilding of Europe got under way at last.

It was the most unambiguously and triumphantly successful of all America's post-war policies. One of the reasons for this was that it was also the most tactful. Marshall Aid was administered by a small group of Americans in Paris, whose principal job was to approve European shopping-lists. Once so approved, dollars were exchanged for European currencies, and with those dollars the Europeans paid for their purchases. In this way American aid, though essential, was almost invisible: ordinary Europeans noticed only that they were dealing with their own authorities; no friction or resentment was created, as would certainly have been the case had the United States tried to administer its aid directly. To be sure, the Europeans were not given any clear cause to be grateful; but then gratitude is a transient and unreliable emotion at the best of times. A more solid *quid pro quo* was provided by the so-called 'counterpart funds' – the vast holdings in European currencies that resulted from the Marshall transactions. They were available to American businessmen wishing to invest in Europe, and as American industrial profits began to pile up there were many such. The economic bonds linking the two continents thus diversified and tightened.

Yet even the Marshall Plan had its drawbacks. In the first place it marked the moment when the USA and the USSR formally and publicly became enemies. Years and years would pass before they found it possible to negotiate seriously again, years during which huge vested interests, with overwhelming stakes in the continuance of the conflict, would emerge. Secondly, what began as a policy of economic containment of Soviet messianism, as promulgated by George Kennan of the State Department, soon modulated into military confrontation. The division of Europe into East and West which the Marshall Plan signalized would soon become a division between military alliances. Third, the way in which the plan was presented to the American people had unfortunate consequences. The administration was chiefly, indeed exclusively, concerned with the Soviet threat to international peace; but anti-communism in the United States tended to be quite as much concerned with a wider range of issues, not all of which could reasonably be connected with the Cold War, and with the imaginary threat of internal subversion. The selling of the Marshall Plan blurred the difference between the two approaches and made the nastier, sillier, more demagogic form of anti-communism respectable. Worse: the intellectual processes behind the formulation, both of the Truman Doctrine and of the Marshall Plan, were deeply confused. The practical instinct of the policy-makers led them to the right policies – to rescue Greece from a communist take-over, to restore Europe to prosperity – but the reasons given, even in the innermost sanctum of the State Department, were fanciful. Dean Acheson, for example, said that a communist victory in Greece might lead to the loss of three continents to Russia. This was pure fantasy, and pointed to an abiding weakness of American diplomacy: its practitioners still found it difficult to recognize reality. Finally, the success of the Marshall Plan not only confirmed America's position as leader of the West but encouraged policy-makers in Washington to undertake bold, ambitious schemes in the high confidence that American strength and will would be sufficient to carry them out. Hysteria at home and over-confidence abroad were the two unhappy states of mind which the designers of the Marshall Plan unintentionally fostered.

At least the plan was not a partisan affair. Indeed it was a saying of the period that politics ought to stop at the water's edge, which explains the prominence of Republicans like Vandenberg and John Foster Dulles in diplomacy. No such partnership was visible in domestic politics. The Republicans had not recaptured Congress to play second fiddle to the Democrats. On the contrary, they acted at times as if they hoped to undo the entire New Deal. Led by their narrow-minded paladin, Senator Taft, they pushed through the Twenty-Second Amendment to the Constitution, which disqualified any candidate from being elected President more than twice. In view of subsequent abuses of Presidential power this revival of the two-term tradition looks a great deal wiser than it did at the time, when Truman denounced it, quite accurately, as a deliberate slur on the memory of Franklin Roosevelt (no one could doubt Truman's disinterestedness, for the amendment did not apply to him). An even more important achievement was the passage of the Taft–Hartley Act in 1947, a law which sharply curtailed the freedom of action, and thus the industrial power, of the labour unions. It outlawed strikes by government employees, for example, banned the closed shop and made the unions responsible for breaches of contract. It required union leaders to swear they were not communists. Above all, it revived the labour injunction by empowering the President to suspend or forbid by court injunction any strike for up to eighty days, the so-called 'cooling-off period', while an agreed solution was sought to whatever problem had arisen. This law could never have got through if the struggles between management and labour, in the post-war period of rapid inflation, had not been so bitter. There had been 5,000 strikes in 1946 alone, and 3,000 in 1947. They had created widespread public resentment. The anti-communist provision was possible because of the savage battles within the CIO and its member unions between communist and anti-communist leaders (men such as Walter Reuther of the United Automobile Workers). At least the unions were at one in denouncing Taft–Hartley. But they have never got it repealed, and it acted as an effective check on union growth in the Sun Belt.

For the rest, the Republicans had little to offer their countrymen save opposition to the administration's proposals, and Red-baiting. The House Committee on Un-American Activities, first set up in 1938, was put on a permanent footing and began a series of investigations and public hearings which initiated a long period of public demoralization, a cause of shame to Americans ever since.[5] The committee members were much more interested in publicity for themselves than in protecting the United States from subversion or respecting the civil liberties of American citizens, not to mention their jobs, reputations and self-respect. The Committee was to have a run of twenty years or so, in the course of which it did incalculable damage and no good. It was an all-too-typical product of Congress in the forties.

President Truman saw an opportunity. Running for election in his own right in 1948 he largely ignored the Republican candidate, Governor Thomas E. Dewey of New York (except that occasionally he abused him, to happy cries of 'Give' em hell, Harry!' – once, monstrously, as a fascist). Instead he spent his time attacking the 'do-nothing' Congress. The experts all agreed that the President had no chance of victory, but he fought a doughty campaign. It was the most purely enjoyable contest of recent times. The candidates were well-matched, and however desperate the state of international relations (the Russians blockaded Berlin in June, which brought on the successful Berlin airlift in retaliation) it was, to the ordinary citizen, the least crisis-laden Presidential year since 1928. It was also the last campaign of the sort which had been traditional since the days of William Jennings Bryan. The conventions were televised, but there were too few households

5 In fairness to the Republicans it should be stated that the committee was revived at the end of the war chiefly by the exertions of Congressman Rankin of Mississippi, a Democrat, and one of the most reactionary members of either house in any generation.

with sets for the new medium to have much effect on the outcome. Truman reached the voters by criss-crossing the country in a train, 'whistle-stopping' in the style of Theodore Roosevelt. Never again! His pugnacity, his good humour, his partisan loyalty and, perhaps, the fact that everyone has a weakness for the underdog (and Dewey was said to look like 'the little man on the wedding-cake') explain the outcome: Truman confounded the experts and defeated Dewey comfortably. He defeated Congress too: the Democrats regained control. In January 1949 he was inaugurated for his first full term, promising a 'Fair Deal' to the American people.

The 'Fair Deal' was a continuation and extension of the New Deal, meant to please those groups – workers, blacks, farmers – whose votes had carried the day for the President. Some of it got through Congress: the minimum legal wage was raised, the benefits of Social Security were extended to ten million more people, a vast programme of slum clearance and federally supported public housing was launched (ultimately, perhaps, to the benefit of the construction industry more than of anyone else, for much of the new housing was so badly built and badly designed that it quickly degenerated into new slums). Some of it did not: proposals for universal medical insurance, a new system of farm subsidies, an anti-lynching law and a Fair Employment Practices bill. Events soon overwhelmed Truman's liberal programme. The 1948 election had not really suited the times. Within his own party Truman had had to fight off two challenges: from Henry Wallace, who eventually ran as a third party candidate, on a 'Progressive' ticket that was little more than a front for the American Communist party; and, more dangerous, from the 'Dixiecrats', Southern Democrats who walked out of the Democratic convention when the Northern liberals, led by the mayor of Minneapolis, Hubert Humphrey, inserted a strong civil rights plank in the party platform. The Dixiecrats put up a fourth candidate, Strom Thurmond of South Carolina, and although they did no fatal damage to Truman, they thereby served notice on him that he might have trouble with the next Congress, in which they would continue to be influential. But as it turned out Truman's second term was dominated not by these domestic difficulties but by crisis abroad. In 1949 the Soviet Union exploded its first atomic bomb, and the Chinese communists drove Chiang Kai-shek and his forces from the mainland to take refuge on the island of Taiwan (or Formosa).

The end of the atomic monopoly caused many Americans to start looking for the spies and traitors who (they assumed) must have made it possible for the Russians to catch up so soon. The assumption was wrong, but it was none the less potent. The episode also decided the administration to enlarge the defence budget and to start work on the hydrogen bomb. This acceleration of the arms race was lamentable, but, given the state of Russo-American relations, was equally inevitable. It illustrated the pattern which the arms race took ever after. The race developed in jerks, according to the state of the nuclear art and the nervousness, which rose and fell, of the great powers. The culmination of the communist revolution in China had equally dramatic results for America, of perhaps an even more ominous kind, which yet do not fit neatly into any pattern.

China had a special place in the outlook of all too many citizens. According to legend, the doctrine of the Open Door had saved the country from the clutches of European imperialism; Sun Yat-sen's revolution in 1911 had appeared to be very much an American affair, inspired by the American ideology; American missionaries and doctors (often the roles were combined) had poured into the country to do it good, to Christianize it, to Westernize it; the fateful dream of profit still haunted many American businessmen; and many American soldiers and airmen had served in China during the war. Finally, Mao Tse-tung was seen as just another Russian puppet. These factors in themselves would have been enough to make it exceedingly difficult for many Americans to accept the communist victory, or to endorse Dean Acheson's assurance that 'the unfortunate but inescapable fact is that the ominous result of the civil war in China was beyond the control of the government of the United States'. Unfortunately their state of mind, that of believers in American omnipotence, to whom, as Acheson observed in his memoirs, every goal unattained was explicable only by incompetence or treason,[6] was to be inflamed and sustained by comparatively accidental matters. The Republicans, for example, saw a heaven-sent opportunity to embarrass the Truman administration: they could accuse it of 'losing China' by weakness and negligence, if not by outright treason. Henry Luce had been born in China and was devoted to Chiang Kai-shek, and perhaps even more to his wife, Madame Chiang, adroit, beautiful and American-educated. Luce had for years propagated the myth that the incompetent Chiang was his country's George Washington, and now he became the lynch-pin of the 'China lobby', a pressure group which dedicated itself wholeheartedly to the task of protecting Chiang from further defeat and, eventually, to the overthrow of 'Red China'. As if all this did not create difficulties enough for the administration, in January 1950 a former State Department official, Alger Hiss, was convicted in the courts of perjury for having denied under oath before the House Un-American Activities Committee (HUAC) that he had once been a Russian agent who had sent copies of confidential state documents to the Soviet Union. The fact that his accuser, Whittaker Chambers, worked for Luce's magazine *Time* inclined the President and his advisers to think that Hiss had been framed (a belief rather hard for most historians to share); but guilty or not, he was a severe embarrassment to the Democrats. He had been close to Dean Acheson, for example, and Acheson was now Secretary of State. The Red-baiters were much encouraged, and began to assert that it was malice domestic, not developments abroad, which explained all they disliked about American foreign policy. Had not Hiss been present at Yalta? Had he not helped to

6 Dean Acheson, *Present at the Creation* (London, 1970), p. 303.

set up the United Nations, in whose Security Council Russia wielded a veto? Was it not probable that he, or some as yet undiscovered traitor, had been responsible for 'the loss of China'? A series of hostile and extremely damaging investigations into the State Department was launched by Congress.

It was a situation made for demagogues. HUAC redoubled its unpleasant activities; but the limelight was soon seized by a latecomer to this particular stage. On 9 February 1950 Senator Joseph R. McCarthy of Wisconsin (1909–57) announced to the world in a speech at Wheeling, West Virginia, that he had in his hand a list of the numerous communists 'known to the Secretary of State' who were still working and making policy in the State Department. And so the great witch-hunt was launched.

The villain of the piece was of an all too familiar type. True, the most notorious demagogues had always previously come from the South, with the exception of the Nazi-sympathizing Father Coughlin, and he was never an office-holder; but McCarthy was otherwise clearly of their kidney. And there has always been something demagogic about even mainstream American politics. If a deliberate attempt to stir up the crowd by character assassination and cries of conspiracy are characteristic of demagogy, then neither Sam Adams, nor Thomas Jefferson, nor Alexander Hamilton, nor Andrew Jackson, and certainly not their associates, were guiltless. They each committed these sins, though they did not make them the sole substance of their politics. Demagogy was a potent force in the 1930s, and but for the success of Franklin Roosevelt might have become really dangerous. The opportunity had if anything grown in the years since then. Previous demagogues had had little solid appeal outside their own states or sections; but twenty years of modern government, modern problems and modern population movements had made the Americans much more homogeneous than ever before, greatly increased the importance of the national government and national politics and, in such devices as radio and television, created a national audience. Thanks to aircraft, a politician in quest of that audience could move about the country far more rapidly and easily. Nationwide magazines like *Time* and *Life*, and the emergence of the syndicated columnist, whose articles would be printed in tens or hundreds of newspapers across the country, had even done something to break down the intense traditional localism of the American press. All this represented opportunity to a demagogue; all he needed as well was an issue; and of those there were plenty in 1950, when the people were bitter and bewildered, not just because of the pace of change in the past two decades but because of the horrible way in which the longed-for post-Hitler peace had turned into the Cold War and then become the prelude to yet another hot war.

None of these reflections exonerate McCarthy. He did enormous damage to his country, both abroad and at home, not all of which has even yet been repaired. He was not, it must be repeated, the only scoundrel to take advantage of public nervousness to drum up a Red scare for his own ends.

But he was incomparably the most able. Not that he was a cold calculator; rather, his genius (for that it undoubtedly was) lay in a certain hot, instinctive cunning which told him how to win power, headlines and a passionately loyal following by manipulating the worst impulses and most entire weaknesses of his fellow-countrymen. He was a liar on a truly amazing scale, telling so many lies, so often, and in such a tangled fashion that Hercules himself could not have completed their refutation, for new falsehoods sprouted faster than old ones could be rebutted. In early life he lost all respect for the pieties and hypocrisies that governed most American politicians and voters, and was therefore able to see quite clearly that the penalties for defying these shibboleths were small, the possible rewards enormous. He lied his way into his first public office, that of circuit judge in Wisconsin; in 1946 he lied his way into the Senate, partly by accusing his opponent in the Republican primary, Robert La Follette Jr, of being corrupt, and partly by insisting that 'Congress needs a tail gunner' – namely McCarthy, who, apart from sitting in a tail gunner's seat when a passenger, on a few occasions, on a military plane in the Pacific during the Second World War, spent his service behind a desk, de-briefing pilots. Never mind: he passed himself off as a wounded war-hero (having injured his leg when falling downstairs, drunk, on a troopship) and won the election. Once in the Senate he pursued his favourite interests, chiefly boozing and gambling, and financed them by taking bribes from corporations that had business in Washington: to use the slang phrase, he was a boodler. He was a palpably unsatisfactory Senator, and by 1950 there were signs that the people of Wisconsin might retire him. He badly needed an issue, and in a rash moment, which they soon greatly regretted, some Catholic acquaintances suggested that he denounce the communist menace. They were thinking of the international crisis, but McCarthy knew better. 'That's it,' he said. 'The government is full of Communists. We can hammer away at them.'

McCarthy knew nothing about communism or the State Department, but he did know that mud sticks, especially if you throw a lot of it. It is doubtful that he ever thought he was doing much harm. He spent his days largely in the company of petty crooks and swindlers, and having no scruples, no respect for law and no concern for reputation (otherwise he would hardly have swaggered so conspicuously as a foul-mouthed, drunken, mendacious brute) probably could not believe that others might have different attitudes, or genuinely suffer if they were traduced. As for the point that his conduct undermined democratic processes at home and fanned hostility to the United States abroad (where many liberals felt that Uncle Sam had at last torn off his disguise: as Richard Rovere says, 'he was the first American ever to be actively hated and feared by foreigners in large numbers'[7]), he ignored it completely. For him it was enough that he had secured his re-election, that money flowed in from anti-communist enthusiasts that

7 Richard H. Rovere, *Senator Joe McCarthy* (New York, 1959; paperback edn, n.d.), p. 123.

he could spend as he pleased, and that he could keep the entire political establishment of the United States in perpetual uproar. He had fun.

His impact on central government is what distinguishes him from the other heroes of the second Red Scare. While HUAC hounded private individuals McCarthy took on the State Department, the army and the Presidency itself. To their eternal shame he was encouraged by his colleagues in the Republican party, now desperate for power. Senator Taft was the son of a Chief Justice of the United States: yet he advised McCarthy, 'If one case doesn't work, try another.' Baser, stupider men in the Senate joined in the cry. First the Truman and then the Eisenhower administration trembled before him; and the press let itself be used as his megaphone. It was as squalid an episode as any in American history.

It bred threefold evil. Least important was the effect on foreign opinion. McCarthyism was of course a marvellous gift to Soviet propagandists. They had long done their best to discredit the United States, abusing it ceaselessly in clichés all their own, such as 'boogie-woogie gangsters' (my favourite). Now the persecution of communists and fellow-travellers and plain citizens of the United States who were neither could easily be trumpeted so that the willing could forget the continuing atrocities of Stalinism. Since 1917 there had been Europeans who resented American power, wealth and leadership; McCarthyism gave them a respectable excuse for expressing their hostility. Less cynical or dishonest elements simply found their doubts confirmed. They disliked the Cold War, did not blame Russia for it exclusively and disliked some of its consequences: the building-up of Germany again (and soon, her rearmament) and the manufacture of the hydrogen bomb. They began to doubt if the country of McCarthy was a safe guardian of nuclear weapons. In this way the seeds of what became a mighty paradox were sown: as the youth of Europe became more and more Americanized, in dress, speech, music, literature, outlook and even in eating habits, it turned away, or thought it did, from American leadership in politics and ideology.

However, in the long run this alienation had surprisingly little impact on events. Much more important was the effect of the great fear[8] on American citizens themselves. Their lives were devastated for four years, and even after the acute phase passed, in 1954–5, there was a long aftermath of uncertainty, anxiety and occasional oppression. Journalists, diplomats, authors, actors (HUAC particularly enjoyed investigating Hollywood, for it thus generated a unique amount of publicity), trades unionists, scientists, scholars were called before Congressional committees and forced to testify against themselves. McCarthy tried to get membership of the Communist party made a crime; he failed, but to be on the safe side many witnesses

8 I take this phrase from David Caute, whose book *The Great Fear* (London, 1978) is probably the fullest and most accurate guide to what happened to Americans during the McCarthy years.

refused to answer questions, invoking their right under the Fifth Amendment not to bear witness against themselves. This did little good: 'taking the Fifth' was interpreted as an admission of guilt, and was often followed by the loss of one's job. Not taking the Fifth did not work either, because the committees would not accept a witness's refusal to tell tales. Many a victim who professed himself or herself willing to talk about their own past, but not about that of other people, ended up in jail for contempt of Congress. A similar fate met those who tried to protect themselves by pleading the First Amendment, supposed to guarantee the rights of free speech and free political activity: they too went to prison for contempt as the courts refused to help. A sort of panic spread through American life. Suspect individuals were blacklisted – that is, diligent private groups denounced them as unfit for employment, at any rate in the jobs they were trained for – and then sacked. In this way many actors fell on hard times. A firm which refused to be bullied into dismissing its employees might be blacklisted itself; a university might find itself cut off from the lucrative government research contracts that were becoming an important part of academic life. So, at any rate, it was feared. Consequently many organizations called in alleged security experts whose function it was to smell out 'subversives'. These experts were as unsavoury a gang of informers as was ever let loose upon the innocent; sometimes their expertise arose from the fact that they had once been communists or communist agents themselves; now they earned a living by denouncing their former associates and anyone else they disapproved of. Sometimes they were former employees of the Federal Bureau of Investigation, who had fallen out with the Director, J. Edgar Hoover. Sometimes they were simple confidence tricksters. Anyway they did enormous harm, since employers were far too ready to leave it to them to say who was or was not worthy of trust. A grey fog of timid conformity settled over American middle-class life. And New York city dismissed a public washroom attendant for past membership of the Communist party. No doubt, if he had continued in employment, he would have corrupted his customers with Soviet soap or Communist lavatory paper.

But the American people, though susceptible to panic, come to their senses eventually. The great fear, like the Red Scare, eventually sank into the past, with all its injustice and suffering. What was not so easy to get over was its impact on the government. This was the third and worst, because longest-lasting, consequence of McCarthyism.

It is never easy to discern a nation's true diplomatic interest, and the United States, as must by now be clear, has always found it particularly difficult. But during the early Truman years the men who shaped American policy were by good fortune exceptionally well fitted for the job. They were perhaps mistaken in seeing Soviet Russia as an aggressive, intriguing enemy, aspiring to world power, like Hitler; but it is hard, perhaps impossible, to believe that any American statesmen, even if Franklin Roosevelt had survived, could have for long taken a different attitude. The United States and the Soviet Union were simply not compatible partners, and, granted that premise, the rest follows. Otherwise there can be no doubt about the merit of Truman's men. Marshall and Acheson in turn headed a State Department that for ability and professionalism has perhaps never been equalled. Their President trusted them and learned from them; although there were blind spots (asked why Latin America was not a participant in the Marshall programme, Truman told his questioner, 'The Latin Americans have a Marshall programme of their own, and it's called the Monroe Doctrine') and, elsewhere in the administration, doctrinaires and incompetents, it can on the whole truthfully be said that they were successful at perceiving the national interest and at shaping policies to realize it. America and the West were safe in their hands; it was they who rebuilt the European economy and set up the Atlantic alliance. Left to themselves they would certainly have accepted the new government in Peking, and they would not have allowed the power of the United States to become the plaything of any particular pressure group or its friends. They believed too easily in the virtue of their country and were perhaps over-impressed by its power; some of them, notably Dean Rusk, one of the Assistant Secretaries of State, believed too devoutly in the need to mount worldwide resistance to communism; but as a whole a team of men of such intelligence would probably not long have let themselves be the victim of any delusion; and among them Dean Acheson, especially, understood the importance of training a generation of worthy successors.

All this was destroyed by the anti-communists. To them the question of China was not so much a political as a religious one. The fall of the quasi-Western, quasi-Christian Chiang government, the 'loss of China' (a country which America had never owned or controlled or found it anything but immensely difficult to influence), was only explicable on the assumption that there were traitors in high places. Joe McCarthy's service was to identify them: Owen Lattimore, for instance, a historian of China, or General Marshall who, said McCarthy, 'would sell his grandmother for any advantage'. (According to Senator Jenner of Indiana, Marshall was not only willing, but eager, to play the role of a front man for traitors.) But it was not only China: all events everywhere were interpreted as manifestations of a worldwide communist conspiracy, mounted and ordered by Josef Stalin. No distinctions were made: liberals, socialists and communists were all alike fiendish; Franklin Roosevelt and the New Deal had been central agents of the conspiracy (McCarthy talked of 'twenty years of treason'). All opponents of Russia, or of Russia's allies, must be worthy of America's friendship, and so the disastrous practice of seeking out and propping up fragile, cruel and incompetent dictatorships was reaffirmed (it had been initiated by the wooing of Chiang Kai-shek). The Presidency was not to be trusted: Senator Bricker of Ohio introduced a Constitutional amendment which would have written isolationism into the Constitution (as one critic put it) by forbidding the President to make non-treaty agreements with foreign powers, and subjecting treaties to such an infinitely drawn-out process of ratification that none in practice could ever come into effect. Senator McCarthy (in pursuit of a private vendetta) started hearings on the loyalty of the army – an action which brought about his ruin, since the hearings were televised and exhibited all too clearly his recklessness, cynicism and brutality, but which, while in progress, did nothing for the morale of the armed services in a time of acute international crisis.

The State Department collapsed under the McCarthyite attack, and the consequence, given the American political system, was inevitable: everybody got into the act. Congressmen, Senators, union leaders (especially George Meany, the ferociously anti-communist head of the AFL), businessmen, editors, clergymen: everyone with an axe to grind felt it his business to settle the foreign policy of the United States in one respect, or in all. They used every lever at their disposal, and, no longer meeting any significant resistance except from each other, got their own way far too often. Politicians running for election or re-election, whether to Congress or the Presidency, found it especially profitable to cultivate 'the three Is' – Ireland, Italy, Israel. The China lobby continued as vigorous as ever. As the international traffic in arms revived, a side-effect of the Cold War, American businessmen and generals were natural lobbyists, not just for continuing weapons research and development, but for their best customers: foreign countries which wished to buy American. Even Presidents in office were not immune to such pressures. President Truman, for example, was convinced that the right policy to pursue with respect to the Jewish survivors of the Holocaust was to allow them to settle in Palestine, and in 1948, needing all the friends he could get, made haste to recognize the state of Israel, born that year. This fateful decision was taken before the destruction of the State Department, but once professional advice was downgraded, once the experts no longer dared offer unpleasant or pessimistic appraisals, for fear of what would happen to them, once, in short, the determination of foreign policy had been taken over by personal hunch (Truman was convinced that Jewish colonization of Palestine went 'hand in hand with the noble policies of Woodrow Wilson, especially the principle of self-determination') and by lobbyists with limited views, no one would ever be in a position to point out how unwise it was, and unhealthy for both parties, to assume (and many soon did) that American and Israeli interests were or would always be identical; or to act on the perception. Not that the Israeli lobby was the only, or the worst, or the least plausible offender. By the end of the fifties the United States was committed to propping up any number of weak and worthless regimes, which by no possible stretch of the imagination could be said to have the sort of claim upon America that Israel had. There was a particularly ripe crop of such regimes in Latin America, notably in Cuba and the Dominican Republic. Unfortunately the imaginations of many Americans politicians are all too flexible when votes are in question. They wanted to please their constituents; they needed funds for their election campaigns; they believed in America's supreme virtue and global omnipotence; where Latin America was concerned, the Monroe Doctrine made a fine theme for unreflecting, assertively nationalistic speeches. Voices in another sense simply could not get a hearing, and one of the preconditions for the disasters of the sixties and seventies had come about. Once more the making of American foreign policy had become the plaything of prejudice, ignorance and selfishness.

However, it would be years before the full measure of the disaster became apparent, for the Marshall generation was still in control in the fifties, and the problems it had to deal with were still the old ones (it was when new ones emerged that the inadequacy of the system would begin to matter). Of these the chief was still, undoubtedly, the question of Marshal Stalin's intentions.

It is difficult to recapture the atmosphere of the late forties, when it seemed self-evident to Washington that Stalin controlled a monolithic world communist movement which had been turned into nothing more than the powerful instrument of Soviet policies. Even then it was not the whole story: Tito's Yugoslavia showed that, in favourable circumstances, a communist country would not automatically toe the Kremlin line, and Stalin's relations with Mao Tse-tung were always difficult. But the belief was so close to reality that the failure to distinguish between communism and Soviet activity was usually of little importance. After the 1948 coup in Czechoslovakia Stalin had imposed a thoroughly tyrannical regime on that country, like those, every bit as oppressive as his own in Russia, which his minions were busy creating in the rest of Eastern Europe. There was every reason to believe that a communist take-over in Western Europe would simply mean more of the same, for the local party leaders (Thorez in France, Togliatti in Italy) were obedient Stalinists; and in a number of test-cases the communists of the world showed themselves indeed to be members of a united movement. For instance, all of them joined in the endless bitter denunciations of Tito, the great heretic. Stalin's desire to crush him was notorious and palpable, and Tito got no aid or comfort from the Communist party of any other nation. Had it not been for the support which the West hastened to offer him, on the principle that my enemy's enemy is my friend, Tito would no doubt have been suppressed as rapidly and thoroughly as Nagy of Hungary was to be in 1956 or Dubček of Czechoslovakia in 1968, when the West was too distracted by troubles of its own to intervene. So it is scarcely surprising that in the late forties the United States and its allies saw themselves as the last guardians of human freedom. They resolved to be strong. There would be no Munich this time: Hitler's successor would be taught caution and good behaviour by all necessary means.

So the invasion of South Korea by North Korea on 25 June 1950 was automatically seen as a deliberate test of Western wills. It was the occupation of the Rhineland, the *Anschluss*, the Sudetenland affair of the Third World War. It was assumed that the North Koreans would never have dared to act without the express authorization of Stalin. The Chinese communists were discounted: they too were supposed to be mere tools of the Kremlin. This was the moment long awaited, long feared. If Stalin were allowed to succeed, the United States would be shamed for ever; worse, the security of Japan and the entire western Pacific would be threatened. Stalin might even be sufficiently encouraged by Western inaction to attempt some feat in Europe. So the line had to be drawn here, now. On 27 June President Truman announced that the United States, acting on behalf of the United Nations, would come to the rescue of the South Korean government and people.

They badly needed such assistance. Korea had been a Japanese colony from the end of the Russo-Japanese War until 1945; it had subsequently been divided, as a purely *ad hoc* measure, along the line of the 38th parallel, which ran across the waist of the peninsula. Neither of the Korean states which emerged had much claim on the respect or liking of the world; both were authoritarian governments; but the Stalinist regime of Kim Il Sung in the North was much better organized for war than the Southern one of Syngman Rhee. The armies of the North very quickly overran the South, until only a perimeter round the port of Pusan, at the toe of the peninsula, remained in non-communist hands.

But the communist forces had neither the material resources nor the military talent available to the Americans. General MacArthur took command in the field for the last time, and in what was perhaps the most daring and brilliant stroke of his entire career launched an amphibious attack at Inchon on the western coast of Korea, deep in the enemy's rear. He ran appalling risks, but the crushing victory which followed more than justified him. With astonishing rapidity the UN forces encircled and defeated the communist army, and the whole of the South was liberated. MacArthur began a rapid pursuit which carried him far north of the 38th parallel. Pyongyang, the North Korean capital, fell on 20 October.

The United States had now achieved its original purpose: South Korea had been rescued from wanton aggression; Stalin, it was to be hoped, had been taught a decisive lesson. Furthermore, it had all been done under the umbrella of the United Nations Organization. By a lucky chance the Soviet Union had been boycotting the sessions of the Security Council when the matter of North Korea's invasion was laid before that body, so it had been possible to get a mandate from the UN of a kind never heard of before or since. Although Americans and South Koreans formed the overwhelming majority of the forces commanded by MacArthur, a great many other nations were also represented (including Britain). The whole affair had proceeded with extraordinary speed and success; it seemed that all that was now needed was a mopping-up operation and the establishment of a new, more defensible border across the peninsula.

Unhappily success went to the policy-makers' heads. The division of Korea into two states was thoroughly artificial and un-historical; besides, would not the people of the North welcome liberation from communism? And might not an even sharper lesson be taught the Kremlin if the original war-aims were extended? If the North Koreans were finally defeated, dazzling possibilities would open. The peninsula might be remade as Japan had been and as a UN resolution of 1947 had prescribed. Besides, military operations north of the 38th parallel were essential if South Korea was to be made secure. The only drawback seemed to be a developing tendency of General MacArthur to act too much on his own. So he was given strict instructions what to avoid: there was to be no military action of any kind across the Korean frontiers with China and the USSR, and non-Korean troops were not to be used in the frontier zones. Harry Truman flew to a conference at Wake Island to make sure that MacArthur understood his orders. But the essence of the matter was all too well expressed in a cable sent by Marshall (by then, Secretary of Defense) to the General: 'We want you to feel unhampered tactically and strategically to proceed north of the 38th parallel.' A resolution of the UN General Assembly had already called for the 'complete independence and unity of Korea'. So MacArthur, seeing the whole peninsula open to him, swept ahead with the same dazzling speed and soon had forces on the Yalu river which formed the border with China: they included US army units, in defiance of orders. The maps published in the newspapers of Europe and America showed the General to be in complete command of Korea, except for some insignificant pockets of resistance in the extreme north. No doubt they would be pinched out in a few days.

Instead there came a counter-attack which sent the UN armies reeling back to the South in what Dean Acheson later called the worst defeat suffered by the US army since first Bull Run. The high command had made the fatal mistake of writing off the Chinese, who had done their best to make their position clear. They had indicated plainly that they could accept the reconquest of the South, but they could not tolerate the loss of the North, any more than the United States had been able to tolerate the original invasion. It was not simply that they would lose face if they allowed an ally to be defeated, or that communism might lose an adherent state. The Chinese also had too much reason to fear that if they allowed the United States to appropriate North Korea they would shortly have to face another Yankee initiative elsewhere. Chiang Kai-shek might be launched on an attempted reconquest of China itself with full American assistance: there was a lot of loose talk going round to that effect. Or the United States might send troops to reinforce France's effort to re-establish her imperial control of Indo-China (it was already subsidizing that effort handsomely). In short, the Chinese looked at the Americans through the same sort of telescope as that which the Americans were pointing at them. They too seemed to see a self-confident aggressor power making the first moves in a campaign that, unless checked, might lead on to world conquest. They too felt that the moment to avert a Third World War was now, the place here.

They noticed that victory had made MacArthur careless. Chinese forces slipped unobserved over the Yalu and broke MacArthur's centre. They achieved total surprise and swept forward as rapidly as their foe had done. Seoul, the South Korean capital, changed hands for the third time (though it was soon won back); and the war changed its character. For the Americans, now under the field command of General Matthew B. Ridgway, rallied; turned; checked the enemy; and then, with agonizing slowness, pushed north again. Only now their mood was sober. It was realized that the war could only be brought to a successful end if the original objective, of saving South Korea, were accepted as all that was attainable. With the assistance of Russian armaments and technical advisers, and China's unlimited man-power, the North Koreans were now unconquerable, since the Americans, or at least the Truman administration, dared not cross the Yalu, either to fight a land battle or to bomb the Chinese industrial centres in Manchuria (it was feared that any such extension of the war might bring in the Soviet Union, with who dared guess what hideous consequences). The moun-tainous terrain of central Korea was perfect for defensive operations. So the war settled down into a long slog, like the Western Front of the First World War. Both sides sent emissaries to Panmunjon to discuss peace terms, but this turned out to be as long a slog as the battles. Weeks turned into months; 1950 gave way to 1951 which gave way to 1952; American casualties mounted; popular dissatisfaction began to grow, dissatisfaction both with the apparently interminable war and the administration that had got bogged down in it.

Truman and the Democrats, in fact, had run out of luck. They had one last great achievement to their name, the creation of the North Atlantic Treaty Organization (NATO) in 1950. In the wake of the Korean emer-gency it had been easy enough to persuade the nations of Western Europe to join with the United States in a new alliance designed to build up military, air and naval forces strong enough to deter and if necessary to fight the USSR successfully. It had also been easy to get the North Atlantic Treaty through the US Senate, and presently General Eisenhower was sent to Paris to be the first Supreme Commander of NATO. He quickly built up a formidable force; and although the United States still provided most of the money and material that the alliance needed, the economic recovery of Europe that the Marshall Plan had fostered had already been successful enough to enable the Europeans to make significant contributions of their own. But this success for the administration was offset by Congressional rejection of most of the Fair Deal and by corruption in the executive. Some of Truman's appointees to office in the lower ranks of the bureaucracy owed their appointment more to the friendship of the President than to their intrinsic fitness for public service, and they allowed themselves to accept presents that were probably meant as bribes. It was all very low-grade, small-time misbehaviour, but muckraking journalists, above all Drew Pearson, who had a much-read, much-dreaded column, 'The Washington

Merry-Go-Round', had a wonderful time making the most of it. As 1952 drew near, it began to seem that a good year for the Republicans was coming at last.

Harry Truman decided not to run for re-election. There were signs that even his own party was getting tired of him (in the New Hampshire Democratic primary election, always the first to be held, more votes went to Senator Kefauver of Tennessee than to the President) and besides he was growing old. For the first time since 1932 the Democrats would have to put up a mere candidate, rather than an actual President, for the people's approval. This was potentially all the more damaging, because the Republicans had found an immensely strong candidate. General Eisenhower had agreed to come home again.

Ike had long been seen and spoken of as a possible President. His immense success as the Allied Commander in Europe during the war was largely attributable to his political skills. He had a hot temper, like George Washington, and like Washington he sometimes found it hard to control; but in public he was always the happy, smiling, friendly, reassuring leader. The only other veteran commander who might have Presidential ambitions was MacArthur; but not only was he much older than Eisenhower, he had also blotted his copybook by his defeat in North Korea and had then displayed persistent insubordination, for which, in April 1951, he was brusquely dismissed. This episode had greatly increased Truman's unpopularity in patriotic circles, and MacArthur was given a hero's welcome when he returned to the United States; but on reflection many Americans found that they did not altogether trust him. He was a great general, but he was also conspicuously rash and arrogant. When he allowed his name to be put forward in the Republican primary in Wisconsin, he was buried in votes for Eisenhower. Nor did the civilian Republicans fare much better. It was pretty clear that, with Ike on the ticket, the GOP (Grand Old Party) would be, at last, unbeatable: the same could not be said for a ticket headed by Senator Taft or by former Governor Stassen of Minnesota. The Republican convention met; there was a short, sharp struggle over credentials; the Eisenhower supporters won; and the General was nominated on the third ballot.

The Democrats responded by nominating their best man, Governor Adlai Stevenson of Illinois (1900–1965). Stevenson had proved himself an effective reforming Governor; he had served before that in the State Department; more than that, he was a speaker of great charm and eloquence, with solid liberal principles and solid understanding of the modern world. He captivated a generation of Democrats, especially the younger ones, and thus saved the party from falling back into the clutches of the Southern conservatives. He prepared the way for the reformers of the Kennedy and Johnson administrations, and, beyond that, for the dissenters who challenged the war in Vietnam. Stevensonian liberalism became as distinct a thread in American political life as, say, Taftite conservatism. But Stevenson never got the Presidency for which he was so well fitted.

The Republicans said it was time for a change, after twenty years, and Truman's retort, 'You never had it so good,' somehow did not seem very effective. They had a string of other issues helping them, above all the war. However, all this was secondary to Ike. When he said that, if elected, he would go to Korea, the people assumed that this meant the war was as good as over. When, on a visit to Wisconsin, McCarthy's base, he not only endorsed the odious Senator for re-election, but suppressed a passage in his speech in which he defended his old friend and patron, General Marshall, against McCarthy's libels, few noticed or cared, and (except for President Truman) most that did forgave him. Stevenson made a generally good impression, but in vain: on election night Eisenhower won by a landslide, carrying every single state outside the Solid South, where, it is to be supposed, party loyalty, rather than a liking for Stevenson's liberalism, carried the day. Three Democratic Senators who had attacked McCarthy were retired by the voters, to the terror of their former brethren. Eisenhower kept his campaign promise and examined the Korean War on the spot. Then he returned to instal an administration of a stripe that nobody in the thirties could ever have expected to see again. Happy days were back for Wall Street.

The Secretary of State, John Foster Dulles, was a corporation lawyer. The Under-Secretary of State had been head of Quaker Oats, Inc. The Secretary of the Treasury, George Humphrey, was the head of Mark Hanna's old firm. The Secretary of Defense, 'Engine Charlie' Wilson, had been the head of General Motors. Big business had recovered its confidence in the prosperity of the forties and early fifties; now it felt ready to take over the country again, and run it on the good old lines.

Unfortunately the Republican party was no longer a very fit instrument for government. McCarthy and his associates in the Senate had their own constituency and let few considerations of party interest or loyalty to the President, as head of the party, restrain them from cultivating it. Even the respectable Republicans were little better than political bankrupts. On domestic affairs, their one notion was to cut taxes and cut back 'big government', regardless of how little this would help the party in the metropolitan areas where national elections were now won or lost. On foreign policy they were only half-repentant isolationists: deeply hostile to Russia, but extremely suspicious of any concrete move to resist her, for in that way America might be dragged into unwanted foreign complications (in this at least they were perfectly right). There was even still a residual suspicion of Great Britain: Senator Knowland, the Republican leader in the Senate after Taft's death in 1953, seems to have believed that it was merely British guile that had involved the United States in two world wars. No doubt there was a case both for government thrift and for caution in American foreign policy, but it was not very convincing as made by this set of rich reactionaries, who had as little concern for the poor and the working class as Andrew Mellon, and as little knowledge of the modern world as Calvin Coolidge.

Furthermore, twenty years as the opposition party had left an ineradicable mark. Congressional Republicans had lost the ability to cooperate with the White House, even when one of their own lived in it; they were imaginatively unable to see and seize the chance they now had of permanently ending the Democrats' long control of Congress. As a result they went through the motions as before, doing all they could to obstruct their President; the policies of Secretary Humphrey plunged the economy into a slight but unpopular recession, which lasted almost throughout the Eisenhower Presidency, and they lost control of Congress again in the autumn of 1954.

Even had they been more equal to the challenge of the times, it might have defeated them, at least in international affairs, where the United States confronted difficulties that entailed choices of an unpleasantness and complexity that transcended the vision of both Democrats and Republicans. It had, indeed, nothing to do with partisan distinctions, and much to do with underlying national attitudes. The issues involved were, as it happened, incarnated in the contrast between those devoted partners, President Eisenhower and Secretary Dulles.

John Foster Dulles was descended from two Secretaries of State and had lived with the ambition of holding that office himself. He was a man of conspicuous faults and limited virtues. In essence he represented the old American missionary zeal. He spoke of containing communism, of rolling it back, of liberating Eastern Europe. These promises alarmed many observers, who did not see how they could be kept without war; but Dulles and his admirers saw no tension between the great twin goals of peace and liberty, for peace could only come, they held, when all the world was free as Americans understood the word. Peace was therefore to be pursued through the assertion of American power and influence, since only these could resist the communist tide and make the world democratic. Dulles, in short, was all too eager to meddle wherever he saw a chance to do so. He was overconfident that he understood whatever was going on. His style was that of a gloomy Presbyterian elder, a Woodrow Wilson without eloquence; but the substance of his policy was militaristic (he was a great believer in military pacts).

Eisenhower, fortunately for the world, was a man of very different temper. He took care to maintain the defences of the United States, in spite of irrational opposition from Congressional Republicans; apart from that his policy was marked by a profound caution, almost a quietism, which allowed him to act promptly and decisively only when the cause of peace could be furthered in no other way. He hoped that patience and reason would bring about a steady improvement in international relations; until they did he was content to play a waiting game. The skill and success of his policy must not be overstated. He connived at the operations by American intelligence (consolidated since 1947 into the Central Intelligence Agency, headed by John Foster Dulles's brother Allen) which overthrew the government of Guatemala so that the operations of the United Fruit Company, an ill-managed American concern, could be safeguarded; he similarly approved the operation which toppled the Iranian nationalist government of Dr Mossadegh and brought back the Shah of Iran from his first exile; in his second term he sent an expeditionary force to restore peace in the Lebanon (a simpler task than it has since become); he made an international issue of the islets of Quemoy and Matsu, off the Chinese mainland, denying control of them to the communists in favour of the Kuomintang. Above all, and most tragically, he did not teach the American people that they could not have both peace and unbridled power. But against that must be set the great facts that he ended the war in Korea and kept the United States out of conflict thereafter, until he left office in 1961; he kept John Foster Dulles under control; he effectively stopped a Franco–British–Israeli invasion of Egypt in 1956; and he launched the policy of *détente* – that is, of actively seeking understanding and agreement with the Soviet Union, of making that the first of diplomatic objectives. Admittedly, he did not pursue that policy with any great success: a big conference in Paris in 1960 collapsed when Russia successfully shot down an American spy-plane that ought to have been kept on the ground at such a delicate juncture; nevertheless, to him belongs the credit of being the first American President to try to bury the Cold War.

On the domestic front Eisenhower did not do so well. He would not act boldly and openly against Joe McCarthy, explaining privately that 'I just will not – I *refuse* – to get into the gutter with that guy.' This left McCarthy free to intensify his persecution of the State Department and to launch a new campaign against the army; luckily for Eisenhower this last enterprise backfired completely, so that in December 1954 the majority of the Senate at last felt brave enough to vote for a motion condemning 'the Senator from Wisconsin, Mr McCarthy' for bringing the Senate 'into dishonour and disrepute'. After that Joe's unique power as a national bully was at an end. Eisenhower burdened himself with the most pious Secretary of Agriculture in American history, Ezra Taft Benson, member of the Council of Twelve of the Church of the Latter-Day Saints (Mormonism was now utterly respectable), who was also the most unpopular with farmers, for he made a determined effort to reduce the size of federal subsidies to agriculture. In other respects the Eisenhower administration was little more than colourless. Its most important action, the Interstate Highway Act of 1956, was undertaken largely at the bidding of a well-organized pressure-group. This Act committed the federal government to spending $33,500,000,000 in fourteen years on building a national network of motor-roads. It was to do more to shape the lives of the American people than any other law passed since 1945. It reinforced the ascendancy of the private car over all other forms of passenger transport; it made continental bus services fully competitive with the already declining railroads; it boosted freight carrying by truck; it gave a great impetus to black emigration from the South, and a huge boost to the automobile, engineering and building industries, thus helping to stimulate the prosperity of the sixties; by encouraging car-ownership it encouraged car utilization, thus stimulating the spread of the population into vast sprawling suburbs, where only the car could get you to work, to the shops, to schools, entertainments and voting-booths; and this change in turn would soon be reflected in political behaviour. Yet it can hardly be pretended that the administration foresaw or desired these results, any more than it did the widespread corruption and faulty construction that went with the hasty building of the highways.

The Eisenhower years were in general ones of comfortable lethargy. When the Soviet Union put the first satellite into space in 1957 the shock to American vanity was almost unbearable; the cry went up that something was badly wrong with American society, American science, American education; it was to take several years for the speed with which the lapse was made good to wipe out this impression. The rifts in the Republican party were obvious, and if time saw off the dinosaurs (McCarthy died in 1957, Knowland disappeared after losing a gubernatorial election in California) it was not bringing forward many bright new Republican faces. True, Nelson Rockefeller, a grandson of old John D., was elected Governor of New York state in 1958, but by this time the GOP was very weary of always taking its cue from the multi-millionaires of the East, who seemed more and more dangerously liberal. That left only the Vice-President, Richard Nixon, whose one certain talent was for a sort of deodorized McCarthyism. He badly wanted the Presidential nomination, and exploited the Vice-Presidency cunningly, carrying out all the routine party chores which bored the President. Nixon, every party-worker knew, would speak for anyone, anywhere. He called in the debts thus incurred in 1960, when he easily won the nomination. He had the rather reluctant blessing of the President; but if he could turn that into a willingness to campaign on his behalf (Ike never much liked campaigning for himself) he would surely be able to glide into the White House, if not in a landslide, at least without great difficulty. Times were not bad; no grave crises obviously threatened; the Democrats, as usual, were deeply divided.

They were not, however, downhearted. The election of 1956 had been a nightmare; Adlai Stevenson had again won the nomination, but had campaigned far less effectively than in 1952, and been beaten even more thoroughly. However, his party had increased its majority in Congress; and in 1958, at the worst point of the Eisenhower recession, had increased it again, enormously. Eisenhower the Invincible was constitutionally barred from running again. Nixon was widely distrusted and disliked (the favourite Democratic joke of the period was a picture of the Vice-President looking shifty, with the slogan underneath, 'Would you buy a used car from this man?'). The economy had still not wholly recovered. Eisenhower's modest and cautious style of leadership had appeared to many as merely timid and incompetent, and the collapse of his peace-seeking ventures at the Paris conference had confirmed the impression. Finally, the Democrats had plenty of energetic and talented candidates.

Of the field, two men looked to the past: Adlai Stevenson, half-reluctant, half-anxious for a third nomination; and Senator Symington, Harry Truman's candidate, who had been one of Truman's Cabinet officers and came from Missouri. These two never looked very likely to get the prize. Three candidates saw themselves as men of the future: Hubert Humphrey, Senator from Minnesota, one of the most energetic and politically creative spirits in Congress; Lyndon Baines Johnson of Texas, Senate Majority Leader, who had given Congress the firm leadership that Eisenhower had refused to supply; and John Fitzgerald Kennedy, junior Senator from Massachusetts. Kennedy won the day. He was young, as politicians go; very handsome, very charming, very able, very rich. He was also a consummate politician. While he demolished Humphrey in the primaries, he quietly rounded up enough support among the old pros of the Democratic party (men like the mayor of Chicago, Richard J. Daley, and John Bailey, the boss of Connecticut) to be sure of defeating the rest, and particularly Johnson, at the convention. Everything went according to plan, and soon nothing was left but the battle with Richard Nixon. It proved a hard tussle; but Nixon's charmlessness, his implausibility as the heir of the smiling, reassuring, authoritative Eisenhower, and half a dozen blunders, of which the worst was to engage in a television debate with Kennedy, which simply gave the rival candidate a chance to get better known, eventually handed the Presidency to Kennedy, who ran a brilliant campaign. He was elected by an almost invisible majority (118,574), but elected he was, and a country which had basked quite happily in the sunny inaction of the Eisenhower era began to feel eager to see what the energetic leadership promised by the new man would amount to. There was a lot needing attention: the ever-deepening rift between the United States and the communist regime which had recently come to power in Cuba; the latest Berlin crisis (the Russians in August 1961 built a wall across the city to stop the flow of refugees from East to West); threatening campaigns by communist guerrillas in Laos and Vietnam; at home, a backlog of long-overdue reforms and, above all, an explosive racial situation. At least one old problem had been solved: though Kennedy had certainly lost votes in some important states because he was a Catholic, he had won them elsewhere for the same reason, and proved in the end that it was no longer necessary to be a Protestant to be President of the United States. So a bad tradition came to an end, and Kennedy stepped forward to take the oath of office. Then he delivered a short inaugural speech. It was an essay in the higher eloquence, well enough for such an occasion though perhaps rather fustian when read in cold blood; its note was stirring, but possibly disconcerting:

Let every nation know, whether it wishes us well or ill, that we shall pay any price, bear any burden, meet any hardship, support any friend, oppose any foe to assure the survival and success of liberty. Let the word go forth from this time and place, to friend and foe alike, that the torch has passed to a new generation of Americans – born in this century, tempered by war, disciplined by a hard and bitter peace, proud of our ancient heritage, and unwilling to witness or permit the slow undoing of human rights to which this Nation has always been committed . . .

Could he mean it? It sounded like a call to a new world war. Well, time would show. Meanwhile it was a moment for joy: joy in the glitter of the new administration, in the high spirits of the President, the beauty of his wife, the obvious intelligence, energy and devotion of his ministers; in the strength and splendour of America at her height, queen and dynamo of the nations. Eisenhower went quietly back to his farm at Gettysburg. Nobody foresaw that his bumbling, peaceful reign would ever be looked back on fondly.

25 Unfinished Business 1954–68

There comes a time when people get tired. We are here this evening to
say to those who have mistreated us so long that we are tired – tired of
being segregated and humiliated, tired of being kicked about by the
brutal feet of oppression. We have no alternative but to protest. For
many years, we have shown amazing patience. We have sometimes given
our white brothers the feeling that we liked the way we were being
treated. But we come here tonight to be saved from that patience that
makes us patient with anything less than freedom and justice.

Martin Luther King, 5 December 1955

The bland smile of American democracy displayed a rotten tooth, or rather
two rotten teeth: the plight of the South and that of the African–Americans.
They were and always had been intimately related, never more so than at
the beginning of the twentieth century, when 85 per cent of 8,800,000
African-Americans lived in the South, a region where the per capita income
was little more than half the national average (if one omitted the trans-
Mississippi South from the calculation, it was *less* than half the national
average). Before the First World War the final touches were put to the Jim
Crow edifice, and in spite of all the brave aspirations to a 'New South' the
region stood supreme in disease, poverty, ignorance, sloth, hunger and
cruelty: in 1900 there were 115 lynchings (nine of whites, 106 of blacks) in
a year when the total number of homicides was 230. Not all the lynchings
occurred in the South, but most of them did. Southern politics appeared
to be immune to the successive challenges of Populism and Progressivism:
however vivacious the reformers, in the end the old order of corruption,
demagogy and reaction, cemented by hatred of the blacks, persisted, it
seemed, unchanged. The South still seemed caught in the trauma of Appomattox: the old Jeffersonian themes of agrarianism and states' rights were
mumbled (or, when necessary, shouted in defiance of the Yankee intruder)
like prayers to a rosary, and with 'the war' formed the staple of most

respectable public discourse. It was a world, it appeared, condemned by itself and fate to permanent exclusion from the American mainstream. The teeth, one might pardonably have assumed, were beyond the skills of the dentist: were past repair and (thanks to Abraham Lincoln) impossible to extract.

Yet this gloomy appearance was necessarily false. Historical change could not spare even the South. Rescue was at hand; the agents of it, war and capitalism.

The First World War served the South in many ways. First, by stimulating a huge demand for unskilled labour and by at the same time cutting off immigration from Europe, it gave the blacks an alternative to cotton-picking. The factories of the North were clamouring for workers; the South supplied them. The 'Great Migration' began: in their thousands the blacks slipped away from the fields to board the trains for Chicago and Detroit. They were seizing the chance to cut the cord which tied them to poverty and the South. Never mind that they would suffer appallingly at the hands of the Northerners; in the end this internal migration would be seen to be the best thing that had happened to their race since the slaves walked away from the plantations. Meanwhile, war necessities poured a flood of wealth and economic stimulus into the South. Her coasts were fringed with shipyards, each building frantically. Soldiers needed cheap, convenient smokes: suddenly the cigarette was big business, and the tobacco farmers were saved. Cotton, needed for explosives, boomed: 'King Cotton is now restored to his throne,' an admirer rejoiced, 'and from fields nodding drowsily in white through the summer he draws royal revenues.' Oil was so much in demand that the problem of overproduction was solved, for the time being at any rate. Vast new coalfields were opened in Kentucky. Army camps sprang up all over the South, bringing with them a huge stimulus to stores and soda-fountains (smoking was not the soldier's only relaxation). The Southern textile industry boomed, and began the rapid advance that was to overtake New England in the post-war period. Ordinary wage-earners – even if they were black – found themselves prosperous as never in their lives before. The South was suddenly alive again; hope was real at last.

It might all have been a bubble, but although there was indeed a recession immediately after the war, and although the perennial problems of Southern agriculture got worse and worse during the twenties, the march, once begun, was not halted, even by the 1929 Crash. During the twenties Northern capital, energetically seeking new investment fields, began to enter the South in unheard-of quantities. Wartime success had opened investors' eyes to the possibilities: they were eager to realize them, and most Southern state governments, mint-new from their Progressive reshaping, were eager to help, especially by advertising the low cost of Southern labour, kept that way by rigid opposition to labour unions and (though they did not say so) by the fomentation of racial rivalry. In the South-West there was an oil boom, characterized by wide-open frontier towns like those of yore, in which the Wild West had its last fling; Coca-Cola, which was manufactured in Atlanta, began its spectacular rise as the world's most popular teenage drink; new commodities such as aluminium and rayon came on swiftly; there was a rising demand for lumber; and the Florida building boom. The result soon showed in the statistics: while the number of wage-earners in manufacturing sank nationally by 9 per cent between 1919 and 1927, it went up in the South by the same amount, and the South's urban population grew more rapidly than that of any other section, though it was still only 32.1 per cent of the area's total in 1930. Southern boosters acclaimed the new vigour and hopefulness of Dixie. It was all very reminiscent of the West a hundred years previously.

All was not gracious in the garden: the boll weevil completed its devastation of the cotton areas in the early twenties, while the mosaic disease threatened the Louisiana sugar industry, and sharecropping continued to spread. But in retrospect the signs of hope seem more important. Certainly they were more important for the Southern blacks, for the ancient agricultural South would never offer them anything other than more of the same tyranny. That was the most compelling reason for the Great Migration; but however many blacks left the South, the number remaining would still be huge, and growing: 8,912,000 in 1920, 9,905,000 in 1940, 11,312,000 in 1960. Even though the Southern black population was slowly dwindling as a proportion of the US black total, African-Americans would never be free and equal until their position in the South had changed fundamentally.

During the twenties the signs suggesting that such a change was on the way multiplied. Such ancient curses as hookworm, malaria, yellow fever and pellagra were eliminated. The last-named, a deficiency disease caused by the country people's too-restricted diet of meal, molasses and salt meat, was not diagnosed until 1906 and not generally recognized as a deficiency disease for another twenty years. Yet it was one of the chief causes of Southern lethargy, of that notorious inability of the poor whites and blacks to work either hard or speedily. Its disappearance was a major blessing, if only for what it implied about improved diets and therefore improved incomes.

Inevitably, the South was badly hit by the Depression. The boosters (who in the twenties had brought about substantial investment in new roads, among other things) were stopped in their tracks. Southern farmers probably suffered worse than any others from the general economic collapse. Forced sales of farm lands were on a gigantic scale (on a single day in April 1932, a quarter of the land of the state of Mississippi was auctioned), banks and railroads collapsed, so did the prices of the great Southern staples, cotton, tobacco and sugar; state governments tottered on the brink of bankruptcy. At some point between 1930 and 1935 tenant farming and sharecropping, those twin certain indicators of economic malaise in the South, became more common than ever before or since. Yet the region almost certainly gained more from the New Deal than any other. This was partly because of the Congressional ascendancy of the South in the newly dominant Democratic party: important partners of FDR like Senator Robinson of Arkansas, the majority leader, or Representative Bankhead of Alabama, Speaker of the House between 1936 and 1940, not to mention Cordell Hull of Tennessee or James Byrnes of South Carolina, were excellently placed to further the interests of their section; and a stream of legislation poured continuously out of Washington to aid the South, the most spectacular item of which, the TVA, rescued from poverty and oblivion the hinterland of five Southern states (Tennessee, Georgia, Florida, Alabama and North Carolina). Still more important, perhaps, was the fact that the nature of the Depression entailed certain remedies, and both the emergency and its cure were marvellously appropriate stimuli to the Southern economy. The collapse of the world market, for example, at last brought about the dethrone- ment of King Cotton. What a century of agrarian reformers had urged in vain was now compelled by disaster. White and black farmers learned alike, the hard way, that their apathetic reliance on cotton could now only ruin them; and while many abandoned agriculture altogether, many diversified into other crops, particularly livestock, which they found to their surprise were much more profitable; while those who stuck to cotton were bailed out by the federal government on condition that they henceforth regulated production with reference to the national, not the international, market. Subsidy, in short, implied federal planning and control; reluctantly the sturdy individualists of Southern agriculture accepted the lesson (the tobacco farmers made a bolt for freedom in the later thirties, but it ended so rapidly in disaster that they returned to the fold with equal speed) and Southern farming began at last to catch up with farming elsewhere in America. Meanwhile the NRA made itself felt in Southern industry, raising wages in cotton manufacturing (and ending the scandal of child labour in the mills), regulating oil production and making possible the unionization, at long last, of the coalmines. The RFC encouraged the development of a paper industry in the region, exploiting the abundant softwoods of the piny barrens. Chemicals rapidly made their way to a leading position in the Southern economy, partly as a side-effect of the rise of the oil industry. The South recovered more rapidly than any other part of the nation from the Depression; by the Second World War it was poised for a spectacular burst of growth. The emergence of new industrial, financial and commercial classes implied that the entire basis of Southern politics would soon be altered.

Meanwhile, for the Southern blacks, transformation had already begun. Their standard of living and their incomes had been so low that relief payments under FERA and WPA meant that they were actually better off – much better off. The point did not go unnoticed. 'Ever since federal relief came in you can't hire a nigger to do anything for you. High wages is ruinin' 'em,' said a North Carolina landlord. 'I wouldn't plough nobody's mule from sunrise to sunset for 50 cents per day when I could get $1.30

for pretending to work on a DITCH,' said a white Georgian farmer. Intense pressure was brought to undo this shocking state of affairs, leading at one moment (in 1937) to the revival of 'something like the slave patrol'[1] which drove blacks to work in the cotton fields. Federal policy accepted the idea that relief payments ought to be lower per capita in the South than elsewhere, just as wages were; but neither this nor any other concession to conservatives could make much difference. The poor of the South, black and white, discovered that higher wages for less work were now available to them, thanks to Uncle Sam; and they were soon ready to think that these good things ought to be available to them on principle. The relief programme reinforced the sturdy patriotism of the Southern poor white. A North Carolina tenant farmer said that whenever he heard the 'Star-Spangled Banner' he got a lump in his throat: 'There ain't no other nation in the world that would have sense enough to think of WPA and all the other As.' The Southern poor black began to look about him, as his Northern kin had already learned to do.

The experience of segregated service in the profoundly racist army of the First World War, of lynching on the home front and of riots in the war's aftermath gave Northern blacks a deep awareness of their oppressed status and an equally deep determination to improve it. Sometimes this determination had bizarre results. One such was the Universal Negro Improvement Association of Marcus Garvey (1887–1940). Garvey was a Jamaican who found his way to the United States in 1916 and in the post-war years gained a huge following by his insistence on the greatness and glory of being black (an attitude that was to return in greatly increased strength in the 1960s, when it was expressed in the slogan 'Black is Beautiful!'). He denounced white Americans as hopelessly corrupt and racist, and urged a return to Africa; meanwhile he urged his followers to build up autonomous black social, economic and military institutions, of which the most celebrated was the Black Star Steamship Line. Unfortunately it caused his downfall: it was commercially unsound, and in 1925 Garvey was sent to prison for using the mails to defraud – he had raised money for his Black Star by post. When he was let out two years later Coolidge deported him as an undesirable alien. Garveyism rapidly faded, to the relief of many black leaders, who found its competition all too effective; but it had enunciated many themes that were to re-emerge forty years later. By an irony of history W. E. B. Du Bois, Garvey's chief opponent, was eventually to adopt one of Garvey's principles: when Ghana became the first of Britain's African colonies to regain its independence Du Bois renounced his American citizenship and went to end his days there.

On the whole there was more promise in the activities of the more sedate black organizations, such as the National Association for the Advancement of Colored People (NAACP), which had been founded in 1909, by Du

1 George Brown Tindall, *The Emergence of the New South* (Baton Rouge, 1967), p. 480.

Bois and others, in the wake of a dreadful race riot at Springfield, Illinois, in the previous year. The NAACP, which was the most important and effective of black pressure groups, was a partnership of blacks and whites, like the old abolitionist movement of which it was self-consciously the heir; and it concentrated on securing African-American advancement through the courts. It made some few gains between the wars, notably by securing the destruction of the 'grandfather clause', which was outlawed by the US Supreme Court in the case of *Lane* v. *Wilson* (1939) and by scoring a first defeat of the white primary in *Nixon* v. *Herndon* (1927); but these victories were more than offset by the loss of *Grovey* v. *Townsend* (1935), in which the Court unanimously acknowledged the legality of a revised, but equally effective, form of the white primary. This was a heavy blow to the NAACP which had invested a great deal of time and money in the case; furthermore, the Association had difficulty in answering the charge, made in 1940 by Ralph Bunche (a black intellectual, later a leading diplomatist), that it was of very little use to the bulk of poor blacks, who had more pressing concerns than their inability to vote: 'The escape that the Negro mass seeks is one from economic deprivation, from destitution and imminent starvation. To these people, appealing for livelihood, the NAACP answers: give them educational facilities, let them sit next to whites in street-cars, restaurants, and theaters. They cry for bread and are offered political cake.'

Yet there were some signs that important changes were at hand. In 1925 A. Philip Randolph (1889–1978) organized the first successful black labour union, the Brotherhood of Sleeping Car Porters and Maids, that after years of struggle succeeded in winning both recognition and wage increases from the Pullman Company. The Republican allegiance of black voters (where there were any – that is, in the North) began to crack in the 1928 election, when Herbert Hoover, very injudiciously, courted the racist vote in the South. In the same year Oscar De Priest of Illinois became the first black man since Reconstruction to be elected to Congress.

All the same, the twenties were a miserable period for blacks north as well as south of the Mason–Dixon line, and the coming of the Depression made matters worse. The accelerated impoverishment of the mass of black workers meant that the black lower middle class of small businessmen – shopkeepers, undertakers and the like – who sold them services could no longer find customers, and they too began to succumb to economic disaster. And at first it did not seem that the New Deal could be of much assistance. Roosevelt could not place black rights high on his agenda, if anywhere at all. The NAACP pressed him, as it had pressed so many Presidents before, to support an anti-lynching bill. He told its head, Walter White, 'I did not choose the tools with which I work . . . Southerners, by reason of the seniority rule in Congress, are chairmen or occupy strategic places on most of the . . . committees. If I come out for the anti-lynching bill now, they will block every bill I ask Congress to pass to keep America from collapsing. I just can't take that risk.' But though they accepted this reasoning, black leaders did not let it discourage them. They took comfort from the fact that FDR had a 'black cabinet', an unofficial body of African-Americans whose advice he sought on matters to do with their race, from the knowledge that Eleanor Roosevelt was on their side, and from the President's words to Mary McLeod Bethune, a member of the black cabinet: 'People like you and me are fighting . . . for the day when a man will be regarded as a man regardless of his race. That day will come, but we must pass through perilous times before we realize it.' They discounted the fact that the TVA accepted Jim Crow restrictions, and that the Federal Housing Authority positively encouraged residential segregation.[2] To them the all-important thing was that the President's policies had saved them from despair and starvation, and they went over to the Democratic party *en bloc*: for instance, in 1934 a black Democrat, Arthur W. Mitchell, replaced the black Republican, De Priest, as Congressman from the first district of Illinois. At the same time, Republicans did not let the growing black vote go without a struggle, which partly explains the rapidly increasing number of blacks in the state legislatures during the thirties. Black judges began to appear here and there in the North. The Roosevelt administration appointed large numbers of African-Americans to executive posts (though not to any very important ones), while its expenditures went not only on relief for individuals but on building hospitals and college buildings for blacks as well. The emergence of the CIO at last opened a way into unionism for large numbers of black industrial workers, who had previously been blocked by the AFL, more because craft unions disliked unskilled workers than because their members disliked blacks. In 1937 the Supreme Court declared that it was legal to picket firms which refused to employ African-Americans.

Then the Second World War transformed the position and prospects of black Americans, just as the First World War had transformed the prospects of the South.

The new conflict, to be sure, also carried on the work of the first. Once more, army camps sprouted everywhere in the South. So did military airfields. Some $4,500,000,000 was spent on war plants in the section, raising its industrial capacity by 40 per cent or so; among the long-term effects were the creation of a pool of skilled workers, another of local capital and yet another of trained managers. Once more the South demonstrated its attractions as a field of investment, and financiers and industrialists took note. There was a renewed rush from the land, a renewed burst of urban growth (bringing many acute problems with it); yet times had never been so good on the farms. The new cities and factories could absorb all that the land could produce. With the return of good times came an acceleration of the reviving conservatism of the farmers: they supported the conservative lobby, the Farm Bureau, ever more enthusiastically, and actively encouraged the dismantling of the Farm Security Administration, which had tried to

2 Harry Truman put a stop to this (see p. 625).

help tenant farmers and sharecroppers. Not that this was too tragic a development: the tenants and sharecroppers were already streaming to the city and the better life (paid for by wartime jobs) that it promised.

What Torified the whites radicalized the blacks, and they made substantial gains in both military and civilian life, though not without anguish. In the services they quickly discovered that they were being treated as second-class citizens, and were equally quick to resent it. Northern blacks, called up in large numbers, found themselves at training-camps in the rural South where these second- or third-generation city-dwellers, these soldiers of freedom (many had joined up with great enthusiasm to fight Hitler) found themselves treated as they never had been in their lives before – treated as their Southern kin were. The contempt, the brutality, the injustice of white supremacy made themselves felt every day. What was particularly hard to bear was the sight of Nazi prisoners of war enjoying facilities, such as railway restaurants and dining-cars, which black American soldiers were forbidden to enter. Nor did these Northerners appreciate segregated quarters within the camps, or segregated everything in nearby towns. Inevitably there was trouble: fights, riots and one full-scale mutiny. The high command came badly out of the story.[3] Not only was segregation in the army preserved, but black units were denied equal opportunity to shine in war: all too often they were given poor training, poor equipment, and were sent to the least promising parts of the battlefield. In spite of this many individual blacks and many black units performed heroically and more than vindicated their claim to equal rights as American soldiers. But the only leading American general who seemed to understand and accept the idea was George Patton, a hot-headed, brilliant commander who welcomed the 761st 'Black Panther' Tank Battalion to his army in Normandy in 1944 in a speech that endured among many veterans' treasured memories:

Men, you are the first Negro tankers ever to fight in the American army. I would never have asked for you if you were not good. I have nothing but the best in my army. I don't care what color you are as long as you go up there and kill those Kraut sons-of-bitches. Everyone has their eyes on you and are expecting great things from you. Most of all, your race is looking forward to your success. Don't let them down, and, damn you, don't let me down!

If you want me you can always find me in the lead tank.

But even an officer corps dominated by men of Southern background and attitudes eventually had to accept that it had a wolf by the ears; in the mere interests of military efficiency concessions had to be made. Officer cadet schools were desegregated in 1940; blacks were admitted to the Marine Corps for the first time and, on an equal footing, to the navy; in the army

---

3 Typical of its attitude was General Eisenhower's comment on segregation in 1948: 'If we attempt to force someone to like someone else, we are just going to get into trouble.'

they were used in a combat role in all theatres (whereas in the First World War they had been confined to a support role, though not in the Civil War); finally, during the crisis of the Battle of the Bulge in December 1944, when the Germans counter-attacked for the last time and for a few days carried all before them, black reinforcements were thrown in wherever they could be of most use and a measure of *de facto* desegregation at the fighting level occurred. It was followed up in January 1945 by the creation of the first formally integrated unit in the history of the army. The implications were plain, and in 1948 President Truman opened all jobs in the armed services to African-Americans and abolished the racial quota, according to which no more blacks would be accepted into uniform than there were, proportionately, in the total population. Finally, during the Korean War, the needs of the battlefield once more took a hand, and under the pressure of events the complete integration of the US army was at last achieved.

The impact of the Second World War on civilian blacks was just as profound, though possibly less visibly dramatic. Progress was determined by two factors: the growing importance of black votes in Northern elections, especially in the great urban-industrial complexes, and by the manpower needs of the nation at war. As a matter of fact, black political leverage had been growing for some time: for example, in 1930 it was largely African-American pressure that defeated Herbert Hoover's nomination of an unacceptable candidate to the Supreme Court. Ten years later A. Philip Randolph spectacularly demonstrated the new muscle of his people. After the outbreak of the war in Europe, the United States economy, as we have seen, moved over to the production of war materials and began to boom. Blacks found it exceedingly hard to get employment in the resuscitated factories. A colour bar unquestionably existed, and denunciations by the President, by the US Office of Education and by the National Defense Advisory Committee did little or nothing to improve matters. So in January 1941 Randolph announced that unless the bar was lifted he would lead a march of blacks on Washington on 1 July, a date unpleasantly near the glorious Fourth, and an event calculated to draw the greatest possible attention to the existence of racial oppression in the leading Western democracy: a propaganda gift to Goebbels. Nothing could have been more divisive or more likely to give a harried administration, struggling to control events as America drifted towards war, enormous political trouble. At the same time the blacks of America responded with huge enthusiasm. Leading New Dealers such as Mayor La Guardia and Mrs Roosevelt were sent to dissuade Randolph, but he was inexorable. At length the President gave in. After conferring with the black leader Roosevelt issued Executive Order 8802, under which every defence contract between the government and industry had to have a clause forbidding racial discrimination in employment, and a committee on fair employment practices was set up to make sure that the clauses were honoured. Randolph called off the march on Washington. But the tactic was not forgotten: Mr Randolph was to live to see it actually used.

Blacks, of course, welcomed 8802; the South did not. One Kentucky journalist tried to make it acceptable to Southern white opinion by arguing that it had nothing to do with racial segregation and by asserting comfortingly that 'all the armies of the world, both of the United Nations and the Axis, could not force upon the South the abandonment of racial segregation'. Like the proposed march, this assertion afforded a glimpse of the future.

The fair employment order and the Fair Employment Practices Committee (FEPC) could not immediately end all prejudicial discrimination by employers; blacks still failed to get all the jobs they were entitled to, or, when employed, to secure earned promotion; but still they made huge advances, as the rapid rise of the black population of such cities as Los Angeles, San Francisco, Chicago and Detroit suggested. The NAACP went on with its war in the courts. It brought unceasing pressure to bear in the attempt to equalize educational opportunities for black and white children in the South, and in particular to equalize teachers' salaries: after winning a crucial case in the Supreme Court, *Gaines* v. *Canada* (1938), in which chief Justice Hughes declared that, to be constitutional, 'separate but equal' facilities (as required by *Plessy* v. *Ferguson*) had to be truly equal, the NAACP was able to lobby so effectively that soon after the end of the war black schoolteachers' salaries in the South had risen to 79 per cent of whites'. *Gaines* thus added appreciably to the cost of maintaining school segregation; it also marked the Supreme Court's first step away from segregationist doctrine. Even more important was another NAACP-inspired decision, *Smith* v. *Allwright* (1944), in which the Court finally declared the white primary to be unconstitutional in any form. This decision did not of itself mean that Southern blacks would now be able to vote. It was only a first step, like *Gaines*. But first steps have to be taken.

These successes owed much to the transformation of the Supreme Court by appointments made during Roosevelt's second and third terms, and even while they were being won blacks were still suffering outrageously at the hands of fellow-citizens. NAACP persistence in pursuing these cases was, however, a sign that blacks were even less willing than they had been after the First World War to endure bad treatment, at least in the North (and the black North, as whites were reminded in 1943, 'has always been the tongue of the black South'). Matters came to a head in Detroit. The great automobile assembly lines had been turned over to the production of tanks, and the whole industry had greatly expanded: by the end of the war it was responsible for 20 per cent of all war production. The wide-open job market had allured many poor blacks as well as whites from the South (50,000 of the one sort, 450,000 of the other). Such an influx, only comparable to what had occurred at the height of the Great Migration and the Industrial Revolution, would in any circumstances have imposed enormous strains on social resources. All over America it proved difficult to house wartime workers, and shanty-towns, 'new Hoovervilles', inevitably grew up to accommodate them. Black and white immigrants were alike unused to city and factory life; the white Southerners brought their traditional hostilities with them and acted upon them; rabblerousers were not lacking. At last, after incessant provocation, the blacks retaliated. On 20 June 1943, after a fist fight between a black man and a white, the races clashed violently all over the city. At length Roosevelt had to declare a state of emergency and send in federal troops to restore order. The trouble ended only after twenty-five blacks and nine whites had been killed, 800 people had been injured, and two million dollars worth of damage had been done to property (most of it belonging to blacks). It was a shocking and depressing affair, but in its way also signified progress: African-Americans had not submitted tamely to oppression, and the violence had dramatically advertised their grievances to the world.

So it can be argued that by the end of the war the blacks had discovered the three weapons with which, in the fifties and sixties, they were to achieve such striking victories: the imaginative use of political and economic pressure; the appeal to the courts and the Constitution; violence. In addition, wartime service and wartime mobility had not only widened black horizons, but made the blacks more conscious of their strength, and of the need for united action. But the immediate post-war period was not one in which these discoveries could be put to use. The majority of the people – the whites – were rejoicing in the return of peace and its opportunities, while in Congress the alliance of reactionaries was rising to the peak of its influence. Social statistics indicated that black folk were continuing to gain ground: black incomes were rising, more workers were skilled or semi-skilled, more were going to university and fewer were earning their living on the land. But such political momentum as the black cause retained was attributable to the actions of the new President. Harry Truman was not untouched by the prejudices of his native state, Missouri, but he was too intelligent and had too lively a sense of decency and justice to let them rule him. Besides, he knew the increasing importance of the black vote to the Democratic party and, above all, to the New Deal, which he was determined to carry to renewed victories. So as well as ordering the desegregation of the armed services he set up a new FEPC, using his executive authority (the wartime FEPC had lapsed after the return of peace, and filibustering Southern Senators made sure that Congress did not revive it on a statutory footing), he forbade the Federal Housing Administration to lend money to racially segregated building projects, and he opened vast numbers of civil service jobs to blacks. He also made various symbolic gestures, calculated to advertise the blacks' cause and his own attachment to it: he proposed a civil rights Act, and appointed Dr Ralph Bunche to be American ambassador to the United Nations. Best of all, perhaps, by defying the Dixiecrats in 1948 and yet managing to get re-elected he showed that the power of the Solid South was waning at last, in the Democratic party and in the nation at large.

If the black vote was worth winning, it was worth competing for: in and after the 1952 election the Republicans were careful to show themselves liberal on the race issue, and won some friends thereby. Eisenhower completed the desegregation of the armed services and followed Truman's policy of making numerous black appointments. But if the African-Americans allowed their progress to wait on the actions of the federal government it would be very slow. So the NAACP stuck to its own line. It tried hard to get the federal courts to declare segregation in schools unconstitutional, and in 1954 it succeeded. In that year the Supreme Court overturned *Plessy* v. *Ferguson* at last. It had been whittling away at that notorious precedent ever since the *Gaines* case; now, under the leadership of the new Chief Justice, Earl Warren of California, a unanimous Court accepted the arguments of the NAACP that 'separate but equal' was a contradiction in terms, and in its decision in the case of *Brown* v. *Topeka Board of Education*,[4] after citing the Fourteenth Amendment, found for the plaintiff. Next year it followed up this finding with a decree that school desegregation should begin everywhere 'with all deliberate speed'. In so doing it touched off a revolution.

The detailed reasoning of the Court need not detain us. Some of it was dictated by the necessity of getting a unanimous bench, which would make the decision sufficiently impressive to public and legal opinion. Some of it was shaped by sociological arguments which nowadays look sadly unconvincing, as sociological arguments tend to do once their time has passed. At least one justice was influenced by the knowledge that segregation damaged America's claim to be the leader of the free world in the Cold War. In short, the legal logic was not impeccable – few of the great decisions of the Warren Court were to be so. It scarcely matters. Essentially the Court was responding to three considerations. First, the rise of the African-American community in numbers, assertiveness and even wealth (there was now a quite large black middle class) required acknowledgement by the law, and if Congress was still unable to make the necessary adjustment then the courts must, for not until he had the sanction of either the legislature or the judiciary could the President – any President – take the initiative. Second, 'separate but equal' had had over sixty years in which to prove itself, and it had proved to be a farce. Even if the Southern States had had the will to provide equal facilities for their black citizens the task would have been beyond their financial resources. As it was, the existence of two parallel school systems proved such a burden that neither was up to much. The Supreme Court may have been philosophically injudicious in declaring that separate schooling was 'inherently' unequal; there could be no doubt that in American circumstances it was in fact wholly unequal and certain

4 It is a pleasing coincidence that, a century or so after 'Brown' and 'Kansas' had figured so largely in the crisis which launched the destruction of slavery, these names should recur in the case which began the destruction of white supremacy. Oliver Brown was a black whose daughter Linda had been denied entrance to a nearby white school. In view of later developments it is ironic that his claim for redress was founded on the fact that Linda had to go a mile by bus to a black school.

to remain so while it lasted. Third, there could be no doubt that a system of unequal, racist, pseudo-education was in 1954 as offensive to the ideals for which America so ostentatiously stood as slavery had been in its day. Mr Justice Frankfurter believed that 'the effect of changes in men's feelings for what is right and just is equally relevant in determining whether a discrimination denies the equal protection of the laws'. The NAACP addressed itself to the consciences of judges well aware that the antics of Joe McCarthy had already made the name of America stink in too many nostrils; well aware, also, of what racist doctrines had led to in Nazi Germany. Such an appeal could hardly fail. As the *Knoxville Journal* put it (a newspaper from the Republican, formerly Unionist, eastern part of Tennessee – but still, a newspaper from the South), 'No citizen, fitted by character and intelligence to sit as a justice of the Supreme Court, and sworn to uphold the Constitution of the United States, could have decided this question other than the way it was decided.'

But of course the process of dismantling segregation could not be plain sailing. For one thing, to attack it in the schools was to attack it everywhere. The structure of white supremacy tottered. The Deep South rose in wrath and came together in fear. It resolved to evade or defeat this decision as it had so many others, and in carrying out this resolution it had, to start with, considerable success. *Brown* v. *Board of Education* turned out to be only the first blow in a new battle in the long, long war.

In the wake of the great decision it was possible for Southern black schoolchildren and college-age students to claim admission to formerly all-white institutions; but making good that claim was another matter. The resources of the enemy seemed to be limitless. The Ku Klux Klan had yet another revival, though not a very effective one (no one could weld it into a single movement); more ominously, the New South expressed itself in the so-called White Citizens' Councils, middle-class affairs ('country club Klans,' somebody said) which tried to draw in the new urban, professional whites (many of whom originated outside Dixie) to the old cause. For a few years, in the Deep South, and especially in Alabama and Mississippi, the Citizens' Councils had great success in creating an atmosphere of intimidation. The old reliable weapon of violence proved its usefulness yet again: in 1955 a black fourteen-year-old, Emmett Till, was lynched in Mississippi. Then there was the legal arm. Perhaps individual cases could be dragged out until the children involved grew up or gave up; perhaps the Citizens' Councils could turn the public schools of the South into private white academies and so evade the law. Worth trying, anyway. Best of all, the instruments of law enforcement might be emasculated. The government in Washington was remote, and unless Congress acted (which, thanks to the ascendancy of white Southern committee chairmen, it was unlikely to do) its powers were too restricted and clumsy to be of much help to blacks, even if President Eisenhower had been eager to act, which he wasn't. Local authorities were easy to intimidate. The stark old questions were once more posed to office-holders and office-seekers, and unless their answer was sufficiently racist – unless they committed themselves to resist integration – they were driven back into private life. Governors, Senators, Congressmen; mayors, sheriffs, commissioners; all got the message, and, with a few brave exceptions such as Senator Estes Kefauver of Tennessee, responded accordingly.

The years of aggressive white reaction which followed the *Brown* decision saw a great many dramatic incidents, of which the best remembered is the attempted desegregation of the school system in Little Rock, Arkansas. This project was undertaken by the local school board in 1957, after securing the approval of the federal courts for its highly deliberate processes. The Citizens' Council led the bitter resistance, which was fanned by the self-serving rhetoric of the state's Governor, Orval Faubus, formerly a racial moderate, who now raised the old cry of 'states' rights' for the old, self-serving reasons. When the school term began on 2 September, Faubus sent in the state's National Guard to preserve order by denying a handful of black children admission to Little Rock High School. This was a flagrant defiance of federal law, and although the National Guard was withdrawn after a few weeks it was replaced by a mob which made matters worse. On 24 September, Eisenhower, very reluctantly, sent in 500 soldiers of the 101st Airborne Division to preserve true order in Little Rock for the rest of the school year. The black children got their education, but in 1958 the High School was closed; Faubus was re-elected governor four times. Arkansas was not, as a matter of fact, a particularly rabid state: its most eminent representative in Congress was Senator J. William Fulbright, who was no bigot, and after 1959 the Little Rock High School was reopened. Elsewhere the white supremacists' tactics were much more successful, if less newsworthy. By 1963 only 9 per cent of the South's bi-racial school districts had been desegregated; and in the Deep South the percentage was much, much less.

Yet Southern resistance, though bitter, prolonged and occasionally murderous, lacked the dynamism of the black movement and therefore, at the last, succumbed to it. An early sign of what was to come was the boycott of buses in Montgomery, Alabama, from December 1955 to December 1956. The boycott was the response of the black community of Montgomery to the arrest of Mrs Rosa Parks for sitting down in one of the front seats of a city bus – seats reserved for whites. Mrs Parks said she felt too tired to do anything else. She was fined $10. But this episode was something the black leadership of the town had been waiting for. The result was a boycott, sustained for nearly a year. The economic impact on the bus company was severe, but more important was the nationwide publicity the boycott received. The two sides battled each other through the courts, but victory came to the blacks when, in November 1956, the US Supreme Court found that all Alabama's laws enforcing segregation on buses were unconstitutional. At 5.55 a.m. on 21 December, slightly more than a year since the boycott started, Martin Luther King Jr, the young black minister who had emerged as his community's most eloquent and inspiring leader, boarded a bus, sat where he chose and got only civility from the white driver. The struggle for racial justice in Alabama was far from over, but this was a famous victory. It served notice to the world that the NAACP path, of patient litigation, was not the only route that African–Americans would take, and that Southern blacks, traditionally far less assertive than those of the North, were now equally ready to take the initiative.

The embodiment of this development, Martin Luther King, was an extraordinary man, the most remarkable, perhaps, of all those prophets thrown up in a few years by the civil rights movement. Born in Atlanta, and with a doctor of theology's degree from Boston University, he combined the traditional fervour of Southern black Christianity with trained philosophical insight. Profoundly influenced by the example of Mohandas Gandhi, who by displaying moral authority (*Satyagraha*) through non-violence had overthrown the British Empire in India, King's peculiar contributions were his perception that the same philosophy and similar tactics could overthrow white supremacy in America, and his ability to dramatize this doctrine for millions. He was not the first to spot the weak point in white armour. Gunnar Myrdal, the Swedish economist, in his classical study of the race problem, *An American Dilemma*, had pointed out that the blacks had a 'powerful tool' in their struggle, 'the glorious American ideals of democracy, liberty, and equality to which America is pledged not only by its political Constitution but also by the sincere devotion of its citizens . . . The whites have all the power, but they are split in their moral personality. Their better selves are with the insurgents. The Negroes do not need any other allies.'[5] Nor was King the first to hold up the ideal of non-violence: his associate during the bus boycott, Bayard Rustin, was a fervent pacifist. But the success of that boycott, and King's leading role in it, gave him such an opportunity as Myrdal and Rustin never had. Black and white liberals, by their millions, and not only within the United States, looked to Montgomery, and heard a voice:

Give us the ballot. Give us the ballot and we will no longer have to worry the federal government about our basic rights . . . We will no longer plead – we will write the proper laws on the books. Give us the ballot and we will get the people judges who love mercy. Give us the ballot and we will quietly, lawfully, and nonviolently, without rancor or bitterness, implement the May 17, 1954, decision of the Supreme Court.[6]

Presently they saw an example. The demands of the Southern blacks were now spreading out to touch every aspect of segregation. On 1 February

5 Gunnar Myrdal, *An American Dilemma* (New York, 1944; 1982 edn), p. 1004.
6 King actually made this speech in Washington, not Montgomery.

1960, two black students in Greensboro, North Carolina, invented the sit-in when they were refused service at a whites-only lunch counter: they returned, day after day, to sit peacefully at the counter and demand service. Their example spread like lightning over the South: the philosophy of *Satyagraha*, of non-violent confrontation, had won thousands of adherents through King's teaching. He became the acknowledged leader of the movement: his organization, the Southern Christian Leadership Conference (SCLC), gave birth to the Student Non-Violent Co-ordinating Committee (SNCC); and finally he himself (having previously had his house dynamited, during the boycott, and suffered malignantly untrue accusations of peculation and tax-evasion) was arrested for sitting-in at a lunch counter in Atlanta, and, on a further trumped-up charge, sentenced to four months' hard labour in a prison camp. It seemed, all too probably, to be a prelude to a lynching. But King had good lawyers, and it was election year: though Eisenhower and Nixon were, as it turned out unwisely, silent, Jack Kennedy and his brother Robert were not: Jack phoned Mrs King, Robert phoned the judge in the case, and King was released next day. The Kennedys had not, actually, had much to do with the release, but they got the credit and the black vote and thereby won their election, a fact they were never to be allowed to forget. The experience did nothing to discourage the hero of the hour: during the next few years Martin Luther King was to go to prison sixteen more times.

The Kennedy intervention showed how central the black question was again becoming to American politics. The last years of the Eisenhower administration had witnessed a gentlemanly competition between Republicans and Democrats for credit with the blacks, which the Democrats had won, largely because of Eisenhower's passivity in the matter. In 1957, the same year as Little Rock, Congress passed the first Civil Rights Act since Reconstruction. It only did so under the joint pressure of Attorney-General Herbert Brownell and Senate Majority Leader Lyndon Johnson, and the act did not amount to very much – its provisions are not worth listing; but it was one more sign that the old South was no longer invincible and that the national government was stirring on the side of the blacks. The same alliance was able to push through a slightly stronger Civil Rights Act in 1960, which increased the powers of the Attorney-General to protect the rights of black citizens to vote, but did not increase them nearly enough. Plenty more remained to be done when John F. Kennedy became President.

Yet Kennedy did not attach any particular urgency to black demands. He favoured them, of course; but he had so much else to do, and, like Franklin Roosevelt, needed the co-operation of a Southern-dominated Congress to do it. He had proclaimed a 'new frontier', in which all America's problems, from her fiscal system to her symphony orchestras, would feel the helpful touch of his creating hand. Besides all that, there was the tangled challenge of foreign affairs. Under Nikita Khrushchev, the Soviet Union's ebullient, rather brutal, unpredictable leader, the Russians were asserting themselves by flaunting their bombs and their nuclear tests in the face of the West, and probing every hint of American weakness (they were also beginning their long quarrel with China, but the importance of this was as yet far from clear). Khrushchev was inclined to think that Kennedy was no more than the beardless boy that Fidel Castro of Cuba had called him, and behaved accordingly. Castro himself was a problem almost as taxing. Before the success of his revolution in 1959, while the dictator Batista ruled, Cuba had been the merest vassal of the United States, and Havana had been treated as if it were no more than an offshore Miami. Hundreds of millions of US dollars had been invested in the place. The revolution then swept away all these tawdry vestiges and undertook the wholesale reconstruction of the island's politics, society and economy. By the time Eisenhower left office, official Washington was convinced that Cuba had become an intolerable affront, a communist state, a Russian satellite in the heart of the American sphere of influence. An expeditionary force of Cuban exiles had been prepared for dispatch against it. Kennedy ordered the enterprise to go ahead. It met total, humiliating disaster at the Bay of Pigs on the Cuban coast on 17 April 1961. This defeat enraged American public opinion and encouraged Khrushchev's adventurism: eighteen months later he secretly began to install nuclear missiles on Cuban soil, an operation which, if successful, would bring the heartlands of the United States into danger. Thanks to the CIA, Washington discovered this threat in time, and Kennedy ordered a blockade of Cuba. For a moment the world held its breath; but then the Soviet ships which were carrying the missiles sheered away rather than challenge the blockade. Americans relaxed, congratulating themselves and their President on having defused the threat of Castro, and thereafter a better respect developed between Kennedy and Khrushchev, so much so that in July 1963 they and the British were able to sign a treaty by which they undertook to conduct no more atmospheric tests of nuclear weapons. The Senate ratified this agreement in September; more than ninety other nations adhered to it; it was immensely popular with American opinion, and seemed likely to guarantee Kennedy's re-election in 1964.

But what was all this to the African-Americans? Their movement had continued to gather and exert strength, but it was clearer and clearer that what was now needed was the fullest backing from the federal government. And Kennedy, during his first eighteen months in office, had shown himself to be little more of a civil rights activist than his predecessor. As he had promised, he issued an order forbidding racial discrimination in all housing projects that received financial assistance, of whatever nature, from the federal government; but though he had said, during his campaign, that it could be done with 'a stroke of the pen', he did not wield that implement until November 1962. He established a Committee on Equal Employment Opportunity, headed by Lyndon Johnson (now the Vice-President), which in a quiet way discouraged racial discrimination by all employers; and he made some highly visible black appointments to federal positions in his gift; but that was all, and even the appointments were offset by the elevation of three notorious racial reactionaries to the federal bench in the Deep South. While Kennedy, like FDR, exuded goodwill to the blacks, their needs did not come very high on his list of priorities, any more than they had on Roosevelt's. But times had changed, and soon his priorities were to change too, in a hurry.

For the civil rights movement, 1961 was the year of the Freedom Rides. These entailed groups of young people travelling through the Deep South by bus, often on the new highways built by the Eisenhower administration; as they went they defied the segregation laws, whether on the buses or in the bus terminals, and in response were met with threats, insults and violence. White Southerners were not only reacting to the threat to white supremacy: they resented the intrusion of these aliens. It was like Reconstruction all over again. The first Freedom Ride, in May 1961, led to the burning of a bus in Anniston, Alabama; a riot in Montgomery; the arrest of the riders in Jackson, Mississippi; and the dispatch of an escort of federal marshals, and then of National Guardsmen, by the US Attorney-General, Robert Kennedy. More and more Freedom Riders followed this example during the next twelve months, and tension rose steadily in the South.

The Kennedys had hoped to channel civil rights energies into the orderly pursuit of voting rights: they heeded King's cry for the ballot. They thought that a sustained campaign to get blacks to vote in the South, especially if it had the covert backing of the administration, would more or less painlessly achieve the necessary transfer of power: after all, the black population of the South in 1960 was 20 per cent of the total, and if it voted its full strength ought to be able to further its interests without any other assistance. Unfortunately this missed the nub. Southern whites had developed a whole battery of weapons to impede the registration of black voters. Unfair literacy tests, delays of all kinds in the process of registration, economic intimidation, physical violence: all were available, all were effective. It was no help, in the Deep South, to have a doctorate, a college education, property or a decent income. It did not help to be a medalled veteran – if your skin was of the wrong colour. The power structure of the Southern states was securely in the hands of the African-Americans' enemies; to change that would require vigorous and specific national action.

The same lesson was rubbed in by the events of the autumn of 1962. A young black, James Meredith, applied for admission to the University of Mississippi. The NAACP had to bring suit in the federal courts to get his right to enrol acknowledged; when he first tried to exercise that right he was turned away by the university authorities and by the Governor of Mississippi in person. When renewed court action – an injunction for contempt – removed these obstacles, Meredith was met by a wild mob. Protected by hundreds of federal marshals and 3,000 federal troops he was eventually able to register as a student at the university, but first there was a spectacular riot which ended with two dead and 375 wounded. True, at the end of it all the university was integrated, and gradually, during the next few years, the rest of the state universities in the South fell into line (not without incident); but it was a maddeningly slow business, and there was no guarantee that there would ever be more than a token handful of black students at these institutions.

So in 1963 a campaign on a monster scale was launched to get justice done to the black citizens of America. 'Free by '63' was the NAACP's slogan (an allusion to the centenary of the Emancipation Proclamation): brisk action was necessary if anything was to be achieved in time. There were signs that the President was moving: in February he sent a message to Congress asking for a law to protect black voting rights. Then in the spring the movement took to the streets in a big way.

The most important demonstrations were those at Birmingham, Alabama. There, Martin Luther King and the SCLC put their Gandhian philosophy to its stiffest test. Birmingham, a huge industrial city, was wholly unreconstructed. It would smash sit-ins and ignore boycotts. So King and his followers marched, in wave upon wave, on the city hall. The streets were filled, day after day, with singing, shouting multitudes, proclaiming 'We Shall Overcome', 'Ain't Gonna Let Nobody Turn Me Round', 'Woke up This Morning with My Mind Stayed on Freedom'. Those who were arrested were quickly replaced, in the end even by children, some no more than six years old. Elsewhere in America the people witnessed, thanks to television, the response of the city authorities. Led by one 'Bull' Connor, the Commissioner of Public Safety, they turned police dogs, fire-hoses and police truncheons on the demonstrators, even the children. King was thrown into jail again, twice. Eventually the businessmen of Birmingham accepted that they could not imprison the whole of the city's black population and agreed to substantial measures of desegregation. It was a triumph of non-violence, but the threat of violence was also effective and might not be contained for ever. On the same day as the desegregation agreement was announced two time-bombs were exploded against black targets, and in consequence a riot exploded in the Birmingham black ghetto: policemen were attacked, white-owned property was burned down. Kennedy sent federal troops to the neighbourhood to take control if there was a further outbreak.

Birmingham was the most spectacular of these springtime convulsions, but by no means the only one. It stimulated others throughout May and June, in the North as well as in the South. In Mississippi a black leader, Medgar Evers, was murdered, as so many others were to be later in that terrible decade. Here and there the Southern white power-structure made concessions under duress, but it was plain that such piecemeal victories would never solve the national problem: national action was needed more than ever. Fortunately the Birmingham disturbances had at last made up the President's mind. He appeared on television to tell the nation, 'We face ... a moral crisis as a country and a people ... It is a time to act in the

Congress, in your state and local legislative body and, above all, in all of our daily lives.' A few days later he sent a comprehensive civil rights bill to Congress.

The conversion of the Kennedy administration to the view that civil rights was a matter of supreme urgency was a notable achievement, but, it soon appeared, too limited. There remained Congress, where the bill was opposed as being far too radical. To stimulate the Senators and Representatives A. Philip Randolph's old idea was resurrected, and a 'March on Washington for Jobs and Freedom' was organized. It was enthusiastically supported by a very broad spectrum of citizens, and on 28 August 1963 more than 200,000 blacks and whites appeared in Washington. It was the largest demonstration so far in the capital's history; its leaders were received by the President (they included not only stalwarts of the movement such as Randolph, King and Roy Wilkins of the NAACP but also Walter Reuther of the United Automobile Workers, who had greatly assisted with the funding and organization of the march); some members of Congress showed themselves sympathetic; but Congress as a whole gave no sign of getting on with the civil rights bill, and the South still threatened a filibuster. Then in September a black church in Birmingham, Alabama, was bombed, four children being killed; and in November President Kennedy was assassinated in Dallas, Texas.

This event hit the world like a thunderbolt of despair. Kennedy had charmed the millions and had indeed 'got America moving again' as he had promised, though signs were beginning to multiply that she might be moving out of control. Of these signs his murder was the most appalling. An official investigating commission, headed by Chief Justice Warren, found that the President had been shot by a solitary psychotic, like Lincoln and McKinley before him; but though its conclusions were sound, the reasoning used to get to them was not – as critics soon pointed out. It took thirty years for further investigation to put Lee Harvey Oswald's guilt beyond reasonable doubt, and meanwhile conspiracy theories of all kinds flourished, weakening American faith both in rationality and in their political system (since, if Kennedy had been killed by conspirators, there must have been a cover-up at the highest levels of government to conceal the fact). And in any case, Kennedy's death was a reminder of all the ugly, chaotic forces in American life that the framework of democracy and Christianity controlled with difficulty; any of them might have brought about the murder, and every bugbear – the CIA, the FBI, organized crime, Fidel Castro, Castro's Cuban enemies – had its accusers.

In 1963 many citizens found it hard to believe that Lyndon Johnson, who now became President, would turn out any better than had Andrew Johnson (no relation) a hundred years previously. Yet although he entirely lacked Kennedy's charm, wit and scepticism – the scepticism which, applied to himself, was an excellent substitute for modesty, being so cool and level-headed – Lyndon Johnson, suspicious, insecure and monstrously egotistical, had certain political skills which Kennedy lacked. He was only nine years Kennedy's senior, but was a far more seasoned politician. He had emerged in Texas in the late thirties, and as a young Congressman had fallen under the spell of FDR (he himself was inclined to insist obsessively on his own initials, LBJ). Like Kennedy, like two generations of Americans in fact, his idea of the Presidency was governed by what he learned from Roosevelt; but he had been much closer to his *beau idéal* than most of them – certainly than Kennedy. As Majority Leader in the Senate he had shown himself a master of parliamentary leadership. He had been rather wasted as Vice-President (the common fate of men in that lofty but unprofitable job), but as President he soon showed that his skills had not been allowed to rust. He knew that it was absolutely necessary that he establish himself, in record time, as the legitimate heir of both Roosevelt and Kennedy, and that he could do so only by overcoming the suspicions that liberals, Northerners and blacks entertained of him as the first Southerner to have attained the Presidency since Reconstruction (except for the expatriate, Woodrow Wilson). Accordingly he brought all his talents to bear, took advantage of the universal mood of grief and repentance which followed the murder, and in an amazingly short time had the entire Kennedy legislative programme, which had been languishing in Congressional committees, hurrying onto the statute book. The civil rights bill, considerably strengthened, was the most important measure thus passed. As revised, it tackled almost all the problems about which Southern blacks had protested so vehemently in the past few years. It gave the US Attorney-General new powers to intervene to protect citizens' rights; it outlawed segregation in public places and in most places of public accommodation – which meant all hotels and motels save the very smallest. On pain of withdrawal of federal funds, it forbade racial discrimination in any federally assisted undertaking whatever. The Office of Education was authorized to help peaceful school desegregation with advice and money; the Civil Rights Commission, set up under the act of 1957, had its life extended and two new federal bodies were set up, the Community Relations Service and the Equal Employment Opportunity Commission, which together showed that the government knew that it was not enough simply to outlaw racial discrimination: for the peace, happiness and progress of America the process of dismantling white supremacy had to be supervised, encouraged and assisted.

The bill became law on 2 July 1964, in nice time for the Presidential election of that year, in which Lyndon Johnson, the bill's architect, would run against Senator Barry Goldwater, who voted against it. Naturally the blacks voted for Johnson, who crushed Goldwater by one of the biggest margins in the history of Presidential elections: he got forty-three million votes to Goldwater's twenty-seven million, and 486 votes in the electoral college to Goldwater's fifty-two. But there was something ominous for blacks in this second set of figures: apart from Goldwater's native Arizona, it consisted entirely of votes from the Deep South – Alabama, Georgia,

Louisiana, Mississippi and South Carolina. The battle was far from won, as was also proved by events during the 'long, hot summer' of 1964, when the Ku Klux Klan asserted itself once more in Mississippi and, besides bombing two dozen black churches and murdering several blacks in the ordinary way, also killed three young civil rights volunteers – one black Mississippian, two white New Yorkers. No one was ever punished for the deaths of these young men: certain fat, cowboy-hatted, grinning, beer-swilling white yokels were brought to trial, but acquitted by white Mississippian jurors.

Meanwhile the drive to register black Southern voters continued, and continued to run into difficulties. Conditions were particularly bad in Selma, Alabama, a town near Montgomery: two more civil rights volunteers (one white, one black) were killed there. The local sheriff thought of a new refinement of brutality: he and his men used electric cattle-prods on demonstrators to make them trot. (This was too much even for the sluggish consciences of some Southern whites: seventy ministers marched to the county courthouse to show their disapproval.) After an embarrassing false start a grand march of protest set off to walk from Selma to Montgomery, led by almost every prominent black in the country, and a good many notable whites too. Four days on the way, it was addressed on its arrival by the two African–American winners of the Nobel Peace Prize, Ralph Bunche, who had won his fifteen years previously for his work in Palestine, and Martin Luther King, who had been awarded his only a few months previously. But the Confederate flag waved over the state capitol, and that very night (25 March 1965) yet another civil rights activist was killed.

The savagery lurking in American life was welling to the surface; but the resources of civilization were not yet exhausted. Reasoning that the only way to end the crisis in the South was by supporting the blacks to the hilt, so that an irreversible defeat could be dealt the white supremacists, Lyndon Johnson sent another civil rights bill to Congress. It was a short, sharp measure, and probably the most effective law of its kind ever passed in American history. It struck down all the instruments of obstruction and delay that the segregationist states had placed in the way of the black voter, and authorized the Attorney-General to send federal registrars into states and counties where he had reason to think that the registration process was being used to deny citizens their voting rights. Congress, which now had an overwhelming liberal majority, thanks to the Johnson landslide in 1964, passed the bill swiftly into law, and almost at once it began to show its value. The threat of federal intervention spurred on some local officials in the Deep South to undertake reform; elsewhere the federal registrars appeared. As a result nearly 250,000 new black voters were registered before the end of 1965, and in the years that followed the black population of the South continued to register itself, at last, in numbers proportionate to its strength. The effect was soon felt in elections; blacks began to appear in state legislatures where they had not been seen since Reconstruction (though it would be ten years before an African-American won a state-wide election in the South); and the way was clear to a fundamental change in American politics and society. In 1976 Jimmy Carter, a white Georgian, would be elected to the Presidency thanks, in large part, to the vote of Southern blacks;[7] racist Southern white politicians would begin to court the black vote; and the castle of white supremacy at last fell into ruin. There was still great hostility and tension between the races, but as the years went on and the South realized that the old demon was gone for ever, there was a quickening of energy and hope. At last spring came again to Dixie.

The race problem had never been confined to the South, but not until the mid-1960s could it be said that it was primarily a non-Southern affair. This change was as unfortunate as the other was encouraging. Black and white Americans in the North and West now discovered that their country had exchanged one trap for another.

It was part of the price to be paid for tolerating the South's backwardness for so long. Everywhere in the second half of the twentieth century, as communications have improved, poor and dispossessed country-dwellers, victims of the huge transformation which has swollen earth's population and devalued ancient ways while tantalizing men with hope, have swarmed into the cities. The shanty-town, the new slum full of former peasants, is the chief architectural monument of our age. So it was in America. For three generations the poor people of the South had been confined in poverty, disease and ignorance, cramped in their beautiful, benighted homeland; but then came capital and technology: tractors and cotton-picking machines to mechanize agriculture, federal highways and Greyhound buses to carry the former cotton-pickers away to the urban mirage. Some went to Houston, Dallas, New Orleans and, most of all, to Atlanta, which consciously planned to become the new capital of the New South; but more headed north, to Chicago, Detroit, New York; or west to Los Angeles. And they found, all too many of them, that urban slums were worse than rural ones.

For the African-Americans arrived too late; or rather, the very circumstances which had enabled them to move to the city enabled others to move away from it. The huge expansion of the American economy during and after the Second World War had expressed itself in the vast expansion of the American suburbs – monuments to our time only less characteristic than the shanty-towns, and infinitely more agreeable; indeed, one of the great civilized achievements of all history. There, surrounded by the nearest thing they could achieve to green lawns (sometimes, because of the hot climate, ivy has to do as a substitute for grass), shaded by the trees prudently planted along all the roadways, in white-painted frame houses that always seem amazingly big to British eyes, air-conditioned, centrally heated, with

7 When I remember what things were like when I first visited America (in 1962) this simple statement of historical fact seems almost incredible, and the clearest proof that progress is really possible.

an ever-growing array of durable toys – washing-machines, washing-up machines, hi-fi systems, plug-in telephones and of course video systems and colour televisions – American families can tell themselves that they have achieved the good life, and can worry that it is not better. It is not just a matter of the upper or professional classes. The great post-war boom, which ran without serious interruption from 1945 to 1973, spread this affluence downwards with astonishing speed and completeness. The abundance of America was available to most Americans. Could it be said to matter that the ownership of America was still concentrated in comparatively few hands when the day was near (it arrived in the late seventies) that there was one automobile for every two persons in the United States?

The automobile was the clue, the *sine qua non*, the sole instrument which made possible the spreading of the suburbs by thousands of square miles, the coming of the suburban shopping malls, the supermarkets, the hyper-markets, the flyovers and freeways which undergirt the new way of life. Eventually the car would become the author of ruin as well as of happiness, when its insatiable need for petrol outstripped even the abundant supply of American oil and, by oversetting the US balance of payments and putting crucial amounts of wealth and power in the hands of foreign suppliers, upset not only domestic tranquillity but the prospects of peace in the world. But in the fifties and sixties no premonition of this development came to disturb the complacency of the prosperous whites.

Instead came the blacks. They moved north, and discovered when they arrived that there was work for most of them (not all), but not the best work; housing, but only the worst; education, but not what they needed. They poured into the inner cities as the whites moved out, so that before long blacks would be in the majority in places such as Washington, DC, and Cleveland, Ohio; but the jobs moved with the original inhabitants. The coming of the blacks, in fact, accelerated a crisis which was already pressing on the cities: the problem of how to finance themselves as industrial and commercial enterprise moved outside their limits. This problem was not made any easier by the persistence of outmoded political arrangements, so that there was, for example, no unitary government for the whole of greater New York, which spreads across three states and half Long Island; and no possibility of governing Chicago as a whole except through the single unifying agency of the Cook County Democratic party, the last of the great urban machines, which was not likely to last for ever. The problem was made worse by the fact that the black incomers became heavy burdens on the welfare system, both local and federal. As the affluent suburbs spread, so did the indigent black slums, in which a way of life, compounded of welfare payments, crime, drugs and exploitation by absentee landlords and all-too-present storekeepers, was mitigated only by such resources as the new city-dwellers could muster for themselves: their racial and family loyalties, their black culture and their religion – perhaps rather their religions, for by 1960 a new movement was very much to the fore, the Nation of

Islam, of which one Elijah Muhammad (*né* Poole) was the Prophet: he taught a complete rejection of Christianity as the creed of the white devils, and insisted on black separatism in every sphere of life. By the time of Kennedy's death it was clear to many observers that the pressing problems of the racial ghettoes and the decaying cities would not wait for very much longer; New York, it might be said, was the nation's biggest problem; but most Americans averted their gaze, or made do with day-to-day grumbling about the rising crime rate.

The explosion of the civil rights movement made this blind attitude untenable. In 1960, 7,560,000 African-Americans lived outside the South: they too had their bitter wrongs, and when the great revolution began were not slow to demand that they be righted. There were rent strikes in the Harlem slums in 1963; next year, rioting, burning, looting, there and in half a dozen other places in the North, because of police brutality. In 1965 the Watts ghetto in Los Angeles exploded. Watts was a rundown area into which more than 80,000 blacks were crammed, suffering congestion that was four times greater than anything elsewhere in the city: restrictive covenants imposed by banks and real-estate agents made it difficult for even the more prosperous to move into better, white areas. There was a high level of unemployment (30 per cent). Buildings, shops and other businesses were mostly owned by absentee whites, who squeezed as much profit out of their property as they could, without regard to general social conditions. In all this Watts was typical of black ghettoes everywhere. It was August; the city sweltered under its blanket of car-generated smog; tempers were fragile. An altercation between a policeman and a young black motorist, in which the cop drew his gun, led to a horrifying outbreak, a riot on the scale of the New York draft riots of 1863, which left thirty-four dead, 1,032 injured, and damaged an estimated forty million dollars worth of property. Next to the bloodshed, the most memorable thing about the riot was the gleeful fashion in which the ghetto-dwellers descended on the shops and looted them of everything worth carrying away. In 1966 there were more riots, East and West, North and South: in Brooklyn, Atlanta, Chicago, Omaha and elsewhere. There had been nothing like these outbreaks since the American Revolution; even the labour troubles of the late nineteenth century had not posed such a fundamental challenge; but it was a challenge without hope. The tall towers of corporate America, glass and steel and concrete, were not going to fall to the siege of any mob, whatever its numbers or its grievances.

The remedies applied to the South proved to be of little use elsewhere. Something could be done for some of the suffering. The Elementary and Secondary Education Act of 1965 was passed to accelerate school deseg-regation, North and South; a pre-school education programme, 'Operation Headstart', began to do something to correct the educational disadvant-ages of the little children of the slums; the courts ruled repeatedly against all schemes of *de facto* school segregation in Northern cities, requiring the school systems to attain the right balance of races in the classroom (whatever that was) by bussing black and white children in all directions, without regard to the principle of the 'neighbourhood school' which most Americans cherished. The Small Business Administration, set up early in the Eisenhower Presidency, was happy to help would-be black entrepreneurs and shopkeepers with cheap loans and technical advice, even on such mundane but essential points as how to keep accounts. In 1968, in the last great law of the Johnson administration, an Open Housing Act was passed, which forbade discrimination in the rental or sale of housing on the basis of race, colour, religion or national origin. But the fundamental evil continued, little affected.

For with the disappearance of white supremacy, the chief purpose of which had always been to maintain a certain kind of class ascendancy in the South, African-Americans found themselves up against a social structure that was just as unyielding, though based on very different considerations. Racial prejudice was among them, for some form of racism is too common in human society for there to be any hope of Americans outgrowing it entirely in one decade. Hating your neighbour is almost as secure a psychological prop as loving him, especially if he differs from you in looks, language or habits. But the organizing social principle which now oppressed the blacks was quite different, and even more basic to human nature; was indeed one of the dominating themes of American history. In a phrase, the Great Migration from the South now came up against the consequences of the Great Migration of the nineteenth century.

The geographical and occupational mobility of American society is so great as sometimes to dazzle and deceive the eye. The educated American middle class does, to a surprising degree, live according to the enlightened ideology of the Founding Fathers and the benevolent ethics of conventional Christianity. Its individual members can be as stupid and selfish as anyone else, but the class as a whole tries to live up to its formal belief in the equality of human rights and the importance of maintaining an open society. The unlimited prosperity of the post-war period and the swelling birth-rate of the forties and fifties greatly increased the size of this class; it was highly active and vocal both politically and culturally; it was from its ranks that the blacks drew their chief white allies; it was this class which helped the black cause financially; and it was the ideology of this class which the leading black organizations made their own, for 'equality of opportunity' was exactly what they wanted.

There was a certain irony in this convergence of the most and the least prosperous Americans; but it was observed without amusement by the bulk of Northern whites. These looked on the commitment of the middle class to equality as fraudulent, for they were well aware that there was very little equality of opportunity between the children of the richer suburbs and the children of the poorer; between the professional and the manual working classes; between the graduates of Harvard University and those who had not even got to high school. To this lower middle class (to call it working class or proletarian would badly distort the truth about American conditions) the point of America had never been equality, or even opportunity; it had been security. These descendants of the Irish, Italians and Slavs knew that their parents and grandparents had come to the United States mostly to escape intolerable conditions at home, and that they had succeeded largely through group solidarity, which had rapidly, but not without great effort, won them ascendancy in certain jobs and certain neighbourhoods: one thinks of the traditional Irish dominance in police forces and fire brigades, and the proliferation of 'Little Italies', 'Little Germanies', and so on. Talented individuals might and did escape from their tribes of origin into the larger world, but for most the satisfying thing about American city life was that each ethnic group had its niche, in which all its members could nest. The melting-pot, beyond a certain point (the acquisition of citizenship, the adoption of the English language), did not melt, or did so only very slowly.[8] It was extremely important to these groups that their monopolistic hold on certain jobs and neighbourhoods, which guaranteed their identity, should be maintained. In Gary, Indiana, for example, there was a hereditary caste of steelworkers, most reluctant to make room for black newcomers, though by the end of the sixties Gary had a black mayor. In nearby Chicago, Irish and Polish neighbourhoods stubbornly clung to their homogeneity, though they were surrounded by areas of equally solid black occupancy. And everywhere there was the need to protect a family's chief investment, its dwelling. When a black tried to move into Levittown, Pennsylvania, his prospective neighbour observed, 'Probably a nice guy, but every time I look at him I see $2,000 drop off the value of my house.'

None of this might have mattered very much if the American city had retained its economic vitality. Instead, for reasons already given, it was beginning to decay at its core, and the arrival of numberless unemployed blacks, who were in many cases unemployable (either because the job market was closed to them or because the demand for unskilled labour was shrinking fast), simply accelerated the decay. Furthermore, the inner city was already under deeply destructive pressure from various quarters. It was being torn down in all directions to make room for motorways, or to enable real-estate developers to make fortunes by putting up more and more gigantic office-blocks or, bitter irony, so that huge areas of monstrously ugly, dispiriting public housing could be erected with subsidies from the

8 In retrospect it seems highly significant that one of the best musical plays of the mid-fifties, *West Side Story*, dealt with the conflicts between immigrant groups (Poles and Puerto Ricans) in New York, though at the time the point was lost because the show was so ostentatiously a re-telling of the sentimental tale of Romeo and Juliet. A few years later, Romeo would have had to be black. It is perhaps also significant that the other great musical success of the fifties, *My Fair Lady*, was an even more sentimental celebration of a girl's escape from the intolerable conditions of an urban slum. Artists are the unacknowledged fortune-tellers of mankind. *West Side Story* even foreshadowed the great youth rebellion of the sixties.

federal government paid under the Housing Act of 1949. Ethnic neighbourhoods began to seem like islands under siege by the tide, or like fortresses isolated from each other by an invading army. If the enemy were allowed to encroach, the neighbourhood shops and small industrial concerns, which gave employment to many and satisfaction to all, would be the first to go. Then the private houses would be demolished, in larger or smaller numbers; those inhabitants who could would move out, hoping to reconstitute their lives elsewhere; and the blacks (or, in New York, the Puerto Ricans) would begin to move in, which would in turn be the signal for the final desperate scramble outwards to the suburbs. The blacks would not inherit a going concern, as the Italians had once inherited the Lower East Side of New York from the Irish, and they from the Yankees. Instead they would fall heir to a vast area of decaying housing, with decaying services and no prospects except of indefinite reliance on welfare. They were not even safe from direct economic exploitation, for many slum landlords continued to exact high rents while doing the absolute minimum of maintenance for their properties. No wonder that crime figures mounted rapidly, or that one of the most usual crimes was now arson. By the mid-seventies large areas of such places as the South Bronx in New York had, literally, been burnt out, and were being allowed to decay into wilderness once more: a wilderness disfigured by the rusting wrecks of cars, the blackened skeletons of shops, schools and houses, and acre upon acre of cracking concrete slabs.

Against conditions such as these the civil rights movement was largely helpless. Its achievements were of inestimable advantage to the black middle class: the number of blacks in professional occupations doubled between 1960 and 1974, and their place in society was increasingly unchallenged. But most blacks were not middle-class; indeed about half of them lived on, or below, or near, the poverty-line, the line below which, statisticians reckoned, their income was inadequate for the necessities of life. It proved exceedingly difficult to find effective means of helping them, though Lyndon Johnson talked of a war on poverty, and A. Philip Randolph proposed a 'Negro Marshall Plan', which would have involved the expenditure of $10,000,000,000 a year for ten years: but even the liberal Congress of the mid-sixties balked at the idea of expenditure on anything like this scale for such a cause (though at the same time it was voting much larger sums for the war in Vietnam) and after the election of Richard Nixon to the Presidency in 1968 it was clearly vain to hope for anything of the kind. Indeed, one of Nixon's advisers tactlessly suggested that the time had come to practise a little 'benign neglect' of black problems. This outraged the black community, but outrage alone was not going to change anything.

The dilemma was most cruelly exposed in the last years of Martin Luther King. With the passage of the Voting Rights Act the first phase in 'the Second Reconstruction' was virtually complete: in political and legal terms blacks now were, or would soon become, formally equal to whites. But their social and economic deprivations were as bad as ever, and it was clearly incumbent on the leaders of 'the Movement' to launch a second phase which would tackle the horrors of black life in the North. At first King tried to apply the Gandhian tactics which had proved so successful in the South, but they did not work. For one thing he had decided that the war in Vietnam was mopping up economic resources that should have been used to improve conditions at home; that it was killing a disproportionate number of black Americans; that it was hideously cruel; and that it might lead to world war. These considerations impelled the winner of the Nobel Peace Prize to denounce the war repeatedly; but in so doing he alienated the administration which was waging it. Lyndon Johnson was a vindictive man who never liked or trusted Martin King; he never again gave more than token countenance and protection to the activities of the SCLC. What this meant became painfully clear when, in 1966, King took his organization to Chicago and launched a series of marches through the all-white suburbs of that city, hoping to bring down the structure of *de facto* housing segregation there, for he reasoned that if the blacks could break out of the ghetto they might find decent jobs, houses and schools waiting for them. His concrete aim was to shame the city of Chicago into living up to its own open-housing ordinances, its own regulations which required, for example, that all rented property should be repainted once a year. He did manage to get a surprising number of concessions out of the city administration, and a large number of paper promises. But the spirit of willing compliance, essential for real progress, was lacking. Richard J. Daley, the mayor, was the last of the great city bosses. He was under no pressure from Washington to work with King. He knew that the black movement itself was splitting, as the younger activists turned away from King and non-violence to the phantasms of 'Black Power' and war on whitey – phantasms which blended all too well into the criminal violence in which the days of all too many young blacks were passed. He felt that his own political power in Chicago was challenged, and in any case he could hardly make concessions to the blacks when the whites on whom he depended politically were showing such bitter hostility to the marchers. The climax came when 200 marchers through the suburb of Cicero (Al Capone's former lordship) were met with an incessant rain of bottles and stones: the inhabitants of Cicero, mostly Polish-Americans, saw the black demonstrators as embodiments and precursors of all the forces which were threatening their way of life: but for the protection of the police and the National Guard, there would certainly have been killings. King withdrew from Chicago, to carry on the struggle elsewhere; then, on 4 April 1968, he was assassinated by yet another of the wretched, half-insane murderers who were so tragically common at that time.

King was killed in Memphis, Tennessee, by a Southern white, James Earl Ray, who was driven on by the racial tensions which had poisoned Southern life for so long; so it can be said that he was martyred in the cause to which he had brought such great gifts and victories. His death – the death of a devoted, wise and eloquent man, who had a sure grasp of the essentials of the tragedy of his times, and who still had much to give his people, white as well as black – was a fearful loss. When the news of the murder hit the nation, 125 cities rose in an unparalleled outbreak of rage, grief and protest. It took 70,000 troops to suppress the rebellion; once more the people of the ghettoes fought, looted and burned; in particular they erupted across Washington, doing immense damage both to the city and to race relations. It was not a commemoration which King would have appreciated, nor did it do anybody any good, although Lyndon Johnson, with characteristic adroitness, used Martin Luther King's death to push the Open Housing Act through Congress, as he had used Jack Kennedy's to push through the 1964 Civil Rights Act. Riot, arson and looting are poor substitutes for a decent standard of living. This was soon so universally accepted that the poor black population began to sink back into apathy, even while the black middle class increased in numbers, prosperity and status.

The next ten years brought no more dramatic gains. It began to seem as if the Second Reconstruction had ended, like the first, with no more than partial success; it began to be feared that yet another century might run before a Third Reconstruction would at last give African-Americans everything in the way of hope and happiness to which they were as much entitled as their more fortunate white fellow-citizens. It was not very surprising that at the Howard University commencement ceremonies in 1978 Thurgood Marshall, once the leading counsel for NAACP, who had led for the plaintiff in *Brown* v. *Board of Education* and then became the first black Justice of the Supreme Court, commented in the grimmest terms on African–American prospects:

Be careful of the people who say, 'You've got it made. Take it easy. You don't need any more help.' Today we have reached the point where people say, 'You've come a long way.' But so have other people come a long way. Has the gap been getting smaller? No. It's getting bigger. People say we're better off today. Better off than what? . . . Don't listen to that myth that [inequality] can be solved . . . or that it has already been solved. Take it from me, it has not been solved.

Poverty and racism: America's most urgent business was still unfinished.

26 The Crisis of the New Order 1963–74

Oh build your ship of death. Oh build it!
for you will need it,
for the voyage of oblivion awaits you.

D. H. Lawrence

Anyone trying to make sense of the story of the American people must notice, I think, that two themes persist. One is continuity: this is a nation which, born in the seventeenth century, has developed along one line ever since. The other is challenge and response: changing times have periodically required radical alterations in the organization of American life. The alterations have seldom or never come in time to avert great troubles, but come they have, so that the great experiment of American freedom has been enabled to continue. The Revolution, the Civil War, the Industrial Revolution, the New Deal, the Second World War: these were the stages by which the American people had evolved; the changes of course by which they avoided shipwreck.

By 1963 nearly two decades had passed since the last of these creative transformations had been completed, and it is far from surprising that then, and in the years since, the new order created during the Roosevelt administrations began to show its imperfections as well as its permanent value. Furthermore, the toils of the Cold War, though inevitable, and justified by results, as communism was eventually discredited and the Soviet Union disappeared, did to a large extent distort the natural evolution of American society, and exacted some monstrous sacrifices which will not be forgotten for a long time and may never be wholly made good. The tragedy of Lyndon Johnson was that while he clearly understood the need for new departures in American domestic policy, he did not accept the even more urgent need for a radical overhaul of foreign policy. Still less did he understand, as Martin Luther King did, that radical change at home – programmes to rescue the country's poor from desperation, for instance –

were dependent on adjustments right across the board. He allowed himself to be imprisoned by the traditions and institutions of the forties and fifties and plunged the United States deep into war, disgrace, economic crisis and political disaster. Things got no better under his immediate successors. Not until outsiders captured the presidency in 1976 and 1980 – outsiders who, from very different points of view, despised the Washington establishment – did the United States begin once more to adjust to new times. The process was still incomplete by the end of the twentieth century; it was a very choppy one at times, even if the eventual outcome was on the whole beneficial to America; and the years between 1963 and 1974, the matter of this chapter, were a time of continual crisis.

It is not true that people learn nothing from history: they are marvellous at learning the wrong lessons. So it must seem, at any rate, to most students of America's war in Vietnam. The story runs like a ghastly parody of the post-1918 tragedy. Once more the American people, mastered by illusion, went down the path to disaster behind leaders even more darkened than themselves. Once more disaster took the form of war; only this time the usual horror of international conflict was deepened by the fact that it was war in the name of an obsolete view of the world and of America's duty in it against peoples who were of the most marginal concern to the real interests of the United States. Against these unoffending strangers America hurled her fullest might, with frightful consequences. The episode was the worst stain on the national honour since slavery.

America's participation in the Indo-Chinese wars was a mistake with many roots, yet the most important single cause can be stated in a sentence. It was the failure to understand the nature and consequences of the great movement which dismantled the European empires. Obsessed with the Cold War, and imagining that all the rest of the world shared their obsession, American policy-makers and their supporters simply did not notice that reality was in large part organized round different concerns, and they forced such facts as could not be denied into their preconceptions, instead of modifying the preconceptions to fit the facts. In 1961 Soviet Russia and Red China were perceived as a united threat to the peace of the world and the liberty of the United States, and were likened to the German danger of the first half of the century. The steady divergence of Russian and Chinese policies was ignored, and when the two great communist powers began openly to quarrel experienced men could be heard warning that it was all a pretence to lull the West into false security. When either Russia or China showed an interest in a particular country or region, that was sufficient proof that an anti-American plot was hatching; and when, as in Indo-China, both powers showed an interest, it was self-evident that the United States was seriously threatened and must go actively to work to defend itself. The idea that a nationalist movement, such as that led against the French Empire in Indo-China by Ho Chi Minh, was exceedingly unlikely to let itself become the simple tool of Soviet or Chinese expansionism was often put forward, but Washington paid no attention to such arguments (which were amply vindicated by events after 1975). Ho Chi Minh, said Washington, was a communist; he was therefore a tool of the Kremlin; he was therefore an enemy of the United States. The syllogism was as perfect in form as it was worthless in content. It served as a substitute for thought in exactly the same way that the Kellogg–Briand pact had so served in the twenties and thirties. Woodrow Wilson would have denounced it as a bad old balance-of-power calculation. Theodore Roosevelt, one would like to think, would have denounced it as a balance-of-power miscalculation. Like isolationism, it rested on a deep unwillingness to accept that the world was never going to dance at Uncle Sam's every whim or share his every prejudice.

The French Empire in Indo-China had been founded in the nineteenth century chiefly to annoy the British and the Germans. It was destroyed beyond possibility of restoration by the Japanese conquest in the Second World War. This was so clear at the time to men on the spot, and was so much in accord with the repeatedly affirmed policy of Franklin Roosevelt, who disliked all European imperialisms, that the American representatives in Indo-China collaborated quite closely with Ho Chi Minh at the end of the war, in the expectation that he would soon be recognized as the ruler of an independent Vietnam. The French, however, deemed otherwise. National vanity and national obstinacy bred in them the illusion that they could repossess Indo-China, and General de Gaulle, the head of the French government at the time (1944–6), committed his country to the attempt, which was persisted in even after the General's sudden abdication in January 1946. His successors immediately came up against the problem which should have made them abandon the policy: France, shattered by the Second World War and its aftermath, was simply not strong enough to subdue her former subjects; nor was it clear what the French people would gain even if the impossible undertaking succeeded. Not for nine years, however, was any French government brave enough to acknowledge the inevitable. Instead ministers looked about for ways of entangling the United States, with its apparently limitless resources, in their enterprise.

The American anti-colonial tradition was so strong, and the war in Indo-China was so exactly the sort of thing that George Washington's Farewell Address had warned against, that the French could never have succeeded in their scheme, but for the Cold War. The Cold War unfortunately made it possible for the United States government to believe the message, constantly in French mouths, that the nationalist movement in Indo-China was simply another manifestation of 'the international communist conspiracy'. Furthermore, co-operation in Indo-China was a small price to pay for getting French co-operation in Europe against Russia. The Truman administration also believed that the USSR was constantly probing the West's will, and would, wherever it detected weakness, mount an offensive. So it was as important to stand firm in Indo-China as in Korea. This explains why, after the 1950 invasion of South Korea, Truman increased aid to the French. For if Stalin was foiled in Korea, he might, with his right hand so to speak, launch an assault in South-East Asia, unless deterred.

So America before long became the chief supplier and paymaster for the French war-effort; but that was still not enough to bring victory. In 1954 the French suffered a complete and humiliating defeat at the siege of Dienbienphu, and it became clear that the game was up. A new French Prime Minister, Pierre Mendès-France, negotiated a more or less graceful withdrawal at a conference of the powers in Geneva. It was a splendid opportunity for the Americans to cut their losses like the French. Unfortunately John Foster Dulles did not see the occasion in those terms. He was depressed and indignant at the French admission of defeat, and at one time hoped to send in American troops as a replacement, or just to stiffen morale. This idea got no support from anyone except the more brutal American admirals and generals, and Dulles was reduced to an attempt to wreck the Geneva conference by a spectacular sulk (he even refused to shake hands with the Chinese premier, Chou En-Lai). The composure of the other participants (Britain, Russia and China, as well as the belligerents) survived his tantrums, and agreement was reached after a month of hard bargaining. To this agreement (known as the Geneva Accords) Dulles refused to put his name. He accepted it as a *fait accompli*, but thereafter lost no opportunity of sabotaging it. For instance, the Accords divided Vietnam into two parts, north and south, pending countrywide elections which were supposed to take place in 1956. Anti-communist Vietnamese fled south, communists fled north. Dulles made this unpromising situation worse by inciting the provisional administration of South Vietnam to refuse to participate in the elections, which were therefore not held; for the Secretary of State believed, no doubt correctly, that such elections would be won by Ho Chi Minh, and thus the communists would take over the whole of Vietnam, which Dulles was determined to prevent. He was convinced that South-East Asia was the Western alliance's weak point and the object of special attention by the fiends in the Kremlin (Stalin was dead, but that made no difference to Dulles). As well as snuffing out the last faint hope that Vietnam could be unified peacefully, he set up a South-East Asia Treaty Organization on the model of NATO. The members, besides the United States, were Britain, France, Australia, New Zealand, Pakistan, Thailand and the Philippines: they pledged themselves to defend each other against any attack, which might have embarrassed them if SEATO had ever amounted to anything solid. But like so many of Dulles's schemes, it was only a castle in the air. It was neither a deterrent nor a defence.

America was now deeply committed to resisting communism in Indo-China, but the point of no return was still some way ahead. This was in part due to President Eisenhower's willingness to rein in John Foster Dulles. A common canard of the time showed Ike viewing the Presidency simply as an agreeable place in which to pass the early years of his retirement, with wonderful opportunities for golf. It was a grotesque exaggeration, but it conveyed a truth, as good caricature always does. Eisenhower had no great sense of mission; prudent passivity was more his line. This attitude left a lot to be desired in domestic affairs, but it had great advantages internationally. Unfortunately Ike was not consistent. He took the struggle against communism very seriously; not only did he permit the CIA to begin the planning which was to end so catastrophically in the Bay of Pigs, he also identified Indo-China as a region where the United States must, if necessary, resist the communists with its own military forces. If any one country of South-East Asia – Laos, for example – fell to the communists, all the rest would tumble over like a row of dominoes. When he met his successor, just before Kennedy's inauguration, he said that the US should send troops into Laos, if necessary. Kennedy was appalled.

Laos was only one of the unpleasant problems which the Kennedy administration inherited. To be sure, the 'missile gap' of which the Democrats had made much during the election campaign of 1960 turned out to be a fiction: the United States was vastly stronger than the Soviet Union in rocketry as in all other forms of sophisticated weaponry. But relations between America and Cuba were abysmal, and the communists were plainly gaining ground in both Laos and Vietnam. The story of the Kennedy administration's struggle with the Cuban difficulty has already been told; its handling of Indo-China displayed the same mixture of shrewdness, idealism and misplaced energy. Laos, the new President soon realized, was beyond all but diplomatic aid; as a result an agreement was negotiated, on the sort of unsatisfactory, compromised, provisional basis which has been known to last for ever, which more or less froze the Laotian civil war. Although the settlement was soon undermined by United States action, it lasted until the collapse of South Vietnam a decade later. It was easy to hope that Kennedy would finesse the Vietnamese problem in the same way. Unhappily he did not see the cases as similar. He believed that the Eisenhower administration had needlessly alienated the South Vietnamese government of Ngo Dinh Diem, and devoted most of such time as he could spare for Vietnam between 1961 and 1963 to reassuring Diem, or trying to. Besides, his Secretary of Defense, Robert McNamara, encouraged him to believe that the problem was essentially a military one, and that for every military problem there was a military answer if you looked for it hard enough. For instance, British success in suppressing the communist guerrilla movement in Malaya during the 1950s was put down to superior training in jungle warfare – superior, that is, to anything which the Americans practised; accordingly a new corps was set up, the so-called Green Berets, which followed the British model. Kennedy was infatuated with this invention, and his ghost must have been pleased to see a Green Beret among the sentinels round his coffin during his lying-in-state; but even if counter-insurgency forces were truly the means to victory in South Vietnam, which is anything but certain, the American armed services were far too conservative in doctrine to give them a fair chance. What the admirals and generals (of the army and air force) believed in was fire-power: they were always anxious to recommend the use of nuclear weapons. They continued in that belief to the end. So Kennedy's hopes for the Green Berets were misplaced; and it was folly to think that hugely increasing the number of American 'advisers' in Vietnam would be very helpful either: 'advisers', led by General Stilwell, had never been able to achieve much with Chiang Kai-shek during the Second World War, or after it either. President Diem was very like Chiang, and eventually Kennedy recognized that the problem was essentially political. Diem was an unmanageable ally, an incompetent ruler, and a hopeless commander in war. In the summer of 1963, when Diem's great unpopularity with his people at last became undeniable, Kennedy realized that he was groping in a minefield in the dark. He acquiesced in a coup against Diem, but was horrified when that resulted in Diem's murder. His own murder came three weeks later. All he had achieved in Vietnam was to lose time and deepen the American commitment. Yet it is only fair to add that the point of no return had still not been passed at the time of his death.

That death was, possibly, the decisive event. During his tenure of office Kennedy had shown himself all too ready to act as leader of the 'Free World' against the communist crusade – he despised his predecessor's comparative inactivity – and he showed little scepticism about Cold War orthodoxies. On the other hand, his three years as President had seasoned him, and his cool intelligence was not one to be content with shibboleths. By contrast, Lyndon Johnson was not only inexperienced in foreign affairs, but distracted by the demands of the job into which he had been so suddenly dropped. He could never shake off a feeling that he had to act as the executor of the dead President's will, so to speak; he dared not seem to betray his memory by abandoning policies (such as the defence of South Vietnam) to which Kennedy seemed to have been committed; besides, he himself believed firmly in the cause, and he could not forget how the Republicans had abused Truman for 'losing' China. So it seemed right to him to assure Henry Cabot Lodge Jr, a leading Republican, even before Kennedy was buried, that 'I am not going to lose Vietnam. I am not going to be the President who saw Southeast Asia go the way China went.' He stuck to this simple view of the business throughout his term of office. Yet he did not at first give Vietnam all his attention. He had to get himself elected President in his own right, and the way to do that, in 1964, was by concentrating on domestic issues. When at last he felt free, in the winter of 1964–5, to turn seriously to Vietnamese affairs, time had run out. The communists were on the verge of total victory over their enemies, and the American government could no longer evade a radical choice: to increase the stakes or give up the game.

Not that the little group of men round the President saw it in quite that way. Their individual choices had been made long before. All their training made it certain that the majority of them would see the decision before them in the most conventional Cold War terms. Dean Rusk, for example, the Secretary of State, Assistant Secretary of State in charge of Far Eastern affairs during the Truman administration, had been a strong believer in the Stalinist conspiracy as an explanation of the invasion of South Korea and as a justification of America's resistance to it. He applied the same reasoning to the Vietnamese case and came up with the same answer. Others may have been more influenced by the memory of McCarthyism: like Lyndon Johnson, they did not want to be persecuted for acquiescing in a Red victory. And they all accepted the blend of rationalizations, commitments and beliefs which made up American global policy. They were staunch anti-communists, sincerely wishing to save the Vietnamese from a fate worse than death. They were uncritically convinced that if America were seen to retreat in Indo-China all faith in her will and power would be shattered everywhere else, even in Europe: some no doubt still dreaded a return to isolationism, the bugbear of their youth, others may have taken note of General de Gaulle's earnest efforts to undermine faith in the American commitment to European defence (the General was back at the head of French affairs and proving as obstructive to American designs as ever). All were sure that the Russians would seize the opportunity presented to them by such American weakness to make gains all over the place. Then there was the so-called 'domino theory' – the belief that if Indo-China fell to communism, so would every other independent state in the East, beginning with Thailand and Malaysia. Finally, there was the question of America's inescapable commitments in the western Pacific: Guam, the Philippines, Taiwan, Japan. Would any of these be safe if the communists drove the United States and its allies off the mainland? Would not success in Saigon lead them on to attack Manila, or Chiang Kai-shek? Victory might make the Reds reckless: a forward defence was best. So all aid should be offered to the Saigon government, just as it had been to Syngman Rhee of South Korea. American military might was now so overwhelming (thanks to the enlightened reforms of Secretary McNamara) that victory ought not to take very long.

President Johnson listened to all these points, and indeed could have made most of them himself: he too was a product of Cold War Washington. They necessarily seemed very persuasive. But as President he was inevitably aware of countervailing pressures; he could not conceal from himself that there was still a choice to be made, by him. His advisers could take comfort in their own righteousness and consistency: he could not. If America were to go to war yet again, her people would demand success. Could he be sure of attaining it?

To unprejudiced bystanders with any knowledge of the reasons for the dismantling of the British Empire and the destruction of the French, the answer, by 1965, was, clearly, No. Essentially, the old imperial relationship between Europe and the rest of the world had failed, not because Europe was impoverished and weakened by war, though that helped, nor, emphatically, because of the rise of Russia and the United States to pre-eminence, but because the subject peoples had rejected their status. They could make it agonizingly expensive, in lives, credit and treasure, for any power which tried to keep them in subjection. The British, more by luck than good management, had perceived this truth in time and retired from the business of empire with comparative ease and dignity. The Dutch had been constrained to follow the British example. The French had defied it, and the result had been two long and cruel wars, in Indo-China and Algeria, both of which had ended in total defeat and one of which (the war in Algeria) had nearly destroyed the French state. During the sixties the same process was at work in the Portuguese Empire – a process which not only brought down that empire at last, but also broke the dictatorship long before set up in Portugal herself by Antonio Salazar. The strength of guerrilla and resistance movements did not lie in their knowledge of the tactics of Mao Tse-tung or in the power of their foreign friends, but in the fact that, so long as they had any weapons (and weapons are shockingly easy to acquire in the late twentieth century), they could make life unbearable for the imperial power. Empire, as had long before been pointed out, in vain, to George III, had to rest, in the last resort, on the consent of the governed; and that consent had been withdrawn. The white man's mission was obsolete. Happy was the United States, which had never taken it up, or rather had never done so in a big way, and retired early from the game (the Philippines had been given full independence on 4 July 1946).

Whatever Washington chose to think, in 1965 it was in reality proposing to assume the imperial role in Indo-China which the French had abandoned. Put in those terms, the proposal to make war on the Vietnamese communist nationalists was plainly ridiculous. There was no reason to think that American public opinion would prove more patient under the loss of blood and money than the French had. The tragedy of the American policy-makers was that they would not see it in those terms. They were conditioned, in part, by a certain chauvinism. They had no respect for the French, or, for that matter, for the Vietnamese (who would soon be known by the unlovely name of 'gooks'), and the United States was bigger and stronger than either France or Vietnam. D. W. Brogan remarked at the time that what they wanted was a respectable word for imperialism; if they could have found it no doubt they would have accepted the reality of their enterprise, though it would still have failed. As it was, they insisted that they were simply playing the hero's part in the great anti-communist crusade, and rebuked their European allies for failing to support them; and they made much of the story that the legitimate government of South Vietnam was the victim of wanton aggression by a foreign power and ought to be resisted in the name of the basic principles of the United Nations. This was a dubious thesis: it was highly doubtful if the Saigon government was in any sense legitimate, especially after the murder in 1963 of President Diem and his replacement with a succession of military dictators; it was quite certain that

North Vietnam was not, in the normal sense, a foreign power; what was happening was essentially an interior matter, a civil war; and the United Nations charter explicitly forbade interference in the internal affairs of member states. To all this the American answer was simple: the war was not a civil war and the North and South Vietnamese were truly different peoples. Attempts were made to bend the facts of history and geography to back up this nonsense.

From the foregoing it should be plain that Lyndon Johnson was almost bound to decide matters the way he did. He did not reflect that Kennedy's most popular deed had been not his handling of the missile crisis (let alone his Vietnamese involvement) but his negotiation of the nuclear test-ban treaty; or that he himself had won the 1964 election by a landslide because the voters thought he was the peace candidate (or, to use the terms made popular by Robert Kennedy, the dove against Barry Goldwater's hawk). Instead he took comfort that in the wake of the Tonkin Gulf incident in the summer of 1964, when it appeared (erroneously) that the North Vietnamese had mounted an unprovoked attack on ships of the US navy, Congress had passed resolutions conferring on the President sweeping powers to do whatever he thought fit in Vietnam. In the spring of 1965 he thought fit to send American soldiers and American bombers to the aid of Saigon. Five thousand US Marines went ashore in March; and the point of no return was passed.

What followed was tragically predictable. At first the Americans seemed to sweep all before them; and indeed the South Vietnamese state which they came to prop up lasted another ten years. But what they wanted was to end the challenge of the communist guerrillas for ever; and it soon became plain to observers that this was beyond their power. Merely to keep the National Liberation Front at bay would be an exhausting and, worst of all, an endless undertaking.

For though the United States was strong, it could not use all its strength. The lesson of the Yalu river had sunk in deep. To invade North Vietnam would be as bad a mistake as it had been to invade North Korea: President Johnson, and President Nixon after him, dared not risk drawing in Chinese or Russian forces. Besides, America was still pursuing the hope of a reconciliation with the Soviet Union, many voices were beginning to urge that it try and make friends with China, and these possibilities were too precious to be sacrificed to the Vietnamese War. It was astonishing enough that Russia and China were so patient with America's activities in the South (perhaps they were glad to see the Yankee wearing himself out and learning an expensive lesson); it would be too much to gamble on their tolerating a move northwards. Anyway, even if they did, such a move might not end the war: the enemy could simply take refuge in China and continue his wearing-down operations from that base. America would have gained nothing. She would simply have shortened her enemy's lines of communication while lengthening her own. And that would be unwise, for China was not the only communist sanctuary. West and south-west of Vietnam were Laos and Cambodia; the NLF ('Viet Cong' to the Americans) had long ago begun to build hidden refuges in the jungles and mountains of the border. American commanders longed to carry out what they called 'hot pursuit' into these areas; but an overt move into Laos would upset the fragile balance of forces there, and Cambodia was a neutral state whose ruler, Prince Norodom Sihanouk, obstinately refused to collaborate with the Americans. His little country was too weak to resist the incursions of the Vietnamese communists; nevertheless Sihanouk was determined to keep as far out of the war as might be. He knew that it would be a first-class calamity if Cambodia got involved, and for a long time he managed to keep her at peace, an amazing feat which deserved more credit than it ever received. The Americans despised Sihanouk, regarding him as corrupt and treacherous; but for the time being they left him alone.

The Viet Cong, then, could not be uprooted and destroyed, and the condition of South Vietnam itself meant that they could not be defeated. Vietnam had suffered atrociously from war ever since the Japanese conquest; by 1965 it was a society lapsing into incoherence. Catholics were at odds with Buddhists, communists with capitalists, civilians with military; the traditional order had largely disappeared. The drift of population from the countryside to the cities, which has characterized so many societies since 1945, had been greatly accelerated by the disruptions of war and had inevitably bred deep hostility between rulers and ruled, between town and country. Now the Americans swamped the economy. The immense inflow of men and equipment; the tidal wave of dollars; the load placed on all the social services of a comparatively undeveloped country by the needs of a highly mechanized, well-paid and pampered army; the opportunities that opened for black marketing and profiteering: all this spelt ruin. The intensification of the war brought with it the cumulative destruction of agriculture, Vietnam's most important source of income, so that it changed from a rice-exporting to a rice-importing nation. Worse, if anything, was the devastation wrought on town life by the surge of wartime inflation. The middle class was largely destroyed; girls were driven into prostitution, boys into crime. The government kept going by bribery, corruption and tyranny. It became harder and harder to see what good the Americans were achieving in Vietnam, and very easy to see the evil. Certainly they were not helping to establish a stable society with manageable problems, one which could resist the communists successfully by its own strength. Critics constantly clamoured for a political solution rather than a military one; the truth was that there was no such solution. The elements of civil society had been destroyed in South Vietnam, and even the victorious communists were to find, in the seventies, that they did not know how to restore them. Still less did the Americans. Military action was all they had to offer: literally a poisonous gift. For a favourite tactic was to spray the jungle with defoliant, destroying the communists' cover, no doubt, but also thereby destroying

6. *South-East Asia, 1954-75*

the natural cover of the soil. The result was massive erosion, a terrible waste of Vietnam's most important asset. Tactics were devised to suit the personal comfort and technological faith of the American fighting man rather than the terrain and the people. The Green Berets were never given a chance. Instead, William Westmoreland, the worst American commander since John Pope (who was beaten at Second Bull Run), wasted his forces on 'search-and-destroy' missions in the jungle. This suited the communists wonderfully, for they knew, and never forgot, that the war would be won or lost in the densely populated areas in the east and south. Consequently they were happy to build up their guerrilla networks among the paddy-fields while the Americans blundered about up-country, 'zapping the Cong', enduring heavy losses of men and material, and alienating the people they were supposed to be helping by their free-fire zones, their forced resettlements, the large numbers of refugees they created, and by their massively destructive weaponry. They hunted guerrillas from the air in helicopters; success was measured in terms of the 'body-count', and if the bodies were all too often those of non-guerrillas, well, as Sherman had said, war is hell. American officers were often poorly trained: this was the fundamental cause of the My Lai massacre in 1968, where some 200 Vietnamese civilians were killed by a force under the unintelligent and inexperienced Lieutenant William Calley. He and his men were acting on the principle that one dead gook was as good as another – they all looked alike in their black pyjamas.

The war had a corrupting effect on the American army. Every effort was made to conceal the My Lai crime: Calley's superior officers, from Westmoreland down, were skilful and successful in evading punishment, and Calley himself was released from prison after only three years, thanks to President Nixon. The army was largely composed of black enlisted men, who had joined up to escape poverty and prejudice, and now felt, with some justice, that their white officers gave them most of the nastiest and most dangerous work to do. Hostility spread: by the end of the war the practice of 'fragging'[1] was fairly widespread – the murder of officers by their men. Hard and soft drugs were plentiful in Saigon, the capital of South Vietnam: addiction became a major problem. Violence, venereal disease, theft and petty crime were commonplace. Morale and discipline came near to collapse, in large part because many of the men could see no sense in the war and were disgusted by its cruelty. It was plausibly estimated that it would take a generation for the US army to recover from Vietnam, if it ever did. Even the ending of the draft in the Nixon Presidency did not bring back the old professional innocence: cadets at West Point and Annapolis were regularly caught cheating in their exams. Relations between men and officers remained poor; notions of how to fight remained rigid. One senior officer, explaining his refusal to change his tactics, commented, 'I'll be damned if I permit the United States Army, its institutions, its doctrine, and its traditions to be destroyed just to win this lousy war.' This was hardly the spirit of Ulysses S. Grant or George Marshall.

On top of all this, American casualties rose rapidly. By the end of Johnson's Presidency 222,351 servicemen had been either killed or wounded. It is not surprising that the war soon became even more unpopular than the Korean War had been. Other factors intensified the anger and disillusionment that would have been felt in any case.

Lyndon Johnson had timed his war unluckily. For one thing, the television age was now full-fledged, and the screens were filled with images of horror. Americans were shown the devastation of the country, the sufferings of the people, the sufferings of their own soldiers. Furthermore, there was no censorship of news dispatches. Perhaps, had the war started suddenly, a censorship could have been imposed, as during the Second World War and Korea, though circumstances were so different that I must doubt it; as it

1 The word derived from fragmentation bombs.

was, the war crept up on America, and by the time the troops got there in force the reporters were already well established. Most of them were ready to take the administration's view of the conflict, but an increasing number were not; and it was these last who gradually came to dominate the presentation of the news, both in print and on television (by contrast, a gung-ho movie, *The Green Berets*, starring John Wayne, was a dismal flop). The impact of all this reportage, both inside and outside America, was devastating, and the reaction of other nations, especially in Europe, reinforced it. Never had the United States been so universally condemned. It was not just a matter of the usual Leftist hostility. Many old and tried friends of America were appalled by what they saw; and even those who supported Johnson's aims were amazed at his blunders over means. The constant stress on the point that unless the United States stood firm in Vietnam its allies would lose faith in it was misguided: before very long the allied governments were asking how they could trust a country that was so reckless, so unreasonable, so incompetent; dared they retain their links to one that was so unpopular?

Johnson might have ridden out the storm if he had been less in earnest (his cynical successor was to show how); or if his enterprise had not coincided with a curious upheaval in American society. Instead, his war reached its peak just as the age group most affected by it came together in what was, for a year or two, a formidable political movement.

It is easy to be unkind about youth in the sixties. At one moment to be twenty-three and an admirer of the Rolling Stones (a popular team of musicians) was, it seemed, sufficient guarantee of private wisdom and public virtue. Certainly there was something maddening, to their elders, in these ignorant, provincial, conceited young people, who from the gilded shelter of universities which their parents' money had bought for them and in many cases built for them (never had the colleges and universities of America raised funds more successfully than during the fifties and early sixties) looked out with absolute intolerance on the modern world and condemned it as unclean. Some of them turned out to be quite as unpleasant and as stupid as what they condemned, like the young zealots in Greenwich Village who blew up themselves and their house while making bombs for blowing up other people. It was nevertheless a great mistake (one which many committed) to dismiss them all as no more than middle-class hooligans.

Young idealists demand a lot of other people; they also demand a lot of themselves. Both propositions are demonstrated by the sixties youth movement, which had originated in the Freedom Riders, when college America had not only discovered, to its horror, just how racialist and brutal parts of the country were, but also that there was effective action it could take to improve matters. While Jack Kennedy was alive it could also believe that the power structure was on its side, or at any rate had been captured by a friend; but Kennedy's murder broke the picture. Even before that event a deep scepticism had been growing; now it had free rein. Alienation from conventional society and its pieties was reinforced by the effects of prosperity. Children, teenagers and college students were now a major consuming group and called a new world into being by their expenditure. Original popular music became the exclusive property of the young in a way that had only been foreshadowed in the past. A youth market was discovered for clothes, cars, books, pictures, records and drugs, and the suppliers catered for it assiduously. The result was a sub-culture which efficiently insulated its exponents from outsiders. Particularly, it insulated them from the men who ran the universities. Words like 'square' (unfashionable, dated) and 'hip' (fashionable, up-to-date) had acquired mystic force, and university administrators were almost by definition square. They were also, it must be allowed, sadly unimaginative, too concerned with the feelings, tastes and prejudices of parents, alumni, state governments and their colleagues, too little with those of their charges. These presidents of institutions with forty or fifty thousand members each proposed to create a world which was not much to the liking of the young. It is not surprising that in the mid-sixties a widespread challenge was mounted, beginning at Berkeley, near San Francisco, the object of which, in so far as something so vast and incoherent could have one, seems to have been to force university teachers and administrators alike to treat their pupils with human interest, and not as mere statistics, useful for extracting public subsidies, otherwise mere raw material for processing. Rebellion against the men in grey suits spread from one campus to another, and then, borne like a virus by American students travelling abroad, reached the institutions of Europe, thus reinforcing the anti-Americanism already stimulated by Vietnam. Then Lyndon Johnson began to send members of this generation, in large numbers, as conscripts to the war.

Conscription, 'the draft', had been a fact of life ever since Pearl Harbor. It had grown harder and harder to administer since the end of the Korean War, for vast though America's commitments were, the growth of her population was vaster still, and certainly not so slow: in 1968 it passed the 200 million mark. During the fifties there were more eligible males of military age than the armed forces knew what to do with, and an elaborate system of reclassification and declassification had grown up, the net effect of which was that on the whole the poor got drafted and the well-off, if they took pains, did not. One of the most popular forms of evasion was the so-called college deferment, by which youths could put off their military service until they had finished their education – which helps to explain the then-common phenomenon of the thirty-year-old American student, whose college days seemed to be endless. General Westmoreland's constant clamour for reinforcements began to change all that. In return the cry went up, 'Hell, No, We Won't Go!'

It is natural enough to dislike conscription, especially if it is likely to send you to dangerous places to be wounded or killed. But the call to serve in

Vietnam was something else again: a war which made less and less sense and (look at the television screen) was ever crueller and more slaughterous. The response was various. Clever lawyers were much in demand to find ways through the draft regulations. The Reserve Officers Training Corps (ROTC), a part-time, federally paid-for officer training system, was expelled from most universities. In a few well-publicized incidents individuals burnt their draft cards (an indictable offence) or other people's draft records. On the whole the main reactions were two.

Tens of thousands of draftees went missing: some left for foreign parts; others tried to lose themselves in the United States itself. Some deserted, others refused to go before their draft boards. The movement reached sufficient dimensions to constitute a major harassment for the military authorities.

Far worse was the political action taken by the majority. The civil rights movement had taught them tactics, and the continuing black movement frequently gave them fresh ideas; the battles over university regulations had shown them their strength. They were still congenitally disorganized; some regarded the whole thing as an excuse for non-stop pot parties; others, survivors of the Old Left, saw it all as a chance to recruit more members for another sort of party – the communist; dissension was endemic among such leaders as the movement threw up. But as they marched, sang, conferred and issued manifestos it became clear that something of great political significance was occurring; and if student protest should link up effectively with the protest of the blacks and the poor, no one knew where it would all end. The professionals watched and worried.

Matters came to a head in 1968. On 30 January the Viet Cong launched the so-called 'Tet' offensive (named after the Buddhist holiday on which it began) which involved American troops in desperate battles for control of their bases at Da Nang and Khe Sanh, the city of Hue and the grounds of the US embassy in Saigon itself. All this was displayed on television, and the lesson was rubbed in by the widely respected television journalist Walter Cronkite, who visited Vietnam and came back appalled by what he had discovered. 'It seems now more certain than ever that the bloody experience of Vietnam is to end in a stalemate,' he said; and LBJ, watching, commented that if he had lost Cronkite he had lost America. It made no difference that the communists were eventually driven from all their targets, with losses much heavier than those of the Americans: the essential intractability of the war had been made clear to all. Senator Eugene McCarthy, Democrat of Minnesota – no relation of the late Senator Joe and formerly a close associate of Vice-President Hubert Humphrey – after waiting in vain for Robert Kennedy to move (Kennedy was universally regarded as his brother's true heir), announced his candidacy for the Democratic Presidential nomination, and in the March primary election in New Hampshire got an astonishing 40 per cent of the vote. That was enough for Kennedy, who promptly (too promptly for decency, said

McCarthy's friends) announced his own candidacy. Lyndon Johnson read the signs of the times; he had long ago decided provisionally not to run for re-election in 1968, and now he hoped, by suspending the bombing of North Vietnam, to open the way to peace negotiations. He accepted that his candidacy would only split the Democrats further and weaken America's negotiating position: on 31 March he announced a suspension of the bombing, asked Hanoi to begin negotiations, and said he would not seek re-election. Hubert Humphrey immediately began to move to inherit his mantle; and then Martin Luther King was killed. The summer of blood had begun.

McCarthy and Kennedy battled against each other in one primary election after another; Kennedy won the early contests, lost Oregon, carried California and, before the news commentators had time to point out that this gave him a good chance to win the Democratic nomination when the convention met at Chicago, was shot dead by yet another witless loner: this time a young Palestinian, who resented the pro-Israeli remarks that Kennedy had made during his campaign. This murder handed the nomination to Hubert Humphrey, since to the masters of the Democratic party such as Mayor Daley McCarthy seemed too lightweight, too capricious, for the job of President. But to the youth movement Humphrey was just Lyndon Johnson's puppet, a liberal who had abandoned his principles in the quest for power. (LBJ's sadistic taste for publicly humiliating Humphrey lent plausibility to this picture.) The fact that both the President and the Vice-President now put the quest for peace in Vietnam at the top of their agenda seemed unimportant compared with their record. The convention suddenly seemed all-important. The movement's leaders warned their followers to stay away – trouble was brewing – and many of them did; but enough went to Chicago, or emerged from the city itself, to make it seem just possible that they could win the nomination for McCarthy. Instead they were brought to battle by Mayor Daley's police, who loathed them because they were dirty, anti-war, sexually uninhibited and politically radical, and didn't belong in Chicago even if they and their parents lived there. The young were driven from the public parks with night sticks and tear gas, attacked in the streets, chased into the hotels. Battle outside the convention hall did nothing to stop Humphrey getting the nomination, but once more television showed its power: the whole country had witnessed what an official report later termed a 'police riot'; the young turned away from the Democrats. So did large numbers of the working class, and the South. This was the outcome of the years of civil rights agitation; of the long, hot summers of riot; most certainly, of the civil rights legislation and the war. The Republican vote climbed from its abysmal depth of 1964, though it was still substantially less than it had been in 1960; the Democratic vote collapsed. This election marked the end of the Solid South: the section put up its own candidate, George Wallace, who had been Governor of Alabama during the worst of the troubles there. Wallace had a knack of appealing to racists by inflammatory words and deeds, without ever letting them hurry him away into unsustainable resistance. For instance, he had vowed to 'stand in the doorway' to prevent the integration of the University of Alabama, but in the end had stepped aside. It was scarcely surprising, given the white South's state of mind, that he carried Alabama, Arkansas, Georgia, Louisiana and Mississippi; or that the Republicans carried every other Southern state except Texas, still loyal to its President, and Maryland, where the black and liberal vote was fully mobilized. Much more ominous for the Democrats was Wallace's showing outside the South: he took more than four million votes, two-thirds of them from manual workers, and thereby ensured that the next President would be the old Republican wheelhorse, Richard Nixon. In terms of popular votes it was the best performance of a third-party candidate since 1924; in terms of electoral votes, the best in American history. The year 1968 was unusual: even the other fringe parties doubled their total vote, though among them, as usual, was the Prohibition party, whose vote was halved. It was a year in which everyone was protesting, it seemed: the South against blacks, the blacks against whites, the young against the war, the Northern working class against the young, and the 70 per cent of Democrats who remained faithful to their party against Richard Nixon.

Nixon had announced that he had a secret plan for ending the war. But as it turned out the war, or at least America's involvement in it, lasted longer under him than it had under Johnson. The secret plan amounted to little more than an impious hope that he could bomb the North Vietnamese to the conference table and to concessions there, while finishing off the communists in the south with a still harsher battle. A procedure was initiated for replacing American fighting men with Vietnamese, but the agony dragged on, indeed spread. The US high command in Vietnam was still obsessed by the idea of dealing the enemy a crushing blow by bombing what was believed to be his command centre in the Parrot's Beak – a triangular area of Cambodia that projected into South Vietnam. Nixon authorized the attack, while doing his utmost to keep it secret from Congress (still controlled by the Democrats), the world and the American people. Hideous damage was done to eastern Cambodia, but the guerrillas were not destroyed. So after a *coup d'état* toppled Prince Sihanouk, Nixon sent troops into Cambodia to try to eliminate the imaginary Viet Cong base on the ground. This enterprise failed, both militarily and politically: the communists now undertook the systematic conquest of Cambodia and Laos, and the non-communist forces were unable to stand up to them, especially in gentle, Buddhist Cambodia. American forces had a larger area to defend than ever, at just the time when their numbers were beginning to be reduced. Their overwhelming bombing offensive (in the end more bombs were dropped on Indo-China than had been dropped in the entire Second World War) pushed on the destruction of South-East Asia, but did not bring military victory any nearer. Morally, the attack on Cambodia was

America's worst crime, for it forced a neutral, peaceful people to experience the horrors of war and generated a uniquely horrible aftermath, when a genocidal communist regime took power for three years. There is reason to believe that the Cambodians eventually suffered more than any of the other peoples of Indo-China; Richard Nixon's legacy. His attack on Cambodia led in 1970 to further widespread student disturbances. During a demonstration at Kent State University in Ohio four students were shot and killed by the National Guard. There was universal outrage on the campuses of America: students, faculty and administrators at last came together to express their indignation. The manual workers who had voted for Wallace did not share this feeling in the least, for they regarded the peace movement as unpatriotic, if not treasonable. However, they also regarded the war as pointless. As one construction worker remarked, on seeing the coffin of an American soldier go by, 'The whole goddamn country of South Vietnam is not worth the life of one American boy, no matter what the hell our politicians tell us.' When the Republicans did badly in the Congressional elections of 1970 and the peace party made striking gains, Nixon realized that he had no choice but to negotiate seriously. Without a settlement he would lose the 1972 Presidential election; and he had no intention of stepping down like LBJ.

He was an even more complex character than his moody, flamboyant, overpowering predecessor. Superficially it might seem that the man and the moment had met when he was elected. Nixon was a seasoned politician, skilled in all the byways, a man particularly good at rallying his own constituency to his support. The small towns and respectable suburbs loved him. He had an even greater opportunity than Eisenhower's, to end an even more unpopular war than the Korean; and, as events would soon prove, could do so without real damage to America's international interests or to his own popularity. But his character blinded him to his chances. To seize them would have required the sort of courage and insight that Lyndon Johnson occasionally displayed. Unfortunately Nixon was almost devoid of insight, and his sense of reality was seriously defective.

Some of this may perhaps be put down to his Quaker background, unlikely though it may seem (there is a certain distance between a man who relied on bombs and one who relies on the inner light). Nixon conducted the Indo-Chinese war with a cold-blooded violence that was certainly remote from Quaker pacifism. As if his attack on Cambodia were not enough, he sent his planes against Hanoi in the heaviest bombing operation of the war at Christmas, 1972, just when peace agreements were about to be signed: he launched this offensive in order to persuade the South Vietnamese government, which he was actively betraying, that America was as reliable an ally as ever. This was scarcely the attitude of George Fox and William Penn.

Nevertheless the distance from Fox to Nixon is shorter than is often supposed. Nixon was intensely introspective, a trait which his upbringing must have encouraged. He was accustomed to rely entirely on his own perceptions; his decisions were mostly taken alone. Morally he was a shallow man: the only precepts he ever mentioned were those he learned from his Quaker mother and his football coach. The rich and honourable tradition of American republicanism meant nothing to him by comparison. He brought with him to his duties as President a festering rancour. He had been poor, so he would never cease to be preoccupied with the rich, envying them, fearing them, craving to be one of them. He had lost the Presidency to John Kennedy, so the latter's good looks, wit and charm became another painful obsession, much intensified after Kennedy's murder sanctified his memory. He had lost the gubernatorial election in California in 1962, and blamed this defeat on a hostile press: 'Congratulations, gentlemen,' he said ungraciously to reporters, 'you won't have Richard Nixon to kick around any more.' (It was a characteristic politician's vanity that he spoke of himself so often in the third person.) Within him was a darkness, that he mistook for the light. Eventually it would destroy him.

First, however, he destroyed enormous numbers of Indo-Chinese, and not a few American soldiers (by the end of American involvement, 56,000 US servicemen had been killed and 270,000 wounded). This policy having proved inadequate, he changed tack radically. Peace, he decided, must be made on what terms could be got; and the United States must be protected from any possible ill-effects of acknowledging defeat by at last coming to terms with the communist government of China.

In executing this policy Nixon had the assistance of the most remarkable diplomatist to emerge in America since 1945. Henry Kissinger, a German Jew, had come to America as a child refugee just before the Second World War. He had made a very successful career at Harvard as an interpreter of international affairs, in large part because, for good and ill, he did not share conventional American attitudes to them. Completely unsentimental and not much interested in ideology, he believed that the balance of power was still the key to understanding the world and that peace could only be brought about by judicious manipulation of that balance. He was a devout believer in the Soviet threat but came to think it was best dealt with by raising up China; and all other diplomatic problems could be made to yield, in the same way, to the logic of power. Just as Russia would not risk quarrelling with China and the United States simultaneously, so all other governments, without exception, could be coerced or bribed into desirable behaviour if reality was made plain to them. To be sure, the business of exhibiting reality was a delicate one; but here Kissinger could rely on his charm, his mastery both of broad issues and of details, his inexhaustible energy, his intellectual ascendancy, and on the wealth and technological superiority of the United States. During his years as Nixon's adviser on national security, and then as Secretary of State (1973–7), he put all these assets to excellent use in shaping American foreign policy and had many triumphs to his name. He did not emerge with clean hands: his responsibility for the devastation of Cambodia was almost as great as Nixon's. He found his President a very trying man to work for, and his enormous vanity cannot have liked the manner in which Nixon claimed the credit for all the successes brought home by Kissinger; but unflinching White House support was absolutely necessary if successes were to be achieved, and Kissinger paid the price for that support: he flinched at nothing. He flattered Nixon outrageously, and outmanoeuvred all rivals for the President's confidence. The outcome seemed to justify him. Nixon made a state visit to China in February 1972; an end to the Vietnamese War was negotiated in the same year, or at least an end to direct American involvement in it (for this Kissinger and his opposite number in the North Vietnamese delegation to the peace talks in Paris, Le Duc Tho, were jointly awarded the Nobel Peace Prize, which Le Duc Tho refused[2]); and when Kissinger turned his negotiating skills to the Middle East, it actually began to seem that progress was at last being made, if only at a glacial rate, towards the settlement of the Arab–Israeli quarrel. In the middle of all this the 1972 Presidential election was held. The Democrats fell further out of favour with the Wallaceites by nominating Senator George McGovern, a noted liberal and anti-war leader: their vote fell off by another two million. Wallace himself was shot and crippled by a would-be assassin and so was out of the race. Nixon was rewarded for Kissinger's achievements by an overwhelming majority: his popular vote increased by fifteen million, and he took all but seventeen of the electoral votes. But although no one suspected it the doom of his administration was already sealed.

Like most modern Presidents, Nixon from the first felt that he had to build up a personal political alliance, without too much regard to party or to the theoretical separation of powers, if he was to achieve anything in office. He regarded his task as much more difficult than that of his predecessors, for he was convinced that most politicians, journalists, civil servants and lawyers were his bitter enemies. The little group that stuck to him during the lean years of the sixties was composed, not of yes-men (the stories of bitter rows within Nixon's official family are legion), but men who were absolutely loyal to their chief, men, and women too, who would let nothing stand in his way. It was said of one of them that he would walk over his grandmother to please the President. It was this group that Nixon brought with him to Washington, and it was attitudes like theirs that he wanted to instil in all those he had to deal with. He would, if he could, fill the executive branch with Nixonians of this stripe, Congress and the judicial bench too. Men of independent spirit were to be crushed; their every move would be regarded as a stroke against the President. All means must be explored for their destruction.

Such a Manichean attitude is profoundly unwise in American politics, where the separated powers are deeply entrenched in law and custom and

2 When the satirist Tom Lehrer heard the news, he retired from business on the grounds that he could no longer compete with actuality.

where the need to compromise, to live and let live, if the system is to work, is almost universally recognized, by the practitioners if not necessarily by their constituents. Nixon should have learned this lesson quite early in his Presidency when he nominated two totally unfit men for appointment to the Supreme Court. He did not ask what their records as jurists might be; it was enough that they were Southern reactionaries (whose appointment would please the racists), who would owe everything to Nixon and so would presumably be loyal, as the Nixonians understood the word. Unfortunately for them the Supreme Court has its own myth, its own constituency, and appointments thereto need the consent of two-thirds of the US Senate present and voting. It proved surprisingly easy for the opposition to block both appointments. Thereafter Nixon put up only respectable names. But he did not make the appropriate inference that there were some things he could not get away with and ought not to try. He had already set another intrigue on foot.

The intricacies of the Watergate affair defy summary. They have anyway been laid bare to the world with a fullness for which even American government, the most indiscreet in history, showed no precedent. The general outline of the business may, however, be summarized at no great length and with no great inaccuracy. The Nixonians carried with them to the White House the conviction that of all their enemies the liberal intellectuals were the worst. There were too many of them in government, and too many even of those outside government were too good at finding things out. The worst case of the kind occurred when Daniel Ellsberg, a former employee of the Defense Department, leaked the so-called Pentagon Papers, an official but secret and appallingly frank history of the Vietnam entanglement, to the *New York Times*. This sort of thing had to stop, for the papers were a great help to the anti-war movement, and their unopposed publication might mean that the secrets of the new Nixon administration would one day be made public too (a foreboding that eventually came true); so a number of 'plumbers' were hired by the White House to stop leaks, if they could, and to spy on the opposition. Chief among them were Gordon Liddy and Howard Hunt, the one a would-be James Bond, the other a science fiction writer. Both had once worked for the CIA and learned some bad habits. Common sense was not either gentleman's strong point. They burgled the office of Daniel Ellsberg's psychiatrist in a vain attempt to find incriminating information; and with a handful of Cuban refugees, whom they had hired like mercenary soldiers, they broke into the offices of the Democratic National Committee in the Watergate building in Washington, hoping to bug the telephones there. They were detected at their labours by a night watchman who sent for the police; and in a few days all the plumbers had been arrested.

The incident could not have come at a more awkward moment: the 1972 election campaign was about to begin, and if Nixon acknowledged responsibility for the plumbers he would hand the Democrats a first-rate issue. So he did all he could to conceal the involvement of Liddy and his men with the White House, thus beginning a process that would eventually wreck his Presidency, send most of his closest associates to jail and imperil the whole American system of government.

At first it seemed that stout denial would do the trick. Of course it would be difficult if any of the arrested men chose to talk, but the White House hoped that silence could be bought with some of the money in the vast treasury accumulated for the election by the Campaign to Re-Elect the President (known to the Democrats, the press and eventually the world as CREEP). Unfortunately not everyone was satisfied. The *Washington Post* put two able young reporters on the story, and began to ask embarrassing questions. The plumbers all pleaded guilty to charges of burglary, but when they came up for sentencing in January 1973 the judge indicated that he suspected a cover-up and said that unless somebody talked the sentences would be extremely heavy. This cracked the nerves of almost all the defendants: they began to confess. The Senate set up a special committee to investigate 'Watergate'. One of the President's men, his counsel, John Dean, who was deeply involved in the cover-up, decided that the game was lost, and started to tell all he knew to the FBI. Richard Nixon began a long rearguard action.

There ensued one of the oddest episodes in American history. While Egypt and Israel went to war again, and the Arab countries imposed an embargo on oil exports to the United States and, after the war, the Organization of Petroleum Exporting Countries raised world oil prices to unheard-of heights, touching off global inflation and depressing world trade; while the South Vietnamese government lurched ever nearer to final defeat, Nixon paid attention only in so far as he thought he could exploit the crises to remain in office. It was no good. In the end the American people and politicians, or most of them, realized that their President had conspired to pervert the course of justice. Impeachment proceedings were started, and it became clear that they would almost certainly succeed if pursued to the end. Eventually Nixon reluctantly faced the facts and resigned from office on 8 August 1974. The manner of his going showed that he still did not realize what he had done, in spite of his legal training, his long political experience and his sainted mother's good advice. He said that he was resigning, the first President in history to do so, because his political base had been destroyed by unprincipled and vindictive enemies. Neither then nor subsequently did he admit that the charges against him were valid, nor did he express any penitence. His misery was obvious, as obvious as his bewilderment; but it was not the misery of an innocent man. He had been too fond of the trappings of his office, both those which he inherited and those which he devised himself. Among the latter was a system of tape-recording which caught every conversation held in the President's various offices. The evidence of the tapes was unanswerable: Nixon, in defiance of his oath to execute the office of President faithfully, and to preserve, protect and defend the constitution of the United States, which included the requirement that he take care that the laws were faithfully executed, had tried very hard to shield the plumbers and the other culprits from justice. The American people could make sense of this and jumped to the conclusion that Nixon had also planned the original Watergate burglary (which, probably, he did not). Nixon was at a loss. The inner light had failed. For it had told him that anything was allowed to the President of the United States and that anything was allowable which helped a man to win an election. It was the faith on which he had acted all his adult life, the faith he had devised from watching the imperial actions of Franklin Roosevelt, Harry Truman and the rest, all of whom had from time to time taken chances with the Constitution. He could see no difference between their cases and his, and so went whining into exile in the luxurious home he had created for himself (partly with taxpayers' money) in California.

His countrymen, dismayed by defeat in war, violent social conflict and now by betrayal of law and democracy at the very heart of their political system, wondered if they could ever trust any President, or politician, or voter again. For if Nixon had perverted public life with his lies and recklessness, who had believed him, and put him into office, and collaborated with him almost to the last? And the bicentenary ('bicentennial' in American) of independence less than two years away!

Fortunately for the Americans, history waits for nothing, not even a fit of national introspection. Nixon was replaced by his Vice-President, Gerald Ford (b. 1913). Ford had for years been the Republican leader in the House of Representatives, and his loftiest ambition had been to win the Speakership. Then, in the summer of 1973, as the Watergate affair reached its climax, Nixon's first Vice-President, Spiro Agnew, was found to have engaged in corrupt practices and had to resign his office, later pleading guilty, by arrangement with the prosecutors, to the least of the charges brought against him.[3] Nixon nominated Ford to replace Agnew, and less than a year later found that by so doing he had picked his own replacement.

Ford was a good-humoured, honest, straightforward man, who did not pretend to genius: as President he consciously modelled himself on Harry Truman, whose reputation as an unpretentious but successful statesman had grown steadily since he left office, even among Republicans. The new President's family was attractive and reassuring: they began to exorcize the cloud of sulky secrecy which had lain over the White House for so long. Ford lost some goodwill by formally pardoning Nixon, for it seemed to many that the ex-President was getting off a great deal too lightly. Nixon did not help matters by trying to get possession of the celebrated tapes: a

---

3 This was a scandal as unprecedented as Watergate itself, but of course it was overshadowed almost entirely by the President's misdeeds. The Nixon administration was certainly accident-prone. As late as 1981 one of its members (Earl Butz, former Secretary of Agriculture) was sent to prison for cheating on his income tax.

special act of Congress had to be passed to thwart him. But it is likely that Ford did the right thing; without the pardon the aftermath of Watergate would probably have been as long-drawn-out and painful as the crisis itself.

27 A World Restored? 1977–89

We were sure that ours was a nation of the ballot, not the bullet, until the murders of John Kennedy, Robert Kennedy, and Martin Luther King Jr. We were taught that our armies were always invincible and our causes always just, only to suffer the agony of Vietnam. We respected the Presidency as a place of honour until the shock of Watergate. We remember when the phrase 'sound as a dollar' was an expression of absolute dependability, until ten years of inflation began to shrink our dollar and our savings. We believed that our nation's resources were limitless until 1973, when we had to face a growing dependence on foreign oil. These wounds are still very deep. They have never been healed.

President Jimmy Carter, 1979

America is back and standing tall.

President Ronald Reagan, 1984

The defeat in Vietnam and the Watergate scandal together marked a watershed in American history. The effects of the two crises would still be felt at the end of the twentieth century, not least because they made the conduct of foreign policy more difficult and presidents less secure in office. People and politicians alike had to take account of these and related changes, and the struggle to contain the after-effects was a major theme of politics from the mid-seventies until the mid-eighties. But to some extent the double crisis hid for too long the importance of America's abiding power, wealth and energy: there was much unnecessary concern and loose talk about national decline. In part this was because, beyond the country's borders, huge historical developments – which the United States, however deeply involved, might influence but could not control – solved some old problems, created some new ones, and cumulatively left the world looking perplexingly different from its appearance in 1945, or even 1976. It was clear only that it was still not a safe world. The lesson of Pearl Harbor held good. As the twenty-first century drew near it became apparent that although America in 2000 would have no less to celebrate than she had had at her bicentenary, still her voyage was going to be endless: no snug haven lay ahead for the ship of state. The task for Americans, as for all the nations, was to fit themselves for the eternal struggle to avoid shipwreck and make the voyage as happy as might be, while avoiding the complacency which had contributed to the wreck of so many actual ships in 1941.

In 1977 few saw the future in precisely these terms. The new president was inclined rather to view the present as one big emergency and the future as marked by a sharp diminution of the promise of American life: he was an early believer in the theme of decline. He had reasons for this comparatively sober outlook which seemed persuasive to him. The expense of the Vietnam War, and Lyndon Johnson's refusal to meet it by raising taxes sufficiently, had led to rapid inflation. This undermined the international monetary system established at Bretton Woods in 1944,[1] for it was based on an American preponderance and power in the world economy, and on an assumption that the dollar was as good as gold, which inflation eroded. In 1971, with the United States beginning to run a large trade deficit, President Nixon ended the dollar's convertibility into gold, which had stood since Franklin Roosevelt's time, and thereby devalued it by 8 per cent. From now on, the world markets would determine the exchange value of the world's currencies at any given moment. Wiseacres shook their heads over the loss of the fixed rate system, but it is doubtful if it could have coped as well as did the floating rate system with the next great economic emergency, the 1973 'oil shock'.

This was a consequence of American presidential politics. Nixon engineered an economic boom in 1972 to secure his re-election, and this boom continued in 1973. The United States imported larger and larger quantities of raw materials, especially oil. America's vast reserves, which had once made her the biggest oil-producing country in the world, were now seriously depleted, and you couldn't drive Cadillacs on water. War again broke out between Egypt and Israel, and the oil-producing countries of the Middle East took action against Israel's great patron. They had been amazingly patient, but they were tired of sacrificing their earnings to the profligate ways of the Americans, of pampering a country which at moments of crisis always supported their bitterest foe. Why should they subsidize the American way of life? Cheap petrol was not one of the rights of man, whatever American consumers thought. So the cartel of producers, the Organization of Petroleum-Exporting Countries (OPEC), increased the price of oil fourfold in December, 1973. Within months the United States was experiencing inflation of more than 12 per cent per annum. The Nixon boom ended, and there was a record crop of bankruptcies in the building

1 See above, p. 577.

industry. A new economic crisis, less dramatic, but as deadly and intractable as the one which began in 1929, engulfed the globe. So far as the United States was concerned there was no immediately obvious remedy.

President Gerald Ford, loyal to the stern tradition of Herbert Hoover, adopted a severely deflationary policy. Americans (headed by the federal government) must abandon extravagance and learn to live within their means. Ford relentlessly vetoed what seemed to him to be the wasteful proposals of Congress (which the Democrats still controlled) and when the city of New York, finding itself on the brink of bankruptcy, appealed to the President for help, he turned it down flat. FORD TO CITY: 'DROP DEAD', said the headline in the *New York Daily News*, and the President could reflect that he had added substantially to the odds against his re-election.[2] Otherwise he achieved nothing. When he left office, unemployment stood at nearly 8 per cent, and the budget deficit was at a destabilizing and record-breaking $66.4 billion.

Given this Republican record, it was reasonable to expect a crushing Democratic victory in 1976. As if inflation and the memory of Watergate were not bad enough, the glittering edifice of Kissinger's foreign policy had collapsed: in 1975 the communists finally conquered Laos, Cambodia and South Vietnam. The last Americans in Saigon fled ignominiously, leaving behind all too many of their collaborators. The victors renamed Saigon 'Ho Chi Minh City' and set up a regime quite as oppressive as those in other communist countries; in Cambodia the Khmer Rouge went much further and, under their morally and intellectually perverted leader Pol Pot, began to massacre their countrymen by the million. Ford did, and probably could do, nothing to help, but America was shamed. In the same year, at Helsinki, agreements were signed with the Soviet Union by which, for the first time, the West recognized Russian hegemony in Eastern Europe as legitimate; the fact that by the same instrument the Russian communists pledged themselves to respect human rights in the Soviet Union did not impress the critics; the undertaking, they complained, was mere words (in this they were eventually proved wrong). So Ford lost to Jimmy Carter, but only by a small margin after all: he took 48 per cent of the popular vote to Carter's 50 per cent, and the winning margin in the electoral college was only 57.

Democrats (especially northerners) might attribute this rather dismal result solely to Carter's lacklustre campaign; in reality it was a warning that the geography of American politics had shifted profoundly. The old Rooseveltian coalition of organized labour, ethnic minorities, liberals and blacks delivered for Carter magnificently, and the total Democratic vote was no more than two million short of Lyndon Johnson's record-setting

2 All the same, Ford made his point. Since the collapse of New York would be extremely bad for business, a consortium of capitalists came together and devised a scheme for both rescuing the city and sorting out its long-mismanaged finances. This was surely better than getting the American taxpayer to meet the bills, which would have removed any inducement for New York to put its house in order.

tally of 1964; but Carter won only because he reclaimed the South, where blacks voted for him because he was a Democrat and, his record showed, wholly committed to civil rights, and whites (but not a majority of them) because he was one of their own: he was the first President elected from the Deep South since the Civil War. Outside the South, the Democrats only carried two states west of the Mississippi – Missouri and Hawaii.[3] Yet California, Texas and Florida were the fastest growing of all the states. The question arose whether the Democrats could ever again win with a candidate from the North-East at the head of their ticket, and whether Jimmy Carter would be adroit and impressive enough in office to ensure his re-election in 1980 by rebuilding his party's strength outside its heartland in the Frostbelt.

'Frostbelt' was a new term, the counterpart of 'the Sunbelt' – that newly powerful region which, by some reckonings, stretched round the southern border of the United States from Virginia to California. The Sunbelt abounded in exuberant self-confidence and new money; it also included the country's greatest oil-producing areas. Reconciling its views with those of the oil-consuming Frostbelt (or Rustbelt, as it was sometimes even more unkindly called, in allusion to its decaying heavy industry) would tax any president, and a Democratic one most of all.

Carter certainly recognized that the times required a new politics, and he supposed that he could supply it. He had demonstrated, by his success in winning the nomination, that even within the Democratic party there was a feeling that the New Deal tradition was of shrinking relevance to modern America. The great bureaucratic state which was one of the legacies of the New Deal, the Second World War and the Cold War had to many eyes become too large, inefficient and corrupt. Carter gloried in being an outsider to Washington and campaigned against its folly and wickedness as demonstrated by Vietnam and Watergate. He promised 'compassion and competence' in government, as a way of getting round the perpetual struggle between liberal Democrats, who supported activist policies, the welfare state and high taxes, and Republicans, still decrying 'big government' and wasteful expenditure, and wanting tax cuts. Before becoming a peanut farmer, and then a politician, Carter had served six years in the navy as an engineer. This training largely determined his outlook: he believed that government, like engineering, was a process of problem-solving, and that problems yielded most readily to those who worked hard and mastered all details (so he tended to immerse himself in one thing at a time, however many other urgent matters were in need of his attention). He looked always for comprehensive solutions, which is fine in principle but not often sensible when you have a country as large and diverse as America to govern and a body as incalculable as Congress to manage: Carter needed to learn the arts of negotiation and compromise, and how to settle for half a loaf (in

3 The Democrats also carried Minnesota, where the Mississippi rises; it was the home state of Carter's Vice-President, Walter Mondale.

some respects he learned the lesson very well). His entire political career before 1976 had been passed in Georgia, and that was not helpful: it took him a long time to learn, if he ever did, that the presidency and Congress were much more complex and recalcitrant organisms than the Georgian governorship and legislature, and that the little knot of faithful Georgians who had helped him get to the White House were inadequate assistants when it came to governing the country. But in other ways his Georgian background was the best thing about Carter. He had been a leader in the new generation of white Southern politicians who had recognized the victory of the civil rights revolution and had insisted that the fact must be accepted generously and finally. His profound religious faith was that of a Southern Baptist, and his spontaneous friendliness was Southern too. He had a slightly corny, hayseed side to him: he once presented the prime minister of Israel with a sign reading 'Shalom, Y'all'. In the spirit of Jefferson he was ostentatiously determined to strip the presidency of ostentation. Ignoring Speaker O'Neill's wise view that 'most people prefer a little pomp in their presidents',[4] he insisted on carrying his own luggage and cut down the number of renditions of the presidential anthem, 'Hail to the Chief'. After his inauguration at the Capitol, instead of driving to the White House in an armoured limousine, he and his family walked the whole way down Pennsylvania Avenue. He had promised reform, if not a revolution; he was going to clean up Washington and demolish the 'Imperial Presidency' (a phrase recently made popular by the historian and liberal activist, Arthur M. Schlesinger Jr). But his unreadiness for the task was perhaps symbolized by the fact that when after his walk he reached the White House and wanted to set to work, he realized that he did not know the way to the Oval Office.

'Poor bastard,' said a leading Democrat four years later. 'He used up all his luck getting here. We've had our victories and defeats, but we've not had a single piece of good luck.' Fair enough, though it has to be remembered that master politicians to some extent make their luck, as Ronald Reagan was to demonstrate. Carter, or any President elected in 1976 – perhaps especially any Democratic President – was bound to have a hard time, so many and so difficult were the problems pressing in upon him. But it is hard to feel that he tackled them in the best way possible. He was overimpressed by such matters as the rise in oil prices, the federal budget deficit and the cost of the welfare state (which automatically increased its expenditure when unemployment rose). He made much of the idea that America had entered 'an age of limits' and should modify its behaviour accordingly – by turning down its central heating and wearing woolly garments indoors, for instance. This merely made him ridiculous. So, like many other presidents, he turned with relief to foreign policy, where he had a comparatively free hand.

In several negotiations he showed himself as masterly as Henry Kissinger.

4 Tip O'Neill, *Man of the House* (London: the Bodley Head, 1988) p. 314.

Trouble had long been brewing in Panama, where the treaty giving the United States the right to build and manage the Canal, and ceding sovereignty over the Canal Zone,[5] was now intolerable to Panamanian opinion. Simple-minded nationalism in the United States took the view that what had been paid for belonged immutably to the purchaser, that the Panama Canal was a monument to the glory of the United States, and that it would not be safe if control were relinquished – suppose a Soviet ally got hold of it? This opinion was strongly held by congressional conservatives of both parties. But Carter knew that the alternative to a settlement was probably bloody conflict, which might destroy the Canal, damage American prestige and be as disruptive politically as the war in Vietnam; so he negotiated treaties with Panama which provided for restoration of Panamanian sovereignty in 2000, joint management until then, and the guarantee of US interests thereafter; he then persuaded the necessary two-thirds majority of the Senate to ratify them. It was a really notable diplomatic achievement, and saved America much trouble. But Carter's finest hour came in 1978 when he holed up in the presidential retreat, Camp David in the hills of Maryland, and talked the president of Egypt, Anwar Sadat, and the prime minister of Israel, Menachem Begin, into making the agreements which soon led to peace between their countries. It was an extraordinary feat, testifying to Carter's intelligence, persistence, honest purpose and goodwill.

These triumphs did little for what should have been his central political concern – the strengthening of his party; but throughout his presidency Carter showed a curious antipathy to party politics, and even to the Democratic party which, after his final defeat, he dismissed as 'an albatross around my neck'. Here again his Southern background probably misled him. The Democratic party of the Solid South in his boyhood could inspire only limited respect, if any; the Southern tradition with which he identified himself was that of Populism, which had been a revolt against the old parties; yet though he may not have realized it, he was perhaps even more influenced by Progressivism, which had always been deeply critical of the party system itself. Carter never seems to have acknowledged that he needed the Democrats at least as much as they needed him. If anything, his diplomacy weakened them: both in 1978 and 1980, senators who had voted for the Panama treaties went down to defeat – targeted by well-organized and well-financed opponents of Carter's policy.

But foreign policy issues are seldom the central ones in American elections. Inflation was much more damaging to the governing party. Everyone agreed that it ought to be tackled, but there was no consensus on what caused it and what would cure it. Liberals wanted government action to push down prices, conservatives wanted to put a ceiling on wages. New economic theorists abounded, agreeing on nothing except the worthlessness of John Maynard Keynes: monetarists wanted to do something about the money-

5 See above, pp. 451–2.

supply, supply-siders wanted to cut back government regulation and expenditure. Workers, particularly those on the West Coast, who watched an immigration rate rising towards the half-million annual mark,[6] began to fear for their jobs and their high wages. Most ominously of all, from a politician's point of view, inflation was inexorably pushing citizens into higher and higher tax-brackets, since neither the state nor the federal bureaucracies could move fast enough to correct this 'bracket creep'. In 1978, in California (where everything started nowadays) a great tax-revolt began. In an age of inflation it was inevitable that the price of real estate should go up. The state of California largely financed itself out of property taxes (since the federal government pre-empted income tax) and accordingly, as many citizens got richer on paper, their tax bills got larger in real life (but at any one moment most of them were not going to realize their notional capital gains by selling their residences, and those who did had to buy replacements, also at inflated prices). So in a referendum Proposition 13 was passed, by a two-to-one margin, which, among other things, cut property taxes by 57 per cent and ordained that in future the state legislature might only increase taxes if it could muster a two-thirds majority. The idea swept the country: it was like the anti-Stamp movement all over again. Property taxes, income taxes, sales taxes were all slashed, and voices were raised to demand that the federal government do likewise, if necessary by constitutional amendment. The state governments lost billions in revenue, and had to cut back expenditure. It was a bad moment for the Democrats, who had been the big-spending party since Franklin Roosevelt became President.

Nor was taxation the only difficulty; perhaps it was not even the most important.[7] For the social turbulence which began in the 1960s had not died away, only changed its character. There was no longer a war, so there was no anti-war movement; there was no longer a single civil rights movement, for most of what the NAACP and the SCLC had hoped to achieve before 1960 had been accomplished: the continuing campaign for full racial equality was now largely to be waged in normal politics, as was shown when northern cities began to elect black mayors[8] and the number of African-American officeholders soared nationally. But there was still a huge range of issues (a new one seemed to be discovered every year) on which the young, the black, women and radicals wanted action, so agitation

6 This was still much less than the annual rate of immigration just before the First World War, and since the total population of the United States had more than doubled, was much less conspicuous. But the local effects – in Florida, for instance, where refugees from Castro's Cuba settled in large numbers – were often dramatic.

7 However much they moan, Americans are not heavily taxed by international standards. They pay proportionately less than the British or the continental European states although, country for country, they are much richer.

8 This was a mixed achievement. It was largely made possible by the migration from the central cities to the suburbs of the mainly white middle class, which took its taxability with it. As a result the new black mayors had to struggle with endless problems of crime, unemployment, bad housing, bad schooling, and so on, without sufficient resources to do so successfully.

was unceasing, was indeed becoming a tradition, even institutionalized in such bodies as the National Organization of Women (founded in 1966). There were still victories aplenty. In 1978 the President of the Mormon church had a vision which at last allowed African-Americans to become Mormon ministers. Laws against the practice of homosexuality melted away, and San Francisco became famous as a city where gays lived in large numbers and made their presence felt politically. But on the other side, as conservatives saw that the challenge was not going to evaporate, the forces of resistance mustered for a long fight; and they began to gain support from a great many ordinary Americans – especially white ethnic men, members of the lower-middle or working class, the backbone of the Democrats – who were beginning to feel threatened by the new activism which seemed to be taking over their party, and who believed that change had gone far enough, that it threatened to become unfair. Their anxiety was sharpened by the effects of inflation in weakening the economy, destroying jobs, and threatening the comfortable way of life that so many had come to take for granted since 1945.

Various episodes epitomized what was happening.

A legacy of the civil rights movement was a vogue for what was known as 'affirmative action'. It was correctly believed that African-Americans had for generations been economically, socially and educationally discriminated against; accordingly, many states adopted a principle of quotas, by which a fixed proportion of university places and of contracts between government and business should go to minority applicants. The intention was good enough; unfortunately it had the logical consequence that white businesses were sometimes denied contracts for which they were the underbidders, and some white applicants were denied university places for which they were better qualified, academically, than their black competitors. This seemed unfair: whites in the 1970s did not see why they should individually be made to pay for the collective sins of their ancestors. The matter came to a head in the case of *Regents of the University of California* v. *Bakke*, which the US Supreme Court decided in 1978. Allan Bakke was a Vietnam veteran who worked for the National Aeronautics and Space Administration (NASA) near San Francisco. In 1972 he applied for admission to the medical school at Davis, California, and was turned down because there was not room for him if the school was to stick to its quota of sixteen reserved places for blacks and Mexican-Americans. In a carefully written majority opinion (Thurgood Marshall voted in the minority) Justice Powell found for Bakke; the medical school had not shown enough flexibility in administering its policy, 'it denied [Bakke] admission and may have deprived him altogether of a medical education'. Powell and the court, in this and later decisions, actually endorsed affirmative action, but the damage was done: in the decades that followed, the Bakke decision was used far and wide as a justification for attacking affirmative action; eventually a law school in Texas in effect resegregated itself. Two rights seemed to have made a wrong, and the Constitution was no help. The courts were scarcely to blame for admitting as much, but the failure of state legislators and university administrators (not to mention the federal government) to work out a generally applicable, practical and democratic solution to the problem made a depressing coda to the great movement of black liberation.

Sexual liberation was another legacy of the mid-twentieth century. Traditionally (and particularly since the early nineteenth century) the United States had been a society where the public and conventional attitude to sexual conduct was stupendously prudish, and all churches, whether Protestant or Catholic, had supported recurrent campaigns to repress any hints at other codes of conduct (Hollywood, for example, though living off sex, was forced to banish all frank or realistic depiction or discussion of it from the movies); but every town of any size had a red-light district where sporting houses and other facilities for illicit entertainment throve, usually under the protection of a corrupt police force. But in their conduct, as the famous Kinsey reports made very clear just after the Second World War,[9] the American people increasingly defied these ancient arrangements. The divorce rate was rising, the number of births outside marriage was soaring, more and more Catholics were ignoring their Church's ban on contraceptive devices. Perhaps the most spectacular example of what was happening occurred in 1969 in New York, when the cops raided the Stonewall Inn, a homosexual bar. To them it was no more than a routine exercise in intimidation and extortion, but the young customers had had enough; they fought back, and for two days the Stonewall riots raged in Greenwich Village. They ended in a gay victory, and suddenly the closet doors banged open right across America. It was an extraordinary inversion of the situation twenty years earlier, at the time of the first Kinsey report, when homosexual conduct was regarded as a sin if not a crime, punished (when discovered) by dismissal, abuse, violent attack or prison. A gay political movement suddenly emerged (the universal adoption of what had previously been a purely slang word was in itself astonishing). The gains it made were soon incontestable, and led to organized demands for more. Perhaps its biggest achievement was to convince most of the young men newly discovering their homosexuality that there was nothing wrong in being gay; instead of agonizing, they could go clubbing. But reaction was not long in announcing itself. The saddest and oddest incident was the double murder in 1978 of the Mayor of San Francisco, George Moscone, who had courted the gay vote, and of Harvey Milk, an avowedly homosexual city councillor.[10] Yet something more significant had happened the previous year, when in a referendum the citizens of Miami

9 Alfred Kinsey *et al.*, *Sexual Behavior in the Human Male* (1948); *Sexual Behavior in the Human Female* (1953). The humans involved were all Americans.
10 The assassin was another city councillor ('supervisor' in the local jargon) who had just resigned, but wanted his job back; Moscone and Milk were refusing to give it to him. He was deranged, working-class, right-wing and homophobic. Moscone was not the first big-city mayor to be assailed: a mayor of New York was wounded in 1910, and a mayor of Chicago was murdered in 1933.

threw out an ordinance banning discrimination in employment and housing on account of people's 'affectional or sexual preference'. The religious fundamentalists, whose leaders during this period were taking an ever-greater interest in politics, rejoiced at this victory over 'child molesters and religious heretics', and were to keep up their campaign for the next twenty years, with intermittent success; but the tide was against them. Nevertheless, homosexuals had been served notice that attitudes inculcated for generations cannot be changed overnight; and already, though they did not know it, the AIDS epidemic was preparing. They were in for a long, grievous struggle.

The central engine of social change in the seventies was undoubtedly the women's movement. Feminism, though an effective intellectual force, was only part of it. The American workforce had never been wholly male, but after 1945 women poured into the labour market, until by 1980 more than half of all adult women had jobs. The number went on rising thereafter. Many of them were married, with small children. This development – a social revolution in itself – was caused partly by the changing needs of the US economy, which was creating more and more service employment, while the number of jobs in manufacturing was static or declining; partly by the wish of American families to maximize their income (and thus enable themselves to take advantage of the ever-expanding market in consumer goods) by bringing home two wage-packets instead of just one; partly by the wish of American women themselves for horizons wider and challenges more stimulating than domesticity alone could provide. The result was an irreversible transformation of marriage, of the family, and of relations between the sexes both in private and working life. The political consequences were just as profound. After the founding of the National Organization of Women, a mass women's movement, dormant since the twenties, mobilized increasing numbers and greatly influenced the views of countless others. NOW and other organizations such as the National Women's Political Caucus concerned themselves specifically with promoting women's involvement in politics, but also pressed for action on a wide range of issues such as equality in education and employment, 'reproductive rights', child care, maternity leave, health care, and women's roles in the armed services. The early 1970s brought major successes, although they were mostly due to judicial decisions rather than to legislation. In 1971 the Supreme Court for the first time found certain kinds of discrimination against women to be violations of federal law and even unconstitutional; in 1972 Congress passed the Equal Rights Amendment, which had first been proposed in 1923;[11] and in 1973, in the *Roe* v. *Wade* decision, the Supreme Court found that restrictive state laws against abortion were unconstitutional. The women's movement seemed to be sweeping all before it.

But it was hardly possible that, in a society which was still so conservative

---

11 'Equality of rights under the law shall not be denied or abridged by the United States or any state on the basis of sex.'

in many respects (though its dynamism made it also a perpetual fount of radical change), this spectacular transformation could be universally accepted. Too much change of too many kinds had already affronted too many Americans; things, they felt, had gone far enough. Prejudices of all kinds had their effect. There was much bitterness against the so-called youth culture, and as it became clear that the newest teenage generation was not going to give up such pleasures as pre-marital sex and smoking marijuana, the religious Right prepared for another battle. There was resentment between the classes, between city, suburb and country, between the races, between West Coast and East Coast and Middle West, between unbelievers, modern believers and fundamentalists. Above all, a great many women and men were simply not prepared to accept the feminist revolution if they could help it.

The Equal Rights Amendment (ERA) was one subject of battle – it finally lapsed in 1982, its supporters having narrowly failed to persuade the necessary number of state legislatures to endorse it – but abortion came to be the central issue, with repercussions far beyond the women's movement. Perhaps it was not surprising: the anti-abortionists genuinely believed that abortion was a form of murder.[12] They ignored the sorry medical record of the years when it was illegal (many doctors, familiar with the results of back-street abortions, had been early supporters of legalization). Their opponents believed that women should be free to choose; anyway, they had no choice but to fight back, if the whole women's movement was not to be exposed as limited and ineffectual. There could be no compromise, for on both sides the question was seen as one of absolute rights, not of practicalities. Matters were not helped when the 'antis' began to turn to violence in their attempts to close down abortion clinics, and their opponents got Congress to strip them of their right to demonstrate near the clinics.

Those particular developments lay far in the future during Jimmy Carter's presidency, but intense pressure was applied to Congress, the courts, the political parties and the President. Carter, the very embodiment of the middle way, who liked to describe himself as an economic conservative and a liberal on social issues, found himself under assault from both sides, who despised his honestly expressed opinion: 'I am personally opposed to abortion ... I am opposed to a constitutional amendment to alter the Supreme Court's decision [in *Roe* v. *Wade*] by prohibiting abortion or giving states local option authority ... I am personally opposed to government spending for abortion services. However, as President, I will be bound by the courts.'[13] It is hard to see that such a sincere Southern Baptist could say more, and he would need the South (where the antis were numerous)

12 But their good faith came into question in the 1990s when it emerged that some anti-abortion women had been known to take advantage of the law and have abortions themselves before returning to the picket-line.

13 Quoted in John Dumbrell, *The Carter Presidency: A Re-evaluation* (Manchester University Press, 1995) p. 71.

to be re-elected; on the other hand, he could not afford to alienate the women activists, now very strong in the Democratic party. At the Democratic convention in 1980, half the delegates were women; before it met, Eleanor Smeal, president of NOW, threatened to support an independent candidate unless the Democrats committed themselves both to making federal funds available for poor women wanting abortions, and to withhold party funds from candidates who did not support ERA: 'We do not feel the commitment level of the past three and a half years has been strong enough to guarantee our support.'[14] Carter might well feel aggrieved: he had supported ERA constantly and effectively, and had appointed more women to posts in the federal government than any of his predecessors. But he knew when he was beaten, and the Democratic platform of 1980 was much more radical than he, the candidate, would have liked. This helped to consolidate conservative opinion round the Republican candidacy of Ronald Reagan.

Abortion alone was not an issue which was going to determine who won the presidential election, but Carter's inability to find an effective position was all too expressive of his central political weakness. It is tempting to say that he was too quiet and unassuming, when what America wanted was a bold leader. He was certainly no Pied Piper. Yet where the issues which at last destroyed him were concerned, he acted boldly and decidedly; too much so, perhaps.

Carter had come to power preaching a new kind of foreign policy, one which eschewed the cynicism (which they called realism) of Nixon and Kissinger, one which insisted on the importance and universality of human rights, one which, in accordance with Carter's constant preferences, sought comprehensive, not piecemeal, solutions. It was a revival of Woodrow Wilson's approach to diplomacy (though Carter never mentioned this predecessor, of whom he was a downmarket version). It was a noble project, but fraught with difficulties, and provoked the same sort of opposition as that which had defeated Wilson; but in the light of subsequent world history it may be seen as prophetic. Even at the time it had its successes. Unfortunately Carter, as with his domestic policies, wanted to have it both ways: as well as human rights he believed in containment, that is in the doctrine that the competition with the Soviet Union was the overriding concern of the United States, necessitating both a 'forward' foreign policy and heavy defence expenditure. This contradiction, blended with Carter's own lack of judgement, was to bring his administration to disaster.

The contradiction was embodied in the rivalry between the Secretary of State, Cyrus Vance, a veteran diplomatist and firm believer in the human rights policy, and Zbigniew Brzezinski, the National Security Adviser, a refugee intellectual of the Kissinger type (he was a Pole) with many of Kissinger's attitudes and opinions. Had Carter been prepared to back either man firmly, or, failing that, to knock heads together until he was master,

14 Ibid., p. 80.

his diplomacy might not have been such a failure (though it must be remembered that the times were such that US policy was bound to be beset with great difficulties). As it was, he did neither, and muddle became the administration's keynote as it blundered from crisis to crisis.

Kissinger had not much overrated the importance of relations with the Soviet Union. In his view the USSR was a 'mature' power which had given up its ideological crusade; Washington could negotiate successfully with Moscow as issues arose. The Carter team was not so sure. Some of its members held that the Russians had never got over the humiliation of the Cuban missile crisis, and had since 1962 made attaining military equality with the US their central objective; on secondary matters they were merely opportunists.[15] Others, led by Brzezinski, believed that the USSR was as intent as ever on extending its power and ideology. In practical consequences these opinions were not very different: both entailed watching the Soviet Union closely and renewing America's military strength – defence expenditure increased steadily during the Carter years. But Carter's central objective, to the degree that he had one, was to safeguard the peace of the world by negotiating arms reduction agreements with Russia, and that could only be achieved if the Americans and the Russians trusted each other. Unfortunately the Carter administration's record might have been calculated to make the Russians suspicious. The Helsinki accords and the human rights policy stimulated resistance in the Soviet Union to communist policies: in particular, large numbers of Jews demanded the right to emigrate to Israel, and when this was refused they staged protests which caught the world's attention. To build on one of the Nixon administration's few unquestionable successes, and also in pursuit of that old mirage, the balance of power, Carter pursued negotiations with China that in 1979 culminated in the exchange of ambassadors with Peking; Russia thought that her two most dangerous enemies were ganging up on her. And the Soviet Union could not resist trying to extend its influence into Africa, supporting the revolutionary Mengistu regime of Ethiopia in its war with Somalia. Carter in his turn grew distrustful. Then, at Christmas 1979, the USSR invaded Afghanistan, and Carter said that his opinion of the Russians had changed more dramatically in a week than it had in 'even the previous two and a half years'. The invasion, he announced, was 'the most serious threat to peace since World War II' (a quite preposterous statement). He resorted to dramatic action. Sales of American grain to the USSR were suspended, America withdrew from the forthcoming Moscow Olympic Games, registration for the draft was reintroduced (but Congress rejected the President's proposal to register women as well as men), a proposed arms limitation treaty was withdrawn from consideration by the Senate, the defence budget was sharply increased, and the independence of 'the Persian Gulf region' was declared to be a vital interest of the United States (because of all that oil). This sabre-rattling

15 In retrospect, this view seems to have been the most perceptive one.

only had four disadvantages: it took no account of the fact that Afghanistan had been a Soviet satellite long before the invasion;[16] it ignored the likelihood (quickly becoming actuality) that the Soviet Union would find that its Afghan adventure was a cruel, unmanageable quagmire, like America's war in Vietnam; it did nothing to free Afghanistan; and it was a total reversal to the purest Cold War attitudes. Carter does not seem to have remembered the restraint that the Soviet Union had shown during the Vietnamese imbroglio; but then, election year had begun in the United States, and his actions improved his standing in the opinion polls. Carter was sufficiently a politician to think that ample justification.

His behaviour raises certain questions. He had swung over entirely to the containment view; in part, perhaps, because that was the only policy which the Washington establishment was able to execute, or even understand. But in part his excitability was a personal trait, reflecting both his evangelical outlook on the world and his taste for bold, if inappropriate, action. He was not by nature a quietist: he had to school himself to practice patience. He lost his cool again, even more disastrously, in the affair of the Tehran hostages.

The Shah of Iran, a long-standing client of the US, was overthrown by his discontented subjects in January 1979. He was replaced by a so-called 'Islamic Republic', which was really a dictatorship of clergy, dominated by the Ayatollah Khomeini, an elderly provincial bigot well characterized by a British journal as 'an old man deaf to pity'. Khomeini and his militants were incompetent at everything except holding on to power, which they did by the usual means of revolutionary terror; before long they blundered into a long war with Iraq which they ought to have won, or at any rate which they ought not to have lost; but lose it they did, after suffering stupendous battlefield casualties because tactics were deemed un-Islamic. Washington should have been able to handle such an opponent, but it turned out that nothing had been learned from the Vietnam experience (at any rate, not by Jimmy Carter). When, during a characteristic revolutionary tumult, a mob overran the US embassy in Tehran and took the occupants prisoner, Carter tried to retaliate dramatically, without considering that in a game of poker it is unwise to raise the stakes when you have a poor hand, unless you are a master bluffer, which he was not. He expelled Iranian students from the United States and froze Iranian assets there. He stopped purchases of Iranian oil. He wrote off the Ayatollah as 'apparently deranged', and referred to the captives ceaselessly as hostages (at this unhappy time the practice of kidnapping Westerners was all too common in the Middle East). He did nothing to calm, everything to increase, the natural alarm and rage of the American people. The Iranians, seeing how highly he valued

16 The Russians only acted because they were afraid of an Islamist takeover in Afghanistan like that which was occurring in Iran; they feared that such a takeover would weaken their prestige in Central Asia and possibly lead to Islamist unrest in the Soviet Union itself.

the prisoners, decided to extort a high price for their release: they demanded, for instance, that the exiled Shah be returned to them for trial and execution, which the Americans could not in honour or prudence possibly agree to. So Carter, over the objections of Secretary Vance, who therefore resigned, sent an airborne force to rescue the hostages. The expedition was calamitously bungled; eight Americans died when their helicopters crashed into each other on the ground. The combination of the embargo on Iranian oil with America's still-increasing demand for energy meant that there was a second 'oil shock': energy prices had already risen by 25 per cent in 1979; in 1980 they rose by 80 per cent. Unemployment and inflation soared, and suddenly there was a deficit in the federal budget of $74 billion.

It is hardly surprising that Carter was not re-elected, the first sitting president to be denied a second term since that other earnest engineer, Herbert Hoover (his critics in the Democratic party had taken to referring to 'Jimmy Hoover'); but he might not have lost so badly if election day had not happened to be the first anniversary of the Iranian hostage-taking. The people turned out and delivered a landslide for Reagan and the Republicans: Carter carried only five states and the District of Columbia, and the Democrats lost control of the Senate for the first time since 1955. The hostages continued in captivity until the very day of Reagan's inauguration, when the patient diplomacy which Cyrus Vance had always favoured finally secured their freedom in return for the unfreezing of the Iranian assets.

Carter's presidency must be reckoned a failure. His successes were few, and not always worth the political price he paid for them. As an outsider he saw clearly certain changes that he wished to bring about in the way that Washington did things, but he did not understand the system well enough to go the best way about achieving this. But his central failure was political. He wanted to move the Democratic party to the right, and could not understand, let alone respect, those many Democrats who resisted the idea: 'My main political problem was with the so-called liberal wing of the Democratic party,' he complained in 1981; but without those liberals he would have fared far worse than he did. He had a tin ear for the music of American politics. 'I have no new dream to set forth today,' he remarked in his inaugural address, and it was all too true. His message was not what the American people wanted to hear. Their native optimism was fundamentally intact, in spite of the Vietnam years; they did not want to be told that 'we cannot afford to live beyond our means'. They preferred to think that the march to the Big Rock-Candy Mountain could be resumed at once, and their new leader had promised that it would be, just as soon as the dismal Democrats were out of office.

Ronald Reagan, like Jimmy Carter, was an outsider and a man of many contradictions; unlike Carter, he knew how to make his inconsistencies work for him. As a young man his good looks, charm and natural aptitude had swiftly led him to Hollywood, where he soon became a star of the second magnitude – he was not in the same league as Clark Gable, John

Wayne and Humphrey Bogart, but he was a conspicuous figure none the less. In a generation when everyone went to the movies, everyone had seen him. He was also drawn from the first to politics, and was active as a leading liberal Democrat during the forties and early fifties (as a sharp observer noticed, even after thirty years as a Republican he remained a cultural Democrat[17]). He first showed his formidable political talent when called before the HUAC. Other liberal witnesses grovelled, or defied their inquisitors with unpleasant results, or betrayed their friends and themselves; Reagan, without doing any of these things, had the committee eating out of his hand. He was then what was known as a 'cold war liberal': in other words, he was firmly anti-communist; but he did not move to the Right until his acting career began to fade and he took a job as a television spokesman for General Electric. Until then he had been an ardent New Dealer, but he made a swift transition, and before long sounded too conservative even for General Electric. When, in 1964, the conservative cause was clearly sliding towards shattering defeat with Barry Goldwater, Reagan cheered up its supporters by delivering what became known as The Speech, in which he stated his new creed with eloquence and conviction but, still more, with warm good humour. It was such a success that a group of Californian millionaires decided to back him for high office. He won the governorship of California in 1966, and was re-elected in 1970. He decided not to run again in 1974, instead devoting himself to the pursuit of the presidency. He did not have an easy time getting the Republican nomination, for there was a general (quite accurate) impression that his economic proposals did not make sense: one rival said that they were all smoke and mirrors, and another (George Bush, later his Vice-President and successor) said they were 'voodoo economics'. And he was elected President chiefly because he was not Jimmy Carter; but then, in 1932, Roosevelt had been elected because he was not Herbert Hoover.

Reagan was sixty-nine on Inauguration Day, 1981; the oldest man, by a wide margin, ever to have been elected President: he was only a few months younger than the runner-up, Eisenhower, had been at his retirement. This was an advantage to him, because it meant that he had lived through all the important phases of American history since the First World War, and profited by the experience. He clung tenaciously to this lived past; he was old-fashioned rather than conservative. His inaugural speech might have been given by a Democrat rather than a Republican; indeed, except for two short pious references to George Washington and Abraham Lincoln, it *was* given by a Democrat, or Democrats, for it consisted of blatant borrowings from the inaugurals of Thomas Jefferson, Franklin Roosevelt and John Kennedy; and it included a gracious tribute to Jimmy Carter (but there was no trace of Lyndon Johnson). It was Jeffersonian in its assertion of states'

17 Lou Cannon, quoted in Hedley Donovan, *Roosevelt to Reagan* (New York, Perennial Library edn, 1987), p. 278, footnote.

rights and distrust of big government, Rooseveltian in its tribute to the forgotten man ('Putting America back to work means putting all Americans back to work.'). Reagan never abandoned his hero-worship of FDR, lavishly celebrating Roosevelt's centenary in 1982 when Congress was barely prepared to notice it at all. He modelled his style on Roosevelt's. He was called the Great Communicator because he too knew how to simplify complex issues and bring them home to ordinary citizens by homely anecdotes; he responded to crises of every kind with eloquence, humour or courage, as necessary ('Honey, I forgot to duck,' he remarked to his wife Nancy just after being shot and wounded by a madman); above all, he understood that Americans best respond to bold and optimistic leadership, which suited him splendidly, as he was by nature a cheerful soul. 'We will not return to the days of hand-wringing, defeatism, decline and despair,' he said in 1984. He was talking of foreign and defence policy, but such was his attitude to everything; like his hero, he held that Americans had nothing to fear but fear itself.

There was no reason to think that the voters in 1980 had meant to register their support for any particular menu of Reaganite policies, but Reagan remembered how Roosevelt in 1933 had exploited his own landslide to do as he thought best. The Republicans had greatly increased their numbers in the House of Representatives, as well as capturing the Senate; the Democrats were demoralized; Reagan convinced both Congress and journalists that he had a mandate, he had momentum; he launched what his fans called 'the Reagan Revolution', just as FDR had launched the New Deal, and for his first year in office won victory after victory on Capitol Hill. Happy days were here again.

But there was one fundamental difference between Reagan and Roosevelt. Roosevelt's programme had been a genuine New Deal. It had been a comprehensive attempt to meet an overwhelming national crisis, the Great Depression, and to restructure the United States, to rescue the 'forgotten man' for good from the selfishness and stupidity of the rich. Now the rich had a chance to strike back. Their attitude was chiefly negative. They wanted to undo what they regarded as the mistakes of the years since Eisenhower; to dismantle the Great Society and all the supplementary legislation of the Nixon and Carter years; some of them wanted to dismantle the New Deal as well; but they had no structures to serve as replacements. They did not think them necessary. As their leader remarked, 'government is not the solution to our problem'.

Still, it was fun to be the government. 'God has given us the papacy: let us enjoy it,' had been the maxim of Pope Leo X. Such was Reagan's attitude too. Hollywood came to Washington. Not since Kennedy had there been an administration so fond of partying (though the President's favourite entertainment was an evening at home with his wife watching television); not since Andrew Jackson had an inauguration announced so decisively that the foundations of American politics had altered. The money, as well as the population, was now in California, and Reagan relied heavily on Californian businessmen and lawyers for the personnel and ideas of his administration. This was not entirely wise, any more than it had been wise for Carter to rely so heavily on his Georgians. It took the Californians some time to discover that the experience of governing the Golden State, even though it was so big, was not sufficient training for running the United States. Mistakes were made, but so had they been under Jackson. On the whole, it was a healthy thing that the West Coast compelled the East Coast to recognize its weight in the Union in matters of taste as well as power. If New York, Boston and Philadelphia found the exuberant enjoyment of wealth vulgar, so much the worse for New York. The Vanderbilts and Astors had not always been known for their restraint.

Reagan had complete faith in his programme. It was time, he said, to shift power and responsibilities back to the states from the federal government, which had swollen enormously in the previous twenty years. Federal taxes should be cut ruthlessly, to free the entrepreneurial spirit of the American people; the budget should be balanced, to stabilize the economy and kill inflation; defence expenditure should be massively increased, to discourage Soviet adventurism; the role of the federal government in supervising and restricting the economy should be severely reduced by a process of deregulation.

It did not take a genius or a political rival to see that this programme was as contradictory as Jimmy Carter's: for instance, it was most unlikely that the budget could be balanced if the Pentagon was let loose to spend as much as it liked on whatever took its fancy. Nor did it really contain any new ideas. Power can always find intellectuals to do its necessary dirty work. As the conservative tide rose during the seventies, magazines, think-tanks and prophets multiplied to give an air of brilliance and innovation to some venerable opinions. True-blue Republicans in the tradition of Herbert Hoover, Robert A. Taft and Gerald Ford had always disliked high taxes, big government and unbalanced budgets; and since the Second World War, which demonstrated how profitable defence-related industry could be, they had always supported big defence budgets. It was gratifying that monetarists and supply-siders and repentant New York communists could give these stale notions a pinchbeck sheen, it was even helpful in the battle for public opinion, but the new bottles held the same old wine. And by 1981 it was not even a strictly Republican vintage any more. Jimmy Carter had believed in increased military spending; Jimmy Carter had tried to introduce deregulation; Jimmy Carter had tried hard to balance the budget in order to curb inflation – and in large part lost the election thereby. The Reagan Revolution was not really revolutionary, and 'Reaganomics' (another favourite term of the period) was a joke.

But as Emerson had long ago remarked, a foolish consistency is the hobgoblin of little minds. Had Reagan been as inept a politician, or as intellectually honest, as Carter, he would probably have met the same fate.

And indeed the first fruit of his stewardship was a renewed recession which strikingly reduced his popularity. But his cheerful faith in himself, his opinions and his country steered him through to overwhelming success. His inconsistencies proved to be a source of great strength, and incidentally laid bare a truth about the place of the United States in the world which showed how badly Carter had misjudged the risks and opportunities before him.

Or perhaps it was just Carter's famous bad luck. By 1982 the machinations of the Organization of Petroleum-Exporting Countries (OPEC) in driving up the price of oil had had what classical economists would have regarded as an absolutely predictable result: the world's producers extracted and sold as much as they could, glut resulted, and the price collapsed. Mr Reagan's experiments were not going to be sabotaged by a renewed energy shortage. And in one important respect, economic policy was largely out of the President's hands. The Federal Reserve System had been given great independence by its founder, Woodrow Wilson, which subsequent legislation had increased. In 1981 its chairman, Paul Volcker, decided that enough was enough: following the strictest monetarist logic he determined to bring inflation under control whatever the cost; he raised interest rates and curtailed credit. The result was a 'strong' dollar. Exports fell and imports rose; America's trading partners used the dollars thus earned to buy into the American economy and to finance the US national debt, which nearly tripled during Reagan's two terms in office. American heavy industry suffered badly in the process; unemployment and bankruptcies stalked the Rustbelt; but millions of new jobs (mostly low-paid ones) were created; overall, Reagan America exuded an air of prosperity, though the profits went overwhelmingly to those who were already rich.

The administration did its bit in helping this process along. The huge military expenditures of Reagan's first term, the huge tax cuts, the huge outlays on unemployment benefits and other such disbursements made necessary by the Volcker squeeze, the drop in revenue consequent on the initial recession, and the failure to cut federal spending significantly (Reagan refused to curtail his defence programme or to touch Social Security benefits, the two biggest items of the federal budget) meant that the deficit soared, from $58 billion in Carter's last year to $221 billion in 1986–7. This was counter-cyclical policy on a heroic scale: Keynes might have gasped, but the effects were just what he might have predicted. The absurdity was that the Reagan administration was full of monetarists and supply-siders. In later years their only excuse would be that their policies would have worked wonderfully, had they been tried.

To sober economists this was the policy of a madhouse. The rich got richer and the poor got poorer, just as in the 1920s; investment slumped, especially in the country's infrastructure; unemployed workers and threatened industries began to clamour for protectionist measures; the Republicans lost control of the Senate in the 1986 elections though Reagan had been re-elected by a crushing majority in 1984. The last detail was probably the most persuasive in inducing the administration to change course. Monetary policy was relaxed – the dollar weakened – foreign funds began to leave the country, and there was a stock market crash in October 1987, which sliced $500 billion off the value of shares. But this was not 1929 all over again. The market soon recovered, and in 1988 the Republicans again won the presidential election (though they did not win back the Senate).

A great truth had inadvertently been demonstrated. The US economy was so big that merely by existing, and however ill it was managed, it created stability in the world economy, from which it was itself the chief beneficiary. It would have taken more perversity than even the Reaganauts were capable of to wreck this happy state of affairs. The difference from the 1920s was that then the United States had been the only solidly prosperous society in the world; in the 1980s it was one among many. So when Uncle Sam messed up his business, others could take advantage. The Japanese, above all, poured their cheap exports into America, and by investing much of their profits there kept the American people (or most of them) employed and comfortable. And in the years after Reagan, under President Bush and President Clinton, when US economic policy gradually corrected itself, the great American engine began once more to make a positive contribution to world trade and to its own continuing prosperity.

Reagan appears to have been well aware that his actual conduct of economic policy bore little resemblance to the expectations of the zealots whom he brought into office. 'It is true I never submitted a balanced budget to Congress,' he remarked soon after his retirement. 'I may be old, but I'm not stupid.' In some ways he was an unsuitable leader for the religious Right. His friends were mostly drawn from the movie world, where morals were easygoing, to say the least; his own first marriage had ended in divorce, and one of the funnier episodes of the 1980 election was the television interview in which Reagan tried to persuade his interviewer and himself that he was a 'born-again' Christian, like Jimmy Carter: even his polished acting technique could not hide his embarrassment. But that did not prevent him from letting his right-wingers loose in every department that mattered to them – education, for example – so that they too had a chance, like the economic evangelists, to discover the immutable realities of American politics.

Their discomfiture was greatest in the Department of the Interior. A legacy of the great westward movement of the nineteenth century was that the federal government was possessed of something like half the land west of the 100th meridian.[18] This was land (much of it intended for homesteading) that the nineteenth-century market had not been able to

18 In some states the federal government owned even more. Eighty-six per cent of Nevada belongs to Uncle Sam, 64 per cent of Utah and Idaho, and 60 per cent of Alaska.

absorb; and beginning with Theodore Roosevelt's presidency (or perhaps with the creation of Yellowstone National Park in 1872) most of it had come to be set aside for conservation purposes, and was to be developed only under strict controls. After 1962, when Rachel Carson published her appalling warning, *Silent Spring*, environmental protection had become a hugely popular cause, making the despoliation of the wilderness ever more difficult. To win votes, the Nixon administration had set up the Environmental Protection Agency (part of the Interior Department, which also administered the public lands), and it had been operating with fair success for nearly ten years when Reagan took office.

Oilmen, timber men, ranchers, developers, mining corporations: these westerners had long been chafing at the ever more stringent federal regulations which prevented them from getting their hands on the vast wealth of various kinds locked up in the national domain, and with the coming of Reagan and his slogan of deregulation they thought that their time had arrived (it was one of the reasons they had voted for him). James Watt, who had once compared environmentalists to Nazis, was made Secretary of the Interior, and said that his mission was to 'mine more, drill more, cut more timber, to use our resources rather than keep them locked up.'[19] Appropriations for the EPA were cut by half, and the agency's new head, Anne Burford, set out to water down, if not to thwart, all the regulations enforcing the environmental laws which had been passed since 1969. Watt had a genius for making enemies, and Burford was a fatally inexperienced administrator, but what really destroyed them was their cavalier assumption that having won a presidential election they could safely ignore the law, defy the environmental movement and cosy up to their business friends. Had Washington been a mere state capital they might have got away with it; but Congress, the federal bureaucracy, the national press and the ever-more active lobbying system easily saw them off. Both had to resign in 1983. They had not really understood the difference between private and public life; when their opinions and activities became embarrassing to the President, they had to go, and the *status quo* was restored. (Burford was replaced by William Ruckelshaus, the EPA's first director). Similar embarrassments occurred elsewhere: the business mentality found it hard to grasp that you do not own the government because you are appointed to it, nor can you ignore the laws against conflict of interest. By 1983, 225 of Reagan's appointees had been investigated for improprieties or even criminality. The great reform foundered amid allegations that Reagan's was the most corrupt administration in American history.

The pattern which has emerged from consideration of Reagan's domestic record appears again when his conduct of foreign policy is examined. Once more the victory of 1980 is seen to have brought to power an eager crowd

19 Quoted in Iwan W. Morgan, *Beyond the Liberal Consensus* (London, Hurst, 1994), pp. 213–14.

of ideologues; once more their excesses threaten the prospects of the administration, and indeed nearly bring about the destruction of the President
himself; once more common sense reasserts itself, and the normal course
of US policy is resumed; but this time there is also an unexpected and
tremendous pay-off, which ensures Ronald Reagan's place in history.

He was in many respects an untypical conservative; what he chiefly seems
to have wanted to conserve were the achievements and attitudes of the
Roosevelt years (even if he sometimes asserted that FDR opposed the
welfare state); but there is little doubt that his anti-communism was strongly
and sincerely held; was, perhaps, his conservatism's essence. He and his
friends judged, rather unfairly, that the United States was not safe from
Soviet aggression while Carter was President, and they interpreted Soviet
policy in the late 1970s, especially the invasion of Afghanistan, as renewed
proof of communist ambition and hostility. What President Reagan
famously called the 'empire of evil' was spreading its wings again, and
America was required to re-commit herself to resistance. The fact that she
had already been doing so under Carter, for example by launching the
extremely expensive Trident nuclear submarine programme, was firmly
ignored, and the defence budget went up by roughly 50 per cent in five
years. (This delighted both the Pentagon and its contractors, many of whom
were generous contributors to Reagan and the Republican party; it was less
welcome to Reagan's economic advisers, who were trying to balance the
budget.) During Reagan's first term, arms limitation talks with the Soviet
Union gradually sank into the sand, not without moments of drama; by
1984 Moscow had abandoned negotiations with Washington as hopeless.
The CIA was once more given its head, and the White House gaily
undertook to defend American and Western interests aggressively, whatever
it took, wherever was necessary (except in South-East Asia). This mode of
conducting the most important business of the United States nearly ended
in complete disaster, for Reagan at any rate.

He himself can largely be blamed for what happened. Henry Kissinger
(who was still occasionally called to the White House to give advice) noticed
that Reagan did not seem much interested in diplomacy; he only paid keen
attention when the subject of his own speeches came up (an actor and his
lines); 'It was as though long-term strategy was something other people
were paid to worry about.'[20] He was a lazy man; next to Roosevelt, his hero
was Calvin Coolidge, and he hung his portrait in the White House; he
joked, 'It's true that hard work never killed anybody, but I figured why take
the chance?' He rationalized his natural distaste for hard work by adopting
the principle that it was his business to lay down the main lines of policy
and then leave his subordinates to get on with carrying it out. Jimmy Carter
had often let himself be swamped by detail, so this attitude had something
to commend it; but Reagan carried it much too far. He was also far too

20 Strobe Talbott, *Deadly Gambits* (London, Pan Books, 1985), p. 76.

casual about questions of legality and constitutionality, which encouraged similar attitudes in his subordinates, as we have already seen. Worst of all, his hands-off style meant that the administration was constantly at feud with itself. Nobody could say with any certainty what its policy was; it depended too much on who had last got the President's attention.

So calamities occurred. In 1983, during an ill-judged intervention in the Lebanon, where a ferocious civil war was raging, 24 US marines were killed when their barracks was blown up. In 1986 Congress and the press discovered that elements in the Reagan administration, in defiance of public commitments to have no dealings with terrorist regimes, and of express Congressional decision, had entered upon an intrigue to sell arms to Iran via Israel; the money resulting from the sale was to be used to subsidize a rebellion in Nicaragua against a left-wing government which Washington right-wingers (including the President) regarded as a dangerous tool of the Soviet Union in Central America. They were as unreasonably obssessed with the *sandinistas* of Nicaragua as the Kennedy brothers had been with Fidel Castro. Reagan at times talked as if he expected a red tide to come lapping at any moment at the borders of Texas. He propped up a particularly unpleasant regime of right-wing thugs in El Salvador, where there was also a civil war; he launched an armed intervention to overthrow a Marxist gang which seized power on the island of Grenada in 1983 (but that looked less like a principled exercise of American power than an attempt to make people forget about the recent disaster in the Lebanon). Public opinion did not share his anxieties; Americans were only anxious lest the President plunge them into another adventure like that in Vietnam. Public opinion was wise: left to himself, Reagan would no doubt have done so and, surreptitiously, that is just what his zealous but thick-headed assistant, Colonel Oliver North, tried to do. In his usual idle way Reagan let things get out of hand; he forgot that he had sworn to uphold and execute the laws. The Iran–Contra[21] caper was as potentially damaging to the Constitution as Watergate itself; but Congress could not bear the thought of dragging itself and the country through the misery of another impeachment, this time of an immensely popular president.[22] It was content to lay bare the truth through a series of reports and investigations, and to let Reagan exhibit himself as a shuffler, if not a liar, when he responded to investigators' questions with such answers as 'I just have no way of recalling anything specific as to what you are asking.'

But once more his luck saved Ronald Reagan from the consequences of his own inefficiency and bad judgement. In 1985 a new generation took command of the Soviet Union in the person of the new Secretary-General

---

21 'Contra' was the name given to the Nicaraguan rebels.
22 Congress was to show a similar reluctance a decade later, when the question of President Clinton's sexual behaviour and possible perjury came to the fore in the most preposterous presidential scandal yet.

of the Communist party, Mikhail Gorbachev. Gorbachev and his associates saw that the old Bolshevik system, which had steadily decayed since its last era of vigour under Khrushchev, could no longer postpone reform if it was not to collapse (they did not see, but in a few years would discover, that it was going to collapse anyway). The arms race in particular, which the Americans under Reagan seemed to want to push even further, technologically, ever more expensively, was a strain that the Soviet Union could no longer support (military expenditure now amounted to nearly a quarter of its total GNP). And Gorbachev, who harboured no aggressive designs himself – in 1987 he pulled the Red Army out of Afghanistan – no longer believed in the American threat, in spite of Reagan's noisy rhetoric. He and his foreign minister, Edvard Shevardnadze, tried to open serious disarmament negotiations with Washington, and this time, most fortunately for the world, met with a positive response.

Reagan had changed, or rather a new side of his character had come to the fore. He was now in his second term, and wanted to be remembered as a statesman who had done something effective to prevent nuclear war, which filled him with genuine horror. (He seems to have been encouraged in this attitude by Nancy Reagan.) His Secretary of State, George Shultz, who was favourably impressed by Gorbachev, outmanoeuvred the hard men who had never believed that any good could come out of Moscow and did not believe it now. The result was a truly spectacular diplomatic process which culminated in a treaty eliminating intermediate-range nuclear forces, signed in Washington by Gorbachev and Reagan in December 1987, and ratified by the Senate in May, after which Reagan paid a wildly successful visit to Moscow. There was much negotiation still to be done by Reagan's successor, George Bush; it would be many months more before the Berlin Wall came down and the Russians began their retreat from Eastern Europe; but these were consequences of the stunning fact that in 1987 the Cold War was abandoned.

It had lasted for forty years, and for thirty years before that relations between Soviet Russia and the West had been thoroughly abnormal. Its evaporation was a great gain not merely for human safety but also for common sense, and although many other individuals and factors helped to bring this victory about, Gorbachev and Reagan undoubtedly deserved the largest share of the credit. The collapse of the Soviet Union itself, signified by Gorbachev's removal from office in December 1991, was perhaps an even more epochal event. The countries of Eastern Europe regained complete freedom of action; large fragments broke off from what had been the Russian empire of the tsars; Russia herself, though still huge, was a superpower no more; instead she had become an ordinary player on the world stage, beset with many appalling problems. For a moment America bestrode the world, apparently a colossus with all the answers to all the questions – political, social and economic.

It was an illusion. The United States still had many perplexities, some of which had been made worse by the Reagan years. The republic's immense enduring strength meant that less than ever would any nation go voluntarily and formally to war with it, though it had so many enemies (in large part acquired by America's blind support for the reckless state of Israel, and in part by its propensity to turn to force rather than diplomacy when difficulties arose) that it was going to be continuously exposed to terrorist attack of various kinds, and to other provocations. The disappearance of the Soviet rival meant that America was actually weaker, at least in the sense that she could no longer discipline her wayward friends or credibly threaten opponents, unless she first won the support of the world community (as happened in the Gulf War of 1991, when the US rescued Kuwait from annexation by Iraq) or was ready to pay the price for acting unilaterally. The twentieth-century world was in this respect too beginning to resemble that of the nineteenth century, with the United States in the central but not supreme role that had once been the British Empire's.

The reversion to an older order was also evident institutionally. Never again would the presidency be as insignificant as it had been under Franklin Pierce or Chester A. Arthur, but now that foreign policy seemed to be less starkly urgent, Congress was much more inclined to interfere in its conception and execution, and the presidency was correspondingly diminished. It did not help that modern presidents seem compulsively determined to dig their own graves (Carter, Reagan, Bush, Clinton . . .) or that the decay of the old party structures, inside and outside Congress, left individual Senators and Congressmen much freer to speak and act as they pleased than they had been since the 1820s. As then, so now: they were more mindful of Buncombe County than ever,[23] and were less amenable to their chieftains – the Speaker, the committee chairmen, the majority and minority leaders as well as the President. From a philosophical point of view, perhaps this was beneficial: most free states today are too centralized for their own good, and the reviving importance of that bizarre, ill-organized, quarrelsome, voluble body called the Congress of the United States, coupled with the continuing vitality of American federalism, may also revive America's claim to be the first of democracies – but only if Congress shows itself equal to its responsibilities, which it may or may not do. Meanwhile it certainly shows that it is as amenable as ever was the millionaires' club to the representations of the great lobbies, for election expenses continue to rise insanely, and money has to be found somehow.

Beyond Washington, with its curious mixture of grand and parochial visions, the American people had to grapple, inconclusively as ever, with problems old or new or both. There was tension between sections, between

---

23 During the Missouri crisis a congressman from North Carolina made an insufferably empty speech in the House of Representatives. He apologized to his colleagues, explaining that he had been speaking only to Buncombe County. This gave two useful words to the language – 'bunkum', and the less specific 'bunk'.

states and the federal government, between cities and suburbs, country and town. If anxiety about race relations was a little reduced, anxiety about immigration was much increased; the problem of crime, the future of the family, the question of addictive drugs (including alcohol and nicotine), the uneven performance of the economy were among many other preoccupying problems. The women's movement, environmentalism and religious fundamentalism still made themselves felt. There were far too many guns distributed among the population, and as a result there were far too many murders. In short, there were plenty of issues for the tried procedures of American democracy to resolve, and whenever one was more or less settled another would arise to take its place. The ship's voyage was indeed endless; but in 1999, looking back, the American people could reasonably feel that they had survived its most dangerous passage; looking forward, they could expect to find themselves equal to whatever challenges a new century and a new millennium might throw at them.

A Note on Further Reading

A full-scale bibliography would be out of place in a history of this nature: it could do nothing that is not better done elsewhere, for instance in the *Harvard Guide to American History* (Cambridge, Mass., Harvard University Press, revised edn, 1974), available in paperback in Britain and an indispensable tool to anyone seriously interested in the subject. Two other books which ought to be in every school or college library where American history is studied are H. S. Commager, *Documents of American History* (Englewood Cliffs, NJ, Prentice-Hall, 9th edn, 2 vols., 1974), and *The Statistical History of the United States* (New York, Basic Books, 1976). I have also found the *Reader's Companion to American History*, edited by Eric Foner and John A. Garraty (Boston, Houghton Mifflin, 1981) most useful. With these volumes at hand anyone can start the study of American history unaided, even by me.

Yet it is only decent for me to list some of the books which I have found especially valuable in preparing this history, particularly those which are lively in thought or style, or both, and which are thus likely to be of special appeal to beginners. It is always as well to start with entertaining works when launching a programme of historical study: before it is over you are certain to have to plough through many boring ones, and it takes time to find out how nevertheless to enjoy them. As Samuel Butler said, always eat a bunch of grapes from the top. Experts will be amazed at my omissions and eccentric emphases, but the list is not meant for them. It is not even meant primarily for examination candidates, but for those capable of enjoying the subject of American history for its own sake.

I have arranged these titles in rough chronological order of subject. Several of them belong to multi-volume works. Readers must not be put off. The art of dipping into such books is well worth acquiring: the most random sampling is likely to bring up pearls. I have given the full details of publisher, place of publication and date, in all cases except that of works so famous that they exist in a multiplicity of acceptable editions;

only occasionally has it seemed worthwhile to indicate a preferred version.

ALVIN M. JOSEPHY (ed.) and WILLIAM BRANDON, *The American Heritage Book of Indians* (New York, Simon & Schuster, 1961).

D. B. QUINN, *England and the Discovery of America 1481–1620* (London, George Allen & Unwin, 1974).

WALLACE NOTESTEIN, *The English People on the Eve of Colonisation* (New York, Harper & Row, 1954).[1]

CHARLES M. ANDREWS, *The Colonial Period of American History* (New Haven, Connecticut, Yale University Press, 4 vols., paperback edn, 1964).

JOHN SMITH, *The General History of Virginia, New England, and the Summer Isles.*

ROBIN BLACKBURN, *The Making of New World Slavery* (London, Verso, 1997).

WILLIAM BRADFORD, *Of Plymouth Plantation*, ed. Samuel Eliot Morison (New York, Alfred Knopf, 1966).

PERRY MILLER, *Errand into the Wilderness* (Cambridge, Mass., Harvard University Press, 1956).

DANIEL BOORSTIN, *The Americans: The Colonial Experience* (New York, Random House, 1958).

JOSEPH E. ILLICK, *Colonial Pennsylvania* (New York, Scribner's, 1976).

FREDERICK JACKSON TURNER, 'The Significance of the Frontier in American History', in *Frontier and Section: Selected Essays*, ed. R. A. Billington (Englewood Cliffs, NJ, Prentice-Hall, 1961).

R. A. BILLINGTON, *Westward Expansion* (New York, Macmillan, 1949).

WINTHROP JORDAN, *White over Black* (Chapel Hill, NC, University of North Carolina Press, 1968).

L. H. GIPSON, *The British Empire Before the American Revolution* (New York, Knopf, 15 vols., 1939–70).

C. M. ANDREWS, *The Colonial Background to the American Revolution* (New Haven, Conn.; London, Yale University Press, revised edn, 1931).

R. R. PALMER, *The Age of the Democratic Revolution* (London, Oxford University Press, 2 vols., 1959–64).

H. S. COMMAGER, *The Empire of Reason* (London, Weidenfeld & Nicolson, 1978).

BENJAMIN FRANKLIN, *Autobiography.*

DOUGLAS SOUTHALL FREEMAN, *George Washington: A Biography* (New York, Scribner's, 7 vols., 1948–57).

MERRILL D. PETERSON, *Thomas Jefferson and the New Nation: A Biography* (New York, Oxford University Press, 1970).

---

1 This is a volume in the admirable New American Nation series. The Americans are fortunate in such enterprises, as they are in the number and quality of their historical reference books; but the New American Nation volumes are quite outstanding.

BERNARD BAILYN, *The Ideological Origins of the American Revolution* (Cambridge, Mass., Harvard University Press, 1967).

BERNHARD KNOLLENBERG, *The Origins of the American Revolution* (New York and London, Macmillan, 1960).

E. S. AND H. M. MORGAN, *The Stamp Act Crisis* (Chapel Hill, NC, University of North Carolina Press, 1953).

IAN CHRISTIE, *Crisis Of Empire* (London, Edward Arnold, 1966).

JOHN SHY, *Toward Lexington* (Princeton, NJ, Princeton University Press, 1965).

BENJAMIN WOODS LABAREE, *The Boston Tea Party* (New York, Oxford University Press, 1964).

PIERS MACKESY, *The War for America* (Cambridge, Mass., Harvard University Press, 1965).

THOMAS JEFFERSON, *Notes on Virginia*.

JOHN HOPE FRANKLIN, *From Slavery to Freedom: A History of Negro Americans* (New York, Knopf, 5th edn, 1980).

MAX FARRAND (ed.), *The Records of the Federal Convention of 1787* (New Haven and London, Yale University Press, paperback edn, 4 vols., 1966).

ALEXANDER HAMILTON, JAMES MADISON, and JOHN JAY, *The Federalist*, ed. Jacob E. Cooke (Middletown, Conn., Wesleyan University Press, 1961).[2]

CARL VAN DOREN, *The Great Rehearsal* (New York, Viking Press, 1948).

RICHARD HOFSTADTER, *The American Political Tradition* (New York, Knopf, 1948).

DANIEL BOORSTIN, *The Americans: The National Experience* (New York, Random House, 1965).

DOUGLASS C. NORTH, *The Economic Growth of the United States, 1790–1860* (Englewood Cliffs, NJ, Prentice-Hall, 1961).

THOMAS C. COCHRAN and WILLIAM MILLER, *The Age of Enterprise: A Social History of Industrial America* (New York, Harper & Row, revised edn, 1961).

GEORGE R. TAYLOR, *The Transportation Revolution 1815–1860* (New York and London, Holt, Rinehart & Winston, 1951).

MARCUS CUNLIFFE, *The Nation Takes Shape, 1789–1837* (Chicago, University of Chicago Press, 1959).

ARTHUR M. SCHLESINGER JR, *The Age of Jackson* (Boston, Little, Brown, 1945).

ROBERT V. REMINI, *The Election of Andrew Jackson* (Philadelphia and New York, J. B. Lippincott, 1963).

ALEXIS DE TOCQUEVILLE, *Democracy in America*, ed. Phillips Bradley (New York, Knopf, 2 vols., 1945).

STANLEY P. HIRSHSON, *The Lion of the Lord: A Biography of Brigham Young* (New York, Knopf, 1969).

2 The only drawback to this otherwise excellent edition is that it does not have an index.

BERNARD DE VOTO, *The Course of Empire* (Boston, Houghton Mifflin, 1952). *Across the Wide Missouri* (Boston, Houghton Mifflin, 1947). *1846: The Year of Decision* (Boston, Houghton Mifflin, 1943).

W. W. FREEHLING, *Prelude to Civil War: The Nullification Crisis in South Carolina, 1816–1836* (New York, Harper & Row, 1966).

KENNETH M. STAMPP, *The Peculiar Institution* (New York, Random House, 1956).

JOHN HOPE FRANKLIN, *The Militant South* (Cambridge, Mass., Harvard University Press, 1956).

EUGENE GENOVESE, *Roll, Jordan, Roll: The World the Slaves Made* (New York, Pantheon Books, 1974).

D. L. DUMOND, *Anti-Slavery* (Ann Arbor, University of Michigan Press, 1961).

MERTON L. DILLON, *The Abolitionists: The Growth of a Dissident Minority* (New York and London, W. W. Norton, 1974).

W. R. BROCK, *Conflict and Transformation: The United States, 1844–1877* (Harmondsworth, Penguin Books, 1973).

MARK TWAIN, *Tom Sawyer.*

MARK TWAIN, *Huckleberry Finn.*

HARRIET BEECHER STOWE, *Uncle Tom's Cabin.*

BRUCE COLLINS, *The Origins of America's Civil War* (London, Arnold, 1981).

ERIC FONER, *Free Soil, Free Labour, Free Men* (New York, Oxford University Press, 1970).

DAVID M. POTTER, *The Impending Crisis* (New York and London, Harper & Row, 1976).

STEPHEN VINCENT BENÉT, *John Brown's Body* (New York, Farrar & Rinehart, 1928).

STEPHEN B. OATES, *With Malice Toward None: The Life of Abraham Lincoln* (London, Allen & Unwin, 1978).

PETER J. PARISH, *The American Civil War* (London, Eyre Methuen, 1975).

JAMES M. MCPHERSON, *Battle Cry of Freedom: the Civil War Era* (New York, Oxford University Press, 1988).

EDMUND WILSON, *Patriotic Gore: Studies in the Literature of the American Civil War* (New York, Oxford University Press, 1962).

KENNETH M. STAMPP, *The Era of Reconstruction* (London, Eyre & Spottiswoode, 1965).

E. L. MCKITRICK, *Andrew Johnson and Reconstruction* (Chicago and London, University of Chicago Press, 1960).

W. E. B. DU BOIS, *Black Reconstruction in America* (London, Frank Cass, 1966).

C. VANN WOODWARD, *The Origins of the New South* (Baton Rouge, Louisiana, Louisiana State University Press and the University of Texas Press, 1951).

W. J. CASH, *The Mind of the South* (New York, Knopf, 1941).

E. C. KIRKLAND, *Industry Comes of Age* (New York, Holt, Rinehart & Winston, 1951).

HENRY JAMES, *Washington Square.*

OSCAR HANDLIN, *Immigration as a Factor in American History* (Englewood Cliffs, NJ, Prentice-Hall, 1959).

MALDWYN A. JONES, *American Immigration* (Chicago and London, University of Chicago, 1960).

PHILIP TAYLOR, *The Distant Magnet* (London, Eyre & Spottiswoode, 1971).

JOHN HIGHAM, *Strangers in the Land: Patterns of American Nativism 1860–1925* (New York, Atheneum, 1963).

STEPHAN THERNSTROM (ed.), *Harvard Encyclopedia of American Ethnic Groups* (Cambridge, Mass.; London, Harvard University Press, 1980).

JAMES BRYCE, *The American Commonwealth.* Edited with an Introduction by Terrence J. McDonald (Bedford Books, 1994).

WILLIAM L. O'RIORDAN, *Plunkitt of Tammany Hall.*

DANIEL BOORSTIN, *The Americans: The Democratic Experience* (New York, Random House, 1973).

HENRY PELLING, *American Labor* (Chicago and London, University of Chicago Press, 1960).

ROBERT H. WIEBE, *The Search for Order, 1877–1920* (New York and London, Macmillan, 1967).

JOHN D. HICKS, *The Populist Revolt* (Minneapolis, University of Minnesota Press, 1931).

LAWRENCE GOODWYN, *The Populist Movement* (New York, Oxford University Press, 1978).

MARK SULLIVAN, *Our Times* (New York, Scribner's, 6 vols., 1926–35).

GEORGE B. TINDALL, *The Emergence of the New South* (Baton Rouge, Louisiana State University and University of Texas, 1967).

C. VANN WOODWARD, *The Strange Career of Jim Crow* (New York, Oxford University Press, 3rd revised edn, 1974).

LINCOLN STEFFENS, *The Shame of the Cities.*

JOHN M. BLUM, *The Republican Roosevelt* (Cambridge, Mass., Harvard University Press, 1954).

PATRICK RENSHAW, *The Wobblies* (London, Eyre & Spottiswoode, 1967).

GEORGE E. MOWRY, *The California Progressives* (Berkeley, University of California Press, 1951).

JOHN M. BLUM, *Woodrow Wilson and the Politics of Morality* (Boston, Little, Brown, 1956).

GEORGE KENNAN, *American Diplomacy 1900–1950* (Chicago, University of Chicago Press, 1951).

BARBARA TUCHMAN, *The Zimmermann Telegram* (New York, Dell, 1958).

GENE SMITH, *When the Cheering Stopped* (London, Hutchinson, 1964).

WILLIAM E. LEUCHTENBURG, *The Perils of Prosperity 1914–1932* (Chicago, University of Chicago Press, 1958).

F. SCOTT FITZGERALD, *The Great Gatsby*.

ANDREW SINCLAIR, *Prohibition* (London, Faber, 1962).

SAMUEL LUBELL, *The Future of American Politics* (Garden City, NY, Doubleday, 2nd revised edn 1956).

J. K. GALBRAITH, *The Great Crash* (London, Hamish Hamilton, 1955).

STUDS TERKEL, *Hard Times: An Oral History of the Great Depression* (New York, Pantheon, 1970).

WILLIAM E. LEUCHTENBURG, *Franklin D. Roosevelt and the New Deal* (New York and London, Harper & Row, 1963).

JAMES MACGREGOR BURNS, *Roosevelt: The Lion and the Fox* (New York, Harcourt, Brace, 1956).

D. W. BROGAN, *The American Political System* (London, Hamish Hamilton, with new introduction, 1943).

DEAN ACHESON, *Morning and Noon* (London, Hamish Hamilton, 1967).

RICHARD POLENBERG, *One Nation Divisible* (Harmondsworth, Penguin Books, 1980).

HERBERT FEIS, *The Road to Pearl Harbor* (Princeton, NJ, Princeton University Press, 1950).

JAMES MACGREGOR BURNS, *Roosevelt: The Soldier of Freedom* (London, Weidenfeld & Nicolson, 1971).

DANIEL YERGIN *Shattered Peace: The Origins of the Cold War and the National Security State* (Harmondsworth, Penguin Books, 1980).

DEAN ACHESON, *Present at the Creation* (London, Hamish Hamilton, 1969).

DAVID CAUTE, *The Great Fear* (London, Secker & Warburg, 1978).

RICHARD H. ROVERE, *Senator Joe McCarthy* (London, Methuen, 1960).

THEODORE H. WHITE, *The Making of the President 1960* (London, Cape, 1962).

TAYLOR BRANCH, *Parting the Waters* (New York, Simon & Schuster, 1988).

DAVID J. GARROW, *Bearing the Cross: Martin Luther King and Southern Christian Leadership Conference* (New York, Morrow, 1986).

MICHAEL HARRINGTON, *The Other America: Poverty in the United States* (Harmondsworth, Penguin Books, revised edn, 1971).

ROBERT F. KENNEDY, *Thirteen Days: The Cuban Missile Crisis* (London, Macmillan, 1969).

GERALD POSNER, *Case Closed: Lee Harvey Oswald and the Assassination of JFK* (London, Warren, 1994).

NEIL SHEEHAN (ed.), *The Pentagon Papers* (Chicago, Quadrangle Books, 1971).

MICHAEL R. BESCHLOSS, *Taking Charge: the Johnson White House Tapes, 1963–1964* (New York, Simon and Schuster, 1998).

GUENTER LEWY, *America in Vietnam* (New York, Oxford University Press, 1978).

J. ANTHONY LUKAS, *Nightmare: The Underside of the Nixon Years* (New York, Viking, 1976).

DAVID P. CALLEO, *The Imperious Economy* (Cambridge, Mass., Harvard University Press, 1982).

MICHAEL FRENCH, *US Economic History Since 1945* (Manchester, Manchester University Press, 1997).

WILLIAM ISSEL, *Social Change in the United States 1945–1983* (London, Macmillan, 1985).

JOHN DUMBRELL, *American Foreign Policy: Carter to Clinton* (London, Macmillan, 1997).

IWAN W. MORGAN, *Beyond the Liberal Consensus: A Political History of the United States Since 1965* (London, Hurst, 1994).

Index